# READINGS FOR WRITERS

## Sixth Edition

Lexington
Institute

10840 South Western Avenue
Chicago, Illinois 60643-3294
(312) 779-3800

# READINGS FOR WRITERS

## Sixth Edition

Jo Ray McCuen

Glendale College

Anthony C. Winkler

Harcourt Brace Jovanovich, Publishers

San Diego   New York   Chicago   Austin   Washington, D.C.
London   Sydney   Tokyo   Toronto

# •• *PREFACE* ••

From its inception, *Readings for Writers* has had an unwavering identity and *raison d'être*, and the Sixth Edition is no exception. It is the only reader that groups every selection under a purposeful label—*advice, discussion,* or *example*. It is a reader whose selections have always exemplified good writing and whose range of interest is broad enough to exert wide appeal. This edition remains true to its ancestral stock, since it differs not one whit from the five before it in this basic make-up.

But it does differ in other evolutionary ways. First, this edition is more streamlined than its predecessors. It now consists of ten chapters instead of thirteen. Dropped from the edition are the separate chapters on writing reports and writing for the sciences. Consigned to an appendix are chapters formerly devoted to writing about literature and to writing the research paper. We have gone from 144 selections in the Fifth Edition to 134 in the Sixth.

Second, for this edition we have expanded our apparatus to take into account the latest research on critical reading. Questions after each selection are now grouped under three headings: "The Facts," "The Strategies," and "The Issues." Questions under "The Facts" test the student's comprehension; those under "The Strategies," the student's understanding of rhetorical techniques; and those under "The Issues," the student's ability to draw inferences and see wider relationships.

Third, we have expanded the "Issues for Critical Thinking" from seven to ten, one for each chapter. Issues now include legalized abortion, nuclear weapons, surrogate mothers, women's liberation, AIDS, college education, crime and punishment, treatment of animals, the existence of God, and sexist language. To each issue we have added a third article to blunt the absolutist flavor suggested by mere pro-and-con positions and to reflect something of the complexity behind all debate.

Fourth, Chapter 6 on development, formerly some 234 pages long, has been restructured and broken down into three separate chapters: "Reporting" (Chapter 6), "Explaining" (Chapter 7), and "Analyzing" (Chapter 8). In these three chapters, we cover the traditional writing strategies of narration and description, illustration and definition, comparison/contrast, division/classification, and causal analysis. (We cover argumentation in Chapter 9.) We have also expanded the number of short stories—there are now eight in this edition—retained the student essays and the glossary, and freshly annotated the sample student research paper to reflect the latest Modern Language Association (MLA) style.

Finally, and certainly not least in the amount of editorial work involved, we have written introductory essays for every chapter, tying together its selections under a single pedagogical theme. We have also updated the biographical headnotes and added an introduction on critical reading. To the research paper section we have added a step-by-step essay explaining the principles of writing and documenting research papers. Two sample papers are included in this edition—one documented in the MLA style, the other in the American Psychological Association (APA) style—both annotated to teach the basic techniques of research paper writing.

Many people have contributed to this edition with helpful suggestions and informed criticisms, and we thank them all. Special thanks are due to Charles L. Bailiff, University of Alabama, Birmingham; Dorothy Bankston, Louisiana State University; Laird H. Barber, University of Minnesota, Morris; Don Barnett, University of Georgia; Claire Betar, California State University, Long Beach; Lynn Dianne Beene, University of New Mexico; Judy Chitlik, Rancho Santiago College; Gordon Curzon, California Polytechnic State University, San Luis Obispo; Dr. Patricia Elder Dean, South Plains College; Elaine Englehardt, Utah Valley Community College; Cecilia Konchar Farr, Brigham Young University; Sara Farris, University of Minnesota, Morris; Susan Gebhardt-Burns, University of Minnesota, Morris; Dr. Patricia Graves, Georgia State University; J. H. Haeger, San Jose State University; Leigh Holmes, Cameron University; Peggy Jolly, University of Alabama at Birmingham; Cecil L. Jorgensen, Weber State College; Dr. I. A. Khan, University of Minnesota, Morris; George Kennedy, Washington State University; Douglas Kilday, University of Wisconsin, Oshkosh; George Klawitter, Viterbo College; James P. McCurry, Carl Sandburg College; Jim Papworth, Brigham Young University; Janice E. Patten, San Jose State University; Joseph Pawlosky, East Central University; Jeanne Purdy, University of Minnesota, Morris; Dr. Matthew Roudané, Georgia State University; Malinda Snow, Georgia State University; Fiona Sohns, West Valley College; Isabel Bonnyman Stanley, East Tennessee State University; Sally Taylor, Brigham Young University; Judy Whitis, Olivet Nazarene University.

Thanks also are due to those at Harcourt Brace Jovanovich who worked on the Sixth Edition: Marlane Miriello, acquisitions editor; Craig Avery, manuscript editor; Sandy Steiner, marketing manager; Melissa Rose and Paula Bryant, production editors; Martha Gilman, designer; Mandy Van Dusen, production manager; and Vicki Kelly, art editor.

Jo Ray McCuen

Anthony C. Winkler

# $=$ •• *CONTENTS* ••$=$

# THEMATIC TABLE OF CONTENTS

# GUIDELINES
# FOR CRITICAL
# READING

Critical reading means reading with a conscious effort to see both sides of an issue, draw valid conclusions, and detect bias. It means burrowing below the immediate reaction we have to a piece and trying to fathom its underlying meaning. This is not the sort of reading we do when we read a detective novel or a pulp magazine bought from a drugstore shelf. But it is the best way to read, although perhaps the most strenuous, because it helps us to learn. Here are ten guidelines to help you read critically.

### 1. Understand what you read.

Reread difficult passages, looking up in a dictionary all the unfamiliar words. You cannot form an opinion of what you have read unless you understand what the author is saying.

### 2. Imagine an opposing point of view for all opinions.

If a writer says that the Arab punishment of cutting off the hands of an embezzler is more humane than the American equivalent of imprisonment, reverse the argument and see what happens. In other words, look for reasons that support the other side.

### 3. Search for biases and hidden assumptions.

Be alert to the biases of the writer. For example, an atheist arguing for abortion will not attribute a soul to the unborn fetus; a devout Catholic will. To ferret out possible biases and hidden assumptions, check the author's age, sex, education, and ethnic background. These and other personal biographical facts might have influenced the opinions expressed in the work, but you cannot know to what extent unless you know something about the author. (That, by the way, is the rationale behind the use of biographical headnotes, which accompany the articles in this book.)

### 4. Separate emotion from fact.

Talented writers frequently color an issue with emotionally charged language, thus casting their opinions in the best possible light. For example, a condemned murderer may be described in sympathetic language that draws attention away from his horrifying crimes. Be alert to sloganeering, to bumpersticker philosophizing about complex issues. Emotion is no solution to complicated problems.

### 5. If the issue is new to you, look up the facts.

If you are reading about an unfamiliar issue, be willing to fill in the gaps in your knowledge with research. For example, if you are reading an editorial that proposes raising home insurance rates for families taking care of foster children, you will want to know why. Is it because foster children do more damage than natural children? Is it because natural parents are apt to file lawsuits against foster parents? You can find answers to these questions by asking representatives of the affected parties: the State Department of Social Services, typical insurance agencies, foster parents associations, the County Welfare Directors Association, any children's lobby, and others. To make a critical judgment you must know, and carefully weigh, the facts.

## 6. Use insights from one subject to illuminate or correct another.

Be prepared to apply what you already know to whatever you read. History can inform psychology; literature can give you insights into geography. For example, if a writer in psychology argues that most oppressed people develop a psychology of defeat that gives them a subconscious desire to be subjugated and makes them prey to tyrants, your knowledge of American history should tell you otherwise. As proof that oppressed people often fight oppression unto death, you can point to the Battle of Fallen Timbers in 1794, the Battle of Tippecanoe in 1811, and the Black Hawk War of 1832—conflicts in which the Indians fought desperately to retain their territories rather than go meekly to the reservations. In other words, you can use what you have learned from history to refute a falsehood from psychology.

## 7. Evaluate the evidence.

Critical readers do not accept evidence at face value. They question its source, its verifiability, its appropriateness. Here are some practical tips for evaluating evidence:

- Verify a questionable opinion by cross-checking with other sources. For example, if a medical writer argues that heavy smoking tends to cause serious bladder diseases in males, check the medical journals for confirmation of this view. Diligent research often turns up a consensus of opinion among the experts in any field.
- Check the date of the evidence. In science, especially, evidence varies from year to year. Before 1987, no one really knew exactly how the immune system worked. Then Susumu Tonegawa, a geneticist at the Massachusetts Institute of Technology, discovered in 1987 how the immune system protects the body from foreign substances by the manufacture of antibodies. In 1980 the evidence would say that the workings of the immune system were a mystery; that evidence would be inaccurate in 1987.
- Use common sense in evaluating evidence. For example, if a writer argues that a child's handwriting can accurately predict his or her life as

an adult, your own experience with human nature should lead you to reject this conclusion as speculative. No convincing evidence exists to corroborate it.

## 8. Ponder the values that give an argument its impetus.

In writing the Declaration of Independence, Thomas Jefferson based his arguments on the value that "all men are created equal." On the other hand, Karl Marx based the arguments of his *Communist Manifesto* on the value that the laborer is society's greatest good. Critical reading means thinking about the values implicit in an argument. For instance, to argue that murderers should be hanged in public to satisfy society's need for revenge is to value revenge over human dignity. On the other hand, to argue that democracy can exist only with free speech is to highly value freedom of speech.

## 9. Look for logical fallacies.

These typical logical flaws occur in a wide range of arguments: the *ad hominem* attack (attacking the person instead of the issue or argument); the *ad populum* appeal (the use of simplistic popular slogans to convince); the *false analogy* (comparing situations that have no bearing on each other); *begging the question* (arguing in circles); and *ignoring the question* (focusing on matters that are beside the point). For a better understanding of logical fallacies, review Chapter Nine, "Argumentation."

## 10. Don't be seduced by bogus claims.

Arguments are often based on unsubstantiated claims. For example, a writer may warn that "recent studies show women becoming increasingly hostile to men." Or, another writer might announce, "Statistics have shown beyond doubt that most well-educated males oppose gun control." You should always remain skeptical of these and similar claims when they are unaccompanied by hard-headed evidence. A proper claim will always be documented with verifiable evidence.

# 1
# DEFINING RHETORIC

## INTRODUCTION: WHAT IS RHETORIC?

Rhetoric is the art of writing persuasively. It is made up of all those strategies and techniques a writer will use to make a case or drive home a point. All of us are occasionally speakers and writers who try to make a point or sway an audience and can therefore benefit from mastering the art of forceful expression.

Many theories exist about the teaching of writing, and many schools of thought contend for the beginner's discipleship. We have our own theory: You learn to write well by first writing less well. If you write long and often enough, eventually you will write better. Then, after an apprenticeship whose length will vary with your particular gifts, you will begin to write well. That is the way one learns to write—by the painful process of effort and error. One learns what works and what does not; one accumulates a certain habit of phrasing and expression. But mainly, one absorbs the underlying technique that is most likely to yield the best writing—namely, constant revision.

The indispensable lessons that rhetoric and its study can teach are many and varied, but the most important of all is the lesson of keeping an eye on the audience. Writers do not write for themselves. Even the solitary diarist conceptualizes a part of the writing self as listener, reader, audience. It is to this attentive part that the words and phrases of a diary are aimed. Some students assume everything about an instructor except this single obvious fact—that he or she is a paid audience for the student's work. It is to the instructor that you must direct your essay, taking into account personal quirks of taste and inclinations that any audience can be expected to have. If you can produce writing that will please the instructor, it is highly likely that you can do the same later for the boss or for the salespeople whom you might one day try to spur on using the written word.

Collected in this chapter are essays and articles that exemplify the collected wisdom as well as contemporary practice of rhetoric. Paul Roberts, in "How to Say Nothing in Five Hundred Words," focuses on the student written essay that most readers of this book will have to write. John E. Jordan gives us a glimpse of the history and usefulness of rhetoric; Martin Luther King, Jr.'s speech shows us a master rhetorician hard at work persuading an audience; stylist Joan Didion tells us how she obliquely approaches her own particular art.

Then, in the arena of debate, we get our first whiff of rhetorical gunpowder. The issue is a volatile one: legalized abortions. We listen to the rhetorical blasts of disputants who clamor for our hearts and minds. The United States Supreme Court justifies its decision to legalize abortions; Linda Bird Francke expresses both her misgivings and support for the practice; and Ronald Reagan, the only sitting U.S. president ever to write and publish an opinion on such a controversial topic while in office, checks in with vigorous opposition.

One learns to write well by constantly revising. But one also absorbs standards and strategies of rhetoric by peering over the shoulders of skilled writers at work. That is what these articles will allow you to do.

=========== •• *ADVICE* •• ===========

**Paul Roberts**

——————— • **HOW TO SAY NOTHING IN** • ———————
    **FIVE HUNDRED WORDS**

*Paul McHenry Roberts (1917–1967) taught college English for over twenty years, first at San Jose State College and later at Cornell University. He wrote several books on linguistics, including* Understanding Grammar *(1954),* Patterns of English *(1956), and* Understanding English *(1958).*

*Freshman composition, like everything else, has its share of fashions. In the 1950s, when this article was written, the most popular argument raging among student essayists was the proposed abolition of college football. With the greater social consciousness of the early 1960s, the topic of the day became the morality of capital punishment. Topics may change, but the core principles of good writing remain constant, and this essay has become something of a minor classic in explaining them. Be concrete, says Roberts; get to the point; express your opinions colorfully. Refreshingly, he even practices what he preaches. His essay is humorous, direct, and almost salty in summarizing the working habits that all good prose writers must cultivate.*

It's Friday afternoon, and you have almost survived another week    1
of classes. You are just looking forward dreamily to the weekend when the English instructor says: "For Monday you will turn in a five-hundred-word composition on college football."

Well, that puts a good hole in the weekend. You don't have any    2
strong views on college football one way or the other. You get rather excited during the season and go to all the home games and find it rather more fun than not. On the other hand, the class has been reading Robert Hutchins in the anthology and perhaps Shaw's

"Eighty-Yard Run," and from the class discussion you have got the idea that the instructor thinks college football is for the birds. You are no fool. You can figure out what side to take.

After dinner you get out the portable typewriter that you got for high school graduation. You might as well get it over with and enjoy Saturday and Sunday. Five hundred words is about two double-spaced pages with normal margins. You put in a sheet of paper, think up a title, and you're off:

#### WHY COLLEGE FOOTBALL SHOULD BE ABOLISHED

> College football should be abolished because it's bad for the school and also for the players. The players are so busy practicing that they don't have any time for their studies.

This, you feel, is a mighty good start. The only trouble is that it's only thirty-two words. You still have four hundred and sixty-eight to go, and you've pretty well exhausted the subject. It comes to you that you do your best thinking in the morning, so you put away the typewriter and go to the movies. But the next morning you have to do your washing and some math problems, and in the afternoon you go to the game. The English instructor turns up too, and you wonder if you've taken the right side after all. Saturday night you have a date, and Sunday morning you have to go to church. (You can't let English assignments interfere with your religion.) What with one thing and another, it's ten o'clock Sunday night before you get out the typewriter again. You make a pot of coffee and start to fill out your views on college football. Put a little meat on the bones.

#### WHY COLLEGE FOOTBALL SHOULD BE ABOLISHED

> In my opinion, it seems to me that college football should be abolished. The reason why I think this to be true is because I feel that football is bad for the colleges in nearly every respect. As Robert Hutchins says in his article in our anthology in which he discusses college football, it would be better if the colleges had race horses and had races with one another, because then the horses would not have to attend classes. I firmly agree with Mr. Hutchins on this point, and I am sure that many other students would agree too.
>
> One reason why it seems to me that college football is bad is that it has become too commercial. In the olden times when people played football just for the fun of it, maybe college football was all right, but they do not play college football just for the fun of it now as they used

to in the old days. Nowadays college football is what you might call a big business. Maybe this is not true at all schools, and I don't think it is especially true here at State, but certainly this is the case at most colleges and universities in America nowadays, as Mr. Hutchins points out in his very interesting article. Actually the coaches and alumni go around to the high schools and offer the high school stars large salaries to come to their colleges and play football for them. There was one case where a high school star was offered a convertible if he would play football for a certain college.

Another reason for abolishing college football is that it is bad for the players. They do not have time to get a college education, because they are so busy playing football. A football player has to practice every afternoon from three to six and then he is so tired that he can't concentrate on his studies. He just feels like dropping off to sleep after dinner, and then the next day he goes to his classes without having studied and maybe he fails the test.

(Good ripe stuff so far, but you're still a hundred and fifty-one words from home. One more push.)

Also I think college football is bad for the colleges and the universities because not very many students get to participate in it. Out of a college of ten thousand students only seventy-five or a hundred play football, if that many. Football is what you might call a spectator sport. That means that most people go to watch it but do not play it themselves.

(Four hundred and fifteen. Well, you still have the conclusion, and when you retype it, you can make the margins a little wider.)

These are the reasons why I agree with Mr. Hutchins that college football should be abolished in American colleges and universities.

On Monday you turn it in, moderately hopeful, and on Friday it comes    4
back marked "weak in content" and sporting a big "D."

This essay is exaggerated a little, not much. The English instructor    5
will recognize it as reasonably typical of what an assignment on college football will bring in. He knows that nearly half of the class will contrive in five hundred words to say that college football is too commercial and bad for the players. Most of the other half will inform him that college football builds character and prepares one for life and brings prestige to the school. As he reads paper after paper all saying the same thing in almost the same words, all bloodless, five hundred words dripping out of nothing, he wonders how he allowed himself to

get trapped into teaching English when he might have had a happy and interesting life as an electrician or a confidence man.

Well, you may ask, what can you do about it? The subject is one on which you have few convictions and little information. Can you be expected to make a dull subject interesting? As a matter of fact, this is precisely what you are expected to do. This is the writer's essential task. All subjects, except sex, are dull until somebody makes them interesting. The writer's job is to find the argument, the approach, the angle, the wording that will take the reader with him. This is seldom easy, and it is particularly hard in subjects that have been much discussed: College Football, Fraternities, Popular Music, Is Chivalry Dead?, and the like. You will feel that there is nothing you can do with such subjects except repeat the old bromides. But there are some things you can do which will make your papers, if not throbbingly alive, at least less insufferably tedious than they might otherwise be.

## AVOID THE OBVIOUS CONTENT

Say the assignment is college football. Say that you've decided to be against it. Begin by putting down the arguments that come to your mind: it is too commercial, it takes the students' minds off their studies, it is hard on the players, it makes the university a kind of circus instead of an intellectual center, for most schools it is financially ruinous. Can you think of any more arguments, just off hand? All right. Now when you write your paper, *make sure that you don't use any of the material on this list*. If these are the points that leap to your mind, they will leap to everyone else's too, and whether you get a "C" or a "D" may depend on whether the instructor reads your paper early when he is fresh and tolerant or late, when the sentence "In my opinion, college football has become too commercial," inexorably repeated, has brought him to the brink of lunacy.

Be against college football for some reason or reasons of your own. If they are keen and perceptive ones, that's splendid. But even if they are trivial or foolish or indefensible, you are still ahead so long as they are not everybody else's reasons too. Be against it because the colleges don't spend enough money on it to make it worthwhile, because it is bad for the characters of the spectators, because the players are forced to attend classes, because the football stars hog all the beautiful women, because it competes with baseball and is therefore un-

American and possibly Communist-inspired. There are lots of more or less unused reasons for being against college football.

Sometimes it is a good idea to sum up and dispose of the trite and  9 conventional points before going on to your own. This has the advantage of indicating to the reader that you are going to be neither trite nor conventional. Something like this:

> We are often told that college football should be abolished because it has become too commercial or because it is bad for the players. These arguments are no doubt very cogent, but they don't really go to the heart of the matter.

Then you go to the heart of the matter.

## TAKE THE LESS USUAL SIDE

One rather simple way of getting into your paper is to take the side  10 of the argument that most of the citizens will want to avoid. If the assignment is an essay on dogs, you can, if you choose, explain that dogs are faithful and lovable companions, intelligent, useful as guardians of the house and protectors of children, indispensable in police work—in short, when all is said and done, man's best friends. Or you can suggest that those big brown eyes conceal, more often than not, a vacuity of mind and an inconstancy of purpose; that the dogs you have known most intimately have been mangy, ill-tempered brutes, incapable of instruction; and that only your nobility of mind and fear of arrest prevent you from kicking the flea-ridden animals when you pass them on the street.

Naturally personal convictions will sometimes dictate your ap-  11 proach. If the assigned subject is "Is Methodism Rewarding to the Individual?" and you are a pious Methodist, you have really no choice. But few assigned subjects, if any, will fall in this category. Most of them will lie in broad areas of discussion with much to be said on both sides. They are intellectual exercises, and it is legitimate to argue now one way and now another, as debaters do in similar circumstances. Always take the side that looks to you hardest, least defensible. It will almost always turn out to be easier to write interestingly on that side.

This general advice applies where you have a choice of subjects. If  12 you are to choose among "The Value of Fraternities" and "My Favorite High School Teacher" and "What I Think About Beetles," by all means plump for the beetles. By the time the instructor gets to your paper, he

will be up to his ears in tedious tales about a French teacher at Bloom-
bury High and assertions about how fraternities build character and
prepare one for life. Your views on beetles, whatever they are, are
bound to be a refreshing change.

Don't worry too much about figuring out what the instructor thinks    13
about the subject so that you can cuddle up with him. Chances are his
views are no stronger than yours. If he does have convictions and you
oppose him, his problem is to keep from grading you higher than you
deserve in order to show he is not biased. This doesn't mean that
you should always cantankerously dissent from what the instructor
says; that gets tiresome too. And if the subject assigned is "My Pet
Peeve," do not begin, "My pet peeve is the English instructor who
assigns papers on 'my pet peeve.'" This was still funny during the
War of 1812, but it has sort of lost its edge since then. It is in general
good manners to avoid personalities.

## SLIP OUT OF ABSTRACTION

If you will study the essay on college football [near the beginning of    14
this essay], you will perceive that one reason for its appalling dullness
is that it never gets down to particulars. It is just a series of not very
glittering generalities: "football is bad for the colleges," "it has become
too commercial," "football is big business," "it is bad for the players,"
and so on. Such round phrases thudding against the reader's brain
are unlikely to convince him, though they may well render him
unconscious.

If you want the reader to believe that college football is bad for the    15
players, you have to do more than say so. You have to display the evil.
Take your roommate, Alfred Simkins, the second-string center. Picture
poor old Alfy coming home from football practice every evening,
bruised and aching, agonizingly tired, scarcely able to shovel the
mashed potatoes into his mouth. Let us see him staggering up to the
room, getting out his econ textbook, peering desperately at it with his
good eye, falling asleep and failing the test in the morning. Let us
share his unbearable tension as Saturday draws near. Will he fail, be
demoted, lose his monthly allowance, be forced to return to the coal
mines? And if he succeeds, what will be his reward? Perhaps a slight
ripple of applause when the third-string center replaces him, a moment of elation in the locker room if the team wins, of despair if it

loses. What will he look back on when he graduates from college? Toil and torn ligaments. And what will be his future? He is not good enough for pro football, and he is too obscure and weak in econ to succeed in stocks and bonds. College football is tearing the heart from Alfy Simkins and, when it finishes with him, will callously toss aside the shattered hulk.

This is no doubt a weak enough argument for the abolition of college    16
football, but it is a sight better than saying, in three or four variations, that college football (in your opinion) is bad for the players.

Look at the work of any professional writer and notice how con-    17
stantly he is moving from the generality, the abstract statement, to the concrete example, the facts and figures, the illustrations. If he is writing on juvenile delinquency, he does not just tell you that juveniles are (it seems to him) delinquent and that (in his opinion) something should be done about it. He shows you juveniles being delinquent, tearing up movie theatres in Buffalo, stabbing high school principals in Dallas, smoking marijuana in Palo Alto. And more than likely he is moving toward some specific remedy, not just a general wringing of the hands.

It is no doubt possible to be *too* concrete, too illustrative or anecdo-    18
tal, but few inexperienced writers err this way. For most the soundest advice is to be seeking always for the picture, to be always turning general remarks into seeable examples. Don't say, "Sororities teach girls the social graces." Say, "Sorority life teaches a girl how to carry on a conversation while pouring tea, without sloshing the tea into the saucer." Don't say, "I like certain kinds of popular music very much." Say, "Whenever I hear Gerber Sprinklittle play 'Mississippi Man' on the trombone, my socks creep up my ankles."

## GET RID OF OBVIOUS PADDING

The student toiling away at his weekly English theme is too often    19
tormented by a figure: five hundred words. How, he asks himself, is he to achieve this staggering total? Obviously by never using one word when he can somehow work in ten.

He is therefore seldom content with a plain statement like "Fast    20
driving is dangerous." This has only four words in it. He takes thought, and the sentence becomes:

In my opinion, fast driving is dangerous.

Better, but he can do better still:

> In my opinion, fast driving would seem to be rather dangerous.

If he is really adept, it may come out:

> In my humble opinion, though I do not claim to be an expert on this complicated subject, fast driving, in most circumstances, would seem to be rather dangerous in many respects, or at least so it would seem to me.

Thus four words have been turned into forty, and not an iota of content has been added.

Now this is a way to go about reaching five hundred words, and if you are content with a "D" grade, it is as good a way as any. But if you aim higher, you must work differently. Instead of stuffing your sentences with straw, you must try steadily to get rid of the padding, to make your sentences lean and tough. If you are really working at it, your first draft will greatly exceed the required total, and then you will work it down, thus: 21

> It is thought in some quarters that fraternities do not contribute as much as might be expected to campus life.
>
> Some people think that fraternities contribute little to campus life.
>
> The average doctor who practices in small towns or in the country must toil night and day to heal the sick.
>
> Most country doctors work long hours.
>
> When I was a little girl, I suffered from shyness and embarrassment in the presence of others.
>
> I was a shy little girl.
>
> It is absolutely necessary for the person employed as a marine fireman to give the matter of steam pressure his undivided attention at all times.
>
> The fireman has to keep his eye on the steam gauge.

You may ask how you can arrive at five hundred words at this rate. Simple. You dig up more real content. Instead of taking a couple of obvious points off the surface of the topic and then circling warily around them for six paragraphs, you work in and explore, figure out the details. You illustrate. You say that fast driving is dangerous, and then you prove it. How long does it take to stop a car at forty and at eighty? How far can you see at night? What happens when a tire blows? What happens in a head-on collision at fifty miles an hour? 22

Pretty soon your paper will be full of broken glass and blood and headless torsos, and reaching five hundred words will not really be a problem.

## CALL A FOOL A FOOL

Some of the padding in freshman themes is to be blamed not on    23
anxiety about the word minimum but on excessive timidity. The student writes, "In my opinion, the principal of my high school acted in ways that I believe every unbiased person would have to call foolish." This isn't exactly what he means. What he means is, "My high school principal was a fool." If he was a fool, call him a fool. Hedging the thing about with "in-my-opinion's" and "it-seems-to-me's" and "as-I-see-it's" and "at-least-from-my-point-of-view's" gains you nothing. Delete these phrases whenever they creep into your paper.

The student's tendency to hedge stems from a modesty that in other    24
circumstances would be commendable. He is, he realizes, young and inexperienced, and he half suspects that he is dopey and fuzzy-minded beyond the average. Probably only too true. But it doesn't help to announce your incompetence six times in every paragraph. Decide what you want to say and say it as vigorously as possible, without apology and in plain words.

Linguistic diffidence can take various forms. One is what we call    25
*euphemism*. This is the tendency to call a spade "a certain garden implement" or women's underwear "unmentionables." It is stronger in some eras than others and in some people than others but it always operates more or less in subjects that are touchy or taboo: death, sex, madness, and so on. Thus we shrink from saying "He died last night" but say instead "passed away," "left us," "joined his Maker," "went to his reward." Or we try to take off the tension with a lighter cliché: "kicked the bucket," "cashed in his chips," "handed in his dinner pail." We have found all sorts of ways to avoid saying *mad*: "mentally ill," "touched," "not quite right upstairs," "feebleminded," "innocent," "simple," "off his trolley," "not in his right mind." Even such a now plain word as *insane* began as a euphemism with the meaning "not healthy."

Modern science, particularly psychology, contributes many poly-    26
syllables in which we can wrap our thoughts and blunt their force. To

many writers there is no such thing as a bad schoolboy. Schoolboys are maladjusted or unoriented or misunderstood or in the need of guidance or lacking in continued success toward satisfactory integration of the personality as a social unit, but they are never bad. Psychology no doubt makes us better men and women, more sympathetic and tolerant, but it doesn't make writing any easier. Had Shakespeare been confronted with psychology, "To be or not to be" might have come out, "To continue as a social unit or not to do so. That is the personality problem. Whether 'tis a better sign of integration at the conscious level to display a psychic tolerance toward the maladjustments and repressions induced by one's lack of orientation in one's environment or—" But Hamlet would never have finished the soliloquy.

Writing in the modern world, you cannot altogether avoid modern    27
jargon. Nor, in an effort to get away from euphemism, should you salt your paper with four-letter words. But you can do much if you will mount guard against those roundabout phrases, those echoing polysyllables that tend to slip into your writing to rob it of its crispness and force.

## BEWARE OF PAT EXPRESSIONS

Other things being equal, avoid phrases like "other things being    28
equal." Those sentences that come to you whole, or in two or three doughy lumps, are sure to be bad sentences. They are no creation of yours but pieces of common thought floating in the community soup.

Pat expressions are hard, often impossible, to avoid, because they    29
come too easily to be noticed and seem too necessary to be dispensed with. No writer avoids them altogether, but good writers avoid them more often than poor writers.

By "pat expressions" we mean such tags as "to all practical intents    30
and purposes," "the pure and simple truth," "from where I sit," "the time of his life," "to the ends of the earth," "in the twinkling of an eye," "as sure as you're born," "over my dead body," "under cover of darkness," "took the easy way out," "when all is said and done," "told him time and time again," "parted the best of friends," "stand up and be counted," "gave him the best years of her life," "worked her fingers to the bone." Like other clichés, these expressions were once forceful. Now we should use them only when we can't possibly think of anything else.

Some pat expressions stand like a wall between the writer and   31
thought. Such a one is "the American way of life." Many student
writers feel that when they have said that something accords with the
American way of life or does not they have exhausted the subject.
Actually, they have stopped at the highest level of abstraction. The
American way of life is the complicated set of bonds between a
hundred and eighty million ways. All of us know this when we think
about it, but the tag phrase too often keeps us from thinking about it.

So with many another phrase dear to the politician: "this great land   32
of ours," "the man in the street," "our national heritage." These may
prove our patriotism or give a clue to our political beliefs, but otherwise they add nothing to the paper except words.

## COLORFUL WORDS

The writer builds with words, and no builder uses a raw material   33
more slippery and elusive and treacherous. A writer's work is a constant struggle to get the right word in the right place, to find that
particular word that will convey his meaning exactly, that will persuade
the reader or soothe him or startle or amuse him. He never succeeds
altogether—sometimes he feels that he scarcely succeeds at all—but
such successes as he has are what make the thing worth doing.

There is no book of rules for this game. One progresses through   34
everlasting experiment on the basis of ever-widening experience.
There are few useful generalizations that one can make about words
as words, but there are perhaps a few.

Some words are what we call "colorful." By this we mean that they   35
are calculated to produce a picture or induce an emotion. They are
dressy instead of plain, specific instead of general, loud instead of
soft. Thus, in place of "Her heart beat," we may write, "her heart
*pounded, throbbed, fluttered, danced.*" Instead of "He sat in his chair," we
may say, "he *lounged, sprawled, coiled.*" Instead of "It was hot," we may
say, "It was *blistering, sultry, muggy, suffocating, steamy, wilting.*"

However, it should not be supposed that the fancy word is always   36
better. Often it is as well to write "Her heart beat" or "It was hot" if
that is all it did or all it was. Ages differ in how they like their prose.
The nineteenth century liked it rich and smoky. The twentieth has
usually preferred it lean and cool. The twentieth century writer, like

all writers, is forever seeking the exact word, but he is wary of sounding feverish. He tends to pitch it low, to understate it, to throw it away. He knows that if he gets too colorful, the audience is likely to giggle.

See how this strikes you: "As the rich, golden glow of the sunset    37
died away along the eternal western hills, Angela's limpid blue eyes looked softly and trustingly into Montague's flashing brown ones, and her heart pounded like a drum in time with the joyous song surging in her soul." Some people like that sort of thing, but most modern readers would say, "Good grief," and turn on the television.

## COLORED WORDS

Some words we would call not so much colorful as colored—that is,    38
loaded with associations, good or bad. All words—except perhaps structure words—have associations of some sort. We have said that the meaning of a word is the sum of the contexts in which it occurs. When we hear a word, we hear with it an echo of all the situations in which we have heard it before.

In some words, these echoes are obvious and discussable. The word    39
*mother*, for example, has, for most people, agreeable associations. When you hear *mother* you probably think of home, safety, love, food, and various other pleasant things. If one writes, "She was like a mother to me," he gets an effect which he would not get in "She was like an aunt to me." The advertiser makes use of the associations of *mother* by working it in when he talks about his product. The politician works it in when he talks about himself.

So also with such words as *home, liberty, fireside, contentment, patriot,*    40
*tenderness, sacrifice, childlike, manly, bluff, limpid.* All of these words are loaded with associations that would be rather hard to indicate in a straightforward definition. There is more than a literal difference between "They sat around the fireside" and "They sat around the stove." They might have been equally warm and happy around the stove, but *fireside* suggests leisure, grace, quiet tradition, congenial company, and *stove* does not.

Conversely, some words have bad associations. *Mother* suggests    41
pleasant things, but *mother-in-law* does not. Many mothers-in-law are heroically lovable and some mothers drink gin all day and beat their children insensible, but these facts of life are beside the point. The point is that *mother* sounds good and *mother-in-law* does not.

Or consider the word *intellectual*. This would seem to be a compli-    42
mentary term, but in point of fact it is not, for it has picked up associations of impracticality and ineffectuality and general dopiness. So
also such words as *liberal, reactionary, Communist, socialist, capitalist,*
*radical, schoolteacher, truck driver, undertaker, operator, salesman, huckster,*
*speculator.* These convey meaning on the literal level, but beyond that—
sometimes, in some places—they convey contempt on the part of the
speaker.

The question of whether to use loaded words or not depends on    43
what is being written. The scientist, the scholar, try to avoid them; for
the poet, the advertising writer, the public speaker, they are standard
equipment. But every writer should take care that they do not substitute for thought. If you write, "Anyone who thinks that is nothing but
a Socialist (or Communist or capitalist)" you have said nothing except
that you don't like people who think that, and such remarks are effective only with the most naive readers. It is always a bad mistake to
think your readers more naive than they really are.

## COLORLESS WORDS

But probably most student writers come to grief not with words that    44
are colorful or those that are colored but with those that have no color
at all. A pet example is *nice*, a word we would find it hard to dispense
with in casual conversation but which is no longer capable of adding
much to a description. Colorless words are those of such general meaning that in a particular sentence they mean nothing. Slang adjectives
like *cool* ("That's real cool") tend to explode all over the language. They
are applied to everything, lose their original force, and quickly die.

Beware also of nouns of very general meaning, like *circumstances,*    45
*cases, instances, aspects, factors, relationships, attitudes, eventualities,* etc.
In most circumstances you will find that those cases of writing which
contain too many instances of words like these will in this and other
aspects have factors leading to unsatisfactory relationships with the
reader resulting in unfavorable attitudes on his part and perhaps
other eventualities, like a grade of "D." Notice also what *etc.* means. It
means "I'd like to make this list longer, but I can't think of any more
examples."

## VOCABULARY

| | | |
|---|---|---|
| contrive (5)* | vacuity (10) | jargon (27) |
| bromides (6) | warily (22) | polysyllables (27) |
| inexorably (7) | diffidence (25) | elusive (33) |
| cogent (9) | euphemism (25) | induce (35) |

# •• *DISCUSSION* ••

### John E. Jordan

# • **RHETORIC** •

*John Emory Jordan (b. 1913) is a professor of English who has taught at both Johns Hopkins University and the University of California, Berkeley. He has published numerous articles in scholarly journals and has written two books,* Thomas De Quincey: Literary Critic *(1952) and* Using Rhetoric *(1956), from which this selection was taken.*

*Jordan describes how we slander rhetoric by downgrading its value. He then gives a historical and etymological definition of rhetoric, argues our need for more of it, and shows how it differs from grammar or usage.*

Some readers will be nearly as surprised to be told that they regularly practice the ancient art of rhetoric as was Molière's famous character to learn that all his life he had been speaking prose. For the word "rhetoric" is likely to be associated vaguely in our memories with elocutionary posturing and to survive chiefly in the pejorative sense of flowery rhetoric. Or remembering that a rhetorical question does not really intend an answer, we may stigmatize rhetoric as suspiciously sophistical. Thus rhetoric may connote to us either something empty or something false, and at any rate something remote from our affairs, all the while that we are using it, well or badly.

1

---

*The number in parentheses denotes paragraph number in which the word is found.

Historically, rhetoric has been much respected and cultivated. Aris- 2
totle wrote a treatise on it, and in Athens of the second century the
sophist, or professor of rhetoric, was one of the leading citizens. Cicero
and Quintilian were famous Roman rhetoricians. Undergraduate education in medieval times consisted chiefly of the *trivium*: grammar,
logic, and rhetoric. Training in rhetoric was an important part of the
university curriculum in the Renaissance, and as late as the nineteenth
century, colleges had departments of rhetoric. Nowadays, aspects of
the subject are distributed among departments of philosophy, psychology, sociology, English, speech, and dramatic arts, and although
deprived of its prominence among the academic disciplines and
scarcely recognized by its old name, rhetoric still continues to be an
important activity.

Etymologically, rhetoric meant the art of oratory; it came to mean 3
the art of science of persuasion. Now it is apparent that we all use
language to persuade—ourselves as well as others. Even if our primary purpose is to express ourselves or to communicate information,
in so far as we have a hearer or reader, we are seeking to persuade him
to take a certain attitude toward what we say. All of the marshaling of
an argument, the structuring of a statement, the shaping of a paragraph, the molding of a sentence, and the choosing of a word toward
a purposeful end is rhetoric.

## THE PLACE OF RHETORIC

Anywhere, except possibly in a Trappist monastery, rhetoric is one 4
of the facts of life. For most people there is a better, more effective way
to speak and write—and a need to know how to find it. On one level
we recognize the success of the smooth talker, although our traditional
image of ourselves as laconic men of action makes us scorn and fear
his verbal felicity. One of the paradoxes of our culture is that we admire
the strong silent types, while the yap of our radio and TV chokes the
ether. We have to realize that an apotheosis of the power of our physical action is not adequate to our needs as individuals or as a nation.
Gradually, I think, we are coming to this awareness. I was asked some
time ago to teach courses in writing at a research corporation because
their scientists, highly trained and intelligent men most of whom were
Ph.D.'s, could not get their discoveries across to the vice presidents!

Quintilian would have said that they needed to study rhetoric. The term has gone out of favor, but the need remains to be able to express our ideas, to communicate our wishes, to sell our concepts. We are recognizing now that the United States is not gaining friends around the world or making known what is really important about our way of life by producing better refrigerators. The Peace Corps program includes, along with training in techniques of irrigation and other operations valuable to undeveloped areas, training in language—in how to talk about democracy with meaning and persuasion. Aristotle would have said that these young people need a course in rhetoric.

A student once protested to me that he did not want to learn to write 5 like Shakespeare. Although I assured him that he was in no such danger, I regretted his attitude, for what he meant was that he did not think it important for him to make any special effort to rise above the routine and trite. Aside from the small group who perennially aspire to write the great American novel, most Americans are modest in their attitude toward writing. They do not expect to write like Shapespeare or even very well at all. If they do not exactly feel the ancestral contempt for the smooth talker, they are likely to leave writing to Bohemian eggheads. One of the interesting phenomena of recent years has been the articulateness of the "beat" fringe of college generations. Student publications have tended to be *avant garde* partly because the solid, conservative elements in the student body did not feel that writing was their business. My scientist students at the research corporation had erroneously felt that writing was not their business. Probably the young people who join the Peace Corps, for the most part, have not realized the extent to which writing and speaking must be their business.

In our culture effective communication is nearly everybody's busi- 6 ness, and from politics to love rhetoric shows a power we must recognize. We Americans tend to scoff at political oratory; nevertheless, we have seen a presidential election influenced materially, perhaps crucially, by a series of television debates. We have never fancied ourselves as great lovers, but we bestow that distinction on the French—a more articulate people. A nation which has built its economy on the persuasion of the "hard sell" and the "soft sell" cannot afford the belittling point of view expressed by one of Alberto Moravia's heroes: "And I am, in fact, inclined to rhetoric—that is, to the substitution of words for deeds.''* Rhetoric *is* action, a more subtle kind of action, by which words often beget deeds.

At one end of its range rhetoric is concerned with the ordering of     7
ideas: Aristotle said that rhetoric was merely popular logic. At the other end it is concerned with the presentation of ideas in language. Except perhaps in symbolic logic, the two ends are interrelated. Because rhetoric is concerned with the best use of language, it has connections with grammar. Some of these relations will appear later in this book, although we shall be concerned primarily with rhetoric.

The use of language is controlled by three factors: grammar, rheto-     8
ric, and usage. Grammar is the science of what is *permissible* in the language, rhetoric is the art of what is *effective*. Grammar concerns itself with the possible ways of saying something, rhetoric with the best way. A writer or speaker in choosing the best way must necessarily select from among the possible ways—he must know grammar. His choice must also be influenced by usage, the pattern of ways in which people actually use the language in any time, place, and circumstance. Over the history of the language, usage is the source of grammar; but in any given circle, usage rarely involves all the grammatical resources of the language.

For a simple example of the way in which these three elements work,     9
suppose that a man wanted to say that he was named John. A Frenchman would find it natural to say, "I call myself John"; an American might say, "My name is John." One is no better than the other absolutely, but in English "I call myself John" would not mean the same thing as "my name is John"; it would suggest an assumed name or some other peculiarity in the situation. "I call myself John" is not ungrammatical, but it is outside the idioms sanctioned by usage. "I John myself call" would be ungrammatical because it would be meaningless; it does not conform to any English pattern. "John is my name," on the other hand, would be a possible English formulation, not essentially different in meaning from "My name is John," but different in emphasis. Modern usage makes no distinction between the two forms, and a choice between them would have to be made entirely on rhetorical grounds—probably on whether "my" was important. Usage

---

*Alberto Moravia, *Conjugal Love* (New York: Signet Books, New American Library of World Literature, Inc., 1961), p. 11.—Ed.

would influence the rhetorical decision, however, in the choice between "I am named John," "I am John," and "I'm John." For here is a
range from formal to informal usage.

    Rhetoric, then, exploits grammar and usage. The writer who seeks   10
the most effective expression must know the resources of the language; he must know the rules of grammar and usage.

## *VOCABULARY*

| | | |
|---|---|---|
| pejorative (1) | marshaling (3) | aspire (5) |
| stigmatize (1) | laconic (4) | avant garde (5) |
| sophistical (1) | felicity (4) | articulate (adj.) (6) |
| sophist (2) | ether (4) | idioms (9) |
| etymologically (3) | apotheosis (4) | |

## *THE FACTS*

1. What is rhetoric? What are its uses?
2. What is the attitude of most Americans toward writing?
3. What three factors determine the use of language?
4. What is the difference between grammar and rhetoric?
5. What influences a writer's rhetorical choices?

## *THE STRATEGIES*

1. What does the first paragraph of this essay accomplish?
2. What contributions to the definition of *rhetoric* do paragraphs 2 and 3
   respectively make?
3. The author writes: "A student once protested to me that he did not want to
   learn to write like Shakespeare. Although I assured him that he was in no
   such danger, I regretted his attitude." What tone does the author use here?
4. With what other element of language does the author contrast rhetoric?
   How does this contrast enhance his definition of rhetoric?

## *THE ISSUES*

1. In your opinion, are Americans suspicious of "smooth talking" and eloquence? If so, what historical reason can you give to account for it?
2. Jordan writes that rhetoric was once a whole discipline taught in a separate
   academic department. Why do you think it became the fragmented subject
   of today?
3. How do you evaluate a speaker's message?
4. In what way do you use language to persuade yourself, as Jordan alleges?

5. How far do you think a writer and speaker should ethically go in the attempt to persuade an audience? What aspect of the mass media is most likely to daily face this ethical boundary?

### SUGGESTIONS FOR WRITING

1. Definitions will frequently give the lexical meaning of a term, state its history, show its function, and give examples of it. Analyze and discuss the structure of this article to show how it systematically does the above.
2. Write an essay that analyzes the word usage of this article and shows how it is aimed at a particular audience.

 *EXAMPLES*

10840 South Western Avenue
Chicago, Illinois 60643-3294
(312) 779-3800

**Martin Luther King, Jr.**

## • I HAVE A DREAM •

*Martin Luther King, Jr. (1929–1968), American clergyman and black civil rights leader, was born in Atlanta and educated at Morehouse College, Crozer Theological Seminary, and Boston University (Ph.D., 1955). A lifelong advocate of nonviolent resistance to segregation, he led a boycott of blacks in Montgomery, Alabama (1955–1956) against the city's segregated bus system and organized a massive march on Washington in 1963, during which he delivered his famous "I Have a Dream" speech. In 1964 he was awarded the Nobel Peace Prize. Dr. King was assassinated April 4, 1968, on the balcony of a motel in Memphis, Tennessee, where he had journeyed in support of the city's striking sanitation workers.*

*In August 1963, more than two hundred thousand blacks and whites gathered peacefully in Washington, D.C., to focus attention on black demands for civil rights. The marchers gathered at the Lincoln Memorial, where Dr. King delivered this impassioned speech.*

Five score years ago, a great American, in whose symbolic shadow we stand today, signed the Emancipation Proclamation. This momentous decree came as a great beacon of light of hope to millions of Negro slaves who had been seared in the flames of withering injustice. It came as a joyous daybreak to end the long night of their captivity.

But one hundred years later, the Negro still is not free. One hundred years later, the life of the Negro is still sadly crippled by the manacles of segregation and the chains of discrimination.

One hundred years later, the Negro lives on a lonely island of poverty in the midst of a vast ocean of material prosperity. One hundred years later, the Negro is still languished in the corners of American society and finds himself an exile in his own land. So we have come here today to dramatize a shameful condition.

In a sense we have come to our nation's capital to cash a check. When the architects of our republic wrote the magnificent words of the Constitution and the Declaration of Independence, they were signing a promissory note to which every American was to fall heir. This note was a promise that all men, yes, black men as well as white men, would be granted the unalienable rights of life, liberty, and the pursuit of happiness.

It is obvious today that America has defaulted on this promissory note insofar as her citizens of color are concerned. Instead of honoring this sacred obligation, America has given the Negro people a bad check; which has come back marked "insufficient funds."

But we refuse to believe that the bank of justice is bankrupt. We refuse to believe that there are insufficient funds in the great vaults of opportunity of this nation. So we have come to cash this check—a check that will give us upon demand the riches of freedom and the security of justice.

We have also come to this hallowed spot to remind America of the fierce urgency of now. This is no time to engage in the luxury of cooling off or to take the tranquilizing drug of gradualism. Now is the time to make real the promises of democracy. Now is the time to rise from the dark and desolate valley of segregation to the sunlit path of racial justice. Now is the time to lift our nation from the quick sands of racial injustice to the solid rock of brotherhood. Now is the time to make justice a reality for all of God's children.

It would be fatal for the nation to overlook the urgency of the movement and to underestimate the determination of the Negro. This sweltering summer of the Negro's legitimate discontent will not pass until there is an invigorating autumn of freedom and equality. 1963 is not an end but a beginning. Those who hope that the Negro needed to blow off steam and will now be content will have a rude awakening if the nation returns to business as usual.

There will be neither rest nor tranquility in America until the Negro   9
is granted his citizenship rights. The whirlwinds of revolt will continue to shake the foundations of our nation until the bright day of justice emerges.

But there is something that I must say to my people who stand on   10
the warm threshold which leads into the palace of justice. In the process of gaining our rightful place we must not be guilty of wrongful deeds.

Let us not seek to satisfy our thirst for freedom by drinking from   11
the cup of bitterness and hatred. We must forever conduct our struggle on the high plane of dignity and discipline. We must not allow our creative protest to degenerate into physical violence. Again and again we must rise to the majestic heights of meeting physical force with soul force.

The marvelous new militancy which has engulfed the Negro com-   12
munity must not lead us to a distrust of all white people, for many of our white brothers, as evidenced by their presence here today, have come to realize that their destiny is tied up with our destiny and they have come to realize that their freedom is inextricably bound to our freedom. This offense we share mounted to storm the battlements of injustice must be carried forth by a biracial army. We cannot walk alone.

And as we walk, we must make the pledge that we shall always   13
march ahead. We cannot turn back. There are those who are asking the devotees of civil rights, "When will you be satisfied?" We can never be satisfied as long as the Negro is the victim of the unspeakable horrors of police brutality.

We can never be satisfied as long as our bodies, heavy with the   14
fatigue of travel, cannot gain lodging in the motels of the highways and the hotels of the cities. We cannot be satisfied as long as the Negro's basic mobility is from a smaller ghetto to a larger one.

We can never be satisfied as long as our children are stripped of   15
their selfhood and robbed of their dignity by signs stating "for whites only." We cannot be satisfied as long as a Negro in Mississippi cannot vote and a Negro in New York believes he has nothing for which to vote. No, we are not satisfied, and we will not be satisfied until justice rolls down like waters and righteousness like a mighty stream.

I am not unmindful that some of you have come here out of excessive    16
trials and tribulation. Some of you have come fresh from narrow jail
cells. Some of you have come from areas where your quest for freedom
left you battered by the storms of persecution and staggered by the
winds of police brutality. You have been the veterans of creative suffering. Continue to work with the faith that unearned suffering is
redemptive.

Go back to Mississippi; go back to Alabama; go back to South Car-    17
olina; go back to Georgia; go back to Louisiana; go back to the slums
and ghettos of the Northern cities, knowing that somehow this situation can, and will be changed. Let us not wallow in the valley of
despair.

So I say to you, my friends, that even though we must face the    18
difficulties of today and tomorrow, I still have a dream. It is a dream
deeply rooted in the American dream that one day this nation will rise
up and live out the true meaning of its creed—we hold these truths to
be self evident, that all men are created equal.

I have a dream that one day on the red hills of Georgia, sons of    19
former slaves and sons of former slave-owners will be able to sit down
together at the table of brotherhood.

I have a dream that one day, even the state of Mississippi, a state    20
sweltering with the heat of injustice, sweltering with the heat of
oppression, will be transformed into an oasis of freedom and justice.

I have a dream my four little children will one day live in a nation    21
where they will not be judged by the color of their skin but by content
of their character. I have a dream today!

I have a dream that one day, down in Alabama, with its vicious    22
racists, with its governor having his lips dripping with the words of
interposition and nullification, that one day, right there in Alabama,
little black boys and black girls will be able to join hands with little
white boys and white girls as sisters and brothers. I have a dream
today!

I have a dream that one day every valley shall be exalted, every hill    23
and mountain shall be made low, the rough places shall be made plain,
and the crooked places shall be made straight and the glory of the Lord
will be revealed and all flesh shall see it together.

This is our hope. This is the faith that I go back to the South with.    24

With this faith we will be able to hew out of the mountain of despair    25
a stone of hope. With this faith we will be able to transform the jan-
gling discords of our nation into a beautiful symphony of brotherhood.

With this faith we will be able to work together, to pray together, to    26
struggle together, to go to jail together, to stand up for freedom together, knowing that we will be free one day. This will be the day when
all of God's children will be able to sing with new meaning—"my
country 'tis of thee; sweet land of liberty; of thee I sing; land where my
fathers died, land of the pilgrim's pride; from every mountain side, let
freedom ring"—and if America is to be a great nation, this must become true.

So let freedom ring from the prodigious hilltops of New Hampshire.    27
Let freedom ring from the mighty mountains of New York.    28
Let freedom ring from the heightening Alleghenies of Pennsylvania.    29
Let freedom ring from the snow-capped Rockies of Colorado.    30
Let freedom ring from the curvaceous slopes of California.    31
But not only that.    32
Let freedom ring from Stone Mountain of Georgia.    33
Let freedom ring from Lookout Mountain of Tennessee.    34
Let freedom ring from every hill and molehill of Mississippi, from    35
every mountainside, let freedom ring.

And when we allow freedom to ring, when we let it ring from every    36
village and hamlet, from every state and city, we will be able to speed
up that day when all of God's children    black men and white men,
Jews and Gentiles, Catholics and Protestants—will be able to join
hands and to sing in the words of the old Negro spiritual. "Free at last,
free at last; thank God Almighty, we are free at last."

## VOCABULARY

| | | |
|---|---|---|
| momentous (1) | invigorating (8) | sweltering (20) |
| manacles (2) | degenerate (11) | interposition (22) |
| languished (3) | militancy (12) | nullification (22) |
| unalienable (4) | inextricably (12) | exalted (23) |
| hallowed (7) | tribulation (16) | prodigious (27) |
| gradualism (7) | redemptive (16) | curvaceous (31) |

## THE FACTS

1. The speech begins "Five score years ago, . . ." Why was this beginning
   especially appropriate?
2. What grievances of black Americans does Dr. King summarize in paragraphs 2 and 3 of this speech?
3. What does Dr. King caution his listeners against in paragraph 11?

4. What attitude toward white people does the speaker urge upon his audience?
5. Although Dr. King speaks out mainly against injustices committed against blacks in the South, he is also critical of the North. What can be inferred from this speech about the living conditions of blacks in the North during the early 1960s?

## THE STRATEGIES

1. One critic has written of this speech that its purpose was to intensify the values of the black movement. What characteristic of its style can you point to that might be said to have served this purpose?
2. Paragraphs 4 through 6 of the speech are linked through the use of an extended analogy. What is this analogy?
3. What common rhetorical device does the speech frequently use to emphasize its points?
4. It is often said that speakers and writers use paragraphs differently. How are the paragraphs of this speech especially adapted for oral delivery? What is the most obvious difference between these paragraphs and the ones a writer might use?
5. What is the function of the brief paragraph 32?

## THE ISSUES

1. Since *black* is a term widely used in the United States to designate people whose skin color may range from dark brown to sepia, what definition of blackness does our society seem implicitly to use?
2. What, in your opinion, is the basis of racial prejudice?
3. Will the United States ever have a black president? Defend your answer.
4. Does prejudice in the United States against black men exceed or equal the prejudice against black women? Explain the difference, if there is one, and justify your answer.
5. What stereotypes do you hold about black people? Write them down along with an explanation of how you arrived at them. Share them with your classmates.

## SUGGESTIONS FOR WRITING

1. Write an essay analyzing the extensive use of metaphors in this speech. Comment on their effectiveness, bearing in mind the audience for whom the speech was intended.
2. Write an essay analyzing the oral style of this speech. Point out specific techniques of phrasing, sentence construction, paragraphing, and so on, that identify this composition as a speech. Suggest how a writer might have alternately phrased some passages if this work had been written to be read rather than delivered.

Joan Didion

# ———— • WHY I WRITE • ————

*Joan Didion (b. 1934) is a California-born writer known for her graceful, pointed style. Educated at the University of California, Berkeley, she has been a feature editor at* Vogue, *a columnist for the* Saturday Review, *and a contributing editor of the* National Review. *Among her books are three novels—*Run River *(1963),* Play It As It Lays *(1971), and* A Book of Common Prayer *(1977)— and a collection of essays,* Slouching Towards Bethlehem *(1969). With her husband, John Gregory Dunne, Didion coauthored the screenplay for the movie* True Confessions.

*Why do writers write? Sooner or later, most writers of note take a stab at explaining the forces that drove them to their art. As might be expected, the explanations are as varied as literary plots and styles. Our favorite is the reply given by Agatha Christie, that past master of the whodunnit, when asked why she wrote murder mysteries: "One does what one can, not what one can't." Didion's explanation of why she writes is adapted from a Regents' lecture delivered by the author at the University of California, Berkeley.*

Of course I stole the title for this talk from George Orwell. One 1
reason I stole it was that I like the sound of the words: *Why I Write.*
There you have three short unambiguous words that share a sound,
and the sound they share is this:

*I*

*I*

*I*

In many ways writing is the act of saying *I*, of imposing oneself 2
upon other people, of saying *listen to me, see it my way, change your mind.*
It's an aggressive, even a hostile act. You can disguise its aggressiveness all you want with veils of subordinate clauses and qualifiers and
tentative subjunctives, with ellipses and evasions—with the whole
manner of intimating rather than claiming, of alluding rather than
stating—but there's no getting around the fact that setting words on
paper is the tactic of a secret bully, an invasion, an imposition of the
writer's sensibility on the reader's most private space.

I stole the title not only because the words sounded right but be- 3
cause they seemed to sum up, in a no-nonsense way, all I have to tell
you. Like many writers I have only this one "subject," this one "area":
the act of writing. I can bring you no reports from any other front. I
may have other interests: I am "interested," for example, in marine

biology, but I don't flatter myself that you would come out to hear me talk about it. I am not a scholar. I am not in the least an intellectual, which is not to say that when I hear the word "intellectual" I reach for my gun, but only to say that I do not think in abstracts. During the years when I was an undergraduate at Berkeley I tried, with a kind of hopeless late-adolescent energy, to buy some temporary visa into the world of ideas, to forge for myself a mind that could deal with the abstract.

In short I tried to think. I failed. My attention veered inexorably back    4 to the specific, to the tangible, to what was generally considered, by everyone I knew then and for that matter have known since, the peripheral. I would try to contemplate the Hegelian dialectic and would find myself concentrating instead on a flowering pear tree outside my window and the particular way the petals fell on my floor. I would try to read linguistic theory and would find myself wondering instead if the lights were on in the bevatron up the hill. When I say that I was wondering if the lights were on in the bevatron you might immediately suspect, if you deal in ideas at all, that I was registering the bevatron as a political symbol, thinking in shorthand about the military-industrial complex and its role in the university community, but you would be wrong. I was only wondering if the lights were on in the bevatron, and how they looked. A physical fact.

I had trouble graduating from Berkeley, not because of this inability    5 to deal with ideas—I was majoring in English, and I could locate the house-and-garden imagery in "The Portrait of a Lady" as well as the next person, "imagery" being by definition the kind of specific that got my attention—but simply because I had neglected to take a course in Milton. For reasons which now sound baroque I needed a degree by the end of that summer, and the English department finally agreed, if I would come down from Sacramento every Friday and talk about the cosmology of "Paradise Lost," to certify me proficient in Milton. I did this. Some Fridays I took the Greyhound bus, other Fridays I caught the Southern Pacific's City of San Francisco on the last leg of its transcontinental trip. I can no longer tell you whether Milton put the sun or the earth at the center of his universe in "Paradise Lost," the central question of at least one century and a topic about which I wrote 10,000 words that summer, but I can still recall the exact rancidity of the butter in the City of San Francisco's dining car, and the way the tinted windows on the Greyhound bus cast the oil refineries around

Carquinez Straits into a grayed and obscurely sinister light. In short my attention was always on the periphery, on what I could see and taste and touch, on the butter, and the Greyhound bus. During those years I was traveling on what I knew to be a very shaky passport, forged papers: I knew that I was no legitimate resident in any world of ideas. I knew I couldn't think. All I knew then was what I couldn't do. All I knew was what I wasn't, and it took me some years to discover what I was.

Which was a writer.                                                                6

By which I mean not a "good" writer or a "bad" writer but simply    7
a writer, a person whose most absorbed and passionate hours are spent arranging words on pieces of paper. Had my credentials been in order I would never have become a writer. Had I been blessed with even limited access to my own mind there would have been no reason to write. I write entirely to find out what I'm thinking, what I'm look-ing at, what I see and what it means. What I want and what I fear. Why did the oil refineries around Carquinez Straits seem sinister to me in the summer of 1956? Why have the night lights in the bevatron burned in my mind for twenty years? *What is going on in these pictures in my mind?*

When I talk about pictures in my mind I am talking, quite specifi-    8
cally, about images that shimmer around the edges. There used to be an illustration in every elementary psychology book showing a cat drawn by a patient in varying stages of schizophrenia. This cat had a shimmer around it. You could see the molecular structure breaking down at the very edges of the cat: the cat became the background and the background the cat, everything interacting, exchanging ions. Peo-ple on hallucinogens describe the same perception of objects. I'm not a schizophrenic, nor do I take hallucinogens, but certain images do shimmer for me. Look hard enough, and you can't miss the shimmer. It's there. You can't think too much about these pictures that shimmer. You just lie low and let them develop. You stay quiet. You don't talk to many people and you keep your nervous system from shorting out and you try to locate the cat in the shimmer, the grammar in the picture.

Just as I meant "shimmer" literally I mean "grammar" literally.    9
Grammar is a piano I play by ear, since I seem to have been out of school the year the rules were mentioned. All I know about grammar is its infinite power. To shift the structure of a sentence alters the

meaning of that sentence, as definitely and inflexibly as the position of a camera alters the meaning of the object photographed. Many people know about camera angles now, but not so many know about sentences. The arrangement of the words matters, and the arrangement you want can be found in the picture in your mind. The picture dictates the arrangement. The picture dictates whether this will be a sentence with or without clauses, a sentence that ends hard or a dying-fall sentence, long or short, active or passive. The picture tells you how to arrange the words and the arrangement of the words tells you, or tells me, what's going on in the picture. *Nota bene:*

It tells you.                                                                  10

You don't tell it.                                                             11

Let me show you what I mean by pictures in the mind. I began "Play    12
It As It Lays" just as I have begun each of my novels, with no notion of "character" or "plot" or even "incident." I had only two pictures in my mind, more about which later, and a technical intention, which was to write a novel so elliptical and fast that it would be over before you noticed it, a novel so fast that it would scarcely exist on the page at all. About the pictures: the first was of white space. Empty space. This was clearly the picture that dictated the narrative intention of the book—a book in which anything that happened would happen off the page, a "white" book to which the reader would have to bring his or her own bad dreams—and yet this picture told me no "story," suggested no situation. The second picture did. This second picture was of something actually witnessed. A young woman with long hair and a short white halter dress walks through the casino at the Riviera in Las Vegas at one in the morning. She crosses the casino alone and picks up a house telephone. I watch her because I have heard her paged, and recognize her name; she is a minor actress I see around Los Angeles from time to time, in places like Jax and once in a gynecologist's office in the Beverly Hills Clinic, but have never met. I know nothing about her. Who is paging her? Why is she here to be paged? How exactly did she come to this? It was precisely this moment in Las Vegas that made "Play It As It Lays" begin to tell itself to me, but the moment appears in the novel only obliquely, in a chapter which begins:

"Maria made a list of things she would never do. She would never:    13
walk through the Sands or Caesar's alone after midnight. She would never: ball at a party, do S-M unless she wanted to, borrow furs from Abe Lipsey, deal. She would never: carry a Yorkshire in Beverly Hills."

That is the beginning of the chapter and that is also the end of the    14
chapter, which may suggest what I meant by "white space."

I recall having a number of pictures in my mind when I began the    15
novel I just finished, "A Book of Common Prayer." As a matter of fact
one of these pictures was of that bevatron I mentioned, although I
would be hard put to tell you a story in which nuclear energy figured.
Another was a newspaper photograph of a hijacked 707 burning on
the desert in the Middle East. Another was the night view from a room
in which I once spent a week with paratyphoid, a hotel room on the
Colombian coast. My husband and I seemed to be on the Colombian
coast representing the United States of America at a film festival (I
recall invoking the name "Jack Valenti" a lot, as if its reiteration could
make me well), and it was a bad place to have fever, not only because
my indisposition offended our hosts but because every night in this
hotel the generator failed. The lights went out. The elevator stopped.
My husband would go to the event of the evening and make excuses
for me and I would stay alone in this hotel room, in the dark. I remember standing at the window trying to call Bogotá (the telephone
seemed to work on the same principle as the generator) and watching
the night wind come up and wondering what I was doing eleven
degrees off the equator with a fever of 103. The view from that window
definitely figures in "A Book of Common Prayer," as does the burning
707, and yet none of these pictures told me the story I needed.

The picture that did, the picture that shimmered and made these    16
other images coalesce, was the Panama airport at 6 A.M. I was in this
airport only once, on a plane to Bogotá that stopped for an hour to
refuel, but the way it looked that morning remained superimposed on
everything I saw until the day I finished "A Book of Common Prayer."
I lived in that airport for several years. I can still feel the hot air when I
step off the plane, can see the heat already rising off the tarmac at 6
A.M. I can feel my skirt damp and wrinkled on my legs. I can feel the
asphalt stick to my sandals. I remember the big tail of a Pan American
plane floating motionless down at the end of the tarmac. I remember
the sound of a slot machine in the waiting room. I could tell you that I
remember a particular woman in the airport, an American woman, a
*norteamericana*, a thin *norteamericana* about 40 who wore a big square
emerald in lieu of a wedding ring, but there was no such woman there.

I put this woman in the airport later. I made this woman up, just as    17
I later made up a country to put the airport in, and a family to run the

country. This woman in the airport is neither catching a plane nor meeting one. She is ordering tea in the airport coffee shop. In fact she is not simply "ordering" tea but insisting that the water be boiled, in front of her, for twenty minutes. Why is this woman in this airport? Why is she going nowhere, where has she been? Where did she get that big emerald? What derangement, or disassociation, makes her believe that her will to see the water boiled can possibly prevail?

"She had been going to one airport or another for four months, one    18 could see it, looking at the visas on her passport. All those airports where Charlotte Douglas's passport had been stamped would have looked alike. Sometimes the sign on the tower would say 'Bienvenidos' and sometimes the sign on the tower would say 'Bienvenue,' some places were wet and hot and others dry and hot, but at each of these airports the pastel concrete walls would rust and stain and the swamp off the runway would be littered with the fuselages of cannibalized Fairchild F-227's and the water would need boiling.

"I knew why Charlotte went to the airport even if Victor did not.    19

"I knew about airports."    20

These lines appear about halfway through "A Book of Common    21 Prayer," but I wrote them during the second week I worked on the book, long before I had any idea where Charlotte Douglas had been or why she went to airports. Until I wrote these lines I had no character called "Victor" in mind: the necessity for mentioning a name, and the name "Victor," occurred to me as I wrote the sentence. *I knew why Charlotte went to the airport* sounded incomplete. *I knew why Charlotte went to the airport even if Victor did not* carried a little more narrative drive. Most important of all, until I wrote these lines I did not know who "I" was, who was telling the story. I had intended until that moment that the "I" be no more than the voice of the author, a 19th-century omniscient narrator. But there it was:

"I knew why Charlotte went to the airport even if Victor did not.    22

"I knew about airports."    23

This "I" was the voice of no author in my house. This "I" was    24 someone who not only knew why Charlotte went to the airport but also knew someone called "Victor." Who was Victor? Who was this narrator? Why was this narrator telling me this story? Let me tell you one thing about why writers write: had I known the answer to any of these questions I would never have needed to write a novel.

## VOCABULARY

unambiguous (1)
tentative (2)
intimating (2)
alluding (2)
sensibility (9)
inexorably (4)
tangible (4)
peripheral (4)

Hegelian (4)
dialectic (4)
bevatron (4)
baroque (5)
cosmology (5)
proficient (5)
rancidity (5)
obscurely (5)

*nota bene* (9)
elliptical (12)
obliquely (12)
reiteration (15)
coalesce (16)
derangement (17)
omniscient (21)

## THE FACTS

1. How is writing a hostile, aggressive act?
2. To what inability in her thinking does Didion ascribe her career as a writer?
3. How does Didion regard grammar?
4. What pictures gave rise to the author's novel, *A Book of Common Prayer*?
5. According to the author, why do writers finally write?

## THE STRATEGIES

1. In the very beginning of her speech, what assumptions does Didion make about her audience? Why is it helpful to a writer or speaker to make similar assumptions about an audience?
2. This "essay" was originally delivered as a speech. What characteristics of its style are distinctly oral rather than literary?
3. How does Didion support her assertion (in paragraph 4) that she was not capable of thinking in abstracts, but only in specifics?
4. Examine paragraphs 6, 10, and 11. What do these paragraphs have in common? How can you account for their unusual structure?
5. What specific detail does Didion use to exemplify her method of composing? How convincing did you find these details?
6. In paragraph 7, Didion qualifies her assertion about discovering that she was a writer by saying that she does not mean a "good" or a "bad" writer. Why do you think she makes this qualification?

## THE ISSUES

1. How does Didion's method of composing differ from yours?
2. What obvious limitations exist in Didion's method of composing that make it impracticable for everyday writing?
3. What overriding purpose seems to be behind Didion's fiction as implied in her method of composition?

4. What advantages do you think a writer would have writing a novel from the viewpoint of "I"?
5. If Didion is right, if writers ply their trade as unconsciously as she implies, do you think that writers perhaps get more credit than they deserve?

### SUGGESTIONS FOR WRITING

1. Write an essay about how easy, hard, pleasurable, agonizing, troublesome, or other it is for you to write.
2. Write an essay of appreciation about any writer's work you especially enjoy. Be specific.

**Ernest Hemingway**

# ——— • A CLEAN, WELL-LIGHTED PLACE • ———

*Ernest Hemingway (1899–1961), one of America's foremost novelists and short-story writers, was born in Oak Park, Illinois, the son of a country doctor. His influence on the evolution of a modern writing style was matchless among twentieth-century writers. Publication in 1926 of his celebrated novel* The Sun Also Rises *accorded Hemingway recognition as a spokesman for the so-called lost generation (as dubbed by Gertrude Stein) of postwar American expatriates living mainly in Paris. His other well-known novels include* A Farewell to Arms *(1929),* For Whom the Bell Tolls *(1940), and* The Old Man and the Sea *(1952). He died by his own hand in 1961.*

*"A Clean, Well-Lighted Place," written in a style of compelling directness characteristic of Hemingway, tells the story of men so rhetorically isolated by a haunting nothingness that they are unable to communicate with one another and even with God.*

It was late and every one had left the café except an old man who    1
sat in the shadow the leaves of the tree made against the electric light. In the day time the street was dusty, but at night the dew settled the dust and the old man liked to sit late because he was deaf and now at night it was quiet and he felt the difference. The two waiters inside the café knew that the old man was a little drunk, and while he was a good client they knew that if he became too drunk he would leave without paying, so they kept watch on him.

"Last week he tried to commit suicide," one waiter said.    2

"Why?"    3

"He was in despair."    4

"What about?"    5

"Nothing."    6

"How do you know it was nothing?"    7

"He has plenty of money."    8

They sat together at a table that was close against the wall near the    9
door of the café and looked at the terrace where the tables were all
empty except where the old man sat in the shadow of the leaves of the
tree that moved slightly in the wind. A girl and a soldier went by in
the street. The street light shone on the brass number on his collar.
The girl wore no head covering and hurried beside him.

"The guard will pick him up," one waiter said.    10

"What does it matter if he gets what he's after?"    11

"He had better get off the street now. The guard will get him. They    12
went by five minutes ago."

The old man sitting in the shadow rapped on his saucer with his    13
glass. The younger waiter went over to him.

"What do you want?"    14

The old man looked at him. "Another brandy," he said.    15

"You'll be drunk," the waiter said. The old man looked at him. The    16
waiter went away.

"He'll stay all night," he said to his colleague. "I'm sleepy now. I    17
never get into bed before three o'clock. He should have killed himself
last week."

The waiter took the brandy bottle and another saucer from the    18
counter inside the café and marched out to the old man's table. He put
down the saucer and poured the glass full of brandy.

"You should have killed yourself last week," he said to the deaf man.    19
The old man motioned with his finger. "A little more," he said. The
waiter poured on into the glass so that the brandy slopped over and
ran down the stem into the top saucer of the pile. "Thank you," the
old man said. The waiter took the bottle back inside the café. He sat
down at the table with his colleague again.

"He's drunk now," he said.    20

"He's drunk every night."    21

"What did he want to kill himself for?"    22

"How should I know."    23

"How did he do it?"    24

"He hung himself with a rope."    25

"Who cut him down?"    26

"His niece."    27

"Why did they do it?"    28

"Fear for his soul."    29

"How much money has he got?"    30

"He's got plenty."    31

"He must be eighty years old."    32

"Anyway I should say he was eighty."    33

"I wish he would go home. I never get to bed before three o'clock.    34
What kind of hour is that to go to bed?"

"He stays up because he likes it."    35

"He's lonely. I'm not lonely. I have a wife waiting in bed for me."    36

"He had a wife once too."    37

"A wife would be no good to him now."    38

"You can't tell. He might be better with a wife."    39

"His niece looks after him. You said she cut him down."    40

"I know."    41

"I wouldn't want to be that old. An old man is a nasty thing."    42

"Not always. This old man is clean. He drinks without spilling. Even    43
now, drunk. Look at him."

"I don't want to look at him. I wish he would go home. He has no    44
regard for those who must work."

The old man looked from his glass across the square, then over at    45
the waiters.

"Another brandy," he said, pointing to his glass. The waiter who    46
was in a hurry came over.

"Finished," he said, speaking with that omission of syntax stupid    47
people employ when talking to drunken people or foreigners. "No
more tonight. Close now."

"Another," said the old man.    48

"No. Finished." The waiter wiped the edge of the table with a towel    49
and shook his head.

The old man stood up, slowly counted the saucers, took a leather    50
coin purse from his pocket and paid for the drinks, leaving half a
peseta tip.

The waiter watched him go down the street, a very old man walking    51
unsteadily but with dignity.

"Why didn't you let him stay and drink?" the unhurried waiter    52
asked. They were putting up the shutters. "It is not half-past two."

"I want to go home to bed." 53

"What is an hour?" 54

"More to me than to him." 55

"An hour is the same." 56

"You talk like an old man yourself. He can buy a bottle and drink 57
at home."

"It's not the same." 58

"No, it is not," agreed the waiter with a wife. He did not wish to be 59
unjust. He was only in a hurry.

"And you? You have no fear of going home before your usual hour?" 60

"Are you trying to insult me?" 61

"No, hombre, only to make a joke." 62

"No," the waiter who was in a hurry said, rising from pulling down 63
the metal shutters. "I have confidence. I am all confidence."

"You have youth, confidence, and a job," the older waiter said. "You 64
have everything."

"And what do you lack?" 65

"Everything but work." 66

"You have everything I have." 67

"No. I have never had confidence and I am not young." 68

"Come on. Stop talking nonsense and lock up." 69

"I am of those who like to stay late at the café," the older waiter said. 70
"With all those who do not want to go to bed. With all those who need
a light for the night."

"I want to go home and into bed." 71

"We are of two different kinds," the older waiter said. He was now 72
dressed to go home. "It is not only a question of youth and confidence
although those things are very beautiful. Each night I am reluctant to
close up because there may be some one who needs the café."

"Hombre, there are bodegas open all night long." 73

"You do not understand. This is a clean and pleasant café. It is well 74
lighted. The light is very good and also, now, there are shadows of the
leaves."

"Good night," said the younger waiter. 75

"Good night," the other said. Turning off the electric light he contin- 76
ued the conversation with himself. It is the light of course but it is
necessary that the place be clean and pleasant. You do not want music.
Certainly you do not want music. Nor can you stand before a bar with
dignity although that is all that is provided for these hours. What did
he fear? It was not fear or dread. It was a nothing that he knew too

well. It was all a nothing and a man was nothing too. It was only that and light was all it needed and a certain cleanness and order. Some lived in it and never felt it but he knew it all was nada y pues nada y nada y pues nada. Our nada who art in nada, nada be thy name thy kingdom nada thy will be nada in nada as it is in nada. Give us this nada our daily nada and nada us our nada as we nada our nadas and nada us not into nada but deliver us from nada; pues nada. Hail nothing full of nothing, nothing is with thee. He smiled and stood before a bar with a shining steam pressure coffee machine.

"What's yours?" asked the barman.                                          77

"Nada."                                                                     78

"Otro loco mas," said the barman and turned away.                           79

"A little cup," said the waiter.                                            80

The barman poured it for him.                                               81

"The light is very bright and pleasant but the bar is unpolished,"          82
the waiter said.

The barman looked at him but did not answer. It was too late at             83
night for conversation.

"You want another copita?" the barman asked.                                84

"No, thank you," said the waiter and went out. He disliked bars and         85
bodegas. A clean, well-lighted café was a very different thing. Now, without thinking further, he would go home to his room. He would lie in the bed and finally, with daylight, he would go to sleep. After all, he said to himself, it is probably only insomnia. Many must have it.

## THE FACTS

1. What did the old man unsuccessfully attempt to do the week before?
2. Why is the younger of the two waiters in such a hurry?
3. Why are the waiters worried about the old man getting drunk?
4. What prayer does the older waiter parody?
5. What does the older waiter think he suffers from?

## THE STRATEGIES

1. Why did Hemingway omit all names for the principal characters of this story? What significance does this omission have on your interpretation of this story?
2. What place, time, and under what conditions does this story unfold? How does Hemingway manage to suggest facts about place, time, and condition with such brief exposition?

3. Along what continuum are the three characters of this short story implicitly arranged? What does Hemingway imply by this arrangement?
4. The younger waiter says, "An old man is a nasty thing," to which the older replies, "Not always. This old man is clean." What do you think the first waiter meant by the "nasty thing" remark?
5. What rhetorical relationship is implied in Hemingway's depiction of the two waiters?

### THE ISSUES

1. What implication about the needs of the elderly does this story make? What, in your opinion, do the elderly need in order to spend their last years in peace and dignity?
2. The young waiter is brusque and rude with the old man. What is Hemingway's attitude toward this impatient waiter? What is your own attitude toward him?
3. "What is an hour?" asks the older waiter. "More to me than to him," the younger replies. Do you think that time passes equally for everyone, no matter what age, as the older waiter implies, or do you agree with the attitude of the younger waiter? Why?
4. What consolation, if any, do you think religion offers the elderly? What effects is the lack of religion likely to have on an elderly person?
5. Should the old man's niece have cut him down for the sake of his soul, or should she have let him die by his own choice? Justify your answer.

### SUGGESTIONS FOR WRITING

1. Write an analysis of the issues about aging and the elderly that are raised in this story.
2. Using this story as principal source, write an analysis of Hemingway's writing style.

# ═══ •• ISSUE FOR CRITICAL •• ═══ THINKING

## Legalized Abortions

On January 22, 1973, the U.S. Supreme Court ruled in *Roe v. Wade* (410 U.S. 113) that a state may not prevent a woman from having an abortion during her first six months of pregnancy. The decision overturned the antiabortion laws of Texas and Georgia and, by implication, other states as well. In the year following that historic decision, 763,476 legal abortions were performed in the United States, one of them on the author of the pro-choice article featured in this debate. Between 1973 and 1981, according to the Centers for Disease Control, 7,614,659 abortions were carried out in the fifty states. Today, well over a million legal abortions are reported each year in the United States.

Since the ruling in *Roe v. Wade*, the topic of legalized abortions has been fiercely debated. Opposition has come mainly from religious groups, based on their convictions about the sanctity of all human life. Proponents argue that it is a woman's right to choose whether or not to abort an unwanted pregnancy and that the state has no business interfering. The first side calls itself "pro-life"; the second, "pro-choice."

In the following selections, we present three sides of this issue. First there is the judgment of the Supreme Court in *Roe v. Wade* itself. A close reading of this decision reveals that the Court did not at all embrace the principle, so ardently proposed by feminists, that a woman has an absolute right "to terminate her pregnancy at any time, in whatever way, and for whatever reason she chooses." Said the Court bluntly: "With this we do not agree." Rather, the Court's decision is founded on a more delicate principle—a woman's right to privacy, which permits her to decide, in consultation with her doctor, whether or not to terminate an unwanted pregnancy.

The second affirmation of this right is made by a writer, Linda Bird Francke, who herself underwent a legal abortion in 1973 and afterward described the experience in a moving article. Published on the opinion page of the *New York Times* under the title, "There Just Wasn't Room in Our Lives for Another Baby," the article generated so many letters that Francke was asked to reply. What started out as an article eventually became a book, *The Ambivalence of Abortion* (1978), whose title reflects Francke's own position on this controversial subject.

Finally, there is the essay by Ronald Reagan, the fortieth president of the United States, which he wrote while in office. President Reagan is decidedly not ambivalent; he is flatly against abortion, which he has opposed in categorical terms since the *Roe v. Wade* decision. His argument against abortion appeals to constitutional law as well as to personal morality.

Few issues of conscience can be severely drawn in black and white, certainly not one as morally complex as abortion. As in all debates, the writers take their stands and make their cases. What is left is for the reader to choose intelligently among them.

## ———— • *FROM ROE V. WADE* • ————
### 410 U.S. 113 (1973)

*The decision below is heavily excerpted with most or all the references to legal precedents excised and much of the technical discussions of subsidiary issues* removed. *Nevertheless, it still demonstrates the reasoning used by the Supreme Court in striking down the Texas law that banned abortions. The decision of the Court, seven to two in favor of overturning the Texas law, was delivered by Justice Harry T. Blackmun.*

## IV

Jane Roe, a single woman who was residing in Dallas County, Texas, instituted this federal action in March 1970 against the District Attorney of the county. She sought a declaratory judgment that the Texas criminal abortion statutes were unconstitutional on their face, and an injunction restraining the defendant from enforcing the statutes. [1]

Roe alleged that she was unmarried and pregnant; that she wished to terminate her pregnancy by an abortion "performed by a competent, licensed physician, under safe, clinical conditions"; that she was unable to get a "legal" abortion in Texas because her life did not appear to be threatened by the continuation of her pregnancy; and that she could not afford to travel to another jurisdiction in order to secure a legal abortion under safe conditions. She claimed that the Texas statutes were unconstitutionally vague and that they abridged her right of personal privacy, protected by the First, Fourth, Fifth, Ninth, and Fourteenth Amendments. . . . [2]

## V

The principal thrust of appellant's attack on the Texas statutes is that they improperly invade a right, said to be possessed by the pregnant woman, to choose to terminate her pregnancy. Appellant would discover this right in the concept of personal "liberty" embodied in the Fourteenth Amendment's Due Process Clause; or in personal, marital, familial, and sexual privacy said to be protected by the Bill of Rights or its penumbras. . . . Before addressing this claim, we feel it desirable briefly to survey, in several aspects, the history of abortion, for such insight as that history may afford us, and then to examine the state purposes and interests behind the criminal abortion laws. [3]

## VI

It perhaps is not generally appreciated that the restrictive criminal abortion laws in effect in a majority of States today are of relatively recent vintage. Those laws, generally proscribing abortion or its attempt at any time during pregnancy except when necessary to pre- [4]

serve the pregnant woman's life, are not of ancient or even of common-law origin. Instead, they derive from statutory changes effected, for the most part, in the latter half of the 19th century.

1. *Ancient attitudes.* These are not capable of precise determination.    5 We are told that at the time of the Persian Empire abortifacients were known and that criminal abortions were severely punished. We are also told, however, that abortion was practiced in Greek times as well as in the Roman Era, and that "it was resorted to without scruple." The Ephesian, Soranos, often described as the greatest of the ancient gynecologists, appears to have been generally opposed to Rome's prevailing free-abortion practices. He found it necessary to think first of the life of the mother, and he resorted to abortion when, upon this standard, he felt the procedure advisable. Greek and Roman law afforded little protection to the unborn. If abortion was prosecuted in some places, it seems to have been based on a concept of a violation of the father's right to his offspring. Ancient religion did not bar abortion.

2. *The Hippocratic Oath.* What then of the famous Oath that has stood    6 so long as the ethical guide of the medical profession and that bears the name of the great Greek (460[?]–377[?]B.C.), who has been described as the Father of Medicine, the "wisest and the greatest practitioner of his art," and the "most important and most complete medical personality of antiquity," who dominated the medical schools of his time, and who typified the sum of the medical knowledge of the past? The Oath varies somewhat according to the particular translation, but in any translation the content is clear: "I will give no deadly medicine to anyone if asked, nor suggest any such counsel; and in like manner I will not give to a woman a pessary to produce abortion," or "I will neither give a deadly drug to anybody if asked for it, nor will I make a suggestion to this effect. Similarly, I will not give to a woman an abortive remedy."

Although the Oath is not mentioned in any of the principal briefs in    7 this case or in *Doe v. Bolton,* . . . it represents the apex of the development of strict ethical concepts in medicine, and its influence endures to this day. Why did not the authority of Hippocrates dissuade abortion practice in his time and that of Rome? The late Dr. Edelstein provides us with a theory: The Oath was not uncontested even in Hippocrates' day; only the Pythagorean school of philosophers frowned upon the related act of suicide. Most Greek thinkers, on the other hand, commended abortion, at least prior to viability. See Plato, Republic, V, 461; Aristotle, Politics, VII, 1335b 25. For the Pythagoreans, however, it was a matter of dogma. For them the embryo was animate from the moment of conception, and abortion meant destruction of a living being. The abortion clause of the Oath, therefore, "echoes Pythagorean doctrines," and "[i]n no other stratum of Greek opinion were such views held or proposed in the same spirit of uncompromising austerity."

Dr. Edelstein then concludes that the Oath originated in a group   8
representing only a small segment of Greek opinion and that it certainly was not accepted by all ancient physicians. He points out that medical writings down to Galen (A.D. 130–200) "give evidence of the violation of almost every one of its injunctions." But with the end of antiquity a decided change took place. Resistance against suicide and against abortion became common. The Oath came to be popular. The emerging teachings of Christianity were in agreement with the Pythagorean ethic. The Oath "became the nucleus of all medical ethics" and "was applauded as the embodiment of truth." Thus, suggests Dr. Edelstein, it is "a Pythagorean manifesto and not the expression of an absolute standard of medical conduct."

This, it seems to us, is a satisfactory and acceptable explanation of   9
the Hippocratic Oath's apparent rigidity. It enables us to understand, in historical context, a long-accepted and revered statement of medical ethics.

3. *The common law.* It is undisputed that at common law, abortion   10
performed *before* "quickening"—the first recognizable movement of the fetus *in utero*,* appearing usually from the 16th to the 18th week of pregnancy—was not an indictable offense. The absence of a common-law crime for pre-quickening abortion appears to have developed from a confluence of earlier philosophical, theological, and civil and canon law concepts of when life begins. These disciplines variously approached the question in terms of the point at which the embryo or fetus became "formed" or recognizably human, or in terms of when a "person" came into being, that is, infused with a "soul" or "animated." A loose consensus evolved in early English law that these events occurred at some point between conception and live birth. This was "mediate animation." Although Christian theology and the canon law came to fix the point of animation at 40 days for a male and 80 days for a female, a view that persisted until the 19th century, there was

---

*"In the uterus."—Ed.

otherwise little agreement about the precise time of formation or animation. There was agreement, however, that prior to this point the fetus was to be regarded as part of the mother, and its destruction, therefore, was not homicide. Due to continued uncertainty about the precise time when animation occurred, to the lack of any empirical basis for the 40–80-day view, and perhaps to Aquinas's definition of movement as one of the two first principles of life, Bracton focused upon quickening as the critical point. The significance of quickening was echoed by later common-law scholars and found its way into the received common law in this country. . . .

Gradually, in the middle and late 19th century the ["]quickening["]     11
distinction disappeared from the statutory law of most States and the degree of the offense and the penalties were increased. By the end of the 1950s, a large majority of the jurisdictions banned abortion, however and whenever performed, unless done to save or preserve the life of the mother. The exceptions, Alabama and the District of Columbia, permitted abortion to preserve the mother's health. Three States permitted abortions that were not "unlawfully" performed or that were not "without lawful justification," leaving interpretation of those standards to the courts. In the past several years, however, a trend toward liberalization of abortion statutes has resulted in adoption, by about one-third of the States, of less stringent laws, . . .

It is thus apparent that at common law, at the time of the adoption     12
of our Constitution, and throughout the major portion of the 19th century, abortion was viewed with less disfavor than under most American statutes currently in effect. Phrasing it another way, a woman enjoyed a substantially broader right to terminate a pregnancy than she does in most States today. At least with respect to the early stage of pregnancy, and very possibly without such a limitation, the opportunity to make this choice was present in this country well into the 19th century. Even later, the law continued for some time to treat less punitively an abortion procured in early pregnancy. . . .

## VIII

The Constitution does not explicitly mention any right of privacy. In     13
a line of decisions, however, going back perhaps as far as *Union Pacific R. Co. v. Botsford*, . . . (1891), the Court has recognized that a right of personal privacy, or a guarantee of certain areas or zones of privacy, does exist under the Constitution. . . .

This right of privacy, whether it be founded in the Fourteenth 14
Amendment's concept of personal liberty and restrictions upon state
action, as we feel it is, or, as the District Court determined, in the
Ninth Amendment's reservation of rights to the people, is broad
enough to encompass a woman's decision whether or not to terminate
her pregnancy. The detriment that the State would impose upon the
pregnant woman by denying this choice altogether is apparent. Specific and direct harm medically diagnosable even in early pregnancy
may be involved. Maternity, or additional offspring, may force upon
the woman a distressful life and future. Psychological harm may be
imminent. Mental and physical health may be taxed by child care.
There is also the distress, for all concerned, associated with the unwanted child, and there is the problem of bringing a child into a family
already unable, psychologically and otherwise, to care for it. In other
cases, as in this one, the additional difficulties and continuing stigma
of unwed motherhood may be involved. All these are factors the
woman and her responsible physician necessarily will consider in
consultation.

On the basis of elements such as these, appellant and some *amici** 15
argue that the woman's right is absolute and that she is entitled to
terminate her pregnancy at whatever time, in whatever way, and for
whatever reason she alone chooses. With this we do not agree. Appellant's arguments that Texas either has no valid interest at all in regulat-
ing the abortion decision, or no reason strong enough to support any
limitation upon the woman's sole determination, are unpersuasive.
The Court's decisions recognizing a right of privacy also acknowledge
that some state regulation in areas protected by that right is appropriate. As noted above, a State may properly assert important interests in
safeguarding health, in maintaining medical standards, and in protecting potential life. At some point in pregnancy, these respective
interests become sufficiently compelling to sustain regulation of the
factors that govern the abortion decision. The privacy right involved,
therefore, cannot be said to be absolute. In fact, it is not clear to us that
the claim asserted by some *amici* that one has an unlimited right to do
with one's body as one pleases bears a close relationship to the right of
privacy previously articulated in the Court's decisions. The Court has
refused to recognize an unlimited right of this kind in the past. . . .

---

*Latin, "friends," from *amicus curiae*, or "friend of the the court," an interested party but not a party to the
case.—Ed.

We, therefore, conclude that the right of personal privacy includes   16
the abortion decision, but that this right is not unqualified and must
be considered against important state interests in regulation. . . .

### IX

A. The appellee and certain *amici* argue that the fetus is a "person"   17
within the language and meaning of the Fourteenth Amendment. In
support of this, they outline at length and in detail the well-known
facts of fetal development. If this suggestion of personhood is established, the appellant's case, of course, collapses, for the fetus's right to
life would then be guaranteed specifically by the Amendment. The
appellant conceded as much on reargument. On the other hand, the
appellee conceded on reargument that no case could be cited that
holds that a fetus is a person within the meaning of the Fourteenth
Amendment.

The Constitution does not define "person" in so many words. Sec-   18
tion 1 of the Fourteenth Amendment contains three references to "person." The first, in defining "citizens," speaks of "persons born or
naturalized in the United States." The word also appears both in the
Due Process Clause and in the Equal Protection Clause. "Person" is
used in other places in the Constitution: . . .

But in nearly all these instances, the use of the word is such that it   19
has application only postnatally. None indicates, with any assurance,
that it has any possible pre-natal application. All this, together with
our observation, *supra*,* that throughout the major portion of the 19th
century prevailing legal abortion practices were far freer than they are
today, persuades us that the word "person," as used in the Fourteenth
Amendment, does not include the unborn. . . . This conclusion, however, does not of itself fully answer the contentions raised by Texas,
and we pass on to other considerations.

B. The pregnant woman cannot be isolated in her privacy. She car-   20
ries an embryo and, later, a fetus, if one accepts the medical definitions
of the developing young in the human uterus. . . . The situation therefore is inherently different from marital intimacy, or bedroom possession of obscene material, or marriage, or procreation, or education,
with which *Eisenstadt* and *Griswold, Stanley, Loving, Skinner* and *Pierce*
and *Meyer* were respectively concerned. As we have intimated above,

---

*Latin, "above."—Ed.

it is reasonable and appropriate for a State to decide that at some point in time another interest, that of health of the mother or that of potential human life, becomes significantly involved. The woman's privacy is no longer sole and any right of privacy she possesses must be measured accordingly.

Texas urges that, apart from the Fourteenth Amendment, life begins    21 at conception and is present throughout pregnancy, and that, therefore, the State has a compelling interest in protecting that life from and after conception. We need not resolve the difficult question of when life begins. When those trained in the respective disciplines of medicine, philosophy, and theology are unable to arrive at any consensus, the judiciary, at this point in the development of man's knowledge, is not in a position to speculate as to the answer.

It should be sufficient to note briefly the wide divergence of thinking    22 on this most sensitive and difficult question. There has always been strong support for the view that life does not begin until live birth. This was the belief of the Stoics. It appears to be the predominant, though not the unanimous, attitude of the Jewish faith. It may be taken to represent also the position of a large segment of the Protestant community, insofar as that can be ascertained; organized groups that have taken a formal position on the abortion issue have generally regarded abortion as a matter for the conscience of the individual and her family. As we have noted, the common law found greater significance in quickening. Physicians and their scientific colleagues have regarded that event with less interest and have tended to focus either upon conception, upon live birth, or upon the interim point at which the fetus becomes "viable," that is, potentially able to live outside the mother's womb, albeit with artificial aid. Viability is usually placed at about seven months (28 weeks) but may occur earlier, even at 24 weeks. The Aristotelian theory of "mediate animation," that held sway throughout the Middle Ages and the Renaissance in Europe, continued to be official Roman Catholic dogma until the 19th century, despite opposition to this "ensoulment" theory from those in the Church who would recognize the existence of life from the moment of conception. The latter is now, of course, the official belief of the Catholic Church. As one brief *amicus* discloses, this is a view strongly held by many non-Catholics as well, and by many physicians. Substantial problems for precise definition of this view are posed, however, by new embryological data that purport to indicate that conception is a "process" over time, rather than an event, and by new medical techniques such as menstrual extraction, the "morning-after" pill, implantation of embryos, artificial insemination, and even artificial wombs. . . .

## X

In view of all this, we do not agree that, by adopting one theory of life, Texas may override the rights of the pregnant woman that are at stake. We repeat, however, that the State does have an important and legitimate interest in preserving and protecting the health of the pregnant woman, whether she be a resident of the State or a nonresident who seeks medical consultation and treatment there, and that it has still *another* important and legitimate interest in protecting the potentiality of human life. These interests are separate and distinct. Each grows in substantiality as the woman approaches term and, at a point during pregnancy, each becomes "compelling."  23

With respect to the State's important and legitimate interest in the health of the mother, the "compelling" point, in the light of present medical knowledge, is at approximately the end of the first trimester. This is so because of the now-established medical fact, referred to above . . . , that until the end of the first trimester mortality in abortion may be less than mortality in normal childbirth. It follows that, from and after this point, a State may regulate the abortion procedure to the extent that the regulation reasonably relates to the preservation and protection of maternal health. Examples of permissible state regulation in this area are requirements as to the qualifications of the person who is to perform the abortion; as to the licensure of that person; as to the facility in which the procedure is to be performed, that is, whether it must be a hospital or may be a clinic or some other place of less-than-hospital status; as to the licensing of the facility; and the like.  24

This means, on the other hand, that, for the period of pregnancy prior to this "compelling" point, the attending physician, in consultation, with his patient, is free to determine, without regulation by the State, that, in his medical judgment, the patient's pregnancy should be terminated. If that decision is reached, the judgment may be effectuated by an abortion free of interference by the State. . . .  25

## *VOCABULARY*

| | | |
|---|---|---|
| penumbras (3) | austerity (7) | detriment (14) |
| proscribing (4) | injunctions (8) | imminent (14) |

| | | |
|---|---|---|
| abortifacients (5) | indictable (10) | procreation (20) |
| pessary (6) | confluence (10) | divergence (22) |
| dissuade (7) | empirical (10) | substantiality (23) |
| viability (7) | punitively (12) | effectuated (25) |
| dogma (7) | encompass (14) | |

## THE FACTS

1. What basic claim did Jane Roe make in her suit to overturn the Texas statute that banned abortions?
2. According to the Supreme Court, exactly when did the laws banning abortion mainly come into effect?
3. What explanation does the Court advance of the Hippocratic Oath's rigid proscription of abortion?
4. What does the Court mean by "quickening"? When does the first sign of quickening generally appear?
5. What theory of life did Texas adopt that the Court disagreed with?

## THE STRATEGIES

1. Why do you think the Court's decision began with a summary of historical attitudes toward abortion?
2. What are some characteristics of its language that give this decision an appropriately formal style?
3. What function is served by the brief paragraph 19?
4. What is the common rhetorical purpose of paragraphs 17 through 19?
5. Throughout the decision the Court cites multiple opinions from a variety of legal and medical experts. Why was this citing of expert opinion necessary in a legal decision supposedly based on an interpretation of the Constitution?

## THE ISSUES

1. Some conservatives argue that the Constitution should be interpreted literally and not in the light of prevailing knowledge and opinion. How do you think the decision in *Roe v. Wade* might have gone had the Court interpreted the Constitution strictly by the letter?
2. What is meant by "ensoulment" as the term applies to the beginning of life? What does ensoulment imply about the nature of human life?
3. Based on your reading of the Constitution, can you think of any inferred right that might entitle a father to have a say in a mother's decision to abort?
4. In a subsequent decision, the Court upheld the sodomy laws of Georgia and decreed that states do have the power to pass and enforce such laws. What, if any, inconsistency do you see between that decision and the one handed down in *Roe v. Wade*?

5. Paragraph 22 discusses the various theories of when life begins. Which theory do you subscribe to, and how does it affect your own views on abortion?

### SUGGESTIONS FOR WRITING

1. Write an essay that carefully examines and sums up the Supreme Court's medical attitude toward pregnancy and the unborn as reflected in this decision. Refer specifically to the decision itself.
2. Write an essay attacking or defending the Court's decision that "person" as used in the Constitution can have only postnatal application.

### Linda Bird Francke

## • THE RIGHT TO CHOOSE •

*Writer and author Linda Bird Francke (b. 1939) was born in New York City and attended Bradford Junior College. She has worked as a contributing editor to* Newsweek *and, since 1972, has been that magazine's general editor for New York City. Her published books include* The Ambivalence of Abortion *(1978), from which this excerpt has been taken, and* Father and Daughters *(1980).*

"Jane Doe," thirty-eight, had an abortion in New York City in 1973. 1 The mother of three children, then three, five, and eleven, Jane had just started a full-time job in publishing. She and her husband, an investment banker, decided together that another baby would add an almost unbearable strain to their lives, which were already overfull. What Jane had not anticipated was the guilt and sadness that followed the abortion. She wrote about the experience shortly thereafter and filed the story away. Three years later she reread it and decided it might be helpful to other women who experience the ambivalence of abortion. The *New York Times* ran it on their Op-Ed page in May 1976. This is what she wrote:

We were sitting in a bar on Lexington Avenue when I told my hus- 2 band I was pregnant. It is not a memory I like to dwell on. Instead of the champagne and hope which had heralded the impending births of the first, second, and third child, the news of this one was greeted with shocked silence and Scotch. "Jesus," my husband kept saying to himself, stirring the ice cubes around and around. "Oh, Jesus."

Oh, how we tried to rationalize it that night as the starting time for 3 the movie came and went. My husband talked about his plans for a career change in the next year, to stem the staleness that fourteen years with the same investment-banking firm had brought him. A new baby would preclude that option.

The timing wasn't right for me either. Having juggled pregnancies and child care with what freelance jobs I could fit in between feedings, I had just taken on a full-time job. A new baby would put me right back in the nursery just when our youngest child was finally school age. It was time for *us*, we tried to rationalize. There just wasn't room in our lives now for another baby. We both agreed. And agreed. And agreed.

How very considerate they are at the Women's Services, known formally as the Center for Reproductive and Sexual Health. Yes, indeed, I could have an abortion that very Saturday morning and be out in time to drive to the country that afternoon. Bring a first morning urine specimen, a sanitary belt and napkins, a money order or $125 cash—and a friend.

My friend turned out to be my husband, standing awkwardly and ill at ease as men always do in places that are exclusively for women, as I checked in at nine A.M. Other men hovered around just as anxiously, knowing they had to be there, wishing they weren't. No one spoke to each other. When I would be cycled out of there four hours later, the same men would be slumped in their same seats, locked downcast in their cells of embarrassment.

The Saturday morning women's group was more dispirited than the men in the waiting room. There were around fifteen of us, a mixture of races, ages and backgrounds. Three didn't speak English at all and a fourth, a pregnant Puerto Rican girl around eighteen, translated for them.

There were six black women and a hodge-podge of whites, among them a T-shirted teenager who kept leaving the room to throw up and a puzzled middle-aged woman from Queens with three grown children.

"What form of birth control were you using?" the volunteer asked each one of us. The answer was inevitably "none." She then went on to describe the various forms of birth control available at the clinic, and offered them to each of us.

The youngest Puerto Rican girl was asked through the interpreter which she'd like to use: the loop, diaphragm, or pill. She shook her head "no" three times. "You don't want to come back here again, do you?" the volunteer pressed. The girl's head was so low her chin rested on her breastbone. "Sí," she whispered.

We had been there two hours by that time, filling out endless forms, giving blood and urine, receiving lectures. But unlike any other group of women I've been in, we didn't talk. Our common denominator, the one which usually floods across language and economic barriers into

4

5

6

7

8

9

10

11

familiarity, today was one of shame. We were losing life that day, not giving it.

The group kept getting cut back to smaller, more workable units, and finally I was put in a small waiting room with just two other women. We changed into paper bathrobes and paper slippers, and we rustled whenever we moved. One of the women in my room was shivering and an aide brought her a blanket.    12

"What's the matter?" the aide asked her. "I'm scared," the woman said. "How much will it hurt?" The aide smiled. "Oh, nothing worse than a couple of bad cramps," she said. "This afternoon you'll be danc- ing a jig."    13

I began to panic. Suddenly the rhetoric, the abortion marches I'd walked in, the telegrams sent to Albany to counteract the Friends of the Fetus, the Zero Population Growth buttons I'd worn, peeled away, and I was all alone with my microscopic baby. There were just the two of us there, and soon, because it was more convenient for me and my hus- band, there would be one again.    14

How could it be that I, who am so neurotic about life that I step over bugs rather than on them, who spend hours planting flowers and vege- tables in the spring even though we rent out the house and never see them, who make sure the children are vaccinated and inoculated and filled with vitamin C, could so arbitrarily decide that this life shouldn't be?    15

"It's not a life," my husband had argued, more to convince himself than me. "It's a bunch of cells smaller than my fingernail."    16

But any woman who has had children knows that certain feeling in her taut, swollen breasts, and the slight but constant ache in her uterus that signals the arrival of a life. Though I would march myself into blisters for a woman's right to exercise the option of motherhood, I discovered there in the waiting room that I was not the modern woman I thought I was.    17

When my name was called, my body felt so heavy the nurse had to help me into the examining room. I waited for my husband to burst through the door and yell "stop," but of course he didn't. I concentrated on three black spots in the acoustic ceiling until they grew in size to the shape of saucers, while the doctor swabbed my insides with antiseptic.    18

"You're going to feel a burning sensation now," he said, injecting Novocaine into the neck of the womb. The pain was swift and severe, and I twisted to get away from him. He was hurting my baby, I reasoned, and the black saucers quivered in the air. "Stop," I cried. "Please stop." He shook his head, busy with his equipment. "It's too late to stop now," he said. "It'll just take a few more seconds."    19

What good sports we women are. And how obedient. Physically the   20
pain passed even before the hum of the machine signaled that the vac-
uuming of my uterus was completed, my baby sucked up like ashes
after a cocktail party. Ten minutes start to finish. And I was back on the
arm of the nurse.

There were twelve beds in the recovery room. Each one had a gaily   21
flowered draw sheet and a soft green or blue thermal blanket. It was all
very feminine. Lying on these beds for an hour or more were the
shocked victims of their sex, their full wombs now stripped clean, their
futures less encumbered.

It was very quiet in that room. The only voice was that of the nurse,   22
locating the new women who had just come in so she could monitor
their blood pressure, and checking out the recovered women who were
free to leave.

Juice was being passed about, and I found myself sipping a Dixie cup   23
of Hawaiian Punch. An older woman with tightly curled bleached hair
was just getting up from the next bed, "That was no goddamn snap,"
she said, resting before putting on her miniskirt and high white boots.
Other women came and went, some walking out as dazed as they had
entered, others with a bounce that signaled they were going right back
to Bloomingdale's.

Finally then, it was time for me to leave. I checked out, making an   24
appointment to return in two weeks for an IUD insertion. My husband
was slumped in the waiting room, clutching a single yellow rose
wrapped in a wet paper towel and stuffed into a baggie.

We didn't talk the whole way home, but just held hands very tightly.   25
At home there were more yellow roses and a tray in bed for me and the
children's curiosity to divert.

It had certainly been a successful operation. I didn't bleed at all for   26
two days just as they had predicted, and then I bled only moderately for
another four days. Within a week my breasts had subsided and the
tenderness vanished, and my body felt mine again instead of the egg-
shell it becomes when it's protecting someone else.

My husband and I are back to planning our summer vacation and his   27
career switch.

And it certainly does make more sense not to be having a baby right   28
now—we say that to each other all the time. But I have this ghost now.
A very little ghost that only appears when I'm seeing something beautiful, like the full moon on the ocean last weekend. And the baby waves
at me. And I wave at the baby. "Of course, we have room," I cry to the
ghost. "Of course, we do."

I am "Jane Doe." Using a pseudonym was not the act of cowardice    29
some have said it was, but rather an act of sympathy for the feelings of
my family. My daughters were too young then to understand what an
abortion was, and my twelve-year-old son (my husband's stepson)
reacted angrily when I even broached the subject of abortion to him.
Andrew was deeply moralistic, as many children are at that age, and
still young enough to feel threatened by the actions of adults; his
replies to my "suppose I had an abortion" queries were devastating.
"I think abortion is okay if the boy and girl aren't married, and they
just made a mistake," he said. "But if you had an abortion, that would
be different. You're married, and there is no reason for you not to have
another baby. How could you just kill something—no matter how little
it is—that's going to grow and have legs and wiggle its fingers?

"I would be furious with you if you had an abortion. I'd lose all    30
respect for you for being so selfish. I'd make you suffer and remind
you of it all the time. I would think of ways to be mean. Maybe I'd give
you the silent treatment or something.

"If God had meant women to have abortions, He would have put    31
buttons on their stomachs."

I decided to wait until he was older before we discussed it again.    32

There were other considerations as well. My husband and I had    33
chosen not to tell our parents about the abortion. My mother was very
ill at the time and not up to a barrage of phone calls from her friends
about "what Linda had written in the newspaper." And there were my
parents-in-law, who had always hoped for a male grandchild to carry
on the family name. So I avoided the confessional and simply wrote
what I thought would be a helpful piece for other women who might
have shared my experience.

The result was almost great enough to be recorded on a seismo-    34
graph. Interpreting the piece as anti-abortion grist, the Right-to-Lifers
reproduced it by the thousands and sent it to everyone on their mailing
lists. In one Catholic mailing, two sentences were deleted from the
article: one that said I was planning to return to the clinic for an IUD
insertion, and the other the quote from a middle-aged woman, "That
was no goddamn snap." Papers around the country and in Canada
ran it, culminating in its appearance in the Canadian edition of the
*Reader's Digest*, whose staff took it upon their editorial selves to delete
the last paragraph about the "little ghost" because they considered it
"mawkish." They also changed the title from "There Just Wasn't Room

in Our Lives for Another Baby" to "A Successful Operation" in hopes that it would change their magazine's pro-abortion image.

Hundreds of letters poured into the *New York Times*, some from Right-to-Lifers, who predictably called me a "murderer," and others from pro-choice zealots who had decided the article was a "plant" and might even have been written by a man. Women wrote about their own abortions, some of which had been positive experiences and some disastrous. One woman even wrote that she wished her own mother had had an abortion instead of subjecting her to a childhood that was "brutal and crushing." Many of the respondents criticized me, quite rightly, for not using birth control in the first place. I was stunned, and so was the *New York Times*. A few weeks later they ran a sampling of the letters and my reply, which follows:

> The varied reactions to my abortion article do not surprise me at all. They are all right. And they are all wrong. There is no issue so fundamental as the giving of life, or the cessation of it. These decisions are the most personal one can ever make and each person facing them reacts in her own way. It is not black-and-white as the laws governing abortion are forced to be. Rather it is the gray area whose core touches our definition of ourselves that produces "little ghosts" in some, and a sense of relief in others.

> I admire the woman who chose not to bear her fourth child because she and her husband could not afford to give that child the future they felt necessary. I admire the women who were outraged that I had failed to use any form of contraception. And I ache for the woman whose mother had given birth to her even though she was not wanted, and thus spent an empty, lonely childhood. It takes courage to take the life of someone else in your own hands, and even more courage to assume responsibility for your own.

> I had my abortion over two years ago. And I wrote about it shortly thereafter. It was only recently, however, that I decided to publish it. I felt it was important to share how one person's abortion had affected her, rather than just sit by while the pro and con groups haggled over legislation.

> The effect has indeed been profound. Though my husband was very supportive of me, and I, I think, of him, our relationship slowly faltered. As our children are girls, my husband anguished at the possibility that I had been carrying a son. Just a case of male macho, many would argue. But still, that's the way he feels, and it is important. I hope we can get back on a loving track again.

Needless to say, I have an IUD now, instead of the diaphragm that is    40
too easily forgotten. I do not begrudge my husband his lack of contra-
ception. Condoms are awkward. Neither do I feel he should have a
vasectomy. It is profoundly difficult for him to face the possibility that
he might never have that son. Nor do I regret having the abortion. I am
just as much an avid supporter of children by choice as I ever was.

My only regret is the sheer irresponsibility on my part to become    41
pregnant in the first place. I pray to God that it will never happen again.
But if it does, I will be equally thankful that the law provides women the
dignity to choose whether to bring a new life into the world or not.

## VOCABULARY

| | | |
|---|---|---|
| ambivalence (1) | encumbered (21) | zealots (35) |
| impending (2) | pseudonym (29) | cessation (36) |
| rationalize (3) | seismograph (34) | haggled (38) |
| preclude (3) | culminating (34) | faltered (39) |
| dispirited (7) | mawkish (34) | |

## THE FACTS

1. The author admits from the beginning that the idea of an abortion made her squeamish. Why, then, did she and her husband go through with it?
2. According to the author, what common denominator existed between the women waiting to have their abortions performed?
3. What discovery did Francke make about herself as she sat in the waiting room?
4. What did the author hope that her husband would do as she was being led into the operating room? If her husband had done what she had hoped, what difference do you think that might have made?
5. What effect did the abortion have on the author and on her relationship with her husband?
6. In the end, for what was the author grateful?

## THE STRATEGIES

1. One of the reasons that this is such a moving piece is because of its deft use of specific details. What are some examples of these details?
2. In paragraph 4, how does the author make it clear that the decision to have an abortion was an agonizing and difficult one for her and her husband?
3. What tone does Francke use in paragraph 5 to describe the abortion clinic? What does her tone reveal about her feelings?

4. What simile does Francke use in paragraph 20 to describe the abortion itself? Is this an effective image? Why or why not?
5. The description of the abortion was originally published as a newspaper article. What characteristics of its style identify it as being written for a newspaper?

## THE ISSUES

1. Should the biological father be consulted in a woman's decision to have an abortion? Why or why not?
2. Francke's twelve-year-old son maintained that he could understand an unmarried woman who made a mistake having an abortion, but not a married woman. What is your view of his opinion?
3. Francke asks: "How could it be that I, who am so neurotic about life that I step over bugs rather than on them, who spend hours planting flowers and vegetables in the spring even though we rent out the house and never see them, who make sure the children are vaccinated and inoculated and filled with vitamin C, could so arbitrarily decide that this life shouldn't be?" What answer can you give to this question?
4. Francke writes that in the waiting room she discovered she was not the modern woman she thought she was. By implication, what is her definition of a modern woman?
5. Since abortion is legal and freely chosen, why do you think the women in the waiting room felt shame, as Francke alleges?

## SUGGESTIONS FOR WRITING

1. Write an essay stating your own views on abortion as persuasively as you can.
2. Write an essay analyzing the imagery and language Francke uses to describe the abortion experience. Deduce what they tell about her own "ambivalent" feelings.

### Ronald Reagan

# —— • ABORTION AND THE CONSCIENCE • ——
# OF THE NATION

*Ronald Reagan (b. 1911), fortieth president of the United States, was born in Tampico, Illinois. A former movie actor, he served six terms as president of the Screen Actors Guild and two terms (1966–1974) as governor of California. He was elected to the presidency in 1980 as the Republican candidate, beating Jimmy Carter in a landslide and becoming the first politician since 1932 to unseat an incumbent President. Reagan won reelection to a second term in 1984 with an unprecedented trouncing of the Democratic challenger, Walter Mondale.*

The 10th Anniversary of the Supreme Court decision in *Roe v. Wade* is a good time for us to pause and reflect. Our nationwide policy of abortion-on-demand through all nine months of pregnancy was neither voted for by our people nor enacted by our legislators—not a single State had such unrestricted abortion before the Supreme Court decreed it to be national policy in 1973. But the consequences of this judicial decision are now obvious: since 1973, more than 15 million unborn children have had their lives snuffed out by legalized abortions. That is over ten times the number of Americans lost in all our nation's wars.

Make no mistake, abortion-on-demand is not a right granted by the Constitution. No serious scholar, including one disposed to agree with the Court's result, has argued that the framers of the Constitution intended to create such a right. Shortly after the *Roe v. Wade* decision, Professor John Hart Ely, now Dean of Stanford Law School, wrote that the opinion "is not constitutional law and gives almost no sense of an obligation to try to be." Nowhere do the plain words of the Constitution even hint at a "right" so sweeping as to permit abortion up to the time the child is ready to be born. Yet that is what the Court ruled.

As an act of "raw judicial power" (to use Justice White's biting phrase), the decision by the seven-man majority in *Roe v. Wade* has so far been made to stick. But the Court's decision has by no means settled the debate. Instead, *Roe v. Wade* has become a continuing prod to the conscience of the nation.

Abortion concerns not just the unborn child, it concerns every one of us. The English poet, John Donne, wrote: ". . . any man's death diminishes me, because I am involved in mankind; and therefore never send to know for whom the bell tolls; it tolls for thee."

We cannot diminish the value of one category of human life—the unborn—without diminishing the value of all human life. We saw tragic proof of this truism last year when the Indiana courts allowed the starvation death of "Baby Doe" in Bloomington because the child had Down's Syndrome.

Many of our fellow citizens grieve over the loss of life that has   6
followed *Roe v. Wade*. Margaret Heckler, soon after being nominated to
head the largest department of our government, Health and Human
Services, told an audience that she believed abortion to be the greatest
moral crisis facing our country today. And the revered Mother Teresa,
who works in the streets of Calcutta ministering to dying people in
her world-famous mission of mercy, has said that "the greatest misery
of our time is the generalized abortion of children."

Over the first two years of my Administration I have closely followed   7
and assisted efforts in Congress to reverse the tide of abortion—efforts
of Congressmen, Senators and citizens responding to an urgent moral
crisis. Regrettably, I have also seen the massive efforts of those who,
under the banner of "freedom of choice," have so far blocked every
effort to reverse nationwide abortion-on-demand.

Despite the formidable obstacles before us, we must not lose heart.   8
This is not the first time our country has been divided by a Supreme
Court decision that denied the value of certain human lives. The *Dred
Scott* decision of 1857 was not overturned in a day, or a year, or even a
decade. At first, only a minority of Americans recognized and de-
plored the moral crisis brought about by denying the full humanity of
our black brothers and sisters; but that minority persisted in their
vision and finally prevailed. They did it by appealing to the hearts and
minds of their countrymen, to the truth of human dignity under God.
From their example, we know that respect for the sacred value of
human life is too deeply engrained in the hearts of our people to
remain forever suppressed. But the great majority of the American
people have not yet made their voices heard, and we cannot expect
them to—any more than the public voice arose against slavery—*until*
the issue is clearly framed and presented.

What, then, is the real issue? I have often said that when we talk   9
about abortion, we are talking about two lives—the life of the mother
and the life of the unborn child. Why else do we call a pregnant woman
a mother? I have also said that anyone who doesn't feel sure whether
we are talking about a second human life should clearly give life the
benefit of the doubt. If you don't know whether a body is alive or dead,
you would never bury it. I think this consideration itself should be
enough for all of us to insist on protecting the unborn.

The case against abortion does not rest here, however, for medical   10
practice confirms at every step the correctness of these moral sensibil-

ities. Modern medicine treats the unborn child as a patient. Medical pioneers have made great breakthroughs in treating the unborn—for genetic problems, vitamin deficiencies, irregular heart rhythms, and other medical conditions. Who can forget George Will's moving account of the little boy who underwent brain surgery six times during the nine weeks before he was born? Who is the *patient* if not that tiny unborn human being who can feel pain when he or she is approached by doctors who come to kill rather than to cure?

11   The real question today is not when human life begins, but, *What is the value of human life?* The abortionist who reassembles the arms and legs of a tiny baby to make sure all its parts have been torn from its mother's body can hardly doubt whether it is a human being. The real question for him and for all of us is whether that tiny human life has a God-given right to be protected by the law—the same right we have.

12   What more dramatic confirmation could we have of the real issue than the Baby Doe case in Bloomington, Indiana? The death of that tiny infant tore at the hearts of all Americans because the child was undeniably a live human being—one lying helpless before the eyes of the doctors and the eyes of the nation. The real issue for the courts was *not* whether Baby Doe was a human being. The real issue was whether to protect the life of a human being who had Down's Syndrome, who would probably be mentally handicapped, but who needed a routine surgical procedure to unblock his esophagus and allow him to eat. A doctor testified to the presiding judge that, even with his physical problem corrected, Baby Doe would have a "nonexistent" possibility for "a minimally adequate quality of life"—in other words, that retardation was the equivalent of a crime deserving the death penalty. The judge let Baby Doe starve and die, and the Indiana Supreme Court sanctioned his decision.

13   Federal law does not allow Federally-assisted hospitals to decide that Down's Syndrome infants are not worth treating, much less to decide to starve them to death. Accordingly, I have directed the Departments of Justice and HHS to apply civil rights regulations to protect handicapped newborns. All hospitals receiving Federal funds must post notices which will clearly state that failure to feed handicapped babies is prohibited by Federal law. The basic issue is whether to value and protect the lives of the handicapped, whether to recognize the sanctity of human life. This is the same basic issue that underlies the question of abortion.

The 1981 Senate hearings on the beginning of human life brought    14
out the basic issue more clearly than ever before. The many medical
and scientific witnesses who testified disagreed on many things, but
not on the *scientific* evidence that the unborn child is alive, is a distinct
individual, or is a member of the human species. They did disagree
over the *value* question, whether to give value to a human life at its
early and most vulnerable stages of existence.

Regrettably, we live at a time when some persons do *not* value all    15
human life. They want to pick and choose which individuals have
value. Some have said that only those individuals with "consciousness
of self" are human beings. One such writer has followed this deadly
logic and concluded that "shocking as it may seem, a newly born infant
is not a human being."

A Nobel Prize winning scientist has suggested that if a handicapped    16
child "were not declared fully human until three days after birth, then
all parents could be allowed the choice." In other words, "quality
control" to see if newly born human beings are up to snuff.

Obviously, some influential people want to deny that every human    17
life has intrinsic, sacred worth. They insist that a member of the human race must have certain qualities before they accord him or her
status as a "human being."

Events have borne out the editorial in a California medical journal    18
which explained three years before *Roe v. Wade* that the social acceptance of abortion is a "defiance of the long-held Western ethic of intrinsic and equal value for every human life regardless of its stage,
condition, or status."

Every legislator, every doctor, and every citizen needs to recognize    19
that the real issue is whether to affirm and protect the sanctity of all
human life, or to embrace a social ethic where some human lives are
valued and others are not. As a nation, we must choose between the
sanctity of life ethic and the quality of life ethic.

I have no trouble identifying the answer our nation has always given    20
to this basic question, and the answer that I hope and pray it will give
in the future. America was founded by men and women who shared a
vision of the value of each and every individual. They stated this vision
clearly from the very start in the Declaration of Independence, using
words that every schoolboy and schoolgirl can recite:

We hold these truths to be self-evident, that all men are created equal, that they are endowed by their Creator with certain unalienable rights, that among these are life, liberty, and the pursuit of happiness.

We fought a terrible war to guarantee that one category of man-    21
kind—black people in America—could not be denied the inalienable rights with which their Creator endowed them. The great champion of the sanctity of all human life in that day, Abraham Lincoln, gave us his assessment of the Declaration's purpose. Speaking of the framers of that noble document, he said:

> This was their majestic interpretation of the economy of the Universe. This was their lofty, and wise, and noble understanding of the justice of the Creator to His creatures. Yes, gentlemen, to all His creatures, to the whole great family of man. In their enlightened belief, nothing stamped with the divine image and likeness was sent into the world to be trodden on . . . They grasped not only the whole race of man then living, but they reached forward and seized upon the farthest posterity. They erected a beacon to guide their children and their children's children, and the countless myriads who should inhabit the earth in other ages.

He warned also of the danger we would face if we closed our eyes    22
to the value of life in any category of human beings:

> I should like to know if taking this old Declaration of Independence, which declares that all men are equal upon principle and making exceptions to it where will it stop. If one man says it does not mean a Negro, why not another say it does not mean some other man?

When Congressman John A. Bingham of Ohio drafted the Four-    23
teenth Amendment to guarantee the rights of life, liberty, and property to all human beings, he explained that *all* are "entitled to the protection of American law, because its divine spirit of equality declares that all men are created equal." He said the rights guaranteed by the amendment would therefore apply to "any human being." Justice William Brennan, writing in another case decided only the year before *Roe v. Wade*, referred to our society as one that "strongly affirms the sanctity of life."

Another William Brennan—not the Justice—has reminded us of the    24
terrible consequences that can follow when a nation rejects the sanctity of life ethic:

> The cultural environment for a human holocaust is present whenever

any society can be misled into defining individuals as less than human and therefore devoid of value and respect.

As a nation today, we have *not* rejected the sanctity of human life. 25 The American people have not had an opportunity to express their view on the sanctity of human life in the unborn. I am convinced that Americans do not want to play God with the value of human life. It is not for us to decide who is worthy to live and who is not. Even the Supreme Court's opinion in *Roe v. Wade* did not explicitly reject the traditional American idea of intrinsic worth and value in all human life; it simply dodged this issue.

The Congress has before it several measures that would enable our 26 people to reaffirm the sanctity of human life, even the smallest and the youngest and the most defenseless. The Human Life Bill expressly recognizes the unborn as human beings and accordingly protects them as persons under our Constitution. This bill, first introduced by Senator Jesse Helms, provided the vehicle for the Senate hearings in 1981 which contributed so much to our understanding of the real issue of abortion.

The Respect Human Life Act, just introduced in the 98th Congress, 27 states in its first section that the policy of the United States is "to protect innocent life, both before and after birth." This bill, sponsored by Congressman Henry Hyde and Senator Roger Jepsen, prohibits the Federal government from performing abortions or assisting those who do so, except to save the life of the mother. It also addresses the pressing issue of infanticide which, as we have seen, flows inevitably from permissive abortion as another step in the denial of the inviolability of innocent human life.

I have endorsed each of these measures, as well as the more difficult 28 route of constitutional amendment, and I will give these initiatives my full support. Each of them, in different ways, attempts to reverse the tragic policy of abortion-on-demand imposed by the Supreme Court ten years ago. Each of them is a decisive way to affirm the sanctity of human life.

We must all educate ourselves to the reality of the horrors taking 29 place. Doctors today know that unborn children can feel a touch within the womb and that they respond to pain. But how many Americans are aware that abortion techniques are allowed today, in all

50 states, that burn the skin of a baby with a salt solution, in an agonizing death that can last for hours?

Another example: two years ago, the *Philadelphia Inquirer* ran a   30
Sunday special supplement on "The Dreaded Complication." The "dreaded complication" referred to in the article—the complication feared by doctors who perform abortions—is the *survival* of the child despite all the painful attacks during the abortion procedure. Some unborn children *do survive the late-term abortions* the Supreme Court has made legal. Is there any question that these victims of abortion deserve our attention and protection? Is there any question that those who *don't* survive were living human beings before they were killed?

Late-term abortions, especially when the baby survives, but is then   31
killed by starvation, neglect, or suffocation, show once again the link between abortion and infanticide. The time to stop both is now. As my Administration acts to stop infanticide, we will be fully aware of the real issue that underlies the death of babies before and soon after birth.

Our society has, fortunately, become sensitive to the rights and   32
special needs of the handicapped, but I am shocked that physical or mental handicaps of newborns are still used to justify their extinction. This Administration has a Surgeon General, Dr. C. Everett Koop, who has done perhaps more than any other American for handicapped children, by pioneering surgical techniques to help them, by speaking out on the value of their lives, and by working with them in the context of loving families. You will not find his former patients advocating the so-called quality of life ethic.

I know that when the true issue of infanticide is placed before the   33
American people, with all the facts openly aired, we will have no trouble deciding that a mentally or physically handicapped baby has the same intrinsic worth and right to life as the rest of us. As the New Jersey Supreme Court said two decades ago, in a decision upholding the sanctity of human life, "a child need not be perfect to have a worthwhile life."

Whether we are talking about pain suffered by unborn children, or   34
about late-term abortions, or about infanticide, we inevitably focus on the humanity of the unborn child. Each of these issues is a potential rallying point for the sanctity of life ethic. Once we as a nation rally around any one of these issues to affirm the sanctity of life, we will see the importance of affirming this principle across the board.

Malcolm Muggeridge, the English writer, goes right to the heart of    35
the matter: "Either life is always and in all circumstances sacred, or
intrinsically of no account; it is inconceivable that it should be in some
cases the one, and in some the other." The sanctity of innocent human
life is a principle that Congress should proclaim at every opportunity.

It is possible that the Supreme Court itself may overturn its abortion    36
rulings. We need only recall that in *Brown v. Board of Education* the
Court reversed its own earlier "separate-but-equal" decision. I believe
if the Supreme Court took another look at *Roe v. Wade*, and considered
the real issue between the sanctity of life ethic and the quality of life
ethic, it would change its mind once again.

As we continue to work to overturn *Roe v. Wade*, we must also con-    37
tinue to lay the groundwork for a society in which abortion is not the
accepted answer to unwanted pregnancy. Pro-life people have already
taken heroic steps, often at great personal sacrifice, to provide for
unwed mothers. I recently spoke about a young pregnant woman
named Victoria, who said, "In this society we save whales, we save
timber wolves and bald eagles and Coke bottles. Yet, everyone wanted
me to throw away my baby." She has been helped by Sav-a-Life, a
group in Dallas, which provides a way for unwed mothers to preserve
the human life within them when they might otherwise be tempted to
resort to abortion. I think also of House of His Creation in Coatesville,
Pennsylvania, where a loving couple has taken in almost 200 young
women in the past ten years. They have seen, as a fact of life, that the
girls are *not* better off having abortions than saving their babies. I am
also reminded of the remarkable Rossow family of Ellington, Connecticut, who have opened their hearts and their home to nine handicapped adopted and foster children.

The Adolescent Family Life Program, adopted by Congress at the    38
request of Senator Jeremiah Denton, has opened new opportunities
for unwed mothers to give their children life. We should not rest until
our entire society echoes the tone of John Powell in the dedication of
his book, *Abortion: The Silent Holocaust*, a dedication to every woman
carrying an unwanted child: "Please believe that you are not alone.
There are many of us that truly love you, who want to stand at your
side, and help in any way we can." And we can echo the always-
practical woman of faith, Mother Teresa, when she says, "If you don't
want the little child, that unborn child, give him to me." We have so

many families in America seeking to adopt children that the slogan "every child a wanted child" is now the emptiest of all reasons to tolerate abortion.

I have often said we need to join in prayer to bring protection to the     39
unborn. Prayer and action are needed to uphold the sanctity of human life. I believe it will not be possible to accomplish our work, the work of saving lives, "without being a soul of prayer." The famous British Member of Parliament, William Wilberforce, prayed with his small group of influential friends, the "Clapham Sect," for *decades* to see an end to slavery in the British empire. Wilberforce led that struggle in Parliament, unflaggingly, because he believed in the sanctity of human life. He saw the fulfillment of his impossible dream when Parliament outlawed slavery just before his death.

Let his faith and perseverance be our guide. We will never recognize     40
the true value of our own lives until we affirm the value in the life of others, a value of which Malcolm Muggeridge says: ". . . however low it flickers or fiercely burns, it is still a Divine flame which no man dare presume to put out, be his motives ever so humane and enlightened."

Abraham Lincoln recognized that we could not survive as a free     41
land when some men could decide that others were not fit to be free and should therefore be slaves. Likewise, we cannot survive as a free nation when some men decide that others are not fit to live and should be abandoned to abortion or infanticide. My Administration is dedicated to the preservation of America as a free land, and there is no cause more important for preserving that freedom than affirming the transcendent right to life of all human beings, the right without which no other rights have any meaning.

## *VOCABULARY*

| | | |
|---|---|---|
| decreed (1) | intrinsic (17) | explicitly (25) |
| truism (5) | posterity (21) | infanticide (27) |
| deplored (8) | myriads (21) | inviolability (27) |
| sensibilities (10) | holocaust (24) | transcendent (41) |
| sanctioned (12) | devoid (24) | |

## *THE FACTS*

1. What constitutional objection to abortion-on-demand does President Reagan raise?

2. To what other decision of the Supreme Court does the President liken the verdict in *Roe v. Wade*? Is this a fair comparison? Why or why not?
3. According to Reagan, what is the real question in the abortion debate?
4. On what important question did witnesses at the 1981 Senate hearings on the beginning of human life disagree?
5. Reagan argues that abortion-on-demand defies the tradition of a long-held western ethic. What is this ethic?
6. According to Reagan, what is the relationship between abortion and infanticide?

## THE STRATEGIES

1. What rhetorical restraints and problems did Reagan face in writing this article? What advantages did he have?
2. The appeal to authority is an ancient and honorable tactic in argument. Where does the President use this tactic and with what effect?
3. Reagan charges that abortion is a variation on infanticide. What support does he offer in his essay of the link between the two? What is your opinion of this reasoning?
4. How does Reagan use rhetorical questions in this essay? Comment on whether or not this use is stylistically effective.

## THE ISSUES

1. Reagan argues that only prayer will advance the anti-abortionist cause. In her article favoring abortion, Linda Bird Francke gives thanks to God that she had a choice. What part does religious belief play in either side of this debate? Should this issue be decided strictly in secular terms, or should religion play a part in the decision? Why or why not?
2. Reagan says that the real question of the abortion debate is the value of human life. In your view, what is the real question of the abortion debate?
3. Abortion seems an issue dominated by moral relativity, with differing concepts of good and evil coming into open conflict. How would a climate of moral absoluteness, in which everyone subscribed to the same views of good and evil, likely affect the abortion debate?
4. In what way may the abortion debate be said to be a battle of competing definitions?
5. Some moral philosophers have said that no one willingly commits evil, for everyone is striving in a personal way for an internally defined good. How may this concept be applied to the abortion debate?

## SUGGESTIONS FOR WRITING

1. Write an essay comparing and contrasting the decision in the *Dred Scott* case, which denied citizenship to blacks, to the decision in *Roe v. Wade,* which legalized abortions.
2. The argument has often been made that if abortions were ruled illegal, then illegal abortionists would rise once again to wreak a terrible carnage among women. Write an essay for or against this argument.

## CHAPTER WRITING ASSIGNMENTS

1. Select any two paragraphs, one from an article in the *Reader's Digest* and another from an article in *The New Yorker.* Analyze the differences in the language (diction, phrasing, sentence style and length of the paragraph) and speculate on the intended audience of each magazine.
2. Compare and contrast Dr. King's speech with the Reagan essay. Focus primarily on the use of language to convey the writer's purpose.
3. Write an essay in which you explain how you signal intimacy and closeness in the language of your own correspondence.
4. Write an essay on the meaning of rhetoric as exemplified by the selections in this chapter.

# 2
# THE WRITER'S VOICE

# INTRODUCTION: WHAT IS A WRITER'S VOICE?

It is unlikely that any reader of this page does not know what "tone of voice" means when applied to human speech. We all possess a range of speaking tones that we unconsciously inflect to signal moods from despair to cheerfulness. What is even more astonishing is that we alter these speaking tones without even thinking, making sophisticated adjustments to them on the spot. A similar technique is also within the power of writers. A letter to a banker will not sound like a *billet-doux* to a lover, and if it does, then either the banker or the lover is in for trouble. In sum, we do not always write in the same style. Yet mysteries persist: What is a writer's style? How does it differ from the writer's voice?

Unless their object is embezzlement or deceit, most writers do not sit down to write consciously in a certain style. They do, however, try to project a certain voice onto the page. Sometimes this voice is deliberately assumed, but often it is chosen for the writer by the psychology of audience and material, by the need and occasion that make the writing necessary.

Here is an example. You, the boss, sit down to write a memo to your employees. Your position goes to your head, and you write:

> Illumination of the overhead fixtures must be extinguished by the final person exiting the premises.

This notice tells the reader two things. First, it tells the reader to turn out the lights before leaving the room. Second, it tells the reader that you are the boss and you say so. That is not the only kind of notice you could have written. You might, for example, have written this equivalent:

> The last person to leave this room must turn out the overhead lights.

This makes the point but you think it also makes you sound awfully humble.

The difference between these two is not one of content, but of tone or style. It is tone of voice when you are composing the memo, for what you tried to do was not write in a certain style but to sound like the boss; to the reader, however, it is your style. Voice goes in; style comes out: that is the formula to remember.

With some justification, many writing teachers approach voice and style as if they are always related to the writer's psychology. If you had confidence in your authority as the boss, if you really felt comfortable with your power, you wouldn't think it necessary to sound like God in every memo you wrote. So if you must sound like the Almighty in your memos, perhaps it is because you really don't feel at ease with the idea of being the boss. Many similar mishaps of voice or style in student papers can be traced to a psychological uncertainty about the material, to an unconfident attitude, or even to the writer's resistance to the assignment.

Behind this line of thinking lurks that age-old advice instructors often hand out to student writers: "Be yourself." Don't try to write in a voice that is not truly your own; don't try to put on airs in your writing. This is genuinely good advice, for the pompous voice affected by the writer always comes out for the reader as a pompous style. As computer programmers say: "Garbage in, garbage out." "Sincerity in, sincerity out" is also a happier truth.

The articles in this chapter grapple with the perennial problem of voice and style. John R. Trimble tells us how to make our writing more readable; F. L. Lucas tries to pinpoint the meaning of style. Then we are treated to a range of highly individualistic styles, from the lyrical broken English of Bartolomeo Vanzetti to the tongue-in-cheek wit of Mark Twain. The chapter ends with a discussion of what is without question the most explosive issue confronting humankind: nuclear weapons and what to do about them.

## •• *ADVICE* ••

### John R. Trimble

## • TIPS FOR INCREASING YOUR • READABILITY

*John R. Trimble (b. 1940) teaches writing at the University of Texas in Austin. His book* Writing with Style *(1975) continues to be a bestseller because it offers practical advice exemplifying all that its author expounds.*

*The essay that follows offers twenty-six tips for promoting an authentic and readable style of writing.*

Write with the assumption that your reader is a companionable friend    1 with a warm sense of humor and an appreciation of simple straight-forwardness.

Write as if you were actually talking to that friend, but talking with    2 enough leisure to frame your thoughts concisely and interestingly.

If you tack these two tips on the wall in front of your writing desk    3 and make a habit of continually glancing at them, I predict that the

readability quotient of your prose style will take a dramatic leap up-
wards. Here are some additional tips:

Substitute the pronoun *that* for *which* wherever possible. The one is    4
conversational, the other bookish. Reserve *which* for those places
where a comma would normally precede it. Example: "The shortage,
which has now reached critical proportions, is likely to remain a problem." Here the *which* clause merely adds some nonessential information and thus functions as a parenthesis. Contrast to: "The shortage
that he spoke of is likely to remain a problem." Here the *that* clause
serves to specify the particular shortage being referred to: hence it
defines or restricts the subject, "shortage," and mustn't be separated
from it by commas. The rule is: if you can remove a clause without
damaging the sense of the sentence, use *which* and a comma before it.

Use occasional contractions. They'll keep you from taking yourself    5
too seriously, tell your reader that you're not a prude, and help you
achieve a more natural, conversational rhythm in your style. The most
popular contractions are those involving *am, are, is,* and *not.* Among
that group the following are especially natural to the ear:

I'm
you're, we're, they're
he's, she's, here's
won't, wouldn't, don't, doesn't, can't

Contractions, though, are like kisses: when bestowed indiscriminately,
they lose their effect, in fact seem cheap. Hold them in reserve. Save
them for when you want to civilize an otherwise barbarous-sounding
sentence like "Let us start now because I will not be in town tomorrow" or "Would you not think a stuffed shirt wrote this sentence?"

If you mean "I," *say* "I." Don't wrap your identity in such pomposi-    6
ties as "the writer" or "one" or "this author" or "we." Reserve "we"
and "our" for those situations where you're referring to both your
reader and yourself—i.e., where there really is more than one of you
involved. Reserve "one" for when you mean "a person," as in "One
would have to be a lawyer to understand that." When referring to the
reader alone, address him as "you," not "the reader." The printed page
already puts enough distance between the two of you. Why add to it?

Use dashes to isolate concluding phrases for emphasis or humorous    7
effect. Pauline Kael* is an artist with the dash. If you . . . read her

---

*Pauline Kael is a well-known motion picture critic.—Ed.

reviews, . . . you'll get an idea of the kind of effects you can achieve with it yourself.

Use dialogue wherever your context warrants it—it's intrinsically    8
dramatic. Also use imagined thoughts. Example:

> Events inexorably force Enobarbus to a decision—an impossible one. It would seem that he's thinking here something like this: "My mind tells me to leave Antony for Rome. My heart tells me to leave Rome for Antony. Both courses of action are right, and both are wrong. To go either way is to deny a central fact of my existence. I am a Roman, but I am also a man. There seems to be only one solution: death. It will eliminate the need to choose."

As a general rule of thumb, if you have written three long sentences    9
in a row, make your fourth a short one. And don't be afraid of the very short sentence. Sometimes even a single word works beautifully, as this example from humorist Gregg Hopkins shows:

> Many American parents have voiced the opinion that today's colleges are veritable breeding grounds for premarital sex. Nonsense. Each year, literally tens of students graduate with their virtue still intact.

The more abstract your argument, the more you should lace it with    10
graphic illustrations, analogies, apt quotations, and concrete details. These are aids not only to your reader's understanding but also to his memory. In fact, he'll probably remember the illustration or analogy far longer than he will the abstract idea itself. If the illustration is a good one, though, he'll often be able to reconstruct the thought with a little effort, so it will have served its purpose twice over.

Keep your adjectives to a minimum. Let strong nouns do the work    11
of adjectives. You'll find that this will simplify your style *and* give it more point. I think that Voltaire overstated the case a bit, though, when he observed, "The adjective is the enemy of the noun." A more sensible maxim is Twain's: "As to the Adjective: when in doubt, strike it out."

Avoid weak (trite) adverbs like *very, extremely, really,* and *terribly.*    12
Instead of saying, "She was very upset by the news," say "She was shattered by the news." The use of *very* and its cognates usually betrays a distrust of the power of the word that follows it. If it's not as strong as you want it, find another word. There always is one.

Use the fewest words possible and the simplest words possible.    13
Occasionally, to be sure, the longer word will be the only right word: it

may express the idea concisely, or contribute just the rhythm and texture wanted, or gratify your reader with the joy of surprise. . . . But be warned: the more you surrender to the temptation to use big words—"gigundas," I call them—the further you are apt to stray from your true feelings and the more you will tend to write a style designed to impress rather than to serve the reader. Also, fancy prose can give a writer the delusion that he's really saying something significant, when it may be that he's using rhetoric defensively to conceal from himself how little he actually has to say. Oratory should never be asked to substitute for accuracy and truth. So, follow Henry Thoreau's famous advice, for your own protection: "Simplify, simplify." This may sound easy. It isn't. "To write simply is as difficult as to be good," sighed Somerset Maugham. Hemingway agreed: "Writing plain English is hard work."

Make sure that each sentence you write is manifestly connected to     14
the ones immediately preceding and following it. There's no other way to achieve smooth continuity.

In a long essay or report, periodically summarize your argument so     15
that your reader will be able to keep his bearings. It's often effective to cast these summaries in the form of brief transitional paragraphs, perhaps only three or four sentences in length. They make a welcome change of pace and serve to graphically separate the stages in your argument.

If you enjoy putting questions to your reader, it's prudent to pose     16
them at the beginning of a paper and answer them. If you put them at the tail end and leave your reader the job of answering them, you may achieve only confusion, not resolution.

Use semicolons to reduce choppiness, particularly when you have     17
several related sentences in parallel structure. Also use them for a change of pace. . . .

Read your prose aloud. *Always* read your prose aloud. If it sounds     18
as if it's come out of a machine or a social scientist's report (which is approximately the same thing), spare your reader and rewrite it.

Instead of always saying "first" and "second," occasionally use the     19
numerals themselves in parentheses. It's a superstition that numerals have no place in serious writing. For proof of this, browse through any major anthology of expository prose—*The Norton Reader*, for example.

Written-out numbers such as *twenty-eight* are unwieldy. Most au-     20
thorities recommend that you use the numerals themselves over 20 and the written form for all numbers under 20. But why write *eighteen*

when it's so much simpler to write *18*? What can possibly be objection-able about *18*? The purist would probably answer: "It lacks the dignity of *eighteen*." Such a person doubtless undresses with the lights out. I recommend that you use the numerals themselves from 10 on and congratulate yourself on your common sense.

If you begin a sentence with *and* or *but* (and you should occasion-   21 ally), don't put a comma after it. You want to speed up your prose with those words, and the comma would simply cancel out any gain. The comma is necessary only if a parenthetical clause immediately follows that first word—e.g., "But, from all the evidence, that proves to be a sound conclusion."

Give free rein to your sense of humor wherever possible. What's   22 called "serious writing" need not be solemn writing. F. L. Lucas, in his excellent book *Style*, observed with characteristic good sense: "No manual of style that I know has a word to say of good humour; and yet, for me, a lack of it can sometimes blemish all the literary beauties and blandishments ever taught."

There's as much psychology in paragraphing properly as in any   23 other aspect of writing. Long paragraphs send off alarms in most readers' minds; very short paragraphs suggest insubstantiality and flightiness; a long succession of medium-length paragraphs indicates no imagination and proves monotonous. Moral: vary your pacing to keep your piece alive and vital, as Dr. Seuss advised.

Choose your title with care. Make it accurately descriptive (leave the   24 "teasing" title to cute writers) and try to give it zing. Remember, it's your reader's introduction to your paper. A pedestrian title is about as welcoming as a burned-out motel sign.

Avoid exclamation points, which have been cheapened by comic-   25 strip cartoonists (who haven't yet discovered the period) and by adver-tising copywriters. . . .

If you've written a paragraph that sounds heavy and tortured, put   26 down your pencil and ask yourself: "If I were actually speaking these thoughts to a friend, how would I probably say them?" Then go ahead and talk them *out loud*, and when you're finished, write down as nearly as you can recall what you said. The chances are good that many of your talked-out sentences will be an improvement over the earlier, labored version of them.

Another tip for the same crisis is this: Take a 10-minute break and   27 read a few paragraphs of a writer whose style you relish. Try to *soak in* that style; try to feel yourself actually writing those paragraphs as you read them. Then say to yourself, "OK, now, how would Blank rewrite my paragraph?" and let yourself go. This usually works. And even when it doesn't, it will at least enable you to gain a fresh perspective on what you've written. That's half the battle right there.

## •• DISCUSSION ••

### F. L. Lucas

## • WHAT IS STYLE? •

*F. L. Lucas (1894–1967) was for many years a distinguished scholar and lecturer at Cambridge. In his teaching, he placed particular emphasis on the classics and on good writing. Lucas tried his hand at virtually every literary form; yet his best work was in the field of literary criticism, where he was prolific. Among his principal works are* The Decline and Fall of the Romantic Ideal *(1934),* Greek Poetry for Everyman *(1951),* Greek Drama for Everyman *(1954), and* The Art of Living *(1959).*

*Style belongs to that category of things about which people commonly say: I don't know what it is but I know what I like. We all think that we can recognize and appreciate style when we see it, but few of us would undertake to define it. Literary style is possibly the most elusive kind of all. In this essay, originally published in March 1960, F. L. Lucas surveys what some famous people have written and said about style, and gives us some suggestions for improving our own.*

When it was suggested to Walt Whitman that one of his works    1
should be bound in vellum, he was outraged—"Pshaw!" he snorted, "—hangings, curtains, finger bowls, chinaware, Matthew Arnold!" And he might have been equally irritated by talk of style; for he boasted of "my barbaric yawp"—he would *not* be literary; his readers should touch not a book but a man. Yet Whitman took the pains to rewrite *Leaves of Grass* four times, and his style is unmistakable. Samuel Butler maintained that writers who bothered about their style became unreadable but he bothered about his own. "Style" has got a bad name by growing associated with precious and superior persons

who, like Oscar Wilde, spend a morning putting in a comma, and the afternoon (so he said) taking it out again. But such abuse of "style" is misuse of English. For the word means merely "a way of expressing oneself, in language, manner, or appearance"; or, secondly, "a *good* way of so expressing oneself"—as when one says, "Her behavior never lacked style."

Now there is no crime in expressing oneself (though to try to impress oneself on others easily grows revolting or ridiculous). Indeed one cannot help expressing oneself, unless one passes one's life in a cupboard. Even the most rigid Communist, or Organization-man, is compelled by Nature to have a unique voice, unique fingerprints, unique handwriting. Even the signatures of the letters on your breakfast table may reveal more than their writers guess. There are blustering signatures that swish across the page like cornstalks bowed before a tempest. There are cryptic signatures, like a scrabble of lightning across a cloud, suggesting that behind is a lofty divinity whom all must know, or an aloof divinity whom none is worthy to know (though, as this might be highly inconvenient, a docile typist sometimes interprets the mystery in a bracket underneath). There are impetuous squiggles implying that the author is a sort of strenuous Sputnik streaking around the globe every eighty minutes. There are florid signatures, all curlicues and danglements and flamboyance, like the youthful Disraeli (though these seem rather out of fashion). There are humble, humdrum signatures. And there are also, sometimes, signatures that are courteously clear, yet mindful of a certain simple grace and artistic economy—in short, of style.

Since, then, not one of us can put pen to paper, or even open his mouth, without giving something of himself away to shrewd observers, it seems mere common sense to give the matter a little thought. Yet it does not seem very common. Ladies may take infinite pains about having style in their clothes, but many of us remain curiously indifferent about having it in our words. How many women would dream of polishing not only their nails but also their tongues? They may play freely on that perilous little organ, but they cannot often be bothered to tune it. And how many men think of improving their talk as well as their golf handicap?

No doubt strong silent men, speaking only in gruff monosyllables, may despise "mere words." No doubt the world does suffer from an endemic plague of verbal dysentery. But that, precisely, is bad style.

And consider the amazing power of mere words. Adolf Hilter was a bad artist, bad statesman, bad general, and bad man. But largely because he could tune his rant, with psychological nicety, to the exact wave length of his audiences and make millions quarrelsome-drunk all at the same time by his command of windy nonsense, skilled statesmen, soldiers, scientists were blown away like chaff, and he came near to rule the world. If Sir Winston Churchill had been a mere speechifier, we might well have lost the war; yet his speeches did quite a lot to win it.

No man was less of a literary aesthete than Benjamin Franklin; yet   5 this tallow-chandler's son, who changed world history, regarded as "a principal means of my advancement" that pungent style which he acquired partly by working in youth over old *Spectators*; but mainly by being Benjamin Franklin. The squinting demagogue, John Wilkes, as ugly as his many sins, had yet a tongue so winning that he asked only half an hour's start (to counteract his face) against any rival for a woman's favor. "Vote for you!" growled a surly elector in his constituency. "I'd sooner vote for the devil!" "But in case your friend should not stand . . . ?" Cleopatra, the ensnarer of world conquerors, owed less to the shape of her nose than to the charm of her tongue. Shakespeare himself has often poor plots and thin ideas; even his mastery of character has been questioned; what does remain unchallenged is his verbal magic. Men are often taken, like rabbits, by the ears. And though the tongue has no bones, it can sometimes break millions of them.

"But," the reader may grumble, "I am neither Hitler, Cleopatra, nor   6 Shakespeare. What is all this to me?" Yet we all talk—often too much; we all have to write letters—often too many. We live not by bread alone but also by words. And not always with remarkable efficiency. Strikes, lawsuits, divorces, all sorts of public nuisance and private misery, often come just from the gaggling incompetence with which we express ourselves. Americans and British get at cross-purposes because they use the same words with different meanings. Men have been hanged on a comma in a statute. And in the valley of Balaclava a mere verbal ambiguity, about *which* guns were to be captured, sent the whole Light Brigade to futile annihilation.

Words can be more powerful, and more treacherous, than we some-   7 times suspect; communication more difficult than we may think. We are all serving life sentences of solitary confinement within our own bodies; like prisoners, we have, as it were, to tap in awkward code to our fellow men in their neighboring cells. Further, when A and B converse, there take part in their dialogue not two characters, as they suppose, but six. For there is A's real self—call it $A_1$; there is also A's picture of himself—$A_2$; there is also B's picture of A—$A_3$. And there are three corresponding personalities of B. With six characters involved even in a simple tête-à-tête, no wonder we fall into muddles and misunderstandings.

Perhaps, then, there are five main reasons for trying to gain some mastery of language:    8

We have no other way of understanding, informing, misinforming, or persuading one another.

Even alone, we think mainly in words; if our language is muddy, so will our thinking be.

By our handling of words we are often revealed and judged. "Has he written anything?" said Napoleon of a candidate for an appointment. "Let me see his *style*."

Without a feeling for language one remains half-blind and deaf to literature.

Our mother tongue is bettered or worsened by the way each generation uses it. Languages evolve like species. They can degenerate; just as oysters and barnacles have lost their heads. Compare ancient Greek with modern. A heavy responsibility, though often forgotten.

Why and how did I become interested in style? The main answer, I suppose, is that I was born that way. Then I was, till ten, an only child running loose in a house packed with books, and in a world (thank goodness) still undistracted by radio and television. So at three I groaned to my mother, "Oh, I *wish* I could read," and at four I read. Now travel among books is the best travel of all, and the easiest, and the cheapest. (Not that I belittle ordinary travel—which I regard as one of the three main pleasures in life.) One learns to write by reading good books, as one learns to talk by hearing good talkers. And If I have learned anything in writing, it is largely from writers like Montaigne, Dorothy Osborne, Horace Walpole, Johnson, Goldsmith, Montesquieu, Voltaire, Flaubert and Anatole France. Again, I was reared on Greek and Latin, and one can learn much from translating Homer or the Greek Anthology, Horace or Tacitus, if one is thrilled    9 by the originals and tries, however vainly, to recapture some of that thrill in English.

But at Rugby I could *not* write English essays. I believe it stupid to torment boys to write on topics that they know and care nothing about. I used to rush to the school library and cram the subject, like a python swallowing rabbits; then, still replete as a postprandial python, I would tie myself in clumsy knots to embrace those accursed themes. Bacon was wise in saying that reading makes a full man; talking, a ready one; writing, an exact one. But writing from an empty head is futile anguish. 10

At Cambridge, my head having grown a little fuller, I suddenly found I *could* write—not with enjoyment (it is always tearing oneself in pieces)—but fairly fluently. Then came the War of 1914–18; and though soldiers have other things than pens to handle, they learn painfully to be clear and brief. Then the late Sir Desmond MacCarthy invited me to review for the *New Statesman:* it was a useful apprentice- ship, and he was delightful to work for. But I think it was well after a few years to stop; reviewers remain essential, but there are too many books one *cannot* praise, and only the pugnacious enjoy amassing enemies. By then I was an ink-addict—not because writing is much pleasure, but because not to write is pain; just as some smokers do not so much enjoy tobacco as suffer without it. The positive happiness of writing comes, I think, from work when done—decently, one hopes, and not without use—and from the letters of readers which help to reassure, or delude, one that so it is. 11

But one of my most vivid lessons came, I think, from service in a war department during the Second World War. Then, if the matter one sent out was too wordy, the communication channels might choke; yet if it was not absolutely clear, the results might be serious. So I emerged, after six years of it, with more passion than ever for clarity and brevity, more loathing than ever for the obscure and the verbose. 12

For forty years at Cambridge I have tried to teach young men to write well, and have come to think it impossible. To write really well is a gift inborn; those who have it teach themselves; one can only try to help and hasten the process. After all, the uneducated sometimes express themselves far better than their "betters." In language, as in life, it is possible to be perfectly correct—and yet perfectly tedious, or odious. The literate last letter of the doomed Vanzetti* was more mov- 13

---

*See p. 91.—Ed.

ing than most professional orators; 18th Century ladies, who should have been spanked for their spelling, could yet write far better letters than most professors of English; and the talk of Synge's Irish peasants seems to me vastly more vivid than the latter styles of Henry James. Yet Synge averred that his characters owed far less of their eloquence to what he invented for them than to what he had overheard in the cottages of Wicklow and Kerry.

> CHRISTY. It's little you'll think if my love's a poacher's, or an earl's itself, when you'll feel my two hands stretched around you, and I squeezing kisses on your puckered lips, till I'd feel a kind of pity for the Lord God in all ages sitting lonesome in His golden chair.
>
> PEGEEN. That'll be right fun, Christy Mahon, and any girl would walk her heart out before she'd meet a young man was your like for eloquence, or talk at all.

Well she might! It's not like that they talk in universities—more's the pity. 14

But though one cannot teach people to write well, one can sometimes teach them to write rather better. One can give a certain number of hints, which often seem boringly obvious—only experience shows they are not. 15

One can say: Beware of pronouns—they are devils. Look at even Addison, describing the type of pedant who chatters of style without having any: 16

> Upon enquiry I found my learned friend had dined that day with Mr. Swan, the famous punster; and desiring *him* to give me some account of Mr. Swan's conversation, *he* told me that *he* generally talked in the Paronomasia, that *he* sometimes gave it to the Ploce, but that in *his* humble opinion *he* shone most in the Antanaclasis.

What a sluttish muddle of *he* and *him* and *his!* It all needs rewording. Far better repeat a noun, or a name, than puzzle the reader, even for a moment, with ambiguous pronouns. Thou shalt not puzzle thy reader. 17

Or one can say: Avoid jingles. The B.B.C. news bulletins seem compiled by earless persons, capable of crying around the globe: "The enemy is *reported* to have seized this im*port*ant *port*, and reinforcements are hurrying up in sup*port*." Any fool, once told, can hear such things to be insupportable. 18

Or one can say: Be sparing with relative clauses. Don't string them together like sausages, or jam them inside one another like Chinese 19 boxes or the receptacles of Buddha's tooth. Or one can say: Don't flaunt jargon, like Addison's Mr. Swan, or the type of modern critic who gurgles more technical terms in a page than Johnson used in all his *Lives* or Sainte-Beuve in thirty volumes. But dozens of such snippety precepts, though they may sometimes save people from writing badly, will help them little toward writing well. Are there no general rules of a more positive kind, and of more positive use?

Perhaps. There *are* certain basic principles which seem to me observed by many authors I admire, which I think have served me and which may serve others. I am not talking of geniuses, who are a law to themselves (and do not always write a very good style, either); nor of poetry, which has different laws from prose; nor of poetic prose, like Sir Thomas Browne's or De Quincey's which is often more akin to poetry; but of the plain prose of ordinary books and documents, letters and talk.    20

The writer should respect truth and himself; therefore honesty. He should respect his readers; therefore courtesy. These are two of the cornerstones of style. Confucius saw it, twenty-five centuries ago: "The Master said, The gentleman is courteous, but not pliable: common men are pliable, but not courteous."    21

First, honesty. In literature, as in life, one of the fundamentals is to find, and be, one's true self. One's true self may indeed be unpleasant (though one can try to better it); but a false self, sooner or later, becomes disgusting—just as a nice plain woman, painted to the eyebrows, can become horrid. In writing, in the long run, pretense does not work. As the police put it, anything you say may be used as evidence against you. If handwriting reveals character, writing reveals it still more. You cannot fool *all* your judges *all* the time.    22

Most style is not honest enough. Easy to say, but hard to practice. A writer may take to long words, as young men to beards—to impress. But long words, like beards, are often the badge of charlatans. Or a writer may cultivate the obscure, to seem profound. But even carefully muddied puddles are soon fathomed. Or he may cultivate eccentricity, to seem original. But really original people do not have to think about being original—they can no more help it than they can help breathing. They do not need to dye their hair green. The fame of Meredith, Wilde or Bernard Shaw might now shine brighter, had they struggled less to be brilliant; whereas Johnson remains great, not merely because his gifts were formidable but also because, with all his prejudice and passion, he fought no less passionately to "clear his mind of cant."    23

Secondly, courtesy—respect for the reader. From this follow several     24
other basic principles of style. Clarity is one. For it is boorish to make
your reader rack his brains to understand. One should aim at being
impossible to misunderstand—though men's capacity for misunderstanding approaches infinity. Hence Molière and Po Chu-i tried their
work on their cooks; and Swift his on his men-servants—"which, if
they did not comprehend, he would alter and amend, until they understood it perfectly." Our bureaucrats and pundits, unfortunately, are
less considerate.

Brevity is another basic principle. For it is boorish, to waste your     25
reader's time. People who would not dream of stealing a penny of
one's money turn not a hair at stealing hours of one's life. But that does
not make them less exasperating. Therefore there is no excuse for the
sort of writer who takes as long as a marching army corps to pass a
given point. Besides, brevity is often more effective; the half can say
more than the whole, and to imply things may strike far deeper than
to state them at length. And because one is particularly apt to waste
words on preambles before coming to the substance, there was sense
in the Scots professor who always asked his pupils—"Did ye remember to tear up that fir-r-st page?"

Here are some instances that would only lose by lengthening.     26

> It is useless to go to bed to save the light, if the result is twins. (Chinese
>    proverb.)
>
> My barn is burnt down—
>    Nothing hides the moon. (Complete Japanese poem.)
>
> Je me regrette.* (Dying words of the gay Vicomtesse d'Houdetot.)
>
> I have seen their backs before. (Wellington, when French marshals
>    turned their backs on him at a reception.)
>
> Continue until the tanks stop, then get out and walk. (Patton to the Twelfth
>    Corps, halted for fuel supplies at St. Dizier, 8/30/44.)

Or there is the most laconic diplomatic note on record: when Philip     26
of Macedon wrote to the Spartans that, if he came within their borders,
he would leave not one stone of their city, they wrote back the one
word—"If."

Clarity comes before even brevity. But it is a fallacy that wordiness     27
is necessarily clearer. Metternich when he thought something he had

*"I shall miss myself."—Ed.

written was obscure would simply go through it crossing out everything irrelevant. What remained, he found, often became clear. Wellington, asked to recommend three names for the post of Commander-in-Chief, India, took a piece of paper and wrote three times— "Napier." Pages could not have been clearer—or as forcible. On the other hand the lectures, and the sentences, of Coleridge became at times bewildering because his mind was often "wiggle-waggle"; just as he could not even walk straight on a path.

But clarity and brevity, though a good beginning, are only a beginning. By themselves, they may remain bare and bleak. When Calvin Coolidge, asked by his wife what the preacher had preached on, replied "Sin," and, asked what the preacher had said, replied, "He was against it," he was brief enough. But one hardly envies Mrs. Coolidge.    28

An attractive style requires, of course, all kinds of further gifts— such as variety, good humor, good sense, vitality, imagination. Variety means avoiding monotony of rhythm, of language, of mood. One needs to vary one's sentence length (this present article has too many short sentences; but so vast a subject grows here as cramped as a djin in a bottle); to amplify one's vocabulary; to diversify one's tone. There are books that petrify one throughout, with the rigidly pompous solemnity of an owl perched on a leafless tree. But ceaseless facetiousness can be as bad; or perpetual irony. Even the smile of Voltaire can seem at times a fixed grin, a disagreeable wrinkle. Constant peevishness is far worse, as often in Swift; even on the stage too much irritable dialogue may irritate an audience, without its knowing why.    29

Still more are vitality, energy, imagination gifts that must be inborn before they can be cultivated. But under the head of imagination two common devices may be mentioned that have been the making of many a style—metaphor and simile. Why such magic power should reside in simply saying, or implying, that A is like B remains a little mysterious. But even our unconscious seems to love symbols; again, language often tends to lose itself in clouds of vaporous abstraction, and simile or metaphor can bring it back to concrete solidity; and, again, such imagery can gild the gray flats of prose with sudden sunglints of poetry.    30

If a foreigner may for a moment be impertinent, I admire the native gift of Americans for imagery as much as I wince at their fondness for slang. (Slang seems to me a kind of linguistic fungus; as poisonous, and as shortlived, as toadstools.) When Matthew Arnold lectured in    31 the United States, he was likened by one newspaper to "an elderly macaw pecking at a trellis of grapes"; he observed, very justly, "How lively journalistic fancy is among the Americans!" General Grant, again, unable to hear him, remarked: "Well, wife, we've paid to see the British lion, but as we can't hear him roar, we'd better go home." By simile and metaphor, these two quotations bring before us the slightly pompous, fastidious, inaudible Arnold as no direct description could have done.

Or consider how language comes alive in the Chinese saying that 32 lending to the feckless is "like pelting a stray dog with dumplings," or in the Arab proverb: "They came to shoe the pasha's horse, and the beetle stretched forth his leg"; in the Greek phrase for a perilous cape—"stepmother of ships"; or the Hebrew adage that "as the climbing up a sandy way is to the feet of the aged, so is a wife full of words to a quiet man"; in Shakespeare's phrase for a little England lost in the world's vastness—"in a great Poole, a Swan's nest"; or Fuller's libel on tall men—"Ofttimes such who are built four stories high are observed to have little in their cockloft"; in Chateaubriand's "I go yawning my life"; or in Jules Renard's portrait of a cat, "well buttoned in her fur." Or, to take a modern instance, there is Churchill on dealing with Russia:

> Trying to maintain good relations with a Communist is like wooing a crocodile. You do not know whether to tickle it under the chin or beat it over the head. When it opens its mouth, you cannot tell whether it is trying to smile or preparing to eat you up.

What a miracle human speech can be, and how dull is most that one 33 hears! Would one hold one's hearers, it is far less help, I suspect, to read manuals on style than to cultivate one's own imagination and imagery.

I will end with two remarks by two wise old women of the civilized 34 18th Century.

The first is from the blind Mme. du Deffand (the friend of Horace 35 Walpole) to that Mlle. de Lespinasse with whom, alas, she was to quarrel so unwisely: "You must make up your mind, my queen, to live with me in the greatest truth and sincerity. You will be charming so long as you let yourself be natural, and remain without pretension and without artifice." The second is from Mme. de Charrière, the Zélide whom Boswell had once loved at Utrecht in vain, to a Swiss girl friend: "Lucinde, my clever Lucinde, while you wait for the Romeos to arrive, you have nothing better to do than become perfect. Have ideas that are clear, and expressions that are simple." *("Ayez des idées nettes et des expressions simples.")* More than half the bad writing in the world, I believe, comes from neglecting those two very simple pieces of advice.

In many ways, no doubt, our world grows more and more complex; sputniks cannot be simple; yet how many of our complexities remain futile, how many of our artificialities false. Simplicity too can be subtle—as the straight lines of a Greek temple, like the Parthenon at Athens, are delicately curved, in order to look straighter still.

36

## *VOCABULARY*

| | | |
|---|---|---|
| curlicues (2) | annihilation (6) | verbose (12) |
| endemic (4) | tête-à-tête (7) | odious (13) |
| aesthete (5) | degenerate (8) | averred (13) |
| tallow-chandler (5) | replete (10) | pedant (16) |
| demagogue (5) | postprandial (10) | |
| gaggling (6) | pugnacious (11) | |

## *THE FACTS*

1. Why, according to the author, did "style" get a bad name?
2. What are the two basic principles of good writing style? What other principles follow from the second?
3. What are some other gifts of an attractive style listed in paragraph 29?
4. What are two common literary devices that have made many a style? According to paragraph 31, who has a particular gift for these devices?
5. Lucas ends his essay with some pertinent advice from two women. Who are they and what is their advice?

## *THE STRATEGIES*

1. What is the difference between "expressing" and "impressing" as discussed in paragraph 2?
2. In paragraph 4 Lucas states that skilled statesmen, soldiers, and scientists were "blown away like chaff" by Adolf Hitler's "windy nonsense." What would happen to Lucas's style if you substituted "drowned" for "blown away"?
3. Paragraph 5 alludes to Benjamin Franklin, John Wilkes, Cleopatra, and Shakespeare as people who owed their charm or success to their verbal style. Whom else can you add to the list? Give reasons for your choices.

4. In paragraph 9 Lucas suggests that people learn to write by reading good books. What purpose is served by the list of nine authors that follows?
5. What is the rhetorical function of paragraph 33?

### THE ISSUES

1. What is the difference, if any, between "class" and "style" when each word is used to designate an individual's personal conduct and mode of living?
2. The author says that we all express a self no matter how hard we may try to efface it. Does it not follow, then, that we all have "style"? Why or why not?
3. Lucas comes from a highly elitist background in which privilege and status dictated advancement and social preferment. How does his definition of style implicitly reflect this background? Or does it?
4. What is your opinion of the adage "Style is the man"? How does it apply or not apply to Lucas's idea of style?
5. Lucas implies that growing up in a world undistracted by radio and television helped him to develop early as a writer and reader. What effect, if any, have radio and television had on your own development as a reader and writer?

### SUGGESTIONS FOR WRITING

1. Lucas's essay was first published as a magazine article in March 1960. Write an essay quoting and evaluating particular passages and opinions to which a modern reader, especially a feminist, might take offense.
2. Write an essay explaining the effect you think the media have had on your own development as a reader and writer. Say how this effect might have been overcome or lessened.

=========  •• *EXAMPLES* ••  =========

Bartolomeo Vanzetti

—— • **REMARKS ON THE LIFE OF SACCO** • ——
**AND ON HIS OWN LIFE AND EXECUTION**

*Bartolomeo Vanzetti (1888–1927) was born of peasant stock in northern Italy, where he worked as a baker's apprentice before migrating to the United States in 1908. In the U.S. he worked as a laborer and became an avowed anarchist. In*

*1920, along with Nicolo Sacco, another Italian immigrant, Vanzetti was arrested for the murder of a guard during a payroll robbery. While in prison awaiting execution, he wrote his autobiography. Maintaining their innocence to the end, and despite the worldwide public protest mounted in their behalf, Sacco and Vanzetti were executed on August 22, 1927.*

*These four paragraphs are assembled from the writings and sayings of Vanzetti. The first two paragraphs are notes from a speech. Vanzetti intended to deliver them in court before his sentencing but was barred from doing so by the judge. The final paragraph is a transcription from an interview given by Vanzetti in April 1927 to Philip D. Strong, a reporter for the North American Newspaper Alliance. The entire excerpt illustrates the lyricism and elegance of simple words cast in idiomatic sentences.*

1    I have talk a great deal of myself but I even forgot to name Sacco. Sacco too is a worker from his boyhood, a skilled worker lover of work, with a good job and pay, a good and lovely wife, two beautiful children and a neat little home at the verge of a wood, near a brook. Sacco is a heart, a faith, a character, a man; a man lover of nature and of mankind. A man who gave all, who sacrifice all to the cause of Liberty and to his love for mankind; money, rest, mundane ambitions, his own wife, his children, himself and his own life. Sacco has never dreamt to steal, never to assassinate. He and I have never brought a morsel of bread to our mouths, from our childhood to today—which has not been gained by the sweat of our brows. Never. His people also are in good position and of good reputation.

2    Oh, yes, I may be more witful, as some have put it, I am a better babbler than he is, but many, many times in hearing his heartful voice ringing a faith sublime, in considering his supreme sacrifice, remembering his heroism I felt small small at the presence of his greatness and found myself compelled to fight back from my throat to not weep before him—this man called thief and assassin and doomed. But Sacco's name will live in the hearts of the people and in their gratitude when Katzmann's* and your bones will be dispersed by time, when your name, his name, your laws, institutions, and your false god are but a *deem rememoring of a cursed past in which man was wolf to the man.* . . .

3    If it had not been for these thing . . . I might have live out my life talking at street corners to scorning men. I might have die, unmarked, unknown, a failure. Now we are not a failure. This is our career and

*Frederick G. Katzmann was the district attorney who prosecuted the case.—Ed.

our triumph. Never in our full life could we hope to do such work for tolerance, for joostice, for man's onderstanding of man as now we do by accident.

Our words—our lives—our pains—nothing! The taking of our   4
lives—lives of a good shoemaker and a poor fish-peddler—all! That last moment belongs to us—that agony is our triumph.


## VOCABULARY

mundane (1)      sublime (2)


## THE FACTS

1. What kind of man does the excerpt make Sacco out to be?
2. What does Vanzetti claim to be better at than Sacco?
3. According to Vanzetti, how might his life have turned out were it not for his trial and conviction?


## THE STRATEGIES

1. The author was an Italian with a frail grasp of the American speech idiom. What effect do his grammatical errors have on the way he expresses himself?
2. How would you characterize the diction of this excerpt? Is it lofty? Plain?
3. Why do some editors include this excerpt in poetry anthologies? What is poetic about it?


## THE ISSUES

1. Because of his beliefs, Vanzetti was labeled a philosophical anarchist. What is a philosophical anarchist?
2. In the final paragraph, Vanzetti calls his impending execution with Sacco "our triumph." What do you think he meant by that?
3. The Sacco and Vanzetti trial was made famous mainly because of the intense media attention it drew. What restrictions, if any, do you think should be imposed on media coverage of sensational criminals and trials? Why? Justify your answer.


## SUGGESTIONS FOR WRITING

1. Copy this excerpt, correcting its grammatical and spelling errors as you go. Add any words that are necessary to make it grammatical. Write a paragraph on which version you think is more effective, the original or the corrected one, giving your reasons.

2. Without doing any further research into Vanzetti, and using this excerpt as your only evidence, write an impressionistic description of the kind of man you think he was. Be specific in your references to passages in the excerpt.

### TERM PAPER SUGGESTION

Write a term paper on the Sacco–Vanzetti trial. Reach your own conclusion as to whether or not it was a fair trial, and support your belief.

**Langston Hughes**

## • SALVATION •

*Langston Hughes (1902–1967) was born in Joplin, Missouri, and educated at Columbia University, New York, and Lincoln University, Pennsylvania. He worked at odd jobs in this country and in France before becoming established as a writer. His lifetime interest was the promotion of black art, history, and causes. In addition to many collections of poetry, Hughes wrote a novel,* Not Without Laughter *(1930), and an autobiography,* The Big Sea *(1940).*

*In this selection from* The Big Sea, *Hughes recounts a dramatic incident from his childhood. The incident is narrated from the perspective of a twelve-year-old boy and demonstrates a skillful writer's use of language to re-create the innocent voice of childhood.*

I was saved from sin when I was going on thirteen. But not really saved. It happened like this. There was a big revival at my Auntie Reed's church. Every night for weeks there had been much preaching, singing, praying, and shouting, and some very hardened sinners had been brought to Christ, and the membership of the church had grown by leaps and bounds. Then just before the revival ended, they held a special meeting for children, "to bring the young lambs to the fold." My aunt spoke of it for days ahead. That night I was escorted to the front row and placed on the mourners' bench with all the other young sinners, who had not yet been brought to Jesus.

My aunt told me that when you were saved you saw a light, and something happened to you inside! And Jesus came into your life! And God was with you from then on! She said you could see and hear and feel Jesus in your soul. I believed her. I had heard a great many old people say the same thing and it seemed to me they ought to know.

So I sat there calmly in the hot, crowded church, waiting for Jesus to come to me.

The preacher preached a wonderful rhythmical sermon, all moans and shouts and lonely cries and dire pictures of hell, and then he sang a song about the ninety and nine safe in the fold, but one little lamb was left out in the cold. Then he said: "Won't you come? Won't you come to Jesus? Young lambs, won't you come?" And he held out his arms to all us young sinners there on the mourners' bench. And the little girls cried. And some of them jumped up and went to Jesus right away. But most of us just sat there.   3

A great many old people came and knelt around us and prayed, old women with jet-black faces and braided hair, old men with work-gnarled hands. And the church sang a song about the lower lights are burning, some poor sinners to be saved. And the whole building rocked with prayer and song.   4

Still I keep waiting to *see* Jesus.   5

Finally all the young people had gone to the altar and were saved, but one boy and me. He was a rounder's son named Westley. Westley and I were surrounded by sisters and deacons praying. It was very hot in the church, and getting late now. Finally Westley said to me in a whisper: "God damn! I'm tired o' sitting here. Let's get up and be saved." So he got up and was saved.   6

Then I was left all alone on the mourners' bench. My aunt came and knelt at my knees and cried, while prayers and songs swirled all around me in the little church. The whole congregation prayed for me alone, in a mighty wail of moans and voices. And I kept waiting serenely for Jesus, waiting, waiting—but he didn't come. I wanted to see him, but nothing happened to me. Nothing! I wanted something to happen to me, but nothing happened.   7

I heard the songs and the minister saying: "Why don't you come? My dear child, why don't you come to Jesus? Jesus is waiting for you. He wants you. Why don't you come? Sister Reed, what is this child's name?"   8

"Langston," my aunt sobbed.   9

"Langston, why don't you come? Why don't you come and be saved? Oh, Lamb of God! Why don't you come?"   10

Now it was really getting late. I began to be ashamed of myself, holding everything up so long. I began to wonder what God thought about Westley, who certainly hadn't seen Jesus either, but who was now sitting proudly on the platform, swinging his knickerbockered   11 legs and grinning down at me, surrounded by deacons and old women on their knees praying. God had not struck Westley dead for taking his name in vain or for lying in the temple. So I decided that maybe to save further trouble, I'd better lie, too, and say that Jesus had come, and get up and be saved.

So I got up.    12

Suddenly the whole room broke into a sea of shouting, as they saw    13
me rise. Waves of rejoicing swept the place. Women leaped in the air. My aunt threw her arms around me. The minister took me by the hand and led me to the platform.

When things quieted down, in a hushed silence, punctuated by a    14
few ecstatic "Amens," all the new young lambs were blessed in the name of God. Then joyous singing filled the room.

That night, for the last time in my life but one—for I was a big boy    15
twelve years old—I cried. I cried, in bed alone, and couldn't stop. I buried my head under the quilts, but my aunt heard me. She woke up and told my uncle I was crying because the Holy Ghost had come into my life, and because I had seen Jesus. But I was really crying because I couldn't bear to tell her that I had lied, that I had deceived everybody in the church, and I hadn't seen Jesus, and that now I didn't believe there was a Jesus any more, since he didn't come to help me.

## VOCABULARY

gnarled (4)                punctuated (14)                ecstatic (14)

## THE FACTS

1. How does Westley's attitude differ from the narrator's? Is Westley more realistic and less gullible, or is he simply more callous and less sensitive than the narrator? Comment.
2. The narrator holds out to the last minute and finally submits to being saved. What is his motive for finally giving in?
3. Who has been deceived in the story? The aunt by the narrator? The narrator by the aunt? Both the narrator and the aunt by the minister? Everybody by the demands of religion? Comment.
4. What insight does the narrator come to at the end of the story? What has he learned?
5. The story is told as a flashback to when Hughes was a boy. What is his attitude toward the experience as he retells it?

## THE STRATEGIES

1. The story is narrated from the point of view of a twelve-year-old boy. What techniques of language are used in the story to create the perspective of a boy? How is the vocabulary appropriate to a boy?
2. In his article on "How to Say Nothing in Five Hundred Words," Paul Roberts urges the use of specific details in writing. How does Hughes make use of such details?
3. The description in paragraph 4 is vivid but compressed. How does Hughes achieve this effect?

## THE ISSUES

1. Marx wrote that "religion . . . is the opium of the people." What is your view of this sentiment? How does it apply or not apply to this excerpt?
2. The little girls were the first to break down and offer themselves to be saved. The last two holdouts were boys. How do you explain this different reaction of the two sexes?
3. What do you think would have likely happened if the narrator had not gone up to be saved?
4. Religions often use ovine terms (*sheep, lamb, flock*) to refer to their congregations. What do you think is the origin of this usage? What does this usage imply about the members?

## SUGGESTIONS FOR WRITING

1. Describe an experience of your own where group pressure forced you into doing something you did not believe in.
2. Write a brief biographical sketch of Westley, fantasizing on the kind of man you believe he grew into and the kind of life he eventually led.

**Richard Lederer**

———— • A HISTORY OF THE WORLD • ————

*Richard Lederer (b. 1938) is a freelance writer and English teacher at St. Paul, a private high school in Concord, New Hampshire. He studied English at Harvard University (M.A., 1962) and received a Ph.D. in English from the University of New Hampshire in 1980. He has published numerous articles in English journals and is the coauthor of the book* Basic Verbal Skills *(1975). Lederer is the author of* Anguished English *(1987). His column, "Looking at Language," appears regularly in the* Concord Monitor, *and his short talks on language are heard on New Hampshire public radio.*

One of the fringe benefits of being an English or history teacher is   1
receiving the occasional jewel of a student blooper in an essay. I have
pasted together the following "history" of the world from certifiably
genuine student bloopers collected by teachers throughout the United
States, from eighth grade through college level. Read carefully, and
you will learn a lot.

The inhabitants of ancient Egypt were called mummies. They lived   2
in the Sarah Dessert and traveled by Camelot. The climate of the Sarah
is such that the inhabitants have to live elsewhere, so certain areas of
the dessert are cultivated by irritation. The Egyptians built the Pyra-
mids in the shape of a huge triangular cube. The Pramids are a range
of mountains between France and Spain.

The Bible is full of interesting caricatures. In the first book of the   3
Bible, Guinesses, Adam and Eve were created from an apple tree. One
of their children, Cain, once asked, "Am I my brother's son?" God
asked Abraham to sacrifice Isaac on Mount Montezuma. Jacob, son of
Isaac, stole his brother's birth mark. Jacob was a patriarch who brought
up his twelve sons to be patriarchs, but they did not take to it. One of
Jacob's sons, Joseph, gave refuse to the Israelites.

Pharaoh forced the Hebrew slaves to make bread without straw.   4
Moses led them to the Red Sea, where they made unleavened bread,
which is bread made without any ingredients. Afterwards, Moses
went up on Mount Cyanide to get the ten commandments. David was
a Hebrew king skilled at playing the liar. He fought with the Philatelists, a race of people who lived in Biblical times. Solomon, one of
David's sons, had 500 wives and 500 porcupines.

Without the Greeks we wouldn't have history. The Greeks invented   5
three kinds of columns—Corinthian, Doric, and Ironic. They also had
myths. A myth is a female moth. One myth says that the mother of
Achilles dipped him in the River Stynx until he became intollerable.
Achilles appears in *The Iliad*, by Homer. Homer also wrote *The Oddity*,
in which Penelope was the last hardship that Ulysses endured on his
journey. Actually, Homer was not written by Homer but by another
man of that name.

Socrates was a famous Greek teacher who went around giving   6
people advice. They killed him. Socrates died from an overdose of
wedlock.

In the Olympic Games, Greeks ran races, jumped, hurled the bis-   7
cuits, and threw the java. The reward to the victor was a coral wreath.

The government of Athens was democratic because people took the law into their own hands. There were no wars in Greece, as the mountains were so high that they couldn't climb over to see what their neighbors were doing. When they fought with the Persians, the Greeks were outnumbered because the Persians had more men.

Eventually, the Ramons conquered the Geeks. History calls people    8
Romans because they never stayed in one place for very long. At Roman banquets, the guests wore garlics in their hair. Julius Caesar extinguished himself on the battlefields of Gaul. The Ides of March murdered him because they thought he was going to be made king. Nero was a cruel tyranny who would torture his poor subjects by playing the fiddle to them.

Then came the Middle Ages. King Alfred conquered the Dames,    9
King Arthur lived in the Age of Shivery, King Harold mustarded his troops before the Battle of Hastings, Joan of Arc was cannonized by Bernard Shaw, and victims of the Black Death grew boobs on their necks. Finally, Magna Carta provided that no free man should be hanged twice for the same offense.

In midevil times most of the people were alliterate. The greatest    10
writer of the time was Chaucer, who wrote many poems and verses and also wrote literature. Another tale tells of William Tell, who shot an arrow through an apple while standing on his son's head.

The Renaissance was an age in which more individuals felt the value    11
of their human being. Martin Luther was nailed to the church door at Wittenberg for selling papal indulgences. He died a horrible death, being excommunicated by a bull. It was the painter Donatello's interest in the female nude that made him the father of the Renaissance. It was an age of great inventions and discoveries. Gutenberg invented the Bible. Sir Walter Raleigh is a historical figure because he invented cigarettes. Another important invention was the circulation of blood. Sir Francis Drake circumcised the world with a 100-foot clipper.

The government of England was a limited mockery. Henry VIII    12
found walking difficult because he had an abbess on his knee. Queen Elizabeth was the "Virgin Queen." As a queen she was a success. When Elizabeth exposed herself before her troops, they all shouted, "hurrah." Then her navy went out and defeated the Spanish Armadillo.

The greatest writer of the Renaissance was William Shakespear.    13
Shakespear never made much money and is famous only because of

his plays. He lived at Windsor with his merry wives, writing tragedies, comedies, and errors. In one of Shakespear's famous plays, Hamlet rations out his situation by relieving himself in a long soliloquy. In another, Lady Macbeth tries to convince Macbeth to kill the King by attacking his manhood. Romeo and Juliet are an example of a heroic couplet. Writing at the same time as Shakespear was Miguel Cervantes. He wrote *Donkey Hote*. The next great author was John Milton. Milton wrote *Paradise Lost*. Then his wife died and he wrote *Paradise Regained*.

During the Renaissance America began. Christopher Columbus was    14
a great navigator who discovered America while cursing about the Atlantic. His ships were called the Nina, the Pinta, and the Santa Fe. Later, the Pilgrims crossed the ocean, and this was known as Pilgrims Progress. When they landed at Plymouth Rock, they were greeted by the Indians, who came down the hill rolling their war hoops before them. The Indian squabs carried porpoises on their back. Many of the Indian heroes were killed, along with their cabooses, which proved very fatal to them. The winter of 1620 was a hard one for the settlers. Many people died and many babies were born. Captain John Smith was responsible for all this.

One of the causes of the Revolutionary Wars was the English put    15
tacks in their tea. Also, the colonists would send their parcels through the post without stamps. During the War, the Red Coats and Paul Revere was throwing balls over stone walls. The dogs were barking and the peacocks crowing. Finally, the colonists won the War and no longer had to pay for taxis.

Delegates from the original thirteen states formed the Contented    16
Congress. Thomas Jefferson, a Virgin, and Benjamin Franklin were two singers of the Declaration of Independence. Franklin had gone to Boston carrying all his clothes in his pocket and a loaf of bread under each arm. He invented electricity by rubbing cats backwards and declared, "A horse divided against itself cannot stand." Franklin died in 1790 and is still dead.

George Washington married Martha Curtis and in due time became    17
the Father of Our Country. Then the Constitution of the United States was adopted to secure domestic hostility. Under the Constitution the people enjoyed the right to keep bare arms.

Abraham Lincoln became America's greatest Precedent. Lincoln's    18
mother died in infancy, and he was born in a log cabin which he built

with his own hands. When Lincoln was President, he wore only a tall silk hat. He said, "In onion there is strength." Abraham Lincoln wrote the Gettysburg Address while traveling from Washington to Gettysburg on the back of an envelope. He also freed the slaves by signing the Emasculation Proclamation, and the Fourteenth Amendment gave the ex-Negroes citizenship. But the Clue Clux Clan would torcher and lynch the ex-Negroes and other innocent victims. It claimed it represented law and odor. On the night of April 14, 1865, Lincoln went to the theater and got shot in his seat by one of the actors in a moving picture show. The believed assinator was John Wilkes Booth, a supposingly insane actor. This ruined Booth's career.

Meanwhile in Europe, the enlightenment was a reasonable time.    19
Voltare invented electricity and also wrote a book called *Candy.* Gravity was invented by Isaac Walton. It is chiefly noticeable in the Autumn, when the apples are falling off the trees.

Bach was the most famous composer in the world, and so was    20
Handel. Handel was half German, half Italian, and half English. He was very large. Bach died from 1750 to the present. Beethoven wrote music even though he was deaf. He was so deaf he wrote loud music. He took long walks in the forest even when everyone was calling for him. Beethoven expired in 1827 and later died for this.

France was in a very serious state. The French Revolution was ac-    21
complished before it happened. The Marseillaise was the theme song of the French Revolution, and it catapulted into Napoleon. During the Napoleonic Wars, the crowned heads of Europe were trembling in their shoes. Then the Spanish gorillas came down from the hills and nipped at Napoleon's flanks. Napoleon became ill with bladder problems and was very tense and unrestrained. He wanted an heir to inherit his power, but since Josephine was a baroness, she couldn't bear children.

The sun never set on the British Empire because the British Empire    22
is in the East and the sun sets in the West. Queen Victoria was the longest queen. She sat on a thorn for sixty-three years. Her reclining years and finally the end of her life were exemplatory of a great personality. Her death was the final event which ended her reign.

The nineteenth century was a time of many great inventions and    23
thoughts. The invention of the steamboat caused a network of rivers to spring up. Cyrus McCormick invented the McCormick raper, which did the work of a hundred men. Samuel Morse invented a code of

telepathy. Louis Pasteur discovered a cure for rabbis. Charles Darwin was a naturalist who wrote the *Organ of the Species*. Madman Curie discovered radium. And Karl Marx became one of the Marx brothers.

The First World War, caused by the assignation of the Arch-Duck by a surf, ushered in a new error in the anals of human history. 24

## THE FACTS

1. "The inhabitants of ancient Egypt were called mummies. They lived in the Sarah Dessert and traveled by Camelot." Who *were* the inhabitants of ancient Egypt, what desert did they live in, and how did they travel?
2. "The Bible is full of interesting caricatures." What is a caricature? What do you suppose the writer really meant to say?
3. "David was a Hebrew king skilled at playing the liar. He fought with the Philatelists, a race of people who lived in Biblical times." What instrument was David skilled at playing? What is a philatelist? With what people did David fight?
4. Of what did Socrates really die?
5. Who was Gutenberg, and what did he really invent?

## THE STRATEGIES

1. The author does not indicate with quotations marks or ellipses that he is quoting from the works of others. What effect does this omission have?
2. What logical and orderly pattern does this "essay" follow?
3. What do the errors and blunders all have in common? How does this common element add to the humor?
4. Aside from the first paragraph, the author adds no identifiable commentary of his own to the essay. Why?
5. On what prerequisite in the reader does this essay's humor depend? How would the essay likely appear to someone completely ignorant of Western history?

## THE ISSUES

1. Do you think that this essay is insulting to students? Justify your answer.
2. In the Chicago *Tribune* of May 25, 1916, Henry Ford was quoted as saying, "History is more or less bunk." Do you agree with his opinion? Of what value is history?
3. The author urges us to read carefully and learn a lot. What do you think he expects us to learn?

4. Some have alleged that students today are worse informed than those of a generation ago. What is your view of this opinion? If you agree, what reasons can you suggest to explain the discrepancy?
5. Should a student who is interested only in vocational training at school still be compelled to take mandatory courses in the humanities and history? Why or why not?

### SUGGESTIONS FOR WRITING

1. Take any ten paragraphs of this essay and rewrite them to correct their historical inaccuracies and grammatical blunders.
2. Attack or defend the proposition that history should be taught to all college students regardless of their academic majors.


Mark Twain

## • ADVICE TO YOUTH •

*Mark Twain, pseudonym of Samuel Langhorne Clemens (1835–1910), American author and humorist, was born in Missouri and spent most of his boyhood in Hannibal, on the Mississippi River, where he was apprenticed to a printer. During his long life, Twain was a printer, a journalist, a Mississippi riverboat pilot, a writer, and a humorous lecturer. He is regarded as the creator of the first modern American novel,* The Adventures of Huckleberry Finn *(1844). Among his many other works are* The Gilded Age *(1873), written with Charles Dudley Warner;* The Adventures of Tom Sawyer *(1876);* The Prince and the Pauper *(1882); and* A Connecticut Yankee in King Arthur's Court *(1889). Toward the end of his life, with the death of his wife and two daughters, Twain became increasingly bitter and misanthropic.*

*Exactly when and where this speech was given is uncertain. Twain wrote in his own hand that it was delivered "about 1882," but his memory for dates was notoriously unreliable. One editor guesses that it was delivered in Boston on April 15, 1882, at a meeting of The Saturday Morning Club, which would have been attended chiefly by young people. The adaptation of one's subject to meet the expectations of an audience, amply illustrated in this speech, is as much a matter of common sense as it is a principle of rhetoric.*

Being told I would be expected to talk here, I inquired what sort of   1
a talk I ought to make. They said it should be something suitable to

youth—something didactic, instructive, or something in the nature of good advice. Very well. I have a few things in my mind which I have often longed to say for the instruction of the young; for it is in one's tender early years that such things will best take root and be most enduring and most valuable. First, then, I will say to you, my young friends—and I say it beseechingly, urgingly—

Always obey your parents, when they are present. This is the best      2 policy in the long run, because if you don't they will make you. Most parents think they know better than you do, and you can generally make more by humoring that superstition than you can by acting on your own better judgment.

Be respectful to your superiors, if you have any, also to strangers,      3 and sometimes to others. If a person offends you, and you are in doubt as to whether it was intentional or not, do not resort to extreme measures; simply watch your chance and hit him with a brick. That will be sufficient. If you shall find that he had not intended any offense, come out frankly and confess yourself in the wrong when you struck him; acknowledge it like a man and say you didn't mean to. Yes, always avoid violence; in this age of charity and kindliness, the time has gone by for such things. Leave dynamite to the low and unrefined.

Go to bed early, get up early—this is wise. Some authorities say get      4 up with the sun; some others say get up with one thing, some with another. But a lark is really the best thing to get up with. It gives you a splendid reputation with everybody to know that you get up with the lark; and if you get the right kind of a lark, and work at him right, you can easily train him to get up at half past nine, every time—it is no trick at all.

Now as to the matter of lying. You want to be very careful about      5 lying; otherwise you are nearly sure to get caught. Once caught, you can never again be, in the eyes of the good and the pure, what you were before. Many a young person has injured himself permanently through a single clumsy and illfinished lie, the result of carelessness born of incomplete training. Some authorities hold that the young ought not to lie at all. That, of course, is putting it rather stronger than necessary; still, while I cannot go quite so far as that, I do maintain, and I believe I am right, that the young ought to be temperate in the use of this great art until practice and experience shall give them that confidence, elegance, and precision which alone can make the accomplishment graceful and profitable. Patience, diligence, painstaking attention to detail—these are the requirements; these, in time, will make the student perfect; upon these, and upon these only, may he rely as the sure foundation for future eminence. Think what tedious years of study, thought, practice, experience, went to the equipment of that peerless old master who was able to impose upon the whole world the lofty and sounding maxim that "truth is mighty and will prevail"— the most majestic compound fracture of fact which any of woman born has yet achieved. For the history of our race, and each individual's experience, are sown thick with evidence that a truth is not hard to kill and that a lie told well is immortal. There is in Boston a monument of the man who discovered anaesthesia; many people are aware, in these latter days, that the man didn't discover it at all, but stole the discovery from another man. Is this truth mighty, and will it prevail? Ah no, my hearers, the monument is made of hardy material, but the lie it tells will outlast it a million years. An awkward, feeble, leaky lie is a thing which you ought to make it your unceasing study to avoid; such a lie as that has no more real permanence than an average truth. Why, you might as well tell the truth at once and be done with it. A feeble, stupid, preposterous lie will not live two years   except it be a slander upon somebody. It is indestructible, then, of course, but that is no merit of yours. A final word: begin your practice of this gracious and beautiful art early—begin now. If I had begun earlier, I could have learned how.

Never handle firearms carelessly. The sorrow and suffering that have been caused through the innocent but heedless handling of firearms by the young! Only four days ago, right in the next farmhouse to the one where I am spending the summer, a grandmother, old and gray and sweet, one of the loveliest spirits in the land, was sitting at her work, when her young grandson crept in and got down an old, battered, rusty gun which had not been touched for many years and was supposed not to be loaded, and pointed it at her, laughing and threatening to shoot. In her fright she ran screaming and pleading toward the door on the other side of the room; but as she passed him he placed the gun almost against her very breast and pulled the trigger! He had supposed it was not loaded. And he was right—it wasn't. So there wasn't any harm done. It is the only case of that kind I ever heard of. Therefore, just the same, don't you meddle with old unloaded firearms; they are the most deadly and unerring things that have ever been created by man. You don't have to take any pains at all with them; you don't have to have a rest, you don't have to have any sights on the gun, you don't have to take aim, even. No, you just pick out a relative and bang away, and you are sure to get him. A youth who can't hit a cathedral at thirty yards with a Gatling gun in three-quarters of an hour, can take up an old empty musket and bag his grandmother every time, at a hundred. Think what Waterloo would have been if one of the armies had been boys armed with old muskets supposed not be loaded, and the other army had been composed of their female relations. The very thought of it makes one shudder.

There are many sorts of books; but good ones are the sort for the      7
young to read. Remember that. They are a great, an inestimable, an unspeakable means of improvement. Therefore be careful in your selection, my young friends; be very careful; confine yourselves exclusively to Robertson's Sermons, Baxter's *Saint's Rest, The Innocents Abroad*, and works of that kind.

But I have said enough. I hope you will treasure up the instructions      8
which I have given you, and make them a guide to your feet and a light to your understanding. Build your character thoughtfully and painstakingly upon these precepts, and by and by, when you have got it built, you will be surprised and gratified to see how nicely and sharply it resembles everybody else's.

## *VOCABULARY*

didactic (1)                    diligence (5)                    eminence (5)

## *THE FACTS*

1. How does Twain recommend answering an offense or insult?
2. What is the gist of Twain's advice about lying?
3. What "lofty and sounding maxim" does Twain call "the most majestic compound fracture of fact which any of woman born has yet achieved"?
4. Who, according to Twain, is an unerring marksman, and with what weapon and target?
5. What general category of books does Twain suggest for the young?

## THE STRATEGIES

1. Twain ends his first paragraph thus: "First, then, I will say to you, my young friends—and I say it beseechingly, urgingly—" What tone is he using here? What is its purpose?
2. Periphrasis is defined as "an indirect, abstract, roundabout method of stating ideas," and is frequently used by writers and speakers for humor. Which sentence in paragraph 5 is an obvious example of periphrasis?
3. Anticlimax is "the arrangement of descriptive or narrative details in such an order that the lesser, the trivial, or the ludicrous confront the reader at the point when he expects something greater and more serious." Which sentence in paragraph 2 meets this definition?
4. Reread paragraph 6. How would you characterize the ending of this story?
5. Twain writes: "A youth who can't hit a cathedral at thirty yards with a Gatling gun in three-quarters of an hour, can take up an old empty musket and bag his grandmother every time, at a hundred." Why does he use the word "bag"?

## THE ISSUES

1. What does this speech imply about Twain's view of human beings? Are adults really as hypocritical when moralizing to the young as Twain implies?
2. Twain says that if the young follow his advice, they will turn out like everybody else. What is everyone else like, according to this speech?
3. Twain's advice is supposedly intended to build character in the young. What is generally meant by "character" nowadays? How does character differ from personality?
4. Toward the end of his life, Twain became bitter and misanthropic in his outlook. What evidence, if any, can you find in this speech that foreshadows this change?
5. "Guns don't kill people; people kill people" is a slogan once favored by the gun lobby. How is this slogan proved or disproved by Twain's story about the grandson who pointed a gun at his elderly grandmother?

## SUGGESTIONS FOR WRITING

1. Analyze and discuss this speech as reflecting Twain's well-known hatred of hypocrisy.
2. Identify, analyze, and discuss Twain's use in this speech of anticlimax as a source of humor and satire.

Kate Chopin

## ────── • THE STORY OF AN HOUR • ──────

*Kate O'Flaherty Chopin (1851–1904), American author, was born in St. Louis of Creole–Irish descent. She married a Louisiana businessman with whom she lived in New Orleans, acquiring an intimate knowledge of Creole and Cajun life that became the theme for many of her stories. Her books include* Bayou Folk *(1894),* A Night in Acadie *(1897), and her controversial novel* The Awakening *(1899), whose direct treatment of female sexuality provoked a storm of criticism and censure. Largely ignored after her death, her work was rediscovered by feminists in the 1960s and reprinted to praise for its literary merit as well as its independence of mind.*

*"The Story of an Hour" tells about a young woman brought face-to-face by a sudden tragedy with her own hidden and forbidden longings. She accepts the truth about herself for an ecstatic instant and then, in a sudden reversal, finds herself stripped of it—with tragic consequences.*

Knowing that Mrs. Mallard was afflicted with a heart trouble, great    1
care was taken to break to her as gently as possible the news of her husband's death.

It was her sister Josephine who told her, in broken sentences, veiled    2
hints that revealed in half concealing. Her husband's friend Richards was there, too, near her. It was he who had been in the newspaper office when intelligence of the railroad disaster was received, with Brently Mallard's name leading the list of "killed." He had only taken the time to assure himself of its truth by a second telegram, and had hastened to forestall any less careful, less tender friend in bearing the sad message.

She did not hear the story as many women have heard the same,    3
with a paralyzed inability to accept its significance. She wept at once, with sudden, wild abandonment, in her sister's arms. When the storm of grief had spent itself she went away to her room alone. She would have no one follow her.

There stood, facing the open window, a comfortable, roomy arm-    4
chair. Into this she sank, pressed down by a physical exhaustion that haunted her body and seemed to reach into her soul.

She could see in the open square before her house the tops of trees    5
that were all aquiver with the new spring life. The delicious breath of rain was in the air. In the street below a peddler was crying his wares.

The notes of a distant song which some one was singing reached her faintly, and countless sparrows were twittering in the eaves.

There were patches of blue sky showing here and there through the clouds that had met and piled above the other in the west facing her window.    6

She sat with her head thrown back upon the cushion of the chair quite motionless, except when a sob came up into her throat and shook her, as a child who has cried itself to sleep continues to sob in its dreams.    7

She was young, with a fair, calm face, whose lines bespoke repression and even a certain strength. But now there was a dull stare in her eyes, whose gaze was fixed away off yonder on one of those patches of blue sky. It was not a glance of reflection, but rather indicated a suspension of intelligent thought.    8

There was something coming to her and she was waiting for it, fearfully. What was it? She did not know; it was too subtle and elusive to name. But she felt it, creeping out of the sky, reaching toward her through the sounds, the scents, the color that filled the air.    9

Now her bosom rose and fell tumultuously. She was beginning to recognize this thing that was approaching to possess her, and she was striving to beat it back with her will—as powerless as her two white slender hands would have been.    10

When she abandoned herself a little whispered word escaped her slightly parted lips. She said it over and over under her breath: "Free, free, free!" The vacant stare and the look of terror that had followed it went from her eyes. They stayed keen and bright. Her pulses beat fast, and the coursing blood warmed and relaxed every inch of her body.    11

She did not stop to ask if it were not a monstrous joy that held her. A clear and exalted perception enabled her to dismiss the suggestion as trivial.    12

She knew that she would weep again when she saw the kind, tender hands folded in death; the face that had never looked save with love upon her, fixed and gray and dead. But she saw beyond that bitter moment a long procession of years to come that would belong to her absolutely. And she opened and spread her arms out to them in welcome.    13

There would be no one to live for during those coming years; she would live for herself. There would be no powerful will bending her in that blind persistence with which men and women believe they have a    14 right to impose a private will upon a fellow-creature. A kind intention or a cruel intention made the act seem no less a crime as she looked upon it in that brief moment of illumination.

And yet she had loved him—sometimes. Often she had not. What did it matter! What could love, the unsolved mystery, count for in face of this possession of self-assertion which she suddenly recognized as the strongest impulse of her being! <sub>15</sub>

"Free! Body and soul free!" she kept whispering. <sub>16</sub>

Josephine was kneeling before the closed door with her lips to the keyhole, imploring for admission. "Louise, open the door! I beg; open the door—you will make yourself ill. What are you doing, Louise? For heaven's sake open the door." <sub>17</sub>

"Go away. I am not making myself ill." No; she was drinking in a very elixir of life through that open window. <sub>18</sub>

Her fancy was running riot along those days ahead of her. Spring days, and summer days, and all sorts of days that would be her own. She breathed a quick prayer that life might be long. It was only yesterday she had thought with a shudder that life might be long. <sub>19</sub>

She arose at length and opened the door to her sister's importunities. There was a feverish triumph in her eyes, and she carried herself unwittingly like a goddess of Victory. She clasped her sister's waist, and together they descended the stairs. Richards stood waiting for them at the bottom. <sub>20</sub>

Some one was opening the front door with a latchkey. It was Brently Mallard who entered, a little travel-stained, composedly carrying his gripsack and umbrella. He had been far from the scene of accident, and did not even know there had been one. He stood amazed at Josephine's piercing cry; at Richards' quick motion to screen him from the view of his wife. <sub>21</sub>

But Richards was too late. <sub>22</sub>

When the doctors came they said she had died of heart disease—of joy that kills. <sub>23</sub>

## VOCABULARY

forestall (2)              tumultuously (10)              importunities (20)
repression (8)

## THE FACTS

1. From what affliction did Mrs. Mallard suffer?
2. What news about her husband did Mrs. Mallard receive?
3. How did Mrs. Mallard initially react to the news about her husband?
4. What was her later reaction after the initial shock had passed?
5. What happened to Mrs. Mallard at the end of the story?

## THE STRATEGIES

1. Why do you think the author tells us in the very beginning of the story about Mrs. Mallard's affliction?
2. Read paragraphs 5 and 6. Given the news that Mrs. Mallard has just heard, what initially strikes a reader as odd and unusual about these paragraphs?
3. In paragraph 10, the author writes that Mrs. Mallard was "beginning to recognize this thing that was approaching to possess her." Why do you think the author chose to refer to Mrs. Mallard's feeling as an external "thing" rather than simply state that this was how she felt?
4. How would you characterize the ending of the story?

## THE ISSUES

1. Why does Mrs. Mallard secretly rejoice over the death of her husband? Do you regard her sentiments as anti-male? Justify your answer.
2. The story was written in the last century. Has marriage changed in our own time to the extent that married people enjoy greater freedom than Mrs. Mallard did? Explain your answer.
3. What kinds of conventional restrictions on the behavior of married people do you think are justified? What limits on personal freedom should marriage place on men and women?
4. Mrs. Mallard admits to sometimes loving her husband. How does this view differ from conventional wisdom about love?
5. What is your opinion of open marriages, in which each individual is perfectly free to do exactly as he or she pleases? Do you regard such marriages as workable? Why or why not?

## SUGGESTIONS FOR WRITING

1. Write an essay exploring the merits and demerits of conventional monogamous marriage.
2. Some sociologists have suggested that polygamous marriages—between several women and one man—should be allowed among the elderly, where women vastly outnumber men. Write an essay discussing this proposal.

Edna St. Vincent Millay

## • YOU WILL BE SORRY •

*Edna St. Vincent Millay (1892–1950), one of the most popular American poets of her era, wrote lyrics characterized by freshness and vigor. Born in Rockland, Maine, she attended Vassar College and spent much of her youth living in bohemian freedom in Greenwich Village, New York. Her collected work includes* A Few Figs from Thistles *(1920) and* The Ballad of the Harp Weaver *(1922). For the latter work she was awarded the Pulitzer Prize.*

*The voice in this sonnet, a poetic form over which Millay achieved absolute mastery, is indignant and angry over a familiar insult inflicted by an unknown someone, but it is also measured and dignified.*

Oh, oh, you will be sorry for that word!
Give back my book and take my kiss instead.
Was it my enemy or my friend I heard,
"What a big book for such a little head!"
Come, I will show you now my newest hat,                    5
And you may watch me purse my mouth and prink!
Oh, I shall love you still, and all of that.
I never again shall tell you what I think.
I shall be sweet and crafty, soft and sly;
You will not catch me reading any more:                     10
I shall be called a wife to pattern by;
And some day when you knock and push the door,
Some sane day, not too bright and not too stormy,
I shall be gone, and you may whistle for me.

### THE FACTS

1. What remark does the speaker of the poem bristle at?
2. What does the speaker say she will never again share with the unknown insulter?
3. What does the speaker threaten?

### THE STRATEGIES

1. What kind of sonnet is this?
2. "Come, I will show you now my newest hat, / And you may watch me purse my mouth and prink!" What tone is the speaker using here?
3. To what does the final couplet of the poem implicitly compare the speaker?

## THE ISSUES

1. Do you think the insult justifies the furious response of the speaker? Why or why not?
2. By implication, who insulted the speaker with the quoted remark? What evidence exists for this conclusion in the poem?
3. Do you think a similar remark might have been made to a man? Why or why not?

## SUGGESTIONS FOR WRITING

1. Write an analysis of this poem or some other poem by Millay. Direct your remarks not only to what the poem says, but also to how it says it.
2. Write a feminist interpretation of this poem.

# •• *ISSUE FOR CRITICAL THINKING* ••

## *Nuclear Weapons*

The control of nuclear weapons is one issue that makes a sham of anyone's pretense to indifference or neutrality. If nuclear weapons should ever be used in a global war, the committed as well as the indifferent among us will be just as efficiently incinerated. Yet for all the periodic hue and cry for missile reductions and nuclear freezes, somehow the arms race still lumbers on like an unleashed beast. Estimates are difficult to verify, but as of 1984 the United States was thought to possess 1,037 intercontinental ballistic missiles, some with individual warhead yields exceeding nine megatons of firepower (one megaton is equal to the explosive force of one million tons of TNT). The Soviet Union was judged to have an arsenal of 1,398 of these behemoth weapons, with comparatively hideous yields. Experts do not have to quibble over the finer details nor even count the submarine-launched missiles possessed by either country to reach this consensus: Both sides have enough nuclear weapons to destroy the entire world several times over. Once, any sane man or woman would think, is surely enough.

No doubt it was such horrifying statistics as these that prompted peace activist Randall Forsberg to propose a nuclear weapons freeze in April of 1980. The issue was debated in the House of Representatives in 1983 and defeated by the narrowest margin, 204 to 202. Since then the U.S. and the Soviet Union have engaged on and off in peace talks, and some inching progress has been made on various schemes for reducing nuclear weapons deployed in Europe.

The direct participants in our debate about nuclear weapons and their control are Roger Fisher and Charlton Heston. Fisher's speech, reproduced here as an argument for control of nuclear weapons, was given before a symposium organized by the Physicians for Social Responsibility in 1981. Heston's own speech was delivered in 1983 to the National Center for Legislative Research. The third voice is that of Mrs. Futaba Kitayama, a Japanese housewife who survived the bombing of Hiroshima. When we remember that the inferno she endured and witnessed was inflicted by a runt of an A-bomb whose yield was estimated at a paltry 20,000 tons of TNT, we cannot even imagine the nightmarish holocaust of a modern one-megaton bomb dropped on a major population center such as Moscow or New York.

**Roger Fisher**

———— • **PREVENTING NUCLEAR WAR** • ————

*Roger Fisher (b. 1922), professor of law at Harvard Law School, was the origi-nator and executive editor of* The Advocates *(1969–1970) and* Arabs and Israelis *(1974–1975), two public television series produced by WGBH in Bos-ton. He is the author of several books, among them* International Conflict for Beginners *(1969) and* International Crises and the Role of Law: Points of Choice *(1978).*

"Preventing Nuclear War"? "Boy, have *you* got a problem." That reaction a few minutes ago to the title of these remarks reminded me of an incident when during World War II, I was a B-17 weather recon-naissance officer. One fine day we were in Newfoundland test-flying a new engine that replaced one we had lost. Our pilot's rank was only that of flight officer because he had been court martialed so frequently for his wild activities; but he was highly skillful. 1

He took us up to about 14,000 feet and then, to give the new engine a rigorous test, he stopped the other three and feathered their propel-lers into the wind. It is rather impressive to see what a B-17 can do on one engine. But then, just for a lark, the pilot feathered the fourth propeller and turned off that fourth engine. With all four propellers stationary, we glided, somewhat like a stone, toward the rocks and forests of Newfoundland. 2

After a minute or so the pilot pushed the button to unfeather. Only   3
then did he remember: In order to unfeather the propeller you had to
have electric power, and in order to have electric power you had to have
at least one engine going. As we were buckling on our parachutes, the
copilot burst out laughing. Turning to the pilot he said, "Boy, have *you*
got a problem!"

As with the crew of that B-17, we're all in this together. Professionals,   4
whether lawyers like myself or doctors like you, tend to put the problem of preventing nuclear war on somebody else's agenda. But
whoever is responsible for creating the danger, we're all on board one
fragile spacecraft. The risk is high. What can we do to reduce it?

There are two kinds of reasons for the high risk: hardware reasons   5
and people reasons. We—and the military—tend to focus on the hardware: nuclear explosives and the means for their delivery. We think
about the terrible numbers of terrible weapons. We count them by the
hundreds, by the thousands and by the tens of thousands. There are
clearly too many. There are too many fingers on the trigger. There are
too many hands through which weapons pass in Europe, in the United
States and in the Soviet Union.

Yes, changes should be made in the hardware. I believe we should   6
stop all nuclear weapons production; we should cut back on our stock-
piles. But even if we should succeed in stopping production, and even
if we should succeed in bringing about significant reductions, there
will still be thousands of nuclear weapons. We keep our attention on
the hardware. The military think it is the answer; we think it is the
problem. In my judgment it is not the most serious problem.

The U.S. Air Force and the U.S. Navy both have enough weapons   7
to blow each other up; and they have disagreements. There are serious
disputes between the Air Force and the Navy: disputes that mean jobs,
careers; disputes that are sometimes more serious in practical consequences than those between the United States and the Soviet Union.
But the two services have learned to fight out their differences before
the Senate Appropriations Committee, before the Secretary of Defense, in the White House and on the football field.

The case of the Navy and the Air Force demonstrates, in a crude   8
way, that the problem is not just in the hardware; it is in our heads. It
lies in the way we think about nuclear weapons. And if the problem
lies in the way we think, then that's where the answer lies. In Pogo's
immortal phrase, "We have met the enemy and they are us."

The danger of nuclear war is so great primarily because of the men-    9
tal box we put ourselves in. We all have working assumptions that
remain unexamined. It is these assumptions that make the world so
dangerous. Let me suggest three sets of mistaken assumptions about:
(1) our goals, that is, the ends we are trying to pursue; (2) the means
for pursuing those ends; and (3) whose job it is to do what.

● First, what are our goals? Internationally, we think we want to    10
"win." We go back to primitive notions of victory. We look at a situation
and we ask, "Who's winning?" But that is an area in which we must
change our thinking. Internationally and domestically, we do not really
want a system in which any one side—even our own—wins all the
time. Yet this concept of "winning"—that there is such a thing and
that it is our dominant objective—is one of our fundamental beliefs.

In fact, like a poker player, we have three kinds of objectives. One is    11
to win the hand. Whatever it is we think we want, we want it now. We
want victory. The second is to be in a good position for future hands.
We want a reputation and chips on the table so that we can influence
future events. In other words, we want power. Our third objective is
not to have the table kicked over, the house burned down, or our
opponent pull a gun. We want peace.

We want victory; we want power; we want peace. Exploding nuclear    12
weapons will not help us achieve any one of them. We have to re-
examine rigorously our working assumption that in a future war we
would want to "win." What do we mean by "win"? What would our
purpose be?

Last spring I gave the officers at the NATO Defense College in Rome    13
a hypothetical war in Europe, and asked them to work out NATO's war
aims. The "war" was presumed to have grown out of a general strike
in East Germany, with Soviet and West German tanks fighting on both
sides of the border. Deterrence had failed. I told the officers: "You are
in charge of the hotline message to Moscow. What is the purpose of
this war? What are you trying to do?" At first they thought they
knew—win! Very simple. But what did that mean? What was the
purpose of the war? They began to realize that NATO did not plan to
conquer the Soviet Union acre by acre as the Allies had conquered
Germany in World War II. They did not plan physically to impose their
will on the Soviet Union. They were seeking a Soviet decision. That
was the only way they could have a successful outcome.

With further thought they reached a second conclusion; they were  14
not going to ask for unconditional surrender. That gave them a specific
task: Just define the Soviet decision that would constitute success for
NATO and that NATO could reasonably expect the Soviet Union to make.
The officers worked through the day considering how the Russians
probably saw their choice, how we wanted them to see it, and what
kind of "victory" for us we could realistically expect the Soviet Union
to agree to.

It turned out that the only plausible objective was to stop the war.  15
"Winning" meant ending the war on acceptable terms. The goal was
some kind of cease-fire, the sooner the better. It was with difficulty
and even pain that some officers discovered that winning meant stopping, even if some Soviet troops remained in West Germany; even with
only a promise to restore the *status quo ante*.*

They found it hard to draft a fair cease-fire that didn't sound like a  16
unilateral Western ultimatum. It might say, "Stop firing at 0100 hours
tomorrow, promise to withdraw, promise to restore the status quo
within 48 hours, and we will meet in Vienna to talk about serious
problems as soon as the status quo is 'more or less' restored." But the
NATO draftsmen did not know whether the Soviets would prefer Geneva to Vienna or whether they wanted 0200 hours instead of 0100
hours, etc.

Someone creatively suggested, "Wouldn't it be a good idea if right  17
now we worked out with the Russians some standby cease-fire terms?
Then in a crisis we wouldn't have to be demanding that they accept
our terms or they demanding that we accept theirs. Let's produce some
cease-fire drafts that we can both accept." One of the other officers
was incredulous: "What did you say? You are going to negotiate the
armistice before the war begins? In that case, why have the war?"

The need to re-examine assumptions about our foreign policy objec-  18
tives is also demonstrated by our self-centered definition of national
security. Typically, political leaders and journalists alike suggest that
the primary goal of foreign policy is national security, and only after
that has been assured should we worry about our relations with the
Soviet Union.

---

*Latin, "In the state in which things were before."—Ed.

Such thinking assumes that we can be secure while the Soviet Union   19
is insecure—that somehow we can be safe while the Soviet Union faces
a high risk of nuclear war. But in any nuclear war between the United
States and the Soviet Union missiles will go both ways. There is no
way we can make the world more dangerous for them without also
making it more dangerous for ourselves. The less secure the Soviets
feel, the more they will be doing about it, and the less secure we will
become. Security is a joint problem.

We must make the Soviet Union share responsibility for our security   20
problem. We should say, "Look, you Russians have to understand why
we built these missiles and how it looks to us when you behave as you
do. You must take some responsibility for helping us deal with our
security problem." Similarly, we must take on responsibility for dealing with their security problem. We cannot make our end of the boat
safer by making the Soviet end more likely to capsize. We cannot
improve our security by making nuclear war more likely for them. We
can't "win" security from nuclear war unless they win it too. Any
contrary assumption is dangerous.

Here I may point out that we in the peace movement do not always   21
practice what we preach. I am always ready to tell friends at the Pentagon that it does no good to call Soviet officials idiots, but am likely to
add, "Don't you see that, you idiot"? We who are concerned with
reducing the risks of war often think that our job is to "win" the war
against hawks. In advancing our interests we assume that our adversaries have none worth considering. But our task is not to win a battle.
Instead, we have to find out what the other side's legitimate concerns
are, and we have to help solve their legitimate problems in order to
solve our own. At every level, domestically and internationally, we
need to re-examine our working assumptions. We are not seeking to
win a war, but to gain a peace.

• A second set of dangerous assumptions are those we make about   22
how to pursue our objectives. The basic mistaken assumption is that
for every problem there is a military solution. We will first try diplo-
macy. We will talk about it; we will negotiate. But if that doesn't solve
the problem we assume that we can always resort to force. We tend to
assume that if we have the will and the courage, and are prepared to
pay the price, then we can always solve the problem by military means.
Wrong. For the world's big problems there is no military solu-

tion. Nuclear war is not a solution. It is worse than any problem it might "solve."

We have mislearned from the past. During World War II the Allies   23
could physically impose a result on Hitler and his country. Acre by acre it was done. But the world has changed. We can no longer impose such a result on any nuclear power. We cannot physically make things happen. The only means we have available is to try to change someone's mind.

There is no way in which nuclear hardware can bring about a phys-   24
ical solution to any problem we face except the population problem. Just as you cannot make a marriage work by dynamite or make a town work by blowing it up, there is no way we can make the world work by using nuclear bombs. When people hear that they say, "Yes, that's true." Yet they go right ahead, operating on the assumption that there are military solutions.

Like Linus in the Charlie Brown comic strip, we cling to our security   25
blanket, military hardware. Both U.S. and Soviet officials clutch their plutonium security blankets as though somehow they offer real security. Somehow, we think, this bomb, this hardware, will give us strength, will protect us. We will be able to avoid the necessity of dealing with the real world. Our assumption is that the problem is simple—it's us against them. We want to believe in a quick fix. It is like cowboys and Indians. Whatever the problem, John Wayne will arrive with his six-guns blazing, and the problem will be solved.

Those are our common assumptions about how to deal with inter-   26
national problems. We operate on them although most of us know they are not true. The fact that conventional weapons remain useful and that conventional wars, such as that between Iraq and Iran, continue, reinforces our mistaken assumptions about the use of nuclear weapons.

We have far better ways to deal with international problems. Break   27
up big problems into manageable pieces. Look at each item on its merits. Sit down side-by-side and discuss it. Don't concentrate on what our adversaries say their positions are, but try to understand and deal with their interests. Communicate and listen. What's in their minds? What's bothering them? How would we feel?

If you were sitting in Moscow and looking off to the left saw Japan   28
thinking of rearming; if you saw your long-time strongest ally, China,

with a 2,000-mile common frontier, now your worst enemy; if you saw Pakistan apparently getting a nuclear bomb; if you heard Western voices saying, "We must help the rebels in Afghanistan"; if you saw American military equipment now in the Gulf, in Saudi Arabia, in Egypt and in Israel; if you saw Greece rejoining NATO and Turkey in the hands of a military government; and if cruise missiles were about to be located in West Germany—how must that all look from Moscow? We should put ourselves in their shoes and understand their problems. The only way we can succeed is to affect their future thinking. The starting point is to understand their present thinking.

Second, we have to invent wise solutions. We have to figure out not just good arguments, but good ways to reconcile our differing interests. And they must participate in that process. There is no way, in any conflict, in which one side can produce the right answer. The understanding that comes from both sides working on a problem, and the acceptability that comes from joint participation in a solution, make any good answer better. We need to engage in joint problem-solving.   29

That same process of working together is equally applicable to our domestic difference. The peace movement is not the only source of wisdom; we are part of the conflict. There are a lot of people in this country who have legitimate concerns about the Soviet Union. We must try to understand these concerns and meet them, not carry on a war. We need to put ourselves in their shoes—in Pentagon shoes. We have to listen as well as talk. With their participation, we will invent better solutions.   30

By this process we will promote joint learning, not just at the intellectual level but at the level of feeling, of emotion, of caring, the level of concern. International conflict is too often dealt with cerebrally, too often dealt with as a hypothetical problem out there. We need not only to apply what we know, but to keep on learning about human behavior, how to affect our own behavior and that of others, not just manipulate it.   31

The danger of nuclear war lies largely within us. It lies in how we think about winning, in how we define success, and in our illusions of being able to impose results.   32

• The danger also comes from my third set of assumptions—about whose job it is to reduce the risk of war. If there were a military solution, there would be a case for leaving it to the military—to policy-science experts, and to professional strategists. Physicians, for exam-   33 ple, have said: "We are just concerned with the medical aspects of nuclear war and will limit ourselves to that area. We will tell you how bad a nuclear war would be. It is somebody else's job to prevent it."

Such statements rest on the assumption that the solution is in the hardware department. But we are not facing a technical military problem "out there." The solution lies right here: in changing our own assumptions and those of other people; in growing up; in abandoning our plutonium security blanket.    34

The Soviet Union and the United States cling to nuclear weapons as symbols of security; other national leaders want them. If someone is clinging to a plutonium blanket which is bad for his health, you do not call in an engineer and say, "Design a better plutonium blanket." The problem is in the heads of those who are clinging to it.    35

There is no one I know who has a professional license in the skills of reducing the risk of nuclear war. Fortunately, however, no professional license is required. But who are those with skills in dealing with psychological problems like denial, like distancing, like turning flesh and blood issues into abstract problems through the use of jargon? Who is likely to notice that people are denying responsibility because a problem seems too overwhelming? Nuclear engineers? I think not.    36

A few minutes ago I left you in a B-17 over the hills of Newfoundland. The co-pilot was saying to the pilot: "Boy, do *you* have a problem." Well, we didn't crash; we weren't all killed. On that plane we had a buck sergeant who remembered that back behind the bomb bay we had a putt-putt generator for use in case we had to land at some emergency air field that did not have any electric power to start the engines. The sergeant found it. He fiddled with the carburetor; wrapped a rope around the flywheel a few times; pulled it and pulled it; got the generator going and before we were down to 3,000 feet we had electricity. The pilot restarted the engines, and we were all safe. Now saving that plane was not the sergeant's job in the sense that he created the risk. The danger we were in was not his fault or his responsibility. But it was his job in the sense that he had an opportunity to do something about it.    37

We professionals tend to define our roles narrowly. I sometimes ask my law students: "What would have been the responsibility of a professional musician judging Nero's performance on the fiddle while Rome burned? Should he limit himself to discussing the music?" A member of the lay public would probably get a bucket and put out the    38 fire. By becoming professionals do we become less responsible? Can we say, "No, I'm a professional. I'm not a firefighter. That's someone else's job."?

Such special knowledge and training as we have may not make it  39
obligatory for us to try to prevent nuclear war. Rather, it gives us an opportunity. My notion of whose job something is is best defined by who has an opportunity. We have an opportunity. I encourage you, as I encourage myself, to use it. The world is at risk. The very danger of nuclear war means that there is more opportunity to make a difference than ever before.

If everyone with any significant power made the right decision every  40
time, that's as near utopia as we can get. There are only three reasons they don't. One is that they are poor decision-makers. Our job is to change them; that is what politics is about. Second, they are operating on bad assumptions, thinking poorly. Our job is to correct their assumptions. And the third possibility is that they are subject to harmful constraints. Our job is to free them from those constraints.

In a simple chart I have put all problems on the left-hand side,  41
divided into those three parts. Across the top are the activities in which we can engage: research on facts and theory; communication in terms of learning ourselves and teaching others; devising things to do (that is, turning a problem into a possible answer, inventing possible proposals or action ideas), getting a proposal onto somebody's agenda; advocating ideas; or doing something ourselves.

To get a wise decision we need good answers *in every box*. No  42
amount of useful research will overcome poor deciders; no number of good deciders will overcome bad assumptions or harmful constraints. Somebody has to invent what's to be done. Somebody has to put it on the agenda. Somebody has to persuade others that it is a good idea and somebody has to do it. All those activities are needed for each category of problem. There is enough to keep all of us busy.

## CHART OF USEFUL ACTIVITIES

Avoiding nuclear war will require wise decision-makers, who make wise assumptions on ends and means, and who are free from harmful constraints. Which part of that problem do you want to work on? Which activity will best harness your interests and abilities? To get wise results someone must devote attention to each box in the matrix. To get a wise decision answers are needed in every box.

| PROBLEMS | ACTIVITIES | | | | | |
|---|---|---|---|---|---|---|
| | Research: facts, theory | Commu-nicate: learn, teach | Devise things to do | Build an agenda | Advocate | Do it yourself |
| Poor deciders | | | | | | |
| Poor thinking on ends on means | | | | | | |
| Harmful constraints | | | | | | |

All of us can do any of those things. No single activity will be  43
sufficient. We need theory on how to reduce instability. We need to
develop knowledge about nuclear war, about the consequences and
about ways to reduce the risks. We need to communicate that knowledge both to the public, who constrain our decision-makers, and to
the people who are making the decisions. We need to communicate
both the bad news and the opportunities for reducing it.

If all we do is deliver bad news and say that there's nothing we can  44
do about it, the bad news does not become operational. We have to
turn that news into something we can do.

My favorite activity is inventing. An early arms control proposal  45
dealt with the problem of distancing that the President would have in
the circumstances of facing a decision about nuclear war. There is a
young man, probably a Navy officer, who accompanies the President.
This young man has a black attache case which contains the codes that
are needed to fire nuclear weapons. I could see the President at a staff
meeting considering nuclear war as an abstract question. He might
conclude: "On SIOP Plan One, the decision is affirmative. Communicate the Alpha line XYZ." Such jargon holds what is involved at a
distance.

My suggestion was quite simple: Put that needed code number in a  46
little capsule, and then implant that capsule right next to the heart of a
volunteer. The volunteer would carry with him a big, heavy butcher
knife as he accompanied the President. If ever the President wanted to
fire nuclear weapons, the only way he could do so would be for him
first, with his own hands, to kill one human being. The President says,

"George, I'm sorry but tens of millions must die." He has to look at someone and realize what death is—what an innocent death is. Blood on the White House carpet. It's reality brought home.

When I suggested this to friends in the Pentagon they said, "My    47 God, that's terrible. Having to kill someone would distort the President's judgment. He might never push the button."

Whether or not that particular idea has any merit, there is lots to do.    48 Action is required to convince the public that it is in our interest to have the Soviets feel secure rather than insecure. Much of the press apparently thinks that the more terrified the Soviets are the more we benefit. The Committee on the Present Danger (perhaps better called the Committee on Increasing the Present Danger) ignores the fact that if we raise the risk of nuclear war for the Soviet Union we also raise it for ourselves.

If you don't know what to do, that's great. That gives you something    49 to do right there. Get some friends together on Saturday morning and generate some ideas. Separate this inventing process from the later process of deciding among them. Identify three or four other people who might make a decision of some significance. What can you do to increase the chance they'll make some desired decision next week? Whoever it is—journalists, congressmen, governors, legislators, newspaper editors, businessmen, a civic organization, a medical association, a friend of President Reagan's, a school teacher, a publisher—what are some things they might do that would illuminate our faulty working assumptions to help establish better ones? Figuring out what to do is itself an excellent activity. In intellectual efforts, as in gunnery, aiming is crucial.

Don't wait to be instructed. Take charge. This is not an organized    50 campaign that someone else is going to run. If you share these concerns, get involved. There is a lot to do to reduce the risk of nuclear war. Reading, writing, talking, perhaps a radio program, or perhaps a letter-writing campaign to your congressman. Tell him, "Grow up. Give up your plutonium security blanket."

But perhaps you are still holding on to your own security blanket,    51 that neat definition of your job. The security blanket most of us cling to is, "Don't blame me. It's not my job to plan nuclear strategy. I'm not responsible for the risk of nuclear war." You can give up that security blanket any time.

The way to enlist support is not to burden others with guilt but to 52 provide them with an opportunity to volunteer. I find it an exciting venture. It is a glorious world outside. There are people to be loved and pleasures to share. We should not let details of past wars and the threat of the future take away the fun and the joy we can have working together on a challenging task. I see no reason to be gloomy about trying to save the world. There is more exhilaration, more challenge, more zest in tilting at windmills than in any routine job. Be involved, not just intellectually but emotionally. Here is a chance to work together with affection, with caring, with feeling. Feel some of your emotions. Don't be uptight. You don't have to be simply a doctor, a lawyer, or a merchant. We are human beings. Be human.

People have struggled all of their lives to clear ten acres of ground 53 or simply to maintain themselves and their family. Look at the opportunity we have. Few people in history have been given such a chance— a chance to apply our convictions, our values, our highest moral goals with such competence as our professional skills may give us. A chance to work with others—to have the satisfaction that comes from playing a role, however small, in a constructive enterprise. It's not compulsory. So much the better. But what challenge could be greater? We have an opportunity to improve the chance of human survival.

In medicine there is a traditional call that strikes a nice balance 54 between duty and opportunity, that invites us to lend a hand with all the skill and compassion we can muster: "Is there a doctor in the house?"

## VOCABULARY

| | | |
|---|---|---|
| reconnaissance (1) | armistice (17) | obligatory (39) |
| deterrence (13) | adversaries (21) | constraints (40) |
| plausible (15) | cerebrally (31) | exhilaration (52) |
| unilateral (16) | hypothetical (31) | compulsory (53) |

## THE FACTS

1. Fisher says that there are two kinds of reasons for the high risk of nuclear war. What are they?
2. What three sets of mistaken assumptions do people make in thinking about nuclear war?

3. In contemplating a possible nuclear war between the United States and the Soviet Union, what did the NATO officers discover about the meaning of "winning"?
4. What does Fisher suggest is a better way of dealing with international problems than stockpiling nuclear weapons?
5. What fault does Fisher see in the way international conflict is presently handled?
6. According to Fisher, whose job is it to try and prevent the occurrence of a nuclear war?
7. What idea did Fisher suggest as a way of overcoming the problem of distancing that a president might face in deciding whether or not to start a nuclear war?

## THE STRATEGIES

1. Although this is one of the longer pieces in the book, only twelve words from it have made the vocabulary list. Why do you think the author uses such a simple and colloquial vocabulary?
2. The anecdote about the B-17 makes an important point. But what other purpose does this anecdote serve?
3. The subject of this speech is divided into three major categories that are systematically covered. How does the author make a clear transition from one category to another?
4. What analogy does Fisher use in paragraph 11 to clarify our dominant objectives in dealing with other nations?
5. Paragraphs 13 through 17 discuss the responses of NATO officers to a hypothetical war problem posed them by Fisher. Essentially, what rhetorical task did the author assign the officers?
6. What is the purpose of paragraph 26 and paragraph 32? What do these two paragraphs have in common?
7. In the first 37 paragraphs of this speech Fisher analyzes the dangerous and mistaken assumptions we have about nuclear weapons. If the first two-thirds of this speech is analytical, how would you characterize the remaining one-third of it?

## THE ISSUES

1. Much has been made about the fanaticism of communists and the communist movement. What is your personal view of communists and their movement? Do you regard worldwide communism as a unified ideology with a single goal, or do you think it an ideology that has been modified in its application to different countries?

2. Fisher claims that we do not want a system in which any one side—even our own—wins all the time. Why not? What is wrong with our side winning all the time?
3. Fisher says that political leaders and journalists typically suggest that the primary goal of foreign policy is national security. What does national security mean to you?
4. What assumption about the Soviets does Fisher seem to be making throughout this speech? How does this assumption tally with your own preconceptions of them?
5. What does Fisher mean by "distancing"? What psychological need does distancing satisfy? How is it used in our everyday lives?

### *SUGGESTIONS FOR WRITING*

1. It has been variously estimated that a nuclear war between the United States and the Soviet Union would inflict some 50 to 100 million casualties immediately on either nation, not to mention the uncountable number of fatalities that would follow from radiation sickness and pestilence. Over what issues do you think such a war worth fighting? Write an essay exploring this problem as you see it.
2. Since the United States already has enough nuclear weapons to destroy the world several times over, should it unilaterally reduce its stockpile of weapons as the author suggests? Write an essay debating this issue.

**Charlton Heston**

## ———— • THE PEACE MOVEMENT • ————

*Charlton Heston (b. 1924) was born in Evanston, Illinois, and educated at Northwestern University. A well-known actor, he is identified in the public mind with such memorable films as* The Ten Commandments *and* Ben Hur, *for which he won an Oscar. But, as the following speech shows, Heston is also an outspoken advocate of conservative political views, one of which is staunch opposition to the Nuclear Freeze movement.*

I was in Los Alamos a few weeks ago, doing a minor chore for the    1
Atomic Testing Laboratory the University of California maintains

there. As I was leaving, they presented me with a sample of a rare mineral . . . trinitite. It was formed instantaneously, thirty-eight years ago, from the sand of the New Mexican desert in the atomic test, code-named "Trinity," that validated the atomic bombs that ended World War II.

I took it home and gave it to my son, Fraser, a fine young man of twenty-seven, because it occurred to me that it was, in a very real sense, his birthstone. In the summer of 1945, when the blast that coalesced the sands of Los Alamos into trinitite was set off, Fraser was unconceived and his mother was still in school. I was in the Aleutian Islands in the 11th Air Force, preparing to invade the main islands of Japan.

If the trinity test had failed, no atomic bombs would have fallen on Hiroshima and Nagasaki, and the hundred and fifty thousand Japanese who died there would have been spared. Some of them, at least. Many, surely, would have been included in the four million Japanese it was estimated would die in the invasion of Japan. "Operation Coronet" it was called. U.S. losses were expected to be one million men. One million men who would not come home, whose children would not be born. I don't know if I would have been among them or not, of course . . . but I'm glad I didn't have to find out. The creation of that lump of trinitite saved the lives of five million people and allowed the creation of ten million more. Perhaps my son lives because we bombed Hiroshima, ten years before he was born.

In the generation of his lifetime, since those stirring days, much has changed. We thought we had defeated tyranny forever and democracy was the bright wave of the future. We were wrong. It is tyranny that floats on a rising tide, and freedom lives only on islands of democracy scattered in a sullen sea. The climate of the blood is chill. . . . It has turned to dark November in the American soul.

"Peace" is the cry on every hand. From politicians sniffing a breeze bearing votes, from scholars and bishops, and earnest journalists, from anxious mothers and frightened school children taught to draw crayola mushroom clouds instead of Easter bunnies, we hear it. "Peace. God, give us peace." Amen to that, surely.

The curious thing is, we *have* peace. Since Hiroshima, there has been no global war. Peace has been preserved for almost thirty-eight years by the nuclear deterrent maintained by the United States and her NATO allies. This force has restrained the only conceivable enemy in such a conflict: the Soviet Union.

Nevertheless, throughout the Western democracies in the last two years, thousands of decent people, chilled by the fear of nuclear war, have concluded that the way to avoid it is to toss away the shield that has protected us from it. War is a terrible thing, to fear it is reasonable, and common to us all. But fear is not a reasonable guide for human actions.

History is. Less than forty-five years ago, we saw the same phenomenon in Europe we see now. The enemy was Hitler then, but the fear of war was just as real. Then, as now, this fear led many to propose the most irrational compromises, the most cringing accommodations. Winston Churchill, out of office and vilified as a war-monger, fought to stem the tide. A rich lady labourite chided him once at dinner. "Tell me, Mr. Churchill," she said. "Why do you try so hard to persuade us that Hitler is a bad man?" "If I do not succeed, Madam," said Churchill, "I'm afraid you will find out." They did.

We may well find out in our time. Meanwhile, many of my countrymen propose as a solution a nuclear freeze, to be negotiated bilaterally between the United States and the Soviet Union. This has been the subject of intense debate in the West, to which we are even now contributing. There has of course been no such debate in the Soviet Union, because there *is* no debate in the Soviet Union. This is not to say that the Soviets have not contributed to the debate. They have, very effectively, but their efforts have been confined to the Western democracies, where a highly sophisticated and well-planned KGB disinformation program has functioned most effectively in the freeze movement in the West. This fact does not reflect on the sincerity of the thousands of people in the West who support a nuclear freeze out of a conviction that it will somehow bring us the peace of the world we all seek. I've heard several of them. There is no doubting the passion they bring to their belief in the freeze as a panacea for peace. I'm very pleased to have been asked to speak on this issue tonight, but I'll try to do so without passion. A few months ago, I heard a man . . . another actor, I'm afraid . . . support the freeze by saying, "No, I haven't *read* anything about it. I don't need to. This is a gut issue." Indeed it is. But you can't think with your guts. You can, of course, think of the search for peace as a moral obligation incumbent on every human being. Let us do that, by all means. A great philosopher . . . Hegel, I think . . . put that best. He said, "The most important of all moral obligations is to think clearly." My hope . . . my passionate hope, if you like . . . is that all of us will do that on this subject.

Without passion, then, and with as much reason as we can muster,   10 let us consider the nuclear freeze. Reason tells us a freeze will not preserve the peace; worse than that, it threatens the peace we enjoy, because it is unnegotiable, unverifiable, and unequal. Let's examine those three negatives in order.

To attempt to negotiate a bilateral freeze treaty with the Soviet Union   11 would, in the first place, derail the American efforts now in progress in Geneva not merely to freeze nuclear arms, but reduce them. It would also fragment the popular support crucial to those negotiations. Indeed, the freeze debate has already done that, a fact not lost on the Soviets. They are unlikely to move in any negotiation until they see how far the debate in this country brings us toward accommodation with the Soviet position. Ignorant as they are of the open function of the democratic process in a free society, and truly unable to comprehend the power of the American media, the Soviets take our debate on this issue merely as a sign of weakness of will and commitment in the American people. That message is false, but it nonetheless echoes in the Kremlin. To a lesser degree, the same message is marked in the NATO countries to whose security we have been committed for two generations, all of them democracies who depend on us for that security.

The difficulties of negotiating with the Soviets are compounded not   12 only by their ignorance of our system, but by our ignorance of theirs. David Satter, a journalist of long experience in Russia, wrote recently on this point. "We are not only different countries," he said, "but different mentalities. The Soviet Union is based on an ideology which claims to be a system of universal explanation. Soviet leaders operate on the assumption that they are infallible. Soviet citizens defer to this authority. In order to fulfill their ideology, the Soviets must *create* reality. Instead, they have created a whole series of mirages imitating democratic institutions . . . trade unions without power, newspapers without information, courts to which there is no recourse, and a parliament without function."

If we cannot penetrate the Soviet mind, nor comprehend Soviet   13 ideology, we still have a valuable guide in considering negotiations with them. We're all familiar with Santayana's dictum, "He who will not study history is doomed to repeat it." If we fail to study the lessons history provides us on the Soviet Union, we face a very unpleasant doom indeed. The nuclear freeze proposal, as even its supporters concede, requires the adherence of the Soviets to the terms of any treaty that might be negotiated. Lenin, the founding father and patron saint of the Soviet state, set Soviet policy on treaties. "Promises are like pie crust," he said. "Made to be broken." They have followed his advice.

To put it succinctly, the Soviets have violated nearly every treaty they have signed since the founding of the Soviet state in 1922, from the League of Nations and the Geneva Convention, through the Atlantic Charter, Yalta, Potsdam, the Four-Power Agreement on Berlin, the United Nations Charter, the Nuclear Test-Ban Treaty, and the Helsinki Human-Rights Agreement, as well as SALT I and II. The several treaties they broke in their brutal invasions of Finland, Hungary, Czechoslovakia, and Afghanistan, and their use of poison gas there, as well as in Laos and Cambodia, revolted the world. This has deterred neither the Soviets nor those eager to undertake yet another treaty with them. The rising evidence linking them to the attempted assassination of the Pope indicates so horrendous a violation of the code by which civilized nations coexist in the world that Western governments can hardly bring themselves to contemplate the consequences. 14

The Soviets did adhere scrupulously to one treaty: their secret pact with Hitler to invade Poland in 1939. Of course, this treaty violated a previous non-aggression pact with Poland, so perhaps we can call that a wash. 15

A nuclear freeze observed by us and broken by the Soviets would be suicidal, I think most would agree. Therefore, on the historical record, it is unnegotiable. 16

All right, what about verification? An ABC/*Washington Post* poll last year indicated that 80 percent of those polled felt the Soviets would try to cheat on a freeze treaty, and 87 percent opposed such a treaty if they *could* cheat. Yet freeze initiatives passed in several states. So much for reason over emotion. 17

Since almost no one will seriously defend the idea that the Soviets can be trusted to keep an agreement on their own, a freeze treaty *depends* on verification. Indeed, most freeze proposals specify a verifiable ban on "the testing and/or production of nuclear weapons or 18 carriers," meaning aircraft. Despite what you may have heard about the uncanny surveillance capacities of our space satellites, they are useless in cloudy weather, or over areas not covered by their orbits. Since those orbits are well known to Soviet intelligence, both as to track and timing, the movement and storage of vehicles, supplies, and equipment, even in open country, can be scheduled to the absence of the satellite. The Soviets routinely exploit these shortfalls in our satellite capacity. Furthermore, design and testing operations are routinely and can entirely be conducted indoors or underground. Satellite surveillance is useless in these circumstances. Lastly, our satellites are vulnerable in ways I will not specify to attacks from an increasingly effective Soviet anti-satellite technology. I've attended classified briefings in recent weeks, both by the Strategic Air Command and at Los Alamos. These briefings specify that our satellites are not adequate to verify Soviet compliance with the terms of a nuclear freeze treaty as outlined here.

That leaves on-site inspection. The answer is simple: "No." The 19 Soviets have never permitted it, have never even been willing to discuss it. Indeed, they cannot. In a country that does not allow freedom of movement to its own citizens, it is politically and ideologically impossible to allow foreign access to strategic installations.

I recognize that neither negotiability nor verification concerns many 20 freeze proponents very much. What electrifies them is the need to *do* it. "The arms race!" . . . or, more often, "the *insane* arms race!" is the rallying cry. The fact is, there *is* no arms race. The Soviets are the only runners at this point. Since 1946, when espionage on their side and traitors on ours gave them a start, they have never *stopped* running. No one worried about nuclear war when we were the only ones who could launch a preemptive first strike, nor even when a balance of power was achieved. Indeed, for the past fifteen years, we've been trying to leave it at that. We have offered and undertaken both bilateral and unilateral bans and moratoriums on the testing and production of nuclear arms. They have without exception been either ignored or broken by the Soviet Union.

Since 1967 we have reduced by some thousands the number of our 21 warheads, while the Soviets have added more than six thousand. Meanwhile, they aid campaigns to prevent the replacement of our aging nuclear armaments with more effective and cleaner weapons systems . . . systems desperately needed. They did this with spectacular success with the enhanced radiation warhead President Carter intended to install at the urging of all his security and defense advisors, as well as the NATO countries it was designed to protect. All this, while they relentlessly build what can only be defined as an offensive war machine.

True, Soviet leaders periodically announce their desire for peace. I   22
point out that Lenin once said, "Ultimately, peace simply means communist world control." I know, it's old-fashioned to quote Lenin now. It's what resourceful editorialists have called "pre-nuclear thinking." Perhaps Leonid Brezhnev is sufficiently up to date for quotation. In Prague, in 1973, he said, "Trust us, comrades. By 1985, we will have achieved our objectives in Western Europe. A decisive shift in the balance of forces will enable us to exert our will." Conversely, Prime Minister Thatcher said last year, "The last war sprang not from an arms race, but from a tyrant's belief that his neighbors lacked the means and the will to resist him."

Ladies and gentlemen, I am not offering you an apocalyptic forecast.   23
I believe in the capacity of mankind and the love of God. Yet, I share the concerns and fears of every person here. We live . . . God knows we always have . . . in an infinitely dangerous world. We'll never get out of it alive. But while we are here, surely reason must tell us to put the infinite treasure of the peace of the world in the hands of those we love, not those we fear.

## *VOCABULARY*

| | | |
|---|---|---|
| validated (1) | incumbent (9) | moratoriums (20) |
| coalesced (2) | recourse (12) | relentlessly (21) |
| vilified (8) | succinctly (14) | apocalyptic (23) |
| disinformation (9) | scrupulously (15) | |
| panacea (9) | preemptive (20) | |

## *THE FACTS*

1. How many Japanese were killed by the blasts at Hiroshima and Nagasaki? How many did Heston estimate would have been killed in an Allied invasion?
2. According to Hegel, what is the most important of all moral obligations?
3. What three reasons does Heston give for opposing a nuclear freeze?
4. According to Heston, what is the difference between the United States and the Soviet Union?

5. What, according to Margaret Thatcher, was the underlying cause of the last world war?

## THE STRATEGIES

1. How does Heston use personal experience and testimony to advance his arguments against a nuclear freeze? How effective is this use?
2. What tone does Heston use to describe those who favor a nuclear freeze? What rhetorical purpose is achieved through the use of this tone? Why is this an effective or ineffective ploy?
3. What historical parallel does Heston draw in his speech? What does he achieve in drawing this parallel?
4. What uses does Heston make of quotations in his speech? How effective is this use?
5. What tone does Heston accomplish by mentioning the classified briefings he received from the Strategic Air Command and the Los Alamos Atomic Testing Laboratory?
6. What does Heston mean by "pre-nuclear thinking" (paragraph 22)? Why do you think he uses this term?

## THE ISSUES

1. Heston quotes a journalist who says that the Soviet Union and the United States are of different mentalities. What is our mentality? What do you regard as the mentality of the Soviets?
2. What is your main source of information about the Soviet Union and its people? How valid is this source?
3. Heston says that no one was worried about a preemptive nuclear strike when the U.S. alone was capable of delivering one. Can this be true? What is your opinion of that statement?
4. What is a moral obligation? What do you think is the most important of all moral obligations?
5. Heston quotes a writer as saying that the Soviet Union is based on an ideology which claims "to be a system of universal explanation." What does "a system of universal explanation" mean? Is U.S. society also based on an ideology, or is the Soviet Union alone in its ideological under-pinnings?

## SUGGESTIONS FOR WRITING

1. During the antinuclear demonstrations of the 1950s and early 1960s, the phrase "Better Red than dead" was a rallying cry for some protesters. Write an essay giving your view on whether you'd rather be Red than dead—or dead than Red.

2. Many young people are very troubled by the nuclear arsenals of the Super-
powers and their ability to destroy the whole world. Write an essay about
the effect these weapons have had on your life and thinking.

### Robert Guillain

# ————— • I THOUGHT MY LAST HOUR • —————
# HAD COME

*Robert Guillain (b. 1908) is the permanent Tokyo correspondent for* Le Monde
*and an acknowledged authority on Far Eastern affairs. He is the author of several
books about the Far East, among them* The Blue Ants: 600 Million Chinese
Under the Red Flag *(1957), and* I Saw Tokyo Burning *(1981), from which
the following excerpt comes.*

*This eyewitness account tells us what it is like to have suffered and survived a
nuclear bombing. Gripping in its stark simplicity and horror, the story is told
by a Japanese housewife who was thirty-three years old on August 6, 1945, the
day Hiroshima was bombed.*

Monday, August 6, 1945, in Hiroshima. A few seconds after 8:15    1
A.M., a flash of light, brighter than a thousand suns, shredded the
space over the city's center. A gigantic sphere of fire, a prodigious blast,
a formidable pillar of smoke and debris rose into the sky: an entire city
annihilated as it was going to work, almost vaporized at the blast's
point zero, irradiated to death, crushed and swept away. Its thousands
of wooden houses were splintered and soon ablaze, its few stone and
brick buildings smashed, its ancient temples destroyed, its schools and
barracks incinerated just as classes and drills were beginning, its
crowded streetcars upended, their passengers buried under the wreck-
age of streets and alleys crowded with people going about their daily
business. A city of 300,000 inhabitants—more, if its large military
population was counted, for Hiroshima was headquarters for the
southern Japan command. In a flash, much of its population, especially in the center, was reduced to a mash of burned and bleeding
bodies, crawling, writhing on the ground in their death agonies, expir-
ing under the ruins of their houses or, soon, roasted in the fire that
was spreading throughout the city—or fleeing, half-mad, with the
sudden torrent of nightmare-haunted humanity staggering toward the

hills, bodies naked and blackened, flayed alive, with charcoal faces and blind eyes.

Is there any way to describe the horror and the pity of that hell? Let a victim tell of it. Among the thousand accounts was this one by a Hiroshima housewife, Mrs. Futaba Kitayama, then aged thirty-three, who was struck down 1900 yards—just over a mile—from the point of impact. We should bear in mind that the horrors she described could be multiplied a hundredfold in the future. 2

"I was in Hiroshima, that morning of August 6. I had joined a team of women who, like me, worked as volunteers in cutting firepaths against incendiary raids by demolishing whole rows of houses. My husband, because of a raid alert the previous night, had stayed at the *Chunichi (Central Japan Journal)*, where he worked. 3

"Our group had passed the Tsurumi bridge, Indian-file, when there was an alert; an enemy plane appeared all alone, very high over our heads. Its silver wings shone brightly in the sun. A woman exclaimed, 'Oh, look—a parachute!' I turned toward where she was pointing, and just at that moment a shattering flash filled the whole sky. 4

"Was it the flash that came first, or the sound of the explosion, tearing up my insides? I don't remember. I was thrown to the ground, pinned to the earth, and immediately the world began to collapse around me, on my head, my shoulders. I couldn't see anything. It was completely dark. I thought my last hour had come. I thought of my three children, who had been evacuated to the country to be safe from the raids. I couldn't move; debris kept falling, beams and tiles piled up on top of me. 5

"Finally I did manage to crawl free. There was a terrible smell in the air. Thinking the bomb that hit us might have been a yellow phosphorus incendiary like those that had fallen on so many other cities, I rubbed my nose and mouth hard with a *tenugui* (a kind of towel) I had at my waist. To my horror, I found that the skin of my face had come off in the towel. Oh! The skin on my hands, on my arms, came off too. From elbow to fingertips, all the skin on my right arm had come loose and was hanging grotesquely. The skin of my left hand fell off too, the five fingers, like a glove. 6

"I found myself sitting on the ground, prostrate. Gradually I registered that all my companions had disappeared. What had happened to them? A frantic panic gripped me, I wanted to run, but where? 7

Around me was just debris, wooden framing, beams and roofing tiles; there wasn't a single landmark left.

"And what had happened to the sky, so blue a moment ago? Now it was as black as night. Everything seemed vague and fuzzy. It was as though a cloud covered my eyes and I wondered if I had lost my senses. I finally saw the Tsurumi bridge and I ran headlong toward it, jumping over the piles of rubble. What I saw under the bridge then horrified me. 8

"People by the hundreds were flailing in the river. I couldn't tell if they were men or women; they were all in the same state: their faces were puffy and ashen, their hair tangled, they held their hands raised and, groaning with pain, threw themselves into the water. I had a violent impulse to do so myself, because of the pain burning through my whole body. But I can't swim and I held back. 9

"Past the bridge, I looked back to see that the whole Hachobori district had suddenly caught fire, to my surprise, because I thought only the district I was in had been bombed. As I ran, I shouted my children's names. Where was I going? I have no idea, but I can still see the scenes of horror I glimpsed here and there on my way. 10

"A mother, her face and shoulders covered with blood, tried frantically to run into a burning house. A man held her back and she screamed, 'Let me go! Let me go! My son is burning in there!' She was like a mad demon. Under the Kojin bridge, which had half collapsed and had lost its heavy, reinforced-concrete parapets, I saw a lot of bodies floating in the water like dead dogs, almost naked, with their clothes in shreds. At the river's edge, near the bank, a woman lay on her back with her breasts ripped off, bathed in blood. How could such a frightful thing have happened? I thought of the scenes of the Buddhist hell my grandmother had described to me when I was little. 11

"I must have wandered for at least two hours before finding myself on the Eastern military parade ground. My burns were hurting me, but the pain was different from an ordinary burn. It was a dull pain that seemed somehow to come from outside my body. A kind of yellow pus oozed from my hands, and I thought that my face must also be horrible to see. 12

"Around me on the parade ground were a number of grade-school and secondary-school children, boys and girls, writhing in spasms of agony. Like me, they were members of the anti–air raid volunteer 13 corps. I heard them crying 'Mama! Mama!' as though they'd gone crazy. They were so burned and bloody that looking at them was insupportable. I forced myself to do so just the same, and I cried out in rage, 'Why? Why these children?' But there was no one to rage at and I could do nothing but watch them die, one after the other, vainly calling for their mothers.

"After lying almost unconscious for a long time on the parade ground, I started walking again. As far as I could see with my failing sight, everything was in flames, as far as the Hiroshima station and the Atago district. It seemed to me that my face was hardening little by little. I cautiously touched my hands to my cheeks. My face felt as though it had doubled in size. I could see less and less clearly. Was I going blind, then? After so much hardship, was I going to die? I kept on walking anyway and I reached a suburban area.     14

"In that district, farther removed from the center, I found my elder sister alive, with only slight injuries to the head and feet. She didn't recognize me at first, then she burst into tears. In a handcart, she wheeled me nearly three miles to the first-aid center at Yaga. It was night when we arrived. I later learned there was a pile of corpses and countless injured there. I spent two nights there, unconscious; my sister told me that in my delirium I kept repeating, 'My children! Take me to my children!'     15

"On August 8, I was carried on a stretcher to a train and transported to the home of relatives in the village of Kasumi. The village doctor said my case was hopeless. My children, recalled from their evacuation refuge, rushed to my side. I could no longer see them; I could recognize them only by smelling their good odor. On August 11, my husband joined us. The children wept with joy as they embraced him.     16

"Our happiness soon ended. My husband, who bore no trace of injury, died suddenly three days later, vomiting blood. We had been married sixteen years and now, because I was at the brink of death myself, I couldn't even rest his head as I should have on the pillow of the dead.     17

"I said to myself, 'My poor children, because of you I don't have the right to die!' And finally, by a miracle, I survived after I had again and again been given up for lost.     18

"My sight returned fairly quickly, and after twenty days I could dimly see my children's features. The burns on my face and hands did not heal so rapidly, and the wounds remained pulpy, like rotten toma-     19 toes. It wasn't until December that I could walk again. When my bandages were removed in January, I knew that my face and hands would always be deformed. My left ear was half its original size. A streak of cheloma, a dark brown swelling as wide as my hand, runs from the side of my head across my mouth to my throat. My right hand is striped with a cheloma two inches wide from the wrist to the little finger. The five fingers on my left hand are now fused at the base. . . ."

## VOCABULARY

prodigious (1)          irradiated (1)          incendiary (3)
vaporized (1)           incinerated (1)         parapets (11)

## THE FACTS

1. What happened to Mrs. Kitayama when she rubbed her nose and mouth with the *tenugui*?
2. Why didn't Mrs. Kitayama also throw herself into the river to cool her injuries?
3. Of what did the gristly scenes after the bombing remind Mrs. Kitayama?
4. Who carried Mrs. Kitayama to the first-aid shelter at Yaga?
5. How did Mrs. Kitayama recognize her children even though she could not see?

## THE STRATEGIES

1. How would you characterize the style of this narrative? How does it contribute to the believability of Mrs. Kitayama's story?
2. In paragraph 6, how does Mrs. Kitayama convey the horror she felt after she rubbed her face with the *tenugui*?
3. Why do you think Mrs. Kitayama mentions the woman's comment about the parachute in paragraph 3? What does this sort of trivial detail convey?
4. What rhetorical figure does Mrs. Kitayama frequently use to suggest the confusion, despair, and stupefaction she felt following the attack?
5. Frequently Mrs. Kitayama uses specific places names of districts in Hiroshima that the general reader simply cannot be expected to know. How does this usage contribute to or detract from her narrative?

## THE ISSUES

1. What can you infer about Mrs. Kitayama the person from the story she tells?
2. Some people deplore accounts that personalize the issue of nuclear arms,

arguing that they play into the hands of our enemies. What is your opinion of this line of argument?

3. Some have argued that we dropped the atomic bomb on Japan rather than on Nazi Germany for racist reasons. What are your own thoughts on that subject?

4. Heston argues, and history mainly agrees, that the atomic bombing of Japan saved millions of American lives that would otherwise have been lost in an invasion attempt. Do you think the toll in actual Japanese lives was justified by the savings in hypothetical American casualties? Why or why not?

5. Would you prefer to survive a global thermonuclear war or be an instant victim of one? Justify your answer.

### SUGGESTIONS FOR WRITING

1. Analyze Mrs. Kitayama's essay for observations and details that give a glimpse into her character and personality. Then write an essay saying what you think she is like, supporting your deductions with quotations from her eyewitness account.

2. Write an essay justifying or condemning the American use of atomic weapons on Japan during World War II.

## CHAPTER WRITING ASSIGNMENTS

1. Contrast the voice of the writer of "What Is Style?" with that of the writer of "Salvation."

2. Present your own ideas on how a writer finds a voice in his or her writing. Apply these ideas to your own writing.

3. Using the wooden style associated with government agencies and bureaucrats, write a report on the aftereffects of a nuclear blast on the city or town in which you live.

# 3
# PURPOSE AND THESIS

# INTRODUCTION: WHAT IS A THESIS?

The thesis of an essay is the writer's main point. It is what the essay intends to prove, assert, or argue. Some theorists claim that an essay's thesis should be as extractable as an almond from its shell, and that one should always be able to sum up the essence of any essay on a postcard. But anyone who regularly reads essays and articles knows that there is considerable variation in the way theses are used. Some essays that are otherwise perfectly clear have an indistinct thesis buried amid the prose. Other essays have a typical postcard-clear thesis. The fact is that professional writers do not write cookie-cutter theses as often as idealists would have us believe.

There are two identifiable kinds of theses that are commonly found in essays. The first is the implicit thesis. It is not plainly spelled out in any single sentence; yet it is still inferable from what the writer has written. Michael Novak's "Buying and Selling Babies" in the Issues section of this chapter offers an example of this kind of thesis. The writer is staunchly against surrogate motherhood, makes a strong moral argument in support of his case, but does not sum up his position in any single sentence to which the orthodox can point.

The second kind of thesis explicitly states the author's position in a single sentence. Usually this sentence occurs at the end of the first paragraph. Students are encouraged and occasionally compelled to use this explicit thesis, which professional writers use only infrequently and seldom with the rigidity of the classroom practice. T. H. Huxley's essay "The Method of Scientific Investigation" uses an explicit thesis as do virtually all the student essays in the appendix of this book.

This variation between theory and the practice in the use of the thesis should not surprise us. Orthodoxy in any discipline is always demanded of the beginner, and the student writer must understandably abide by rhetorical conventions that the professional will flout. Once you have written a number of essays, you will no doubt be able to focus and follow through on a main point without first writing it down in an explicit thesis. But the hard fact is that many beginners cannot. They wander and stray from the point if they do not clearly and distinctly write it down. That is why students are encouraged to use explicit theses.

The essays in this chapter illustrate how various writers use theses to help them maintain and achieve focus. Sheridan Baker dispenses some clever advice about how a writer may derive rhetorical energy from a well-chosen thesis; Harry Crosby and George Estey tell us why the thesis is necessary and how it helps both reader and writer. Huxley's essay begins with an utterly explicit thesis; Richard Selzer's vignette ends on one. The other essays show us the real-world practice, in which the thesis is implied by the focus of the essay rather than trumpeted in an opening paragraph.

Rhetorical techniques are only a means to an end, not an end in themselves. The end purpose of any written work is to communicate with an audience, and one conventional means of doing this is to make your main point crystal clear in an explicit thesis. Doing so will help you stick to the point while helping your reader follow your thinking.

# •• *ADVICE* ••

### Sheridan Baker

## • **THE THESIS** •

*Sheridan Baker (b. 1918) is presently professor of English at the University of Michigan and has been a Fulbright lecturer. He has edited several works by the eighteenth-century novelist Henry Fielding, including* Joseph Andrews, Shamela, *and* Tom Jones. *Baker's two rhetorics,* The Practical Stylist *(1962) and* The Complete Stylist *(1976), are widely used in colleges throughout the United States.*

*In this excerpt from* The Complete Stylist, *Baker advises the student to state clearly, in a sharp-edged thesis, the controlling purpose of the essay.*

You can usually blame a bad essay on a bad beginning. If your essay    1
falls apart, it probably has no primary idea to hold it together. "What's the big idea?" we used to ask. The phrase will serve as a reminder that you must find the "big idea" behind your several smaller thoughts and musings before you start to write. In the beginning was the *logos*, says the Bible—the idea, the plan, caught in a flash as if in a single word. Find your *logos*, and you are ready to round out your essay and set it spinning.

The big idea behind our ride in the speeding car was that in adoles-    2
cence, especially, the group can have a very deadly influence on the individual. If you had not focused your big idea in a thesis, you might have begun by picking up thoughts at random, something like this:

Everyone thinks he is a good driver. There are more accidents caused by young drivers than any other group. Driver education is a good beginning, but further practice is very necessary. People who object to driver education do not realize that modern society, with its suburban pattern of growth, is built around the automobile. The car becomes a way of life and a status symbol. When a teen-ager goes too fast he is probably only copying his own father.

A little reconsideration, aimed at a good thesis-sentence, could turn ₃ this into a reasonably good beginning:

> Modern society is built on the automobile. Every child looks forward to the time when he can drive; every teen-ager, to the day when his father lets him take out the car alone. Soon he is testing his skill at higher and higher speeds, especially with a group of friends along. One final test at extreme speeds usually suffices. The teen-ager's high-speed ride, if it does not kill him, will probably open his eyes to the deadly dynamics of the group.

Thus the central idea, or thesis, is your essay's life and spirit. If your ₄ thesis is sufficiently firm and clear, it may tell you immediately how to organize your supporting material and so obviate elaborate planning. If you do not find a thesis, your essay will be a tour through the miscellaneous. An essay replete with scaffolds and catwalks—"We have just seen this; now let us turn to this"—is an essay in which the inherent idea is weak or nonexistent. A purely expository and descriptive essay, one simply about "Cats," for instance, will have to rely on outer scaffolding alone (some orderly progression from Persia to Siam) since it really has no idea at all. It is all subject, all cats, instead of being based on an idea *about* cats.

## THE ARGUMENTATIVE EDGE

### Find Your Thesis

The *about*-ness puts an argumentative edge on the subject. When ₅ you have something to say *about* cats, you have found your underlying idea. You have something to defend, something to fight about: not just "Cats," but "The cat is really man's best friend." Now the hackles on all dog men are rising, and you have an argument on your hands. You have something to prove. You have a thesis.

"What's the big idea, Mac?" Let the impudence in that time-honored ₆ demand remind you that the best thesis is a kind of affront to somebody. No one will be very much interested in listening to you deplete the thesis "The dog is man's best friend." Everyone knows that already.

Even the dog lovers will be uninterested, convinced that they know better than you. But the cat . . .

So it is with any unpopular idea. The more unpopular the viewpoint   7 and the stronger the push against convention, the stronger the thesis and the more energetic the essay. Compare the energy in "Democracy is good" with that in "Communism is good," for instance. The first is filled with platitudes, the second with plutonium. By the same token, if you can find the real energy in "Democracy is good," if you can get down through the sand to where the roots and water are, you will have a real essay, because the opposition against which you generate your energy is the heaviest in the world: boredom. Probably the most energetic thesis of all, the greatest inner organizer, is some tired old truth that you cause to jet with new life, making the old ground green again.

To find a thesis and put it into one sentence is to narrow and define   8 your subject to a workable size. Under "Cats" you must deal with all felinity from the jungle up, carefully partitioning the eons and areas, the tigers and tabbies, the sizes and shapes. The minute you proclaim the cat the friend of man, you have pared away whole categories and chapters, and need only think up the arguments sufficient to overwhelm the opposition. So, put an argumentative edge on your subject—and you will have found your thesis.

Simple exposition, to be sure, has its uses. You may want to tell   9 someone how to build a doghouse, how to can asparagus, how to follow the outlines of relativity, or even how to write an essay. Performing a few exercises in simple exposition will no doubt sharpen your insight into the problems of finding orderly sequences, of considering how best to lead your readers through the hoops, of writing clearly and accurately. It will also illustrate how much finer and surer an argument is.

You will see that picking an argument immediately simplifies the   10 problems so troublesome in straight exposition: the defining, the partitioning, the narrowing of the subject. Actually, you can put an argumentative edge on the flattest of expository subjects. "How to build a doghouse" might become "Building a doghouse is a thorough introduction to the building trades, including architecture and mechanical engineering." "Canning asparagus" might become "An asparagus patch is a course in economics." "Relativity" might become "Relativity is not so inscrutable as many suppose." You have simply assumed that you have a loyal opposition consisting of the uninformed, the scornful, or both. You have given your subject its edge; you have limited and organized it at a single stroke. Pick an argument, then, and you will automatically be defining and narrowing your subject, and all the partitions you don't need will fold up. Instead of dealing with things, subjects, and pieces of subjects, you will be dealing with an idea and its consequences.

## Sharpen Your Thesis

Come out with your subject pointed. Take a stand, make a judgment    11
of value. Be reasonable, but don't be timid. It is helpful to think of your thesis, your main idea, as a debating question—"Resolved: Old age pensions must go"—taking out the "Resolved" when you actually write the subject down. But your resolution will be even stronger, your essay clearer and tighter, if you can sharpen your thesis even further— "Resolved: Old age pensions must go because——." Fill in that blank and your worries are practically over. The main idea is to put your whole argument into one sentence.

Try for instance: "Old age pensions must go because they are mak-    12
ing people irresponsible." I don't know at all if that is true, and neither will you until you write your way into it, considering probabilities and alternatives and objections, and especially the underlying assumptions. In fact, no one, no master sociologist or future historian, can tell absolutely if it is true, so multiplex are the causes in human affairs, so endless and tangled the consequences. The basic assumption—that irresponsibility is growing—may be entirely false. No one, I repeat, can tell absolutely. But by the same token, your guess may be as good as another's. At any rate, you are now ready to write. You have found your *logos*.

Now you can put your well-pointed thesis-sentence on a card on    13
the wall in front of you to keep from drifting off target. But you will now want to dress it for the public, to burnish it, and make it comely. Suppose you try:

> Old age pensions, perhaps more than anything else, are eroding our heritage of personal and familial responsibility.

But is this true? Perhaps you had better try something like:

> Despite their many advantages, old age pensions may actually be eroding our heritage of personal and familial responsibility.

This is really your thesis, and you can write that down on a scrap of paper too.

### *VOCABULARY*

| | | |
|---|---|---|
| obviate (4) | inherent (4) | platitudes (7) |
| replete (4) | affront (5) | multiplex (12) |

## ═══ •• *DISCUSSION* •• ═══

**Harry Crosby and George Estey**

## ── • THE CONTROLLING CONCEPT • ──

*Harry Herbert Crosby (b. 1919) is professor of American literature and rhetoric at Boston University. George Fisher Estey (b. 1924) is professor of English literature and rhetoric at the same university. They are coauthors of* College Writing: The Rhetorical Imperative *(1968) and* Just Rhetoric *(1972). Estey is also coeditor of two anthologies,* Non-Violence: A Reader in the Ethics of Action *(1971) and* Violence: A Reader in the Ethics of Action *(1971).*

*In this selection from* College Writing, *the authors supply appropriate examples and commentary to demonstrate how a thesis works.*

"A speech has two parts. You must state your thesis, and you must prove it."

— ARISTOTLE

Most of the writing in serious magazines, in military, professional, political, scientific, and literary reports, in college term papers, and in all other forms of nonfiction prose is composed of a mixture of definitive and generative sentences. Each composition has at its core a generative sentence that is the broadest or most complex idea in the work. It is this sentence that gives unity and purpose to the total effort.

That prose literature has unity is easily seen by examining almost any book or magazine article. Thomas Macaulay, in *The History of England from the Accession of James II* (1849–1861), does not merely present a vivid and detailed history of England from the reign of James II to the death of William III; he tried to prove that England under the influence of a Whig government and the Protestant religion was the best of all possible worlds. Another famous work of history, Frederick Jackson Turner's speech at the American Historical Association's meeting in Chicago in 1893, "The Significance of the Frontier in American History," set out to prove that America is the product of a series of developments accompanying the new type of frontier.

Almost invariably the central idea is expressly stated. The monu-  3
mental *Main Currents in American Thought,* by Vernon L. Parrington, contains in its introduction this sentence:

> I have undertaken to give some account of the genesis and develop-
> ment in American letters of certain germinal ideas that have come to be
> reckoned traditionally American—how they came into being here, how
> they were exposed, and what influence they have exerted in determin-
> ing the form and scope of our characteristic ideals and institutions.

This is Professor Parrington's purpose statement; it controls the en-  4
tire work. The work is divided into three volumes, and each volume is broken into books. Part One of the first book in Volume I is called "The Puritan Heritage." Preceding it is a brief introduction that ends with the book's thesis or generative statement: "The Puritan was a contribution of the old world, created by the rugged idealism of the English Reformation; the Yankee was a product of native conditions, created by practical economics."

Thorstein Veblen's *The Theory of the Leisure Class* (1899) attempts to  5
prove that the leisure class represents a continuing maladjustment of modern institutions that causes a reversion to an archaic scheme of life. He expresses this idea in a thesis sentence in the first chapter of his work.

Shorter prose literature also has the characteristic of stating the  6
central idea. Francis Bacon's essay "Of Studies" begins, "Studies serve for delight, for ornament, and for ability," thus giving the reader cause to anticipate three reasons why study is valuable. "The Method of Scientific Investigation," an essay by Thomas Henry Huxley,* contains in its introduction the sentence, "The method of scientific investigation is nothing but the expression of the necessary mode of working of the

---

*Huxley's essay begins on page 151.—Ed.

human mind"; the rest of the essay describes the scientific method and shows why the human mind must use the method to arrive at sound ideas. In an article in the *Saturday Evening Post* (July 13, 1957), a testy English baron, Lord Conesford, put his thesis in his title, "You Americans Are Murdering the Language," and you can anticipate what followed. In a *New Yorker* article (December 16, 1950), John Hersey wrote, "This conference caused frightful headlines all over the world about the possible use of the atomic bomb in Korea and China, and it also provided a hair-raising example of how bad news can be manufactured." Hersey's statement is another example of the generative sentence that predicts and obligates the rest of the article.

This characteristic of good writing is known to skilled readers. According to Mortimer Adler and almost every other reading expert, the first requirement of effective reading is that you must be able to put in a single sentence the central message or thesis of the material you are reading. Very often, when skilled students read a book, they underline certain passages. This is a good technique—if the proper sections are selected. Too often, students underline only the sections they find interesting. The single sentence that should be underlined is the thesis or purpose statement of the book, its generative sentence. Almost every author, either in the introduction, the first chapter, or the final chapter, sums up his central idea. When you locate the sentence you aid comprehension. Take, for instance, the very difficult *Education of Henry Adams*. Many readers start out with Chapter 1; instead, they should begin with the preface, for in it are found these two sentences: "Except in the abandoned sphere of dead languages, no one has discussed what part of education has, in his personal experience, turned out to be useful, and what not. This volume attempts to discuss it." From these sentences the reader has a frame on which to hang all subsequent material. Reviewers frequently have misunderstood Adams's purpose; in spite of its title, they have perceived his book to be an autobiography and have criticized it because it makes no reference to such personal matters as his marriage and the suicide of his wife.

As Walter Pater has said, one of the delights of reading worthwhile prose is to detect the point of the composition, and then to follow an orderly mind through the content that must follow. If the thesis is not established and the content does not fulfill its obligation, we do not have effective, valuable writing.

## VOCABULARY

| | | |
|---|---|---|
| definitive (1) | expressly (3) | idealism (4) |
| generative (1) | monumental (3) | reversion (5) |
| accession (2) | genesis (3) | mode (6) |
| Whig (2) | germinal (3) | |

## THE FACTS

1. What synonym do the authors use for *thesis*?
2. According to the authors, what is the purpose of a thesis?
3. What did Thomas Macaulay try to prove in *The History of England from the Accession of James II* (1849–1861)?
4. What, according to Mortimer Adler and other reading experts, is the first requirement of effective reading?
5. What mistake do student readers often make when they underline sections of a book?

## THE STRATEGIES

1. What is the thesis of this essay and where is it to be found?
2. What technique do Crosby and Estey mainly use to prove their own thesis?
3. What do the authors accomplish by referring to Mortimer Adler in paragraph 7?
4. What two words in the first paragraph require defining before this essay can be understood?

## THE ISSUES

1. What is a definitive sentence? What is a generative sentence?
2. The essay alludes to an article titled "You Americans Are Murdering the Language," written by an English baron. This charge has been made repeatedly against Americans by the English. What is your opinion of this charge? How can anyone murder a language?
3. What part of your own education in English so far have you found most valuable? What part least valuable?
4. Crosby and Estey quote Walter Pater on the delights of reading worthwhile prose. What delights have you discovered from your own reading?

## SUGGESTIONS FOR WRITING

1. Locate and copy down the thesis of at least three books in the library. This thesis must be stated expressly in one sentence. Follow Crosby and Estey's suggestion of checking the preface or introduction in each book.

2. Using any article from this book, supply the following: (a) a thesis, (b) a controlling question as thesis, (c) a statement of purpose as thesis.

## •• *EXAMPLES* ••

### T. H. Huxley

## • THE METHOD OF SCIENTIFIC • INVESTIGATION

*Thomas Henry Huxley (1825–1895) was an English biologist who also popularized science in the Victorian era. He was the principal proponent of Darwin's theories and coined the word* agnostic *to describe his own religious beliefs. Among his best-known works are* Evolution and Ethics *(1893),* Collected Essays *(1893–1894), and* Scientific Memoirs *(1898–1902).*

*In a series of closely knit paragraphs from his* Autobiography and Selected Essays *(1910), Huxley explains the logical processes of deduction and induction, indicating that these terms are merely technical names for thought habits we all use.*

The method of scientific investigation is nothing but the expression of the necessary mode of working of the human mind. It is simply the mode at which all phenomena are reasoned about, rendered precise and exact. There is no more difference, but there is just the same kind of difference, between the mental operations of a man of science and those of an ordinary person, as there is between the operations and methods of a baker or of a butcher weighing out his goods in common scales and the operation of a chemist in performing a difficult and complex analysis by means of his balance and finely graduated weights. It is not that the action of the scales in the one case and the balance in the other differ in the principles of their construction or manner of working; but the beam of one is set on an infinitely finer axis than the other, and of course turns by the addition of a much smaller weight.

You will understand this better, perhaps, if I give you some familiar    2
example. You have all heard it repeated, I dare say, that men of science
work by means of induction and deduction, and that by the help of
these operations, they, in a sort of sense, wring from Nature certain
other things, which are called natural laws and causes, and that out of
these, by some cunning skill of their own, they build up hypotheses
and theories. And it is imagined by many that the operations of the
common mind can be by no means compared with these processes,
and that they have to be acquired by a sort of special apprenticeship to
the craft. To hear all these large words, you would think that the mind
of a man of science must be constituted differently from that of his
fellow men; but if you will not be frightened by terms, you will discover that you are quite wrong, and that all these terrible apparatus
are being used by yourselves every day and every hour of your lives.

There is a well-known incident in one of Molière's* plays, where the    3
author makes the hero express unbounded delight on being told that
he has been talking prose during the whole of his life. In the same
way, I trust that you will take comfort, and be delighted with yourselves, on the discovery that you have been acting on the principles of
inductive and deductive philosophy during the same period. Probably
there is not one here who has not in the course of the day had occasion
to set in motion a complex train of reasoning, of the very same kind,
though differing of course in degree, as that which a scientific man
goes through in tracing the causes of natural phenomena.

A very trivial circumstance will serve to exemplify this. Suppose    4
you go into a fruiterer's shop, wanting an apple—you take one up,
and, on biting, you find it is sour; you look at it, and see that it is hard,
and green. You take up another one and that too is hard, green, and
sour. The shop man offers you a third; but, before biting it, you examine it, and find that it is hard and green, and you immediately say
that you will not have it, as it must be sour, like those that you have
already tried.

Nothing can be more simple than that, you think; but if you will    5
take the trouble to analyze and trace out into its logical elements what
has been done by the mind, you will be greatly surprised. In the first
place, you have performed the operation of induction. You found, that,

---

*Pen name of Jean-Baptiste Poquelin (1622–1673), French playwright.—Ed.

in two experiences, hardness and greenness in apples went together with sourness. It was so in the first case, and it was confirmed by the second. True, it is a very small basis, but still it is enough to make an induction from; you generalize the facts, and you expect to find sourness in apples where you get hardness and greenness. You found upon that a general law, that all hard and green apples are sour; and that, so far as it goes, is a perfect induction. Well, having got your natural law in this way, when you are offered another apple which you find is hard and green, you say, "All hard and green apples are sour; this apple is hard and green, therefore this apple is sour." That train of reasoning is what logicians call a syllogism and has all its various parts and terms—its major premise, its minor premise, and its conclusion. And, by the help of further reasoning, which, if drawn out, would have to be exhibited in two or three other syllogisms, you arrive at your final determination: "I will not have that apple." So that, you see, you have, in the first place, established a law by induction, and upon that you have founded a deduction and reasoned out the special conclusion of the particular case. Well now, suppose, having got your law, that at some time afterwards, you are discussing the qualities of apples with a friend; you will say to him, "It is a very curious thing—but I find that all hard and green apples are sour!" Your friend says to you, "But how do you know that?" You at once reply, "Oh, because I have tried them over and over again and have always found them to be so." Well, if we were talking science instead of common sense, we should call that an experimental verification. And, if still opposed, you go further and say, "I have heard from the people in Somersetshire and Devonshire, where a large number of apples are grown, that they have observed the same thing. It is also found to be the case in Normandy, and in North America. In short, I find it to be the universal experience of mankind wherever attention has been directed to the subject." Whereupon your friend, unless he is a very unreasonable man, agrees with you and is convinced that you are quite right in the conclusion you have drawn. He believes, although perhaps he does not know he believes it, that the more extensive verifications are—that the more frequently experiments have been made and results of the same kind arrived at—that the more varied the conditions under which the same results are attained, the more certain is the ultimate conclusion, and he disputes the question no further. He sees that the experiment has been tried under all sorts of conditions, as to time, place, and people, with the same result; and he says with you, therefore, that the law you have laid down must be a good one, and he must believe it.

In science we do the same thing; the philosopher exercises precisely the same faculties, though in a much more delicate manner. In scientific inquiry it becomes a matter of duty to expose a supposed law to every possible kind of verification and to take care, moreover, that this is done intentionally and not left to a mere accident, as in the case of the apples. And in science, as in common life, our confidence in a law is in exact proportion to the absence of variation in the result of our experimental verifications. For instance, if you let go your grasp of an article you may have in your hand, it will immediately fall to the ground. That is a very common verification of one of the best established laws of nature—that of gravitation. The method by which men of science established the existence of that law is exactly the same as that by which we have established the trivial proposition about the sourness of hard and green apples. But we believe it in such an extensive, thorough, and unhesitating manner because the universal experience of mankind verifies it, and we can verify it ourselves at any time; and that is the strongest possible foundation on which any natural law can rest.

## VOCABULARY

| | | |
|---|---|---|
| phenomena (1) | theories (2) | premise (5) |
| analysis (1) | apparatus (2) | faculties (6) |
| induction (2) | exemplify (4) | inquiry (6) |
| deduction (2) | logicians (5) | variation (6) |
| hypotheses (2) | syllogism (5) | |

## THE FACTS

1. What logical operations do scientists use to wring conclusions from nature?
2. What is experimental verification?
3. What is one of nature's best established laws?
4. What is one of the most widely used formulas of deductive reasoning?
5. What is the strongest possible foundation upon which any natural law can rest?

## *THE STRATEGIES*

1. What are some of the techniques Huxley uses here to make clear his explanation of the scientific method?
2. What is the thesis of Huxley's essay and where is it stated? What is the advantage of this placement of the thesis?
3. What is the purpose of the allusion to the character in Molière's play?
4. What advantage does the author derive from informally addressing his reader as "you"?

## *THE ISSUES*

1. What do you suppose would be the disadvantage of a life lived entirely by inductive reasoning? The disadvantage of one lived entirely by deduction?
2. What, if anything, is wrong with this syllogism?
   All redheads are passionate.
   This person is a redhead.
   This person is passionate.
3. The author refers repeatedly to "scientific man" and to "man of science" throughout his essay. What effect do you think these exclusively masculine terms would have on a female reader with scientific ambitions and talent?
4. How does the concept of evolution and natural selection—cornerstone ideas of Darwinism—affect your own religious beliefs?
5. At least one writer has suggested that the emergence of superstition marked the beginning of rationality and inductive thinking among primitive peoples. How might induction lead to superstition?

## *SUGGESTIONS FOR WRITING*

1. Write a summary of a notable experiment made by some famous scientist. (Examples: Madame Curie, Kepler, Galileo, Darwin, Newton.)
2. Describe the inductive logic that led you to some important conclusion in your life.

### Richard Selzer

# • A MAN OF LETTERS •

*Richard Selzer (b. 1928) was born in Troy, New York, and educated at Union College, at Albany Medical School, and at Yale University. Since 1960 he has been practicing as a general surgeon in New Haven, Connecticut, while also serving on the faculty of the Yale School of Medicine. His essays and short stories dealing with the field of medicine have attracted a wide and loyal audience. Of particular note is his short-story collection entitled* Rituals of Surgery (1974).

*Many instructors insist that students place their theses in the first paragraph of their papers. This is a reasonable requirement to make of a beginning writer, who depends on the guidance of an explicit thesis to develop a topic. However, professional writers labor under no such rule. In this excerpt, a poignant tale about a stricken English professor, the thesis—which the story has carefully developed—appears at the very end.*

A man of letters lies in the intensive care unit. A professor, used to words and students. He has corrected the sentences of many. He understands punctuation. One day in his classroom he was speaking of Emily Dickinson when suddenly he grew pale, and a wonder sprang upon his face, as though he had just, for the first time, *seen* something, understood something that had eluded him all his life. It was the look of the Wound, the struck blow that makes no noise, but happens in the depths somewhere, unseen. His students could not have known that at that moment his stomach had perforated, that even as he spoke, its contents were issuing forth into his peritoneal cavity like a horde of marauding goblins. From the blackboard to the desk he reeled, fell across the top of it, and turning his face to one side, he vomited up his blood, great gouts and gobbets of it, as though having given his class the last of his spirit, he now offered them his fluid and cells.

In time, he was carried to the operating room, this man whom I had known, who had taught me poetry. I took him up, in my hands, and laid him open, and found from where he bled. I stitched it up, and bandaged him, and said later, "Now you are whole."

But it was not so, for he had begun to die. And I could not keep him from it, not with all my earnestness, so sure was his course. From surgery he was taken to the intensive care unit. His family, his students were stopped at the electronic door. They could not pass, for he had entered a new state of being, a strange antechamber where they may not go.

For three weeks he has dwelt in that House of Intensive Care, punctured by needles, wearing tubes of many calibers in all of his orifices, irrigated, dialyzed, insufflated, pumped, and drained . . . and feeling every prick and pressure the way a lover feels desire spring acutely to his skin.

In the room a woman moves. She is dressed in white. Lovingly she measures his hourly flow of urine. With hands familiar, she delivers oxygen to his nostrils and counts his pulse as though she were telling beads. Each bit of his decline she records with her heart full of grief, shaking her head. At last, she turns from her machinery to the simple touch of the flesh. Sighing, she strips back the sheet, and bathes his limbs.

The man of letters did not know this woman before. Preoccupied with dying, he is scarcely aware of her presence now. But this nurse is his wife in his new life of dying. They are close, these two, intimate, depending one upon the other, loving. It is a marriage, for although they own no shared past, they possess this awful, intense present, this matrimonial now, that binds them as strongly as any promise.

A man does not know whose hands will stroke from him the last bubbles of his life. That alone should make him kinder to strangers.

## VOCABULARY

| | | |
|---|---|---|
| eluded (1) | gouts (1) | orifices (4) |
| perforated (1) | gobbets (1) | dialyzed (4) |
| peritoneal (1) | antechamber (3) | insufflated (4) |
| marauding (1) | calibers (4) | |

## THE FACTS

1. What happened to the man of letters during his class?
2. What relationship existed between Selzer and the man of letters?
3. Who becomes the makeshift wife of the man of letters?
4. According to Selzer, what alone should make us kinder to strangers?

## THE STRATEGIES

1. What paragraph contains the thesis of the essay? Do you think this is an effective place for the thesis?
2. What two kinds of language does the author combine in this essay? Why?
3. In paragraph 4, what is the effect of capitalizing "House of Intensive Care"?
4. In paragraph 5, if you substituted *legs* for *limbs*, what would be lost?

### THE ISSUES

1. In some hospitals, the man of letters might have been denied treatment and sent to a public hospital unless he could prove that he was fully insured or otherwise able to pay. What is your opinion of this state of affairs?
2. Why is it ironic that the man of letters should have been explicating Emily Dickinson at the moment of his attack?
3. Other than the one suggested at the end of this essay, what other reason can you think of for being kinder to strangers?
4. Why do you think Selzer says, "Now you are whole"? (See paragraph 2.) What do you think of this sentiment in the context of the essay?

### SUGGESTIONS FOR WRITING

1. Write an essay that analyzes Selzer's use of poetic imagery and figurative language in "A Man of Letters." Refer specifically to the figure of speech you are analyzing and comment on its effectiveness.
2. Write an account of your stay in a hospital or an experience at the doctor's office. Try to include as many details as possible. Place your thesis at the end of the essay as a conclusive summary of the experience.

### Flannery O'Connor

## ———— • A GOOD MAN IS HARD TO FIND • ————

*Flannery O'Connor (1925–1964) was a Christian humanist writer and a member of the so-called southern renaissance in American literature. She was born in Savannah, Georgia, and educated at the Woman's College of Georgia and the State University of Iowa. Her best-known stories, written from an orthodox Catholic perspective, are contained in* A Good Man Is Hard to Find and Other Stories *(1953) and* Everything That Rises Must Converge *(1956).*

*We do not usually think of a story as having a thesis, but we almost always think of a story as having a point. The point of this story—its thesis—is hinted at in its title, from which it proceeds with grim, irresistible logic.*

The grandmother didn't want to go to Florida. She wanted to visit some of her connections in east Tennessee and she was seizing at every chance to change Bailey's mind. Bailey was the son she lived with, her only boy. He was sitting on the edge of his chair at the table, bent over the orange sports section of the *Journal*. "Now look here, Bailey," she said, "see here, read this," and she stood with one hand on her thin hip and the other rattling the newspaper at his bald head. "Here this fellow that calls himself The Misfit is aloose from the Federal Pen and headed toward Florida and you read here what it says he did to these people. Just you read it. I wouldn't take my children in any direction with a criminal like that aloose in it. I couldn't answer to my conscience if I did."

Bailey didn't look up from his reading so she wheeled around then   2 and faced the children's mother, a young woman in slacks, whose face was as broad and innocent as a cabbage and was tied around with a green headkerchief that had two points on the top like a rabbit's ears. She was sitting on the sofa, feeding the baby his apricots out of a jar. "The children have been to Florida before," the old lady said. "You all ought to take them somewhere else for a change so they would see different parts of the world and be broad. They never have been to east Tennessee."

The children's mother didn't seem to hear her but the eight-year-old   3 boy, John Wesley, a stocky child with glasses, said, "If you don't want to go to Florida, why dontcha stay at home?" He and the little girl, June Star, were reading the funny papers on the floor.

"She wouldn't stay at home to be queen for a day," June Star said   4 without raising her yellow head.

"Yes and what would you do if this fellow, The Misfit, caught you?"   5 the grandmother asked.

"I'd smack his face," John Wesley said.   6

"She wouldn't stay at home for a million bucks," June Star said.   7 "Afraid she'd miss something. She has to go everywhere we go."

"All right, Miss," the grandmother said. "Just remember that the   8 next time you want me to curl your hair."

June Star said her hair was naturally curly.   9

The next morning the grandmother was the first one in the car,   10 ready to go. She had her big black valise that looked like the head of a hippopotamus in one corner, and underneath it she was hiding a basket with Pitty Sing, the cat, in it. She didn't intend for the cat to be left alone in the house for three days because he would miss her too much and she was afraid he might brush against one of the gas burners and accidentally asphyxiate himself. Her son, Bailey, didn't like to arrive at a motel with a cat.

She sat in the middle of the back seat with John Wesley and June   11 Star on either side of her. Bailey and the children's mother and the baby

sat in front and they left Atlanta at eight forty-five with the mileage on
the car at 55890. The grandmother wrote this down because she
thought it would be interesting to say how many miles they had been
when they got back. It took them twenty minutes to reach the outskirts
of the city.

The old lady settled herself comfortably, removing her white cotton     12
gloves and putting them up with her purse on the shelf in front of the
back window. The children's mother still had on slacks and still had
her head tied up in a green kerchief, but the grandmother had on a
navy blue straw sailor hat with a bunch of white violets on the brim
and a navy blue dress with a small white dot in the print. Her collars
and cuffs were white organdy trimmed with lace and at her neckline
she had pinned a purple spray of cloth violets containing a sachet. In
case of an accident, anyone seeing her dead on the highway would
know at once that she was a lady.

She said she thought it was going to be a good day for driving,     13
neither too hot nor too cold, and she cautioned Bailey that the speed
limit was fifty-five miles an hour and that the patrolmen hid themselves behind billboards and small clumps of trees and sped out after
you before you had a chance to slow down. She pointed out interesting
details of the scenery: Stone Mountain; the blue granite that in some
places came up to both sides of the highway; the brilliant red clay
banks slightly streaked with purple; and the various crops that made
rows of green lace-work on the ground. The trees were full of silver-
white sunlight and the meanest of them sparkled. The children were
reading comic magazines and their mother had gone back to sleep.

"Let's go through Georgia fast so we won't have to look at it much,"     14
John Wesley said.

"If I were a little boy," said the grandmother, "I wouldn't talk about     15
my native state that way. Tennessee has the mountains and Georgia
has the hills."

"Tennessee is just a hillbilly dumping ground," John Wesley said,     16
"and Georgia is a lousy state too."

"You said it," June Star said.     17

"In my time," said the grandmother, folding her thin veined fingers,     18
"children were more respectful of their native states and their parents
and everything else. People did right then. Oh look at the cute little
pickaninny!" she said and pointed to a Negro child standing in the
door of a shack. "Wouldn't that make a picture, now?" she asked and

they all turned and looked at the little Negro out of the back window. He waved.

"He didn't have any britches on," June Star said.                              19

"He probably didn't have any," the grandmother explained. "Little     20
niggers in the country don't have things like we do. If I could paint, I'd paint that picture," she said.

The children exchanged comic books.                                           21

The grandmother offered to hold the baby and the children's mother     22
passed him over the front seat to her. She sat him on her knee and bounced him and told him about the things they were passing. She rolled her eyes and screwed up her mouth and stuck her leathery thin face into his smooth bland one. Occasionally he gave her a faraway smile. They passed a large cotton field with five or six graves fenced in the middle of it, like a small island. "Look at the graveyard!" the grandmother said, pointing it out. "That was the old family burying ground. That belonged to the plantation."

"Where's the plantation?" John Wesley asked.                                  23

"Gone With the Wind," said the grandmother. "Ha. Ha."                         24

When the children finished all the comic books they had brought,     25
they opened the lunch and ate it. The grandmother ate a peanut butter sandwich and an olive and would not let the children throw the box and the paper napkins out the window. When there was nothing else to do they played a game by choosing a cloud and making the other two guess what shape it suggested. John Wesley took one the shape of a cow and June Star guessed a cow and John Wesley said, no, an automobile, and June Star said he didn't play fair, and they began to slap each other over the grandmother.

The grandmother said she would tell them a story if they would     26
keep quiet. When she told a story, she rolled her eyes and waved her head and was very dramatic. She said once when she was a maiden lady she had been courted by a Mr. Edgar Atkins Teagarden from Jasper, Georgia. She said he was a very good-looking man and a gentleman and that he brought her a watermelon every Saturday afternoon with his initials cut in it, E. A. T. Well, one Saturday, she said, Mr. Teagarden brought the watermelon and there was nobody at home and he left it on the front porch and returned in his buggy to Jasper, but she never got the watermelon, she said, because a nigger boy ate it when he saw the initials, E. A. T.! This story tickled John Wesley's funny bone and he giggled and giggled but June Star didn't think it

was any good. She said she wouldn't marry a man that just brought her a watermelon on Saturday. The grandmother said she would have done well to marry Mr. Teagarden because he was a gentleman and had bought Coca-Cola stock when it first came out and that he had died only a few years ago, a very wealthy man.

They stopped at The Tower for barbecued sandwiches. The Tower    27
was a part stucco and part wood filling station and dance hall set in a clearing outside of Timothy. A fat man named Red Sammy Butts ran it and there were signs stuck here and there on the building and for miles up and down the highway saying, TRY RED SAMMY'S FAMOUS BARBECUE. NONE LIKE FAMOUS RED SAMMY'S! RED SAM! THE FAT BOY WITH THE HAPPY LAUGH! A VETERAN! RED SAMMY'S YOUR MAN!

Red Sammy was lying on the bare ground outside The Tower with    28
his head under a truck while a gray monkey about a foot high, chained to a small chinaberry tree, chattered nearby. The monkey sprang back into the tree and got on the highest limb as soon as he saw the children jump out of the car and run toward him.

Inside, The Tower was a long dark room with a counter at one end    29
and tables at the other and dancing space in the middle. They all sat down at a board table next to the nickelodeon and Red Sam's wife, a tall burnt-brown woman with hair and eyes lighter than her skin, came and took their order. The children's mother put a dime in the machine and played "The Tennessee Waltz," and the grandmother said that tune always made her want to dance. She asked Bailey if he would like to dance but he only glared at her. He didn't have a naturally sunny disposition like she did and trips made him nervous. The grandmother's brown eyes were very bright. She swayed her head from side to side and pretended she was dancing in her chair. June Star said play something she could tap to so the children's mother put in another dime and played a fast number and June Star stepped out onto the dance floor and did her tap routine.

"Ain't she cute?" Red Sam's wife said, leaning over the counter.    30
"Would you like to come be my little girl?"

"No I certainly wouldn't," June Star said. "I wouldn't live in a    31
broken-down place like this for a million bucks!" and she ran back to the table.

"Ain't she cute?" the woman repeated, stretching her mouth    32
politely.

"Aren't you ashamed?" hissed the grandmother.                      33

Red Sam came in and told his wife to quit lounging on the counter   34
and hurry up with these people's order. His khaki trousers reached
just to his hip bones and his stomach hung over them like a sack of
meal swaying under his shirt. He came over and sat down at a table
nearby and let out a combination sigh and yodel. "You can't win," he
said. "You can't win," and he wiped his sweating red face off with a
gray handkerchief. "These days you don't know who to trust," he said.
"Ain't that the truth?"

"People are certainly not nice like they used to be," said the grand-  35
mother.

"Two fellers come in here last week," Red Sammy said, "driving a    36
Chrysler. It was a old beat-up car but it was a good one and these boys
looked all right to me. Said they worked at the mill and you know I let
them fellers charge the gas they bought? Now why did I do that?"

"Because you're a good man!" the grandmother said at once.         37

"Yes'm, I suppose so," Red Sam said as if he were struck with this   38
answer.

His wife brought the orders, carrying the five plates all at once    39
without a tray, two in each hand and one balanced on her arm. "It isn't
a soul in this green world of God's that you can trust," she said. "And
I don't count nobody out of that, not nobody," she repeated, looking
at Red Sammy.

"Did you read about that criminal, The Misfit, that's escaped?"     40
asked the grandmother.

"I wouldn't be a bit surprised if he didn't attact this place right here,"   41
said the woman. "If he hears about it being here, I wouldn't be none
surprised to see him. If he hears it's two cent in the cash register, I
wouldn't be a tall surprised if he . . ."

"That'll do," Red Sam said, "Go bring these people their Co'-Colas,"   42
and the woman went off to get the rest of the order.

"A good man is hard to find," Red Sammy said. "Everything is        43
getting terrible. I remember the day you could go off and leave your
screen door unlatched. Not no more."

He and the grandmother discussed better times. The old lady said    44
that in her opinion Europe was entirely to blame for the way things
were now. She said the way Europe acted you would think we were
made of money and Red Sam said it was no use talking about it, she

was exactly right. The children ran outside into the white sunlight and looked at the monkey in the lacy chinaberry tree. He was busy catching fleas on himself and biting each one carefully between his teeth as if it were a delicacy.

They drove off again into the hot afternoon. The grandmother took    45
cat naps and woke up every few minutes with her own snoring. Outside of Toombsboro she woke up and recalled an old plantation that she had visited in this neighborhood once when she was a young lady. She said the house had six white columns across the front and that there was an avenue of oaks leading up to it and two little wooden trellis arbors on each side in front where you sat down with your suitor after a stroll in the garden. She recalled exactly which road to turn off to get to it. She knew that Bailey would not be willing to lose any time looking at an old house, but the more she talked about it, the more she wanted to see it once again and find out if the little twin arbors were still standing. "There was a secret panel in this house," she said craftily, not telling the truth but wishing that she were, "and the story went that all the family silver was hidden in it when Sherman came through but it was never found . . ."

"Hey!" John Wesley said. "Let's go see it! We'll find it! We'll poke all    46
the woodwork and find it! Who lives there? Where do you turn off at? Hey Pop, can't we turn off there?"

"We never have seen a house with a secret panel!" June Star    47
shrieked. "Let's go to the house with the secret panel! Hey Pop, can't we go see the house with the secret panel!"

"It's not far from here, I know," the grandmother said. "It wouldn't    48
take over twenty minutes."

Bailey was looking straight ahead. His jaw was as rigid as a horse-    49
shoe. "No," he said.

The children began to yell and scream that they wanted to see the    50
house with the secret panel. John Wesley kicked the back of the front seat and June Star hung over her mother's shoulder and whined desperately into her ear that they never had any fun even on their vacation, that they could never do what THEY wanted to do. The baby began to scream and John Wesley kicked the back of the seat so hard that his father could feel the blows in his kidney.

"All right!" he shouted and drew the car to a stop at the side of the    51
road. "Will you all shut up? Will you all just shut up for one second? If you don't shut up, we won't go anywhere."

"It would be very educational for them," the grandmother    52
murmured.

"All right," Bailey said, "but get this: This is the only time we're    53
going to stop for anything like this. This is the one and only time."

"The dirt road that you have to turn down is about a mile back," the    54
grandmother directed. "I marked it when we passed."

"A dirt road," Bailey groaned.    55

After they had turned around and were headed toward the dirt    56
road, the grandmother recalled other points about the house, the
beautiful glass over the front doorway and the candle-lamp in the hall.
John Wesley said that the secret panel was probably in the fireplace.

"You can't go inside this house," Bailey said. "You don't know who    57
lives there."

"While you all talk to the people in front, I'll run around behind and    58
get in a window," John Wesley suggested.

"We'll all stay in the car," his mother said.    59

They turned onto the dirt road and the car raced roughly along in a    60
swirl of pink dust. The grandmother recalled the times when there
were no paved roads and thirty miles was a day's journey. The dirt
road was hilly and there were sudden washes in it and sharp curves
on dangerous embankments. All at once they would be on a hill,
looking down over the blue tops of trees for miles around, then the
next minute, they would be in a red depression with the dust-coated
trees looking down on them.

"This place had better turn up in a minute," Bailey said, "or I'm    61
going to turn around."

The road looked as if no one had traveled on it in months.    62

"It's not much farther," the grandmother said and just as she said it,    63
a horrible thought came to her. The thought was so embarrassing that
she turned red in the face and her eyes dilated and her feet jumped
up, upsetting her valise in the corner. The instant the valise moved,
the newspaper top she had over the basket under it rose with a snarl
and Pitty Sing, the cat, sprang onto Bailey's shoulder.

The children were thrown to the floor and their mother, clutching    64
the baby, was thrown out the door onto the ground; the old lady was
thrown into the front seat. The car turned over once and landed right-
side-up in a gulch off the side of the road. Bailey remained in the
driver's seat with the cat—gray-striped with a broad white face and an
orange nose—clinging to his neck like a caterpillar.

As soon as the children saw they could move their arms and legs,    65
they scrambled out of the car, shouting, "We've had an ACCIDENT!"
The grandmother was curled up under the dashboard, hoping she was
injured so that Bailey's wrath would not come down on her all at once.
The horrible thought she had had before the accident was that the
house she had remembered so vividly was not in Georgia but in
Tennessee.

Bailey removed the cat from his neck with both hands and flung it    66
out the window against the side of a pine tree. Then he got out of the
car and started looking for the children's mother. She was sitting
against the side of the red gutted ditch, holding the screaming baby,
but she only had a cut down her face and a broken shoulder. "We've
had an ACCIDENT!" the children screamed in a frenzy of delight.

"But nobody's killed," June Star said with disappointment as the    67
grandmother limped out of the car, her hat still pinned to her head but
the broken front brim standing up at a jaunty angle and the violet
spray hanging off the side. They all sat down in the ditch, except the
children, to recover from the shock. They were all shaking.

"Maybe a car will come along," said the children's mother hoarsely.    68

"I believe I have injured an organ," said the grandmother, pressing    69
her side, but no one answered her. Bailey's teeth were clattering. He
had on a yellow sport shirt with bright blue parrots designed in it and
his face was as yellow as the shirt. The grandmother decided that she
would not mention that the house was in Tennessee.

The road was about ten feet above and they could see only the tops    70
of the trees on the other side of it. Behind the ditch they were sitting
in there were more woods, tall and dark and deep. In a few minutes
they saw a car some distance away on top of a hill, coming slowly as if
the occupants were watching them. The grandmother stood up and
waved both arms dramatically to attract their attention. The car continued to come on slowly, disappeared around a bend and appeared
again, moving even slower, on top of the hill they had gone over.
It was a big black battered hearselike automobile. There were three
men in it.

It came to a stop just over them and for some minutes, the driver    71
looked down with a steady expressionless gaze to where they were
sitting, and didn't speak. Then he turned his head and muttered something to the other two and they got out. One was a fat boy in black
trousers and a red sweat shirt with a silver stallion embossed on the

front of it. He moved around on the right side of them and stood staring, his mouth partly open in a kind of loose grin. The other had on khaki pants and a blue striped coat and a gray hat pulled down very low, hiding most of his face. He came around slowly on the left side. Neither spoke.

The driver got out of the car and stood by the side of it, looking down at them. He was an older man than the other two. His hair was just beginning to gray and he wore silver-rimmed spectacles that gave him a scholarly look. He had a long creased face and didn't have on any shirt or undershirt. He had on blue jeans that were too tight for him and was holding a black hat and a gun. The two boys also had guns.    72

"We've had an ACCIDENT!" the children screamed.    73

The grandmother had the peculiar feeling that the bespectacled man was someone she knew. His face was as familiar to her as if she had known him all her life but she could not recall who he was. He moved away from the car and began to come down the embankment, placing his feet carefully so that he wouldn't slip. He had on tan and white shoes and no socks, and his ankles were red and thin. "Good afternoon," he said. "I see you all had you a little spill."    74

"We turned over twice!" said the grandmother.    75

"Oncet," he corrected. "We seen it happen. Try their car and see will it run, Hiram," he said quietly to the boy with the gray hat.    76

"What you got that gun for?" John Wesley asked. "Whatcha gonna do with that gun?"    77

"Lady," the man said to the children's mother, "would you mind calling them children to sit down by you? Children make me nervous. I want all you all to sit down right together there where you're at."    78

"What are you telling us what to do for?" June Star asked.    79

Behind them the line of woods gaped like a dark open mouth. "Come here," said their mother.    80

"Look here now," Bailey began suddenly, "we're in a predicament! We're in . . ."    81

The grandmother shrieked. She scrambled to her feet and stood staring. "You're The Misfit!" she said, "I recognized you at once!"    82

"Yes'm," the man said, smiling slightly as if he were pleased in spite of himself to be known, "but it would have been better for all of you, lady, if you hadn't of reckernized me."    83

Bailey turned his head sharply and said something to his mother    84 that shocked even the children. The old lady began to cry and The Misfit reddened.

"Lady," he said, "don't you get upset. Sometimes a man says things    85
he don't mean. I don't reckon he meant to talk to you thataway."

"You wouldn't shoot a lady, would you?" the grandmother said and    86
removed a clean handkerchief from her cuff and began to slap at her eyes with it.

The Misfit pointed the toe of his shoe into the ground and made    87
a little hole and then covered it up again. "I would hate to have to," he said.

"Listen," the grandmother almost screamed, "I know you're a good    88
man. You don't look a bit like you have common blood. I know you must come from nice people!"

"Yes mam," he said, "finest people in the world." When he smiled    89
he showed a row of strong white teeth. "God never made a finer woman than my mother and my daddy's heart was pure gold," he said. The boy with the red sweat shirt had come around behind them and was standing with his gun at his hip. The Misfit squatted down on the ground. "Watch them children, Bobby Lee," he said. "You know they make me nervous." He looked at the six of them huddled together in front of him and he seemed to be embarrassed as if he couldn't think of anything to say. "Ain't a cloud in the sky," he remarked, looking up at it. "Don't see no sun but don't see no cloud neither."

"Yes, it's a beautiful day," said the grandmother. "Listen," she said,    90
"you shouldn't call yourself The Misfit because I know you're a good man at heart. I can just look at you and tell."

"Hush!" Bailey yelled. "Hush! Everybody shut up and let me han-    91
dle this!" He was squatting in the position of a runner about to sprint forward but he didn't move.

"I pre-chate that, lady," The Misfit said and drew a little circle in the    92
ground with the butt of his gun.

"It'll take a half a hour to fix this here car," Hiram called, looking    93
over the raised hood of it.

"Well, first you and Bobby Lee get him and that little boy to step    94
over yonder with you," The Misfit said, pointing to Bailey and John Wesley, "The boys want to ast you something," he said to Bailey. "Would you mind stepping back in them woods there with them?"

"Listen," Bailey began, "we're in a terrible predicament! Nobody    95
realizes what this is," and his voice cracked. His eyes were as blue and intense as the parrots in his shirt and he remained perfectly still.

The grandmother reached up to adjust her hat brim as if she were    96
going to the woods with him but it came off in her hand. She stood
staring at it and after a second she let it fall on the ground. Hiram
pulled Bailey up by the arm as if he were assisting an old man. John
Wesley caught hold of his father's hand and Bobby Lee followed. They
went off toward the woods and just as they reached the dark edge,
Bailey turned and supporting himself against a gray naked pine trunk,
he shouted, "I'll be back in a minute, Mamma, wait on me!"

"Come back this instant!" his mother shrilled but they all disap-    97
peared into the woods.

"Bailey Boy!" the grandmother called in a tragic voice but she found    98
she was looking at The Misfit squatting on the ground in front of her.
"I just know you're a good man," she said desperately. "You're not a
bit common!"

"Nome, I ain't a good man," The Misfit said after a second as if he    99
had considered her statement carefully, "But I ain't the worst in the
world neither. My daddy said I was a different breed of dog from my
brothers and sisters. 'You know,' Daddy said, 'it's some that can live
their whole life out without asking about it and it's others has to know
why it is, and this boy is one of the latters. He's going to be into
everything!'" He put on his black hat and looked up suddenly and
then away deep into the woods as if he were embarrassed again. "I'm
sorry I don't have on a shirt before you ladies," he said, hunching his
shoulders slightly. "We buried our clothes that we had on when we
escaped and we're just making do until we can get better. We borrowed
these from some folks we met," he explained.

"That's perfectly all right," the grandmother said. "Maybe Bailey    100
has an extra shirt in his suitcase."

"I'll look and see terrectly," The Misfit said.    101

"Where are they taking him?" the children's mother screamed.    102

"Daddy was a card himself," The Misfit said. "You couldn't put    103
anything over on him. He never got in trouble with the Authorities
though. Just had the knack of handling them."

"You could be honest too if you'd only try," said the grandmother.    104
"Think how wonderful it would be to settle down and live a comfortable life and not have to think about somebody chasing you all
the time."

The Misfit kept scratching in the ground with the butt of his gun as    105
if he were thinking about it. "Yes'm, somebody is always after you,"
he murmured.

The grandmother noticed how thin his shoulder blades were just behind his hat because she was standing up looking down on him. "Do you ever pray?" she asked. <sub></sub> 106

He shook his head. All she saw was the black hat wiggle between his shoulder blades. "Nome," he said. 107

There was a pistol shot from the woods, followed closely by another. Then silence. The old lady's head jerked around. She could hear the wind move through the tree tops like a long satisfied insuck of breath. "Bailey Boy!" she called. 108

"I was a gospel singer for a while," The Misfit said. "I been most everything. Been in the arm service, both land and sea, at home and abroad, been twicet married, been an undertaker, been with the rail-roads, plowed Mother Earth, been in a tornado, seen a man burnt alive oncet," and looked up at the children's mother and the little girl who were sitting close together, their faces white and their eyes glassy; "I even seen a woman flogged," he said. 109

"Pray, pray," the grandmother began, "pray, pray . . ." 110

"I never was a bad boy that I remember of," The Misfit said in an almost dreamy voice, "but somewheres along the line I done some-thing wrong and got sent to the penitentiary. I was buried alive," and he looked up and held her attention to him by a steady stare. 111

"That's when you should have started to pray," she said. "What did you do to get sent to the penitentiary that first time?" 112

"Turn to the right, it was a wall," The Misfit said, looking up again at the cloudless sky. "Turn to the left, it was a wall. Look up it was a ceiling, look down it was a floor. I forget what I done, lady. I set there and set there, trying to remember what it was I done and I ain't recalled it to this day. Oncet in a while, I would think it was coming to me, but it never come." 113

"Maybe they put you in by mistake," the old lady said vaguely. 114

"Nome," he said. "It wasn't no mistake. They had the papers on me." 115

"You must have stolen something," she said. 116

The Misfit sneered slightly. "Nobody had nothing I wanted," he said. "It was a head-doctor at the penitentiary said what I had done was kill my daddy but I known that for a lie. My daddy died in nine-teen ought nineteen of the epidemic flu and I never had a thing to do with it. He was buried in the Mount Hopewell Baptist churchyard and you can go there and see for yourself." 117

"If you would pray," the old lady said, "Jesus would help you."   118

"That's right," The Misfit said.   119

"Well then, why don't you pray?" she asked trembling with delight   120
suddenly.

"I don't want no hep," he said, "I'm doing all right by myself."   121

Bobby Lee and Hiram came ambling back from the woods. Bobby   122
Lee was dragging a yellow shirt with bright blue parrots in it.

"Throw me that shirt, Bobby Lee," The Misfit said. The shirt came   123
flying at him and landed on his shoulder and he put it on. The grandmother couldn't name what the shirt reminded her of. "No, lady," The
Misfit said while he was buttoning it up, "I found out the crime don't
matter. You can do one thing or you can do another, kill a man or take
a tire off his car, because sooner or later you're going to forget what it
was you done and just be punished for it."

The children's mother had begun to make heaving noises as if she   124
couldn't get her breath. "Lady," he asked, "would you and that little
girl like to step off yonder with Bobby Lee and Hiram and join your
husband?"

"Yes, thank you," the mother said faintly. Her left arm dangled   125
helplessly and she was holding the baby, who had gone to sleep, in
the other. "Hep that lady up, Hiram," The Misfit said as she struggled
to climb out of the ditch, "and Bobby Lee, you hold onto that little
girl's hand."

"I don't want to hold hands with him," June Star said. "He reminds   126
me of a pig."

The fat boy blushed and laughed and caught her by the arm and   127
pulled her off into the woods after Hiram and her mother.

Alone with The Misfit, the grandmother found that she had lost her   128
voice. There was not a cloud in the sky nor any sun. There was nothing
around her but woods. She wanted to tell him that he must pray. She
opened and closed her mouth several times before anything came out.
Finally she found herself saying, "Jesus, Jesus," meaning, Jesus will
help you, but the way she was saying it, it sounded as if she might
be cursing.

"Yes'm," The Misfit said as if he agreed, "Jesus thrown everything   129
off balance. It was the same case with Him as with me except He hadn't
committed any crime and they could prove I had committed one because they had the papers on me. Of course," he said, "they never
shown me my papers. That's why I sign myself now. I said long ago,

you get you a signature and sign everything you do and keep a copy of it. Then you'll know what you done and you can hold up the crime to the punishment and see do they match and in the end you'll have something to prove you ain't been treated right. I call myself The Misfit," he said, "because I can't make what all I done wrong fit what all I gone through in punishment."

There was a piercing scream from the woods, followed closely by a     130
pistol report. "Does it seem right to you, lady, that one is punished a heap and another ain't punished at all?"

"Jesus!" the old lady cried. "You've got good blood! I know you     131
wouldn't shoot a lady! I know you come from nice people! Pray! Jesus, you ought not to shoot a lady, I'll give you all the money I've got!"

"Lady," The Misfit said, looking beyond her far into the woods,     132
"there never was a body that give the undertaker a tip."

There were two more pistol reports and the grandmother raised her     133
head like a parched old turkey hen crying for water and called, "Bailey Boy, Bailey Boy!" as if her heart would break.

"Jesus was the only One that ever raised the dead." The Misfit     134
continued, "and He shouldn't have done it. He thrown everything off balance. If He did what He said, then it's nothing for you to do but throw away everything and follow Him, and if He didn't, then it's nothing for you to do but enjoy the few minutes you got left the best way you can—by killing somebody or burning down his house or doing some other meanness to him. No pleasure but meanness," he said and his voice had become almost a snarl.

"Maybe He didn't raise the dead," the old lady mumbled, not know-     135
ing what she was saying and feeling so dizzy that she sank down in the ditch with her legs twisted under her.

"I wasn't there so I can't say He didn't," The Misfit said. "I wisht I     136
had of been there," he said, hitting the ground with his fist. "It ain't right I wasn't there because if I had of been there I would of known. Listen lady," he said in a high voice, "if I had of been there I would of known and I wouldn't be like I am now." His voice seemed about to crack and the grandmother's head cleared for an instant. She saw the man's face twisted close to her own as if he were going to cry and she murmured, "Why you're one of my babies. You're one of my own children!" She reached out and touched him on the shoulder. The Misfit sprang back as if a snake had bitten him and shot her three times through the chest. Then he put his gun down on the ground and took off his glasses and began to clean them.

Hiram and Bobby Lee returned from the woods and stood over the    137
ditch, looking down at the grandmother who half sat and half lay in a
puddle of blood with her legs crossed under her like a child's and her
face smiling up at the cloudless sky.

Without his glasses, The Misfit's eyes were red-rimmed and pale    138
and defenseless-looking. "Take her off and throw her where you
thrown the others," he said, picking up the cat that was rubbing itself
against his leg.

"She was a talker, wasn't she?" Bobby Lee said, sliding down the    139
ditch with a yodel.

"She would of been a good woman," The Misfit said, "if it had been    140
somebody there to shoot her every minute of her life."

"Some fun!" Bobby Lee said.    141

"Shut up, Bobby Lee," The Misfit said. "It's no real pleasure in life."    142

## VOCABULARY

| | | |
|---|---|---|
| asphyxiate (10) | dilated (63) | ambling (122) |
| sachet (12) | jaunty (67) | parched (133) |
| bland (22) | embossed (71) | |

## THE FACTS

1. Why didn't the grandmother want to go to Florida? Where did she want to go instead?
2. Why does the family turn off onto the lonely dirt road?
3. What caused the accident?
4. For what crime was the Misfit sent to the penitentiary?
5. Why does he call himself "The Misfit"?

## THE STRATEGIES

1. The Misfit is mentioned in the first paragraph. Why does O'Connor introduce him so early?
2. What does the initial dialogue between the grandmother and the children accomplish?
3. In paragraph 70 the Misfit's automobile is described as "a big black battered hearselike automobile." What is O'Connor doing in this description?
4. At a climactic part of the story, the grandmother has a sudden dramatic recognition of responsibility. When does it occur? Whom does it involve?
5. In paragraph 80 O'Connor writes: "Behind them the line of woods gaped like a dark open mouth." What does this description accomplish? What does it signal to the reader?

## THE ISSUES

1. The Misfit and his cronies commit cold-blooded murder on a family of six. What prerequisite, if any, do you think must necessarily exist before a person is capable of murder? If you think no prerequisite is necessary, do you also think anyone is capable of cold-blooded murder? Justify your answer.
2. What punishment would you regard as just and fitting for the Misfit and his henchmen?
3. Some commentators have said that the children are brats, pure and simple, while others have argued that they are rather typical. What is your opinion of the children and their behavior?
4. One interpretation argues that the Misfit is the devil and the grandmother a Christian who confronts him. What is your opinion of this interpretation?
5. What do you think the grandmother meant when she said to the Misfit, "Why you're one of my babies. You're one of my own children!" Why do you think the Misfit killed her when she said that?

## SUGGESTIONS FOR WRITING

1. Write an essay analyzing the techniques used by the author to foreshadow the family's fatal encounter with the Misfit. Make specific references to scenes and images and include as many quoted passages as necessary to prove your case.
2. Write an essay interpreting this story.

### Sara Teasdale

# • BARTER •

*Sara Teasdale (1884–1933) was an American poet who wrote several volumes of highly personal lyrics, including* Rivers to the Sea *(1915) and* Strange Victory *(1933). She committed suicide at the age of 48.*

*Theses are used mainly in essays and articles and other prose works. Yet some poems, such as this one, are arranged around a core idea which, in its expression and development, functions much the same as the thesis in an essay.*

> Life has loveliness to sell,
>     All beautiful and splendid things,
> Blue waves whitened on a cliff,
>     Soaring fire that sways and sings,
> And children's faces looking up,
> Holding wonder like a cup.

5

Life has loveliness to sell,
   Music like a curve of gold,
Scent of pine trees in the rain,
   Eyes that love you, arms that hold,         10
And for your spirit's still delight,
Holy thoughts that star the night.

Spend all you have for loveliness,
   Buy it and never count the cost;
For one white singing hour of peace        15
   Count many a year of strife well lost,
And for a breath of ecstasy
Give all you have been, or could be.

## THE FACTS

1. What examples of life's loveliness does the first stanza present?
2. To which senses do the images of life's loveliness in the second stanza appeal?
3. What advice does the author give in the third stanza?

## THE STRATEGIES

1. If you had to sum up the theme of this poem in a thesis, what would it be?
2. What is the rhyme scheme of this poem?
3. The first stanza ends on a simile. On what figure of speech does the second stanza end? What is the difference between this figure and the one at the end of the first stanza?

## THE ISSUES

1. The poet exhorts us to spend all we have for loveliness. What do you think is worth spending your all to have?
2. How does the fact that the author took her own life affect your interpretation or reading of this poem?
3. Percy Bysshe Shelley (1792–1822), the English poet, declared in an essay that poets are the "unacknowledged legislators of the world." How may that idea be applied to the poem? In what way may this poem be said to legislate?

## SUGGESTIONS FOR WRITING

1. The *carpe diem* poem is one that exhorts the philosophy "Let us eat and drink, for tomorrow we shall die." Write an essay comparing or contrasting the theme of this poem with the *carpe diem* philosophy.

2. What is the most precious quality that life has to offer you? For the author, it is loveliness. Write an essay about the thing in life that you value above all else.

## ══════ •• *ISSUE FOR CRITICAL* •• ══════
## *THINKING*
### *Surrogate Mothers*

Before the celebrated case of Baby M., most of us probably never dreamed that surrogate mothers existed. The case began in 1985 when Mary Beth Whitehead,* a 29-year-old homemaker from Brick Town, New Jersey, signed a contract with William and Elizabeth Stern, a biochemist and a pediatrician, to bear them a child in return for a $10,000 fee. Mrs. Stern was said to be suffering a mild case of multiple sclerosis that would be aggravated by the complications of childbirth. Whitehead was artificially inseminated with sperm from William Stern and bore him a healthy daughter on March 27, 1986.

But then Whitehad had second thoughts. She pleaded with the Sterns to allow her to keep the baby for a week, then tried to amend the contract to allow her to have the baby one weekend a month and two weeks every summer. The Sterns refused and went to court to enforce the original contract. With the complicity of her husband, Richard, Whitehead fled with the child to the home of her mother in Holiday, Florida. Eventually the Sterns tracked down their lost child, regained possession, and a court case ensued. In an effort to protect the privacy of the disputed infant, the court gave her the pseudonym "Baby M.," and so the case was named.

Although the initial decree went against the Whiteheads and custody of the child was granted to the Sterns, on February 3, 1988, the New Jersey Supreme Court unanimously reversed the lower court, ruling that commercial surrogate-mother contracts amounted to "baby selling" and were illegal. The Sterns were allowed to keep the child but Whitehead could either file for another custodial hearing or at least secure lifelong visitation rights. "The surrogate contract creates, it is based upon, principles that are directly contrary to the objectives of our laws," wrote Chief Justice Robert Wilentz. "It guarantees separation of a child from its mother; it looks to adoption regard-

---

*Whitehead has divorced and remarried and now uses the name Mary Beth Whitehead-Gould.

less of suitability; it totally ignores the child; it takes the child from the mother regardless of her wishes and her maternal fitness, and it does all of this, it accomplishes all of its goals, through use of money."*

Surrogate motherhood is the flip side of the abortion issue. Over a million babies are aborted every year in the United States, a country in which some three and a half million infertile couples are desperate for children. Adoption agencies are so swamped with applicants that a seven-year wait is considered routine. Some estimates say that for every adoptable infant there are ten thousand eager couples on waiting lists.

Among the issues raised by the Baby M. case is this primal one: Are surrogate contracts moral? Decidedly not, says conservative columnist Michael Novak, who invokes comparisons to slavery and baby trafficking. Others worry that such arrangements will create a caste of poor "breeder women" paid to have children for the husbands of their more affluent sisters who do not wish to endure the discomforts of childbearing. A spokesman for the other side is Mona Field, a sociologist whose research has focused on surrogate mothering and other aspects of childbearing. James Risen reminds us that any surrogate arrangement must also include another party—the husband of the surrogate mother—who is often ignored by everyone else.

This is one issue that may be settled by advancements in reproductive technology, if not by public opinions and the courts. The prospect of true "test-tube" babies, gestated in the laboratory rather than in a human uterus, is looming larger. Advances in microscopic surgery offer hope that one day an ovum may be removed from an infertile woman, fertilized by her husband's sperm, and reinserted into her womb for a "natural pregnancy." Until that day, however, we have surrogate mothers and the troubling moral issues they raise.

**Michael Novak**

# ——— • BUYING AND SELLING BABIES: • ———
# LIMITATIONS ON THE MARKETPLACE

*Michael Novak (b. 1933) is a teacher and writer affiliated with Notre Dame University and the American Enterprise Institute, for which he is the Director of Social and Political Studies. He was born in Johnstown, Pennsylvania, and*

---

*Quoted in "Court Bans Surrogate Contracts, But Lets Father Keep 'Baby M,'" *Atlanta Constitution*, February 4, 1988.

*educated at Stonehill College (A.B. 1956); Gregorian University of Rome, Italy (B.T. 1958); Catholic University; and Harvard University (M.A. 1965). He is the author of numerous works including* Belief and Unbelief *(1965) and* Will It Liberate?. Questions about Liberation Theology *(1986).*

Many of us would have thought that it is against American law     1
to buy or sell human beings—something beneath the dignity of human beings.

Many of us would have thought that moral relativism would go     2
so far in our society, and that in the end some things would be universally seen to be simply and absolutely wrong. The discussion around Baby M., therefore, gave us all a rude jolt.

Begin with the terms of the contract, which skillful lawyers carefully     3
explained in advance to the mother of Baby M., Mary Beth Whitehead. First of all, the "charitable agency" that arranged this contract received $7,500 up front, non-refundable. Next, Mrs. Whitehead was presented with the following six-point offer: (1) all risks belonged to her; if anything went wrong with her or the baby during the pregnancy, she was to receive *nothing*: (2) in case of miscarriage, she was to receive *nothing*; (3) between the sixteenth and twentieth week, her baby would have to be tested for "physiological abnormalities"; at this point, (4) if "physiological abnormalities" were discovered, she would be obliged "upon demand of William Stern" to have an abortion; (5) if the abortion were demanded by William Stern, William Stern would pay her a big-hearted $1,000; and (6) with the delivery and surrender of a healthy baby for possession by the Sterns, Mrs. Whitehead would receive—at the point of sale—$10,000.

To me, it is almost inconceivable that the courts could decide such a     4
case merely on the strength of existing contract law. Is not such a contract immoral on its face? Is it any more than trafficking in human life, as slavery was? If a slave woman brought forth a baby, could it not have also been bought? Was such a contract not considered, even long ago, morally repugnant?

Actually, the contract for Baby M. was worse than a contract for a     5
slave. For it was carried through by a series of understandable but grotesque deceptions. These deceptions are understandable because they are so widespread in contemporary consciousness. One sympathizes with the Sterns and the Whiteheads and others who participated. But one is under no necessity to accept the ways in which they

deceived themselves about human reality and the human heart. May they all live happily ever after, even as the rest of us draw lessons from the deceptions so clearly dramatized before our eyes.

The first deception was that of Mr. and Mrs. Stern. Mrs. Stern, 6 according to at least one source, wanted a baby but faced a medical risk in bearing it, while Mr. Stern wanted a baby of *his own* even apart from the woman to whom he was married. Is it not a deception to believe you can become parents by purchase? Such surrogacy is banned by law in the [United Kingdom], for fear of just such monetary exploitation.

The second deception was that of a Manhattan clinical psychologist 7 who testified before the New Jersey Court: "In both structural and functional terms, Mr. and Mrs. Stern's role as parents to Baby M. was achieved by a surrogate uterus and not a surrogate mother." This is absurd. Take the uterus out of Mrs. Whitehead if you think it will structurally and functionally achieve a baby without her. To separate Mrs. Whitehead's *uterus* from her *self* merely by verbal agility is an outrage, not only to common sense but to the dignity of Mrs. White-head. It is a scholastic deception to think that a human child is produced by a uterus alone, not by a human person.

The third deception was to argue that Mrs. Whitehead was less 8 worthy to be the mother than Mrs. Stern, whether on financial or on psychological grounds. No babies in history have chosen their parents. If Mrs. Whitehead is a threat to Baby M., why were her other two children not also taken away from her by the courts? If she was not a threat, then the only distinction between Baby M. and her two siblings appears to be that she was bought, while the other two were not.

"But Mrs. Whitehead signed a contract," some may claim. That is 9 to beg the point. Can *any* contract to buy or to sell a human being be valid?

It was a deception for Mr. Stern to insert the clause on abortion, 10 while later saying he would value the human dignity of his new child. Had she been "physiologically abnormal" at five months, he would have had her killed. He said so in the contract.

It was a deception for some spokespersons to say that compassion 11 for the desire of the Sterns to have their own baby (*his* own baby, not *hers*) entitled them to buy one. There are hundreds of thousands of babies to adopt, although admittedly not enough for all who would adopt them.

Solely for the contracts involved, not counting legal fees, the Sterns    12
paid $17,500. So it is a further, broadly held deception in this society
that babies are *unwanted*. Babies are desperately wanted in this society.

Perhaps, you will say, the Sterns should have persuaded a woman    13
they knew who wished to have an abortion to have that child for them.
They might even have offered to pay her expenses. Genetically, true
enough, the child would not have been Mr. Stern's. (But Mr. Whitehead, though Baby M. was not *his*, fell in love with the infant the
moment he saw her in his wife's arms.) And some might say that the
offer to pay a woman's expenses for not having an abortion, and,
instead, carrying the baby to term, would have been *like* paying Mrs.
Whitehead. On the contrary, it might have been seen as paying a
ransom to redeem an infant hostaged to death.

At birth, of course, that mother, too—like Mrs. Whitehead—might    14
have decided that the precious infant, no longer an abstraction on a
legal pad, once it nestles at her breast, could *not* be given up. So it is
that humanity breaks through the paper on which legal contracts pur-
porting to bind human lives are written.

As readers of *Commonweal* must know by now, I am in favor of free    15
economics and markets, constrained by law (the political system) and
by moral judgment (the moral-cultural system). This very conception,
however, this *novus ordo seclorum*,* shows that the market is a mechanism designed to function only within limits. As I believe in limited
government, so I believe in limited markets. It is simply not the case
that everything is permitted or that everything has a price. Among the
priceless things of our experience are human infants. Certainly our
own, but not only our own.

Based upon concepts fundamental to our political economy—based    16
upon inalienable rights endowed in persons by their Creator—the law
ought to discourage such surrogate parenting, except in certain rare
cases. (There may be exceptional circumstances, more or less intra-
familial, in which such surrogacy makes human sense.) In any case,
the right of the natural mother to change her mind and to keep the
child, as she would in adoption proceedings, must be protected.

We are coming to see that the long-devalued concept "natural,"    17
difficult as it is to define, perennially makes its legitimacy felt. There
are three reasons for this. First, the entire human race is more and

---

*Latin, "A new order of the ages." It is the motto on the Great Seal of the United States.—Ed.

more being seen as interdependent and subject to one single standard of respect for human rights. Second, new scientific knowledge and technical skills offer so many possibilities that, more and more, the impulse to establish the limits that define who we are—our self-appropriated nature—is becoming a self-conscious imperative. Third, our attempts to live by a merely emotive ethic, more or less make-it-yourself, have led to so many disasters that the limits of experimentation are becoming more clearly and more publicly defined, by a growing consensus. The "laws of nature and of nature's God" slowly make themselves known to us through experience and misadventure; thus does nature instruct us in history.

As the state is limited, as markets are limited, so also, it seems, the    18
natural law governing human happiness is less and less obscure; its outlines are emerging from the mist. In a fog, as Chesterton once wrote, to recognize the edges of the cliff is liberty, and vagueness is tyranny.

### VOCABULARY

| | | |
|---|---|---|
| purporting (14) | self-appropriated (17) | misadventure (17) |
| perennially (17) | consensus (17) | |

### THE FACTS

1. According to the contract between the Sterns and Mrs. Whitehead, what would Mrs. Whitehead have received if she had miscarried?
2. If the baby had shown "physiological abnormalities" in the uterus, what would the Sterns's contract have obliged Mrs. Whitehead to do?
3. What is the attitude in the United Kingdom concerning surrogate motherhood? Why does this attitude exist?
4. What testimony given by a Manhattan clinical psychologist does the author find absurd?
5. What sole distinction does Novak find between Baby M. and Mrs. Whitehead's other two children?

### THE STRATEGIES

1. Whose side does Novak plainly take in summarizing the terms of the Baby M. contract in paragraph 3? How does he make his feelings clear?
2. What rhetorical technique does Novak use in paragraph 4 to make his point that surrogate contracts are immoral?

3. What argumentative strategy does Novak use in paragraph 8 when he asks why Mrs. Whitehead's own children were not also taken away from her?
4. What argumentative technique is Novak using in the brief paragraph 9?
5. What technique does Novak use to tie together the discussions in paragraphs 6, 7, 8, 10, and 11?

## THE ISSUES

1. In what way can the conflict between the Sterns and Mrs. Whitehead be seen as a class conflict?
2. In the contract with Mrs. Whitehead, William Stern reserved the right to demand of her an abortion if tests showed that she was carrying an abnormal child. What inferences can you draw about Stern from this clause?
3. In what way may surrogate motherhood be said to resemble slavery? In what way may it be said to be entirely different from slavery?
4. How does surrogate fatherhood (artificial insemination) differ ethically from surrogate motherhood? What are your own views on surrogate fatherhood?
5. What are your views on the Baby M. case? Was the court right in awarding custody of the child to the Sterns and denying visitation rights to Mrs. Whitehead? Why or why not?

## SUGGESTIONS FOR WRITING

1. Write an essay comparing or contrasting surrogate motherhood with slavery.
2. Write an essay in which you argue the opposite point of view to Novak's: that a contract is a contract and that Mrs. Whitehead should be made to keep her part of the bargain.

Mona Field

# • SURROGATE MOTHERHOOD •

### For the Good of the Few

*Mona Field (b. 1953) is an instructor in Social Science at Glendale College. A graduate of Immaculate Heart College and California State University at Los Angeles, she is a member of the Faculty Association Board of Governors for California Community Colleges. Recently she has concentrated her research on surrogate mothering and other aspects of childbearing.*

Marian and Craig, a couple in their mid-thirties, decided to have a    1
child. After four years of multiple sperm counts, hormone treatments,
and exploratory surgeries, they knew the bitter truth: Marian's long
usage of an IUD had badly scarred her Fallopian tubes. She could
never conceive. Their second choice was to adopt, but after adding
their names to the thousands already crammed on eligible lists of
adoption agencies, they were faced with a seven-year wait for a baby
or, as was more likely, never getting one. Their dream of parenting
finally came true at a center for surrogate motherhood that matched
them with Denise, a healthy, warmhearted woman who became the
surrogate for their daughter, Tricia.

The experience of Marian and Craig is typical of childless couples    2
who turn to surrogate centers for help. Surrogate motherhood is
nearly always a last resort to which desperation and the almost mystical urge to have a child have driven them. Yet today this last-resort
option is pointlessly faced with the threat of being legislated out of
existence.

The process of surrogate mothering is legally and medically uncom-    3
plicated, if not ethically so. An infertile couple contracts with a healthy,
fertile woman who, in return for medical expenses and a fee, consents
to be artificially inseminated with sperm from the husband. If pregnancy results, the surrogate carries and delivers the baby for the biological father and adoptive mother.

For all the apparent straightforwardness of this arrangement, how-    4
ever, moralists raise some worrying questions: Is the wife truly infertile? Can the surrogate mother really give up a baby she has carried
in her womb for nine months? Will the child grow up feeling abandoned by its biological mother? Will the surrogate's own children not
fear that they too may be given away?

Many of these questions haunted the infamous "Baby M." episode    5
in which a surrogate mother, Mary Beth Whitehead, a twenty-nine-
year-old homemaker, decided to keep the baby she had agreed to have
for William Stern, a forty-two-year-old biochemist, and his pediatrician wife who could not bear her own children because she suffered a
mild form of multiple sclerosis. The case wound up in an ugly court
fight that resulted in the baby being awarded to the Sterns and Whitehead having limited visitation rights.

But far from being typical of surrogate experiences, the "Baby M."    6
episode is more accurately an isolated and anomalous case in which

everything went wrong. The vast majority of surrogacy arrangements are successful: the infertile couple gets a much-wanted child; the surrogate is rewarded with money and the satisfaction of giving a priceless gift to a childless couple. Michael Balboni, the Long Island attorney who researched the surrogate mother issue for the New York Bar Association, found that fewer than one percent of the known six hundred to seven hundred surrogate mothers nationwide have had second thoughts and tried to keep their children.

Nor is surrogacy unprecedented in history. When Sarah was unable    7
to bear a child for Abraham, her husband, she told him to go to her handmaiden Hagar. "Mary was a surrogate for God" says Jenny Cassem pointedly, a twenty-eight-year-old California mother of five who has served as a surrogate. But if it was a rarity in ancient times, surrogate mothering is markedly on the increase today and for obvious reasons: three and a half million couples in America are classified as infertile. Add to this number the untold thousands likely to be rendered infertile by environmental pollution, sexually transmitted diseases, and the fad of delayed childbearing, and the projected demand for surrogate mothers becomes painfully clear.

The answer to this need is not legislation outlawing surrogate moth-    8
erhood, but sensible regulations that permit consenting adults to arrive at equitable surrogacy contracts. Better screening procedures are needed, for example, to prevent a recurrence of the Baby M. tragedy. Commonsense regulations are needed to prevent the creation of a class of poor "breeder women," which some critics have darkly prophesied as the inevitable outcome of surrogacy. While a scant 14 percent of those surveyed by the Gallup Organization think that no woman who is merely afraid to bear her own child should enter into a surrogate contract, 63 percent do favor surrogacy for cases of medical infertility. One ironic consequence of legislation against surrogates would most likely be to replace the fabled "back-room butchers" who thrived before legalized abortions with an outlawed caste of "back-room breeders."

Intensive application procedures for both surrogates and infertile    9
couples and limits on the number of times a woman can serve as a surrogate, are among two sensible safeguards that can protect the participants in a surrogate contract. The siblings' emotional health can be ensured by laws that forbid any woman whose own children are under ten to act as a surrogate. The assumption is that a child ten or

older can understand the pregnancy of a mother and accept fully the idea of giving the baby to its father and "new" mother.

Ironically, much of the opposition to surrogacy may soon become  10
moot because of the development of alternate methods of reproduction for infertile couples. Through ovum transplant an infertile woman can be implanted with a donated ovum. With microlaparoscopy surgery an egg from the ovary of an "infertile" woman can be removed, fertilized with the husband's sperm, and reinserted into her uterus for a nearly "natural" pregnancy. The prospect of true "test-tube" babies grown in the lab rather than gestated inside a human uterus is looming larger.

These innovations should be seen as potential bonuses for human-  11
kind, not as threats. But until the tide of technological innovation brings these promises within reach of the desperate childless couple, surrogate motherhood is presently the best available option. Let us confront its challenges and respond with sensitivity, caring, and wisdom, not with needless and intrusive laws designed to tell consenting adults what is "best for them."

## VOCABULARY

anomalous (6)

## THE FACTS

1. What is surrogate motherhood?
2. What worrying questions about surrogate motherhood do moralists raise?
3. According to Field, how may the Baby M. case be accurately described?
4. What, according to Field, is the answer to the need for surrogate mothers?
5. Why may much of the opposition to surrogate motherhood soon become moot?

## THE STRATEGIES

1. What does the anecdote in paragraph 1 about Marian and Craig contribute to Field's argument for surrogate motherhood?
2. Where does Field define surrogate motherhood? How does she define this term?
3. Writers of arguments are expected to anticipate and refute the opposition. Where and how does Field anticipate and refute her opposition in this article?

4. Novak raised a pointed moral objection to surrogacy, which Field all but ignores. Why do you think she fails to address this issue in her argument?
5. In paragraph 10 the author puts such common words as *infertile* and *natural* in quotation marks. Why? What is she hinting at with these marks?

### THE ISSUES

1. Opponents of surrogacy fear that women who are afraid to have their own children will be tempted to hire poor "breeder" women as substitutes. Do you think this fear is justified? Why or why not?
2. What role, if any, do you think class differences play in surrogate contracts?
3. Later in life the children of adopted parents often become intensely curious about their natural parents. Do you think the child of a surrogate mother is likely to feel the same way? Why or why not?
4. Should the government be paternalistic and tell people what is "best for them," passing laws accordingly?
5. What, if any, moral objections can you foresee to true "test tube" babies?

### SUGGESTIONS FOR WRITING

1. Write an essay arguing for or against the notion that the use of surrogate mothers is likely to create a "breeder caste" of poorer women.
2. Write an essay predicting the possible effects the child of a surrogate mother might encounter in later life.

James Risen

# • SURROGATES' SPOUSES •

## The Other Men

*James Risen (b. 1955) was born in Cincinnati, Ohio, and educated at Brown University (B.A., 1977). A senior staff writer with the Detroit bureau of the* Los Angeles Times *since 1984, he was formerly on the staff of the Detroit Free Press.*

For Vernon Blanc, the words come hard. He's just an ordinary guy, a 25-year-old Denny's Restaurant manager, and he finds it a little tough to explain something as intimate and complicated as why he is about to let his wife, Michelle, become pregnant by another man.    1

It could happen any time now.    2

Earlier this month, Michelle Blanc, 24, went to a doctor's office near her home in Mount Clemens, Mich., for the first of a series of artificial    3 inseminations. In all likelihood, she will soon become pregnant for an East Coast couple who will pay her $10,000 to bear the husband's child. She will thus cross the line from conventional wife to surrogate mother.

And, after countless fights and threats of divorce, Vernon Blanc is    4 letting her do it.

"At first, I wouldn't even consider it. I wouldn't talk to her about it.    5 As a matter of fact, we almost got into a divorce about it because I was so against it," Blanc said slowly. "I had made up my mind that I didn't want my wife having children for somebody else. I thought the whole deal was just out of this world, strange. I had made up my mind that I was going to take Brittany [their 2-year-old daughter] and leave."

Yet just two months after Michelle first shocked and angered him    6 with the news that she had already contacted a surrogate parenthood clinic, Vernon Blanc has reluctantly given in. He said he was won over after he learned more about the process, and after he met some couples who had tried every other way to have children.

He also admitted that he had, in a sense, simply caved in to his    7 wife's surprisingly strong stand: "She set her mind on this surrogate-parenting thing, and there's just no stopping her."

## MOST MOTHERS MARRIED

Given the potential for such a wide range of marriage-threatening    8 problems, it may seem surprising that any American man would agree to let his wife be a surrogate mother. Yet about 600 women, most of whom are married, have already borne children under such arrangements.

What is perhaps even more startling is just how many of the hus-    9 bands of those women seem to be happily married, middle-class men with good jobs and otherwise normal home lives—men who don't appear to be desperate for the $10,000 fees their wives will earn. Most husbands said the money was not the reason they gave their approval. "You can't do this for the money . . . I can think of a lot of other ways to make $10,000," said Eric Pressler, a 28-year-old systems programmer in Canton, Ohio, whose wife, Peggy, was a surrogate.

## BABY M STIRRED DEBATE

Ever since Mary Beth Whitehead and the Baby M case last winter    10 sparked nationwide debate over the ethics of surrogate motherhood, the focus of attention has been on the surrogate mothers, the desperate, childless couples who hire them and the babies born from their contracts.

Most of the women who become surrogate mothers are married    11
themselves—yet their husbands have been all but lost in the background.

"We need to acknowledge the obvious—that we're not just dealing    12
with a surrogate mother and an infertile couple," said Hilary Hanafin, a staff psychologist at the Center for Surrogate Parenting in Beverly Hills, one of the country's largest programs.

Still, many such clinics seem to have given short shrift to the hus-    13
bands of surrogates; these men have been left virtually to themselves to figure out how to cope with one of the strangest, and potentially most difficult, experiences that a modern American family can have.

With no biological ties to the children born from the surrogate pro-    14
cess, the husbands of surrogates have had to deal with the unusual emotional trauma of turning over the most private aspects of their married lives to strangers.

First, they must agree to abstain from sexual relations with their    15
wives during the months the women are being inseminated, to ensure the paternity of the child. Then, they must help their wives get through pregnancies that they have had nothing to do with. Ultimately, they must endure the emotionally complex time when their wives come home from the hospital without new babies of their own.

Clearly, many marriages wouldn't survive such stress; Hanafin    16
notes that there have been two divorces so far among her center's surrogates.

"If you had a weak marriage, this could be awful," said Rodney    17
Cage, a 32-year-old flooring contractor in Canyon Country, Calif., whose wife, Kim, 31, had just given birth as a surrogate.

## WHY THEY GO ALONG

Hanafin, who is conducting one of the nation's first studies of sur-    18
rogates and their families, said that the typical husband earns $32,000 a year, and usually the surrogate mother also holds down a full-time job.

So, these are men with comfortable lives—husbands one might least    19
expect to agree to something so controversial.

Why do they let their wives do it?                                              20

Many of them, such as Vernon Blanc, acknowledge that they initially   21
gave their approval only to placate their wives, although most clinics
won't accept women as surrogates unless they have their husbands'
written permission.

"I would automatically reject a woman if she didn't have her hus-   22
band's support and consent," said Noel Keane, an attorney who runs
the country's largest surrogate parenthood program in Dearborn,
Mich. "But—consenting in the sense that they are 100% sure of what
their wives are doing? I'm sure many of them are not."

Some men who eventually become ardent supporters of the process   23
as a way to help childless couples at first hate the idea of their wives
getting involved.

But many find that their wives have become virtually obsessed with   24
the idea. Most of these women enjoy being pregnant. At the same
time, they may be a little bored with everyday life and see it as a way
to do something unusual, something that will set them apart. Their
husbands, confronted with mounting pressure, often simply give in
to save their marriages.

"In the beginning," he basically said 'do what you want,' just to shut   25
me up," 26-year-old Peggy Pressler said of her husband, Eric. "I don't
think he felt I would really go through with it."

Mark Johnston, 33, a campground manager in northern Michigan   26
who eventually became an advocate of surrogate parenthood, recalled:
"We had some psychological testing when we got into the program,
and the psychologist kept asking me, 'why are you going to let your
wife [Marilyn] do this?' I said to the psychologist, 'I'm not letting her
do it, she's just doing it.' I thought the woman was crazy. Honest to
Pete, I thought she had lost her marbles. . . . I considered it baby-
selling at first."

Hanafin said that most surrogates' husbands she has studied fall   27
into one of two groups—those who are opposed to the idea but go
along because they have always been supportive of their wives, and
those who agree because they "owe her one."

Some husbands acknowledged that they agreed at first only as a   28
way of repaying their wives for past transgressions or to make up for
career opportunities their wives had lost earlier because of commitments to them.

Melia Josephson, for instance, wanted to be a police officer, but Mark   29

Josephson, a 31-year-old Moreno Valley, Calif., contractor, wouldn't let her. Just two weeks before she was to graduate from police training, Mark told her to quit or face divorce.

She quit, but didn't give up her dream of doing something unique ³⁰ with her life. Three years later, she decided that being a surrogate mother might fill the bill.

"She started looking into the program, and I thought to myself, ³¹ you've got to be kidding," Mark recalled. "I didn't say much, and whatever I did say was very negative. But then she started meeting couples, and it just started going farther and farther, and she really hadn't asked me, one way or another, what I wanted to do. It was more or less, 'hey, this is what I'm going to do.'"

Melia added: "I was doing this with or without him. I hoped I would ³² have his support, but I told him he had stopped me once in my life from doing something I really wanted to do—I really wanted to be a police officer—and he wasn't going to stop me again."

Melia, 30, eventually became the third woman in the world to act as ³³ a surrogate by being implanted with an embryo produced from the eggs and sperm of the couple who hired her.

Some husbands agree because they see a way to satisfy the wife's ³⁴ deep need to become pregnant again without taking on the financial burden of a second, third or fourth child. Almost all women who become surrogates report having easy, enjoyable pregnancies, and about one-third of the surrogates' husbands surveyed by Hanafin had had vasectomies to avoid having more children.

Rodney Cage, a father of two, recently had a vasectomy, but his ³⁵ wife, Kim, now wants to have a second child as a surrogate.

"I love being pregnant. I could be pregnant 12 months out of the ³⁶ year," said Kim. "I feel like a whole woman when I'm pregnant. And Rodney knows it. But we didn't want any more kids, because we feel two is enough. Kids are expensive these days."

Once their wives do get involved, many husbands seem to become ³⁷ much more committed to the idea of surrogate parenting. A large proportion of them are men who deeply love their own children and are heavily involved in raising them, and they sympathize with the plight of the childless men once they meet them.

## SYMPATHY FOR THE CHILDLESS

Dr. Betsy Aigen, a psychologist who runs the Surrogate Mother ³⁸ Program in New York City, said that other husbands of surrogates have relatives or close friends who are infertile, so they can easily identify with the childless couples.

After the husbands begin to take a more active role in the surrogate    39 process, their marriages seem to get stronger. Their wives come to rely heavily on them during their pregnancies.

"Without him, I couldn't have been a surrogate mother," Donna    40 Regan, 24, said of her husband, Rich, a 32-year-old Detroit machine operator. "You can't go off and do something this unique, that you know you are going to get a lot of backlash about, unless you have someone very strong sitting behind you saying, 'go ahead, it's OK, don't listen to what these people are saying, you made your choice and it's all right.'"

## FAMILIES MAY BE FRIENDS

The husbands who handle the situation most successfully appear to    41 be those who have always had close relationships with their wives, and who are self-confident enough not to feel jealous or inadequate as a result of their wives' pregnancies.

Men who are able to develop friendships with the infertile couples    42 who hire their wives also become very strong supporters of surrogate parenthood. Mark and Marilyn Johnston and their children, for instance, frequently visit the couple for whom Marilyn, 34, was a surrogate. Mark has even urged her to have a second child for them.

"When the baby was born, and we were all at the hospital together,    43 I was excited for the guy," said Mark Johnston. "So I opened my big mouth right there and said let's do it again."

Many husbands also insist they are not jealous of the fathers, since    44 the surrogate pregnancies are achieved artificially.

"It's not like there was any form of adultery involved. It was purely    45 technical, so the fact that she was having a baby for another man never really bothered me," said Chris Dodson, 31, a Long Beach, Calif., refinery worker whose 27-year-old wife, Janey, is about to give birth as a surrogate. "I guess I just feel good enough about our relationship that I'm not threatened by that."

Still, even the most accepting husbands sometimes have nagging    46 doubts, and all of them object to the intrusions into their personal lives. Some have had to abstain from sex with their wives for a year or longer, because so many inseminations were required before pregnancy was achieved.

"I don't like abstinence," Eric Pressler said with a sigh. "I think it    47
does intrude," added Vern Blanc. "That part of it does interrupt my
life style."

Some husbands also conceded that they would be concerned if their    48
wives wanted to break their contracts and keep the babies; they say
that would indicate their wives had strong emotional ties unrelated to
their marriages.

"I wasn't jealous, because I knew she didn't have an attachment to    49
the man, and I knew there was no sexual relationship," said Pressler.
"But I told her if she wanted to keep the child, I wouldn't support her."

Other husbands noted that their parents and in-laws are often    50
strongly opposed to surrogate parenthood, and this can lead to damaging rifts between generations.

Blanc said that his wife, Michelle, will no longer visit his parents    51
because of their hostile stand on the issue.

Meanwhile, many husbands are deeply concerned about the medi-    52
cal risks to their wives. (AIDS testing is now routine at surrogate clinics, to protect the surrogates.) "What happens if she gets sick? . . .
What if she can't have any more children as a result of this? What are
we going to do if we decide later we want more children?" Blanc asked.

Some surrogates and their husbands also privately complain that    53
they feel compelled to mislead their medical insurers about their pregnancies. Since such a birth is not covered by the infertile couple's
insurance, they usually rely on their own family coverage to pay for
their hospital stays. But, uncertain of how their insurers would react,
they usually do not inform them that they are acting as surrogates.

Other husbands also remain uncertain about the long-range impact    54
on their own children, who are aware of pregnancy even at a very early
age. Today, most are still very young and seem to be taking it in stride,
but no one really knows how they will be affected later by the knowledge that a half-sibling was turned over to another family.

That was why Mark Josephson would allow Melia to be surrogate    55
only by being implanted with the other couple's embryo—she would
then have no direct biological or genealogical connection to the child,
would not really be the "natural mother."

"If she had been a surrogate in the regular way, I think that would    56
have taken away the special mother relationship she has with her own
children," said Josephson. "I think it had the possibility of infringing
on my life, and hers, years later. How would our children feel if that
person came to the door 18 years later saying [to Melia] 'You're

my mom'? That's another side of the surrogate program that people haven't seen yet."

Right now, Vern Blanc has a more immediate dilemma—how to get through Michelle's surrogate pregnancy. 57

"I remember when she was pregnant with Brittany, I walked around and people said, 'Oh, your wife is pregnant, what are you going to name it?' I just don't know what I'm going to say yet. I haven't figured that one out. 58

"I also made a few comments to Michelle—that when she has her morning sickness, she should call the couple and complain to them. This is their program. They should have to go through it." 59

## VOCABULARY

placate (21)                    transgressions (28)

## THE FACTS

1. What does Risen find especially startling about the backgrounds of husbands of surrogate women?
2. Why do most husbands agree to let their wives become surrogate mothers?
3. What do most of the surrogate mothers have in common?
4. According to one researcher, into what two groups do most husbands of surrogate mothers generally fall?
5. What happens to the marriage once the husband of the surrogate woman agrees to take a more active role in the process?

## THE STRATEGIES

1. Based on the paragraphing and the language, for what source do you think this article was originally written? For what audience?
2. What kind of specific detail does Risen mainly use in making his points?
3. How does Risen end the article? How is the ending related to the beginning?
4. What device to aid with the division of the article does Risen use that a college essayist cannot? What do you think this device adds to the organization of the article?
5. Risen covers the topic while striking a pose of strict neutrality. How does he manage to inform without taking sides in the debate?

## THE ISSUES

1. Why do you think so many clinics have given short shrift to the husbands of surrogate mothers?

2. In what way is the plight of the husband of a surrogate mother similar to that of the father of an aborted child?
3. What do you think would be most difficult about being a surrogate mother or the husband of one?
4. A few women are implanted with the embryo from the childless couple while others contribute an egg that is artificially inseminated with the sperm of a childless man. Do you think an ethical difference exists between these two processes? Justify your answer.
5. Biologists say that the world population is fast approaching the point at which widespread famine and pestilence are possible. In light of this fact, do you think too much is made of the surrogacy issue? Justify your answer.

## SUGGESTIONS FOR WRITING

1. Write an essay in which you demonstrate that this article is really a short, informal term paper. Justify your arguments with quotations from the article itself.
2. Write an essay stating your opposition to, or your support for, the surrogate motherhood program.

## CHAPTER WRITING ASSIGNMENTS

1. Convert one of the following general subjects into a suitable thesis:
   (a) college          (d) politics
   (b) parents          (e) sports
   (c) motion pictures  (f) work
   Now develop your thesis into a well-supported, unified five-hundred-word essay.
2. Using the thesis of any one of the essays in this chapter, develop your own essay. Do not lose sight of your thesis.

# 4
# PLANNING AND ORGANIZING

## INTRODUCTION: PLANNING AND ORGANIZING

To plan and organize an essay means to work it out on paper ahead of the actual writing. It is an effort that all writers do not make equally. Some plan their work in exquisite detail and with complicated outlines; others do not plan at all but merely sit down and write. In between are those who occasionally jot down insights on scraps of paper and are content with that. Plainly, the need for planning and organizing an essay is likely to vary as much with the writer's personality as with the content of the subject. Absolutes are difficult to find and textbook advice tricky to dispense on this subject.

However, there is one well-known pitfall ahead for those who believe in advance planning of a writing project: plans have an irritating tendency to seem ironclad once they have been made. No matter what new information one finds, or what fresh breezes of inspiration blow, one feels a nagging loyalty to the plan and is loath to betray it. This is a foolish persistence and must be ignored. If you find a better way of treating your subject as you write, a way not anticipated by your plan, you must be prepared to scrap the plan and take the better way.

If you must make a plan, the next question is, What kind? In the past, planning an essay meant making a cumbersome outline of it, with branching levels more intricate than a family tree. Outlining is still recommended for complicated or difficult subjects, and especially for research papers, but it is not the only kind of plan now available to writers. You can make a jot list, which is simply a list of the order of topics you intend to cover. You can plan by writing a series of topic sentences that anticipate your paragraphs. You can plan by making a sketch of your essay's topics and showing ideas that branch off them. This sketch can be as fanciful as you like and may even resemble the flowchart of a systems analyst. The point is to get something down on paper about your subject. What format you use is less important to this generation of English teachers than it was to their ancestors.

Whether you write with or without an advance plan, the essays in this chapter will give you a glimpse into the enviable organization achieved by some writers. In the Advice section Edward T. Thompson, a *Reader's Digest* editor, tells us how that magazine achieves its renowned simplicity. In the Discussion section we chuckle through a true-to-life story by Samuel H. Scudder that makes an important point about organizing. Then we are treated to two superbly organized essays in the Examples section—the first by E. M. Forster, the second by Alan Simpson—that demonstrate how complicated subjects can be expressed in elegant literary forms (such as the short story by James Thurber and the sonnet by Shakespeare). The Issues section focuses on women's liberation, giving us three views of this hotly debated topic.

All of us know a well-organized essay when we read one. What we cannot know is how the author managed to organize it so well. For some authors, organization means an advance plan and a careful plotting of topics. Other writers like to hack their way through the forest of a subject with the path ahead not too clearly lighted nor the thicket too plainly shown. The desired object in either case is the same. How one gets there is a matter of temperamental difference.

═══════════ •● *ADVICE* ●• ═══════════

**Edward T. Thompson**

──────── • **HOW TO WRITE CLEARLY** • ────────

*Edward Thorwald Thompson (b. 1928) was born in Milwaukee and educated at MIT. Since 1976 he has been editor in-chief of* Reader's Digest.

*Whatever you may think of the* Reader's Digest—*there are those who love it and those who hate it—you cannot say that its mishmash of self-help, optimistic, and heartwarming articles is written in a disorganized way. In fact, the* Digest *is known above all else for its clear (some would say simplistic) style of writing. The editor of this venerable popular publication, in the article below, offers some specific advice on how to organize your ideas and express them on paper.*

If you are afraid to write, don't be.  1

If you think you've got to string together big fancy words and high-  2
flying phrases, forget it.

To write well, unless you aspire to be a professional poet or novelist,  3
you only need to get your ideas across simply and clearly.

It's not easy. But it *is* easier than you might imagine.  4

There are only three basic requirements:  5

First, you must *want* to write clearly. And I believe you really do, if  6
you've stayed this far with me.

Second, you must be willing to *work hard.* Thinking means work—  7
and that's what it takes to do anything well.

Third, you must know and follow some *basic guidelines.*  8

If, while you're writing for clarity, some lovely, dramatic or inspired    9
phrases or sentences come to you, fine. Put them in.

But then with cold, objective eyes and mind ask yourself: "Do they    10
detract from clarity?" If they do, grit your teeth and cut the frills.

## FOLLOW SOME BASIC GUIDELINES

I can't give you a complete list of "dos and don'ts" for every writing    11
problem you'll ever face.

But I can give you some fundamental guidelines that cover the most    12
common problems.

### 1. Outline what you want to say.

I know that sounds grade-schoolish. But you can't write clearly un-    13
til, *before you start,* you know where you will stop.

Ironically, that's even a problem in writing an outline (i.e., knowing    14
the ending before you begin).

So try this method:    15

- On 3"x5" cards, write—one point to a card—all the points you need to make.
- Divide the cards into piles—one pile for each group of points *closely related* to each other. (If you were describing an automobile, you'd put all the points about mileage in one pile, all the points about safety in another, and so on).
- Arrange your piles of points in a sequence. Which are most important and should be given first or saved for last? Which must you present before others in order to make the others understandable?
- Now, *within* each pile, do the same thing—arrange the *points* in logical, understandable order.

There you have your outline, needing only an introduction and    16
conclusion.

This is a practical way to outline. It's also flexible. You can add, delete    17
or change the location of points easily.

### 2. Start where your readers are.

How much do they know about the subject? Don't write to a level    18
higher than your readers' knowledge of it.

CAUTION: Forget that old—and wrong—advice about writing to a    19
12-year-old mentality. That's insulting. But do remember that your
prime purpose is to *explain* something, not prove that you're smarter
than your readers.

### 3. Avoid jargon.

Don't use words, expressions, phrases known only to people with    20
specific knowledge or interests.

Example: A scientist, using scientific jargon, wrote, "The biota ex-    21
hibited a one hundred percent mortality response." He could have
written: "All the fish died."

### 4. Use familiar combinations of words.

A speech writer for President Franklin D. Roosevelt wrote, "We are    22
endeavoring to construct a more inclusive society." F. D. R. changed it
to, "We're going to make a country in which no one is left out."

CAUTION: By familiar combinations of words, I *do not* mean incorrect    23
grammar. *That* can be *un*clear. Example: John's father says he can't go
out Friday. (Who can't go out? John or his father?)

### 5. Use "first-degree" words.

These words immediately bring an image to your mind. Other    24
words must be "translated" through the first-degree word before you
see the image. Those are second/third-degree words.

| First-degree words | Second/third-degree words |
|---|---|
| face ——————— | visage, countenance |
| stay ——————— | abide, remain, reside |
| book ——————— | volume, tome, publication |

First-degree words are usually the most precise words, too.    25

### 6. Stick to the point.

Your outline—which was more work in the beginning—now saves    26
you work. Because now you can ask about any sentence you write:
"Does it relate to a point in the outline? If it doesn't, should I add it to
the outline? If not, I'm getting off the track." Then, full steam ahead—
on the main line.

## 7. Be as brief as possible.

Whatever you write, shortening—*condensing*—almost always   27
makes it tighter, straighter, easier to read and understand.

Condensing, as *Reader's Digest* does it, is in large part artistry. But it   28
involves techniques that anyone can learn and use.

- *Present your points in logical* ABC *order:* Here again, your outline
  should save you work because, if you did it right, your points
  already stand in logical ABC order—A makes B understandable, B
  makes C understandable and so on. To write in a straight line is
  to say something clearly in the fewest possible words.
- *Don't waste words telling people what they already know:* Notice how
  we edited this: "Have you ever wondered how banks rate you as
  a credit risk? ~~You know, of course, that it's some combination of
  facts about your income, your job, and so on. But actually,~~ Many
  banks have a scoring system. . . ."
- *Cut out excess evidence and unnecessary anecdotes:* Usually, one fact
  or example (at most, two) will support a point. More just belabor
  it. And while writing about something may remind you of a good
  story, ask yourself: "Does it *really help* to tell the story, or does it
  slow me down?"

(Many people think *Reader's Digest* articles are filled with anecdotes.   29
Actually, we use them sparingly and usually for one of two reasons:
either the subject is so dry it needs some "humanity" to give it life; or
the subject is so hard to grasp, it needs anecdotes to help readers
understand. If the subject is both lively and easy to grasp, we move
right along.)

- *Look for the most common word wasters:* windy phrases.

| Windy phrases | Cut to . . . |
|---|---|
| at the present time | now |
| in the event of | if |
| in the majority of instances | usually |

- *Look for passive verbs you can make active:* Invariably, this produces
  a shorter sentence. "The cherry tree *was* chopped down by
  George Washington." (Passive verb and nine words.) "George

Washington *chopped* down the cherry tree." (Active verb and seven words.)

- *Look for positive/negative sections from which you can cut the negative:* See how we did it here: "The answer ~~does not rest with carelessness or incompetence. It lies largely in~~'s having enough people to do the job."
- Finally, to write more clearly by saying it in fewer words: when you've finished, stop.

---

## ·• *DISCUSSION* •·

### Samuel H. Scudder

## • TAKE THIS FISH AND LOOK AT IT •

*Samuel H. Scudder (1837–1911) was an American scientist who was educated at Williams College and Harvard University. His main scientific contributions were in the study of butterflies and Orthoptera (an order of insects that includes grasshoppers and crickets). He was one of the most learned and productive entomologists of his day.*

*Most of us tend to look at things without really seeing what is there. In everyday life this lack of observation may not be noticed, but in science it would be considered a serious failing. Scudder was a student of Louis Agassiz (1807–1873), the distinguished Harvard professor of natural history who used to subject his students to a rigorous but useful exercise in minute observation. The following is Scudder's account of one such exercise.*

It was more than fifteen years ago that I entered the laboratory of Professor Agassiz, and told him I had enrolled my name in the Scientific School as a student of natural history. He asked me a few questions about my object in coming, my antecedents generally, the mode in which I afterwards proposed to use the knowledge I might acquire, and, finally, whether I wished to study any special branch. To the latter I replied that, while I wished to be well grounded in all departments of zoology, I purposed to devote myself specially to insects.

"When do you wish to begin?" he asked.                                    2

"Now," I replied.                                                        3

This seemed to please him, and with an energetic "Very well!" he          4
reached from a shelf a huge jar of specimens in yellow alcohol. "Take
this fish," he said, "and look at it; we call it a haemulon; by and by I
will ask what you have seen."

With that he left me, but in a moment returned with explicit instruc-     5
tions as to the care of the object entrusted to me.

"No man is fit to be a naturalist," said he, "who does not know how        6
to take care of specimens."

I was to keep the fish before me in a tin tray, and occasionally          7
moisten the surface with alcohol from the jar, always taking care to
replace the stopper tightly. Those were not the days of ground-glass
stoppers and elegantly shaped exhibition jars; all the old students will
recall the huge neckless glass bottles with their leaky, wax-besmeared
corks, half eaten by insects, and begrimed with cellar dust. Entomol-
ogy was a cleaner science than ichthyology, but the example of the
Professor, who had unhesitatingly plunged to the bottom of the jar to
produce the fish, was infectious; and though this alcohol had a "very
ancient and fishlike smell," I really dared not show any aversion within
these sacred precincts, and treated the alcohol as though it were pure
water. Still I was conscious of a passing feeling of disappointment, for
gazing at a fish did not commend itself to an ardent entomologist. My
friends at home, too, were annoyed when they discovered that no
amount of eau-de-Cologne would drown the perfume which haunted
me like a shadow.

In ten minutes I had seen all that could be seen in that fish, and        8
started in search of the Professor—who had, however, left the Museum; and when I returned, after lingering over some of the odd
animals stored in the upper apartment, my specimen was dry all over.
I dashed the fluid over the fish as if to resuscitate the beast from a
fainting fit, and looked with anxiety for a return of the normal sloppy
appearance. This little excitement over, nothing was to be done but to
return to a steadfast gaze at my mute companion. Half an hour
passed—an hour—another hour; the fish began to look loathsome. I
turned it over and around; looked it in the face—ghastly; from behind,
beneath, above, sideways, at a three-quarters' view—just as ghastly. I
was in despair; at an early hour I concluded that lunch was necessary;

so, with infinite relief, the fish was carefully replaced in the jar, and for an hour I was free.

On my return, I learned that Professor Agassiz had been at the Museum, but had gone, and would not return for several hours. My fellow-students were too busy to be disturbed by continued conversation. Slowly I drew forth that hideous fish, and with a feeling of desperation again looked at it. I might not use a magnifying-glass; instruments of all kinds were interdicted. My two hands, my two eyes, and the fish: it seemed a most limited field. I pushed my finger down its throat to feel how sharp the teeth were. I began to count the scales in the different rows, until I was convinced that was nonsense. At last a happy thought struck me—I would draw the fish; and now with surprise I began to discover new features in the creature. Just then the Professor returned.   9

"That is right," said he; "a pencil is one of the best of eyes. I am glad to notice, too, that you keep your specimen wet, and your bottle corked."   10

With these encouraging words, he added:   11

"Well, what is it like?"   12

He listened attentively to my brief rehearsal of the structure of parts whose names were still unknown to me: the fringed gill-arches and movable operculum; the pores of the head, fleshy lips and lidless eyes; the lateral line, the spinous fins and forked tail; the compressed and arched body. When I finished, he waited as if expecting more, and then, with an air of disappointment:   13

"You have not looked very carefully; why," he continued more earnestly, "you haven't even seen one of the most conspicuous features of the animal, which is plainly before your eyes as the fish itself; look again, look again!" and he left me to my misery.   14

I was piqued; I was mortified. Still more of that wretched fish! But now I set myself to my task with a will, and discovered one new thing after another, until I saw how just the Professor's criticism had been. The afternoon passed quickly; and when, towards its close, the Professor inquired:   15

"Do you see it yet?"   16

"No," I replied, "I am certain I do not, but I see how little I saw before."   17

"That is next best," said he, earnestly, "but I won't hear you now;   18 put away your fish and go home; perhaps you will be ready with a better answer in the morning. I will examine you before you look at the fish."

This was disconcerting. Not only must I think of my fish all night,    19
studying, without the object before me, what this unknown but most visible feature might be; but also, without reviewing my discoveries, I must give an exact account of them the next day. I had a bad memory; so I walked home by Charles River in a distracted state, with my two perplexities.

The cordial greeting from the Professor the next morning was reas-    20
suring; here was a man who seemed to be quite as anxious as I that I should see for myself what he saw.

"Do you perhaps mean," I asked, "that the fish has symmetrical    21
sides with paired organs?"

His thoroughly pleased "Of course! Of course!" repaid the wakeful    22
hours of the previous night. After he had discoursed most happily and enthusiastically—as he always did—upon the importance of this point, I ventured to ask what I should do next.

"Oh, look at your fish!" he said, and left me again to my own    23
devices. In a little more than an hour he returned, and heard my new catalogue.

"That is good, that is good!" he repeated; "but that is not all; go    24
on"; and so for three long days he placed that fish before my eyes, forbidding me to look at anything else, or to use any artificial aid. "Look, look, look," was his repeated injunction.

This was the best entomological lesson I ever had—a lesson whose    25
influence has extended to the details of every subsequent study; a legacy the Professor had left to me, as he has left it to so many others, of inestimable value, which we could not buy, with which we cannot part.

A year afterward, some of us were amusing ourselves with chalking    26
outlandish beasts on the Museum blackboard. We drew prancing star-fishes; frogs in mortal combat; hydra-headed worms; stately craw-fishes, standing on their tails, bearing aloft umbrellas; and grotesque fishes with gaping mouths and staring eyes. The Professor came in shortly after, and was as amused as any at our experiments. He looked at the fishes.

"Haemulons, every one of them," he said; "Mr. ——— drew them."    27

True; and to this day, if I attempt a fish, I can draw nothing but 28
haemulons.

The fourth day, a second fish of the same group was placed beside 29
the first, and I was bidden to point out the resemblances and differences between the two; another and another followed, until the entire
family lay before me, and a whole legion of jars covered the table and
surrounding shelves; the odor had become a pleasant perfume; and
even now, the sight of an old, six-inch, worm-eaten cork brings fra-
grant memories.

The whole group of haemulons was thus brought in review; and, 30
whether engaged upon the dissection of the internal organs, the preparation and examination of the bony framework, or the description of
the various parts, Agassiz's training in the method of observing facts
and their orderly arrangement was ever accompanied by the urgent
exhortation not to be content with them.

"Facts are stupid things," he would say, "until brought into connec- 31
tion with some general law."

At the end of eight months, it was almost with reluctance that I left 32
these friends and turned to insects; but what I had gained by this
outside experience has been of greater value than years of later investigation in my favorite groups.

## *VOCABULARY*

| | | |
|---|---|---|
| antecedents (1) | resuscitate (8) | catalogue (23) |
| explicit (5) | interdicted (9) | injunction (24) |
| entomology (7) | operculum (13) | inestimable (25) |
| ichthyology (7) | spinous (13) | hydra-headed (26) |
| aversion (7) | piqued (15) | exhortation (30) |

## *THE FACTS*

1. What kind of fish was Scudder asked to examine?
2. What did Agassiz call "one of the best of eyes"?
3. What important feature did Scudder discover about his fish after a night's
   rest and a second look?
4. What was the best entomological lesson that Scudder ever learned from
   Agassiz?
5. When, according to Agassiz, did facts cease to be stupid things?

## THE STRATEGIES

1. What is the level of diction used in this essay? What kind of audience is it aimed at?
2. This is not the kind of essay that lends itself to outlining, but it does follow a pattern. What is the pattern that gives organization to the essay?
3. Despite the academic and scientific setting of this experience, humor abounds. How is this humor achieved? Point out specific examples.
4. Which passage do you consider the most descriptive in terms of details supplied? Explain your selection.

## THE ISSUES

1. What relevance does Scudder's experience have to organizing an essay?
2. What characteristic do good writers and good scientists share?
3. Why would drawing the fish have helped Scudder to see it better?
4. What is a fact? What is a general law? How do they differ?
5. If drawing an object helps a science student see it more clearly, what might a student of English composition do to help him or her more clearly understand or see a certain subject?

## SUGGESTIONS FOR WRITING

1. Following Scudder's example, write about an experience in which one of your teachers taught you an important lesson. Relate the experience according to an organized sequence.
2. Write an essay in which you start with the thesis, "Facts are stupid things until brought into connection with some general law." Illustrate this thesis with examples from your own experience.

# ══════ •• EXAMPLES •• ══════

### E. M. Forster

# ───── • MY WOOD • ─────

*E. M. Forster (1879–1969) was a British novelist, essayist, and short-story writer whose work first won wide recognition in 1924, with the publication of his* Passage to India. *In 1946 Forster was made an honorary fellow of King's*

*College, Cambridge, where he lived until his death. Among his many other works
are* Howard's End *(1910) and* Two Cheers for Democracy *(1951), a collection
of his essays.*

*"My Wood," a superbly organized short essay, investigates the effect of property
ownership on the individual and society.*

A few years ago I wrote a book which dealt in part with the difficul-    1
ties of the English in India. Feeling that they would have had no difficulties in India themselves, the Americans read the book freely. The
more they read it the better it made them feel, and a cheque to the
author was the result. I bought a wood with the cheque. It is not a
large wood—it contains scarcely any trees, and it is intersected, blast
it, by a public footpath. Still, it is the first property that I have owned,
so it is right that other people should participate in my shame, and
should ask themselves, in accents that will vary in horror, this very
important question: What is the effect of property upon the character?
Don't let's touch economics; the effect of private ownership upon the
community as a whole is another question—a more important question, perhaps, but another one. Let's keep to psychology. If you own
things, what's their effect on you? What's the effect on me of my wood?

In the first place, it makes me feel heavy. Property does have this    2
effect. Property produces men of weight, and it was a man of weight
who failed to get into the Kingdom of Heaven. He was not wicked,
that unfortunate millionaire in the parable, he was only stout; he stuck
out in front, not to mention behind, and as he wedged himself this
way and that in the crystalline entrance and bruised his well-fed
flanks, he saw beneath him a comparatively slim camel passing
through the eye of a needle and being woven into the robe of God. The
Gospels all through couple stoutness and slowness. They point out
what is perfectly obvious, yet seldom realized: that if you have a lot of
things you cannot move about a lot, that furniture requires dusting,
dusters require servants, servants require insurance stamps,* and the
whole tangle of them makes you think twice before you accept an
invitation to dinner or go for a bathe in the Jordan. Sometimes the
Gospels proceed further and say with Tolstoy that property is sinful;

*In England.—Ed.

they approach the difficult ground of asceticism here, where I cannot follow them. But as to the immediate effects of property on people, they just show straightforward logic. It produces men of weight. Men of weight cannot, by definition, move like the lightning from the East unto the West, and the ascent of a fourteen-stone bishop into a pulpit is thus the exact antithesis of the coming of the Son of Man. My wood makes me feel heavy.

In the second place, it makes me feel it ought to be larger.     3

The other day I heard a twig snap in it. I was annoyed at first, for I     4 thought that someone was blackberrying, and depreciating the value of the undergrowth. On coming nearer, I saw it was not a man who had trodden on the twig and snapped it, but a bird, and I felt pleased. My bird. The bird was not equally pleased. Ignoring the relation between us, it took fright as soon as it saw the shape of my face, and flew straight over the boundary hedge into a field, the property of Mrs. Henessy, where it sat down with a loud squawk. It had become Mrs. Henessy's bird. Something seemed grossly amiss here, something that would not have occurred had the wood been larger. I could not afford to buy Mrs. Henessy out, I dared not murder her, and limitations of this sort beset me on every side. Ahab did not want that vineyard—he only needed it to round off his property, preparatory to plotting a new curve—and all the land around my wood has become necessary to me in order to round off the wood. A boundary protects. But—poor little thing—the boundary ought in its turn to be protected. Noises on the edge of it. Children throw stones. A little more, and then a little more, until we reach the sea. Happy Canute! Happier Alexander! And after all, why should even the world be the limit of possession? A rocket containing a Union Jack, will, it is hoped, be shortly fired at the moon. Mars. Sirius. Beyond which . . . But these immensities ended by saddening me. I could not suppose that my wood was the destined nucleus of universal dominion—it is so very small and contains no mineral wealth beyond the blackberries. Nor was I comforted when Mrs. Henessy's bird took alarm for the second time and flew clean away from us all, under the belief that it belonged to itself.

In the third place, property makes its owner feel that he ought to do     5 something to it. Yet he isn't sure what. A restlessness comes over him, a vague sense that he has a personality to express—the same sense which, without any vagueness, leads the artist to an act of creation.

Sometimes I think I will cut down such trees as remain in the wood, at other times I want to fill up the gaps between them with new trees. Both impulses are pretentious and empty. They are not honest movements towards money-making or beauty. They spring from a foolish desire to express myself and from an inability to enjoy what I have got. Creation, property, enjoyment form a sinister trinity in the human mind. Creation and enjoyment are both very good, yet they are often unattainable without a material basis, and at such moments property pushes itself in as a substitute, saying, "Accept me instead—I'm good enough for all three." It is not enough. It is, as Shakespeare said of lust, "The expense of spirit in a waste of shame": it is "Before, a joy proposed; behind, a dream." Yet we don't know how to shun it. It is forced on us by our economic system as the alternative to starvation. It is also forced on us by an internal defect in the soul, by the feeling that in property may lie the germs of self-development and of exquisite or heroic deeds. Our life on earth is, and ought to be, material and carnal. But we have not yet learned to manage our materialism and carnality properly; they are still entangled with the desire for ownership, where (in the words of Dante) "Possession is one with loss."

And this brings us to our fourth and final point: the blackberries.    6

Blackberries are not plentiful in this meagre grove, but they are    7 easily seen from the public footpath which traverses it, and all too easily gathered. Foxgloves, too—people will pull up the foxgloves, and ladies of an educational tendency even grub for toad stools to show them on the Monday in class. Other ladies, less educated, roll down the bracken in the arms of their gentlemen friends. There is a paper, there are tins. Pray, does my wood belong to me or doesn't it? And, if it does, should I not own it best by allowing no one else to walk there? There is a wood near Lyme Regis, also cursed by a public footpath, where the owner has not hesitated on this point. He has built high stone walls on each side of the path, and has spanned it by bridges, so that the public circulate like termites while he gorges on the blackberries unseen. He really does own his wood, this able chap. Dives in Hell did pretty well, but the gulf dividing him from Lazarus could be traversed by vision, and nothing traverses it here. And perhaps I shall come to this in time. I shall wall in and fence out until I really taste the sweets of property. Enormously stout, endlessly avaricious, pseudo-creative, intensely selfish, I shall weave upon my forehead the quadruple crown of possession until those nasty Bolshies come and take it off again and thrust me aside into the outer darkness.

### THE FACTS

1. What intersects Forster's wood and is a source of annoyance to him?
2. What is the first effect Forster's wood had on him?
3. What or whom did Forster discover on his property when he heard a twig snap?
4. According to Forster, what does property make an owner feel he ought to do with it?
5. What does Forster think he will eventually do with his wood?

### THE STRATEGIES

1. What are the obvious divisions in the topics and subtopics of this essay? Make an outline showing the thesis, main points, and subtopics of the essay.
2. Read the last sentence of paragraph 2. What is the purpose of this sentence?
3. What is the purpose of paragraph 3?
4. What tone does Forster use throughout this essay? Do you regard his tone as mocking, serious, ironic? Justify your answer.
5. In paragraph 4 Forster writes: ''Happy Canute! Happier Alexander!'' What is this figure of speech called? Why is Alexander happier than Canute?

### THE ISSUES

1. What point does Forster make obliquely in his discussion about the bird?
2. What effect does ownership have on you? Is Forster exaggerating here or have you experienced these same effects that he describes?
3. What useful benefits, if any, do you think society gains from ownership of private property?
4. What do you think Dante meant by, ''Possession is one with loss''? Interpret this statement.
5. ''Our life on earth is, and ought to be, material and carnal.'' What is your opinion of this statement? How do you think our life on earth ought to be?

### SUGGESTIONS FOR WRITING

1. Write an analysis of the tone of this essay, carefully supporting your points with quotations from the work itself.
2. Write an essay on the benefits of property ownership.

Alan Simpson

## ——————— • *from* THE MARKS OF AN • ———————
## EDUCATED MAN

*Alan Simpson (b. 1912), former president of Vassar College, was born in England but became a naturalized citizen of the United States in 1954. He was educated at Oxford University and Harvard University and was a professor of history at the University of Chicago from 1946 to 1964. His books include* Puritanism in Old and New England *(1961) and* Readings in the Formulation of American Policy *(1949), of which he was coeditor.*

*Simpson's description of an educated man goes back to the Renaissance ideal that placed equal stress on the mental, moral, and physical excellence of human beings.*

Any education that matters is *liberal*. All the saving truths and healing graces that distinguish a good education from a bad one or a full education from a half-empty one are contained in that word. Whatever ups and downs the term "liberal" suffers in the political vocabulary, it soars above all controversy in the educational world. In the blackest pits of pedagogy the squirming victim has only to ask, "What's liberal about this?" to shame his persecutors. In times past a liberal education set off a free man from a slave or a gentleman from laborers and artisans. It now distinguishes whatever nourishes the mind and spirit from the training which is merely practical or professional or from the trivialities which are no training at all. Such an education involves a combination of knowledge, skills, and standards.

So far as knowledge is concerned, the record is ambiguous. It is sufficiently confused for the fact-filled freak who excels in quiz shows to have passed himself off in some company as an educated man. More respectable is the notion that there are some things which every educated man ought to know; but many highly educated men would cheerfully admit to a vast ignorance, and the framers of curriculums have differed greatly in the knowledge they prescribe. If there have been times when all the students at school or college studied the same things, as if it were obvious that without exposure to a common body of knowledge they would not be educated at all, there have been other times when specialization ran so wild that it might almost seem as if educated men had abandoned the thought of ever talking to each other once their education was completed.

If knowledge is one of our marks, we can hardly be dogmatic about the kind or the amount. A single fertile field tilled with care and imagination can probably develop all the instincts of an educated man. However, if the framer of a curriculum wants to minimize his risks, he can invoke an ancient doctrine which holds that an educated man ought to know a little about everything and a lot about something.     3

The "little about everything" is best interpreted these days by those who have given most thought to the sort of general education an informed individual ought to have. More is required than a sampling of the introductory courses which specialists offer in their own disciplines. Courses are needed in each of the major divisions of knowledge—the humanities, the natural sciences, and social sciences—which are organized with the breadth of view and the imaginative power of competent staffs who understand the needs of interested amateurs. But, over and above this exciting smattering of knowledge, students should bite deeply into at least one subject and taste its full flavor. It is not enough to be dilettantes in everything without striving also to be craftsmen in something.     4

If there is some ambiguity about the knowledge an educated man should have, there is none at all about the skills. The first is simply the training of the mind in the capacity to think clearly. This has always been the business of education, but the way it is done varies enormously. Marshalling the notes of a lecture is one experience; the opportunity to argue with a teacher is another. Thinking within an accepted tradition is one thing; to challenge the tradition itself is another. The best results are achieved when the idea of the examined life is held firmly before the mind and when the examination is conducted with the zest, rigor, and freedom which really stretches everyone's capacities.     5

The vital aid to clear thought is the habit of approaching everything we hear and everything we are taught to believe with a certain skepticism. The method of using doubt as an examiner is a familiar one among scholars and scientists, but it is also the best protection which a citizen has against the cant and humbug that surround us.     6

To be able to listen to a phony argument and to see its dishonesty is surely one of the marks of an educated man. We may not need to be     7 educated to possess some of this quality. A shrewd peasant was always well enough protected against imposters in the market place, and we have all sorts of businessmen who have made themselves excellent judges of phoniness without the benefit of a high-school diploma; but this kind of shrewdness goes along with a great deal of credulity. Outside the limited field within which experience has taught the peasant or the illiterate businessman his lessons, he is often hopelessly gullible. The educated man, by contrast, has tried to develop a critical faculty for general use, and he likes to think that he is fortified against imposture in all its forms.

It does not matter for our purposes whether the imposter is a deliberate liar or not. Some are, but the commonest enemies of mankind are the unconscious frauds. Most salesmen under the intoxication of their own exuberance seem to believe in what they say. Most experts whose *expertise* is only a pretentious sham behave as if they had been solemnly inducted into some kind of priesthood. Very few demagogues are so cynical as to remain undeceived by their own rhetoric, and some of the worst tyrants in history have been fatally sincere. We can leave the disentanglement of motives to the students of fraud and error, but we cannot afford to be taken in by the shams. 8

We are, of course, surrounded by shams. Until recently the schools were full of them—the notion that education can be had without tears, that puffed rice is a better intellectual diet than oatmeal, that adjustment to the group is more important than knowing where the group is going, and that democracy has made it a sin to separate the sheep from the goats. Mercifully, these are much less evident now than they were before Sputnik startled us into our wits. 9

In front of the professor are the shams of the learned fraternity. There is the sham science of the social scientist who first invented a speech for fuddling thought and then proceeded to tell us in his lock-jawed way what we already knew. There is the sham humanism of the humanist who wonders why civilization that once feasted at his table is repelled by the shredded and desiccated dishes that often lie on it today. There is the sham message of the physical scientist who feels that his mastery of nature has made him an expert in politics and morals, and there are all the other brands of hokum which have furnished material for satire since the first quacks established themselves in the first cloisters. 10

If this is true of universities with their solemn vows and limited    11
temptations, how much truer is it of the naughty world outside, where
the prizes are far more dazzling and the only protection against humbug is the skepticism of the ordinary voter, customer, reader, listener,
and viewer? Of course, the follies of human nature are not going to be
exorcised by anything that the educator can do, and I am not sure that
he would want to exorcise them if he could. There is something irresistibly funny about the old Adam, and life would be duller without
his antics. But they ought to be kept within bounds. We are none the
better for not recognizing a clown when we see one.

The other basic skill is simply the art of self-expression in speech    12
and on paper. A man is uneducated who has not mastered the elements of clean forcible prose and picked up some relish for style.

It is a curious fact that we style everything in this country—our cars,    13
our homes, our clothes—except our minds. They still chug along like
a Model T—rugged, persevering, but far from graceful.

No doubt this appeal for style, like the appeal for clear thinking, can    14
be carried too far. There was once an American who said that the only
important thing in life was "to set a chime of words ringing in a few
fastidious minds." As far as can be learned, he left this country in a
huff to tinkle his little bell in a foreign land. Most of us would think
that he lacked a sense of proportion. After all, the political history of
this country is full of good judgment expressed in bad prose, and the
business history has smashed through to some of its grandest
triumphs across acres of broken syntax. But we can discard some of
these frontier manners without becoming absurdly precious.

The road ahead bristles with obstacles. There is the reluctance of    15
many people to use one word where they can get away with a half-
dozen or a word of one syllable if they can find a longer one. No one
has ever told them about the first rule in English composition: every
slaughtered syllable is a good deed. The most persuasive teachers of
this maxim are undoubtedly the commercial firms that offer a thousand dollars for the completion of a slogan in twenty-five words. They
are the only people who are putting a handsome premium on economy
of statement.

There is the decay of the habit of memorizing good prose and good    16
poetry in the years when tastes are being formed. It is very difficult to
write a bad sentence if the Bible has been a steady companion and

very easy to imagine a well-turned phrase if the ear has been tuned on enough poetry.

There is the monstrous proliferation of gobbledy-gook in govern-    17
ment, business, and the professions. Take this horrible example of verbal smog.

> It is inherent to motivational phenomena that there is a drive for more gratification than is realistically possible, on any level or in any type of personality organization. Likewise it is inherent to the world of objects that not all potentially desirable opportunities can be realized within a human life span. Therefore, any personality must involve an organi-zation that allocates opportunities for gratification, that systematizes precedence relative to the limited possibilities. The possibilities of grat-ification, simultaneously or sequentially, of all need-dispositions are se-verely limited by the structure of the object system and by the intra-systemic incompatibility of the consequences of gratifying them all.

What this smothered soul is trying to say is simply, "We must pick and choose, because we cannot have everything we want."

Finally, there is the universal employment of the objective test as    18
part of the price which has to be paid for mass education. Nothing but the difficulty of finding enough readers to mark essays can condone a system which reduces a literate student to the ignoble necessity of "blackening the answer space" when he might be giving his mind and pen free play. Though we have managed to get some benefits from these examinations, the simple fact remains that the shapely prose of the Declaration of Independence or the "Gettysburg Address" was never learned under an educational system which employed objective tests. It was mastered by people who took writing seriously, who had good models in front of them, good critics to judge them, and an endless capacity for taking pains. Without that sort of discipline, the arts of self-expression will remain as mutilated as they are now.

The standards which mark an educated man can be expressed in    19
terms of three tests.

The first is a matter of sophistication. Emerson put it nicely when he    20
talked about getting rid of "the nonsense of our wigwams." The wig-wam may be an uncultivated home, a suburban conformity, a crass patriotism, or a cramped dogma. Some of this nonsense withers in the classroom. More of it rubs off by simply mixing with people, provided they are drawn from a wide range of backgrounds and exposed within

a good college to a civilized tradition. An educated man can be judged by the quality of his prejudices. There is a refined nonsense which survives the raw nonsense which Emerson was talking about.

The second test is a matter of moral values. Though we all know [21] individuals who have contrived to be both highly educated and highly immoral, and though we have all heard of periods in history when the subtlest resources of wit and sophistication were employed to make a mockery of simple values, we do not really believe that a college is doing its job when it is simply multiplying the number of educated scoundrels, hucksters, and triflers.

The health of society depends on simple virtues like honesty, de- [22] cency, courage, and public spirit. There are forces in human nature which constantly tend to corrupt them, and every age has its own vices. The worst feature of ours is probably the obsession with violence. Up to some such time as 1914, it was possible to believe in a kind of moral progress. The quality which distinguished the Victorian from the Elizabethan was a sensitivity to suffering and a revulsion from cruelty which greatly enlarged the idea of human dignity. Since 1914 we have steadily brutalized ourselves. The horrors of modern war, the bestialities of modern political creeds, the uncontrollable vices of modern cities, the favorite themes of modern novelists—all have conspired to degrade us. Some of the corruption is blatant. The authors of the best sellers, after exhausting all the possibilities of sex in its normal and abnormal forms and all the variations of alcoholism and drug addiction, are about to invade the recesses of the hospitals. A clinical study of a hero undergoing the irrigation of his colon is about all there is left to gratify a morbid appetite.

Some of the corruption is insidious. A national columnist recently [23] wrote an article in praise of cockfighting. He had visited a cockfight in the company of Ernest Hemingway. After pointing out that Hemingway had made bullfighting respectable, he proceeded to describe the terrible beauty of fierce indomitable birds trained to kill each other for the excitement of the spectators. Needless to say, there used to be a terrible beauty about Christians defending themselves against lions or about heretics being burned at the stake, and there are still parts of the world where a public execution is regarded as a richly satisfying feast. But for three or four centuries the West taught itself to resist these excitements in the interest of a moral idea.

Educators are needlessly squeamish about their duty to uphold    24
moral values and needlessly perplexed about how to implant them.
The corruptions of our times are a sufficient warning that we cannot
afford to abandon the duty to the homes and the churches, and the
capacity which many institutions have shown to do their duty in a
liberal spirit is a sufficient guaranty against bigotry.

Finally, there is the test imposed by the unique challenge of our own    25
times. We are not unique in suffering from moral confusion—these
crises are a familiar story—but we are unique in the tremendous ac-
celeration of the rate of social change and in the tremendous risk of a
catastrophic end to all our hopes. We cannot afford educated men who
have every grace except the gift for survival. An indispensable mark of
the modern educated man is the kind of versatile, flexible mind that
can deal with new and explosive conditions.

With this reserve, there is little in this profile which has not been    26
familiar for centuries. Unfortunately, the description which once sufficed to suggest its personality has been debased in journalistic currency. The "well-rounded man" has become the organization man, or
the man who is so well rounded that he rolls wherever he is pushed.
The humanists who invented the idea and preached it for centuries
would recoil in contempt from any such notion. They understood the
possibilities of the whole man and wanted an educational system
which would give the many sides of his nature some chance to develop
in harmony. They thought it a good idea to mix the wisdom of the
world with the learning of the cloister, to develop the body as well
as the mind, to pay a great deal of attention to character, and to neglect no art which could add to the enjoyment of living. It was a spacious idea which offered every hospitality to creative energy. Anyone
who is seriously interested in liberal education must begin by redis-
covering it.

## VOCABULARY

| | | |
|---|---|---|
| pedagogy (1) | dilettantes (4) | demagogues (8) |
| artisans (1) | humbug (6) | humanism (10) |
| ambiguous (2) | cant (6) | desiccated (10) |
| dogmatic (3) | gullible (7) | hokum (10) |
| amateurs (4) | credulity (7) | cloisters (10) |

exorcise (11)            proliferation (17)        squeamish (24)
fastidious (14)          gobbledy-gook (17)        unique (25)
precious (14)            sophistication (20)       versatile (25)
maxim (15)               blatant (22)

## THE FACTS

1. How does Simpson define liberal education at the start of his essay?
2. In which paragraph is the first skill of the educated person discussed? What is this skill and what does it enable one to do?
3. At what point does Simpson introduce the second skill of the educated man? What is it?
4. What tests of an educated man does the author propose? Make an outline of his discussion of these tests.
5. List the obstacles to proper written and spoken communications that Simpson cites. In which paragraph are they described?
7. In his final paragraph, whom does Simpson hold up as an example of truly educated men? What virtues did they exhibit?

## THE STRATEGIES

1. What contrast is developed in paragraph 1? Find other contrasts in other paragraphs.
2. How are the beautiful balance and coherence of paragraphs 9 and 10 achieved?
3. In what way do the opening sentences of paragraphs 4, 9, and 10 provide transitions from the preceding paragraphs?
4. Simpson makes free use of metaphors in his essay. How effective are the following? Comment on each.
   a. sheep and goats (paragraph 9)
   b. feast and dishes (paragraph 10)
   c. to smash across acres of broken syntax (paragraph 14)
   d. a road bristling with obstacles (paragraph 15)
   e. journalistic currency (paragraph 26)
5. Into what major topics does Simpson divide his discussion of a liberal education? How is this division sustained throughout this essay?

## THE ISSUES

1. What courses offered by your college could be regarded as part of a liberal education? What courses could be regarded as mere training? Name at least three courses that fit each description.

2. Simpson claims that a liberal education exposes students to standards. When applied to literature, do you agree that standards can and must be absolute, or are they relative to time, place, and circumstance?
3. Based on Simpson's definition of a liberal education, must a liberal education inevitably be elitist, or can it be egalitarian? Justify your answer.
4. In paragraph 25 Simpson argues that the modern educated person must have a versatile and flexible mind that can "deal with new and explosive conditions." What are three potentially explosive conditions in modern society?
5. In an aside in paragraph 18, the author concedes that we have managed to get good benefits from objective tests. What kind of good benefits do you think he has in mind? What are the advantages of objective tests over written ones?

### SUGGESTIONS FOR WRITING

1. Write an essay describing a person whom you consider truly educated. Be specific about his or her characteristics.
2. What pitfalls attend the lack of a liberal education? Write an essay enumerating these pitfalls. Organize your essay around two or three major points that are in turn subdivided.
3. Write a sentence outline delineating your personal college curriculum and what educational values you expect to get out of it.

### TERM PAPER SUGGESTION

Write a research paper based on the unique contribution to education made by one of the following Renaissance humanists: Desiderius Erasmus, Thomas More, John Colet, John Milton.

**James Thurber**

# • THE CATBIRD SEAT •

*James Thurber (1894–1963) was an American humorist, cartoonist, and social commentator. His contributions to* The New Yorker *made him immensely popular. Among his best-known works are* My Life and Hard Times *(1933),* Fables for Our Time *(1940), and* The Thurber Carnival *(1945), from which this selection was taken.*

*A conventional, well-behaved office clerk suddenly finds his job threatened by an aggressive, loud-mouthed "special adviser to the president." To protect his job, this unobtrusive little man resorts to a most unusual crime.*

Mr. Martin bought the pack of Camels on Monday night in the most crowded cigar store on Broadway. It was theatre time and seven or eight men were buying cigarettes. The clerk didn't even glance at Mr. Martin, who put the pack in his overcoat pocket and went out. If any of the staff at F & S had seen him buy the cigarettes, they would have been astonished, for it was generally known that Mr. Martin did not smoke, and never had. No one saw him. [1]

It was just a week to the day since Mr. Martin had decided to rub out Mrs. Ulgine Barrows. The term "rub out" pleased him because it suggested nothing more than the correction of an error—in this case an error of Mr. Fitweiler. Mr. Martin had spent each night of the past week working out his plan and examining it. As he walked home now he went over it again. For the hundredth time he resented the element of imprecision, the margin of guesswork that entered into the business. The project as he had worked it out was casual and bold, the risks were considerable. Something might go wrong anywhere along the line. And therein lay the cunning of his scheme. No one would ever see in it the cautious, painstaking hand of Erwin Martin, head of the filing department at F & S, of whom Mr. Fitweiler had once said, "Man is fallible but Martin isn't." No one would see his hand, that is, unless it were caught in the act. [2]

Sitting in his apartment, drinking a glass of milk, Mr. Martin reviewed his case against Mrs. Ulgine Barrows, as he had every night for seven nights. He began at the beginning. Her quacking voice and braying laugh had first profaned the halls of F & S on March 7, 1941 (Mr. Martin had a head for dates). Old Roberts, the personnel chief, had introduced her as the newly appointed special adviser to the president of the firm, Mr. Fitweiler. The woman had appalled Mr. Martin instantly, but he hadn't shown it. He had given her his dry hand, a look of studious concentration, and a faint smile. "Well," she had said, looking at the papers on his desk, "are you lifting the oxcart out of the ditch?" As Mr. Martin recalled that moment, over his milk, he squirmed slightly. He must keep his mind on her crimes as a special adviser, not on her peccadillos as a personality. This he found difficult [3] to do, in spite of entering an objection and sustaining it. The faults of the woman as a woman kept chattering on in his mind like an unruly witness. She had, for almost two years now, baited him. In the halls, in the elevator, even in his own office, into which she romped now and then like a circus horse, she was constantly shouting these silly questions at him. "Are you lifting the oxcart out of the ditch? Are you tearing up the pea patch? Are you hollering down the rain barrel? Are you scraping around the bottom of the pickle barrel? Are you sitting in the catbird seat?"

It was Joey Hart, one of Mr. Martin's two assistants, who had ex-  4 plained what the gibberish meant. "She must be a Dodger fan," he had said. "Red Barber announces the Dodger games over the radio and he uses those expressions—picked 'em up down South." Joey had gone on to explain one or two. "Tearing up the pea patch" meant going on a rampage; "sitting in the catbird seat" meant sitting pretty, like a batter with three balls and no strikes on him. Mr. Martin dismissed all this with an effort. It had been annoying, it had driven him near to distraction, but he was too solid a man to be moved to murder by anything so childish. It was fortunate, he reflected as he passed on to the important charges against Mrs. Barrows, that he had stood up under it so well. He had maintained always an outward appearance of polite tolerance. "Why, I even believe you like the woman," Miss Paird, his other assistant, had once said to him. He had simply smiled.

A gavel rapped in Mr. Martin's mind and the case proper was re-  5 sumed. Mrs. Ulgine Barrows stood charged with willful, blatant, and persistent attempts to destroy the efficiency and system of F & S. It was competent, material, and relevant to review her advent and rise to power. Mr. Martin had got the story from Miss Paird, who seemed always able to find things out. According to her, Mrs. Barrows had met Mr. Fitweiler at a party, where she had rescued him from the embraces of a powerfully built drunken man who had mistaken the president of F & S for a famous retired Middle Western football coach. She had led him to a sofa and somehow worked upon him a monstrous magic. The aging gentleman had jumped to the conclusion there and then that this was a woman of singular attainments, equipped to bring out the best in him and in the firm. A week later he had introduced her into F & S as his special adviser. On that day confusion got its foot in the door. After Miss Tyson, Mr. Brundage, and Mr. Bartlett had been fired and Mr. Munson had taken his hat and stalked out, mailing in his resignation later, old Roberts had been emboldened to speak to Mr. Fitweiler. He mentioned that Mr. Munson's department had been "a little disrupted" and hadn't they perhaps better resume the old system there? Mr. Fitweiler had said certainly not. He had the greatest faith in Mrs. Barrows' ideas. "They require a little seasoning, a little seasoning, is all," he had added. Mr. Roberts had given it up. Mr. Martin reviewed in detail all the changes wrought by Mrs. Barrows. She had begun chipping at the cornices of the firm's edifice and now she was swinging at the foundation stones with a pickaxe.

Mr. Martin came now, in his summing up, to the afternoon of Monday, November 2, 1942—just one week ago. On that day, at 3 P.M., Mrs. Barrows had bounced into his office. "Boo!" she had yelled. "Are you scraping around the bottom of the pickle barrel?" Mr. Martin had looked at her from under his green eyeshade, saying nothing. She had begun to wander about the office, taking it in with her great, popping eyes. "Do you really need *all* these filing cabinets?" she had demanded suddenly. Mr. Martin's heart had jumped. "Each of these files," he had said, keeping his voice even, "plays an indispensable part in the system of F & S." She had brayed at him, "Well, don't tear up the pea patch!" and gone to the door. From there she had bawled, "But you sure have got a lot of fine scrap in here!" Mr. Martin could no longer doubt that the finger was on his beloved department. Her pickaxe was on the upswing, poised for the first blow. It had not come yet; he had received no blue memo from the enchanted Mr. Fitweiler bearing nonsensical instructions deriving from the obscene woman. But there was no doubt in Mr. Martin's mind that one would be forthcoming. He must act quickly. Already a precious week had gone by. Mr. Martin stood up in his living room, still holding his milk glass. "Gentlemen of the jury" he said to himself, "I demand the death penalty for this horrible person."

The next day Mr. Martin followed his routine, as usual. He polished his glasses more often and once sharpened an already sharp pencil, but not even Miss Paird noticed. Only once did he catch sight of his victim; she swept past him in the hall with a patronizing "Hi!" At five-thirty he walked home, as usual, and had a glass of milk, as usual. He had never drunk anything stronger in his life—unless you could count ginger ale. The late Sam Schlosser, the S of F & S, had praised Mr. Martin at a staff meeting several years before for his temperate habits. "Our most efficient worker neither drinks nor smokes," he had said. "The results speak for themselves." Mr. Fitweiler had sat by, nodding approval.

Mr. Martin was still thinking about that red-letter day as he walked over to the Schrafft's on Fifth Avenue near Forty-sixth Street. He got there, as he always did, at eight o'clock. He finished his dinner and the financial page of the *Sun* at a quarter to nine, as he always did. It was his custom after dinner to take a walk. This time he walked down Fifth Avenue at a casual pace. His gloved hands felt moist and warm, his forehead cold. He transferred the Camels from his overcoat to a jacket pocket. He wondered, as he did so, if they did not represent an unnecessary note of strain. Mrs. Barrows smoked only Luckies. It was his idea to puff a few puffs on a Camel (after the rubbing-out), stub it out in the ashtray holding her lipstick-stained Luckies, and thus drag a small red herring across the trail. Perhaps it was not a good idea. It would take time. He might even choke, too loudly.

Mr. Martin had never seen the house on West Twelfth Street where Mrs. Barrows lived, but he had a clear enough picture of it. Fortunately, she had bragged to everybody about her ducky first-floor apartment in the perfectly darling three-story red-brick. There would be no doorman or other attendants; just the tenants of the second and third floors. As he walked along, Mr. Martin realized that he would get there before nine-thirty. He had considered walking north on Fifth Avenue from Schrafft's to a point from which it would take him until ten o'clock to reach the house. At that hour people were less likely to be coming in or going out. But the procedure would have made an awkward loop in the straight thread of his casualness, and he had abandoned it. It was impossible to figure when people would be entering or leaving the house, anyway. There was a great risk at any hour. If he ran into anybody, he would simply have to place the rubbing-out of Ulgine Barrows in the inactive file forever. The same thing would hold true if there were someone in her apartment. In that case he would just say that he had been passing by, recognized her charming house, and thought to drop in.

It was eighteen minutes after nine when Mr. Martin turned into Twelfth Street. A man passed him, and a man and a woman, talking. There was no one within fifty paces when he came to the house, halfway down the block. He was up the steps and in the small vestibule in no time, pressing the bell under the card that said "Mrs. Ulgine

Barrows." When the clicking in the lock started, he jumped forward against the door. He got inside fast, closing the door behind him. A bulb in a lantern hung from the hall ceiling on a chain seemed to give a monstrously bright light. There was nobody on the stair, which went up ahead of him along the left wall. A door opened down the hall in the wall on the right. He went toward it swiftly, on tiptoe.

"Well, for God's sake, look who's here!" bawled Mrs. Barrows, and her braying laugh rang out like the report of a shotgun. He rushed past her like a football tackle, bumping her. "Hey, quit shoving!" she said, closing the door behind them. They were in her living room, which seemed to Mr. Martin to be lighted by a hundred lamps. "What's after you?" she said. "You're as jumpy as a goat." He found he was unable to speak. His heart was wheezing in his throat. "I— yes," he finally brought out. She was jabbering and laughing as she started to help him off with his coat. "No, no," he said. "I'll put it here." He took it off and put in on a chair near the door. "Your hat and gloves, too," she said. "You're in a lady's house." He put his hat on top of the coat. Mrs. Barrows seemed larger than he had thought. He kept his gloves on. "I was passing by," he said. "I recognized—is there anyone here?" She laughed louder than ever. "No," she said, "we're all alone. You're as white as a sheet, you funny man. Whatever *has* come over you? I'll mix you a toddy." She started toward a door across the room. "Scotch-and-soda be all right? But say, you don't drink, do you?" She turned and gave him her amused look. Mr. Martin pulled himself together. "Scotch-and-soda will be all right," he heard himself say. He could hear her laughing in the kitchen.

Mr. Martin looked quickly around the living room for the weapon. He had counted on finding one there. There were andirons and a poker and something in a corner that looked like an Indian club. None of them would do. It couldn't be that way. He began to pace around. He came to a desk. On it lay a metal paper knife with an ornate handle. Would it be sharp enough? He reached for it and knocked over a small brass jar. Stamps spilled out of it and it fell to the floor with a clatter. "Hey," Mrs. Barrows yelled from the kitchen, "are you tearing up the pea patch?" Mr. Martin gave a strange laugh. Picking up the knife, he tried its point against his left wrist. It was blunt. It wouldn't do.

When Mrs. Barrows reappeared, carrying two highballs, Mr. Martin, standing there with his gloves on, became acutely conscious of the fantasy he had wrought. Cigarettes in his pocket, a drink prepared for him—it was all too grossly improbable. It was more than that; it was impossible. Somewhere in the back of his mind a vague idea stirred, sprouted. "For heaven's sake, take off those gloves," said Mrs. Barrows. "I always wear them in the house," said Mr. Martin. The idea began to bloom, strange and wonderful. She put the glasses on a coffee table in front of a sofa and sat on the sofa. "Come over here, you odd little man," she said. Mr. Martin went over and sat beside her. It was difficult getting a cigarette out of the pack of Camels, but he managed it. She held a match for him, laughing. "Well," she said, handing him a drink, "this is perfectly marvellous. You with a drink and a cigarette."

Mr. Martin puffed, not too awkwardly, and took a gulp of the highball. "I drink and smoke all the time," he said. He clinked his glass against hers. "Here's nuts to that old windbag, Fitweiler," he said, and gulped again. The stuff tasted awful, but he made no grimace. "Really, Mr. Martin," she said, her voice and posture changing, "you are insulting our employer." Mrs. Barrows was now all special adviser to the president. "I am preparing a bomb," said Mr. Martin, "which will blow the old goat higher than hell." He had only had a little of the drink, which was not strong. It couldn't be that. "Do you take dope or something?" Mrs. Barrows asked coldly. "Heroin," said Mr. Martin. "I'll be coked to the gills when I bump that old buzzard off." "Mr. Martin!" she shouted, getting to her feet. "That will be all of that. You must go at once." Mr. Martin took another swallow of his drink. He tapped his cigarette out in the ashtray and put the pack of Camels on the coffee table. Then he got up. She stood glaring at him. He walked over and put on his hat and coat. "Not a word about this," he said, and laid an index finger against his lips. All Mrs. Barrows could bring out was "Really!" Mr. Martin put his hand on the doorknob. "I'm sitting in the catbird seat," he said. He stuck his tongue out at her and left. Nobody saw him go. 14

Mr. Martin got to his apartment, walking, well before eleven. No one saw him go in. He had two glasses of milk after brushing his teeth, and he felt elated. It wasn't tipsiness, because he hadn't been tipsy. Anyway, the walk had worn off all effects of the whiskey. He got in bed and read a magazine for a while. He was asleep before midnight. 15

Mr. Martin got to the office at eight-thirty the next morning, as usual. At a quarter to nine, Ulgine Barrows, who had never before arrived at work before ten, swept into his office. "I'm reporting to Mr. 16

Fitweiler now!" she shouted. "If he turns you over to the police, it's no more than you deserve!" Mr. Martin gave her a look of shocked surprise. "I beg your pardon?" he said. Mrs. Barrows snorted and bounced out of the room, leaving Miss Paird and Joey Hart staring after her. "What's the matter with that old devil now?" asked Miss Paird. "I have no idea," said Mr. Martin, resuming his work. The other two looked at him and then at each other. Miss Paird got up and went out. She walked slowly past the closed door of Mr. Fitweiler's office. Mrs. Barrows was yelling inside, but she was not braying. Miss Paird could not hear what the woman was saying. She went back to her desk.

Forty-five minutes later, Mrs. Barrows left the president's office and went into her own, shutting the door. It wasn't until half an hour later that Mr. Fitweiler sent for Mr. Martin. The head of the filing department, neat, quiet, attentive, stood in front of the old man's desk. Mr. Fitweiler was pale and nervous. He took his glasses off and twiddled them. He made a small, bruffing sound in his throat. "Martin," he said, "you have been with us more than twenty years." "Twenty-two, sir," said Mr. Martin. "In that time," pursued the president, "your work and your—uh—manner have been exemplary." "I trust so, sir," said Mr. Martin. "I have understood, Martin," said Mr. Fitweiler, "that you have never taken a drink or smoked." "That is correct, sir," said Mr. Martin. "Ah, yes." Mr. Fitweiler polished his glasses. "You may describe what you did after leaving the office yesterday, Martin," he said. Mr. Martin allowed less than a second for his bewildered pause. "Certainly, sir," he said. "I walked home. Then I went to Schrafft's for dinner. Afterward I walked home again. I went to bed early, sir, and read a magazine for a while. I was asleep before eleven." "Ah, yes," said Mr. Fitweiler again. He was silent for a moment, searching for the proper words to say to the head of the filing department. "Mrs. Barrows," he said finally, "Mrs. Barrows has worked hard, Martin, very hard. It grieves me to report that she has suffered a severe breakdown. It has taken the form of a persecution complex accompanied by distressing hallucinations." "I am very sorry, sir," said Mr. Martin. "Mrs. Barrows is under the delusion," continued Mr. Fitweiler, "that you visited her last evening and behaved yourself in an—uh—unseemly manner." He raised his hand to silence Mr. Martin's little pained outcry. "It is the nature of these psychological diseases," Mr. Fitweiler said, "to fix upon the least likely and most innocent party as the—

uh—source of persecution. These matters are not for the lay mind to grasp, Martin. I've just had my psychiatrist, Dr. Fitch, on the phone. He would not, of course, commit himself, but he made enough generalizations to substantiate my suspicions. I suggested to Mrs. Barrows, when she had completed her—uh—story to me this morning, that she visit Dr. Fitch, for I suspected a condition at once. She flew, I regret to say, into a rage, and demanded—uh—requested that I call you on the carpet. You may not know, Martin, but Mrs. Barrows had planned a reorganization of your department—subject to my approval, of course, subject to my approval. This brought you, rather than anyone else, to her mind—but again that is a phenomenon for Dr. Fitch and not for us. So, Martin, I am afraid Mrs. Barrows' usefulness here is at an end." "I am dreadfully sorry, sir," said Mr. Martin.

It was at this point that the door to the office blew open with the suddenness of a gas-main explosion and Mrs. Barrows catapulted through it. "Is the little rat denying it?" she screamed. "He can't get away with that!" Mr. Martin got up and moved discreetly to a point beside Mr. Fitweiler's chair. "You drank and smoked at my apartment," she bawled at Mr. Martin, "and you know it! You called Mr. Fitweiler an old windbag and said you were going to blow him up when you got coked to the gills on your heroin!" She stopped yelling to catch her breath and a new glint came into her popping eyes. "If you weren't such a drab, ordinary little man," she said, "I'd think you'd planned it all. Sticking your tongue out, saying you were sitting in the catbird seat, because you thought no one would believe me when I told it! My God, it's really too perfect!" She glared at Mr. Fitweiler. "Can't you see how he has tricked us, you old fool? Can't you see his little game?" But Mr. Fitweiler had been surreptitiously pressing all the buttons under the top of his desk and employees of F & S began pouring into the room. "Stockton," said Mr. Fitweiler, "you and Fishbein will take Mrs. Barrows to her home. Mrs. Powell, you will go with them." Stockton, who had played a little football in high school, blocked Mrs. Barrows as she made for Mr. Martin. It took him and Fishbein together to force her out of the door into the hall, crowded with stenographers and office boys. She was still screaming imprecations at Mr. Martin, tangled and contradictory imprecations. The hubbub finally died out down the corridor.

"I regret that this has happened," said Mr. Fitweiler. "I shall ask you to dismiss it from your mind, Martin." "Yes, sir," said Mr. Martin,

18

19

anticipating his chief's "That will be all" by moving to the door. "I will dismiss it." He went out and shut the door, and his step was light and quick in the hall. When he entered his department he had slowed down to his customary gait, and he walked quietly across the room to the W20 file, wearing a look of studious concentration.

## VOCABULARY

| | | |
|---|---|---|
| fallible (2) | patronizing (7) | exemplary (17) |
| appalled (3) | temperate (7) | hallucinations (17) |
| peccadillos (3) | red herring (8) | unseemly (17) |
| romped (3) | ducky (9) | catapulted (18) |
| gibberish (4) | monstrously (10) | surreptitiously (18) |
| edifice (5) | wheezing (11) | imprecations (18) |
| indispensable (6) | grossly (13) | |
| obscene (6) | bruffing (17) | |

## THE FACTS

1. What is the origin of the colorful expressions that Mrs. Barrows constantly uses?
2. What is Mrs. Barrows's title in the firm of F & S?
3. Why does Mr. Martin finally decide to "rub out" Mrs. Barrows?
4. What shocking disclosures does Mr. Martin reveal to Mrs. Barrows on his surprise visit to her apartment?
5. What is the outcome of Mrs. Barrows's accusations against Mr. Martin?

## THE STRATEGIES

1. The organization of the story falls naturally into four divisions: (a) the trial and verdict of Mrs. Barrows, (b) preparation for the crime, (c) change of plan and perpetration of the crime, (d) result of the crime. Summarize what happens in each of these segments.
2. Early in the story the author tells us that Mr. Martin plans to kill Mrs. Barrows. Why does this announcement not eliminate suspense from the story?
3. What is the emotional climax of the story?
4. How does Thurber prepare us for Mr. Fitweiler's incredulous reaction to Mrs. Barrows's story about Mr. Martin? Why are we amused but not surprised at Mr. Fitweiler's reaction?

## THE ISSUES

1. What obvious contrasts between Mr. Martin and Mrs. Barrows does Thurber draw?
2. What is your view of the morality of Mr. Martin's actions? Was he justified in his extreme steps or not?
3. How does Mrs. Barrows's character reinforce an ancient sexual stereotype about women? How would you characterize this stereotype?
4. Would this story, if set in an office today rather than in the 1940s, be as believable? Why or why not?
5. Reverse the characters of Mrs. Barrows and Mr. Martin. She is now the fastidious head of the filing department, he the brassy opportunist who has ingratiated himself in the good graces of the boss, Fitweiler. Does the story still work? Why or why not?

## SUGGESTIONS FOR WRITING

1. Choose one of your close friends and write a short caricature by exaggerating his or her traits.
2. Write an essay analyzing the humorous devices used by Thurber in the story "The Catbird Seat." Pay attention to such factors as character, plot reversal, and style.

### William Shakespeare

# —— • THAT TIME OF YEAR (SONNET 73) • ——

*William Shakespeare (1564–1616) is generally acknowledged as the greatest literary genius of the English language. Born in Stratford-on-Avon, England, he was the son of a prosperous businessman, and probably attended grammar schools in his native town. In 1582, Shakespeare married Anne Hathaway, who was eight years his senior, and who bore him three children. The legacy of his writing includes thirty-six plays, one hundred fifty-four sonnets, and five long poems.*

*The English or Shakespearean sonnet is composed of three quatrains of four lines each and a concluding couplet of two, rhyming* abab cdcd efef gg. *There is usually a correspondence between the units marked off by the rhymes and the development of the thought. The three quatrains, for instance, may represent three different images or three questions from which a conclusion is drawn in the final couplet. As a result, the sonnet is one of the most tightly organized poetic forms used.*

That time of year thou mayst in me behold
When yellow leaves, or none, or few, do hang
Upon those boughs which shake against the cold,
Bare ruined choirs where late the sweet birds sang.
In me thou see'st the twilight of such day                                    5
As after sunset fadeth in the west,
Which by and by black night doth take away,
Death's second self, that seals up all in rest.
In me thou see'st the glowing of such fire,
That on the ashes of his youth doth lie                                       10
As the deathbed whereon it must expire,
Consumed with that which it was nourished by.
This thou perceivest, which makes thy love more strong,
To love that well which thou must leave ere long.

## THE FACTS

1. In the first quatrain what image does the poet focus on? What relationship does this image have to the speaker?
2. In the second quatrain the speaker shifts to another image. What is it and what relationship does it bear to him?
3. In the third quatrain yet another image is introduced. What is the image and how does it relate to the speaker? What rather complex philosophical paradox is involved?
4. The final couplet states the poet's thesis (or theme). What is that thesis? State it in your own words.

## THE STRATEGIES

1. The entire poem is organized around three analogies. State them in three succinct sentences.
2. The three images in the poem are presented in a particular order. Do you see any reason for this order?
3. In lines 3 and 4, what effect do the words "cold / Bare ruined choirs" have on the rhythm and meter?
4. In line 2, what would be the result of substituting "hang" for "do hang"?
5. What is the antecedent of "this" in line 13?

## THE ISSUES

1. What can you deduce about the speaker and his frame of mind from this poem?

2. Some wag once said, "Youth is wasted on the young." How might that witticism be applied to this poem?
3. Why should a student whose major is, say, business and who has no interest whatsoever in literature be forced to take classes in which poems such as this one are studied?
4. Shakespeare has been called surprisingly modern in his outlook. What about this poem would seem to justify that observation?

## SUGGESTIONS FOR WRITING

1. In two or three well-developed paragraphs, answer the question, "What is the single worst aspect of old age?"
2. Write an essay in which you outline the way you plan to make your own old age as pleasant and fulfilling as possible.

# •• *ISSUE FOR CRITICAL* ••
# *THINKING*

## *Women's Liberation*

The Constitution of the United States contains no clause specifically guaranteeing the rights of women. Women at the time of the Constitutional Convention could not own property, engage in business, or even assume control over their own children, the law of man and the law of God as interpreted by men demanding their utter subjugation to husbands or fathers. So it was understandable that Abigail Adams and Mercy Otis Warren, two feminists of that era, would urge just such a constitutional provision for the liberation of women upon George Washington and Thomas Jefferson, to no avail. In 1972 an attempt was made to correct this oversight by passage of the Equal Rights Amendment. But the amendment could not win ratification by the thirty-eight states it needed to become law. Its failure marked a typical chapter in the struggle for women's liberation, which has always proceeded by fits and starts, making gains here, losing ground there.

According to the statisticians, women do not earn as much as men; they do not occupy positions of power commensurate with their numbers; they do not have the "clout" of men in the boardroom, backroom, or clubroom, triumphing only in the cloakroom, where a woman attendant is more likely to be found than a man. There has never been a woman president in the history of the United States; only a handful of women serve in the Congress;

fewer still serve in state gubernatorial offices. In some cantons of Switzer-land—certainly a modern and developed country by any measure—women still do not have the right to vote.

The three selections on this issue span the range of history and attitudes one would expect to find on such a subject. In Joseph Sobron's article, "The Cruel Logic of Liberation," we see the viewpoint of a conservative male. Sobron is irked that women insist on retaining the right to abort a pregnancy without consulting the father, and he believes he has caught them in a moral and logical inconsistency. Next we hear from Abigail Abbott Bailey, a New England housewife of the eighteenth century whose tyrannical husband de-veloped a sick obsession for their daughter. Finally, we hear from Judy Syfers, whose "I Want a Wife" is considered by some as a manifesto for the modern feminist movement.

Women can point to real achievements and gains won in recent years. But are these gains enough to compensate for the inequalities that still persist? Will the final battle for complete and total equality ever be won, and if so, at what cost? Most of us can ask the questions. Few of us have any good answers.

Joseph Sobron

# • THE CRUEL LOGIC OF • LIBERATION

*Joseph Sobron (b. 1946) is a freelance writer, syndicated with United Press. He is a senior editor for* National Review *and a contributing editor to* Human Life. *He has written articles and essays for numerous magazines such as* Har-per's *and* The American Spectator.

Maybe it would be an exaggeration to say that men have only them-selves to blame for feminism. But I think there's something in it.     1

One of the big (and ugly) feminist issues is abortion. I recently got     2
into a debate with a feminist who contended that men should have no say in the matter, that it was strictly a women's concern. Very well, I rejoined: in that case women shouldn't be able to file paternity suits.

Why not? she demanded. Because, I said, if motherhood is going to     3
be optional, then no woman who chooses it should be able to impose the consequence of her choice on an unwilling man. If a pregnant woman has nine months in which to decide whether to bear a child,

during which time she need neither consult nor inform the father (even if he's her husband) and during which time he can't have any say in the matter, it seems grossly unfair to require him to support the child she alone decided to bring into this world.

Put otherwise, we have disjoined sex from procreation. Officially, a  4
human fetus is no longer a human being: no objective social penalty attaches to killing it. It's now a matter of law that a sexual act can't commit a woman to motherhood: she can repudiate the consequences of her act. (It's "her body.") So it seems like an illogical residue of an older code to say that the same act that commits her to nothing can simultaneously commit her partner to fatherhood. The paternity suit is a vestige of the code that presumed that the whole point of sex, not to mention the foreseeable result, was reproduction. If women shouldn't be burdened with unwanted children, neither should men. Especially not at the whim of the woman.

My interlocutor was distressed by this line of argument, but she had  5
no reply. So I tried it out on a radio broadcast. The only answer I got was that my logic was cruel. But the logic wasn't particularly mine and, besides, a syllogism is under no obligation to be humanitarian: abortion is nasty, so we shouldn't be surprised if the consistent application of its rationale turns out to be equally nasty.

Which was exactly the point I set out to make. I agree that people  6
shouldn't be forced to have unwanted children. But once they've begotten a child, they have a child. If either party has a "right" to renounce it, the other should have the same right. Or there is no such right, for anyone.

I feel compassion for the woman who is distressed by her preg-  7
nancy. But I also feel compassion for the man who can't prevent his child from being aborted, and above all for the child, who has least choice in the matter. As far as that goes, I feel compassion for the poor girl, herself seduced and abandoned, who abandons her infant. But I don't therefore approve of the act that merely passes the injustice along to an innocent party.

A good deal of contemporary feminism (by no means all of it) can  8
be traced to the sense of modern life's injustice to woman. Abortion is inherent in the sexual revolution: we were promised a cheap intimacy, an intimacy without commitment, by erotic utopians like Hugh Hefner.

But like most revolutions and utopias, the sexual one went awry.  9

The burden of it fell most heavily on women; when accidents happen, they happen to women. That is not a good reason for making the children pay. It's an excellent reason for doing something else: namely, challenging the dogmatic premises of sexual "liberation."

Correct me if I'm wrong but my strong impression is that the new    10
morality hasn't increased the sum total of human bliss. The rates of divorce, abortion and venereal disease are up, up, up, and the pornography trade that has bought Hefner his jet planes and mansions seems to me to testify not to more romance but to more intense loneliness, of a somewhat morbid and sordid kind.

It's time to insist that the promises of the sexual utopians have been    11
as false as those of the social utopians, and as disastrous. If we haven't noticed this, maybe it's because the disasters have occurred on a smaller scale.

## VOCABULARY

disjoined (4)          vestige (4)          dogmatic (9)
procreation (4)        interlocutor (5)

## THE FACTS

1. According to Sobron, why shouldn't women be able to file paternity suits?
2. What was the only reply Sobron claimed to have gotten when he tried out his argument on a radio show?
3. To what can a good deal of contemporary feminism be traced, according to the author?
4. What, according to Sobron, did erotic utopians like Hugh Hefner promise us?
5. What does Sobron think the pornography trade actually brought us?

## THE STRATEGIES

1. What characteristics identify this article as an opinion column?
2. Why doesn't Sobron use quotations marks in paragraph 3 to enclose the direct speech?
3. Why does Sobron use quotations marks in the parenthetical remark in paragraph 4?
4. What rhetorical mode is Sobron evidently practicing in paragraphs 8 and 9?

## THE ISSUES

1. Do you think that women should not be able to file paternity suits if men have no right to intervene in their decisions to have an abortion? Why or why not?
2. What is your opinion of Sobron's logic?
3. In your view, what rights should the father have in a woman's decision to have or not have an abortion?
4. What is your opinion of Sobron's argument that people like Hugh Hefner are to be blamed for the present difficulties of women?
5. What relationship, if any, do you think pornography has with divorce, abortion, and venereal disease rates?

## SUGGESTIONS FOR WRITING

1. Write an essay analyzing the logic of Sobron's argument.
2. Write an essay either for or against the concepts and principles of feminism.

Abigail Abbot Bailey

# —— • DIARY OF AN ABUSED WIFE • ——

*Abigail Abbot Bailey (1746–1815) of Concord, New Hampshire, married Asa Bailey in 1767 and bore him seventeen children. The family settled in Landaff, New Hampshire, where Asa Bailey achieved prominence as a landowner and town selectman and fought in the Revolutionary War. After the episodes described in this selection, Abigail was granted a "bill of divorcement" from Asa in 1792. She died at the home of her son Asa in Bath, New Hampshire, after an attack of "lung fever."*

*The painful experiences related by this eighteenth-century housewife are perhaps more typical of domestic life in our own turbulent time than in the colonial era. Her story of a powerless wife at the mercy of a cruel husband who has become sexually obsessed with his own daughter is distressingly familiar. Found among Abigail's possessions after her death, the manuscript was turned over to the Reverend Ethan Smith of Haverhill, New Hampshire, who edited it for publication in 1815 under the conviction that "few lives of christians, in modern days, have afforded such rare materials for instructive biography."*

December, 1788. Mr. B. began to behave in a very uncommon man-  1
ner: he would rise in the morning, and after being dressed, would seat

himself in his great chair, by the fire, and would scarcely go out all day. He would not speak, unless spoken to; and not always then. He seemed like one in the deepest study. If a child came to him, and asked him to go to breakfast, or dinner, he seemed not to hear: then I would go to him, and must take hold of him, and speak very loudly, before he would attend; and then he would seem like one waking from sleep. Often when he was eating, he would drop his knife and fork, or whatever he had in his hand, and seemed not to know what he was doing. Nor could he be induced to give any explanation of his strange appearance and conduct. He did not appear like one senseless, or as though he could not hear, or speak. His eyes would sparkle with the keen emotions of his mind.

I had a great desire to learn the cause of this strange appearance 2 and conduct. I at first hoped it might be concern for his soul; but I was led to believe this was not the case. He continued thus several days and nights, and seemed to sleep but little.

One night, soon after we had retired to bed; he began to talk very 3 familiarly, and seemed pleasant. He said, now I will tell you what I have been studying upon all this while: I have been planning to sell our farm, and to take our family and interest, and move to the westward, over toward the Ohio country, five or six hundred miles; I think that is a much better country than this; and I have planned out the whole matter. Now I want to learn your mind concerning it; for I am unwilling to do any thing contrary to your wishes in things so important as this. He said he wished to gain my consent, and then he would consult the children, and get their consent also. I was troubled at his proposal; I saw many difficulties in the way. But he seemed much engaged, and said he could easily remove all my objections. I told him it would be uncertain what kind of people we should find there; and how we should be situated relative to gospel privileges. He said he had considered all those things; that he well knew what kind of minister, and what people would suit me; and he would make it his care to settle where those things would be agreeable to me, and that in all things he would seek as much to please me, as himself. His manner was now tender and obliging: and though his subject was most disagreeable to me, yet I deemed it not prudent to be hasty in discovering too much opposition to his plans. I believe I remarked, that I must submit the matter to him. If he was confident it would be for the interest of the family, I could not say it would not be thus; but really I could not at present confide in it.

He proceeded to say, that he would take one of our sons, and one 4 daughter, to go first with him on this tour, to wait on him; and that he probably should not return to take the rest of the family under a year from the time he should set out. He said he would put his affairs in order, so that it should be as easy and comfortable for me as possible, during his absence.

Soon after, Mr. B. laid this his pretended plan before the children; 5 and after a while he obtained their consent to move to the westward. They were not pleased with the idea, but wished to be obedient, and to honor their father. Thus we all consented, at last, to follow our head and guide, wherever he should think best; for our family had ever been in the habit of obedience: and perhaps never were more pains taken to please the head of a family, than had ever been taken in our domestic circle.

But alas! words fail to set forth the things which followed! All this 6 pretended *plan* was but a specious cover to infernal designs. Here I might pause, and wonder, and be silent, humble, and astonished, as long as I live! A family, which God had committed to my head and husband, as well as to me, to protect and train up for God, must now have their peace and honor sacrificed by an inhuman parent, under the most subtle and vile intrigues, to gratify the most contemptible passion! I had before endured sorrowful days and years, on account of the follies, cruelties, and base incontinency of him who vowed to be my faithful husband. But all past afflictions vanish before those which follow. But how can I relate them? Oh tell it not in Gath! Must I record such grievousness against the husband of my youth?

> Oft as I try to tell the doleful tale,
> My quivering lips and faltering tongue do fail:
> Nor can my trembling hand, or feeble pen,
> Equal the follies of this worst of men!

I have already related that Mr. B. said he would take one of our sons, 7 and one daughter, to wait on him in his distant tour, before he would take all the family. After he had talked of this for a few days, he said he had altered his plan; he would leave his son, and take only his daughter: he could hire what men's help he needed: his daughter must go and cook for him. He now commenced a new series of conduct in relation to this daughter, whom he selected to go with him, in order (as he pretended) to render himself pleasing and familiar to her, so that she might be willing to go with him, and feel happy: for though, as a father, he had a right to command her to go, yet (he said) he would so conduct toward her, as to make her cheerful and well pleased to go with him. A great part of the time he now spent in the room where she was spinning; and seemed shy of me, and of the rest of the family. He seemed to have forgotten his age, his honor, and all decency, as well as all virtue. He would spend his time with this daughter, in telling idle stories, and foolish riddles, and singing songs to her, and sometimes before the small children, when they were in that room. He thus pursued a course of conduct, which had the most direct tendency to corrupt young and tender minds, and lead them the greatest distance from every serious subject. He would try to make his daughter tell stories with him; wishing to make her free and sociable, and to erase from her mind all that fear and reserve, which he had ever taught his children to feel toward him. He had ever been sovereign, severe and hard with his children, and they stood in the greatest fear of him. His whole conduct, toward this daughter especially, was now changed, and became most disagreeable.

For a considerable time I was wholly at a loss what to think of his 8 conduct, or what his wish or intentions could be. Had such conduct appeared toward any young woman beside his own young daughter, I should have had no question what he intended: but as it now was, I was loth to indulge the least suspicion of base design. His daily conduct forced a conviction upon my alarmed and tortured mind, that his designs were the most vile. All his tender affections were withdrawn from the wife of his youth, the mother of his children. My room was deserted, and left lonely. His care for the rest of the family seemed abandoned, as well as all his attention to his large circle of worldly business. Every thing must lie neglected, while this one daughter engrossed all his attention.

Though all the conduct of Mr. B. from day to day, seemed to dem- 9 onstrate my apprehension, that he was determined, and was continually plotting, to ruin this poor young daughter, yet it was so intolerably crossing to every feeling of my soul to admit such a thought, that I strove with all my might to banish it from my mind, and to disbelieve the possibility of such a thing. I felt terrified at my own thoughts upon the subject; and shocked that such a thing should enter my mind. But the more I labored to banish those things from my mind, the more I found it impossible to annihilate evident facts. Now my grief was dreadful. No words can express the agitations of my soul: From day to day they tortured me, and seemed to roll on with a resistless power. I was constrained to expect that he would accomplish his wickedness: And such were my infirmities, weakness and fears, (my circumstances being very difficult) that I did not dare to hint any thing of my fears to him, or to any creature. This may to some appear strange; but with me it was then a reality. I labored to divert his mind from his follies, and to turn his attention to things of the greatest importance. But I had the mortification to find that my endeavors were unsuccessful.

I soon perceived that his strange conduct toward this daughter was    10
to her very disagreeable. And she shewed as much unwillingness to be in the room with him, as she dared. I often saw her cheeks bedewed with tears, on account of his new and astonishing behavior. But as his will had ever been the law of the family, she saw no way to deliver herself from her cruel father. Such were her fears of him, that she did not dare to talk with me, or any other person, upon her situation: for he was exceedingly jealous of my conversing with her, and cautioning her. If I ever dropped words, which I hoped would put her upon her guard, or inquired the cause of her troubles, or what business her father had so much with her? if I was ever so cautious, he would find it out, and be very angry. He watched her and me most narrowly; and by his subtle questions with her, he would find out what I had said, during his absence. He would make her think I had informed him what I had said, and then would be very angry with me: so that at times I feared for my life. I queried with myself which way I could turn. How could I caution a young daughter in such a case? My thoughts flew to God for relief, that the Father of mercies would protect a poor helpless creature marked out for a prey; and turn the heart of a cruel father from every wicked purpose.

After a while Mr. B's conduct toward this daughter was strangely    11
altered. Instead of idle songs, fawning and flattery, he grew very angry with her; and would wish her dead, and buried: and he would correct her very severely. It seemed, that when he found his first line of conduct ineffectual, he changed his behavior, felt his vile indignation moved, and was determined to see what he could effect by tyranny

and cruelty. He most cautiously guarded her against having any free conversation with me, or any of the family, at any time; lest she should expose him. He would forbid any of the children going with her to milking. If, at any time, any went with her, it must be a number; so that nothing could be said concerning him. He would not suffer her to go from home: I might not send her abroad on any occasion. Never before had Mr. B. thus confined her, or any of his children. None but an eye witness can conceive of the strangeness of his conduct from day to day, and of his plans to conceal his wickedness, and to secure himself from the light of evidence.* . . .

The black cloud, rising like a storm of hail, had rolled on, and had    12 gathered over my head. I clearly saw that Mr. B. entertained the most vile intentions relative to his own daughter. Whatever difficulty attended the obtaining of legal proof, yet no remaining doubt existed in my mind, relative to the existence of his wickedness: and I had no doubt remaining of the violence, which he had used; and hence arose his rage against her. It must have drawn tears of anguish from the eyes of the hardest mortals, to see the barbarous corrections, which he, from time to time, inflicted on this poor young creature; and for no just cause. Sometimes he corrected her with a rod; and sometimes with a beach stick, large enough for the driving of a team; and with such sternness and anger sparkling in his eyes, that his visage seemed to resemble an infernal; declaring, that if she attempted to run from him again, she should never want but one correction more; for he would whip her to death! This his conduct could be for no common disobedience; for she had ever been most obedient to him in all lawful commands. It seemed as though the poor girl must now be destroyed under his furious hand. She was abashed, and could look no one in the face.

---

*Editor, 1815: The discreet reader will repeatedly wonder that this pious sufferer did not look abroad for help against so vile a son of Beliel, and avail herself of the law of the land, by swearing the peace against him. Her forbearance does indeed seem to have been carried to excess. But when we consider her delicate situation at this time; her peaceable habits from youth; her native tenderness of mind; her long fears of a tyranical cruel husband; her having, at no time of her sufferings, seen all that we now see of his abominable character, as a reason why he should have been brought to justice; her wishes and hopes that he might be brought to reformation; her desires not to have the family honor sacrificed; and the difficulty of exhibiting sufficient evidence against a popular, subtle man, to prove such horrid crimes;—these things plead much in her behalf. After all, it will be difficult to resist the conviction, which will be excited in the course of these memoirs, that Mrs. B. did truly err, in not having her husband brought to justice. The law is made for the lawless and disobedient.

Among the many instances of his wickedly correcting her, I shall    13
mention one. One morning Mr. B. rose from bed, while it was yet
dark. He immediately called this daughter, and told her to get up. She
obeyed. And as she knew her daily business, she made up her fire in
her room, and sat down to her work. He sat by the fire in the kitchen.
As my door was open, I carefully observed his motions. He sat looking
into the fire for some time, as though absorbed in his thoughts. It soon
grew light. The small children arose, and came round the fire. He
looked round like one disappointed and vexed. He sprang from his
chair, and called his daughter, whom he first called. She left her work
in her room, and came immediately to him. In great rage, and with a
voice of terror, he asked why she did not come to him, when he first
called her? She respectfully told him that he called her to get up, which
she immediately did, and went to her work. But she said she did not
hear him call her to come to him. He seized his horse whip, and said,
in a rage, he would make her know that when he called her, she should
come to him. He then fell to whipping her without mercy. She cried,
and begged, and repeated her assertion, that she did not know he
called her to come to him. She had done as he told her. She got up,
and went to her work. But he was not in the least appeased. He continued to whip her, as though he were dealing with an ungovernable
brute; striking over her head, hands, and back; nor did he spare
her face and eyes; while the poor girl appeared as though she must
die. No proper account could he ever be prevailed on to give of this
conduct.

None can describe the anguish of my heart on the beholding of such    14
scenes. How pitiful must be the case of a poor young female, to be
subjected to such barbarous treatment by her own father; so that she
knew of no way of redress!

It may appear surprising that such wickedness was not checked by    15
legal restraints. But great difficulties attend in such a case. While I was
fully convinced of the wickedness, yet I knew not that I could make
legal proof. I could not prevail upon this daughter to make known to
me her troubles; or to testify against the author of them. Fear, shame,
youthful inexperience, and the terrible peculiarities of her case, all
conspired to close her mouth against affording me, or any one, proper
information. My soul was moved with pity for her wretched case: and
yet I cannot say I did not feel a degree of resentment, that she would

not, as she ought, expose the wickedness of her father, that she might be relieved from him, and he brought to due punishment. But no doubt his intrigues, insinuations, commands, threats, and parental influence, led her to feel that it was in vain for her to seek redress.

My circumstances, and peculiar bodily infirmities, at that time, were [16] such as to entitle a woman to the tenderest affection and sympathies of a companion. On this account, and as Mr. B. was exceedingly stern, and angry with me for entertaining hard thoughts of him, I felt unable to do any thing more for the relief of my poor daughter. My hope in God was my only support. And I did abundantly and earnestly commit my cause to him. I felt confident that he would, in his own time, and as his infinite wisdom should determine, grant relief. . . .

Sept. 15, 1789. . . . The next morning I took an opportunity with [17] Mr. B. alone to have solemn conversation. My health being now restored, I thought it high time, and had determined, to adopt a new mode of treatment with Mr. B. I calmly introduced the subject, and told him, plainly and solemnly, all my views of his wicked conduct, in which he had long lived with his daughter. He flew into a passion, was high, and seemed to imagine, he could at once frighten me out of my object. But I was carried equally above fear, and above temper. Of this I soon convinced him, I let him know, that the business I now had taken in hand, was of too serious a nature, and too interesting, to be thus disposed of, or dismissed with a few angry words. I told him I should no longer be turned off in this manner; but should pursue my object with firmness, and with whatever wisdom and ability God might give me; and that God would plead my cause, and prosper my present undertaking, as he should see best. I reminded Mr. B. of my long and unusually distressing illness; how he had treated me in it; how wicked and cruel he had been to the wife of his youth; how unable I had been to check him in that awful wickedness, which I knew he had pursued; that all my inexpressible griefs and solemn entreaties had been by him trampled under foot.

I therefore had not known what to do better than to wait on God as [18] I had done, to afford me strength and opportunity to introduce the means of his effectual control. This time I told him had arrived. And now, if God spared my life, (I told Mr. B.) he should find a new leaf turned over;—and that I would not suffer him to go on any longer as he had done. I would now soon adopt measures to put a stop to his abominable wickedness and cruelties. For this could and ought to be done. And if I did it not, I should be a partaker of his sins, and should aid in bringing down the curse of God upon our family.

By this time Mr. B. had become silent. He appeared struck with    19
some degree of fear. He, by and by, asked me what I intended or expected to do, to bring about such a revolution as I had intimated? whether I knew what an awful crime I had laid to his charge? which he said could not be proved. He wished to know whether I had considered how difficult it would be for me to do any such thing against him? as I was under his legal control; and he could overrule all my plans as he pleased. I told him, I well knew I had been placed under his lawful government and authority, and likewise under his care and protection. And most delightful would it have been to me, to have been able quietly and safely to remain there as long as I lived. Gladly would I have remained a kind, faithful, obedient wife to him, as I had ever been. But I told Mr. B. he *knew* he had violated his marriage covenant; and hence had forfeited all legal and just right and authority over me; and I should convince him that I well knew it. I told him I was not in any passion. I acted on principle, and from long and mature consideration. And though it had ever been my greatest care and pleasure (among my earthly comforts) to obey and please him; yet by his most wicked and cruel conduct, he had compelled me to undertake this most undesirable business—of stopping him in his mad career; and that I now felt strength, courage and zeal to pursue my resolution. And if my life was spared, he would find that I should bring something to pass, and probably more than he now apprehended.

As to what I could prove against him, I told Mr. B. he knew not how    20
much evidence I had of his unnatural crimes, of which I had accused him, and of which *he knew he was guilty*. I asked him why he should not expect that I should institute a process against him, for that most horrid conduct, which he had long allowed himself to pursue, and with the most indecent and astonishing boldness? I told him I well knew that he was naturally a man of sense; and that his conscience now fully approved of my conduct.

Mr. B. seeing me thus bold and determinate, soon changed his    21
countenance and conduct. He appeared panic-struck; and he soon became mild, sociable and pleasant. He now made an attempt, with all his usual subtlety, and flatteries, to induce me to relinquish my design. He pretended to deny the charge of incest. But I told him I had

no confidence in his denial of it; it was therefore in vain! Upon this he said, he really did not blame, or think hard of me, for believing him guilty of this sin. He said, he knew he had behaved foolishly; and had given me full reason to be jealous of him; and he repeated that he did not at all think hard of me for entertaining the views which I had of him. He then took the Bible, and said, he would lay his hand upon it, and swear that he was not guilty of the crime laid to his charge. Knowing what I did, I was surprised and disgusted at this impious attempt. I stepped towards him, and in a resolute and solemn manner begged of him to forbear! assuring him, that such an oath could not undo or alter real facts, of which he was conscious. And this proceeding, I assured him, would be so far from giving me any satisfaction, that it would greatly increase the distress of my soul for him in his wickedness. Upon this he forbore, and laid his Bible aside.

Mr. B. now said, he was very sorry he had given me so much reason    22
to think such things of him; and that he had so far destroyed my confidence in him as a man of truth. He then begged of me to forgive all that was past; and he promised that he would ever be kind and faithful to me in future, and never more give me reason to complain of him for any such conduct. I told him, if I had but evidence of his real reformation, I could readily forgive him as a fellow creature, and could plead with God to forgive him. But as to my living with him in the most endearing relation any longer, after such horrid crimes, I did not see that I *could*, or *ought* to do it! He then anxiously made some remarks upon the consequences of my refusing to remain his wife, and seeking a separation from him. These he seemed unable to endure. I remarked, that I well knew it was no small thing for a husband and wife to part, and their family of children to be broken up; that such a separation could not be rendered expedient or lawful, without great sin indeed: and that I would not be the cause of it, and of breaking up our family, for *all the world*. But, said I, you have done all in your power to bring about such a separation, and to ruin and destroy our family. And I meet it as my duty now to do all in my power to save them from further destruction. . . .

[*Abigail Bailey determines to seek a separation from her husband, and rather*    23
*than be brought to trial, he agrees. He also agrees to a 50/50 property settle-*
*ment to which end he arranges to sell his farm to Captain Gould of Granville,*
*New York, for 500 pounds. To complete this bargain, Abigail Bailey consents*
*to travel with her husband to Granville, a journey that should take three days.*]

Monday, March 19 [1792]

After we had proceeded several miles, Mr. B. threw off the mask at    24
once, and kept me no longer in the dark, at least relative to what was
*not* the object of his journey, that it was not what he had ever said. He
told me, we are now in the State of New York, and now you must be
governed by the laws of this State, which are far more suitable to
govern such women as you, than are the laws of New Hampshire. He
added, that he was not going to Granville; nor had he ever intended to
go thither, or to trade with Capt. Gould. But all this plan, he said, he
had laid, to lead me off from home, that he might get me away from
the circle of the Abbots, and Brocks, and my connexions; and then see
if he could not bring me to terms, that would better suit himself. And
now, if I would drop all that was past, and concerning which I had
made so much noise; and would promise never to make any more rout
about any of those things; and to be a kind and obedient wife to him,
without any more ado; it was well! If not, he would proceed accordingly. He said, unless I would thus engage, he would drive on among
strangers, till that sleigh, and those horses were worn out! He went on
conversing in this way. Sometimes he would speak of carrying me to
the Ohio; sometimes of taking me among the Dutch people, where, he
said, I could not understand a word of their language. And then he
would talk of taking me to Albany, or where he could sell me on board
a ship. He assured me that I should never return home again. He said
he had been cunning enough to get me away from home; and now he
believed he should be crafty enough to keep me away. I might *cry*, he
added, as much as I pleased; but I could not help myself. If I should
try to escape from him, he said, he was as long headed as I was; and I
might well expect that he could outwit me. Mr. B. said that his brothers, D. and F. and also E.F., were all confederate with him in this plan.
And if I should by any means escape from him, and get home, he had
empowered his brother D. to keep all the interest out of my hands,
and to advertise me in his name, forbidding all persons harboring or
trusting me.

[*In New York, Abigail Bailey contracts smallpox and the illness brings her*    25
*near death. Mr. B. leaves her in this condition and returns to New Hampshire*
*to sell his farm. Left on her own, Abigail Bailey decides she must, even in her*
*weakened condition, attempt the 270 mile journey back by herself. She leaves*
*on horseback on May 24 and finds food and lodging at taverns and homes*
*along the way. Those who are shocked to find a woman traveling alone are*

*quick to offer assistance when they hear her story. After a series of "kind providences," she finds herself six days later almost out of New York state.*]

The next morning I crossed the river; not as a captive, or in fear of falling through the ice, as when I came over it before. I well remembered the wormwood and the gall, when I was dragged over it by the man who vaunted over me, and seemed to rejoice in the imagination, that no power could take me out of his hands. I now saw it is safe trusting in that God, who, when the wicked deal proudly, Is above them. Finding myself safely on the east side of the North river, I felt a confidence that God, who had thus far delivered, would, in due time, bring me out of all my distresses. . . .     26

This day I must get my horse shod. I had set out from Unadilla with less than one dollar in money. While I was thinking of this subject, a young gentleman rode up and went on with me with naked hands. I told him I thought he needed a pair of gloves. He said he did, and meant to have a pair as soon as he could find them. I took a good pair out of my saddlebags, which I had provided on purpose to help bear my expenses in the way. They just fitted his hand. He paid me a generous price for them, and some refreshment beside. Now I had plenty of money for shoeing my horse. I called and got it done. The blacksmith asked but a moderate price, and gave me dinner. Thus I lived on a series of mercies. From Sabbath morning till Wednesday night, I had been kept, nights and days, without cost, for me or my horse. Wednesday night I put up in a tavern near Salem court house. Here they were so kind as to take for my reckoning such articles as I had to spare.     27

Thursday, May 31, I set forward. I crossed the line of the state, into Vermont. I remembered the terrors of my mind, when I was told, that now I was in the state of New York, and was threatened with horrid treatment. I rejoiced that God had thus far broken the rod of the oppressor: and I gave him thanks for his great goodness. . . .     28

[*After arriving home, Abigail Bailey enlists the aid of her brothers and swears a warrant against her husband. Before he is arrested however, he is able to persuade an associate, Captain White, to flee with the Bailey children and property. White is intercepted in his attempt. Asa Bailey, under the threat of a public trial for his crimes, agrees to a property settlement. He is allowed to*     29

*depart with his three oldest sons (who later return to their mother), leaving
the other children with her.*]

I was at Gen. B.'s, when Mr. B. was brought there under keepers. It <sub>30</sub> was indeed a solemn sight to me. Here was the man, who had been the husband of my youth, whom I had tenderly loved, as my companion, in years past, now a prisoner of civil justice, and at my prosecution. But his most obstinate and persevering wickedness had rendered it necessary. And I thought I might hope that the situation of my family might now be altered for the better. . . .

Thus I have sketched some of the most important events of my life, <sub>31</sub> through which God, in his deep and holy providence, caused me to pass, from the time I entered the family state, A.D. 1767, in the twenty-second year of my age,—till A.D. 1792, when I was in my forty-seventh year. Great trials, and wonderful mercies have been my lot, from the hands of my Heavenly Father.

[*Abigail Bailey was eventually granted a "bill of divorcement" and Asa* <sub>32</sub> *Bailey left Landaff. After arranging for her children to be "put out in regular and good households," she joined the family of a minister in a neighboring town. In the last years of her life, she lived with various of her children and died of "lung fever" while with the family of her son Asa in Bath, New Hampshire.*]

## VOCABULARY

| | | |
|---|---|---|
| induced (1) | agitations (9) | intimated (19) |
| specious (6) | constrained (9) | covenant (19) |
| incontinency (6) | abashed (12) | relinquish (21) |
| engrossed (8) | appeased (13) | impious (21) |
| annihilate (9) | redress (14) | expedient (22) |

## THE FACTS

1. To what does Abigail at first attribute her husband's strange periods of brooding silence?
2. Where does the husband propose to move his entire family?
3. After a while, how does Mr. B.'s conduct toward his daughter change?
4. To what state does Mr. B. lure Abigail and for what purpose?
5. Where does Mr. B. last appear in this chronicle and in what condition?

## THE STRATEGIES

1. Bearing in mind that this excerpt was written not by a scholar but by an eighteenth-century housewife, how does it differ in style and grammar from what you would expect to find today in the diary of the writer's modern counterpart?
2. Why does Abigail resort to poetry in paragraph 6 as she struggles to express her anguish and grief?
3. In paragraph 6 Abigail exclaims, "Oh tell it not in Gath!" What does this mean? What does the use of this odd expression reveal about her?
4. "Now I want to learn your mind concerning it; for I am unwilling to do any thing contrary to your wishes in things so important as this." How would a modern writer punctuate this sentence from paragraph 3?
5. "Of this I soon convinced him, I let him know, that the business I now had taken in hand, was of too serious a nature, and too interesting, to be thus disposed of, or dismissed with a few angry words" (Paragraph 17). What does "interesting" mean in this context? What other word might a modern writer use?

## THE ISSUES

1. How might a modern reader or observer interpret Mr. B.'s initial withdrawal, long stretches of silence, and sleeplessness? How does Abigail seem to interpret these symptoms?
2. What can a modern reader deduce about the structure of a colonial family from Abigail's account?
3. Read the footnote comment on page 240, which was inserted in 1815 by the editor, the Reverend Ethan Smith. Do you agree with his judgment about Abigail that "her forbearance does indeed seem to have been carried to excess"? In your opinion, what could Abigail have done that she failed to do?
4. Would a modern housewife who finds herself and her family in a similar situation today be better able to escape the clutches of a Mr. B.?
5. Throughout the excerpt, Abigail persists in calling her estranged husband "Mr. B.," even after he appears before her accompanied by his keepers. What does this odd formality say about her and, by inference, other colonial women?

## SUGGESTIONS FOR WRITING

1. Write an essay analyzing Abigail's personality and character, supporting your inferences and points with quotations from her diary.
2. Write an essay detailing what advantages a modern woman in a similar circumstance would have in fending off the aggressions of a cruel husband.

Investigate the facilities available to battered women in your community and mention them in your essay.

**Judy Syfers**

—————————— • **I WANT A WIFE** • ——————————

*Judy Syfers (b. 1937) was born in San Francisco and educated at the University of Iowa, where she earned a B.F.A. in painting (1962). In 1973, her feminist convictions led her to Cuba to study class relationships as a means of understanding how social change can occur. Presently employed as a secretary, and doing occasional freelance writing, she calls herself a "disenfranchised (and fired) housewife."*

I belong to that classification of people known as wives. I am a Wife. And, not altogether incidentally, I am a mother.    1

Not too long ago a male friend of mine appeared on the scene fresh    2
from a recent divorce. He had one child, who is, of course, with his ex-wife. He is obviously looking for another wife. As I thought about him while I was ironing one evening, it suddenly occurred to me that I, too, would like to have a wife. Why do I want a wife?

I would like to go back to school so that I can become economically    3
independent, support myself, and, if need be, support those dependent on me. I want a wife who will work and send me to school. And while I am going to school I want a wife to take care of my children. I want a wife to keep track of the children's doctor and dentist appointments. And to keep track of mine, too. I want a wife to make sure that my children eat properly and are kept clean. I want a wife who will wash the children's clothes and keep them mended. I want a wife who is a good nurturant attendant to my children, who arranges for their schooling, makes sure they have an adequate social life with their peers, takes them to the park, the zoo, etc. I want a wife who takes care of the children when they are sick, a wife who arranges to be around when the children need special care, because, of course, I cannot miss classes at school. My wife must arrange to lose time at work and not lose the job. It may mean a small cut in my wife's income from time to time, but I guess I can tolerate that. Needless to say, my wife will arrange and pay for the care of the children while my wife is working.

I want a wife who will take care of *my* physical needs. I want a wife  4
who will keep the house clean. A wife who will pick up after me. I
want a wife who will keep my clothes clean, ironed, mended, replaced
when need be, and who will see to it that my personal things are kept
in their proper place so that I can find what I need the minute I need
it. I want a wife who cooks the meals, a wife who is a *good* cook. I want
a wife who will plan the menus, do the necessary shopping, prepare
the meals, serve them pleasantly, and then do the cleaning up while I
do my studying. I want a wife who will care for me when I am sick
and sympathize with my pain and loss of time from school. I want a
wife to go along when our family takes a vacation so that someone can
continue to care for me and my children when I need a rest and change
of scene.

I want a wife who will not bother me with rambling complaints  5
about a wife's duties. But I want a wife who will listen to me when I
feel the need to explain a rather difficult point I have come across in
my course of studies. And I want a wife who will type my papers for
me when I have written them.

I want a wife who will take care of the details of my social life. When  6
my wife and I are invited out by my friends, I want a wife who will
take care of the babysitting arrangements. When I meet people at
school that I like and want to entertain, I want a wife who will have
the house clean, prepare a special meal, serve it to me and my friends,
and not interrupt when I talk about the things that interest me and my
friends. I want a wife who will have arranged that the children are fed
and ready for bed before my guests arrive so that the children do not
bother us. I want a wife who takes care of the needs of my guests so
that they feel comfortable, who makes sure that they have an ashtray,
that they are passed the hors d'oeuvres, that they are offered a second
helping of the food, that their wine glasses are replenished when
necessary, that their coffee is served to them as they like it.

And I want a wife who knows that sometimes I need a night out by  7
myself.

I want a wife who is sensitive to my sexual needs, a wife who makes  8
love passionately and eagerly when I feel like it, a wife who makes
sure that I am satisfied. And, of course, I want a wife who will not
demand sexual attention when I am not in the mood for it. I want a
wife who assumes the complete responsibility for birth control, because I do not want more children. I want a wife who will remain

sexually faithful to me so that I do not have to clutter up my intellectual life with jealousies. And I want a wife who understands that *my* sexual needs may entail more than strict adherence to monogamy. I must, after all, be able to relate to people as fully as possible.

If, by chance, I find another person more suitable as a wife than the  9 wife I already have, I want the liberty to replace my present wife with another one. Naturally, I will expect a fresh, new life; my wife will take the children and be solely responsible for them so that I am left free.

When I am through with school and have a job, I want my wife to  10 quit working and remain at home so that my wife can more fully and completely take care of a wife's duties.

My God, who *wouldn't* want a wife?  11

## VOCABULARY

nurturant (3)                entail (8)                adherence (8)
replenished (6)

## THE FACTS

1. According to Syfers, what dual role does a wife play in the family?
2. What physical needs of the husband does the wife take care of?
3. What does Syfers say about the sexual expectations and behavior of husbands?
4. According to the author, what details of a husband's social life are wives responsible for?

## THE STRATEGIES

1. What part does hyperbole or exaggeration play in this essay?
2. How would you characterize the tone of this essay?
3. What pronoun does the author use to refer to a "wife"? Why?
4. How and where does the author use italics in this essay? To what effect?

## THE ISSUES

1. Do you think Syfers has fairly characterized the expectations men have of their wives, or has she grossly exaggerated?
2. Syfers's article was first published in 1970 and has since then been hailed as a classic manifesto of the feminist movement. Do you think her criticisms still apply today, or have things between men and women changed so much that they are now dated?

3. Would you want a spouse, male or female, as obliging and eager to please as the one Syfers parodies in her essay? Why or why not?
4. What qualities and characteristics would you expect to find in the perfect spouse?

### SUGGESTIONS FOR WRITING

1. Write a similar essay, from a man's point of view, about wanting a husband.
2. Write a serious essay describing your ideal mate.
3. Write an essay telling why you would not want a wife like the one Syfers has described.

## CHAPTER WRITING ASSIGNMENTS

1. Write a well-organized essay revealing the methods you use to impose order and structure on your daily life.
2. After looking up biographical information on Shakespeare, write a brief, chronologically organized essay on his life.

# 5
# DEVELOPING PARAGRAPHS

## INTRODUCTION: WRITING PARAGRAPHS

Imagine a book without paragraphs. Imagine pages and pages of prose with no visual breaks to mark new ideas, no familiar indentation found in present books. Such a book would strike us as hideous to read and difficult to get through, its ideas buried in a jungle of words to be dug out only with the most persistent effort. There are a few such books around, but thankfully they do not sell well enough to be assigned as college texts. And so we are spared grappling with them.

The paragraph is an idea whose time came almost with the dawn of writing. As Richard Weaver tells us in his essay, paragraphs were once identified with marginal marks inserted by medieval scribes who saw the usefulness of notifying the reader of the appearance of a new idea or a new twist on an old one. Since then the familiar indentation has replaced the marginal mark, and paragraphs are everywhere to be found as staple divisions of the written word.

Master the paragraph, learn to write it with style and grace and dash, and you have mastered a unit of prose rivaled in popularity only by the sentence. Although a difficult medium for many student writers, the paragraph and its writing improve with practice. Once you have written a few hundred paragraphs for teachers of various disciplines, the form will become nearly second nature to you. For there is a rhythm of the paragraph that must be learned as well as a sixth sense for inserting transitions and specific details in the right place. But these are skills that ripen with practice.

The materials in this chapter are a varied lot. First is an article by A. M. Tibbetts and Charlene Tibbetts that explains the promise paragraph writers implicitly make to readers. Then Richard Weaver gives us a glimpse into the history and evolution of the paragraph as a literary form. Following these two articles are paragraphs that demonstrate the versatility and subtlety of the form.

The chapter ends with a discussion of the polarizing issue of AIDS and how society ought to react to this latest epidemic. We listen to the words of a man dying of AIDS, to the misgivings of bewildered singles who worry how to tell the healthy partner from the infected, to the opinion of a psychiatrist-turned-columnist who questions why we are spending such massive sums on researching a disease whose scope is limited and whose prevention is certain if safe-sex practices are followed. More questions are raised by this debate than can be presently answered, underscoring again that ours is a complex, enigmatic world.

=========== •• *ADVICE* ••===========

A. M. Tibbetts and Charlene Tibbetts

——• **WRITING SUCCESSFUL PARAGRAPHS** •——

*Arnold M. Tibbetts (b. 1927) has taught English at the University of Iowa, Western Illinois University, Vanderbilt University, and the University of Illinois, Urbana. His wife, Charlene Tibbets (b. 1921), is professor of English at the University of Illinois, Urbana. The Tibbettses are coauthors of* Strategies of Rhetoric *(1969), from which this excerpt was taken.*

*The proverbial warning "Don't promise more than you can give" applies to writing as well as to everyday life. The basis of a good paragraph, say the authors, is a promise that is made in the topic sentence and then carried out in the specific detail. In this excerpt, the authors demonstrate with examples how to make and keep your "paragraph promises."*

A paragraph is a collection of sentences that helps you fulfill your thesis (theme promise). Itself a small "theme," a paragraph should be clearly written and specific; and it should not wander or make irrelevant remarks. Each paragraph should be related in some way to the theme promise. Here are suggestions for writing successful paragraphs:

1. *Get to the point of your paragraph quickly and specifically.*

Don't waste time or words in stating your paragraph promise. Consider this good example of getting to the point—the writer is explaining the ancient Romans' technique for conquering their world:

> The technique of expansion was simple. *Divide et impera* [divide and conquer]: enter into solemn treaty with a neighbouring country, foment internal disorder, intervene in support of the weaker side on the pretense that Roman honour was involved, replace the legitimate ruler with a puppet, giving him the status of a subject ally; later, goad him into rebellion, seize and sack the country, burn down the temples, and carry off the captive gods to adorn a triumph. Conquered territories were placed under the control of a provincial governor-general, an ex-commander-in-chief who garrisoned it, levied taxes, set up courts of

summary justice, and linked the new frontiers with the old by so-called Roman roads—usually built by Greek engineers and native forced labour. Established social and religious practices were permitted so long as they did not threaten Roman administration or offend against the broad-minded Roman standards of good taste. The new province presently became a springboard for further aggression.—Robert Graves, "It Was a Stable World"

Graves makes his promise in the first nine words, in which he mentions the "simple" technique the Romans had for "dividing" and "conquering" in order to expand their empire. Suppose Graves had started his paragraph with these words: 3

> The technique of expansion was interesting. It was based upon a theory about human nature that the Romans practically invented. This theory had to do with how people reacted to certain political and military devices which . . .

Do you see what is wrong? Since the beginning sentences are so vague, the paragraph never gets going. The writer can't fulfill a promise because he hasn't made one. Another example of a poor paragraph beginning: 4

> The first step involves part of the golf club head. The club head has removable parts, some of which are metal. You must consider these parts when deciding how to repair the club.

Specify the beginning of this paragraph and get to the point quicker: 5

> Your first step in repairing the club head is to remove the metal plate held on by Phillips screws.

This solid, specific paragraph beginning gives your reader a clear promise which you can fulfill easily without wasting words. (Observe, by the way, that specifying a writer's stance—as we did in the last example—can help you write clearer paragraph beginnings.) 6

2. *Fulfill your reader's expectation established by the paragraph promise.*

Do this with specific details and examples—explain as fully as you can. Example: 7

> The next thing is to devise a form for your essay. This, which ought to be obvious, is not. I learned it for the first time from an experienced newspaperman. When I was at college I earned extra pocket- and book-money by writing several weekly columns for a newspaper. They were

usually topical, they were always carefully varied, they tried hard to be witty, and (an essential) they never missed a deadline. But once, when I brought in the product, a copy editor stopped me. He said, "Our readers seem to like your stuff all right; but we think it's a bit amateurish." With due humility I replied, "Well, I am an amateur. What should I do with it?" He said, "Your pieces are not coherent; they are only sentences and epigrams strung together; they look like a heap of clothespins in a basket. Every article ought to have a shape. Like this" (and he drew a big letter S on his pad) "or this" (he drew a descending line which turned abruptly upward again) "or this" (and he sketched a solid central core with five or six lines pushing outward from it) "or even this" (and he outlined two big arrows coming into collision). I never saw the man again, but I have never ceased to be grateful to him for his wisdom and for his kindness. Every essay must have a shape. You can ask a question in the first paragraph, discussing several different answers to it till you reach one you think is convincing. You can give a curious fact and offer an explanation of it: a man's character (as Hazlitt did with his fives champion), a building, a book, a striking adventure, a peculiar custom. There are many other shapes which essays can take; but the principle laid down by the copy editor was right. Before you start you must have a form in your mind; and it ought to be a form felt in paragraphs or sections, not in words or sentences—so that, if necessary, you could summarize each paragraph in a single line and put the entire essay on a postcard.—Gilbert Highet, "How to Write an Essay"

Highet makes a promise in the first three sentences, and in the   8
remaining sentences he specifically fulfills it.

### 3. *Avoid fragmentary paragraphs.*

A fragmentary paragraph does not develop its topic or fulfill its   9
promise. A series of fragmentary paragraphs jumps from idea to idea
in a jerky and unconvincing fashion:

My freshman rhetoric class is similar in some ways to my senior English class in high school, but it is also very different.

In my English class we usually had daily homework assignments that were discussed during the class period. If we were studying grammar, the assignments were to correct grammatical errors in the text. If we were studying literature, we were supposed to read the material and understand its ideas.

In rhetoric class, we do basically the same things, except that in the readings we are assigned, we look much deeper into the purpose of the author.

In my English class . . .

Fragmentary paragraphs are often the result of a weak writer's    10
stance.

4. *Avoid irrelevancies in your paragraphs.*

The italicized sentence does not fit the development of this para-    11
graph:

> We need a better working atmosphere at Restik Tool Company. The
> workers must feel that they are a working team instead of just individ-
> uals. If the men felt they were part of a team, they would not misuse the
> special machine tools, which now need to be resharpened twice as often
> as they used to be. *Management's attitude toward the union could be improved
> too.* The team effort is also being damaged by introduction of new prod-
> ucts before their bugs have been worked out. Just when the men are
> getting used to one routine, a new one is installed, and their carefully
> created team effort is seriously damaged.

As with the fragmentary paragraph, the problem of irrelevancies in    12
a paragraph is often the result of a vague writer's stance. The paragraph above does not seem to be written for any particular reader.

### *VOCABULARY*

foment (2)                    topical (7)                    epigrams (7)

# ═══════ •• *DISCUSSION* •• ═══════

### Richard M. Weaver

# ────── • THE FUNCTION OF THE • ──────
# PARAGRAPH

*Richard M. Weaver (1910–1973) was, for many years, a professor of English at
the University of Chicago. He wrote several books on rhetoric, including* A
Concise Handbook of English *(1968) and* A Rhetoric and Handbook
*(1967).*

*What follows gives a brief history of the paragraph and explains its function as a visual aid that signals the beginning of a new thought.*

The mind naturally looks for lines of division in anything it is considering. By these it is enabled to take in, or understand, because understanding is largely a matter of perceiving parts and their relationships. The paragraph is a kind of division, and paragraphing is a way of separating out the parts of a composition. Standing between the sentence as a unit at one end of the scale and the section or chapter at the other, the paragraph has the useful role of organizing our thoughts into groups of intermediate size.     1

The usefulness of a visual aid to division was recognized long before paragraphs were set off as they are today. In medieval manuscripts, which do not have the sort of indentation that we employ now, a symbol was written in the margin to mark a turn in the thought; and the word "paragraph" means "something written beside." Where the medieval scribe used a symbol, we use indentation. But the purpose served is the same, and that is to advise the reader that a new set of thoughts is beginning.     2

A paragraph may therefore be understood as a visible division of the subject matter. The division is initially a convenience to the reader, as it prepares him to turn his attention to something new. But beyond this, most paragraphs have an internal unity, and they can be analyzed as compositions in miniature.     3

Occasionally one finds paragraphs which are compositions in the sense that they are not parts of a larger piece of writing. These occur in the form of single-paragraph statements, themes, and even stories, which are complete and which are not related to anything outside themselves. They will naturally reflect the rules of good composition if they are successful writing. They will have unity, coherence, and emphasis. They will be about something; they will make a progression, and they will have a major point.     4

Substantially the same may be said about paragraphs which are parts of a composition. They will have a relative self-containment, or basic unity and coherence, and they will emphasize some point or idea. Therefore what we have said about the composition in its entirety may be said with almost equal application of single paragraphs within the larger piece. Especially is it true that the subject must be reasonably     5 definite and that the development must follow some plan, although the possible plans of development are various.

The point to be carried in mind is that the relative independence of the paragraph rests upon something. The paragraph is not a device marked off at mechanical intervals simply because it is felt that the reader needs a change. He does need a change, but the place of the change must be related to the course of the thought. Where that changes significantly, a new paragraph begins. It is a signal that something else is starting. This may be a different phase of the subject, an illustration, a qualification, a change of scale, or any one of a large number of things which can mark the course of systematic thinking about a subject. 6

## VOCABULARY

intermediate (1)          miniature (3)                systematic (6)
scribe (2)                self-containment (5)

## THE FACTS

1. Weaver describes the paragraph as an intermediary. Between what two parts does it stand?
2. What is the root meaning of the word "paragraph"?
3. What does Weaver mean when he calls the paragraph a composition in miniature?
4. The paragraph does not occur at regular intervals. When does it occur?
5. What does Weaver consider the requirements for a good paragraph?

## THE STRATEGIES

1. Does Weaver follow his own rule about when paragraphs should occur? See the last half of paragraph 6.
2. In paragraph 4, through what means is coherence achieved?
3. What is the topic sentence of paragraph 6?

## THE ISSUES

1. How do the paragraphs used by newspapers and popular magazines differ from those used in academic writing?
2. What do you find to be most difficult about writing coherent and complete paragraphs?

3. Aside from paragraphs, what other visual aids do you find useful in reading and understanding a written work?

# •• *EXAMPLES* ••

## *Paragraphs with the Topic Sentence at the Beginning*

### Edith Hamilton

## • *from* THE LESSONS OF THE PAST •

*Edith Hamilton (1867–1963) was an American classicist, educator, and writer. Her writing career began after retirement, and at the age of eighty she started giving public addresses and lectures. When she was ninety, she was made an honorary citizen of Greece. Among her books are* The Greek Way *(1942),* The Roman Way *(1932), and* Witness to the Truth: Christ and His Interpreters *(1948).*

Basic to all the Greek achievement was freedom. The Athenians were the only free people in the world. In the great empires of antiquity—Egypt, Babylon, Assyria, Persia—splendid though they were, with riches beyond reckoning and immense power, freedom was unknown. The idea of it never dawned in any of them. It was born in Greece, a poor little country, but with it able to remain unconquered no matter what manpower and what wealth were arrayed against her. At Marathon and at Salamis overwhelming numbers of Persians had been defeated by small Greek forces. It had been proved that one free man was superior to many submissively obedient subjects of a tyrant. Athens was the leader in that amazing victory, and to the Athenians freedom was their dearest possession. Demosthenes said that they would not think it worth their while to live if they could not do so as free men, and years later a great teacher said, "Athenians, if you deprive them of their liberty, will die."

## VOCABULARY

| reckoning | Salamis | Demosthenes |
| arrayed | submissively | |
| Marathon | tyrant | |

## THE FACTS

1. Were you convinced of the truth of the topic sentence after reading the paragraph? If so, what convinced you?
2. In what way are free men superior to those who are submissively obedient to a tyrant?

## THE STRATEGIES

1. What is the topic sentence of the paragraph?
2. Who is the "great teacher" alluded to?

## THE ISSUES

1. Hamilton writes that freedom was basic to the Greek achievement. What does freedom mean to you in a political context?
2. According to Hamilton, it has been proved that one free man is superior to many submissively obedient subjects. Why do you think this is so?

**William Somerset Maugham**

## • PAIN •

*English author William Somerset Maugham (1874–1965) wrote short stories, novels, plays, and books of criticism. His successful plays include* The Circle *(1921),* Our Betters *(1923), and* The Constant Wife *(1927). His most famous novel is his semiautobiographical account of a young physician with a clubfoot,* Of Human Bondage *(1919).*

No more stupid apology for pain has ever been devised than that it elevates. It is an explanation due to the necessity of justifying pain from the Christian point of view. Pain is nothing more than the signal given by the nerves that the organism is in circumstances hurtful to it; it would be as reasonable to assert that a danger signal elevates a train.

But one would have thought that the ordinary observation of life was enough to show that in the great majority of cases, pain, far from refining, has an effect which is merely brutalising. An example in point is the case of hospital in-patients: physical pain makes them self-absorbed, selfish, querulous, impatient, unjust and greedy; I could name a score of petty vices that it generates, but not one virtue. Poverty also is pain. I have known well men who suffered from that grinding agony of poverty which befalls persons who have to live among those richer than themselves; it makes them grasping and mean, dishonest and untruthful. It teaches them all sorts of detestable tricks. With moderate means they would have been honourable men, but ground down by poverty they have lost all sense of decency.

## VOCABULARY

querulous

## THE FACTS

1. According to Maugham, why do some people think it necessary to justify pain?
2. What is Maugham's view of pain?
3. Aside from the pain of physical illness, what other cause of pain is there?

## THE STRATEGIES

1. What analogy does Maugham use in refuting the view that pain elevates?
2. What example does Maugham give to support his view of pain?
3. The paragraph discusses two causes of pain. What transitional word does Maugham use to move the discussion from the one cause to the other?

## THE ISSUES

1. Maugham says that he cannot name a single virtue that pain produces. What virtue is pain generally thought to produce?
2. What is the distinction between pain and suffering?
3. Maugham writes that to say pain elevates is as reasonable as asserting that "a danger signal elevates a train." What is fundamentally false about this analogy?

Chief Joseph of the Nez Percé

## ———— • I AM TIRED OF FIGHTING • ————
### (Surrender Speech)

*Chief Joseph (1840?–1904) was the leader of the Nez Percé tribe of Sahaptin Indians, who lived along the Snake River in Idaho and Oregon. In 1877, under Chief Joseph, the tribe fought the United States government in a desperate attempt to preserve their land. Eventually, the Indians lost their struggle and were forced to retreat to the border of Canada.*

I am tired of fighting. Our chiefs are killed. Looking Glass is dead. Toohulsote is dead. The old men are all dead. It is the young men who say no and yes. He who led the young men is dead. It is cold and we have no blankets. The little children are freezing to death. My people, some of them, have run away to the hills and have no blankets, no food. No one knows where they are—perhaps they are freezing to death. I want to have time to look for my children and see how many of them I can find. Maybe I shall find them among the dead. Hear me, my chiefs, I am tired. My heart is sad and sick. From where the sun stands I will fight no more forever.

### THE FACTS

1. According to this speech, what nonmilitary factor contributed most to the decision of Chief Joseph to surrender?
2. Who was left among the Nez Percé to say no and yes?

### THE STRATEGIES

1. On what word do most of the sentences of this paragraph end? What is the effect of this repeated ending?
2. How would you characterize the language used in this speech? Formal? Informal? Colloquial? What effect do you think the speaker achieves in his diction?
3. What are some examples of poetic constructions that add to the stateliness and dignity of this speech? Translate them literally and say what is lost in the translation.

## THE ISSUES

1. How are Indians portrayed in popular literature and films? How has this portrayal affected your impression of them?
2. Historians agree that the Indians got short shrift at the hands of the encroaching white settlers. What responsibility, if any, do the descendants of the victors have to the descendants of the vanquished Indians?


### Will Durant

# • THE POLITICAL CAUSES OF •
# THE DECAY OF ROME

*Will Durant (1885–1981) was an American historian and essayist. His book* The Story of Philosophy *(1926), an immediate best seller, blazed a trail for popularized history. Later, in collaboration with his wife, Ariel, he completed ten volumes of* The Story of Civilization *(1935–1967).*

*In this tightly organized, detailed paragraph, Durant discusses some of the reasons for the fall of Rome.*

The political causes of decay were rooted in one fact—that increasing despotism destroyed the citizen's civic sense and dried up statesmanship at its source. Powerless to express his political will except by violence, the Roman lost interest in government and became absorbed in his business, his amusements, his legion, or his individual salvation. Patriotism and the pagan religion had been bound together, and now together decayed. The Senate, losing ever more of its power and prestige after Pertinax, relapsed into indolence, subservience, or venality; and the last barrier fell that might have saved the state from militarism and anarchy. Local governments, overrun by imperial *correctores** and *exactores,*[†] no longer attracted first-rate men. The responsibility of municipal officials for the tax quotas of their areas, the rising expense of their unpaid honors, the fees, liturgies, benefactions, and games expected of them, the dangers incident to invasion and class war, led to a flight from office corresponding to the flight from taxes,

---

*Improvers (bureaucrats).—Ed.

[†]Tax collectors, superintendents.—Ed.

factories, and farms. Men deliberately made themselves ineligible by debasing their social category; some fled to other towns; some became farmers, some monks. In 313 Constantine extended to the Christian clergy that exemption from municipal office, and from several taxes, which pagan priests had traditionally enjoyed; the Church was soon swamped with candidates for ordination, and cities complained of losses in revenue and senators; in the end Constantine was compelled to rule that no man eligible for municipal position should be admitted to the priesthood. The imperial police pursued fugitives from political honors as it hunted evaders of taxes or conscription; it brought them back to the cities and forced them to serve; finally it decreed that a son must inherit the social status of his father, and must accept election if eligible to it by his rank. A serfdom of office rounded out the prison of economic caste.

## VOCABULARY

| | | |
|---|---|---|
| despotism | anarchy | ordination |
| indolence | liturgies | conscription |
| subservience | benefactions | serfdom |
| venality | debasing | |

## THE FACTS

1. The author writes that the political causes of decay were rooted in one fact. What was this fact?
2. Why did local governments no longer attract first-rate men?
3. What exemption did Constantine grant in 313?

## THE STRATEGIES

1. What is the topic sentence of this paragraph?
2. What purpose does the final sentence in the paragraph serve?

## THE ISSUES

1. Durant writes that statesmanship was dried up at its source because despotism destroyed the Roman citizen's civic sense. What disincentives against serving in government exist in our own society?
2. Does our own government, in your opinion, attract first-rate candidates for service? Justify your answer.

*Paragraphs with the Topic Sentence at the End*

W. T. Stace

——————— • **MAN AGAINST DARKNESS** • ———————

*Walter Terrence Stace (1886–1967) was an English naturalist and philosopher known for his ability to translate complex theories into terms that appealed to a general reader. An authority on Hegel, Stace was the author of numerous books, among them* A Critical History of Greek Philosophy *(1920) and* The Philosophy of Hegel *(1924).*

The picture of meaningless world, and a meaningless human life, is, I think, the basic theme of much modern art and literature. Certainly it is the basic theme of modern philosophy. According to the most characteristic philosophies of the modern period from Hume in the eighteenth century to the so-called positivists of today, the world is just what it is, and that is the end of all inquiry. There is no reason for its being what it is. Everything might just as well have been quite different, and there would have been no reason for that either. When you have stated what things are, what things the world contains, there is nothing more which could be said, even by an omniscient being. To ask any question about why things are thus, or what purpose their being so serves, is to ask a senseless question, because they serve no purpose at all. For instance, there is for modern philosophy no such thing as the ancient problem of evil. For this once famous question pre-supposes that pain and misery, though they seem so inexplicable and irrational to us, must ultimately subserve some rational purpose, must have their places in the cosmic plan. But this is nonsense. There is no such overruling rationality in the universe. Belief in the ultimate irrationality of everything is the quintessence of what is called the modern mind.

## *VOCABULARY*

positivists                     subserve                     quintessence
omniscient

## THE FACTS

1. What is the basic theme of much modern art and literature?
2. How do the most characteristic philosophies of the modern era view the world?
3. Why is there in modern philosophy no such thing as the ancient problem of evil?

## THE STRATEGIES

1. Stace is known for expressing complex ideas with clarity. In this example, how does he make clear the complex views of modern philosophy?
2. From whose point of view is this paragraph mainly written? How can you tell?
3. "Begging the question" is the logical name given to an argument that assumes as proved the very thing that is in dispute. Is the attitude of modern philosophy toward evil an example of begging the question? Why, or why not?

## THE ISSUES

1. What is your opinion of modern philosophy, as Stace summarizes it, that ascribes everything to irrationality? How does this philosophy square with your own beliefs?
2. What is the ancient problem of evil?
3. What imaginable purpose can evil possibly serve? If evil did not exist, would it have to be invented?

### Mark Van Doren

## •  WHAT IS A POET?  •

*Mark Van Doren (1894–1973), American poet and critic, was born in Illinois and educated at Columbia University, where he later won renown as a dedicated teacher. He was the author of many books, among them* American and British Literature since 1890 *(1939, written with his brother Carl);* Collected Poems, 1922–1938 *(1939, Pulitzer Prize); and* The Last Days of Lincoln *(1959).*

Here is the figure we have set up. A pale, lost man with long, soft hair. Tapering fingers at the ends of furtively fluttering arms. An air of abstraction in the delicate face, but more often a look of shy pain as some aspect of reality—a real man or woman, a grocer's bill, a train, a load of bricks, a newspaper, a noise from the street—makes itself manifest. He is generally incompetent. He cannot find his way in a city, he forgets where he is going, he has no aptitude for business, he is childishly gullible and so the prey of human sharks, he cares nothing for money, he is probably poor, he will sacrifice his welfare for a whim, he stops to pet homeless cats, he is especially knowing where children are concerned (being a child himself), he sighs, he sleeps, he wakes to sigh again. The one great assumption from which the foregoing portrait is drawn is an assumption which thousands of otherwise intelligent citizens go on. It is the assumption that the poet is more sensitive than any other kind of man, that he feels more than the rest of us and is more definitely the victim of his feeling.

## VOCABULARY

gullible

## THE FACTS

1. What do we expect a poet to look like?
2. What kind of personality do we expect a poet to have?
3. What one great assumption do we make about poets?

## THE STRATEGIES

1. What is Van Doren attempting to do in this paragraph? What single word could you use to describe the type of portrait he is sketching?
2. Van Doren writes: "A pale, lost man with long, soft hair. Tapering fingers at the ends of furtively fluttering arms." Grammatically, what do these two assertions have in common? What effect do they contribute to the description?
3. A *catalogue* is a list of things or attributes. Where in this paragraph does the author obviously use a catalogue?

## THE ISSUES

1. Given the characteristics traditionally identified as masculine and feminine, which would you expect a poet to be—more masculine than feminine, or vice versa? Why?
2. What, in your mind, is a poet? Does your definition of a poet differ substantially from the description given by Van Doren? In what way?
3. Of what use is poetry in the modern world?

Lewis Thomas, M.D.

## • ON DISEASE •

*Lewis Thomas (b. 1913) was born in New York and educated at Princeton and Harvard. Dr. Thomas is president of the Memorial Sloan-Kettering Cancer Center in New York and an essayist who has been praised for his lucid style. His essays have been published in three collections,* The Lives of a Cell *(1974, National Book Award),* The Medusa and the Snail *(1979), and* Late Night Thoughts on Listening to Mahler's Ninth Symphony *(1983).*

We were all reassured, when the first moon landing was ready to be made, that the greatest precautions would be taken to protect the life of the earth, especially human life, against infection by whatever there might be alive on the moon. And, in fact, the elaborate ceremony of lunar asepsis was performed after each of the early landings; the voyagers were masked and kept behind plate glass, quarantined away from contact with the earth until it was a certainty that we wouldn't catch something from them. The idea that germs are all around us, trying to get at us, to devour and destroy us, is so firmly rooted in modern consciousness that it made sense to think that strange germs, from the moon, would be even scarier and harder to handle.

### VOCABULARY

asepsis                           quarantined

### THE FACTS

1. What were we all reassured about before the first moon landing was made?
2. What idea about germs is firmly rooted in our consciousness?

### THE STRATEGIES

1. What specific detail does the author use to support his assertion that an elaborate ceremony of asepsis was performed after each of the lunar landings?
2. Assuming that the paragraph is representative of the style of the whole essay, what kind of audience do you think the essay was orginally written for?

## THE ISSUES

1. Do you trust medical doctors to the extent that you implicitly follow their advice? Why or why not?
2. Which disease do you fear the most? Why?

### Robert Frost

# • THE FLOOD •

*Robert Frost (1874–1963) was a lecturer, poet, and teacher. When he was nine-teen and working in a mill in Lawrence, Massachusetts, the* Independent *accepted and published "My Butterfly, An Elegy"—the poem that began Frost's career as one of America's great poets. Rugged New England farm life was the inspiration for many of his poems.*

Blood has been harder to dam back than water.
Just when we think we have it impounded safe
Behind new barrier walls (and let it chafe!),
It breaks away in some new kind of slaughter.
We choose to say it is let loose by the devil;                    5
But power of blood itself releases blood.
It goes by might of being such a flood
Held high at so unnatural a level.
It will have outlet, brave and not so brave.
Weapons of war and implements of peace                           10
Are but the points at which it finds release.
And now it is once more the tidal wave
That when it has swept by leaves summits stained.
Oh, blood will out. It cannot be contained.

## VOCABULARY

impounded                            chafe

## THE FACTS

1. What interpretation can be given to Frost's mention of a flood of blood?
2. What is meant by the statement "power of blood itself releases blood"?

3. What is the "tidal wave" Frost refers to? Why does it leave summits stained?

## THE STRATEGIES

1. In poetry, the stanza serves a similar purpose as the paragraph. That being the case, what do you consider the topic sentence of this poem? Is it stated more than once?
2. Both water and blood are mentioned in this poem. Which of these words is used literally and which symbolically?

## THE ISSUES

1. What is the theme of this poem?
2. In writing about blood Frost says: ". . . implements of peace / Are but the points at which it finds release." What can this line possibly mean?

# ═══ •• ISSUE FOR CRITICAL •• ═══
# THINKING
## AIDS

AIDS is an acronym for acquired immune deficiency syndrome, a disease first noticed by doctors among homosexual men in the late 1970s. Since then it has been linked to a retrovirus identified by American researchers as HTLV-3 and by French researchers as LAV. Over twenty-three thousand people have died from the disease, which has a nearly one hundred percent mortality rate. Some estimates say that more than one and a half million people may already have the virus, with the preponderant majority of cases occurring among male homosexuals and intravenous drug users. The disease is difficult for epidemiologists to track because infection progresses slowly with few or no symptoms in the initial stages, and incubation can take as long as seven or more years after exposure. Among homosexual men the primary means of transmission is through anal intercourse; among drug users, the disease is spread by sharing contaminated needles.

What should we do about AIDS? Find a cure, one would think. But the issue is not that clear-cut or simple. First, a cure has proven elusive. The retrovirus is submicroscopic, mutates often, and is difficult to combat medically. Second, the disease competes for research funds against even more lethal killers to which the entire population is at risk—cancer and heart disease are among the primary examples. Complicating the problem is the identification of AIDS in the public's consciousness as a lifestyle disease, and this association of AIDS with minority groups some find abhorrent has transformed the national debate about the disease into an argument over morality. Gay-rights activists claim that the government has been deliberately dilatory in funding research on AIDS precisely because it strikes mainly homosexuals.

The three writers who tackle this issue approach the subject from exotically different perspectives. Vincent Coppola focuses on the epidemic of fear that AIDS has sparked among heterosexuals—ironically, the very group least at risk for the disease. Hank Koehn, now deceased as a result of AIDS, tells us graphically what it is like to be in the grips of the disease. Charles Krauthammer argues that AIDS has already drained too much of the national resources, given its limited effect and preventable nature.

As usual, these contending opinions raise more questions than they answer. Perhaps the profoundest issue they raise is not what we should do about AIDS, but what is the nature and extent of our compassion and love for those who have been stricken by this killing epidemic.

### Vincent Coppola

## •  THE PARTY'S OVER  •

*Vincent Coppola (b. 1947) was born in New York and educated at City College of New York and Columbia University (M.A., 1977). A senior writer for* Atlanta Magazine *since July 1987, he was formerly a writer with* Newsweek. *He has won a* Page One *award from the Newspaper Guild for science reporting.*

*The main article is followed by its two short companion pieces, "The Testing Dilemma" and "Troubled Voices," both by Coppola.*

They sat there, two sultry orchids in the perfumed hothouse that is    1
élan* on a busy night. Donna, auburn-haired and full of figure, wore a clingy, purple dress; she had lived in New York and New Orleans before moving to Atlanta. Cindy was every Northern boy's dream of a Southern girl, sparkly blue eyes and feathered blond hair, a cheerleader's body sheathed in a tight turquoise dress set off by matching spike-heeled shoes. They were savvy and sassy, career-oriented, open and

---

*A trendy nightclub in an affluent Atlanta suburb.—Ed.

funny, the kind of women married guys convince themselves don't exist—and single guys hesitate to approach. Women who make otherwise sane and settled men want to send the wife and kids off to visit her folks in Knoxville.

Both were recently divorced; neither was involved in a relationship. Work filled their days, but loneliness nibbled at the edges of their lives. They had come, they said, to dance and have a few drinks, to ease the tensions of the job and the burdens of single parenthood. They had come, driven like so many of us, in the hope of meeting that special someone. That hope seemed more distant and fragile than ever. There was hesitation in their eyes and a nervousness behind their smiles. They looked past the schools of slick-haired and Armani-attired predators who circled their table looking for an opening.  2

They were frightened to death of AIDS.  3

The fear might be groundless—the deadly epidemic does not appear to be moving rapidly into the general population—but it is real. It is threatening the nonstop party that has been underway in Atlanta for the past 20 years. The lines may be as long as ever outside the Buckhead* bars, and the after-hours action as frantic, but the last thought after the last drink on the couch is no longer, "Will he respect me in the morning?"  4

"In the past, your pride was hurt," says Donna. "Now you can die. . . . It's not that my morality has changed. My dread of the *A-word* has increased."  5

AIDS—acquired immune deficiency syndrome—is a disease that reaches beyond its victims. It has created a new medical category, the worried well, who suffer from a new syndrome: 'FRAIDS. They're everywhere in Atlanta: pinstriped professionals visiting doctors and therapists; suddenly meek good ol' boys calling anonymously to the AIDS hotline; guilt-driven husbands and unfaithful wives surreptitiously visiting clinics to be tested for the virus.  6

Donna, 39, is worried about "a mistake I may have made three years ago." A bisexual lover? An intravenous drug user? She won't explain. "You used to see those signs—SPEED KILLS," she says reaching for her drink. "Now it's SEX KILLS." Cindy, 26, is concerned about men she hasn't yet met. "How can you even tell if a guy's been a homosexual?" she asks bleakly.  7

---

*A Midtown suburb of affluent homes and expensive restaurants and bars.—Ed.

For that matter, how can you tell if he's been with a woman who's  8
been with a bisexual infected with the virus? Of if that perky sorority
sister has slept with a fraternity brother who had sex with an infected
prostitute the last time Georgia played in the Sugar Bowl? The per-
mutations are endless and terrifying. When you go to bed with someone, say the experts, every sexual partner in that person's past is
climbing in with you.

Both women have drastically reduced their sexual contacts. "I was  9
much more willing to have brief encounters, brief friendships," says
Donna, a sales manager with a national corporation. She pauses. "Listen, most women don't want one night stands, but it often works out
that way." She has dated "at least 20" men in the past year and gone to
bed "with three or four." Cindy won't cite statistics; she's "dated a lot,
but only gone to bed with very, very few." Even those nag at her. "So
you date a guy for two months before going to bed with him. You let
feelings come into play. Then you do it and hope to God. . . . But
who's going to stop in a moment of passion and say 'Let's take a test'?"

"It does no good to ask these questions," agrees Donna. "A person's  10
sexual history is unknowable. Besides, how can you trust a man's
answers? . . . I personally would never go for a test. If I were positive,
it would signal the end of my life. I don't *think* I am, but who knows?
I'm getting older. Who needs this grief?"

"The sexual revolution got out of hand," says Cindy. "People screw-  11
ing whoever they wanted, whenever they wanted. There's nothing
wrong with sexuality, but it's wrong to pick up someone, screw them
and leave them somewhere." As she speaks, she is joined by George,
a bulky man in a shiny brown suit with matching tie and yellow pocket
handkerchief. George, who resembles the fighter Gerrie Coetzee,
whisks Cindy off to the dance floor. They return; he finds the conversation none-too-promising. He begins to murmur earnestly into Cindy's ear; the murmur quickly graduates to a nuzzle.

"Tell me," asks Donna with a laugh. "Does this look like a man who  12
is worried about AIDS?"

We are living in what will certainly be called the AIDS Era, as surely  13
as we lived through the Vietnam Era. (In a few years, the epidemic
will have claimed more lives than that unhappy war.) Like Vietnam,
AIDS is cutting across every segment of society. It is divisive and de-
structive and may be, ultimately, unbeatable. A disease has become
part of the national consciousness. Moralists debate its "meaning"

from the lecturn and pulpit. (Have you ever heard anyone trying to "justify" cancer?) AIDS is the subject of cocktail party concern and tabloid gossip. It has already taken its place beside nuclear war in the nightmares of our children. "I haven't heard an AIDS joke in a long time," says Emory student Christie Constantino. "AIDS will affect everyone in the long run. It already has—we're all worried about it."

AIDS has become more than a devastating disease caused by a mind-    14
less agent existing on the borderline between the animate and the inanimate, between life and non-life. AIDS *is* more, linking as it does, sex with painful death, pitting as it does, traditional morality against two decades of sexual and personal liberation. AIDS raises, as Georgia State University sociologist Jackie Boles puts it, that ultimately troubling question: "Did Mom and Dad really know what was best for us?"

According to a national survey conducted last summer by the *Los*    15
*Angeles Times*, nearly one in five Americans has radically changed his lifestyle (i.e. sexual behavior) because of fear of AIDS—a threefold increase since 1985. Most of the changes have been in the 18-to-24 age group, and among those who reported multiple sexual partners in the year preceding the poll. More than 10 percent of those surveyed said they had personally known someone who tested positive, contracted, or died from AIDS. The disease is now the second most-feared—after cancer—in the nation.

"Many of my patients are absolutely, astronomically frightened,"    16
says Dr. Steven Morganstern, a well-known Atlanta urologist. "AIDS is something they know I can't cure." But Morganstern's patients are typically not AIDS victims or risk group members. He's treating world-weary college students convinced that commonplace urinary tract infections are "something lethal." He's working with a 32-year-old banker, symptomatic, yet free of any infection, a victim of what Morganstern calls the "galloping guilts." And then there's the psychiatrist. "He comes in and says 'Steve, I trust you to the nth degree. I screwed this girl four months ago, and now I'm terrified. Please help me. Tell me what to do.' And this is from an M.D.! A psychiatrist!"

Morganstern is also seeing the darker side: gay patients who test    17
positive for HIV (human immunodeficiency virus, the agent that causes AIDS) "and continue to go out." He's convinced many people are indulging in reckless sexual behavior that will accelerate the spread of

AIDS into the general population. He mentions a man he's treating for genital warts (caused by human papilloma virus, which has been linked to cervical cancer in women). "This guy walks in and starts bragging about the chicks he's going to bed with. . . . 'This divorcée . . . this 23-year-old . . . this nurse.' I'm standing there amazed! He's a walking social indignity! He knows what he has, and he knows he's putting every one of those women at risk.

"Sex is an extremely strong human drive," Morganstern continues,    18 groping for an explanation. "Sometimes it overrides rational behavior." The doctor has put together a bit of safe sex dialogue he'd like incorporated into everyone's single's bar repertoire, a mantra to be endlessly repeated in the AIDS Era:

"I'm free of disease. Are you? I wouldn't want to transmit anything    19 to you. I know you wouldn't want to transmit anything to me. Have you used IV drugs? Have you engaged in bisexual or homosexual activity? Do you have herpes? Do you have syphilis? Do you have warts?"

"Forget being swept away," he mutters with the wisdom of a man    20 who has spent too many years looking directly at other people's mistakes and malfunctions. "When you meet someone in a bar and they want to go to bed with you, and you want to go to bed with them, remember, as fresh and exciting as that moment seems, it's happened before—to both of you."

Heterosexual victims—men and women infected through sexual    21 contact with someone with AIDS or at risk for the disease—account for about 4 percent of all cases. (In Georgia there have been just 18 of these cases.) The overwhelming majority have been black and Hispanic women living in the Northeast and Florida whose sex partners were drug abusers. Nationwide, more than 40,500 persons have contracted AIDS; more than 23,000 have died; 1.5 million more may be infected with the virus, their fate uncertain. Ninety percent of these have been gay or bisexual men or IV drug abusers. Hemophilia- and blood transfusion-associated cases make up 3 percent of the total; unknowns, patients for whom information is incomplete (due to death, refusal to be interviewed, etc.) make up the final 3 percent of all adult cases. "We're not seeing a dramatic shift in the kinds of cases," says Dr. Harold Jaffe, chief of AIDS epidemiology at the U.S. Centers for Disease Control in Atlanta.

In recent studies of heterosexuals seeking treatment at sexually    22
transmitted disease clinics, none of 300 surveyed in Seattle tested positive for the AIDS virus; in Denver only one of 1,000 had been exposed.
In Atlanta, only one of 92 prostitutes surveyed in a year-long study
was infected. "This suggests very, very low rates in the general population," says Jaffe.

Yet, the panic grows. Talk to any nurse in town about the fear on the    23
hospital wards. (The CDC recently reported three health care workers
had been infected, apparently by patients' blood coming in contact
with minor skin abrasions or acne.) AIDS can incubate for years; the
virus spreads silently without symptoms. By some estimates, heterosexuals will comprise 9 percent of the 270,000 AIDS cases predicted for
1991. No one knows how many seemingly healthy people are infected
with, or passing the virus to, others. And what can you say for sure
about that seemingly healthy person standing next to you at the bar,
or smiling at you across the crowded floor of the health club?

Harvey is convinced he's going to get AIDS. He's not gay or bisexual    24
and doesn't inject himself with illicit drugs. He is a construction
worker who believes—despite all his precautions—that infected vaginal secretions will penetrate his scraped and scratched hands and
perhaps he will die. His fear drove him to Atlanta's first safe sex party
for heterosexual males held last August. Harvey, a trim, dark-haired
man in his late 20s, wanted information on "hand condoms"—known
to the rest of the world as surgical gloves.

Safe sex parties—organized by AID Atanta, a nonprofit organization    25
that ministers to AIDS patients and others affected by the disease—
provide instruction and advice on how to avoid becoming infected or
passing the virus on to others. The mood may be light, but the message is blunt and deadly serious. Nearly 2,000 gay men in Atlanta have
attended these functions. (Estimates of AIDS virus infection in Atlanta's
gay community run as high as 30 percent.) In the last year, nervous
heterosexual women—mostly professionals in their 20s—have begun
to sign up. "The big fear among women," says Lynn Hampton, one of
the organizers, "is 'How do I suggest using a condom? He'll think I
think he's gay or I'm a slut.' Rather than suggesting, many are abstain-
ing from sex."

The condom is king in the AIDS Era—a must for all but the most    26
secure sexual partners. Atlanta pharmacies all report higher condom

sales, with young women increasingly making purchases. The big seller is the traditional latex condom ($4 to $7 a dozen), but the upscale crowd is opting for lambskin ($25 per dozen), clearly the BMW of prophylactics. "It's the folks on Habersham Road* that want the lamb-skins," says Steve Falkenhainer, manager of the King's pharmacy in Peachtree Battle shopping center.

At the safe sex party, a candy bowl contained condoms of various    27
textures and qualities (lubricated, ribbed, receptacled); later they were distributed as favors.

Harvey got to try on his hand condoms ("kinda kinky"), recom-    28
mended for those who practice "mutual masturbation." (The AIDS virus has been cultured from vaginal secretions and pre-ejaculatory fluids.) "In Atlanta, chances are you will never meet a woman who has AIDS," said Hampton, but no one seemed to hear. When one party goer offered statistics that suggested the incidence of AIDS virus infection among heterosexuals who are neither members nor the sex partners of high-risk groups is one per 100,000 or lower, he was accused of having a bad attitude.

"This is war," said Harvey. "When I go into battle, I go prepared."    29
In truth, Harvey had already surrendered. He later admitted he had given up sex entirely because of AIDS.

The real surprise at the party was David. He was tall and curly-    30
haired, a handsome, virile and sophisticated man, a lady-killer by anyone's measure. He announced he'd been tested for the AIDS virus and was negative. "Why were you tested?" someone asked. "I'm a practicing bisexual," he replied. The room fell silent. David was a living example of the bridge everyone is worried about, a pathway that could introduce AIDS into the heterosexual pool. In Minnesota, for example, one third of the AIDS cases have been bisexual men. At least two women in a Minneapolis swingers' club were infected by such men.

David is not the stereotypical bisexual—a male who marries and    31
raises a family because it is what society demands, but is sexually and emotionally attracted to men.

David loves women, and sleeps with them without telling them he    32
is bisexual.

---

*An affluent area.—Ed.

If AIDS does explode into the straight population, Atlanta may well be Ground Zero. Georgia is first nationwide in gonorrhea cases, fifth in the number of teen pregnancies. There are an estimated 3,000 drug addicts in Atlanta and a booming, convention-driven prostitute trade. Atlanta's whores may not yet be infected with the AIDS virus, but fully 50 percent of them admit to using IV drugs. One of them admitted to having 5,000 sexual contacts. On Cypress Street, feral packs of male hustlers—many of them drug users—service the furtive needs of bi-sexual men, some of whom return to prosperous suburbs to join wives and children at Little League games. Many of these drug abusing hustlers have girlfriends who are prostitutes. "AIDS is a sexually trans-mitted disease," says Ken South, the former director of AID Atlanta, "and Georgia is a sexually active state. This isn't just a half dozen queers in Midtown having sex. Atlanta is a cauldron for infection."    33

Elaine sits in the living room of the elegant Tudor home. She is trim and attractive—tanned and toned to perfection. The air conditioner hums softly in the background. The lawn beyond the windows sweeps abruptly downward to Habersham Road. This is another Atlanta, sep-arated from the mundane, workaday city by distance only money can measure. "I fear AIDS," she says with a little shiver. "It's out there." She tries to remember when the uneasiness began. Perhaps when her dentist, then her electrolysist, began wearing gloves.    34

"At parties," she says, "you know how you always talk about sex, religion, and politics—those three categories. AIDS is now a category."    35

She's read a lot, but like most people doesn't believe everything the government is telling her about the epidemic. She knows the disease is not supposed to be spread by casual contact. "[But] what if someone cuts himself in a restaurant and it's transmitted?" she asks. Elaine and her husband, George, travel a good deal. "We have a lot of friends in New York," she says. "Everybody there knows someone who's got it, who's died from it. The feeling has filtered down."    36

She's worried about her children, both still preadolescents. She bought material for them to read. "Terrific stuff," she says. "I want them to be educated."    37

George takes many business trips. "I tell him 'You better not fool around.' It's playful and joking. He tells me the same. I know he's safe. . . ."    38

Elaine says she has a lot of friends, successful career women, divorced or never married, approaching 40. "They've been fooling around since their 20s. They've banged a lot of eyes out. Now they're terrified."    39

And then she reveals one of Buckhead's open secrets: another pathway for AIDS. "I know firsthand that a lot of men are seeing hookers. I'm talking about high-class hookers. It's a way of life around here. They're in unhappy relationships with their wives. This is how they cope.    40

"We'll pay for it," she laughs. "Us poor Buckhead wives."    41

There is something more that makes Atlanta particularly susceptible to the terrors—real and imagined—of AIDS. Something beyond the reach of statistics and epidemiological surveys. Something to do with youth, sex, money, power and expectation. The perception of a once-tired city reborn and shaped in the image of tens of thousands of young people who were drawn here: rural Southerners escaping the choking grasp of small-town life; Northerners fleeing the bleak realities of the Rust Belt; blacks realizing the barriers were finally lifted; college kids eager to embark on life's first adventures. A desire for life in the fast lane . . . a sense of limits to exceed and new horizons to explore.    42

An illusion, perhaps, but one powerful enough to make Atlanta one of the premier party towns in America for two decades. "It was personified liberation," says Boles. "People came to *Hotlanta*. Young, ambitious, good-looking people who wanted to be free." And they were. Bars and clubs sprouted like weeds—Billy's and Harrison's, élan and Limelight, Carlos McGee's, Fitzgerald's, Zazu's, a hundred others, some with a half-life as short as plutonium 232 and about as explosive. Music played; whiskey flowed. Drugs were everywhere, easing the way past other barriers.    43

"Sex was safe for the first time," says Boles. "If you got some disease, you got a shot of penicillin. You had birth control. You had cars. These happy occurrences all came at once. . . . All of a sudden sex was a natural, biological thing, like breathing. The more you do it, the healthier you are. Sex kept down psychoses and neuroses, cleaned out your pores, regulated your heartbeat. If you were overweight or drank too much, have sex. Sex could be substituted for all these other drives. Wasn't that wonderful?    44

"Nobody ever died from too much sex.     45

"And then," continues Boles, "things started going wrong. Women     46
weren't using birth control; illegitimate births began to soar. Women
got STDs* from too many partners. They became sterile. You had
herpes."

And the lonely weight of all the one-night stands, and all the shame-     47
less, nameless encounters began to build. The foundations of newly
liberated Atlanta suddenly seemed cracked and shaky; the old Atlanta,
the bedrock, guilt-driven, Bible Belt town, began to stir and rumble.
AIDS was suddenly among us.

People began to die from sex.     48

There have been 864 cases of AIDS recorded in Georgia. Eighty per-     49
cent of them are in Atlanta; 508 have died. By 1991, there will be 5,000
people in the city dying of AIDS.

"Human beings always try to get meaning out of what is happen-     50
ing," says Boles. "Why do we suddenly have a plague? The obvious
lessons are being drawn, too easily I think: perhaps sex is not natural
after all; maybe sex is dangerous and has to be controlled. If not, we're
going to have chaos."

Roy Griffen knows chaos firsthand. The blue-eyed, 34-year-old     51
Alabamian with the baseball catcher's body is living everyone
else's nightmare. He has AIDS. Hospitalized four times in the past
two years because of a debilitating diarrhea caused by an obscure
parasite known as cryptosporida, Griffen recovered only to develop
pneumocystis carinii pneumonia (the deadliest AIDS-related infection)
last January.

"Don't call me an AIDS victim," he says sipping a root beer. "No one     52
mugged me and gave me AIDS. I went out and got it myself."

When he speaks, there is an old man's wheeze in his voice. His face     53
is flushed and once again he has begun to cough up yellow-green
sputum—all signs of recurrent pneumonia. Once, he worked outdoors and did all kinds of manual labor.

That seems such a long time ago. Now he admits he can't walk two     54
blocks without getting out of breath. Like so many other young people, Griffen came to Atlanta chasing a dream. Not to corner the real
estate market or make partner in a big law firm. Griffen, a modest man

---

*Sexually transmitted diseases.—Ed.

whose roots run deep in the rocky soil of northern Alabama, wanted to be a landscaper. That and nothing more. He wasn't gay until he was 26 years old. He'd married his childhood sweetheart, spent six years in the Air Force, even got in a year of college. He was the first on either side of his family to finish high school.

Deep down, he knew he was different. He loved Marilyn dearly and    55
never strayed as long as they were married. He understood just how different he was in one of those strange flashes of insight: "My wife and I were shopping. I realized we were both looking at the same man." It troubled him.

"I was raised to believe that gays were dirty old men in the bushes,"    56
he says. "I was not that way. So I told myself I mustn't be gay. It was a very slow process coming to terms with these feelings."

He told his wife the marriage was over. "She blamed herself," he    57
says. "I said 'If you were Dolly Parton, I'd still feel the same way.'" Griffen "came out" eight years ago and enjoyed his new-found sexual freedom.

"I tired of that very quickly," he says. "I wanted to settle into a real    58
lifestyle."

He must have been infected almost immediately.    59

Griffen arrived in Atlanta in 1984, the AIDS virus already singing in    60
his blood. He began working with a landscaper learning the trade. Within a year he began to get sick. "I knew I had AIDS long before they told me," he says. "I was hoping it was something else." He wanted to die at home. He was a Southerner and this is what Southerners have always done. "My grandfather was an invalid for nine years and we took care of him. We never thought of a nursing home," he says. Griffen wanted to stay in an old trailer next to his grandmother's house. "I was very sick. I had no insurance. One of my aunts told the rest of my family I had AIDS. She said she could tell from my voice."

They turned him away.    61

"My family is afraid of AIDS. They live in a very rural area. People    62
would mark them. They'd be outcasts."

This is what he says now. At the time, he tried to kill himself. A year    63
ago he met Bud; both men were suffering from ARC, or AIDS-related complex, a debilitating assortment of symptoms and so-called "opportunistic infections" that are often precursors to full-blown AIDS. The two men grew close. Sex was never an issue.

"I've had no sex drive for a long, long time," says Griffen. Bud    64 died early on a Sunday morning in June—in the same bed Roy now sleeps in.

He is alone much of the time. Some of his friends have abandoned   65
him. He understands. "For them to deal with me, they have to deal with AIDS," he says. "They don't want that."

Griffen doesn't want to die among strangers in Grady Hospital.* He   66
is counting on the staff of AID Atlanta to be with him, but still, on those dark and haunted nights, he grows afraid.

He is not sorry for the way he has lived his life. "I'm a much better   67
person for having been gay," he says. "I've had to deal with bigotry and oppression, but I realized my true feelings and acted upon them. Not too many people can say that. . . . I guess I've not been successful by the world's standards, but I'm successful by mine. I'm a Christian. I have faith. I am at peace with myself.

"But," he adds, "it's a funny thing. To some people I'm the scum of   68
the earth."

With the faith that so often comforts the dying, Griffen believes   69
some good can come out of a plague. "A higher power may be working here to remind us that we have to interact with each other as human beings and not sex objects," he says. Dr. Morganstern agrees. "The sensual thing was getting out of hand. There is going to be a refocusing of sexual attitudes."

Others worry that the main consequence of the epidemic will be a   70
swing back to the sexual repression of the '50s, before the drawing of sexual liberation in the '60s. Sensing these attitudinal changes, politicians are now beginning to evaluate what the situation means for them. Privately, many epidemiologists worry that AIDS is becoming politicized. "There is no doubt that increased funding is coming, in part, because of heterosexual fear," says the CDC's Jaffe. "We have to wonder if the money will be spent wisely. Will heterosexual hysteria feed demands for more testing, quarantine and other repressive measures?

"AIDS is so terrible, we don't want anybody to take a risk and get it,"   71
continues Jaffe. "But the major problem continues to be infected drug abusers and their sex partners—people who don't read newspaper editorials and have lots of other problems in their lives. . . . The panic

*Atlanta's public hospital.—Ed.

will grow worse. The feeling out there is for more restrictive policies. Political leaders sense what the public wants. If it is not what the public health community is giving them, then the politicians will take over."

It is not surprising that people want assurance in a time of pesti-  72
lence. When science and medicine cannot provide guarantees, per-haps the law will. Others simply don't want the party to end. "We're really upset," says one divorce-scarred and whiskey-soaked veteran, "because sex is our favorite activity."

"The thinking is," counters Ken South, the former AID Atlanta di-  73
rector, "as long as I know everyone who's positive and everyone who's negative, I can be safe. But it isn't the responsibility of the state to lock up infected people and protect the poor uninfecteds. It's defensive driving. Every sexually active American is going to have to practice safe sex . . . wear rubbers. They don't want to do it. They don't want to change. They don't like it."

So the party goes on, though the hour is late and the floor is not  74
as crowded as it once was. Maybe it will take, as psychologist Dr. Catherine Blusiewicz puts it, "the death of the first heterosexual movie star from AIDS" to halt it completely.

It goes on because very, very few straight Americans—outside doc-  75
tors, health care types and grieving family members—have ever seen an AIDS victim in the horrible final stages of disease.

The party goes on because all of us want love but many have come  76
to accept something less: sex as the synonym for love. The party goes on because sexual behavior is almost impossible to modify. Blusiewicz cites one of her patients, "an extremely sexually active 16-year-old girl," who is convinced that AIDS will destroy the human race. But, says the therapist, "in terms of how she behaves sexually, it has no input."

On the other side of the generation gap stands Lane, a 50-year-old  77
divorced grandfather and a fixture at the bar of the Creekside Cafe. Lane does not believe AIDS will penetrate his magic circle of lawyers, businessmen and media types. He's not particularly concerned. "To have it hit you," he says, "you got to know somebody it nailed."

He says this though he's slept with 12 women in the last year and  78
used a condom with only two. He says this despite the fact that Mary, one of his dates, is so frightened of AIDS she fled in terror from a portrait *painted* by an AIDS victim (just a touch away!). Another of his

dates recently threw a news clipping on AIDS in front of him saying, "Since my divorce, you're the only man I slept with. If I got it, it has to be you."

Not to worry, says Lane. "If it does hit, it will be the meat market    79
places, the bars with loud music and plastic people. . . . Obviously, I
consider myself real."

The question occurs: "But for how much longer?"    80

(Some names in this story have been changed where requested by the
individuals interviewed.)

# THE TESTING DILEMMA

Completely Confidential AIDS TESTING. No name or identification
required. Buckhead location. Call 261-9327 for information.
> —ADVERTISEMENT, *ATLANTA CONSTITUTION*, JULY 1987

When you call you are told to ask for Cathy. Cathy doesn't exist. The    1
name alerts nurses and technicians at the Piedmont Minor Emergency
Clinic that you, an anonymous person, are requesting a very special
test—one which determines whether you've been exposed to the virus
that causes the acquired immune deficiency syndrome.

When you arrive, there is no waiting. Let the lucky folks with splin-    2
tered bones and jagged lacerations sit in the waiting room. You are
escorted straight to the lab and given five pages of AIDS information to
read. A technician carefully draws 5 cubic centimeters of your blood
and assigns you a number. You're probably worried even if you're
among the 10 percent coming in for premarital testing. You ask lots of
questions: "How long does it take for antibodies to the virus to appear
in my blood?" "What does it mean to be positive?" "Will I get AIDS?"
The last question, of course, cannot be answered.

If you are really nervous, you ask the nurse if the needle she's using    3
is sterile. "It's funny," says Selena Colvin, the clinic's head nurse. "I'm
doing an AIDS test on them and they want to know if my needles are
sterile."

The whole thing takes about 20 minutes. Your blood is stoppered    4 and centrifuged (to separate out the sera) and wrapped in a plastic transport bag along with a requisition sheet listing your number. A courier comes by to pick up the specimen; it is driven to International Clinical Laboratories' Doraville facility, logged onto a computer, then flown to a Nashville laboratory where the actual testing (an almost fully automated procedure) takes place.

At the Piedmont Minor Emergency Clinic, you pay $80 (always in cash). No charts are written up; no medical records established. The typical clients (75 percent) are white males and females with college backgrounds. If male, you are between 40 and 50 years old. You are likely to be heterosexual. If you are blatantly gay, the nurses may try to remember your face and number and make friendly bets on you.

You might be the accountant in your late 40s who had an affair with his secretary. You've done this before, of course—the office affairs— but suddenly you don't trust this woman. You ask how you should break the news to your wife if you test positive. As an afterthought, you wonder if you should tell the secretary.

Perhaps, you're the pretty, dark-haired woman in your early 30s who arrives in a business suit and carrying a brief case. You haven't had a relationship in years—maybe you've been too busy with a career. You've met a new guy you really like. You don't want to sleep with him until you know for sure.

You might be the clean-cut man, mid-20s, coming in for premarital testing. You've had other lovers (female). Now that you're getting married, you want to be certain. There might be children to consider. Besides, didn't President Reagan himself recommend routine premarital testing for the AIDS virus? So you use your own name (*never, ever do that*) because you have nothing to hide. And you mail in a claim to your insurance company for reimbursement. And your insurance is canceled. And you are labeled high risk. And, says nurse Colvin, who heard this very story from a doctor at another testing site, "You'll never be able to get medical insurance again."

After five days, the courier brings back your results. You call the clinic and give them your ID number. If you're a risk group member, you are terrified. Ice water is coursing through your veins. Everyone else is just plain scared. You recall the information sheet given you when you first showed up at the clinic. One of the topics was "Should I take the test?" And the nurse specifically asked how the results might affect your life. You wish you had paid more attention.

If your test is negative, the nurse tells you so right over the phone. You breathe real deep and say things like, "It's abstinence for me." If you are positive, the test will be run at least twice and a final, very reliable test called the Western blot will confirm the results. You then are referred to a doctor who will attempt to calm and counsel you over the phone. Of course, he will fail, because at that moment, you are inconsolable. And doing it over the phone is ineffective at best, inhuman at worst. 10

If you were the young man who tempted fate and gambled with death by allowing the nurses to assign you the identification number 13, you lost. 11

Your test came back positive. 12

# TROUBLED VOICES

The phones ring constantly, 12 hours a day, seven days a week. Answering them is never easy. Volunteers at AID Atlanta's Info-Line are often plunged headlong into the nightmare world of dying or newly diagnosed AIDS victims. Begun four years ago to provide AIDS information, the hotline has become much more: a crisis intervention mechanism, a shoulder to cry on, a no-nonsense authority on safe sex and risk reduction. 1

On a recent Friday morning, Ellen Lappa, a self-proclaimed "tennis-playing Dunwoody housewife," was working the phones. Calls ranged from the tragic to the absurd, from a man with "a friend with some symptoms," to a guy afraid to put his hemorrhoid-troubled backside on a public toilet. Following is a random selection from the log of calls that came in on Lappa's watch, along with a few of her responses. Think of it as a quick peek at Atlanta's AIDS-troubled psyche: 2

**Caller No. 1:** (White male, rural accent.) "Is there a chance of getting AIDS from deep kissing or wet kissing?" 3
**Lappa:** "It's highly unlikely." 4

**Caller No. 2:** (Ambulance driver.) "Can AIDS be transmitted by per-   5
spiration? What if I got a patient who was violent and sweaty? I'd have
to be real careful, right?"

**Lappa:** "It would take about a quart of perspiration in your blood-   6
stream to infect you."

**Caller:** "Well, I was watching this basketball game . . . I saw these   7
kids, all soaking and rubbing against each other. It got me to thinking . . ."

**Caller No. 3:** (Gay white male.) "I have shingles (herpes zoster, a   8
painful inflammation of the nerve endings caused by a viral infection).
Someone told me it was a precursor to AIDS. But everybody in my
family has shingles. I need to know for sure."

**Caller No. 4:** (White female, rich Southern accent.) "I read where   9
one of the first symptoms is swelling of the lymph glands. Can you tell
me a little bit about that? My glands have been swollen since Monday.
I haven't been with anybody but my husband in six years, but I've
become a little paranoid. I'm sure you understand . . ."

**Caller No. 5:** (Black male, scared, not doing a good job hiding it.) "I   10
had sex with a woman in December. A friend just told me she has AIDS.
Her roommate put her out on the street . . . I can't find her . . . My
wife has this rash. Her doctor says something funny's going on."

**Caller No. 6:** (White female, blue-collar, nervous.) "How soon   11
would you know if you were infected with AIDS. . . . On Monday, I
went to bed with this guy who's . . . not my husband. He's a very
promiscuous person. My fear is exposing my husband. This is my
fault and I don't want to risk anyone else's life. Do you see where I'm
coming from? A few years ago, this wasn't such a problem. . . . Hell,
I don't even know what test to go for."

**Lappa:** (Explains that it can take as long as six months for antibodies   12
to the AIDS virus to appear in the bloodstream after infection. Therefore, it could take that long for any reliable test results. She tries a
joke.) "Tell your husband you were bitten by a mosquito. Really, you're
going to drive yourself crazy."

**Caller:** (Not amused.) "So, it's sort of a 'hang in there' thing? . . . 13
My husband's a workaholic. We only have sex on Saturday night. It's already Friday. . . ."

**Caller No. 7:** (White male, business type.) "My brother lives in San 14
Francisco. He told me he's had swollen glands for two years. He says everybody out there has them. He's the only brother I have. I don't want to lose him. [Long pause.] He's coming to Atlanta for Thanksgiving. There are children involved. I understand there's no risk from casual contact. Is that right? Should my children be allowed to touch and hug him?"
**Lappa:** "He'll need lots of hugs. Feel perfectly comfortable with him 15
coming to visit for the holidays."

**Caller No. 8:** (Airline pilot.) "I'm worried about my copilot. He's 16
screwing everything in sight."

**Caller No. 9:** (White woman, upper-class.) "Honey, I just want to 17
find out how prevalent this is in the heterosexual community, because several years ago, I had an affair."

**Caller No. 10:** (Young white male, giddy, obviously calling from a 18
pay phone.) "Is oral sex safe?"
**Lappa:** "Not a hundred percent safe, but . . ." 19
**Caller:** (Interrupting with a laugh.) "I won't go into the details, but 20
I can promise you it won't happen again!"
**Lappa:** "How well do you know this . . . woman?" 21
**Caller:** (Laughing crazily.) "Hell, I don't even know her name!" 22

**Caller No. 11:** (Gay white male.) "My name is Phil and I've just 23
learned my best friend has AIDS. Please tell me what I can do. . . ."

## *VOCABULARY*

| | | |
|---|---|---|
| surreptitiously (6) | furtive (18) | precursors (63) |
| permutations (8) | feral (33) | repressive (70) |
| mantra (18) | mundane (34) | inconsolable |
| repertoire (18) | debilitating (51) | (10, "Testing") |

## THE FACTS

1. What new category of sufferers has the AIDS epidemic created?
2. Why, according to Coppola, are heterosexuals' fears of AIDS probably groundless?
3. What generalization is true of most heterosexual victims of AIDS?
4. According to epidemiologists, what inroads is the AIDS epidemic making into the heterosexual population?
5. Why, according to Coppola, should you never use your real name when being tested for AIDS?

## THE STRATEGIES

1. What kind of specific detail does Coppola primarily use in documenting the views and opinions in the main article?
2. How does Coppola manage to engage our interest in his opening paragraphs? Comment on the opening he uses.
3. What do paragraphs 3 and 61 of "The Party's Over" have in common?
4. In paragraph 1 Coppola writes: "Women who make otherwise sane and settled men want to send the wife and kids off to visit her folks in Knoxville." What grammatical construction is this, and what justification does the author have for its use?
5. "If AIDS does explode into the straight population, Atlanta may well be Ground Zero" (paragraph 33). What does this metaphor mean, and where does it come from?

## THE ISSUES

1. Coppola mentions "safe sex" parties. What do you think is "unsafe" sex?
2. What were some of the justifications people in the article used for not altering their lifestyles? Were these justifications dealt with adequately in the article?
3. Do you think that the AIDS epidemic is likely to usher in a 1950s-style sexual repressiveness? Why or why not?
4. The author asks: "Have you ever heard anyone trying to 'justify' cancer?" (paragraph 13) Why do you think AIDS seems to occupy a special place in the ongoing moral debate?
5. Based on what you know about AIDS, do you regard its terrors as real or imagined?

## SUGGESTIONS FOR WRITING

1. Write an essay on the effects AIDS has had on people in your community.

2. Write an essay in which you argue for or against one of the following:
   a. Disclosure of persons testing positively for AIDS.
   b. Quarantining of AIDS patients.
   c. More financial support for AIDS research.

Hank E. Koehn

———— • **MY PASSAGE THROUGH AIDS** • ————

*Hank Koehn (1933–1987) was born in Newark, New Jersey, and was educated at New York University and Columbia University. Chairman of the Trimtab Consulting Group and a former vice president and director of the futures research division of Security Pacific Bank, Koehn was regarded as a pioneering futurist in the banking industry. His frank article about life with AIDS, first published in the* Los Angeles Times *(August 14, 1987), provoked hundreds of telephone calls and letters from around the country. Koehn died of AIDS in September 1987.*

My world came to an end in the San Jose air terminal on Friday,   1
Feb. 27.

I had been in the San Jose area on a two-day business trip, which   2
like most of my out-of-town visits consisted of speaking engagements.
While waiting for my return flight to Los Angeles, I made a phone call.

A week earlier my doctor had convinced me that I should have a test   3
for the human immuno-deficiency virus. Like other men, I had initially
rejected the idea. I suppose, like many others, I was avoiding the
information that I already suspected. That Friday, my call was to find
out the test results. The doctor informed me they were positive.

I knew then that I had AIDS.   4

With almost clinical detachment, I made an appointment to visit   5
him early the following week. I had been having difficulty using my
left hand, and for several weeks had assumed it was due to a possible
pulled shoulder muscle. At my doctor's office at the end of that visit, I
almost casually mentioned the problem.

### A BRAIN SCAN

After several questions, he said the difficulty could be an indication   6
of a serious problem; it seemed there might be brain damage as a result
of the now-active AIDS virus in my body. Within minutes, a magnetic
resonance scan of my brain was scheduled for the next afternoon.

The scan consisted of placing my head and shoulders inside a tube- 7
like device that seemed to belong on a "Star Trek" movie set. Within a
day it would indicate that there was a lesion on the right side of my
brain. The lesion, the doctor said, could be the result of a tumor or,
more probably, a direct attack by the AIDS virus on my brain. His coolly
efficient explanation transmitted a subconscious emotional message: I
had a terminal condition. My future consisted of certain death.

I was to be hospitalized for a complete diagnosis. Much to my doc- 8
tor's displeasure, I delayed entering the hospital while I turned over
my client commitments to an associate and visited my attorney to
arrange matters should I not leave the hospital alive. On the day I left
home, I took a final look at my budding liquidambar tree and thought
it highly probable I would never see it with all of its leaves.

I had not been in a hospital for more than 50 years, but it was not 9
unpleasant. Still, the multitude of tests did little to change my outlook.
They indicated that the brain lesion was due to a toxoplasmosis infection. This protozoan is usually present in all of us, but our immune
systems keep it in check. In my case, the infection in my brain was
slowly taking away my ability to use my left hand and arm. Dressing
and daily living became a one handed exercise.

On the day I was to leave the hospital, I had my first seizure. My 10
arm and hand jumped around for about 15 seconds as a result of "short
circuit" signals from the infected area of the brain. I was terrified.

I was told this could become a common event (it did) and I received 11
my first capsule of the drug Dilantin. I left the hospital convinced that
my days among the living were indeed numbered. The doctors were
surprised I was so calm, but I did not feel cheated and could therefore
face my impending demise calmly. I resolved to get on with it, deciding
two things: First, I most likely would not live beyond the end of the
year; second, when I thought it was time to die, I would merely get
into bed and stay there.

These feelings and an all-encompassing resignation remained with 12
me for several weeks. I was calm in the face of an accepted certainty. I
also decided I would no longer be able to work. For one thing, I
couldn't bear the thought of having a seizure in front of a group in the
middle of a lecture. But I also felt I would be rejected when word got
out that I had AIDS. I was sure most of my clients would be appalled at
learning about my choice of life style.

Once I decided to stop work, my feelings took two directions at 13
once. First, I discovered I had lost self-worth; indeed, I found I had

little personal identity outside my work life. Second, I lost interest in the outside world. As a futurist and social observer, I had spent most of my time watching and reading about change. Now, I found I had empty days. To fill the time, I began to sleep all day, and all night. I would stare at nothing on the ceiling for many hours. Everything, including reading, became too much of an effort. Since my days were numbered, nothing seemed worthwhile.

In a way, it was all very comfortable; I was well cared for at home. In retrospect, the frightening fact was, I was very content doing nothing. And since I had a relatively strong personality, there was almost no one to challenge my deep feeling of resignation. It seemed the civilized approach to my remaining life.    14

During this time, the only trips I took outside my home were to my doctors for blood tests. My medication routine had been established. I took pills seven times a day and adjusted to sleeping in small packets of time. I also attempted to fulfill a few out-of-town trips. That activity ended in emotional disaster when I had seizures aboard aircraft and once while passing through security at the Oakland airport.    15

All of this made my continued resignation to dying very easy.    16

Then one day while talking with a friend, I asked again if he didn't think I had become too resigned too easily. Together we explored this thought. I became convinced I had given up too quickly, even if it were an obvious course of action. From that point on I began to explore the alternative.    17

I had been receiving counseling to stabilize my emotional state, even though I felt I was stable without help. To my surprise I found, upon reflection, that my inner needs were spiritual or metaphysical. When I mentioned this to more friends, I found that during illness they had reached the same conclusions in their own lives. They suggested I read several books, including one written by Louise L. Hay, a metaphysical healer who had been working successfully with cancer and AIDS patients. Her Wednesday night meetings in Plummer Park in West Hollywood had become legends in the gay community.    18

I acquired several of her tapes, purchased other meditation tapes at the Bodhi Tree bookstore on Melrose Avenue, and played them several times a day. Slowly I began to understand that my future was in my own hands—actually, *mind* is a better word.    19

It's strange when you consider that, as a futurist, I told my clients: "If you can dream it, you can do it." Louise Hay reminded me that    20 each of us has the capacity to invent tomorrow by the thoughts we have today.

Through the tapes, I began to believe I could play a major role in     21
healing myself.

## TRIP TO THE OCEAN

I also developed an unexplained but insatiable urge to visit the     22
ocean. The need was so real that my lover, Jim Hill, and I went to stay
in a Laguna Beach hotel directly overlooking the surf. As I sat in a
lounge chair staring down at the water, the pattern of the waves slowly
began to relax my mind and I realized why I had wanted to come to
the sea. My mind began to float and I recalled a long-forgotten thought
from early childhood: how abandoned I had felt as an only child who
was separated from his parents at a young age. This feeling of abandonment would be repeated in my teen years and as an adult with two
relationships that failed.

My overpowering fear, now as a man with AIDS, was that I would     23
once again be abandoned. This sudden, ocean-induced awareness was
a shock. I hadn't realized I thought in those terms; at least I couldn't
consciously recall that I had. I returned home resolved to learn more
about myself, and healing myself.

The attempt to reach my inner mind and understand its abilities and     24
effects on my life became a challenge. Indeed, it would prove to be the
biggest challenge I had ever encountered. To my amazement, many of
my friends had also attempted to mentally influence their health and
well-being. They suggested a considerable number of books on the
self-healing process.

As I reached deep inside myself for understanding and direction,     25
there were many moments of feelings of success. There were many
more moments of failure. But I continued on, reminding myself that
for many decades, I had shaped my work career through personal
determination—and been successful at it.

## A DIFFERENT PERSON

It became clear, then, that whoever I became at the end of my spiri-     26
tual odyssey, I would be far different from the person first diagnosed
with AIDS in February. It was also obvious that it was time for me to

make a passage or transition in my life. I felt that having AIDS could be turned into a positive experience.

During the months since that initial diagnosis, I found, for the first 27 time in my life, that I cried easily. I cried not out of fear but as an emotional expression, an outlet for pent-up anger and frustration, and as a response to the kindness of my friends.

I never thought so many people, including business associates and 28 clients, would come forward so openly expressing their love for me. Dozens of callers expressed love and hope and encouragement. To date, no one has been appalled by the knowledge of my preferred life style of the past 20 years. I have deeply felt the love of others who I never thought would call and say "We love you." This all created a sadness in me because I had never understood how they felt about me.

With that came a frequently overpowering feeling of loneliness; very 29 often it felt as if I were all alone in a strange dark place. And I developed an almost-desperate need to be hugged and held close, as if I were a small child.

It was a time of new feelings that were almost beyond my control. 30 But slowly I began to realize that no matter how uncertain my life seemed, there could be a future. I could still exercise some control over my existence.

The last few months have involved the steady loss of my ability to 31 move my left arm, use my left hand and use my left leg. Over a period of 120 days, I watched my disability grow until I could no longer move freely under normal circumstances. I progressively became more crippled and more useless. Standing up became a high risk; I fell on objects around my home. Canes were useless, and manipulating a wheelchair became a one-armed event.

## NEEDING HELP AT HOME

I was being transformed from an independent person into someone 32 who could no longer walk alone, someone who needed help to shower and to get to bed at night. The massive change in so short a time left me confused and surprised at my feelings; they seemed to belong to someone I didn't know, a new individual I was not prepared to either understand or control. Even the closet full of executive suits now seemed to belong to someone else.

Frequently, I would wake in the morning still believing I could hop    33
out of bed and jump into the shower. Obviously, I had not adjusted to
my new body and I wondered how long memories of the past would
seem to represent a nonexisting present reality. I wondered when the
present reality would dissolve the memories and actions of more than
50 years.

AIDS is perceived as altering the life of one person. This is not the    34
whole truth. As the patient becomes slowly dependent upon someone
else, finally needing help all day, all week, the disease slowly destroys
the quality of life for two people. The care-giver of the AIDS patient is
also held hostage by the disease.

The sickness is relentless, trapping two or more people in a round    35
of simple but necessary tasks. If there is one thing worse than having
AIDS, it is watching and caring for the person who has it. The significant other can do little but wonder, "How long will this go on?" The
patient watches while the life of the care-giver becomes less in the
name of love and more a self-imposed duty. It is difficult to say who is
the victim and who hurts the most. Joy seems to slowly vanish in the
eyes of both. Life becomes increasingly restrictive; the disease domi-
nates every discussion and action. Freedom for both vanishes.

The overriding challenge is how I can be less of a burden on my    36
care-giver. Accepting care is something that almost must be learned.
Understanding limitations also must be learned. Expectations must be
adjusted to a new reality.

AIDS is a very new disease and most doctors are very confused about    37
its treatment. Most have not been trained generally to accept the patient as full partner in the healing process. The patient is seen as a
mechanical device to be repaired; the tools are surgery and chemicals.

I don't believe, however, that we have any choice but to take charge    38
of our healing. The criteria for selecting a doctor should be: Will you
accept me as a partner in my quest for wellness?

Doctors are especially insensitive to the effect of new drugs. The    39
doctor's challenge with an AIDS patient seems to be to keep you alive
until a cure is discovered. Regrettably, hospitals also go along with
this, in their competitive attitude toward who has the largest market
share of AIDS patients. The AIDS patient, with insurance, is clearly a
cash cow. The AIDS patient is also today's leper, the focal point of
attitudes similar to those of 100 years ago.

Those attitudes, unfortunately, extend to corporate America as a    40 whole. What we're seeing in the AIDS crisis is a social destabilizer, an event that is changing the future of the world. Yet, most businesses do not have an AIDS policy; they treat it on a case-by-case basis. They view AIDS as a homosexual disease and pretend that no one on their staff could ever get it. They're not facing up to it.

Over five months I have learned slowly how to help myself and take     41 responsibility for my healing. By talking to others I have received information on therapies and drugs with which to fight the disease. How others cope with the challenge also gives me clues and direction in my own search for maintaining a civilized level of life.

Now, my preferred life of 54 years is gone. Even if I were to go into     42 remission or be given a cure, that life is over. My concern with my spiritual needs and my metaphysical well-being is now central to my existence. I also empathize with terminally ill cancer patients and the helpless feelings of the elderly as they are forced to depend on others for their daily existence.

I'm not sure what I'll be like when I complete this passage. But I do     43 know I will be very different, able to accept my needs and the love of others.

## VOCABULARY

demise (11)                    insatiable (22)                    odyssey (26)
retrospect (14)

## THE FACTS

1. What were the first symptoms of Koehn's AIDS infection?
2. How did Koehn initially react to the news that he had AIDS?
3. How was Koehn affected when he decided to stop work?
4. What happened to Koehn aboard an aircraft and as he was passing through security at the Oakland airport?
5. How did Koehn's business associates and clients react to the news that he had AIDS?

## THE STRATEGIES

1. How would you characterize the tone of this essay? How does the tone contribute to the essay's overall impact?
2. Paragraph 4 consists of a short, single sentence. Why?

3. Reread paragraphs 11 and 13. How does Koehn organize and marshal the points of these paragraphs? What does this technique reveal about him?
4. What kind of rhetorical difficulties do you think Koehn faced in deciding to do an article about having AIDS? What do you think he accomplished in writing it?
5. How is the ending of this essay tied in with its beginning?

## THE ISSUES

1. From this article, what inferences can you make about Koehn as a person? How does the article predispose you to feel about him?
2. Does the knowledge that Koehn was a homosexual affect your reaction to his article?
3. What is your attitude toward homosexuality?
4. "If you can dream it, you can do it" (paragraph 38). This was advice the author used to give his clients. Do you agree with it? Why or why not?
5. In the same paragraph, Koehn writes, "The criteria for selecting a doctor should be: Will you accept me as a partner in my quest for wellness?" What do you think is likely to be the attitude of most doctors toward being judged by this criterion?

## SUGGESTIONS FOR WRITING

1. Infer the character and personality of the writer from what he tells us about himself in this article. Sum up your impression of him in an overall thesis, then prove it in an essay that uses quotations from the article as evidence.
2. Gay-rights activists have argued that the government was slow to respond to the AIDS epidemic because of a homophobic aversion to their lifestyle. Write an essay arguing for or against this viewpoint.

**Charles Krauthammer**

# • AIDS RESEARCH DOES DESERVE • FUNDING, BUT THERE ARE OTHER FATAL DISEASES, TOO

*Charles Krauthammer (b. 1950) was born in New York City and educated at McGill University (B.A., 1970) and Harvard Medical School (M.D., 1975) where he was trained as a psychiatrist. He is a senior editor at the* New Republic, *an essayist for* Time, *and a syndicated columnist for the* Washington Post.

*In 1987 he was awarded the Pulitzer Price for distinguished commentary. He is the author of* Cutting Edges: Making Sense of the 1980's *(1985).*

AIDS is public health enemy No. 1, says President Reagan. It is on    1
every front page, on every candidate's lips. Everyone agrees: We need
to do more. Sen. Robert Dole has the presidential candidate's standard
AIDS formulation, calling for spending "whatever resources [are] necessary to get the job done."

"Whatever resources"? When politicians are unanimous on any is-    2
sue, it is time to pause. Sen. Al Gore has called for a "Manhattan
Project" on AIDS. Why should the fight against AIDS be the exclusive
beneficiary of a massive government effort?

Because AIDS is fatal? Since 1981, AIDS has killed about 20,000 Amer-    3
icans. Heart disease kills 65,000 every month. Because AIDS strikes
young people in the prime of their lives? Schizophrenia, which afflicts
1,650,000 Americans, is also a disease of young people.

It is not good politics to come out against an AIDS cure, but it is    4
worth asking the question: Why should AIDS be a privileged disease—
federally protected, as it were—while other diseases, many of which
cause suffering in many more Americans, are not?

The only possible answer is that AIDS is such an explosive threat to    5
society that it must be stopped now. The key to this claim is that AIDS
is breaking through to the general population. But the latest numbers
indicate otherwise. AIDS remains largely confined to two groups: male
homosexuals and intravenous drug abusers. They continue to account
for 9 out of 10 AIDS cases. Heterosexual transmission accounts for no
more than 4 percent of cases.

A Berkeley study presented in Washington at the Third Interna-    6
tional Conference on AIDS demonstrates how difficult heterosexual
transmission really is. It showed that women whose partners had AIDS
needed a very large number of sexual contacts before contracting the
disease. For example, of women who had sex more than 600 times with
an AIDS patient, only one in three contracted the disease.

Of the two major risk groups, drug abusers are not organized. Gays    7
are. Gay-rights groups have turned AIDS into a political issue. They
have two principal demands on the government: immediate cure and
no testing. And they have not been reticent about their wishes. During
the Washington conference, there were many demonstrations. A sit-

down outside the White House featured chants of "Reagan, Reagan, too little, too late." Pamphlets distributed at the conference urged the booing of administration officials who proposed testing. And booed they were, despite the fact that the proposals they offered—testing prisoners, couples about to marry, and aliens seeking entry to the United States—were moderate and reasonable.

Gays have every right to lobby for AIDS. But the general public has 8 an equal right to question their sense of entitlement. Other groups have other diseases, some just as terrible, some more so. Medical claims on society, like nonmedical claims, must be tested against each other. Yet the AIDS constituency has been adamant in demanding special protection.

Where does this sense of entitlement come from? After all, unlike, 9 say, a brain tumor, AIDS is preventable. We know exactly how to contract it and exactly how to prevent it. Preventative measures are not particularly complicated. Moreover, they are all within the power of the individual to control. With rare exceptions, contracting AIDS, like contracting lung cancer, requires the collaboration of the victim.

This does not mean that AIDS victims deserve neither our compas- 10 sion nor our support. It does mean that those who claim that AIDS victims deserve special compassion and special support have some explaining to do. They have not done it.

On Capitol Hill, when money is preferentially funneled to a partic- 11 ular disease in the news, cynics call it the "disease-of-the-month club" syndrome. AIDS is turning into the disease of the decade. It is hard to speak dispassionately about AIDS without getting booed. AIDS deserves funding and its victims our care.

But AIDS is not the pandemic its publicists would like us to believe, 12 nor does it merit its privileged position at the head of every line of human misfortunes that make claims on our resources, attention and compassion. It is a disease. You would not know it from reading the papers, but there are others.

## *VOCABULARY*

| | | |
|---|---|---|
| reticent (7) | syndrome (11) | pandemic (12) |
| adamant (8) | | |

## THE FACTS

1. According to Krauthammer, how does the president characterize AIDS?
2. Which disease kills 65,000 Americans every month?
3. To which two groups, according to Krauthammer, is AIDS mainly confined?
4. What is the key to the claim that AIDS is a potentially explosive threat to society?
5. What two principal demands on the government do gay-rights groups make?

## THE STRATEGIES

1. This article was originally published as a newspaper column. What are some of the characteristics of language and style that identify it as a column?
2. What was the Manhattan Project? What does Senator Gore mean by the use of this term to describe a national effort to combat AIDS?
3. Krauthammer repeatedly asks questions to which he immediately replies. Why is the question a rather good device for use in a newspaper column such as this?
4. What contribution to the article does its title make?
5. What kind of evidence does Krauthammer use to support his points? How convincing is it?

## THE ISSUES

1. Krauthammer asks the question, Why should AIDS be a privileged disease? What reply can you give to this question?
2. If AIDS were definitely shown *not* to be spreading beyond its two primary host groups—male homosexuals and intravenous drug abusers—what do you think federal policy ought to be toward funding efforts for a cure?
3. Where in this article does Krauthammer come perilously close to blaming those who have contracted AIDS for their own disease? What is your opinion of this viewpoint?
4. Some commentators claim that the spread of AIDS can be stopped if homosexuals would only practice sexual abstinence or engage in so-called safe sex. What is your opinion of the suggestion?
5. What is your opinion of the charge, made by some fundamentalist Christian groups, that AIDS is God's vengeance against biblically forbidden sex practices?

## SUGGESTIONS FOR WRITING

1. Write an essay justifying the claim that AIDS is public health enemy number one.

2. Write an essay arguing for or against mandatory testing for AIDS.

## CHAPTER WRITING ASSIGNMENTS

1. Select one of the following topics and develop it into a unified, coherent, and complete paragraph:
   a. Carelessness can do more harm than lack of knowledge.
   b. Today the prevailing mood on the campus is one of. . . . (Fill in the words you think apply.)
   c. Many cars are still not designed for safety.
   d. Kissing is an odd, overly romanticized act.
   e. A plagiarized paper has several bad effects.
   f. Buying term papers from a commercial source is an unethical act.
2. List the particular details that you would use to write a convincing paragraph on the following topic sentences:
   a. Sarcastic people are unpleasant to be around.
   b. I like the security of dating the same person (or, I like the freedom of dating different persons).
   c. Yuppies have gotten bad press and a bad name.
   d. Children and fools speak the truth.
   e. Common sense is . . . (define it).

# INTRODUCTION TO THE PATTERNS OF DEVELOPMENT

Behind the rhetorical modes or patterns in composition is this simple idea: To write about a subject, you must first have thought about it, and this systematic thinking can be translated into an idealized pattern. For example, you might choose to tell a story about your subject (**narration**); to describe it (**description**); to give examples of it (**example**); to define it (**definition**); to compare it to something else (**comparison and contrast**); to break it down into its constituent parts (**division and classification**); or to say what its known causes or effects are (**causal analysis**). Superimposing one of these seven abstract modes or patterns on your subject will make writing about it easier.

Each of these rhetorical modes is a composite of specific writing and organizing techniques that can be isolated and taught. All narrations are alike, whether they tell a story about aliens from Mars or about facing up to a bully. All descriptions draw on common organizing and focusing techniques, no matter what they describe. If you are writing a comparison and contrast, for example, you know that you must alternate back and forth between the compared items and that you must insert suitable transitions so your reader can follow this movement. If you are defining, you know that there are specific techniques to be used in a definition. Knowing that a subject is to be approached a certain way also endows a writer's purpose with a refreshing narrowness. For what is especially bedeviling to the writer is not necessarily the complexity of a subject, but the infinity of possible approaches suggested by the blank sheet of paper.

The advice that instructors often give beginning writers is, "Narrow your subject." Writing by rhetorical modes allows you to limit and narrow your *approach* to a subject. You say, "I'm going to divide and classify this subject," and you have an abstract pattern in mind that you can follow. You say, "I'm going to analyze cause," and you also have an abstract pattern to follow. In either case, you are not left dangling between "What shall I say?" and "How shall I say it?" You know how to say it in the abstract. What's left is the application of the ideal pattern to your particular subject.

Here is an example, the subject of guilt as developed in the seven most widely used rhetorical patterns. Notice how the writer's focus shifts with the use of each new pattern.

The Editors

# ——— • PATTERNS OF DEVELOPMENT FOR • ——— THE SUBJECT "GUILT"

## 1. NARRATION

I was seven years old when I first became aware of the terrible power of guilt. For piling our toys into the toy box, Mother had rewarded my brother and me with five shiny pennies each. If I had had ten pennies instead of just five, I could have bought a gingerbread man with raisin eyes and sugar-frosted hair. The image danced in my head all day, until, finally, I crept into my brother's room and stole his five pennies. The next morning, as my brother and I were dressing to go to school, I hid all ten pennies in the pocket of my coat, cramming one of my father's handkerchiefs on top of them. As my brother and I lined up in front of Mother to be kissed goodbye, she looked at my bulging pocket with amazement. "What on earth do you have in your pocket?" she asked. "It's nothing," I said as offhandedly as I could. "It's nothing at all." Bewildered, but too busy to investigate any further, Mother kissed me goodbye. I ran out the door and down our gravel path as fast as my feet could carry me. But the farther from home I got, the more miserable I became. The shiny pennies in my pocket felt oppressively like one-ton boulders. And I was haunted by the idea that I had become a thief. Forgotten was the gingerbread man, for whose sake I had stolen my brother's pennies. Finally, unable to bear my horrible feeling of guilt, I ran back home to blurt out my crime to my mother.

## 2. DESCRIPTION

Never before had Pedro experienced such a depth of despair and such a sense of isolation. He began to avoid those nearest to him, returning their friendly greetings with rough and indifferent replies. Often he sat in his room staring vacantly into space with hollow eyes. His hands were cold and clammy most of the time; yet his forehead burned hot with a mysterious fever. Terrible nightmares haunted his sleep, causing him to rise out of bed in the middle of the night, overcome with terror. When strangers at the store asked him a simple question such as "Where is the thread?" or "Have you any molasses?"

he would read silent accusations in their eyes and his hands would tremble. He had become a man tormented by guilt.

## 3. EXAMPLE

Seneca once said, "Every guilty person is his own hangman." The truth of this observation can be illustrated by the lives of countless villains. One such is Macbeth, from Shakespeare's tragedy of the same name. At the instigation of his wife, Macbeth kills the king of Scotland and usurps his throne—an act of treachery for which Macbeth and his wife suffer torments of guilt. Lady Macbeth develops an obsession that her hands are stained with blood, and she wanders somnambulistically through the castle trying vainly to cleanse them. Before he murders the king, Macbeth hallucinates a dagger floating in the air. Later, after his assassins murder Banquo, Macbeth is tormented by hallucinations of Banquo's ghost. Eventually, Lady Macbeth commits suicide. Macbeth is killed during a rebellion of his noblemen, which is brought about—in the main—by the excesses to which his guilt has driven him.

## 4. DEFINITION

Guilt is the remorse that comes from an awareness of having done something wrong. The origin of guilt is psychological. From childhood, we have all been conditioned by family and society to act within defined standards of reasonableness and decency. Gradually, over a period of years, these standards are internalized and modified to become the core of what is called "conscience." When we do something that violates these internalized standards, we feel guilty. If we have been brought up in a religious environment, we feel an added measure of guilt when we break what we think is a divine commandment. Whenever we don't play according to our internalized rules, we feel miserable, and this misery is what guilt is all about.

## 5. COMPARISON AND CONTRAST

Although the two words may seem to share some connotations, *guilt* is not a synonym for *blame*. Guilt must be felt; blame must be assessed. Guilt implies self-reproach that comes from an internal consciousness of wrong. Blame hints at fault that has been externally assessed. A man may suffer guilt yet be entirely exonerated of blame; conversely, he may be blamed and yet feel no guilt. In short, while guilt is a feeling, blame is a judgment—and that is the chief distinction between the two.

## 6. DIVISION AND CLASSIFICATION

The Bible identifies three kinds of guilt: guilt of the unpardonable sin, redeemable guilt, and guilt of innocence. First, the guilt of the unpardonable sin belongs to any being who has become so steeped in evil that a change for good is no longer possible. Lucifer is said to have committed this sin by which he cut himself off eternally from Yahweh, the source of all good. Second, redeemable guilt is guilt that can be erased because it belongs to one whose heart is not incorrigibly corrupt, but which has weakened temporarily under the pressure of temptation. King David, for instance, murdered Uriah in order to marry Bathsheba, Uriah's wife. But despite this sin, David was a noble king with a thirst for righteousness; he was redeemable. Finally, the guilt of innocence is the guilt that Jesus bore when he decided to be crucified for the collective wrong of mankind even though he was, of all men, most innocent. In other words, Jesus died as if he were guilty when, in fact, his character was free from any trace of evil.

## 7. CAUSAL ANALYSIS

Guilt is caused by the failure of the will. The human mind, according to Freudian theory, is delicately balanced between the drive for instant gratification that comes from the id, and the desire for regulation and postponement that originates in the superego, which is sometimes identified with what we call the conscience. The function of the will is to mediate between these two desires. When the individual succumbs to temptation, the forces of the id have triumphed over the repression of the superego. But the superego fights back by tormenting the self with regret—in short, by evoking feelings of guilt. The stricter the superego, or conscience, the harsher the toll in guilt and the greater the person suffers. Whoever allows the will to fail must therefore pay for the gratification of the libido's urges in the coin of guilt.

These seven rhetorical modes allow us to teach idealized writing forms and techniques. You will not always use them, and you will most likely use them less and less consciously as your writing skills mature. But, in the beginning, you will find it easier to approach a writing assignment from the viewpoint of a specific mode rather than to invent a wholly original form for every essay.

# 6
# REPORTING

Narration and Description

=== •• *ADVICE* ••===

## HOW TO WRITE A NARRATION

If there is a rhetorical mode that can be said to be inborn in some people, it is narration. Most of us think we can tell a good story, and almost all of us have tried our hand at narration. Granted our stories may have been oral and told on the front porch to family and friends, but a story is a story and the techniques for telling one orally or in writing are essentially similar. Briefly and in order of importance, they are as follows:

### 1. Have a point.

The point of a story is what endows it with movement—with a beginning, a middle, and an end. If your story has no point it will also seem to have no movement, to go nowhere, to become bogged down and stagnant. Good storytellers always begin with a point in mind. They want to show how absent-minded Uncle Mickey has become; they wish to prove that "haste make waste." From this beginning the story should proceed without pause or slip. Sometimes a storyteller will even begin by telling us the point of the story, an admission that is often helpful to both writer and reader. A classic example of a story that begins by telling us its point is George Orwell's "Shooting an Elephant."

> One day something happened which in a roundabout way was enlightening. It was a tiny incident in itself, but it gave me a better glimpse than I had had before of the real nature of imperialism—the real motives for which despotic governments act.

This tells us what to expect. As we read on, we expect the author to deliver what he has advertised.

Have a point and stick to it—that age-old advice often given by writing teachers definitely applies to narration.

### 2. Pace your story.

Fiction tells lies about time. It has to. Real time is not always action-packed, does not always carry us to the dizzying brink or make us feel the throb of life. In fact, time is usually humdrum and dull in real life. But no reader wants a story to trudge through uneventful hours. What the reader wants is for the dull and humdrum to disappear in the puff of a sentence, and for the focus of the story always to be on time that is eventful and exciting. The technique of doing this is known as **pacing**.

All storytellers pace their materials to focus only on eventful periods and to ignore all inconsequential stretches in between. In the following example, taken from "We're Poor," an entire season disappears in a single paragraph:

> I didn't go back to school that fall. My mother said it was because I was sick. I did have a cold the week that school opened; I had been playing in the gutters and had got my feet wet, because there were holes in my shoes. . . . As long as I had to stay in the house anyway, they were all right.
>
> I stayed cooped up in the house, without any companionship. . . .

In "We're Poor" the author, Floyd Dell, learns from a Christmas experience that his family is destitute. The story consequently spends a good deal of time and attention on that climactic Christmas Eve during which the narrator makes this discovery. But the inconsequential months of the preceding fall are quickly dismissed in a paragraph.

### 3. Tell the story from a consistent point of view.

The point of view of a story is the angle from which it is told. This angle may be personal and intimate, a narrator being referred to by the pronoun *I*. Or it may be an omniscient point of view, in which the author is like a camera sweeping over the scene and pausing briefly to focus over the shoulders of selective characters. In any case, you must always stay in character when telling a story, and you must always remain consistent to the viewpoint from which you are telling it.

Here is an example of the omniscient point of view in a narration. It comes from "R.M.S. *Titanic*," Hanson Baldwin's gripping narration of the tragic maiden voyage of that ship. Baldwin is describing a lookout's first glimpse of the iceberg that was to doom the ocean liner:

> Out of the dark she came, a vast, dim, white, monstrous shape, directly in the *Titanic*'s path. For a moment Fleet doubted his eyes. But she was a deadly reality, this ghastly *thing*. Frantically, Fleet struck three bells—*something dead ahead*. He snatched the telephone and called the bridge:
>
> "Iceberg! Right ahead!"

The entire scene is shown from the viewpoint of Frederick Fleet, the lookout in the crow's nest. When the author describes the iceberg as a "ghastly thing" with a "monstrous shape" we willingly believe that so the iceberg must have appeared to Fleet as it loomed out of the icy night.

On the other hand, consider this excerpt taken from Beryl Markham's vivid childhood memoir, "Praise God for the Blood of the Bull":

> I lean for a moment on my spear peering outward at what is nothing, and then turn toward my thorn tree.

"Are you here, Lakwani?"
*Arap* Maina's voice is cool as water on shaded rocks.
"I am here, Maina."
He is tall and naked and very dark beside me. His shuka is tied around his left forearm to allow his body freedom to run.
"You are alone, and you have suffered, my child."
"I am all right, Maina, but I fear for Buller. I think he may die."
*Arap* Maina kneels on the earth and runs his hand over Buller's body.
*"He has been seriously and perhaps mortally wounded, Lakwani, but do not permit your mind to be too obsessed with any imaginary deficiencies or self-recriminations on your part. I conjecture that your lance has rescued him from a certain death, and God will recompense you for that. . . ."*

If the final paragraph sounds bizarre to you in the context of the excerpt, it should. We have altered the dialogue (and added italics to clearly distinguish it from Markham's words) to dramatize what we mean by a lapse in consistency. In the final paragraph Maina suddenly and inexplicably shifts from the simple speech of a native African to the pompous, long-winded speech of a British magistrate. A character in a narrative must always speak more or less the same way throughout and cannot lurch from one style of talk to another as we have made Maina do. Make your characters consistent and your narrative will seem believable.

## 4. Insert appropriate details.

Details are indispensable to narrative writing and can make the difference between boredom and delight in a reader. No one can teach you the art of including captivating details, but common sense tells us that you are more likely to include the absolutely right details if you write your narrations about what you truly know. Here, for example, in Beryl Markham's description of a warthog, we get the feeling that the writer has had personal experience with the animals:

> I know animals more gallant than the African warthog, but none more courageous. He is the peasant of the plains—the drab and dowdy digger in the earth. He is the uncomely but intrepid defender of family, home, and bourgeois convention, and he will fight anything of any size that intrudes upon his smug existence. Even his weapons are plebeian—curved tusks, sharp, deadly, but not beautiful, used inelegantly for rooting as well as for fighting.

We get this same feeling of authenticity from the details of this paragraph:

> Sunday dawned fair and clear. The *Titanic* steamed smoothly toward the west, faint streamers of brownish smoke trailing from her funnels. The purser held services in the saloon in the morning; on the steerage deck aft the immigrants were playing games and a Scotsman was puffing "The Campbells Are Coming" on his bagpipes in the midst of the uproar.

Yet we know that Baldwin was not aboard the *Titanic* and could not possibly have seen these things for himself. Lacking this personal experience, how did he manage to write such a convincing account? The answer is by doing his homework diligently. He pored over descriptions and transcripts left behind by survivors. His details are right not because they are informed by personal experience, but because he did the necessary research.

If you cannot write about what you know, the next best thing is to know about what you write. The advice to always research your subject before writing about it cannot be imparted too strongly. Even veteran fiction writers do not simply plunge into their narrations without doing the spadework necessary to make their scenes authentic. And while personal experience is probably the best basis for a narration, adequate and detailed research can be every bit as good.

=========== •• *EXAMPLES* •• ===========

**Beryl Markham**

——— • **PRAISE GOD FOR THE BLOOD** • ———
**OF THE BULL**

*Beryl Markham (1902–1986), an English aviator, grew up on her father's farm in East Africa, where she was allowed to roam freely and hunt with the native children. After working (at eighteen) as a racehorse trainer, she became a flyer and qualified for a commercial pilot's license. Markham was the first person to fly the North Atlantic from England to Nova Scotia, a feat that made world headlines in 1936. Her published books are her autobiography,* West with the Night *(1942), and* The Splendid Outcasts *(1987), a short-story collection.*

*This excerpt from* West with the Night *is a stirring narration about a wild boar hunt. What distinguishes it from other adventure narratives—aside from its wonderfully lyrical descriptive style—is that it was written by a woman recollecting an experience from her childhood.*

*Arap** Maina clasped the gourd of blood and curdled milk in both     1
hands and looked toward the sun. He chanted in a low voice:

---

*According to Mary S. Lovell in *Straight on Till Morning: The Biography of Beryl Markham* (St. Martin's Press, 1987, p. 330), and as noted by others, Markham or her original editor miscast the Swahili title *arap* as "Arab," among other words. We have ventured to correct this throughout the selection.—Eds.

'Praise God for the blood of the bull which brings strength to our    2
loins, and for the milk of the cow which gives warmth to the breasts
of our lovers.'

He drank deeply of the gourd then, let his belch roll upward from    3
his belly and resound against the morning silence. It was a silence that
we who stood there preserved until *arap* Maina had finished, because
this was religion; it was the ritual that came before the hunt. It was the
Nandi custom.

'Praise God for the blood of the bull,' we said, and stood before the    4
singiri, and waited.

Jebbta had brought the gourds for *arap* Maina, for *arap* Kosky, and    5
for me. But she looked only at me.

'The heart of a Murani is like unto stone,' she whispered, 'and his    6
limbs have the speed of an antelope. Where do you find the strength
and the daring to hunt with them, my sister?'

We were as young as each other, Jebbta and I, but she was a Nandi,    7
and if the men of the Nandi were like unto stone, their women were
like unto leaves of grass. They were shy and they were feminine and
they did the things that women are meant to do, and they never
hunted.

I looked down at the ankle-length skins Jebbta wore, which rustled    8
like taffeta when she moved, and she looked at my khaki shorts and
lanky, naked legs.

'Your body is like mine,' she said; 'it is the same and it is no stronger.'    9
She turned, avoiding the men with her eyes, because that too was law,
and went quickly away tittering like a small bird.

'The blood of the bull . . .' said *arap* Maina.    10

'We are ready.' *Arap* Kosky drew his sword from its scabbard and    11
tested its blade. The scabbard was of leather, dyed red, and it hung on
a beaded belt that encircled narrow and supple hips. He tested the
blade and put it back into the red scabbard.

'By the sacred womb of my mother, we will kill the wild boar today!'    12

He moved forward behind *arap* Maina with his broad shield and his    13
straight spear, and I followed *arap* Kosky with my own spear that was
still new and very clean, and lighter than theirs. Behind me came
Buller with no spear and no shield, but with the heart of a hunter and
jaws that were weapons enough. There were the other dogs, but there
was no dog like Buller.

We left the singiri with the first light of the sun warming the roofs    14
of the huts, with cattle, goats, and sheep moving along the trails that
led to open pastures—fat cattle, pampered cattle, attended as always
by the young, uncircumcised boys.

There were cows, steers, and heifers—liquid brown eyes, wet,    15
friendly nostrils, slobbery mouths that covered our legs with sticky
fluid as *arap* Maina pushed the stupid heads aside with his shield.

There were the pungent stench of goat's urine and a hot, comforting    16
odour seeping through the hides of the cattle, and light on the long
muscles of *arap* Maina and *arap* Kosky.

There was the whole of the day ahead—and the world to hunt in.    17

His little ritual forgotten now, *arap* Maina was no longer stern. He    18
laughed when *arap* Kosky or I slipped in the cattle dung that littered
our path, and shook his spear at a big black bull busy tearing up the
earth with his hooves. 'Take care of your people and dare not insult
me with a barren cow this year!'

But, for the most part, we ran silently in single file skirting the edge    19
of the dense Mau Forest, wheeling north to descend into the Rongai
Valley, its bottom a thousand feet below us.

Eight weeks had passed since the end of the heavy rains and the    20
grass in the valley had already reached the height of a man's knee. The
ears had begun to ripen in patches. Looking down upon it, the whole
was like a broad counterpane dyed in rust and yellow and golden
brown.

We filed along our path, almost invisible now, through the fresh-    21
smelling leleshwa bush, avoiding with quick turns and careful leaps
the stinging nettle and the shrubs that were armed with thorns. Buller
ran at my heels with the native dogs spread fanwise behind.

Halfway down the slope of the valley a bevy of partridges rose from    22
the grass and wheeled noisily into the sky. *Arap* Maina lifted his spear
almost imperceptibly; *arap* Kosky's long muscles were suddenly rigid.
Watching him, I froze in my tracks and held my breath. It was the
natural reaction of all hunters—that moment of listening after any
alarm.

But there was nothing. The spear of *arap* Maina dipped gently, the    23
long muscles of *arap* Kosky sprang again to life, Buller flicked his
stubby tail, and we were off again, one behind another, with the warm
sunlight weaving a pattern of our shadows in the thicket.

The heat of the valley rose to meet us. Singing cicadas, butterflies   24
like flowers before a wind fluttered against our bodies or hovered over
the low bush. Only small things that were safe in the daylight moved.

We had run another mile before the cold nose of Buller nudged   25
against my leg and the dog slipped quickly past me, past the two
Murani, to plant himself, alert and motionless, in the centre of
our path.

'Stop.' I whispered the word, putting my hand on *arap* Kosky's   26
shoulder. 'Buller has scented something.'

'I believe you are right, Lakweit!' With a wave of his hand *arap* Kosky   27
ordered the pack of native dogs to crouch. In that they were well
trained. They pressed their lean bellies on the ground, cocked their
ears, but scarcely seemed to breathe.

*Arap* Maina, sensing the need for free action, began laying down his   28
shield. The fingers of his left hand still touched the worn leather of its
handle, his legs were still bent at the knee, when a male reed-buck
bounded high into the air more than fifty yards away.

I saw *arap* Kosky's body bend like a bow and watched his spear fly   29
to his shoulder, but he was too late. The spear of *arap* Maina flashed in
a quick arc of silver light and the reed-buck fell with the hard point
sunk deep under his heart. Not even his first frantic bound had been
completed before *arap* Maina's arm had brought him down.

'Karara-ni! The hand of our leader is swifter than the flight of an   30
arrow and stronger than the stroke of a leopard.'

Heaping praise on *arap* Maina, *arap* Kosky ran toward the fallen   31
reed-buck, the sword from his red leather sheath drawn for the kill.

I looked at *arap* Maina's slender arms with their even, flat muscles   32
and saw no visible sign of such immense strength. *Arap* Maina, like
*arap* Kosky, was tall and lithe as a young bamboo, and his skin glowed
like an ember under a whisper of wind. His face was young and hard,
but there was soft humour in it. There was love of life in it—love for
the beauty and usefulness of his spear.

The spear was made of pliant steel tempered and forged by the   33
metallist of his own tribe. But it was also more than that.

To each Murani his spear is a symbol of his manhood, and as much   34
a part of himself as the sinews of his body. His spear is a manifestation
of his faith; without it he can achieve nothing—no land, no cattle, no
wives. Not even honour can be his until that day comes, after his
circumcision, when he stands before the gathered members of his

tribe—men and women of all ages, from manyattas as scattered as the seeds of wild grass—and swears allegiance to them and to their common heritage.

He takes the spear from the hands of the ol-oiboni and holds it, as he will always hold it while there is strength in his arms and no cloud of age before his eyes. It is the emblem of his blood and his breeding, and possessing it, he is suddenly a man.

Possessing it, it is never afterward beyond his reach.

*Arap* Maina placed his left foot on the reed-buck and carefully drew out his spear.

'I do not know, it may have struck a bone,' he said.

He ran bloody fingers along the sharp edges of the weapon and let a little smile twist his lips. 'By the will of God, the metal is not chipped! My spear is unhurt.' He stooped to pluck a handful of grass and wiped the blood from the bright, warm steel.

*Arap* Kosky and I had already begun to skin the animal, using our 'bushman's friends.' There was not much time to waste, because our real hunt for the wild boar had not yet begun. But still the meat of the reed-buck would provide food for the dogs.

'The sun has hit the valley,' said *arap* Maina; 'if we do not hurry the pigs will have gone in all directions like rolling weeds in a wind.'

*Arap* Kosky buried his fingers along the walls of the reed-buck's stomach, tearing it from the animal's frame.

'Hold this, Lakwani,' he said, 'and help me separate the intestines for the dogs.'

I took the slippery, jelly-like stomach in my hands and held it while I kneeled over the reed-buck.

'Maina, I still don't know how you managed to throw in time from the position you were in!'

*Arap* Kosky smiled.

'He is a Murani, Lakwani—and a Murani must always throw in time. Otherwise, some day a dangerous animal might charge swifter than the spear. Then, instead of mourning his death, our girls would laugh and say he should have stayed at home with the old men!'

*Arap* Maina leaned down and cut a chunk of meat from the cleanly skinned buck. He handed it to me for Buller. The rest, he and *arap* Kosky left to the native mongrels.

Buller trotted a short distance away from the kill, dropped his reward in a little pool of shade, and regarded his snarling cousins with

exquisite disdain. In the language that he spoke, and only I understood, he said quite clearly (with just a tinge of Swahili accent), 'By the
noble ancestry of my bull terrier father, those animals behave like the
wild dog!'

'And now,' said *arap* Maina, moving away from the carnage, 'we    50
must make ready for the hunt.'

The two Murani wore ochre-coloured shukas, each falling loosely    51
from a single knot on the left shoulder, and each looking somewhat
like a scanty Roman toga. They untied the knots now, wrapped the
shukas prudently around their waists, and stood in the sun, the muscles in their backs rippling under their oiled skins like fretted water
over a stony bed.

'Who can move freely with clothes on his body?' *arap* Kosky said as    52
he helped *arap* Maina with the leather thong that bound his braided
headdress in place. 'Who has seen the antelope run with rags upon
his back to hinder his speed!'

'Who indeed?' said *arap* Maina, smiling. 'I think sometimes you    53
babble like a demented goat, Kosky. The sun is high and the valley still
lies below us—and you speak to Lakwani of antelope wearing shukas!
Take up your spears, my friends, and let us go.'

Single file again, with *arap* Maina in the lead, then *arap* Kosky, then    54
myself, and Buller just behind, we ran on down into the valley.

There were no clouds and the sun stared down on the plain making    55
heat waves rise from it like flames without colour.

The Equator runs close to the Rongai Valley, and, even at so high an    56
altitude as this we hunted in, the belly of the earth was hot as live ash
under our feet. Except for an occasional gust of fretful wind that flattened the high, corn-like grass, nothing uttered—nothing in the valley
stirred. The chirrup-like drone of grasshoppers was dead, birds left
the sky unmarked. The sun reigned and there were no aspirants to
his place.

We stopped by the red salt-lick that cropped out of the ground in    57
the path of our trail. I did not remember a time when the salt-lick was
as deserted as this. Always before it had been crowded with grantii,
impala, kongoni, eland, water-buck, and a dozen kinds of smaller
animals. But it was empty today. It was like a marketplace whose flow
and bustle of life you had witnessed ninety-nine times, but, on your
hundredth visit, was vacant and still without even an urchin to tell
you why.

I put my hand on *arap* Maina's arm. 'What are you thinking, Maina?    58
Why is there no game today?'

'Be quiet, Lakweit, and do not move.'    59

I dropped the butt of my spear on the earth and watched the two    60
Murani stand still as trees, their nostrils distended, their ears alert to
all things. *Arap* Kosky's hand was tight on his spear like the claw of an
eagle clasping a branch.

'It is an odd sign,' murmured *arap* Maina, 'when the salt-lick is    61
without company!'

I had forgotten Buller, but the dog had not forgotten us. He had not    62
forgotten that, with all the knowledge of the two Murani, he still knew
better about such things. He thrust his body roughly between *arap*
Maina and myself, holding his black wet nose close to the ground.
And the hairs along his spine stiffened. His hackles rose and he
trembled.

We might have spoken, but we didn't. In his way Buller was more    63
eloquent. Without a sound, he said, as clearly as it could be said—
'Lion.'

'Do not move, Lakweit.' *Arap* Kosky stepped closer to me.    64

'Steady, Buller,' I whispered to the dog, trying to soothe his rising    65
belligerence.

Our eyes followed the direction of *arap* Maina's eyes. He was staring    66
into a small grass-curtained donga a few yards from the edge of the
salt-lick.

The lion that stood in the donga was not intimidated by *arap* Maina's    67
stare. He was not concerned with our number. He swung his tail in
easy arcs, stared back through the wispy grass, and his manner said,
'I am within my rights. If you seek a battle, what are we waiting for?'

He moved slowly forward, increasing the momentum of his tail,    68
flaunting his thick black mane.

'Ach! This is bad! He is angry—he wants to attack!' *Arap* Maina    69
spoke in an undertone.

No animal, however fast, has greater speed than a charging lion    70
over a distance of a few yards. It is a speed faster than thought—faster
always than escape.

Under my restraining hand I felt the muscles of Buller knot and    71
relax, in a surging flow of mounting fury. Buller's mind had reached
its blind spot. Uncontrolled, he would throw himself in gallant suicide
straight at the lion. I dug my fingers into the dog's coat and held tight.

*Arap* Maina's appearance was transformed. His face had taken on a    72
sullen, arrogant expression, his square, bold jaw jutted forward. His
eyes dimmed almost dreamily and sank behind high, shiny cheek-
bones. I watched the muscles on his neck swell like those on the neck
of an angry snake, and saw flecks of white froth appear in the corners
of his mouth. Passive and rigid he stared back at the lion.

He raised his shield at last, as if to make sure it was still in his hand,    73
and let his spear arm drop to his side to preserve all of its power for
whatever might come.

He knew that if the lion attacked, his own skill and *arap* Kosky's    74
would, in the end, prove sufficient—but not before at least one of us
had been killed or badly mauled. *Arap* Maina was more than a Murani;
he was a leader of Murani, and as such he must be able to think as well
as to fight. He must be capable of strategy.

Watching him still, as he in turn watched the lion, I knew that he    75
had a plan of action.

'Observe his eyes,' he said; 'he thinks very hard of many things. He    76
believes that we also think of those same things. We must show him
that we are fearless as he himself is fearless, but that his desires are
not our desires. We must walk straight past him firmly and with courage, and we must shame his anger by laughter and loud talk.'

*Arap* Kosky's brow was dotted with small bubbles of sweat. A slight    77
flicker of a smile crept over his face.

'Yes, true enough! The lion thinks of many things. I too think of    78
many things, and so does Lakweit. But your plan is a good one. We
will try it.'

*Arap* Maina lifted his head a little higher, turning it only enough to    79
keep the lion within the scope of his vision. He placed one sinewy leg
in front of the other, and stiffly, like a man walking the trunk of a tree
that bridges a chasm, he began to move. One after another, we followed. My hand still lay upon Buller's neck, but *arap* Kosky let the dog
and me slip past him to walk between the two Murani.

'Stay close to me, Lakweit'—*arap* Maina's voice was anxious. 'I fear    80
for you when it is not possible to see you.'

*Arap* Kosky burst suddenly into forced laughter.    81

'There is a tale about a rhino who needed a needle to do her hus-    82
band's sewing . . .' he began.

'So she borrowed one from the porcupine . . .' said *arap* Kosky.    83

'And swallowed it,' I contributed. 'I have heard that tale before,    84
Kosky!'

The Murani laughed louder. 'But perhaps our friend the lion has    85
not. Look at him. He is listening!'

'But not laughing,' said *arap* Maina. 'He moves as we move. He    86
comes closer!'

The lion had stalked out of the donga. Now, as we walked, we could    87
see that he guarded the slain body of a large kongoni. Smears of blood
were fresh on his forelegs, his jowls, and his chest. He was a lone
hunter—an individualist—a solitary marauder. His tail had stopped
swinging. His great head turned exactly in ratio to the speed of our
stride. The full force of the lion-smell, meaty, pungent, almost inde-
scribable, struck against our nostrils.

'Having swallowed the needle . . .' said *arap* Kosky.    88

'Silence—he attacks!'    89

I do not know who moved with greater speed—*arap* Maina or the    90
lion. I believe it must have been *arap* Maina. I think the Murani anticipated the charge even before the lion moved, and because of that, it
was a battle of wills instead of weapons.

The lion rushed from the fringe of the donga like a rock from    91
a catapult. He stopped like the same rock striking the walls of a
battlement.

*Arap* Maina was down on his left knee. Beside him was *arap* Kosky.    92
Each man, with his shield, his spear, and his body, was a fighting
machine no longer human, but only motionless and precise and coldly
ready. Buller and I crouched behind them, my own spear as ready as I
could make it in hands that were less hot from the sun than from
excitement and the pounding of my heart.

'Steady, Buller.'    93

'Do not move, Lakweit.'    94

The lion had stopped. He stood a few strides from *arap* Maina's    95
buffalo-hide shield, stared into *arap* Maina's eyes challenging him over
the top of it, and swung his tail like the weight of a clock. At that
moment I think the ants in the grass paused in their work.

And then *arap* Maina stood up.    96

I do not know how he knew that that particular instant was the right    97
instant or how he knew that the lion would accept a truce. It may have
been accomplished by the sheer arrogance of *arap* Maina's decision to

lower his shield, even if slightly, and to rise, no longer warlike, and to beckon us on with superb and sudden indifference. But however it was, the lion never moved.

We left him slicing the tall grass with his heavy tail, the blood of the kongoni drying on his coat. He was thinking many things.                                    98

And I was disappointed. Long after we had continued our trot toward the place where we knew there would be warthog, I thought how wonderful it would have been if the lion had attacked and I had been able to use my spear on him while he clawed at the shields of the two Murani, and how later they might have said, 'If it hadn't been for you, Lakweit . . . !'                                                      99

But then, I was very young.                                                        100

We ran until we reached the Molo River.                                           101

The river took its life from the Mau Escarpment and twisted down into the valley and gave life, in turn, to mimosa trees with crowns as broad as clouds, and long creepers and liana that strangled the sunlight and left the riverbank soothing and dark.                                 102

The earth on the bank was damp and pitted with footprints of the game that followed a web-work of thin trails to drink at dawn, leaving the racy smell of their droppings and their bodies in the air. The river forest was narrow and cool and vibrant with the songs of multi-coloured birds, and clotted with bright flowers that scorned the sun.          103

We laid down our weapons and rested under the trees and drank the chilled water, making cups with our hands.                                    104

*Arap* Maina lifted his face from the edge of the river and smiled gently. 'My mouth was like unto ashes, Lakweit,' he said, 'but truly this water is even sweeter than Jebbta's carefully brewed tembo!'        105

'It is sweeter,' said *arap* Kosky, 'and at this moment it is more welcome. I promise you, my stomach had turned almost sour with thirst!'     106

Looking at me, *arap* Maina laughed.                                              107

'Sour with thirst, he says, Lakweit! Sour, I think, with the sight of the lion at the salt-lick. Courage lives in a man's stomach, but there are times when it is not at home—and then the stomach is sour!'              108

*Arap* Kosky stretched his lithe, straight limbs on the tangled grass and smiled, showing teeth white as sun-cured bone. 'Talk lives in a man's head,' he answered, 'but sometimes it is very lonely because in the heads of some men there is nothing to keep it company—and so talk goes out through the lips.'                                              109

I laughed with both of them and pressed my shoulders comfortably 110 against the tree I leaned upon and looked through a chink in the ceiling of the forest at a vulture flying low.

'Maina, you know, I hate those birds. Their wings are separated like 111 a lot of small snakes.'

'As you say, Lakwani, they are creatures of evil omen—messengers 112 of the dead. Too cowardly to slay for themselves, they are satisfied with the stinking flesh from another man's kill.' *Arap* Maina spat, as if to clean his mouth after talking of unpleasant things.

Buller and the native dogs had gone into the river and wallowed in 113 the cool black muck along its banks. Buller returned now, sleek with slime, dripping and happy. He waited until he had the two Murani and me easily within range and then shook himself with a kind of devilish impudence and stood wagging his stump tail as we wiped water and mud from our faces.

'It is his way of making a joke,' said *arap* Kosky, looking at his 114 spattered shuka.

'It is also his way of telling us to move,' said *arap* Maina. 'The hunter 115 who lies on his back in the forest has little food and no sport. We have spent much time today at other things, but the warthog still waits.'

'What you say is true.' *Arap* Kosky rose from the grass. 'The warthog 116 still waits, and who is so without manners as to keep another waiting? Surely Buller is not. We must take his advice and go.'

We went up the riverbank, falling into single file again, and 117 threaded our way through a labyrinth of silver-grey boulders and rust-red anthills, shaped variously like witches caps or like the figures of kneeling giants or like trees without branches. Some of the anthills were enormous, higher than the huts we lived in, and some were no higher than our knees. They were scattered everywhere.

'Seek 'em out, Buller!' 118

But the dog needed no urging from me. He knew warthog country 119 when he saw it and he knew what to do about it. He rushed on ahead followed by the native mongrels running in a little storm of their own dust.

I know animals more gallant than the African warthog, but none 120 more courageous. He is the peasant of the plains—the drab and dowdy digger in the earth. He is the uncomely but intrepid defender of family, home, and bourgeois convention, and he will fight anything of any size that intrudes upon his smug existence. Even his weapons are plebeian—curved tusks, sharp, deadly, but not beautiful, used inelegantly for rooting as well as for fighting.

He stands higher than a domestic pig when he is full grown, and   121
his hide is dust-coloured and tough and clothed in bristles. His eyes are small and lightless and capable of but one expression—suspicion. What he does not understand, he suspects, and what he suspects, he fights. He can leap into the air and gut a horse while its rider still ponders a strategy of attack, and his speed in emerging from his hole to demonstrate the advantage of surprise is almost phenomenal.

He is not lacking in guile. He enters his snug little den (which is   122
borrowed, not to say commandeered, from its builder, the ant-bear) tail foremost so that he is never caught off guard. While he lies thus in wait for the curiosity or indiscretion of his enemy to bring him within range, he uses his snout to pile a heap of fine dust inside the hole. The dust serves as a smoke screen, bursting into a great, enshrouding billow the moment the warthog emerges to battle. He understands the tactical retreat, but is incapable of surrender, and if a dog is less than a veteran, or a man no more than an intrepid novice, not the only blood spilled will be the warthog's.

These facts were always in my mind when Buller hunted with us,   123
as he always did. But there was never any question of leaving him. It would have been like preventing a born soldier from marching with his regiment or like denying a champion fighter the right to compete in the ring on the grounds that he might be hurt. So Buller always came, and often I worried.

He ran ahead now, flanked by native dogs. The two Murani and I   124
spread out fanwise, running behind.

Our first sign of warthog was the squeal of a baby surprised in a   125
patch of grass by one of the mongrels. The squeal was followed by what seemed to be the squeals of all the baby warthogs in Africa, blended, magnified, and ear-splitting. Panic-stricken, the little pigs ran in all directions, like mice in the dream of a tabby cat. Their tails, held straight and erect, whisked through the grass as if so many bul-rushes had come to life to join in a frantic dance—a mad and some-what gay dance, but hardly as abandoned as it appeared, because the squeals were not without intent or meaning. They were meant for the small, alert ears of their father, who, when he came, would come with murder aforethought.

And come he did. None of us quite knew from where, but in the midst of the bedlam the grass in front of *arap* Maina parted as if cleaved by a scythe, and a large boar, blind with rage, plunged from it straight at the Murani.

If Buller had not run ahead after his own quarry, things might have happened differently. As it was, there was more amusement than tragedy in what did happen.

The boar was larger than average, and the bigger they are the tougher they are. Their hides are tough as boot-leather and nothing less than a spear thrust in a vital part will stop them.

*Arap* Maina was ready and waiting. The boar lunged, the Murani side-stepped, the spear flashed—and the boar was gone. But not alone. Behind him, spitting the flying dust, swearing in Nandi and in Swahili, ran *arap* Maina assisted by two of his mongrels—all of them following, with their eyes and their legs, the drunkenly swaying shaft of *arap* Maina's spear, its point lodged fast and solid between the shoulders of the boar.

*Arap* Kosky and I began to follow, but we couldn't laugh and run at the same time, so we stopped running and watched. In less than a minute the dogs, the man, and the warthog had found the horizon and disappeared behind it like four fabulous characters in search of Æsop.

We turned and trotted in the direction Buller had taken, listening to his deep, excited barks which came at regular intervals. After covering about three miles, we found him at the side of a large hole where he had run his warthog to ground.

Buller stood gazing at the dusty opening in silence, as if hoping the warthog would be such a fool as to think that since there were no more barks, there was no more dog. But the warthog was not taken in. He would emerge in his own good time, and he knew as well as Buller did that no dog would enter an occupied pig-hole and expect to come out alive.

'That's a good boy, Buller!' As usual, I was relieved to find him still unhurt, but the moment I spoke, he broke his strategic silence and demanded, with much tail-wagging and a series of whining barks, that the warthog be roused from his den and be brought back to battle.

More than once every inch of Buller's body had been ripped open in deep, ugly gashes on such pig-hunts, but at least he had lately learned not to go for the boar's head which, in the end, is fatal for any dog. Until now I had always managed to reach the scene of conflict in time to spear the warthog. But I might not always be so lucky.

I moved carefully to the back of the opening while *arap* Kosky stood     135
far to one side.

'If only we had some paper to rustle down the hole, Kosky . . .'     136

The Murani shrugged. 'We will have to try other tricks, Lakweit.'     137

It seems silly, and perhaps it is, but very often, after every other     138
method had failed, we had enticed warthogs into the open, long before they were quite ready to attack, simply by rustling a scrap of paper over the entrance of their holes. It was not always easy to get so limited an article as paper in East Africa at that time, but when we had it, it always worked. I haven't any idea of why it worked. Poking a stick through the hole never did, nor shouting into it, nor even using smoke. To the warthog, I think, the paper made a sound that was clearly insulting—comparable perhaps to what is known here and there nowadays as a Bronx cheer.

But we had no paper. We tried everything else without the least     139
success, and decided finally, in the face of Buller's contempt, to give it up and find out what had happened to *arap* Maina on his quest for the vanished spear.

We were leaving the scene of our mutual discouragement when *arap*     140
Kosky's curiosity overcame his natural caution. He bent down in front of the dark hole and the warthog came out.

It was more like an explosion than an attack by a wild pig. I could     141
see nothing through the thick burst of dust except extremities—the tail of the boar, the feet of *arap* Kosky, the ears of Buller, and the end of a spear.

My own spear was useless in my hands. I might thrust at the     142
warthog only to strike the dog or the Murani. It was an unholy tangle with no end, no beginning, and no opening. It lasted five seconds. Then the warthog shot from the tumbling mass like a clod from a whirlwind and disappeared through a corridor of anthills with Buller just behind slashing at the fleeing grey rump.

I turned to *arap* Kosky. He sat on the ground in a puddle of his own     143
blood, his right thigh cut through as if it had been hacked with a sword. He pressed a fold of his shuka against the wound and stood up. Buller's bark grew fainter, echoing through the forest of anthills.

The boar had won the first battle—and might win the second, unless
I hurried.

'Can you walk, Kosky? I must follow Buller. He may get killed.'    144

The Murani smiled without mirth. 'Of course, Lakweit! This is noth-    145
ing—except reward for my foolishness. I will go back to the singiri
slowly and have it attended to. It is best that you lose no time and
follow Buller. Already the sun is sinking. Go now, and run quickly!'

I clasped the round shaft of the spear tight in my hand and ran with    146
all my strength. For me—because I was still a child—this was a heart-
sinking experience. So many thoughts flashed through my mind.
Would my strength hold out long enough to save Buller from the tusks
of the boar? What had become of *arap* Maina, and why had I ever left
him? How would poor Kosky get home? Would he bleed too badly on
the way?

I ran on and on, following the barely audible bark of Buller, and the    147
few drops of blood clinging at intervals to the stalks of grass or soaking
into the absorbent earth. It was either Buller's blood or the warthog's.
Most likely it was both.

'Ah-yey, if I could only run a little faster!'    148

I must not stop for a minute. My muscles begin to ache, my legs    149
bleed from the 'wait-a-bit' thorns and the blades of elephant grass. My
hand, wet with perspiration, slips on the handle of my spear. I stumble, recover, and run on as the sound of Buller's bark grows louder,
closer, then fades again.

The sun is going and shadows lay like broad hurdles across my    150
path. Nothing is of any importance to me except my dog. The boar is
not retreating; he is leading Buller away from me, away from my help.

The blood spoor grows thicker and there is more of it. Buller's bark    151
is weak and irregular, but a little nearer. There are trees now jutting
from the plain, large, solitary, and silent.

The barking stops and there is nothing but the blood to follow. How    152
can there be so much blood? Breathless and running still, I peer ahead
into the changing light and see something move in a patch of turf
under a flat-topped thorn tree.

I stop and wait. It moves again and takes colour—black and white    153
and splattered with red. It is silent, but it moves. It is Buller.

I need neither breath nor muscles to cover the few hundred yards to    154 the thorn tree. I am suddenly there, under its branches, standing in a welter of blood. The warthog, as large as any I have ever seen, six times as large as Buller, sits exhausted on his haunches while the dog rips at its belly.

The old boar sees me, another enemy, and charges once more with    155
magnificent courage, and I sidestep and plunge my spear to his heart. He falls forward, scraping the earth with his great tusks, and lies still. I leave the spear in his body, turn to Buller, and feel tears starting to my eyes.

The dog is torn open like a slaughtered sheep. His right side is a    156
valley of exposed flesh from the root of his tail to his head, and his ribs show almost white, like the fingers of a hand smeared with blood. He looks at the warthog, then at me beside him on my knees, and lets his head fall into my arms. He needs water, but there is no water anywhere, not within miles.

'Ah-yey! Buller, my poor, foolish Buller!'    157

He licks my hand, and I think he knows I can do nothing, but    158
forgives me for it. I cannot leave him because the light is almost gone now and there are leopards that prowl at night, and hyenas that attack only the wounded and helpless.

'If only he lives through the night! If only he lives through the night!'    159

There is a hyena on a near hill who laughs at that, but it is a coward's    160
laugh. I sit with Buller and the dead boar under the thorn tree and watch the dark come closer.

The world grows bigger as the light leaves it. There are no bound-    161
aries and no landmarks. The trees and the rocks and the anthills begin to disappear, one by one, whisked away under the magical cloak of evening, I stroke the dog's head and try to close my eyes, but of course I cannot. Something moves in the tall grass, making a sound like the swish of a woman's skirt. The dog stirs feebly and the hyena on the hill laughs again.

I let Buller's head rest on the turf, stand up, and pull my spear from    162
the body of the boar. Somewhere to the left there is a sound, but I do not recognize it and I can see only dim shapes that are motionless.

I lean for a moment on my spear peering outward at what is nothing,    163
and then turn toward my thorn tree.

'Are you here, Lakwani?'    164

*Arap* Maina's voice is cool as water on shaded rocks.    165

'I am here, Maina.'    166

He is tall and naked and very dark beside me. His shuka is tied   167
around his left forearm to allow his body freedom to run.

'You are alone, and you have suffered, my child.'   168

'I am all right, Maina, but I fear for Buller. I think he may die.'   169

*Arap* Maina kneels on the earth and runs his hands over Buller's   170
body. 'He is badly hurt, Lakwani—very badly hurt—but do not grieve
too much. I think your spear has saved him from death, and God will
reward you for that. When the moon shines at midnight, we will carry
him home.'

'I am so happy that you have come, Maina.'   171

'How is it Kosky dared to leave you alone? He has betrayed the trust   172
I had in him!'

'Do not be angry with Kosky. He is badly hurt. His thigh was ripped   173
by the warthog.'

'He is no child, Lakweit. He is a Murani, and he should have been   174
more careful, knowing I was not there. After I recovered my spear, I
turned back to find you. I followed the blood on the grass for miles—
and then I followed Buller's barking. If the direction of the wind had
been wrong, you would still be alone. Kosky has the brains of the one-
eyed hare!'

'Ah-yey! What does it matter now, Maina? You are here, and I am   175
not alone. But I am very cold.'

'Lakwani, lie down and rest. I will keep watch until it is light enough   176
for us to go. You are very tired. Your face has become thin.'

He cuts handfuls of grass with his sword and makes a pillow, and I   177
lie down, clasping Buller in my arms. The dog is unconscious now and
bleeding badly. His blood trickles over my khaki shorts and my thighs.

The distant roar of a waking lion rolls against the stillness of the   178
night, and we listen. It is the voice of Africa bringing memories that
do not exist in our minds or in our hearts—perhaps not even in our
blood. It is out of time, but it is there, and it spans a chasm whose
other side we cannot see.

A ripple of lightning plays across the horizon.   179

'I think there will be a storm tonight, Maina.'   180

*Arap* Maina reaches out in the darkness and puts his hand on my   181
forehead. 'Relax, Lakwani; and I will tell you an amusing fable about
the cunning little Hare.'

He begins very slowly and softly, 'The Hare was a thief . . . In the   182
night he came to the manyatta . . . He lied to the Cow, and told her

that her Calf would die if she moved . . . Then he stood up on his hind legs and began sucking the milk from the Cow's milk bag . . . The other . . .'

But I am asleep.                                                                183

## VOCABULARY

| | | |
|---|---|---|
| resound (3) | belligerence (65) | guile (122) |
| bevy (22) | marauder (87) | commandeered (122) |
| imperceptibly (22) | impudence (113) | intrepid (122) |
| emblem (35) | dowdy (120) | bedlam (126) |
| exquisite (49) | bourgeois (120) | enticed (138) |
| aspirants (56) | plebeian (120) | welter (154) |

## THE FACTS

1. With what customary ceremony does a Nandi hunt begin?
2. What were the Nandi women like?
3. What is a Murani? Of what significance is his spear to a Murani?
4. According to the author, how do the Nandi women react to the news that a warrior has been killed on the hunt?
5. Why was the salt lick deserted?

## THE STRATEGIES

1. The dialogue throughout is rather flowery. Why? What effect do you think the author achieves by not rendering the exchanges in more colloquial speech?
2. Throughout the narration, Markham uses many local words and phrases such as *singiri, leleshwa,* and *oloiboni* which are to be found in no ordinary dictionary. What does this word choice add to her narrative?
3. Examine the description in paragraphs 14 through 16. To which of our senses does the author's description appeal? What effect does this appeal have on her description?
4. What use does Markham make of personification in her narration? Point to a specific example and comment on its effectiveness.
5. At paragraph 149, the tense of the narrative suddenly shifts. Why do you think the author does this? What does the shift in tenses add to her tale?

## THE ISSUES

1. Markham implies that Jebbta, the Nandi girl, was jealous because Markham was allowed to hunt with the men while Nandi women were not. Why

do you think the Nandi hunters allowed Markham to accompany them
when they would not take their own women on a hunt?

2. Based on the details of this story, what implied justification do you think
the Nandi had for banning women from the hunt?

3. What division of labor exists in our own society between men and women?
Why is it necessary, or not necessary anymore, for men and women of our
society to have different kinds of jobs?

4. Where in our own society is a strict division of labor between the sexes still
observed? What is the justification for it?

5. What advantages do you think Markham enjoyed in her free African upbringing that are denied to girls reared in our own society? What disadvantages can you perceive in such an upbringing?

## SUGGESTIONS FOR WRITING

1. Write a narration about any experience that made you badly afraid.
2. Write an argument for or against hunting for sport.
3. Tell the story of an exciting hunt or fishing trip you've taken.

### George Orwell

# —————— • SHOOTING AN ELEPHANT • ——————

*George Orwell (1903–1950) was the pseudonym of Eric Arthur Blair. Born in
India and educated at Eton, he served with the imperial police in Burma and
fought on the republican side in the Spanish civil war. Orwell published two
influential novels,* Animal Farm *(1945) and* Nineteen Eight-four *(1949). He
is widely admired for the crisp, lucid prose style of his essays.*

*George Orwell writes in a style that has been described as having "singular
directness and honesty." In this selection he relates an incident that occurred
while he was with the imperial police in Burma.*

In Moulmein, in Lower Burma, I was hated by large numbers of    1
people—the only time in my life that I have been important enough
for this to happen to me. I was sub-divisional police officer of the town,
and in an aimless, petty kind of way anti-European feeling was very
bitter. No one had the guts to raise a riot, but if a European woman
went through the bazaars alone somebody would probably spit betel
juice over her dress. As a police officer I was an obvious target and
was baited whenever it seemed safe to do so. When a nimble Burman
tripped me up on the football field and the referee (another Burman)

looked the other way, the crowd yelled with hideous laughter. This happened more than once. In the end the sneering yellow faces of young men that met me everywhere, the insults hooted after me when I was at a safe distance, got badly on my nerves. The young Buddhist priests were the worst of all. There were several thousand of them in the town and none of them seemed to have anything to do except stand on the street corners and jeer at Europeans.

All this was perplexing and upsetting. For at that time I had already     2
made up my mind that imperialism was an evil thing and the sooner I chucked up my job and got out of it the better. Theoretically—and secretly, of course—I was all for the Burmese and all against their oppressors, the British. As for the job I was doing, I hated it more bitterly than I can perhaps make clear. In a job like that you see the dirty work of Empire at close quarters. The wretched prisoners hud- dling in the stinking cages of the lock-ups, the grey, cowed faces of the long-term convicts, the scarred buttocks of the men who had been flogged with bamboos—all these oppressed me with an intolerable sense of guilt. But I could get nothing into perspective. I was young and ill-educated and I had had to think out my problems in the utter silence that is imposed on every Englishman in the East. I did not even know that the British Empire is dying, still less did I know that it is a great deal better than the younger empires that are going to supplant it. All I knew was that I was stuck between my hatred of the empire I served and my rage against the evil-spirited little beasts who tried to make my job impossible. With one part of my mind I thought of the British Raj as an unbreakable tyranny, as something clamped down, in *saecula saeculorum*,* upon the will of prostrate peoples; with another part I thought that the greatest joy in the world would be to drive a bayonet into a Buddhist priest's guts. Feelings like these are the normal by-products of imperialism; ask any Anglo-Indian official, if you can catch him off duty.

One day something happened which in a roundabout way was     3
enlightening. It was a tiny incident in itself, but it gave me a better glimpse than I had had before of the real nature of imperialism—the real motives for which despotic governments act. Early one morning the sub-inspector at a police station the other end of the town rang me up on the 'phone and said that an elephant was ravaging the bazaar.

*Latin, "for ever and ever."—Ed.

Would I please come and do something about it? I did not know what I could do, but I wanted to see what was happening and I got on to a pony and started out. I took my rifle, an old .44 Winchester and much too small to kill an elephant, but I thought the noise might be useful *in terrorem*.* Various Burmans stopped me on the way and told me about the elephant's doings. It was not, of course, a wild elephant, but a tame one which had gone "must." It had been chained up, as tame elephants always are when their attack of "must" is due, but on the previous night it had broken its chain and escaped. Its mahout, the only person who could manage it when it was in that state, had set out in pursuit, but had taken the wrong direction and was now twelve hours' journey away, and in the morning the elephant had suddenly reappeared in the town. The Burmese population had no weapons and were quite helpless against it. It had already destroyed some-body's bamboo hut, killed a cow and raided some fruit-stalls and de-voured the stock; also it had met the municipal rubbish van and, when the driver jumped out and took to his heels, had turned the van over and inflicted violences upon it.

The Burmese sub-inspector and some Indian constables were wait-  4
ing for me in the quarter where the elephant had been seen. It was a very poor quarter, a labyrinth of squalid bamboo huts, thatched with palm-leaf, winding all over a steep hillside. I remember that it was a cloudy, stuffy morning at the beginning of the rains. We began questioning the people as to where the elephant had gone and, as usual, failed to get any definite information. That is invariably the case in the East; a story always sounds clear enough at a distance, but the nearer you get to the scene of events the vaguer it becomes. Some of the people said that the elephant had gone in one direction, some said that he had gone in another, some professed not even to have heard of any elephant. I had almost made up my mind that the whole story was a pack of lies, when we heard yells a little distance away. There was a loud, scandalized cry of "Go away, child! Go away this instant!" and an old woman with a switch in her hand came round the corner of a hut, violently shooing away a crowd of naked children. Some more women followed, clicking their tongues and exclaiming; evidently there was something that the children ought not to have seen. I rounded the hut and saw a man's dead body sprawling in the mud.

---

*Latin, "as a warning."—Ed.

He was an Indian, a black Dravidian coolie, almost naked, and he could not have been dead many minutes. The people said that the elephant had come suddenly upon him round the corner of the hut, caught him with its trunk, put its foot on his back and ground him into the earth. This was the rainy season and the ground was soft, and his face had scored a trench a foot deep and a couple of yards long. He was lying on his belly with arms crucified and head sharply twisted to one side. His face was coated with mud, the eyes wide open, the teeth bared and grinning with an expression of unendurable agony. (Never tell me, by the way, that the dead look peaceful. Most of the corpses I have seen looked devilish.) The friction of the great beast's foot had stripped the skin from his back as neatly as one skins a rabbit. As soon as I saw the dead man I sent an orderly to a friend's house nearby to borrow an elephant rifle. I had already sent back the pony, not wanting it to go mad with fright and throw me if it smelt the elephant.

The orderly came back in a few minutes with a rifle and five car- 5 tridges, and meanwhile some Burmans had arrived and told us that the elephant was in the paddy fields below, only a few hundred yards away. As I started forward practically the whole population of the quarter flocked out of the houses and followed me. They had seen the rifle and were all shouting excitedly that I was going to shoot the elephant. They had not shown much interest in the elephant when he was merely ravaging their homes, but it was different now that he was going to be shot. It was a bit of fun to them, as it would be to an English crowd; besides they wanted the meat. It made me vaguely uneasy. I had no intention of shooting the elephant—I had merely sent for the rifle to defend myself if necessary—and it is always unnerving to have a crowd following you. I marched down the hill, looking and feeling a fool, with the rifle over my shoulder and an ever-growing army of people jostling at my heels. At the bottom, when you got away from the huts, there was a metalled road and beyond that a miry waste of paddy fields a thousand yards across, not yet ploughed but soggy from the first rains and dotted with coarse grass. The elephant was standing eight yards from the road, his left side towards us. He took not the slightest notice of the crowd's approach. He was tearing up bunches of grass, beating them against his knees to clean them and stuffing them into his mouth.

I had halted on the road. As soon as I saw the elephant I knew with 6 perfect certainty that I ought not to shoot him. It is a serious matter to shoot a working elephant—it is comparable to destroying a huge and costly piece of machinery—and obviously one ought not to do it if it can possibly be avoided. And at that distance, peacefully eating, the elephant looked no more dangerous than a cow. I thought then and I think now that his attack of "must" was already passing off; in which case he would merely wander harmlessly about until the mahout came back and caught him. Moreover, I did not in the least want to shoot him. I decided that I would watch him for a little while to make sure that he did not turn savage again, and then go home.

But at that moment I glanced round at the crowd that had followed me. It was an immense crowd, two thousand at the least and growing every minute. It blocked the road for a long distance on either side. I looked at the sea of yellow faces above the garish clothes—faces all happy and excited over this bit of fun, all certain that the elephant was going to be shot. They were watching me as they would watch a conjurer about to perform a trick. They did not like me, but with the magical rifle in my hands I was momentarily worth watching. And suddenly I realized that I should have to shoot the elephant after all. The people expected it of me and I had got to do it; I could feel their two thousand wills pressing me forward, irresistibly. And it was at this moment, as I stood there with the rifle in my hands, that I first grasped the hollowness, the futility of the white man's dominion in the East. Here was I, the white man with his gun, standing in front of the unarmed native crowd—seemingly the leading actor of the piece; but in reality I was only an absurd puppet pushed to and fro by the will of those yellow faces behind. I perceived in this moment that when the white man turns tyrant it is his own freedom that he destroys. He becomes a sort of hollow, posing dummy, the conventionalized figure of a sahib. For it is the condition of his rule that he shall spend his life in trying to impress the "natives," and so in every crisis he has got to do what the "natives" expect of him. He wears a mask, and his face grows to fit it. I had got to shoot the elephant. I had committed myself to doing it when I sent for the rifle. A sahib has got to act like a sahib; he has got to appear resolute, to know his own mind and do definite things. To come all that way, rifle in hand, with two thousand people marching at my heels, and then to trail feebly away, having done nothing—no, that was impossible. The crowd would laugh at me. And my whole life, every white man's life in the East, was one long struggle not to be laughed at.

But I did not want to shoot the elephant. I watched him beating his    8
bunch of grass against his knees, with that preoccupied grandmoth-
erly air that elephants have. It seemed to me that it would be murder
to shoot him. At that age I was not squeamish about killing animals,
but I had never shot an elephant and never wanted to. (Somehow it
always seems worse to kill a *large* animal.) Besides, there was the
beast's owner to be considered. Alive, the elephant was worth at least
a hundred pounds; dead, he would only be worth the value of his
tusks, five pounds, possibly. But I had got to act quickly. I turned to
some experienced-looking Burmans who had been there when we
arrived, and asked them how the elephant had been behaving. They
all said the same thing: he took no notice of you if you left him alone,
but he might charge if you went too close to him.

It was perfectly clear to me what I ought to do. I ought to walk up    9
to within, say, twenty-five yards of the elephant and test his behavior.
If he charged, I could shoot; if he took no notice of me, it would be safe
to leave him until the mahout came back. But also I knew that I was
going to do no such thing. I was a poor shot with a rifle and the ground
was soft mud into which one would sink at every step. If the elephant
charged and I missed him, I should have about as much chance as a
toad under a steam-roller. But even then I was not thinking particularly
of my own skin, only of the watchful yellow faces behind. For at that
moment, with the crowd watching me, I was not afraid in the ordinary
sense, as I would have been if I had been alone. A white man mustn't
be frightened in front of "natives"; and so, in general, he isn't frightened. The sole thought in my mind was that if anything went wrong
those two thousand Burmans would see me pursued, caught, trampled on and reduced to a grinning corpse like that Indian up the hill.
And if that happened it was quite probable that some of them would
laugh. That would never do. There was only one alternative. I shoved
the cartridges into the magazine and lay down on the road to get a
better aim.

The crowd grew very still, and a deep, low, happy sigh, as of people    10
who see the theatre curtain go up at last, breathed from innumerable
throats. They were going to have their bit of fun after all. The rifle was
a beautiful German thing with cross-hair sights. I did not then know
that in shooting an elephant one would shoot to cut an imaginary bar
running from ear-hole to ear-hole. I ought, therefore, as the elephant
was sideway on, to have aimed straight at his ear-hole; actually I aimed

several inches in front of this, thinking the brain would be further forward.

When I pulled the trigger I did not hear the bang or feel the kick—    11
one never does when a shot goes home—but I heard the devilish roar of glee that went up from the crowd. In that instant, in too short a time, one would have thought, even for the bullet to get there, a mysterious, terrible change had come over the elephant. He neither stirred nor fell, but every line of his body had altered. He looked suddenly stricken, shrunken, immensely old, as though the frightful impact of the bullet had paralyzed him without knocking him down. At last, after what seemed a long time—it might have been five seconds, I dare say—he sagged flabbily to his knees. His mouth slobbered. An enormous senility seemed to have settled upon him. One could have imagined him thousands of years old. I fired again into the same spot. At the second shot he did not collapse but climbed with desperate slowness to his feet and stood weakly upright, with legs sagging and head drooping. I fired a third time. That was the shot that did for him. You could see the agony of it jolt his whole body and knock the last remnant of strength from his legs. But in falling he seemed for a moment to rise, for as his hind legs collapsed beneath him he seemed to tower upward like a huge rock toppling, his trunk reaching skywards like a tree. He trumpeted, for the first and only time. And then down he came, his belly towards me, with a crash that seemed to shake the ground even where I lay.

I got up. The Burmans were already racing past me across the mud.    12
It was obvious that the elephant would never rise again, but he was not dead. He was breathing very rhythmically with long rattling gasps, his great mound of a side painfully rising and falling. His mouth was wide open—I could see far down into caverns of pale pink throat. I waited for a long time for him to die, but his breathing did not weaken. Finally I fired my two remaining shots into the spot where I thought his heart must be. The thick blood welled out of him like red velvet, but still he did not die. His body did not even jerk when the shots hit him, the tortured breathing continued without a pause. He was dying, very slowly and in great agony, but in some world remote from me where not even a bullet could damage him further. I felt that I had got to put an end to that dreadful noise. It seemed dreadful to see the great beast lying there, powerless to move and yet powerless to die, and not even to be able to finish him. I sent back for my small rifle and

poured shot after shot into his heart and down his throat. They seemed to make no impression. The tortured gasps continued as steadily as the ticking of a clock.

In the end I could not stand it any longer and went away. I heard 13 later that it took him half an hour to die. Burmans were bringing dahs and baskets even before I left, and I was told they had stripped his body almost to the bones by the afternoon.

Afterwards, of course, there were endless discussions about the 14 shooting of the elephant. The owner was furious, but he was only an Indian and could do nothing. Besides, legally I had done the right thing, for a mad elephant has to be killed, like a mad dog, if its owner fails to control it. Among the Europeans opinion was divided. The older men said I was right, the younger men said it was a damn shame to shoot an elephant for killing a coolie, because an elephant was worth more than any damn Coringhee coolie. And afterwards I was very glad that the coolie had been killed; it put me legally in the right and it gave me a sufficient pretext for shooting the elephant. I often wondered whether any of the others grasped that I had done it solely to avoid looking a fool.

## *VOCABULARY*

| | | |
|---|---|---|
| supplant (2) | labyrinth (4) | conventionalized (7) |
| prostrate (2) | squalid (4) | resolute (7) |
| despotic (3) | garish (7) | pretext (14) |

## *THE FACTS*

1. Which class of Burmese did Orwell despise most of all?
2. What would likely happen to a white woman who went through the bazaars alone?
3. What is Orwell's opinion of the younger empires that were going to supplant the British Empire?
4. What is invariably the case with stories set in the East?
5. According to Orwell, what is a condition of white rule over the empire?

## *THE STRATEGIES*

1. Orwell writes: "They had not shown much interest in the elephant when he was merely ravaging their homes, but it was different now that he was going to be shot." What tone is he using here?

2. Why does Orwell use Latin phrases? What purpose do they have in the story?
3. The story is told in two tenses: the past and the present. What effect does this have on its telling?
4. Orwell encloses some remarks in parentheses in paragraphs 4 and 8. Why are these remarks set off in this way?
5. What analogy does Orwell use in paragraph 10 to describe his feelings about the crowd gathered to see him kill the elephant? Is this an appropriate analogy? Explain.

## THE ISSUES

1. What is the value of a role and of role playing in the relationships of everyday life?
2. What are the obvious disadvantages of role playing?
3. How would you characterize Orwell's attitude toward the empire he serves?
4. How do you think the author might have behaved, and what do you think he might have done, if he had had other Europeans with him when he met the elephant?
5. What circumstances of today's life might similarly make someone, say a student, feel impelled to behave in a way contrary to his or her better judgment?

## SUGGESTIONS FOR WRITING

1. Analyze and discuss "Shooting an Elephant" as a story about the abstract versus the particular.
2. Write an essay entitled "I Wore a Mask, and My Face Grew to Fit It."

### Hanson W. Baldwin

## • R.M.S. *TITANIC* •

*Hanson W. Baldwin (b. 1903) was born in Baltimore and educated at the United States Naval Academy. He resigned from active naval service in 1927 and eventually became military and naval correspondent for the* New York Times. *He has written innumerable articles and books on military affairs.*

*"R.M.S. Titanic" is a straightforward but compelling narrative of one of the worst ocean-liner disasters in history. Avoiding both interpretation and emotion, the narrator nevertheless vividly recreates the sequence of events leading up to the disaster.*

The White Star liner *Titanic*, largest ship the world had ever known,    1
sailed from Southampton on her maiden voyage to New York on
April 10, 1912. The paint on her strakes was fair and bright; she was
fresh from Harland and Wolff's Belfast yards, strong in the strength of
her forty-six thousand tons of steel, bent, hammered, shaped and
riveted through the three years of her slow birth.

There was little fuss and fanfare at her sailing; her sister-ship, the    2
*Olympic*—slightly smaller than the *Titanic*—had been in service for
some months and to her had gone the thunder of the cheers.

But the *Titanic* needed no whistling steamers or shouting crowds to    3
call attention to her superlative qualities. Her bulk dwarfed the ships
near her as longshoremen singled up her mooring lines and cast off
the turns of heavy rope from the dock bollards. She was not only the
largest ship afloat, but was believed to be the safest. Carlisle, her
builder, had given her double bottoms and had divided her hull into
sixteen water-tight compartments, which made her, men thought, unsinkable. She had been built to be and had been described as a gigantic
lifeboat. Her designers' dreams of a triple-screw giant, a luxurious,
floating hotel, which could speed to New York at twenty-three knots,
had been carefully translated from blue prints and mold loft lines at
the Belfast yards into a living reality.

The *Titanic*'s sailing from Southampton, though quiet, was not    4
wholly uneventful. As the liner moved slowly toward the end of her
dock that April day, the surge of her passing sucked away from the
quay the steamer *New York*, moored just to seaward of the *Titanic*'s
berth. There were sharp cracks as the manila mooring lines of the *New
York* parted under the strain. The frayed ropes writhed and whistled
through the air and snapped down among the waving crowd on the
pier; the *New York* swung toward the *Titanic*'s bow, was checked and
dragged back to the dock barely in time to avert a collision. Seamen
muttered, thought it an ominous start.

Past Spithead and the Isle of Wight the *Titanic* steamed. She called    5
at Cherbourg at dusk and then laid her course for Queenstown. At
1:30 P.M. on Thursday, April 11, she stood out of Queenstown harbor,
screaming gulls soaring in her wake, with 2,201 persons—men,
women, and children—aboard.

Occupying the Empire bedrooms and Georgian suites of the first-    6
class accommodations were many well-known men and women—

Colonel John Jacob Astor and his young bride; Major Archibald Butt, military aide to President Taft, and his friend, Frank D. Millet, the painter; John B. Thayer, vice-president of the Pennsylvania Railroad, and Charles M. Hayes, president of the Grand Trunk Railway of Canada; W. T. Stead, the English journalist; Jacques Futrelle, French novelist; H. B. Harris, theatrical manager, and Mrs. Harris; Mr. and Mrs. Isidor Straus; and J. Bruce Ismay, chairman and managing director of the White Star line.

Down in the plain wooden cabins of the steerage class were 706    7
immigrants to the land of promise, and trimly stowed in the great holds was a cargo valued at $420,000: oak beams, sponges, wine, calabashes, and an odd miscellany of the common and the rare.

The *Titanic* took her departure on Fastnet Light and, heading into    8
the night, laid her course for New York. She was due at Quarantine the following Wednesday morning.

Sunday dawned fair and clear. The *Titanic* steamed smoothly toward    9
the west, faint streamers of brownish smoke trailing from her funnels. The purser held services in the saloon in the morning; on the steerage deck aft the immigrants were playing games and a Scotsman was putting "The Campbells Are Coming" on his bagpipes in the midst of the uproar.

At 9 A.M. a message from the steamer *Caronia* sputtered into the    10
wireless shack:

> Captain, *Titanic*—Westbound steamers report bergs growlers and field ice in 42 degrees N. to 51 degrees W. 12th April.
>
> Compliments—Barr.

It was cold in the afternoon; the sun was brilliant, but the *Titanic*,    11
her screws turning over at 75 revolutions per minute, was approaching the Banks.

In the Marconi cabin Second Operator Harold Bride, ear-phones    12
clamped on his head, was figuring accounts; he did not stop to answer when he heard *MWL*, Continental Morse for the nearby Leyland liner, *Californian*, calling the *Titanic*. The *Californian* had some message about three icebergs; he didn't bother then to take it down. About 1:42 P.M. the rasping spark of those days spoke again across the water. It was the *Baltic*, calling the *Titanic*, warning her of ice on the steamer track. Bride took the message down and sent it up to the bridge. The officer-

of-the-deck glanced at it; sent it to the bearded master of the *Titanic*, Captain E. C. Smith, a veteran of the White Star service. It was lunch time then; the Captain, walking along the promenade deck, saw Mr. Ismay, stopped, and handed him the message without comment. Ismay read it, stuffed it in his pocket, told two ladies about the icebergs, and resumed his walk. Later, about 7:15 P.M., the Captain requested the return of the message in order to post it in the chart room for the information of officers.

Dinner that night in the Jacobean dining room was gay. It was bitter on deck, but the night was calm and fine; the sky was moonless but studded with stars twinkling coldly in the clear air.    13

After dinner some of the second-class passengers gathered in the saloon, where the Reverend Mr. Carter conducted a "hymn sing-song." It was almost ten o'clock and the stewards were waiting with biscuits and coffee as the group sang:    14

> "O, hear us when we cry to Thee
> For those in peril on the sea."

On the bridge Second Officer Lightoller—short, stocky, efficient—was relieved at ten o'clock by First Officer Murdoch. Lightoller had talked with other officers about the proximity of ice; at least five wireless ice warnings had reached the ship; lookouts had been cautioned to be alert; captains and officers expected to reach the field at any time after 9:30 P.M. At 22 knots, its speed unslackened, the *Titanic* plowed on through the night.    15

Lightoller left the darkened bridge to his relief and turned in. Captain Smith went to his cabin. The steerage was long since quiet; in the first and second cabins lights were going out; voices were growing still, people were asleep. Murdoch paced back and forth on the bridge, peering out over the dark water, glancing now and then at the compass in front of Quartermaster Hichens at the wheel.    16

In the crow's nest, Lookout Frederick Fleet and his partner, Leigh, gazed down at the water, still and unruffled in the dim, starlit darkness. Behind and below them the ship, a white shadow with here and there a last winking light; ahead of them a dark and silent and cold ocean.    17

There was a sudden clang. "Dong-dong. Dong-dong. Dong-dong. Dong!" The metal clapper of the great ship's bell struck out 11:30.    18

Mindful of the warnings, Fleet strained his eyes, searching the darkness for the dreaded ice. But there were only the stars and the sea.

In the wireless room, where Phillips, first operator, had relieved    19
Bride, the buzz of the *Californian's* set again crackled into the earphones:

CALIFORNIAN: "Say, old man, we are stuck here, surrounded by ice."
TITANIC: "Shut up, shut up; keep out. I am talking to Cape Race; you
are jamming my signals."

Then, a few minutes later—about 11:40 . . .    20

## II

Out of the dark she came, a vast, dim, white, monstrous shape,    21
directly in the *Titanic's* path. For a moment Fleet doubted his eyes. But
she was a deadly reality, this ghastly *thing*. Frantically, Fleet struck
three bells—*something dead ahead*. He snatched the telephone and
called the bridge:
"Iceberg! Right ahead!"    22
The first Officer heard but did not stop to acknowledge the message.    23
"Hard-a-starboard!"    24
Hichens strained at the wheel; the bow swung slowly to port. The    25
monster was almost upon them now.

Murdoch leaped to the engine-room telegraph. Bells clanged. Far    26
below in the engine-room those bells struck the first warning. Danger!
The indicators on the dial faces swung round to "Stop!" Then "Full
speed astern!" Frantically the engineers turned great valve wheels;
answered the bridge bells. . . .

There was a slight shock, a brief scraping, a small list to port. Shell    27
ice—slabs and chunks of it—fell on the foredeck. Slowly the *Titanic*
stopped.

Captain Smith hurried out of his cabin.    28
"What has the ship struck?"    29
Murdoch answered, "An iceberg, sir. I hard-a-star-boarded and re-    30
versed the engines, and I was going to hard-a-port around it, but she
was too close. I could not do any more. I have closed the water-tight
doors."
Fourth Officer Boxhall, other officers, the carpenter, came to the    31

bridge. The Captain sent Boxhall and the carpenter below to ascertain the damage.

A few lights switched on in the first and second cabins; sleepy     32
passengers peered through porthole glass; some casually asked the stewards:

"Why have we stopped?"     33

"I don't know, sir, but I don't suppose it is anything much."     34

In the smoking room a quorum of gamblers and their prey were still     35
sitting round a poker table; the usual crowd of kibitzers looked on. They had felt the slight jar of the collision and had seen an eighty-foot ice mountain glide by the smoking room windows, but the night was calm and clear, the *Titanic* was "unsinkable"; they hadn't bothered to go on deck.

But far below, in the warren of passages on the starboard side for-     36
ward, in the forward holds and boiler rooms, men could see that the *Titanic's* hurt was mortal. In No. 6 boiler room, where the red glow from the furnaces lighted up the naked, sweaty chests of coal-blackened firemen, water was pouring through a great gash about two feet above the floor plates. This was no slow leak; the ship was open to the sea; in ten minutes there were eight feet of water in No. 6. Long before then the stokers had raked the flaming fires out of the furnaces and had scrambled through the water-tight doors into No. 5 or had climbed up the long steel ladders to safety. When Boxhall looked at the mailroom in No. 3 hold, twenty-four feet above the keel, the mailbags were already floating about in the slushing water. In No. 5 boiler room a stream of water spurted into an empty bunker. All six compartments forward of No. 4 were open to the sea; in ten seconds the iceberg's jagged claw had ripped a three-hundred-foot slash in the bottom of the great *Titanic*.

Reports came to the bridge; Ismay in dressing gown ran out on deck     37
in the cold, still starlit night, climbed up the bridge ladder.

"What has happened?"     38

Captain Smith: "We have struck ice."     39

"Do you think she is seriously damaged?"     40

Captain Smith: "I'm afraid she is."     41

Ismay went below and passed Chief Engineer William Bell fresh     42
from an inspection of the damaged compartments. Bell corroborated the Captain's statement; hurried back down the glistening steel ladders to his duty. Man after man followed him—Thomas Andrews, one

of the ship's designers, Archie Frost, the builder's chief engineer, and his twenty assistants—men who had no posts of duty in the engine-room but whose traditions called them there.

On deck, in corridor and stateroom, life flowed again. Men, women    43
and children awoke and questioned; orders were given to uncover the lifeboats; water rose into the firemen's quarters; half-dressed stokers streamed up on deck. But the passengers—most of them—did not know that the *Titanic* was sinking. The shock of the collision had been so slight that some were not awakened by it; the *Titanic* was so huge that she must be unsinkable; the night was too calm, too beautiful, to think of death at sea.

Captain Smith half ran to the door of the radio shack. Bride, partly    44
dressed, eyes dulled with sleep, was standing behind Phillips, waiting.

"Send the call for assistance."    45

The blue spark danced: "CQD—CQD—CQD—CQ—"    46

Miles away Marconi men heard. Cape Race heard it, and the steam-    47
ships *La Provence* and *Mt. Temple*.

The sea was surging into the *Titanic*'s hold. At 12:20 the water burst    48
into the seamen's quarters through a collapsed fore and aft wooden bulkhead. Pumps strained in the engine-rooms—men and machinery making a futile fight against the sea. Steadily the water rose.

The boats were swung out—slowly; for the deck hands were late in    49
reaching their stations, there had been no boat drill, and many of the crew did not know to what boats they were assigned. Orders were shouted; the safety valves had lifted, and steam was blowing off in a great rushing roar. In the chart house Fourth Officer Boxhall bent above a chart, working rapidly with pencil and dividers.

12:25 A.M. Boxhall's position is sent out to a fleet of vessels: "Come    50
at once; we have struck a berg."

To the Cunarder *Carpathia* (Arthur Henry Rostron, Master, New    51
York to Liverpool, fifty-eight miles away): "It's a CQD, old man. Position 41-46 N.; 50-14 W."

The blue spark dancing: "Sinking; cannot hear for noise of steam."    52

12:30 A.M. The word is passed: "Women and children in the boats."    53
Stewards finish waking their passengers below; life-preservers are tied on; some men smile at the precaution. "The *Titanic* is unsinkable." The *Mt. Temple* starts for the *Titanic*; the *Carpathia* with a double-watch in her stokeholds, radios, "Coming hard." The CQD changes the course

of many ships—but not of one; the operator of the *Californian*, nearby, has just put down his ear-phones and turned in.

The CQD flashes over land and sea from Cape Race to New York; newspaper city rooms leap to life and presses whir. 54

On the *Titanic*, water creeps over the bulkhead between Nos. 5 and 6 firerooms. She is going down by the head; the engineers—fighting a losing battle—are forced back foot by foot by the rising water. Down the promenade deck, Happy Jock Hume, the bandsman, runs with his instrument. 55

12:45 A.M. Murdock, in charge on the starboard side, eyes tragic, but calm and cool, orders boat No. 7 lowered. The women hang back; they want no boat ride on an ice-strewn sea; the *Titanic* is unsinkable. The men encourage them, explain that this is just a precautionary measure: "We'll see you again at breakfast." There is little confusion; passengers stream slowly to the boat deck. In the steerage the immigrants chatter excitedly. 56

A sudden sharp hiss—a streaked flare against the night; Boxhall sends a rocket toward the sky. It explodes, and a parachute of white stars lights up the icy sea. "God! Rockets!" The band plays ragtime. 57

No. 8 is lowered, and No. 5. Ismay, still in dressing gown, calls for women and children, handles lines, stumbles in the way of an officer, is told to "get the hell out of here." Third Officer Pitman takes charge of No. 5; as he swings into the boat Murdoch grasps his hand. "Good-by and good luck, old man." 58

No. 6 goes over the side. There are only twenty-eight people in a lifeboat with a capacity of sixty-five. 59

A light stabs from the bridge; Boxhall is calling in Morse flashes, again and again, to a strange ship stopped in the ice jam five to ten miles away. Another rocket drops its shower of sparks above the ice-strewn sea and the dying ship. 60

1:00 A.M. Slowly the water creeps higher; the fore ports of the *Titanic* are dipping into the sea. Rope squeaks through blocks; lifeboats drop jerkily seaward. Through the shouting on the decks comes the sound of the band playing ragtime. 61

The "Millionaires' Special" leaves the ship—boat No. 1, with a capacity of forty people, carries only Sir Cosmo and Lady Duff Gordon and ten others. Aft, the frightened immigrants mill and jostle and rush for a boat. An officer's fist flies out; three shots are fired in the air, and 62 the panic is quelled. . . . Four Chinese sneak unseen into a boat and hide in its bottom.

1:20 A.M. Water is coming into No. 4 boiler room. Stokers slice and  63
shovel as water laps about their ankles—steam for the dynamos, steam for the dancing spark! As the water rises, great ash hoes rake the flaming coals from the furnaces. Safety valves pop; the stokers retreat aft, and the water-tight doors clang shut behind them.

The rockets fling their splendor toward the stars. The boats are more  64
heavily loaded now, for the passengers know the *Titanic* is sinking. Women cling and sob. The great screws aft are rising clear of the sea. Half-filled boats are ordered to come alongside the cargo ports and take on more passengers, but the ports are never opened—and the boats are never filled. Others pull for the steamer's light miles away but never reach it; the lights disappear, the unknown ship steams off.

The water rises and the band plays ragtime.  65

1:30 A.M. Lightoller is getting the port boats off; Murdoch the star-  66
board. As one boat is lowered into the sea a boat officer fires his gun along the ship's side to stop a rush from the lower decks. A woman tries to take her Great Dane into a boat with her; she is refused and steps out of the boat to die with her dog. Millet's "little smile which played on his lips all through the voyage" plays no more; his lips are grim, but he waves good-by and brings wraps for the women.

Benjamin Guggenheim, in evening clothes, smiles and says, "We've  67
dressed up in our best and are prepared to go down like gentlemen."

1:40 A.M. Boat 14 is clear, and then 13, 16, 15 and C. The lights still  68
shine, but the *Baltic* hears the blue spark say, "Engine-room getting flooded."

The *Olympic* signals. "Am lighting up all possible boilers as fast  69
as can."

Major Butt helps women into the last boats and waves good-by to  70
them. Mrs. Straus puts her foot on the gunwale of a lifeboat, then she draws back and goes to her husband: "We have been together many years; where you go I will go." Colonel John Jacob Astor puts his young wife in a lifeboat, steps back, taps cigarette on fingernail: "Good-by, dearie; I'll join you later."

1:45 A.M. The foredeck is under water, the fo'c'sle head almost  71
awash; the great stern is lifted high toward the bright stars; and still the band plays. Mr. and Mrs. Harris approach a lifeboat arm in arm.

Officer: "Ladies first, please."                                                72

Harris bows, smiles, steps back: "Of course, certainly; ladies first."          73

Boxhall fires the last rocket, then leaves in charge of boat No. 2.              74

2:00 A.M. She is dying now; her bow goes deeper, her stern higher.              75
But there must be steam. Below in the stokeholds the sweaty firemen
keep steam up for the flaring lights and the dancing spark. The glowing coals slide and tumble over the slanted grate bars; the sea pounds
behind that yielding bulkhead. But the spark dances on.

The *Asian* hears Phillips try the new signal—SOS.                              76

Boat No. 4 has left now; boat D leaves ten minutes later. Jacques              77
Futrelle clasps his wife: "For God's sake, go! It's your last chance; go!"
Madame Futrelle is half-forced into the boat. It clears the side.

There are about 660 people in the boats, and 1,500 still on the sink-          78
ing *Titanic*.

On top of the officers' quarters men work frantically to get the two           79
collapsibles stowed there over the side. Water is over the forward part
of A deck now; it surges up the companionways toward the boat deck.
In the radio shack, Bride has slipped a coat and lifejacket about Phillips
as the first operator sits hunched over his key, sending—still sending—"41-46 N.; 50-14 W. CQD—CQD—SOS—SOS—"

The Captain's tired white face appears at the radio-room door;                 80
"Men, you have done your full duty. You can do no more. Now, it's
every man for himself." The Captain disappears—back to his sinking
bridge, where Painter, his personal steward, stands quietly waiting for
orders. The spark dances on. Bride turns his back and goes into the
inner cabin. As he does so, a stoker, grimed with coal, mad with fear,
steals into the shack and reaches for the lifejacket on Phillips' back.
Bride wheels about and brains him with a wrench.

2:10 A.M. Below decks the steam is still holding, though the pressure          81
is falling—rapidly. In the gymnasium on the boat deck the athletic
instructor watches quietly as two gentlemen ride the bicycles and another swings casually at the punching bag. Mail clerks stagger up the
boat-deck stairways, dragging soaked mail sacks. The spark still
dances. The band still plays—but not ragtime:

> "Nearer my God to Thee,
> Nearer to Thee . . ."

A few men take up the refrain; others kneel on the slanting decks to          82
pray. Many run and scramble aft, where hundreds are clinging above

the silent screws on the great uptilted stern. The spark still dances and the lights still flare; the engineers are on the job. The hymn comes to its close. Bandmaster Hartley, Yorkshireman violinist, taps his bow against a bulkhead, calls for "Autumn" as the water curls about his feet, and the eight musicians brace themselves against the ship's slant. People are leaping from the decks into the nearby water—the icy water. A woman cries, "Oh, save me, save me!" A man answers, "Good lady, save yourself. Only God can save you now." The band plays "Autumn":

> "God of Mercy and Compassion!
> Look with pity on my pain . . ."

The water creeps over the bridge where the *Titanic's* master stands; 　83
heavily he steps out to meet it.

2:17 A.M. "CQ—" The *Virginian* hears a ragged, blurred CQ, then 　84
an abrupt stop. The blue spark dances no more. The lights flicker out; the engineers have lost their battle.

2:18 A.M. Men run about blackened decks; leap into the night; are 　85
swept into the sea by the curling wave which licks up the *Titanic's* length. Lightoller does not leave the ship; the ship leaves him; there are hundreds like him, but only a few who live to tell of it. The funnels still swim above the water, but the ship is climbing to the perpendicular; the bridge is under and most of the foremast; the great stern rises like a squat leviathan. Men swim away from the sinking ship; others drop from the stern.

The band plays in the darkness, the water lapping upward: 　86

> "Hold me up in mighty waters,
> Keep my eyes on things above,
> Righteousness, divine atonement,
> Peace and everlas . . ."

The forward funnel snaps and crashes into the sea; its steel tons 　87
hammer out of existence swimmers struggling in the freezing water. Streams of sparks, of smoke and steam, burst from the after funnels. The ship upends to 50—to 60 degrees.

Down in the black abyss of the stokeholds, of the engine-rooms, 　88
where the dynamos have whirred at long last to a stop, the stokers and the engineers are reeling against hot metal, the rising water clutching at their knees. The boilers, the engine cylinders, rip from their bed plates; crash through bulkheads; rumble—steel against steel.

The *Titanic* stands on end, poised briefly for the plunge. Slowly she 89
slides to her grave—slowly at first, and then more quickly—quickly—
quickly.

2:20 A.M. The greatest ship in the world has sunk. From the calm, 90
dark waters, where the floating lifeboats move, there goes up, in the
white wake of her passing, "one long continuous moan."

## III

The boats that the *Titanic* had launched pulled safely away from the 91
slight suction of the sinking ship, pulled away from the screams that
came from the lips of the freezing men and women in the water. The
boats were poorly manned and badly equipped, and they had been
unevenly loaded. Some carried so few seamen that women bent to the
oars. Mrs. Astor tugged at an oar handle; the Countess of Rothes took
a tiller. Shivering stokers in sweaty, coal-blackened singlets and light
trousers steered in some boats; stewards in white coats rowed in others. Ismay was in the last boat that left the ship from the starboard
side; with Mr. Carter of Philadelphia and two seamen he tugged at the
oars. In one of the lifeboats an Italian with a broken wrist—disguised
in a woman's shawl and hat—huddled on the floor boards, ashamed
now that fear had left him. In another rode the only baggage saved
from the *Titanic*—the carry-all of Samuel L. Goldenberg, one of the
rescued passengers.

There were only a few boats that were heavily loaded; most of those 92
that were half empty made but perfunctory efforts to pick up the
moaning swimmers, their officers and crew fearing they would endanger the living if they pulled back into the midst of the dying. Some
boats beat off the freezing victims; fear-crazed men and women struck
with oars at the heads of swimmers. One woman drove her fist into
the face of a half-dead man as he tried feebly to climb over the gunwale. Two other women helped him in and stanched the flow of blood
from the ring-cuts on his face.

One of the collapsible boats, which had floated off the top of the 93
officers' quarters when the *Titanic* sank, was an icy haven for thirty or
forty men. The boat had capsized as the ship sank; men swam to it,
clung to it, climbed upon its slippery bottom, stood knee-deep in
water in the freezing air. Chunks of ice swirled about their legs; their
soaked clothing clutched their bodies in icy folds. Colonel Archibald
Gracie was cast up there. Gracie who had leaped from the stern as the

*Titanic* sank; young Thayer who had seen his father die; Lightoller who had twice been sucked down with the ship and twice blown to the surface by a belch of air; Bride, the second operator, and Phillips, the first. There were many stokers, half-naked; it was a shivering company. They stood there in the icy sea, under the far stars, and sang and prayed—the Lord's Prayer. After a while a lifeboat came and picked them off, but Phillips was dead then or died soon afterward in the boat.

Only a few of the boats had lights; only one—No. 2—had a light  94
that was of any use to the *Carpathia*, twisting through the ice-field to the rescue. Other ships were "coming hard" too; one, the *Californian*, was still dead to opportunity.

The blue sparks still danced, but not the *Titanic*'s. *La Provence* to  95
*Celtic*: "Nobody has heard the *Titanic* for about two hours."

It was 2:40 when the *Carpathia* first sighted the green light from  96
No. 2 boat; it was 4:10 when she picked up the first boat and learned that the *Titanic* had foundered. The last of the moaning cries had just died away then.

Captain Rostron took the survivors aboard, boatload by boatload.  97
He was ready for them, but only a small minority of them required much medical attention. Bride's feet were twisted and frozen; others were suffering from exposure; one died, and seven were dead when taken from the boats, and were buried at sea.

It was then that the fleet of racing ships learned they were too late;  98
the *Parisian* heard the weak signals of *MPA*, the *Carpathia*, report the death of the *Titanic*. It was then—or soon afterward, when her radio operator put on his ear-phones—that the *Californian*, the ship that had been within sight as the *Titanic* was sinking, first learned of the disaster.

And it was then, in all its white-green majesty, that the *Titanic*'s  99
survivors saw the iceberg, tinted with the sunrise, floating idly, pack-ice jammed about its base, other bergs heaving slowly nearby on the blue breast of the sea.

## IV

But it was not until later that the world knew, for wireless then was  100
not what wireless is to-day, and garbled messages had nourished a hope that all of the *Titanic*'s company were safe. Not until Monday evening, when P. A. S. Franklin, Vice-President of the International

Mercantile Marine Company, received relayed messages in New York that left little hope, did the full extent of the disaster begin to be known. Partial and garbled lists of the survivors; rumors of heroism and cowardice; stories spun out of newspaper imagination, based on a few bare facts and many false reports, misled the world, terrified and frightened it. It was not until Thursday night, when the *Carpathia* steamed into the North River, that the full truth was pieced together.

Flashlights flared on the black river when the *Carpathia* stood up to      101
her dock. Tugs nosed about her; shunted her toward Pier 54. Thirty thousand people jammed the streets; ambulances and stretchers stood on the pier; coroners and physicians waited.

In mid-stream the Cunarder dropped over the *Titanic*'s lifeboats;      102
then she headed toward the dock. Beneath the customs letters on the pier stood relatives of the 711 survivors, relatives of the missing— hoping against hope. The *Carpathia* cast her lines ashore; stevedores looped them over bollards. The dense throngs stood quiet as the first survivor stepped down the gangway. The woman half-staggered—led by customs guards—beneath her letter. A "low wailing" moan came from the crowd; fell, grew in volume, and dropped again.

Thus ended the maiden voyage of the *Titanic*. The lifeboats brought      103
to New York by the *Carpathia*, a few deck chairs and gratings awash in the icefield off the Grand Banks 800 miles from shore, were all that was left of the world's greatest ship.

## V

The aftermath of weeping and regret, of recriminations and investi-      104
gations, dragged on for weeks. Charges and countercharges were hurled about; the White Star line was bitterly criticized; Ismay was denounced on the floor of the Senate as a coward, but was defended by those who had been with him on the sinking *Titanic* and by the Board of Trade investigation in England.

It was not until weeks later, when the hastily convened Senate inves-      105
tigation in the United States and the Board of Trade report in England had been completed, that the whole story was told. The Senate investigating committee, under the chairmanship of Senator Smith, who was attacked in both the American and British press as a "backwoods politician," brought out numerous pertinent facts, though its proceedings verged at times on the farcical. Senator Smith was ridiculed for his lack of knowledge of the sea when he asked witnesses, "Of what

is an iceberg composed?" and "Did any of the passengers take refuge in the water-tight compartments?" The Senator seemed particularly interested in the marital status of Fleet, the lookout, who was saved. Fleet, puzzled, growled aside, "Wot questions they're arskin' me!"

The report of Lord Mersey, Wreck Commissioner in the British Board of Trade's investigation, was tersely damning. 106

The *Titanic* had carried boats enough for 1,178 persons, only one-third of her capacity. Her sixteen boats and four collapsibles had saved but 711 persons; 400 people had needlessly lost their lives. The boats had been but partly loaded; officers in charge of launching them had been afraid the falls would break or the boats buckle under their rated loads; boat crews had been slow in reaching their stations; launching arrangements were confused because no boat drill had been held; passengers were loaded into the boats haphazardly because no boat assignments had been made. 107

But that was not all. Lord Mersey found that sufficient warnings of ice on the steamer track had reached the *Titanic*, that her speed of 22 knots was "excessive under the circumstances," that "in view of the high speed at which the vessel was running it is not considered that the lookout was sufficient," and that her master made "a very grievous mistake"—but should not be blamed for negligence. Captain Rostron of the *Carpathia* was highly praised. "He did the very best that could be done." The *Californian* was damned. The testimony of her master, officers, and crew showed that she was not, at the most, more than nineteen miles away from the sinking *Titanic* and probably no more than five to ten miles distant. She had seen the *Titanic*'s lights; she had seen the rockets; she had not received the CQD calls because her radio operator was asleep. She had attempted to get in communication with the ship she had sighted by flashing a light, but vainly. 108

"The night was clear," reported Lord Mersey, "and the sea was smooth. When she first saw the rockets the *Californian* could have pushed through the ice to the open water without any serious risk and so have come to the assistance of the *Titanic*. Had she done so she might have saved many if not all of the lives that were lost. 109

"She made no attempt." 110

## VOCABULARY

| | | |
|---|---|---|
| strakes (1) | loft (3) | Empire (6) |
| bollards (3) | ominous (4) | steerage (7) |

| calabashes (7) | Marconi (12) | warren (36) |
| funnels (9) | promenade (12) | gunwale (70) |
| purser (9) | Jacobean (13) | recriminations (104) |
| growlers (10) | quorum (35) | tersely (106) |

## THE FACTS

1. What kind of ship was the *Titanic*? From where did she embark and where was she headed when the collision occurred?
2. When Lord Mersey, Wreck Commissioner in the British Board of Trade's investigation, finally gave his report, what were some of the most damning judgments?
3. Following is a list of the key personnel on the *Titanic*. What was each person's position or job?

| | | |
| --- | --- | --- |
| Smith | Murdoch | Bell |
| Phillips | Pitman | Andrews |
| Bride | Fleet | Frost |
| Ismay | Leigh | Hartley |
| Carlisle | Hichens | Hume |
| Lightoller | Boxhall | Painter |

4. Why were the passengers unconcerned when the *Titanic* first hit the iceberg?
5. Who was the first to realize that the *Titanic* was mortally wounded?
6. What do you consider the most moving moments described in this chronicle? Why?

## THE STRATEGIES

1. What unifying principle did Baldwin use to unfold the story of the sinking of the *Titanic*?
2. At what point in the narration does the story seem suddenly to burst into exciting action? How is this excitement conveyed?
3. What is the reason for a one-line paragraph like paragraph 65?
4. In paragraph 90, Baldwin uses personification. How?
5. The narration is divided into five parts. What is the general subject of each part?

## THE ISSUES

1. Many feminists reject out of hand the "women and children first" rule that was used to evacuate passengers from the stricken *Titanic*. Why do you think feminists oppose this rule?
2. "The *Titanic* was the incarnation of man's arrogance in equating size with

security. . . ." writes one commentator. Does this equation between size and security still persist today? What is your opinion of it?

3. Some commentators trace the emergence of public distrust of science and technology to the sinking of the *Titanic*. What does the public seem to distrust about science and technology? What do you distrust?

4. If there were a maritime disaster today, do you think the "women and children first" rule would be applied during evacuation? Should it?

5. Recently, the grave of the *Titanic* was found and pictures taken of the site. Do you think salvagers should be allowed to raise memorabilia and artifacts from the wreck? Why or why not?

### SUGGESTIONS FOR WRITING

1. From memory, write a three-hundred-word summary of the sinking of the *Titanic*, referring to as many events and people as you can remember from having read the selection.

2. Write a five-hundred-word chronological narration of one of the most dangerous adventures in your life. Start slowly, then gradually speed up the narration by piling event on event, as does Baldwin.

### Floyd Dell

—————————— • WE'RE POOR • ——————————

*Floyd Dell (1887–1969) was a prolific writer, an editor, and a champion of pacifist and radical causes. In the 1920s and 1930s, he wrote ten novels, six books of nonfiction, a number of plays, and* Homecoming (1933), *his auto-biography.*

*In the following narrative from Dell's autobiography, a child discovers to his shame and humiliation that he and his family are poor.*

That fall, before it was discovered that the soles of both my shoes were worn clear through, I still went to Sunday school. And one time the Sunday-school superintendent made a speech to all the classes. He said that these were hard times, and that many poor children weren't getting enough to eat. It was the first that I had heard about it. He asked everybody to bring some food for the poor children next Sunday. I felt very sorry for the poor children.

Also, little envelopes were distributed to all the classes. Each little boy and girl was to bring money for the poor, next Sunday. The pretty

Sunday-school teacher explained that we were to write our names, or have our parents write them, up in the left-hand corner of the little envelopes. . . . I told my mother all about it when I came home. And my mother gave me, the next Sunday, a small bag of potatoes to carry to Sunday school. I supposed the poor children's mothers would make potato soup out of them. . . . Potato soup was good. My father, who was quite a joker, would always say, as if he were surprised, "Ah! I see we have some nourishing potato soup today!" It was so good that we had it every day. My father was at home all day long and every day, now; and I liked that, even if he was grumpy as he sat reading Grant's "Memoirs." I had my parents all to myself, too; the others were away. My oldest brother was in Quincy, and memory does not reveal where the others were: perhaps with relatives in the country.

Taking my small bag of potatoes to Sunday school, I looked around    3
for the poor children; I was disappointed not to see them. I had heard about poor children in stories. But I was told just to put my contribution with the others on the big table in the side room.

I had brought with me the little yellow envelope, with some money    4
in it for the poor children. My mother had put the money in it and sealed it up. She wouldn't tell me how much money she had put in it, but it felt like several dimes. Only she wouldn't let me write my name on the envelope. I had learned to write my name, and I was proud of being able to do it. But my mother said firmly, no, I must not write my name on the envelope; she didn't tell me why. On the way to Sunday school I had pressed the envelope against the coins until I could tell what they were; they weren't dimes but pennies.

When I handed in my envelope, my Sunday-school teacher noticed    5
that my name wasn't on it, and she gave me a pencil; I could write my own name, she said. So I did. But I was confused because my mother had said not to; and when I came home, I confessed what I had done. She looked distressed. "I told you not to!" she said. But she didn't explain why. . . .

I didn't go back to school that fall. My mother said it was because I    6
was sick. I did have a cold the week that school opened; I had been playing in the gutters and had got my feet wet, because there were holes in my shoes. My father cut insoles out of cardboard, and I wore those in my shoes. As long as I had to stay in the house anyway, they were all right.

I stayed cooped up in the house, without any companionship. We    7 didn't take a Sunday paper any more, but the Barry *Adage* came every week in the mails; and though I did not read small print, I could see the Santa Clauses and holly wreaths in the advertisements.

There was a calendar in the kitchen. The red days were Sundays and 8 holidays; and that red 25 was Christmas. (It was on a Monday, and the two red figures would come right together in 1893; but this represents research in the World Almanac, not memory.) I knew when Sunday was, because I could look out of the window and see the neighbor's children, all dressed up, going to Sunday school. I knew just when Christmas was going to be.

But there was something queer! My father and mother didn't say a 9 word about Christmas. And once, when I spoke of it, there was a strange, embarrassed silence; so I didn't say anything more about it. But I wondered, and was troubled. Why didn't they say anything about it? Was what I had said I wanted (memory refuses to supply that detail) too expensive?

I wasn't arrogant and talkative now. I was silent and frightened. 10 What was the matter? Why didn't my father and mother say anything about Christmas? As the day approached, my chest grew tighter with anxiety.

Now it was the day before Christmas. I couldn't be mistaken. But 11 not a word about it from my father and mother. I waited in painful bewilderment all day. I had supper with them, and was allowed to sit up for an hour. I was waiting for them to say something. "It's time for you to go to bed," my mother said gently. I had to say something.

"This is Christmas Eve, isn't it?" I asked, as if I didn't know. 12

My father and mother looked at one another. Then my mother 13 looked away. Her face was pale and stony. My father cleared his throat, and his face took on a joking look. He pretended he hadn't known it was Christmas Eve, because he hadn't been reading the papers. He said he would go downtown and find out.

My mother got up and walked out of the room. I didn't want my 14 father to have to keep on being funny about it, so I got up and went to bed. I went by myself without having a light. I undressed in the dark and crawled into bed.

I was numb. As if I had been hit by something. It was hard to 15 breathe. I ached all through. I was stunned—with finding out the truth.

My body knew before my mind quite did. In a minute, when I could 16 think, my mind would know. And as the pain in my body ebbed, the pain in my mind began. I knew. I couldn't put it into words yet. But I knew why I had taken only a little bag of potatoes to Sunday school that fall. I knew why there had been only pennies in my little yellow envelope. I knew why I hadn't gone to school that fall—why I hadn't any new shoes—why we had been living on potato soup all winter. All these things, and others, many others, fitted themselves together in my mind, and meant something.

Then the words came into my mind and I whispered them into the    17
darkness:

"We're poor!"    18

That was it. I was one of those poor children I had been sorry for,    19
when I heard about them in Sunday school. My mother hadn't told me. My father was out of work, and we hadn't any money. That was why there wasn't going to be any Christmas at our house.

Then I remembered something that made me squirm with shame—    20
a boast. (Memory will not yield this up. Had I said to some Nice little boy, "I'm going to be President of the United States"? Or to a Nice little girl: "I'll marry you when I grow up"? It was some boast as horribly shameful to remember.)

"We're poor." There in bed in the dark, I whispered it over and over    21
to myself. I was making myself get used to it. (Or—just torturing myself, as one presses the tongue against a sore tooth? No, memory says not like that—but to keep myself from ever being such a fool again: suffering now, to keep this awful thing from ever happening again. Memory is clear on that; it was more like pulling the tooth, to get it over with—never mind the pain, this will be the end!)

It wasn't so bad, now that I knew. I just hadn't known! I had thought    22
all sorts of foolish things: that I was going to Ann Arbor—going to be a lawyer—going to make speeches in the Square, going to be President. Now I knew better.

I had wanted (something) for Christmas. I didn't want it, now. I    23
didn't want anything.

I lay there in the dark, feeling the cold emotion of renunciation. (The    24
tendrils of desire unfold their clasp on the outer world of objects, withdraw, shrivel up. Wishes shrivel up, turn black, die. It is like that.)

It hurt. But nothing would ever hurt again. I would never let myself    25
want anything again.

I lay there stretched out straight and stiff in the dark, my fists 26
clenched hard upon Nothing. . . .

In the morning it had been like a nightmare that is not clearly re- 27
membered—that one wishes to forget. Though I hadn't hung up any
stocking, there was one hanging at the foot of my bed. A bag of
popcorn, and a lead pencil, for me. They had done the best they could,
now they realized that I knew about Christmas. But they needn't have
thought they had to. I didn't want anything.

### VOCABULARY

arrogant (10)              renunciation (24)              tendrils (24)

### THE FACTS

1. How did the author first react to the news that there were poor children in the world? What does his reaction say about him?
2. Why did the author's mother not want him to write his name on the contribution envelope?
3. How did Dell's father generally react to adversity?
4. Before he discovered that he was one of the poor children, what were the author's ambitions?
5. What gifts did the author get for Christmas?

### THE STRATEGIES

1. In the opening sentence of this narrative, Dell writes: "That fall, before it was discovered that the soles of both my shoes were worn clear through, I still went to Sunday school." What do you call the construction "it was discovered"? What is the dramatic justification for using such a construction in this selection?
2. In paragraph 2, Dell supplies many clues to his true condition. What are these clues? How do they function in the story?
3. Read the definition of *pacing* on pages 312–13. How does the pacing of paragraphs 6 and 8 advance the story line?
4. Examine paragraph 15. What technique does Dell use here to heighten the climactic moment of the narrative?
5. What purpose do you think Dell had in making paragraphs 22 through 26 so terse and skimpy?
6. The narrative is recounted in simple words assembled into short sentences. Why? What do you think the author was trying to convey?

## THE ISSUES

1. How did the sudden knowledge of his family's poverty affect the author's dreams and ambitions? How do you think it might have affected his self-image?
2. How do you suppose Dell's father and mother must have felt when their son discovered that they had been trying to conceal Christmas from him?
3. What kind of person is the father? How would you characterize him?
4. What role should government play in helping those who are poor and out of work?
5. What effect do you think television, with its constant barrage of commercials, has on poor children today?

## SUGGESTIONS FOR WRITING

1. Write a short narrative essay about one of your special Christmas memories.
2. When did you first learn that there were poor people in the world? Write a narration describing the experience.

**Robert Hayden**

——————— • **THOSE WINTER SUNDAYS** • ———————

*Robert Hayden (1913–1980) was born in Detroit, attended the University of Michigan, and taught at Fisk University. His* Ballad of Remembrance *was awarded a prize at the 1966 World Festival of Negro Arts held in Dakar, Senegal.*

*The following poem recounts a childhood memory.*

> Sundays too my father got up early
> and put his clothes on in the blueblack cold,
> then with cracked hands that ached
> from labor in the weekday weather made
> banked fires blaze. No one ever thanked him.          5
> I'd wake and hear the cold splintering, breaking.
> When the rooms were warm, he'd call,
> and slowly I would rise and dress,
> fearing the chronic angers of that house,
> Speaking indifferently to him,                        10
> who had driven out the cold
> and polished my good shoes as well.

What did I know, what did I know
of love's austere and lonely offices?

## THE FACTS

1. What did the narrator's father do on Sundays?
2. How did the narrator react to his father in the morning?
3. How would you characterize the narrator's attitude as he looks back on this time with his father?

## THE STRATEGIES

1. What poetic form is this narration framed in? (Hint: Count the number of lines.)
2. The author writes about his father: "No one ever thanked him." Why do you think he chose to put it this way? Why not simply say "I never thanked him"?
3. The poet writes: "I'd wake and hear the cold splintering, breaking." What kind of figure of speech is this?
4. Examine the sentences in the poem. How many are there? What is the technique of running a sentence into several lines without an end-stop or break called?

## THE ISSUES

1. What kind of work do you suppose the speaker's father did? How can his probable occupation be deduced from the poem?
2. What are "love's austere and lonely offices"? What other examples can you give of them?

## SUGGESTIONS FOR WRITING

1. Write an analysis of this poem.
2. Narrate an incident from your own childhood that involved your relationship with a parent.

### Edgar Allan Poe

# ———— • THE CASK OF AMONTILLADO • ————

*Edgar Allan Poe (1809–1849) was an American poet, short-story writer, and critic known for many carefully crafted works that emphasize the beauty of the macabre, the horrible, the grotesque, and the mysterious. Poe is also the originator of the modern detective story; two of his most famous in this genre are*

*"The Murders in the Rue Morgue" and "The Purloined Letter." His poems are well known, among which are "The Raven" and "Annabel Lee." "The Cask of Amontillado" was first published in 1846.*

The thousand injuries of Fortunato I had borne as I best could; but when he ventured upon insult, I vowed revenge. You, who so well know the nature of my soul, will not suppose, however, that I gave utterance to a threat. *At length* I would be avenged; this was a point definitively settled—but the very definitiveness with which it was resolved, precluded the idea of risk. I must not only punish, but punish with impunity. A wrong is unredressed when retribution overtakes its redresser. It is equally unredressed when the avenger fails to make himself felt as such to him who has done the wrong.    1

It must be understood, that neither by word nor deed had I given Fortunato cause to doubt my good-will. I continued, as was my wont, to smile in his face, and he did not perceive that my smile *now* was at the thought of his immolation.    2

He had a weak point—this Fortunato—although in other regards he was a man to be respected and even feared. He prided himself on his connoisseurship in wine. Few Italians have the true virtuoso spirit. For the most part their enthusiasm is adopted to suit the time and opportunity—to practise imposture upon the British and Austrian *millionnaires*. In painting and gemmary Fortunato, like his country-men, was a quack—but in the matter of old wines he was sincere. In this respect I did not differ from him materially: I was skilful in the Italian vintages myself, and bought largely whenever I could.    3

It was about dusk, one evening during the supreme madness of the carnival season, that I encountered my friend. He accosted me with excessive warmth, for he had been drinking much. The man wore motley. He had on a tight-fitting parti-striped dress, and his head was surmounted by the conical cap and bells. I was so pleased to see him, that I thought I should never have done wringing his hand.    4

I said to him: "My dear Fortunato, you are luckily met. How remark-ably well you are looking to-day! But I have received a pipe of what passes for Amontillado, and I have my doubts."    5

"How?" said he. "Amontillado? A pipe? Impossible! And in the middle of the carnival!"    6

"I have my doubts," I replied; "and I was silly enough to pay the    7 full Amontillado price without consulting you in the matter. You were not to be found, and I was fearful of losing a bargain."

"Amontillado!"                                                                                                   8

"I have my doubts."                                                                                           9

"Amontillado!"                                                                                                   10

"And I must satisfy them."                                                                                 11

"Amontillado!"                                                                                                   12

"As you are engaged, I am on my way to Luchesi. If any one has a     13
critical turn, it is he. He will tell me——"

"Luchesi cannot tell Amontillado from Sherry."                                               14

"And yet some fools will have it that his taste is a match for your     15
own."

"Come, let us go."                                                                                            16

"Whither?"                                                                                                        17

"To your vaults."                                                                                               18

"My friend, no; I will not impose upon your good nature. I perceive     19
you have an engagement. Luchesi——"

"I have no engagement;—come."                                                                  20

"My friend, no. It is not the engagement, but the severe cold with     21
which I perceive you are afflicted. The vaults are insufferably damp.
They are encrusted with nitre."

"Let us go, nevertheless. The cold is merely nothing. Amontillado!     22
You have been imposed upon. And as for Luchesi, he cannot distinguish Sherry from Amontillado."

Thus speaking, Fortunato possessed himself of my arm. Putting on     23
a mask of black silk, and drawing a *roquelaire** closely about my person,
I suffered him to hurry me to my palazzo.

There were no attendants at home; they had absconded to make     24
merry in honor of the time. I had told them that I should not return
until the morning, and had given them explicit orders not to stir from
the house. These orders were sufficient, I well knew, to insure their
immediate disappearance, one and all, as soon as my back was turned.

I took from their sconces two flambeaux, and giving one to Fortu-     25
nato, bowed him through several suites of rooms to the archway that
led into the vaults. I passed down a long and winding staircase, requesting him to be cautious as he followed. We came at length to the

---

*Roquelaure; a cloak.—Ed.

foot of the descent, and stood together on the damp ground of the
catacombs of the Montresors.

The gait of my friend was unsteady, and the bells upon his cap    26
jingled as he strode.

"The pipe?" said he.    27

"It is farther on," said I; "but observe the white web-work which    28
gleams from these cavern walls."

He turned toward me, and looked into my eyes with two filmy orbs    29
that distilled the rheum of intoxication.

"Nitre?" he asked, at length.    30

"Nitre," I replied. "How long have you had that cough?"    31

"Ugh! ugh! ugh!—ugh! ugh! ugh!—ugh! ugh! ugh!—ugh! ugh!    32
ugh!—ugh! ugh! ugh!"

My poor friend found it impossible to reply for many minutes.    33

"It is nothing," he said, at last.    34

"Come," I said, with decision, "we will go back; your health is    35
precious. You are rich, respected, admired, beloved; you are happy, as
once I was. You are a man to be missed. For me it is no matter. We will
go back; you will be ill, and I cannot be responsible. Besides, there is
Luchesi——"

"Enough," he said; "the cough is a mere nothing; it will not kill me.    36
I shall not die of a cough."

"True—true," I replied; "and, indeed, I had no intention of alarming    37
you unnecessarily; but you should use all proper caution. A draught
of this Medoc will defend us from the damps."

Here I knocked off the neck a bottle which I drew from a long row    38
of its fellows that lay upon the mould.

"Drink," I said, presenting him the wine.    39

He raised it to his lips with a leer. He paused and nodded to me    40
familiarly, while his bells jingled.

"I drink," he said, "to the buried that repose around us."    41

"And I to your long life."    42

He again took my arm, and we proceeded.    43

"These vaults," he said, "are extensive."    44

"The Montresors," I replied, "were a great and numerous family."    45

"I forget your arms."    46

"A huge human foot d'or, in a field azure; the foot crushes a serpent    47
rampant whose fangs are imbedded in the heel."

"And the motto?"     48

*"Nemo me impune lacessit."** 49

"Good!" he said.     50

The wine sparkled in his eyes and the bells jingled. My own fancy     51
grew warm with the Medoc. We had passed through walls of piled
bones, with casks and puncheons intermingling, into the inmost recesses of the catacombs. I paused again, and this time I made bold to
seize Fortunato by an arm above the elbow.

"The nitre!" I said; "see, it increases. It hangs like moss upon the     52
vaults. We are below the river's bed. The drops of moisture trickle
among the bones. Come, we will go back ere it is too late. Your
cough——"

"It is nothing," he said; "let us go on. But first, another draught of     53
the Medoc."

I broke and reached him a flagon of De Grâve. He emptied it at a     54
breath. His eyes flashed with a fierce light. He laughed and threw the
bottle upward with a gesticulation I did not understand.

I looked at him in surprise. He repeated the movement—a gro-     55
tesque one.

"You do not comprehend?" he said.     56

"Not I," I replied.     57

"Then you are not of the brotherhood."     58

"How?"     59

"You are not of the masons."     60

"Yes, yes," I said; "yes, yes."     61

"You? Impossible! A mason?"     62

"A mason," I replied.     63

"A sign," he said.     64

"It is this," I answered, producing a trowel from beneath the folds     65
of my *roquelaire*.

"You jest," he exclaimed, recoiling a few paces. "But let us proceed     66
to the Amontillado."

"Be it so," I said, replacing the tool beneath the cloak, and again     67
offering him my arm. He leaned upon it heavily. We continued our
route in search of the Amontillado. We passed through a range of low
arches, descended, passed on, and descending again, arrived at a deep

---

*"No one harms me with impunity."—Ed.

crypt, in which the foulness of the air caused our flambeaux rather to glow than flame.

At the most remote end of the crypt there appeared another less spacious. Its walls had been lined with human remains, piled to the vault overhead, in the fashion of the great catacombs of Paris. Three sides of this interior crypt were still ornamented in this manner. From the fourth the bones had been thrown down, and lay promiscuously upon the earth, forming at one point a mound of some size. Within the wall thus exposed by the displacing of the bones, we perceived a still interior recess, in depth about four feet, in width three, in height six or seven. It seemed to have been constructed for no especial use within itself; but formed merely the interval between two of the colossal supports of the roof of the catacombs, and was backed by one of their circumscribing walls of solid granite.    68

It was in vain that Fortunato, uplifting his dull torch, endeavored to pry into the depth of the recess. Its termination the feeble light did not enable us to see.    69

"Proceed," I said; "herein is the Amontillado. As for Luchesi——"    70

"He is an ignoramus," interrupted my friend, as he stepped unsteadily forward, while I followed immediately at his heels. In an instant he had reached the extremity of the niche, and finding his progress arrested by the rock, stood stupidly bewildered. A moment more and I had fettered him to the granite. In its surface were two iron staples, distant from each other about two feet, horizontally. From one of these depended a short chain, from the other a padlock. Throwing the links about his waist, it was but the work of a few seconds to secure it. He was too much astounded to resist. Withdrawing the key I stepped back from the recess.    71

"Pass your hand," I said, "over the wall; you cannot help feeling the nitre. Indeed it is *very* damp. Once more let me *implore* you to return. No? Then I must positively leave you. But I must first render you all the little attentions in my power."    72

"The Amontillado!" ejaculated my friend, not yet recovered from his astonishment.    73

"True," I replied; "the Amontillado."    74

As I said these words I busied myself among the pile of bones of which I have before spoken. Throwing them aside, I soon uncovered a quantity of building stone and mortar. With these materials and with    75 the aid of my trowel, I began vigorously to wall up the entrance of the niche.

I had scarcely laid the first tier of the masonry when I discovered 76 that the intoxication of Fortunato had in a great measure worn off. The earliest indication I had of this was a low moaning cry from the depth of the recess. It was *not* the cry of a drunken man. There was then a long and obstinate silence. I laid the second tier, and the third, and the fourth; and then I heard the furious vibrations of the chain. The noise lasted for several minutes, during which, that I might hearken to it with the more satisfaction, I ceased my labors and sat down upon the bones. When at last the clanking subsided, I resumed the trowel, and finished without interruption the fifth, the sixth, and the seventh tier. The wall was now nearly upon a level with my breast. I again paused, and holding the flambeaux over the mason-work, threw a few feeble rays upon the figure within.

A succession of loud and shrill screams, bursting suddenly from the 77 throat of the chained form, seemed to thrust me violently back. For a brief moment I hesitated—I trembled. Unsheathing my rapier, I began to grope with it about the recess; but the thought of an instant reassured me. I placed my hand upon the solid fabric of the catacombs, and felt satisfied. I reapproached the wall. I replied to the yells of him who clamored. I re-echoed—I aided—I surpassed them in volume and in strength. I did this, and the clamorer grew still.

It was now midnight, and my task was drawing to a close. I had 78 completed the eighth, the ninth, and the tenth tier. I had finished a portion of the last and the eleventh; there remained but a single stone to be fitted and plastered in. I struggled with its weight; I placed it partially in its destined position. But now there came from out the niche a low laugh that erected the hairs upon my head. It was succeeded by a sad voice, which I had difficulty in recognizing as that of the noble Fortunato. The voice said—

"Ha! ha! ha!—he! he!—a very good joke indeed—an excellent jest. 79 We will have many a rich laugh about it at the palazzo—he! he! he!— over our wine—he! he! he!"

"The Amontillado!" I said. 80

"He! he! he!—he! he! he!—yes, the Amontillado. But is it not getting 81 late? Will not they be awaiting us at the palazzo, the Lady Fortunato and the rest? Let us be gone."

"Yes," I said, "let us be gone." 82

*"For the love of God, Montresor!"* 83

"Yes," I said, "for the love of God!" 84

But to these words I hearkened in vain for a reply. I grew impatient. 85
I called aloud:

"Fortunato!" 86

No answer. I called again: 87

"Fortunato!" 88

No answer still. I thrust a torch through the remaining aperture and 89
let it fall within. There came forth in return only a jingling of the bells.
My heart grew sick—on account of the dampness of the catacombs. I
hastened to make an end of my labor. I forced the last stone into its
position; I plastered it up. Against the new masonry I re-erected the
old rampart of bones. For the half of a century no mortal has disturbed
them. *In pace requiescat!*\*

## VOCABULARY

| | | |
|---|---|---|
| ventured (1) | parti-striped (4) | rheum (29) |
| utterance (1) | surmounted (4) | draught (37) |
| precluded (1) | conical (4) | mould (38) |
| impunity (1) | pipe (5) | gesticulation (54) |
| wont (2) | insufferably (21) | crypt (67) |
| immolation (2) | nitre (21) | promiscuously (68) |
| connoisseurship (3) | sconces (25) | circumscribing (68) |
| virtuoso (3) | flambeaux (25) | ejaculated (73) |
| imposture (3) | distilled (29) | aperture (89) |

## THE FACTS

1. What is the reason for Montresor's anger with Fortunato?
2. What time of year does the story take place? How does this detail add to the story?
3. Fortunato is described as an honorable and respected man. Does he have any obvious character flaws? If so, what are they?
4. How does Montresor make sure that Fortunato steps into the final crypt?
5. How does the story end?

---

\*"He rests in peace."—Ed.

## THE STRATEGIES

1. What mood does Poe create throughout the story? How is this mood achieved?
2. How is the narrative paced? Is the story effectively plotted? Give reasons for your answer.
3. What ironies add to the general quality of the narrative?
4. What is the meaning of the story's title?
5. What terms in the story convey that the action probably takes place during the Italian Renaissance among members of the aristocracy?

## THE ISSUES

1. From the beginning, the narrator tells us that he wanted to seek revenge with impunity. Do you believe that he achieved his goal? Why or why not?
2. No clear reason is given for Montresor's intense hatred of Fortunato; yet some clues exist. What are they? Speculate imaginatively on what might have happened.
3. Why does the revenge plot work?
4. What is the dominant impression left by the narrator? What symbolic role does he play?
5. What is the theme of the story? State it in one sentence.

## SUGGESTIONS FOR WRITING

1. Narrate an incident in your life when you sought revenge (or did *not* seek revenge) for something someone did to you. Use the outcome of the event as the theme of your narration.
2. Write an essay in which you give reasons why seeking revenge is not (or *is*) in society's best interest.
3. Narrate a historical event in which revenge played a major role. Comment on the lesson to be learned.

## •• *ADVICE* ••

## HOW TO WRITE A DESCRIPTION

Focus and concentration contribute more to a vivid description than either the size of the writer's vocabulary or the heedless splattering of the page with adjectives. Here is an example of what we mean. The author, Charles Reade, in this excerpt from *The Cloister and the Hearth*, is describing a medieval inn partly through the eyes, but mainly through the nose, of a weary traveler:

> In one corner was a travelling family, a large one; thence flowed into the common stock the peculiar sickly smell of neglected brats. Garlic filled up the interstices of the air. And all this with closed window, and intense heat of the central furnace, and the breath of at least forty persons.
>
> They had just supped.
>
> Now Gerard, like most artists, had sensitive organs, and the potent effluvia struck dismay into him. But the rain lashed him outside, and the light and the fire tempted him in.
>
> He could not force his way all at once through the palpable perfumes, but he returned to the light again and again like a singed moth. At last he discovered that the various smells did not entirely mix, no fiend being there to stir them around. Odor of family predominated in two corners; stewed rustic reigned supreme in the center; and garlic in the noisy group by the window. He found, too, by hasty analysis, that of these the garlic described the smallest aerial orbit, and the scent of reeking rustic darted farthest—a flavor as if ancient goats, or the fathers of all foxes, had been drawn through a river, and were here dried by Nebuchadnezzar.

What is characteristic about this vivid description is its focus. Instead of trying to give us a sweeping view of the dingy inn, the writer zooms in on how bad it smells. The stink of the inn is the **dominant impression** of this description, and the writer's every word, image, and metaphor aims only to serve up this stench to our nostrils.

## 1. Focus on a dominant impression.

Vivid descriptions invariably focus on a single dominant impression and unremittingly deliver it. Nothing distracts from the dominant impression; every word and image is devoted to rendering it keener and sharper. By *dominant impression* we mean a feature of the scene that is characteristic of it. Not all scenes have strikingly characteristic features, and writers must often steep themselves in the aura of a place before they can sum it up in a dominant impression. But some scenes will give off a dominant impression that leaps out at you. For example, a freeway at rush hour is anything but a scene of placidity. Usually it is a tangled skein of cars jockeying for position or trying to nose from one lane into another. To describe a freeway scene at rush hour, you should word your dominant impression to take in the madcap antics of the drivers, the choking fumes of the cars, the background grind and roar of traffic. You might write, as your dominant impression, "The San Diego Freeway at rush hour is a bedlam of traffic noise, choking fumes, and aggressive drivers." Then you would support that dominant impression with specific images and details.

The dominant impression of your description should be the heart of the person, place, or scene you are attempting to describe. If you are describing an elderly aunt who is dull, use her dullness as your dominant impression. If you are writing a description of a Christmas shopping scene, word your dominant impression to show the frazzled throng of weary shoppers, the harried sales clerks, the dazzling glitter of Christmas lights. What you must not try to do in your dominant impression is to account for every speck in the scene you are describing. For example, among the streaming throngs in the department store at Christmas, there are bound to be a few souls who are calm and composed and seemingly immune to the shopping frenzy. But since these lucky few are not at all representative of the overall scene, you should leave them out lest they water down the description. So, if your sister is mainly a bundle of nerves, that is how you should paint her on the page, even if you have glimpsed her occasionally in rare moments of serenity.

## 2. Use images in your descriptions.

Most of us know the basics about imagery, especially the simile and the metaphor. We know that the simile is an image based on an explicit comparison. For example, in "The King of the Birds," Flannery O'Connor describes the crest of a peabiddy with this simile: "This looks at first like a bug's antennae and later like the head feathers of an Indian." On the other hand, we also know that the metaphor is an image based on an indirect comparison with no obvious linking word such as "as" or "like" used to cement it. For example, in "Once More to the Lake," E. B. White uses metaphors to describe a thunderstorm: "Then the kettle drum, then the snare, then the bass drum and cymbals, then crackling light against the dark, and the gods grinning and licking their chops in the hills." This is how a thunderstorm seems to the writer—it makes noises *like* many drums and flashes wicked lights against the hills that look *like* gods licking their chops. Even though the writer omits the "like" that might have made the comparison explicit, we still get the picture.

Aside from these basic images, which every writer occasionally uses, there are some other hard-won lessons about descriptive imagery that can be imparted. The first is this: Vivid images do not miraculously drip off the pen but are usually the result of the writer's reworking the material repeatedly. If nothing original or fresh occurs to you after you've sat at your desk for a scant few minutes trying to write a description, all it means is that you haven't sat long enough or worked hard enough. Reread what you have written. Try to picture in your mind the person, place, or thing you are struggling to describe. Cut a word here; replace another there; persistently scratch away at what you have written and you'll soon be astonished at how much better it begins to sound.

The second lesson to impart about writing vivid images is summed up in the adage, "Less is more." Overdoing a descriptive passage is not only possible, it is very likely. If you are unhappy with a description you have written, instead of stuffing it with more adjectives, try taking some out. Here is an example of a bloated and overdone description; it is from *Delina Delaney* by Amanda McKittrick Ros. The speaker is trying his utmost to describe his feelings as he says goodbye to his sweetheart:

> I am just in time to hear the toll of a parting bell strike its heavy weight of appalling softness against the weakest fibers of a heart of love, arousing and tickling its dormant action, thrusting the dart of evident separation deeper into its tubes of tenderness, and fanning the flame, already unextinguishable, into volumes of blaze.

This is, of course, wretched stuff. One can see the writer huffing and puffing at the pen as she tries desperately to infuse her hero's words with passion. She fails awfully from too much effort.

### 3. Appeal to all the reader's senses.

Most of us are so unabashedly visual that we are tempted to deliver only looks in our descriptions. But there is usually much more to a scene than its looks. You could also write about how it sounds, smells, or feels to the touch. The best descriptions draw on all kinds of images and appeal to as many senses as are appropriate. Here is an example from Elspeth Huxley's *The Flame Trees of Thika*. The writer is describing a World War I troop train leaving an African station at night carrying soldiers to the front:

> The men began to sing the jingle then that was so popular then—"Marching to Tabora"; and the shouts and cheers, the whistles, the hissing and chugging of the engine, filled the station as a kettle fills with steam. Everything seemed to bubble over; men waved from windows; Dick gave a hunting cry; the red hair of Pioneer Mary flared under a lamp; the guard jumped into his moving van; and we watched the rear light of the last coach vanish, and heard the chugging die away. A plume of sparks, a long coil of dancing fireflies, spread across the black ancient shoulder of the crater Menegai; and gradually the vast digesting dark of Africa swallowed up all traces of that audacious grub, the hurrying train.

This description is a mixture of appeals to our senses of sight and sound. The men sing and cheer, and the engine chugs and hisses. We see Pioneer Mary's red hair and the sparks from the train's engine. We are regaled with a clever simile, "filled the station as a kettle fills with steam"; and treated to a riveting metaphor, "the vast digesting dark of Africa swallowed up all traces of that audacious grub, the hurrying train." And did the author really just sit down and calmly mine this rich descriptive vein without effort? We do not know for certain, but most likely not. If her experience is at all typical, she hit this mother-lode of imagery only after persistent and labored digging.

## •• *EXAMPLES* ••

### Etty Hillesum

## • LETTER FROM A NAZI • CONCENTRATION CAMP

*Etty Hillesum (1914–1943) was a Dutch Jew who perished at Auschwitz. She had studied law and then languages at the University of Amsterdam. At the outbreak of World War II, she was living in Amsterdam, where she first began keeping the diary from which this excerpt was taken. In 1942, the Nazis began rounding up Dutch Jews and sending them to a camp in Westerbork, East Holland, for transportation to the Auschwitz extermination camp. Etty could have avoided capture through the influence of her friends, but she chose instead to go and suffer with her people. She was shipped to Auschwitz on September 7, 1943. As the train pulled out of Westerbork, she threw a postcard out the window which was later found by farmers. It read: "We have left the camp singing." Etty died at Auschwitz along with her father, mother, and brother Mischa. Her other brother, Jaap, died on the way back to Holland.*

*Since its publication in 1981,* The Interrupted Life: The Diaries of Etty Hillesum *has taken Europe by storm. It has sold over 150,000 copies and has been reprinted fourteen times. Translations of the diaries have been published in Germany, France, Norway, Finland, Denmark, Sweden, Canada, Italy, and Great Britain. This excerpt is taken from a letter written by Etty to friends in Amsterdam. It is a harrowing description of a terror-filled night when Jews at the Westerbork camp were selected for shipment by rail to the gas chambers of Auschwitz.*

24 August 1943

There was a moment when I felt in all seriousness that, after this night, it would be a sin ever to laugh again. But then I reminded myself that some of those who had gone away had been laughing, even if only a handful of them this time . . . There will be some who will laugh now and then in Poland, too, though not many from this transport, I think.

When I think of the faces of that squad of armed, green-uniformed   2
guards—my God, those faces! I looked at them, each in turn, from behind the safety of a window, and I have never been so frightened of anything in my life as I was of those faces. I sank to my knees with the words that preside over human life: And God made man after His likeness. That passage spent a difficult morning with me.      .

I have told you often enough that no words and images are adequate   3
to describe nights like these. But still I must try to convey something of it to you. One always has the feeling here of being the ears and eyes of a piece of Jewish history, but there is also the need sometimes to be a still, small voice. We must keep one another in touch with everything that happens in the various outposts of this world, each one contributing his own little piece of stone to the great mosaic that will take shape once the war is over.

After a night in the hospital barracks, I took an early morning walk   4
past the punishment barracks, and prisoners were being moved out. The deportees, mainly men, stood with their packs behind the barbed wire. So many of them looked tough and ready for anything. An old acquaintance—I didn't recognise him straightaway, a shaven head often changes people completely—called out to me with a smile, 'If they don't manage to do me in, I'll be back.'

But the babies, those tiny piercing screams of the babies, dragged   5
from their cots in the middle of the night . . . I have to put it all down quickly, in a muddle because if I leave it until later I probably won't be able to go on believing that it really happened. It is like a vision, and drifts further and further away. The babies were easily the worst.

And then there was that paralysed young girl, who didn't want to   6
take her dinner plate along and found it so hard to die. Or the terrified young boy: he had thought he was safe, that was his mistake, and when he realised he was going to have to go anyway, he panicked and ran off. His fellow Jews had to hunt him down—if they didn't find him, scores of others would be put on the transport in his place. He was caught soon enough, hiding in a tent, but 'notwithstanding' . . . 'notwithstanding', all those others had to go on transport anyway, as a deterrent, they said. And so, many good friends were dragged away by that boy. Fifty victims for one moment of insanity. Or rather: he didn't drag them away—our commandant did, someone of whom it is

sometimes said that he is a gentleman. Even so, will the boy be able to live with himself, once it dawns on him exactly what he's been the cause of? And how will all the other Jews on board the train react to him? That boy is going to have a very hard time. The episode might have been overlooked, perhaps, if there hadn't been so much unnerving activity over our heads that night. The commandant must have been affected by that too. '*Donnerwetter,* some flying tonight!' I heard a guard say as he looked up at the stars.

People still harbour such childish hopes that the transport won't get    7
through. Many of us were able from here to watch the bombardment of a nearby town, probably Emden. So why shouldn't it be possible for the railway line to be hit too, and for the train be stopped from leaving? It's never been known to happen yet, but people keep hoping it will with each new transport and with never-flagging hope . . .

The evening before that night, I walked through the camp. People    8
were grouped together between the barracks, under a grey, cloudy sky. 'Look, that's just how people behave after a disaster, standing about on street corners discussing what's happened,' my companion said to me. 'But that's what makes it so impossible to understand,' I burst out. 'This time, it's *before* the disaster!'

Whenever misfortune strikes, people have a natural instinct to lend    9
a helping hand and to save what can be saved. Tonight I shall be 'helping' to dress babies and to calm mothers and that is all I can hope to do. I could almost curse myself for that. For we all know that we are yielding up our sick and defenceless brothers and sisters to hunger, heat, cold, exposure and destruction, and yet we dress them and escort them to the bare cattle trucks—and if they can't walk we carry them on stretchers. What is going on, what mysteries are these, in what sort of fatal mechanism have we become enmeshed? The answer cannot simply be that we are all cowards. We're not that bad. We stand before a much deeper question . . .

In the afternoon I did a round of the hospital barracks one more    10
time, going from bed to bed. Which beds would be empty the next day? The transport lists are never published until the very last moment, but some of us know well in advance that our names will be down. A young girl called me. She was sitting bolt upright in her bed, eyes wide open. This girl has thin wrists and a peaky little face. She is partly paralysed, and has just been learning to walk again, between

two nurses, one step at a time. 'Have you heard? I have to go.' We look at each other for a long moment. It is as if her face has disappeared, she is all eyes. Then she says in a level, grey little voice, 'Such a pity, isn't it? That everything you have learned in life goes for nothing.' And, 'How hard it is to die.' Suddenly the unnatural rigidity of her expression gives way and she sobs, 'Oh, and the worst of it all is having to leave Holland!' And, 'Oh, why wasn't I allowed to die before . . .' Later, during the night, I saw her again, for the last time.

There was a little woman in the wash-house, a basket of dripping    11
clothes on her arm. She grabbed hold of me. She looked deranged. A flood of words poured over me, 'That isn't right, how can that be right, I've got to go and I won't even be able to get my washing dry by tomorrow. And my child is sick, he's feverish, can't you fix things so that I don't have to go? And I don't have enough things for the child, the rompers they sent me are too small, I need the bigger size, oh, it's enough to drive you mad. And you're not even allowed to take a blanket along, we're going to freeze to death, you didn't think of that, did you? There's a cousin of mine here, he came here the same time I did, but he doesn't have to go, he's got the right papers. Couldn't you help me to get some, too? Just say I don't have to go, do you think they'll leave the children with their mothers, that's right, you come back again tonight, you'll help me then, won't you, what do you think, would my cousin's papers . . . ?'

If I were to say that I was in hell that night, what would I really be    12
telling you? I caught myself saying it aloud in the night, aloud to myself and quite soberly, 'So that's what hell is like.' You really can't tell who is going and who isn't this time. Almost everyone is up, the sick help each other to get dressed. There are some who have no clothes at all, whose luggage has been lost or hasn't arrived yet. Ladies from the 'Welfare' walk about doling out clothes, which may fit or not, it doesn't matter so long as you've covered yourself with something. Some old women look a ridiculous sight. Small bottles of milk are being prepared to take along with the babies, whose pitiful screams punctuate all the frantic activity in the barracks. A young mother says to me almost apologetically, 'My baby doesn't usually cry, it's almost as if he can tell what's happening.' She picks up the child, a lovely baby about eight months old, from a makeshift crib and smiles at it, 'If you don't behave yourself, mummy won't take you along with her!' She tells me about some friends, 'When those men in green came to fetch

them in Amsterdam, their children cried terribly. Then their father said, "If you don't behave yourselves, you won't be allowed to go in that green car, this green gentleman won't take you." And that helped—the children calmed down.' She winks at me bravely, a trim, dark little woman with a lively, olive-skinned face, dressed in long grey trousers and a green woollen sweater, 'I may be smiling, but I feel pretty awful.' The little woman with the wet washing is on the point of hysterics. 'Can't you hide my child for me? Go on, please, won't you hide him, he's got a high fever, how can I possibly take him along?' She points to a little bundle of misery with blonde curls and a burning, bright-red little face. The child tosses about in his rough wooden cot. The nurse wants the mother to put on an extra woollen sweater, tries to pull it over her dress. She refuses, 'I'm not going to take anything along, what use would it be . . . my child.' And she sobs, 'They take the sick children away and you never get them back.'

Then a woman comes up to her, a stout working-class woman with   13
a kindly snub-nosed face, draws the desperate mother down with her on to the edge of one of the iron bunk beds and talks to her almost crooningly, 'There now, you're just an ordinary Jew, aren't you, so you'll just have to go, won't you . . . ?'

A few beds further along I suddenly catch sight of the ash-grey,   14
freckled face of a colleague. She is squatting beside the bed of a dying woman who has swallowed some poison and who happens to be her mother . . .

'God Almighty, what are you doing to us?' The words just escape   15
me. Over there is that affectionate little woman from Rotterdam. She is in her ninth month. Two nurses try to get her dressed. She just stands there, her swollen body leaning against her child's cot. Drops of sweat run down her face. She stares into the distance, a distance into which I cannot follow her, and says in a toneless, worn-out voice, 'Two months ago I volunteered to go with my husband to Poland. And then I wasn't allowed to, because I always have such difficult confinements. And now I do have to go . . . just because someone tried to run away tonight.' The wailing of the babies grows louder still, filling every nook and cranny of the barracks, now bathed in ghostly light. It is almost too much to bear. A name occurs to me: Herod.

On the stretcher, on the way to the train, her labour pains begin,   16
and we are allowed to carry the woman to hospital instead of to the goods train, which, this night, seems a rare act of humanity . . .

I pass the bed of the paralysed girl. The others have helped to dress    17
her. I never saw such great big eyes in such a little face. 'I can't take it
all in,' she whispers to me. A few steps away stands my little hunch-
backed Russian woman, I told you about her before. She stands there
as if spun in a web of sorrow. The paralysed girl is a friend of hers.
Later she said sadly to me, 'She doesn't even have a plate, I wanted to
give her mine but she wouldn't take it, she said, "I'll be dead in ten
days' time anyway, and then those horrible Germans will get it." '

She stands there in front of me, a green silk kimono wrapped round    18
her small, misshapen figure. She has the very wise, bright eyes of a
child. She looks at me for a long time in silence, searchingly, and then
says, 'I would like, oh, I really would like, to be able to swim away in
my tears.' And, 'I long so desperately for my dear mother.' (Her mother
died a few months ago from cancer, in the washroom near the WC. At
least she was left alone there for a moment, left to die in peace.) She
asks me with her strange accent in the voice of a child that begs for
forgiveness, 'Surely God will be able to understand my doubts in a
world like this, won't He?' Then she turns away from me, in an almost
loving gesture of infinite sadness, and throughout the night I see the
misshapen, green, silk-clad figure moving between the beds, doing
small services for those about to depart. She herself doesn't have to
go, not this time anyway . . .

I'm sitting here squeezing tomato juice for the babies. A young    19
woman sits beside me. She appears ready and eager to leave, and is
beautifully turned out. It is something like a cry of liberation when she
exclaims, arms flung wide, 'I'm embarking on a wonderful journey, I
might find my husband.' A woman opposite cuts her short bitterly,
'I'm going as well, but I certainly don't think it's wonderful.' I remembered admitting the young woman beside me. She has only been here
for a few days and she came from the punishment block. She seems so
level-headed and independent, with a touch of defiance about her
mouth. She has been ready to leave since the afternoon, dressed in a
long pair of trousers and a woollen jumper and cardigan. Next to her
on the floor stands a heavy rucksack and a blanket roll. She is trying
to force down a few sandwiches. They are mouldy. 'I'll probably get
quite a lot of mouldy bread to eat,' she laughs. 'In prison I didn't eat
anything at all for days.' A bit of her history in her own words: 'My
time wasn't far off when they threw me into prison. And the taunts
and the insults! I made the mistake of saying that I couldn't stand, so

they made me stand for hours, but I managed it without making a sound.' She looks defiant. 'My husband was in the prison as well. I won't tell you what they did to him! But my God, he was tough! They sent him through last month. I was in my third day of labour and couldn't go with him. But how brave he was!' She is almost radiant.

'Perhaps I shall find him again.' She laughs defiantly. 'They may   20
drag us through the dirt, but we'll come through all right in the end!' She looks at the crying babies all round and says, 'I'll have good work to do on the train, I still have lots of milk.'

'What, you here as well?' I suddenly call out in dismay. A woman   21
turns and comes up between the tumbled beds of the poor wailing babies, her hands groping round her for support. She is dressed in a long, black old-fashioned dress. She has a noble brow and white, wavy hair piled up high. Her husband died here a few weeks ago. She is well over eighty, but looks less than sixty. I always admired her for the aristocratic way in which she reclined on her shabby bunk. She answers in a hoarse voice, 'Yes, I'm here as well, they wouldn't let me share my husband's grave.'

'Ah, there she goes again!' It is the tough little ghetto woman who is   22
racked with hunger the whole time because she never gets any parcels. She has seven children here. She trips pluckily and busily about on her little short legs. 'All I know is I've got seven children and they need a proper mother, you can be sure of that!'

With nimble gestures she is busy stuffing a jute bag full of her   23
belongings.

'I'm not leaving anything behind, my husband was sent through   24
here a year ago and my two oldest boys have been through as well.' She beams, 'My children are real treasures!' She bustles about, she packs, she's busy, she has a kind word for everyone who goes by. A plain, dumpy ghetto woman with greasy black hair and little short legs. She has a shabby, short-sleeved dress on, which I can imagine her wearing when she used to stand behind the washtub, back in Jodenbreestraat. And now she is off to Poland in the same old dress, a three days' journey with seven children. 'That's right, seven children, and they need a proper mother, believe me!'

You can tell that the young woman over there is used to luxury and   25
that she must have been very beautiful. She is a recent arrival. She had gone into hiding to save her baby. Now she is here, through treachery, like so many others. Her husband is in the punishment barracks. She

looks quite pitiful now. Her bleached hair has black roots with a green-ish tinge. She has put on many different sets of underwear and other clothing all on top of one another—you can't carry everything by hand, after all, particularly if you have a little child to carry as well. Now she looks lumpy and ridiculous. Her face is blotchy. She stares at everyone with a veiled, tentative gaze, like some defenceless and aban-doned young animal.

What will this young woman, already in a state of collapse, look like  26 after three days in an overcrowded goods wagon with men, women, children and babies all thrown together, bags and baggage, a bucket in the middle their only convenience?

Presumably they will be sent on to another transit camp, and then  27 on again from there.

We are being hunted to death right through Europe . . .  28

I wander in a daze through other barracks. I walk past scenes that  29 loom up before my eyes in crystal-clear detail, and at the same time seem like blurred age-old visions. I see a dying old man being carried away, reciting the Sh'ma* to himself . . .

Slowly but surely six o'clock in the morning has arrived. The train  30 is due to depart at eleven, and they are starting to load it with people and luggage. Paths to the train have been staked out by men of the *Ordedienst*, the Camp Service Corps. Anyone not involved with the transport has to keep to barracks. I slip into one just across from the siding. 'There's always been a splendid view from here . . .' I hear a cynical voice say. The camp has been cut in two halves since yester-day by the train: a depressing series of bare, unpainted goods wagons in the front, and a proper carriage for the guards at the back. Some of the wagons have paper mattresses on the floor. These are for the sick. There is more and more movement now along the asphalt path beside the train.

Men from the 'Flying Column' in brown overalls are bringing the  31 luggage up on wheelbarrows. Among them I spot two of the comman-dant's court jesters: the first is a comedian and a song-writer. Some time ago his name was down, irrevocably, for transport, but for several nights in a row he sang his lungs out for a delighted audience, includ-ing the commandant and his retinue. He sang 'Ich kann es nicht ver-

---

*Sh'ma*: "Hear O Israel: the Lord our God, the Lord is one."

stehen, dass die Rosen blühen' ('I know not why the roses bloom') and other topical songs. The commandant, a great lover of art, thought it all quite splendid. The singer got his 'exemption'. He was even allocated a house where he now lives behind red-checked curtains with his peroxide-blonde wife; who spends all her days at a mangle in the boiling hot laundry. Now here he is, dressed in khaki overalls, pushing a wheelbarrow piled high with the luggage of his fellow Jews. He looks like death warmed up. And over there is another court jester: the commandant's favourite pianist. Legend has it that he is so accomplished that he can play Beethoven's Ninth as a jazz number, which is certainly saying something . . .

Suddenly there are a lot of green-uniformed men swarming over the 32 asphalt. I can't imagine where they have sprung from. Knapsacks and guns over their shoulders. I study their faces. I try to look at them without prejudice.

I can see a father, ready to depart, blessing his wife and child and 33 being himself blessed in turn by an old rabbi with a snow-white beard and the profile of a fiery prophet. I can see . . . ah, I can't begin to describe it all . . .

On earlier transports, some of the guards were simple, kindly types 34 with puzzled expressions, who walked about the camp smoking their pipes and speaking in some incomprehensible dialect, and one would have found their company not too objectionable on the journey. Now I am transfixed with terror. Oafish, jeering faces, in which one seeks in vain for even the slightest trace of human warmth. At what fronts did they learn their business? In what punishment camps were they trained? For after all this is a punishment, isn't it? A few young women are already sitting in a goods wagon. They hold their babies on their laps, their legs dangling outside—they are determined to enjoy the fresh air as long as possible. Sick people are carried past on stretchers. After all, it is meant as a punishment. I almost find myself laughing, the disparity between the guards and the guarded is too absurd. My companion at the window shudders. Months ago he was brought here from Amersfoort, in bits and pieces. 'Oh, yes, that's what those fellows were like,' he says. 'That's what they looked like.'

A couple of young children stand with their noses pressed to the 35 windowpane. I listen in to their earnest conversation, 'Why do those nasty, horrid men wear green, why don't they wear black? Bad people wear black, don't they?' 'Look over there, that man is really sick!' A shock of grey hair above a rumpled blanket on a stretcher. 'Look, there's another sick one . . .'

And, pointing at the green uniforms, 'Look at them, now they're 36 laughing!' 'Look, look, one of them's already drunk!'

More and more people are filling up the spaces in the goods wa- 37 gons. A tall, lonely figure paces the asphalt, a briefcase under his arm. He is the head of the so-called *Antragstelle,* the camp 'appeals depart-ment'. He strives right up to the last moment to get people out of the commandant's clutches. Horse-trading here always continues until the train has actually pulled out. It's even been known for him to manage to free people from the moving train. The man with the briefcase has the brow of a scholar, and tired, very tired shoulders. A bent, little old woman, with a black, old-fashioned hat on her grey, wispy hair, bars his way, gesticulating and brandishing a bundle of papers under his nose. He listens to her for a while, then shakes his head and turns away, his shoulders sagging just a little bit more. This time it won't be possible to get many people off the train in the nick of time. The commandant is annoyed. A young Jew has had the effrontery to run away. One can't really call it a serious attempt to escape—he ab-sconded from the hospital in a moment of panic, a thin jacket over his blue pyjamas, and in a clumsy, childish way took refuge in a tent where he was picked up quickly enough after a search of the camp. But if you are a Jew you may not run away, may not allow yourself to be stricken with panic. The commandant is remorseless. As a reprisal, and with-out warning, scores of others are being sent on the transport with the boy, including quite a few who had thought they were firmly at anchor here. This system happens to believe in collective punishment. And all those planes overhead couldn't have helped to improve the com-mandant's mood, though that is a subject on which he prefers to keep his own counsel.

The goods wagons are now what you might call full. But that's what 38 you think. God Almighty, does all this lot have to get in as well? A large new group has turned up. The children are still standing with their noses glued to the windowpane, they don't miss a thing . . . 'Look over there, a lot of people are getting off, it must be too hot in the train.' Suddenly one of them calls out, 'Look, the commandant!'

He appears at the end of the asphalt path, like a famous star making 39 his entrance during a grand finale. This near-legendary figure is said to be quite charming and so well-disposed towards the Jews. For the commandant of a camp for Jews he has some strange ideas. Recently he decided that we needed more variety in our diet, and we were promptly served marrowfat peas—just once—instead of cabbage. He could also be said to be our artistic patron here, and is a regular at all our cabaret nights. On one occasion he came three times in succession to see the same performance and roared with laughter at the same old jokes each time. Under his auspices, a male choir has been formed that sang 'Bei mir bist du schön' on his personal orders. It sounded very moving here on the heath, it must be said. Now and then he even invites some of the artistes to his house and talks and drinks with them into the early hours. One night not so long ago he escorted an actress back home, and when he took his leave of her he offered her his hand, just imagine, his hand! They also say that he specially loves children. Children must be looked after. In the hospital they even get a tomato each day. And yet many of them seem to die all the same . . . I could go on quite a bit longer about 'our' commandant. Perhaps he sees himself as a prince dispensing largesse to his many humble subjects. God knows how he sees himself. A voice behind me says, 'Once upon a time we had a commandant who used to kick people off to Poland. This one sees them off with a smile.'

He now walks along the train with military precision, a relatively    40
young man who has 'arrived' early in his career, if one may call it that. He is absolute master over the life and death of Dutch and German Jews here on this remote heath in Drenthe Province. A year ago he probably had not the slightest idea that it so much as existed. I didn't know about it myself, to tell the truth. He walks along the train, his grey, immaculately brushed hair just showing beneath his flat, light-green cap. That grey hair, which makes such a romantic contrast with his fairly young face, sends many of the silly young girls here into raptures, although they dare not, of course, express their feelings openly. On this cruel morning his face is almost iron-grey. It is a face that I am quite unable to read. Sometimes it seems to me to be like a long thin scar in which grimness mingles with joylessness and hypocrisy. And there is something else about him, halfway between a dapper hairdresser's assistant and a stage-door Johnny. But the grimness and the rigidly forced bearing predominate. With military step he walks along the goods wagons, bulging now with people. He is inspecting his troops: the sick, infants in arms, young mothers and shaven-

headed men. A few more ailing people are being brought up on stretchers, he makes an impatient gesture, they're taking too long about it. Behind him walks his Jewish secretary, smartly dressed in fawn riding breeches and brown sports jacket. He has the sporty demeanour yet vacuous expression of the English whisky drinker. Suddenly they are joined by a handsome brown gun-dog, where from heaven knows. With studied gestures the fawn secretary plays with it, like something from a picture in an English society paper. The green squad stare at him goggle-eyed. They probably think—though think is a big word—that some of the Jews here look quite different from what their propaganda sheets have led them to believe. A few Jewish big-shots from the camp now also walk along the train. 'Trying to air their "importance",' mutters someone behind me. 'Transport Boulevard,' I say. 'Could one ever hope to convey to the outside world what has happened here today?' I ask my companion. The outside world probably thinks of us as a grey, uniform, suffering mass of Jews, and knows nothing of the gulfs and abysses and subtle differences that exist between us. They could never hope to understand.

The commandant has now been joined by the *Oberdienstleiter,* the 41
head of the Camp Service Corps. The *Oberdienstleiter* is a German Jew of massive build, and the commandant looks slight and insignificant by his side. Black top-boots, black cap, black army coat with yellow star. He has a cruel mouth and a powerful neck. A few years ago he was still a digger in the outworkers' corps. When the story of his meteoric rise is written up later, it will be an important historical account of the mentality of our age. The light-green commandant with his military bearing, the fawn, impassive secretary, the black bully-boy figure of the *Oberdienstleiter,* parade past the train. People fall back around them, but all eyes are on them.

My God, are the doors really being shut now? Yes, they are. Shut 42
on the herded, densely packed, mass of people inside. Through small openings at the top we can see heads and hands, hands that will wave to us later when the train leaves. The commandant takes a bicycle and rides once again along the entire length of the train. Then he makes a brief gesture, like royalty in an operetta. A little orderly comes flying up and deferentially relieves him of the bicycle. The train gives a piercing whistle, and 1,020 Jews leave Holland.

This time the quota was really quite small, all considered: a mere 43
thousand Jews, the extra twenty being reserves, for it is always possi-

ble, indeed quite certain this time, that a few will die or be crushed to death on the way. So many sick people and not a single nurse . . .

The tide of helpers gradually recedes; people go back to their sleep- 44 ing quarters. So many exhausted, pale and suffering faces. One more piece of our camp has been amputated. Next week yet another piece will follow. This is what has been happening now for over a year, week in, week out. We are left with just a few thousand. A hundred thousand Dutch members of our race are toiling away under an unknown sky or lie rotting in some unknown soil. We know nothing of their fate. It is only a short while, perhaps, before we find out, each one of us in his own time, for we are all marked down to share that fate, of that I have not a moment's doubt. But I must go now and lie down and sleep for a little while. I am a bit tired and dizzy. Then later I have to go to the laundry to track down the face cloth that got lost. But first I must sleep. As for the future, I am firmly resolved to return to you after my wanderings. In the meantime, my love once again, you dear people.

## VOCABULARY

| | | |
|---|---|---|
| mosaic (3) | transfixed (34) | reprisal (37) |
| deranged (11) | disparity (34) | auspices (39) |
| makeshift (12) | gesticulating (37) | largesse (39) |
| misshapen (18) | brandishing (37) | predominate (40) |
| tentative (25) | effrontery (37) | vacuous (40) |
| irrevocably (31) | absconded (37) | deferentially (42) |
| retinue (31) | remorseless (37) | |

## THE FACTS

1. Which biblical passage haunted the narrator throughout the ordeal? How can that passage be reconciled with the horror and brutality she describes in her letter?
2. What reprisal did the behavior of the frightened boy bring down on the inmates of the camp?
3. The author finds it impossible to understand the behavior of the inmates as the list of prisoners to be shipped is announced. Historians agree with her: most Jews were perplexingly placid when faced with their own probable extermination. Why do you think that Jewish prisoners accepted their fate so calmly and went without a struggle?
4. What about the newest guards transfixed the narrator with horror?

5. How did the commandant's court jester save himself from being shipped to the gas chambers?

## THE STRATEGIES

1. In paragraph 12, the author abruptly switches the tense of her narrative. What does this switch add to her narration?
2. This letter was a private communication from Etty Hillesum to an unknown friend. Other than merely communicating with a friend, what do you think was her purpose in writing it?
3. In describing her feelings of self-loathing at helping to dress the babies and calm the mothers for the trip, the author writes: "What is going on, what mysteries are these, in what sort of fatal mechanism have we become enmeshed? The answer cannot simply be that we are all cowards. We're not that bad. We stand before a much deeper question . . ." Why do you think she used ellipses here? What deeper question could she have in mind?
4. What is unintentionally ironic in the juxtaposed descriptions of the *Oberdienstleiter* and the camp commandant in paragraph 41?

## THE ISSUES

1. At the beginning of her description, Hillesum tells us that some of the Jewish victims of Nazi oppression were laughing as they departed for the concentration camps. Is this description realistic? Why or why not?
2. If you had witnessed acts of savagery that were historically significant—as a hostage, for example—do you think it would be important to write down those events? Or would it be better for everyone if you simply let the memories fade? Why or why not?
3. In paragraph 41, Hillesum mentions that the meteoric rise of the *Oberdienstleiter* will someday be narrated in writing that will serve as a historical account of the "mentality of our age." What does the author mean?
4. During the postwar legal trials of certain Nazi offenders, the defense often stated that these men were simply carrying out orders—that is, "doing their jobs." What is your view of this defense?
5. Despite the overwhelmingly large body of evidence, many young Germans do not believe that the concentration camps actually existed, attributing stories about them to Allied propaganda. Why do you think they do this?

## SUGGESTIONS FOR WRITING

1. Write an essay explaining why it is necessary or unnecessary to keep memories of the Nazi concentration camps alive.

2. What obligation does a citizen have in the face of wicked or unjust commands from the State? Write an essay on this question.

H. L. Mencken

# ———— • THE LIBIDO FOR THE UGLY • ————

*Henry Louis Mencken (1880–1956) was an editor, author, and critic. He began his journalism career on the* Baltimore Morning Herald *and later became editor of the* Baltimore Evening Herald. *From 1906 until his death, he was on the staff of the* Baltimore Sun *(or* Evening Sun*). In 1924, with George Jean Nathan, Mencken founded the* American Mercury *and served as its editor from 1925 to 1933. Mencken's writing was chiefly devoted to lambasting the smug, conventional attitudes of the middle class. Among his numerous works is* The American Language, *Mencken's monumental study of the American idiom, first published in 1919.*

*Few writers have such an eye for colorful detail as the incomparable Mencken, at his best when he's railing against physical ugliness or storming against a tradition he dislikes. In the essay that follows, Mencken turns his literary wrath against the ugliness of the industrial heartland of America.*

On a Winter day some years ago, coming out of Pittsburgh on one of the expresses of the Pennsylvania Railroad, I rolled eastward for an hour through the coal and steel towns of Westmoreland county. It was familiar ground; boy and man, I had been through it often before. But somehow I had never quite sensed its appalling desolation. Here was the very heart of industrial America, the center of its most lucrative and characteristic activity, the boast and pride of the richest and grandest nation ever seen on earth—and here was a scene so dreadfully hideous, so intolerably bleak and forlorn that it reduced the whole aspiration of man to a macabre and depressing joke. Here was wealth beyond computation, almost beyond imagination—and here were human habitations so abominable that they would have disgraced a race of alley cats.

I am not speaking of mere filth. One expects steel towns to be dirty. What I allude to is the unbroken and agonizing ugliness, the sheer revolting monstrousness, of every house in sight. From East Liberty to Greensburg, a distance of twenty-five miles, there was not one in sight from the train that did not insult and lacerate the eye. Some were so bad, and they were among the most pretentious—churches, stores, warehouses, and the like—that they were downright startling; one blinked before them as one blinks before a man with his face shot away. A few linger in memory, horrible even there: a crazy little church just west of Jeannette, set like a dormer-window on the side of a bare, leprous hill; the headquarters of the Veterans of Foreign Wars at another forlorn town, a steel stadium like a huge rat-trap somewhere further down the line. But most of all I recall the general effect—of hideousness without a break. There was not a single decent house within eye-range from the Pittsburgh suburbs to the Greensburg yards. There was not one that was not misshapen, and there was not one that was not shabby.

The country itself is not uncomely, despite the grime of the endless 3 mills. It is, in form, a narrow river valley, with deep gullies running up into the hills. It is thickly settled, but not noticeably overcrowded. There is still plenty of room for building, even in the larger towns, and there are very few solid blocks. Nearly every house, big and little, has space on all four sides. Obviously, if there were architects of any professional sense or dignity in the region, they would have perfected a chalet to hug the hillsides—a chalet with a high-pitched roof, to throw off the heavy Winter snows, but still essentially a low and clinging building, wider than it was tall. But what have they done? They have taken as their model a brick set on end. This they have converted into a thing of dingy clapboards, with a narrow, low-pitched roof. And the whole they have set upon thin, preposterous brick piers. By the hundreds and thousands these abominable houses cover the bare hillsides, like gravestones in some gigantic and decaying cemetery. On their deep sides they are three, four and even five stories high; on their low sides they bury themselves swinishly in the mud. Not a fifth of them are perpendicular. They lean this way and that, hanging on to their bases precariously. And one and all they are streaked in grime, with dead and eczematous patches of paint peeping through the streaks.

Now and then there is a house of brick. But what brick! When it is 4 new it is the color of a fried egg. When it has taken on the patina of the mills it is the color of an egg long past all hope or caring. Was it necessary to adopt that shocking color? No more than it was necessary to set all of the houses on end. Red brick, even in a steel town, ages with some dignity. Let it become downright black, and it is still sightly, especially if its trimmings are of white stone, with soot in the depths and the high spots washed by the rain. But in Westmoreland they prefer that uremic yellow, and so they have the most loathsome towns and villages ever seen by mortal eye.

I award this championship only after laborious research and incessant prayer. I have seen, I believe, all of the most unlovely towns of the world; they are all to be found in the United States. I have seen the mill towns of decomposing New England and the desert towns of Utah, Arizona and Texas. I am familiar with the back streets of Newark, Brooklyn and Chicago, and have made scientific explorations to Camden, N.J. and Newport News, Va. Safe in a Pullman, I have whirled through the gloomy, God-forsaken villages of Iowa and Kansas, and the malarious tide-water hamlets of Georgia. I have been to Bridgeport, Conn., and to Los Angeles. But nowhere on this earth, at home or abroad, have I seen anything to compare to the villages that huddle along the line of the Pennsylvania from the Pittsburgh yards to Greensburg. They are incomparable in color, and they are incomparable in design. It is as if some titanic and aberrant genius, uncompromisingly inimical to man, had devoted all the ingenuity of Hell to the making of them. They show grotesqueries of ugliness that, in retrospect, become almost diabolical. One cannot imagine mere human beings concocting such dreadful things, and one can scarcely imagine human beings bearing life in them.

Are they so frightful because the valley is full of foreigners—dull, insensate brutes, with no love of beauty in them? Then why didn't these foreigners set up similar abominations in the countries that they came from? You will, in fact, find nothing of the sort in Europe—save perhaps in the more putrid parts of England. There is scarcely an ugly village on the whole Continent. The peasants, however poor, somehow manage to make themselves graceful and charming habitations, even in Spain. But in the American village and small town the pull is always toward ugliness, and in that Westmoreland valley it has been yielded to with an eagerness bordering upon passion. It is incredible that mere ignorance should have achieved such masterpieces of horror.

On certain levels of the American race, indeed, there seems to be a positive libido for the ugly, as on other and less Christian levels there is a libido for the beautiful. It is impossible to put down the wallpaper that defaces the average American home of the lower middle class to mere inadvertence, or to the obscene humor of the manufacturers.

Such ghastly designs, it must be obvious, give a genuine delight to a certain type of mind. They meet, in some unfathomable way, its obscure and unintelligible demands. They caress it as "The Palms" caresses it, or the art of the movie, or jazz. The taste for them is as enigmatical and yet as common as the taste for dogmatic theology and the poetry of Edgar A. Guest.

Thus I suspect (though confessedly without knowing) that the vast    8
majority of the honest folk of Westmoreland county, and especially the 100% Americans among them, actually admire the houses they live in, and are proud of them. For the same money they could get vastly better ones, but they prefer what they have got. Certainly there was no pressure upon the Veterans of Foreign Wars to choose the dreadful edifice that bears their banner, for there are plenty of vacant buildings along the track-side, and some of them are appreciably better. They might, indeed, have built a better one of their own. But they chose that clapboarded horror with their eyes open, and having chosen it, they let it mellow into its present shocking depravity. They like it as it is: beside it, the Parthenon would no doubt offend them. In precisely the same way the authors of the rat-trap stadium that I have mentioned made a deliberate choice. After painfully designing and erecting it, they made it perfect in their own sight by putting a completely impossible pent-house, painted a staring yellow, on top of it. The effect is that of a fat woman with a black eye. It is that of a Presbyterian grinning. But they like it.

Here is something that the psychologists have so far neglected: the    9
love of ugliness for its own sake, the lust to make the world intolerable. Its habitat is the United States. Out of the melting pot emerges a race which hates beauty as it hates truth. The etiology of this madness deserves a great deal more study than it has got. There must be causes behind it; it arises and flourishes in obedience to biological laws, and not as a mere act of God. What, precisely, are the terms of those laws? And why do they run stronger in America than elsewhere? Let some honest *Privat Dozent* in pathological sociology apply himself to the problem.

### VOCABULARY

| | | |
|---|---|---|
| lucrative (1) | uremic (4) | enigmatical (7) |
| aspiration (1) | malarious (5) | dogmatic (7) |

| | | |
|---|---|---|
| macabre (1) | aberrant (5) | Parthenon (8) |
| lacerate (2) | inimical (5) | etiology (9) |
| dormer-window (2) | grotesqueries (5) | *Privat Dozent* (9) |
| clapboards (3) | insensate (6) | pathological (9) |
| eczematous (3) | libido (7) | |
| patina (4) | inadvertence (7) | |

## THE FACTS

1. What area of the country does this essay describe?
2. What is the principal occupation of the region?
3. Mencken not only criticizes the architecture of the region, he suggests an alternative. What sort of architecture does he think suited to this region?
4. On what does Mencken blame the ugliness he describes?
5. What are Mencken's views of the villages in Europe? In his view, how do they compare with American towns?

## THE STRATEGIES

1. A good description focuses on a dominant impression, and develops it. Examine the second paragraph. What is the dominant impression here?
2. Examine the third paragraph. What dominant impression does Mencken focus on in his description of the buildings?
3. What aspect of the ugliness does paragraph 4 deal with?
4. "I have seen, I believe, all of the most unlovely towns of the world; they are all to be found in the United States." Why does he say *unlovely* rather than *ugly*? Which is more effective? Why?
5. "And one and all they are streaked in grime, with dead and eczematous patches of paint peeping through the streaks." What comparison is implied in this metaphor?

## THE ISSUES

1. One of the most vigilant civic groups in the United States today is that of the environmentalists—men and women determined to preserve historical buildings, wilderness areas, sea coasts, and public parks. What importance do you attribute to the efforts of these people? What do you think would happen if they no longer cared?
2. Mencken seems to feel that while architectural ugliness on any scale is lamentable, it is especially insulting when the edifice is pretentious. Do you agree with Mencken's view? Why or why not?
3. What stretch of highway in the U.S. is charmingly beautiful and stands in total contrast to Mencken's description of the houses in Westmoreland

County? Describe such a stretch in detail, focusing on architectural characteristics.
4. Do you agree with Mencken that Americans are psychologically obsessed with ugliness? If you agree, try to find reasons for this obsession. If you disagree, prove that Mencken is wrong by citing instances in which typical Americans have promoted beauty and good taste.
5. If you were to oversee a development of beautiful homes, what aesthetic requirements would you insist on? Describe the development in concrete terms.

## SUGGESTIONS FOR WRITING

1. Write an essay describing the town or city you live in.
2. Write an analysis of Mencken's diction in this essay, paying particular attention to his use of adjectives.

### E. B. White

## ———— • ONCE MORE TO THE LAKE • ————

*Elwyn Brooks White (1899–1985) was one of the wittiest and most admired observers of contemporary American society. As a member of* The New Yorker *magazine staff, he wrote a number of essays for the section called "Talk of the Town," and some of these essays have been collected in* The Wild Flag *(1946). With James Thurber, he wrote* Is Sex Necessary? *(1929). Some of his other well-known works include* One Man's Meat *(1942),* Here Is New York *(1949), and two beloved children's books,* Stuart Little *(1945) and* Charlotte's Web *(1952).*

*This is an essay that ends with a bang, not a whimper. The writer tackles what might seem at first glance a humdrum subject—an annual vacation trip to a lake—and describes in evocative and lovely prose the carefree summer days he spent hiking and fishing with his son. Then, at the very end, the trap is sprung.*

*August 1941*

One summer, along about 1904, my father rented a camp on a lake    1
in Maine and took us all there for the month of August. We all got ringworm from some kittens and had to rub Pond's Extract on our arms and legs night and morning, and my father rolled over in a canoe with all his clothes on; but outside of that the vacation was a success and from then on none of us ever thought there was any place in the

world like that lake in Maine. We returned summer after summer—always on August 1 for one month. I have since become a salt-water man, but sometimes in summer there are days when the restlessness of the tides and the fearful cold of the sea water and the incessant wind that blows across the afternoon and into the evening make me wish for the placidity of a lake in the woods. A few weeks ago this feeling got so strong I bought myself a couple of bass hooks and a spinner and returned to the lake where we used to go, for a week's fishing and to revisit old haunts.

I took along my son, who had never had any fresh water up his nose   2
and who had seen lily pads only from train windows. On the journey over to the lake I began to wonder what it would be like. I wondered how time would have marred this unique, this holy spot—the coves and streams, the hills that the sun set behind, the camps and the paths behind the camps. I was sure that the tarred road would have found it out, and I wondered in what other ways it would be desolated. It is strange how much you can remember about places like that once you allow your mind to return into the grooves that lead back. You remember one thing, and that suddenly reminds you of another thing. I guess I remembered clearest of all the early mornings, when the lake was cool and motionless, remembered how the bedroom smelled of the lumber it was made of and of the wet woods whose scent entered through the screen. The partitions in the camp were thin and did not extend clear to the top of the rooms, and as I was always the first up I would dress softly so as not to wake the others, and sneak out into the sweet outdoors and start out in the canoe, keeping close along the shore in the long shadows of the pines. I remembered being very careful never to rub my paddle against the gunwale for fear of disturbing the stillness of the cathedral.

The lake had never been what you would call a wild lake. There   3
were cottages sprinkled around the shores, and it was in farming country although the shores of the lake were quite heavily wooded. Some of the cottages were owned by nearby farmers, and you would live at the shore and eat your meals at the farmhouse. That's what our family did. But although it wasn't wild, it was a fairly large and undisturbed lake and there were places in it that, to a child at least, seemed infinitely remote and primeval.

I was right about the tar: it led to within half a mile of the shore. But   4
when I got back there, with my boy, and we settled into a camp near a

farmhouse and into the kind of summertime I had known, I could tell that it was going to be pretty much the same as it had been before—I knew it, lying in bed the first morning smelling the bedroom and hearing the boy sneak quietly out and go off along the shore in a boat. I began to sustain the illusion that he was I, and therefore, by simple transposition, that I was my father. This sensation persisted, kept cropping up all the time we were there. It was not an entirely new feeling, but in this setting it grew much stronger. I seemed to be living a dual existence. I would be in the middle of some simple act, I would be picking up a bait box or laying down a table fork, or I would be saying something and suddenly it would be not I but my father who was saying the words or making the gesture. It gave me a creepy sensation.

We went fishing the first morning. I felt the same damp moss cov-   5 ering the worms in the bait can, and saw the dragonfly alight on the tip of my rod as it hovered a few inches from the surface of he water. It was the arrival of this fly that convinced me beyond any doubt that everything was as it always had been, that the years were a mirage and that there had been no years. The small waves were the same, chucking the rowboat under the chin as we fished at anchor, and the boat was the same boat, the same color green and the ribs broken in the same places, and under the floorboards the same fresh water leavings and débris—the dead helgramite, the wisps of moss, the rusty discarded fishhook, the dried blood from yesterday's catch. We stared silently at the tips of our rods, at the dragonflies that came and went. I lowered the tip of mine into the water, tentatively, pensively dislodging the fly, which darted two feet away, poised, darted two feet back, and came to rest again a little farther up the rod. There had been no years between the ducking of this dragonfly and the other one—the one that was part of memory. I looked at the boy, who was silently watching his fly, and it was my hands that held his rod, my eyes watching. I felt dizzy and didn't know which rod I was at the end of.

We caught two bass, hauling them in briskly as though they were   6 mackerel, pulling them over the side of the boat in a businesslike manner without any landing net, and stunning them with a blow on the back of the head. When we got back for a swim before lunch, the lake was exactly where we had left it, the same number of inches from the dock, and there was only the merest suggestion of a breeze. This seemed an utterly enchanted sea, this lake you could leave to its own devices for a few hours and come back to, and find that it had not stirred, this constant and trustworthy body of water. In the shallows, the dark, water-soaked sticks and twigs, smooth and old, were undulating in clusters on the bottom against the clean ribbed sand, and the track of the mussel was plain. A school of minnows swam by, each minnow with its small individual shadow, doubling the attendance, so clear and sharp in the sunlight. Some of the other campers were in swimming, along the shore, one of them with a cake of soap, and the water felt thin and clear and unsubstantial. Over the years there had been this person with the cake of soap, this cultist, and here he was. There had been no years.

Up to the farmhouse to dinner through the teeming dusty field, the road under our sneakers was only a two-track road. The middle track was missing, the one with the marks of the hooves and the splotches of dried, flaky manure. There had always been three tracks to choose from in choosing which track to walk in; now the choice was narrowed down to two. For a moment I missed terribly the middle alternative. But the way led past the tennis court, and something about the way it lay there in the sun reassured me; the tape had loosened along the backline, the alleys were green with plantains and other weeds, and the net (installed in June and removed in September) sagged in the dry noon, and the whole place steamed with midday heat and hunger and emptiness. There was a choice of pie for dessert, and one was blueberry and one was apple, and the waitresses were the same country girls, there having been no passage of time, only the illusion of it as in a dropped curtain—the waitresses were still fifteen; their hair had been washed, that was the only difference—they had been to the movies and seen the pretty girls with the clean hair.

Summertime, oh, summertime, pattern of life indelible with fadeproof lake, the wood unshatterable, the pasture with the sweetfern and the juniper forever and ever, summer without end; this was the background, and the life along the shore was the design, the cottages with their innocent and tranquil design, their tiny docks with the flagpole and the American flag floating against the white clouds in the blue sky, the little paths over the roots of the trees leading from camp to camp and the paths leading back to the outhouses and the can of lime for sprinkling, and at the souvenir counters at the store the miniature birch-bark canoes and the postcards that showed things looking a little better than they looked. This was the American family at play,

escaping the city heat, wondering whether the newcomers in the camp
at the head of the cove were "common" or "nice," wondering whether
it was true that the people who drove up for Sunday dinner at the
farmhouse were turned away because there wasn't enough chicken.

It seemed to me, as I kept remembering all this, that those times and    9
those summers had been infinitely precious and worth saving. There
had been jollity and peace and goodness. The arriving (at the beginning of August) had been so big a business in itself, at the railway
station the farm wagon drawn up, the first smell of the pine-laden air,
the first glimpse of the smiling farmer, and the great importance of the
trunks and your father's enormous authority in such matters, and the
feel of the wagon under you for the long ten-mile haul, and at the top
of the last long hill catching the first view of the lake after eleven
months of not seeing this cherished body of water. The shouts and
cries of the other campers when they saw you, and the trunks to be
unpacked, to give up their rich burden. (Arriving was less exciting
nowadays, when you sneaked up in your car and parked it under a
tree near the camp and took out the bags and in five minutes it was all
over, no fuss, no loud wonderful fuss about trunks.)

Peace and goodness and jollity. The only thing that was wrong now,    10
really, was the sound of the place, an unfamiliar nervous sound of the
outboard motors. This was the note that jarred, the one thing that
would sometimes break the illusion and set the years moving. In those
other summertimes all motors were inboard; and when they were at a
little distance, the noise they made was a sedative, an ingredient of
summer sleep. They were one-cylinder and two-cylinder engines, and
some were make-and-break and some were jump-spark, but they all
made a sleepy sound across the lake. The one-lungers throbbed and
fluttered, and the twin-cylinder ones purred and purred, and that was
a quiet sound, too. But now the campers all had outboards. In the
daytime, in the hot mornings, these motors made a petulant, irritable
sound; at night in the still evening when the afterglow lit the water,
they whined about one's ears like mosquitoes. My boy loved our
rented outboard, and his great desire was to achieve single-handed
mastery over it, and authority, and he soon learned the trick of choking
it a little (but not too much), and the adjustment of the needle valve.
Watching him I would remember the things you could do with the old
one-cylinder engine with the heavy flywheel, how you could have it
eating out of your hand if you got really close to it spiritually. Motor-

boats in those days didn't have clutches, and you would make a landing by shutting off the motor at the proper time and coasting in with a dead rudder. But there was a way of reversing them, if you learned the trick, by cutting the switch and putting it on again exactly on the final dying revolution of the flywheel, so that it would kick back against compression and begin reversing. Approaching a dock in a strong following breeze, it was difficult to slow up sufficiently by the ordinary coasting method, and if a boy felt he had complete mastery over his motor, he was tempted to keep it running beyond its time and then reverse it a few feet from the dock. It took a cool nerve, because if you threw the switch a twentieth of a second too soon you would catch the flywheel when it still had speed enough to go up past center, and the boat would leap ahead, charging bull-fashion at the dock.

We had a good week at the camp. The bass were biting well and the    11
sun shone endlessly, day after day. We would be tired at night and lie down in the accumulated heat of the little bedrooms after the long hot day and the breeze would stir almost imperceptibly outside and the smell of the swamp drift in through the rusty screens. Sleep would come easily and in the morning the red squirrel would be on the roof, tapping out his gay routine. I kept remembering everything, lying in bed in the mornings—the small steamboat that had a long rounded stern like the lip of a Ubangi, and how quietly she ran on the moonlight sails, when the older boys played their mandolins and the girls sang and we ate doughnuts dipped in sugar, and how sweet the music was on the water in the shining night, and what it had felt like to think about girls then. After breakfast we would go up to the store and the things were in the same place—the minnows in a bottle, the plugs and spinners disarranged and pawed over by the youngsters from the boys' camp, the Fig Newtons and the Beeman's gum. Outside, the road was tarred and cars stood in front of the store. Inside, all was just as it had always been, except there was more Coca-Cola and not so much Moxie and root beer and birch beer and sarsaparilla. We would walk out with the bottle of pop apiece and sometimes the pop would backfire up our noses and hurt. We explored the streams, quietly, where the turtles slid off the sunny logs and dug their way into the soft bottom; and we lay on the town wharf and fed worms to the tame bass. Everywhere we went I had trouble making out which was I, the one walking at my side, the one walking in my pants.

One afternoon while we were at that lake a thunderstorm came up.    12

It was like the revival of an old melodrama that I had seen long ago
with childish awe. The second-act climax of the drama of the electrical
disturbance over a lake in America had not changed in any important
respect. This was the big scene, still the big scene. The whole thing
was so familiar, the first feeling of oppression and heat and a general
air around camp of not wanting to go very far away. In midafternoon
(it was all the same) a curious darkening of the sky, and a lull in
everything that had made life tick; and then the way the boats suddenly swung the other way at their moorings with the coming of a
breeze out of the new quarter, and the premonitory rumble. Then the
kettle drum, then the snare, then the bass drum and cymbals, then
crackling light against the dark, and the gods grinning and licking
their chops in the hills. Afterward the calm, the rain steadily rustling
in the calm lake, the return of light and hope and spirits, and the
campers running out in joy and relief to go swimming in the rain, their
bright cries perpetuating the deathless joke about how they were getting simply drenched, and the children screaming with delight at the
new sensation of bathing in the rain, and the joke about getting
drenched linking the generations in a strong indestructible chain. And
the comedian who waded in carrying an umbrella.

When the others went swimming my son said he was going in, too.     13
He pulled his dripping trunks from the line where they had hung all
through the shower and wrung them out. Languidly, and with no
thought of going in, I watched him, his hard little body, skinny and
bare, saw him wince slightly as he pulled up around his vitals the
small, soggy, icy garment. As he buckled the swollen belt, suddenly
my groin felt the chill of death.     .

## VOCABULARY

| | | |
|---|---|---|
| incessant (1) | pensively (5) | sedative (10) |
| desolated (2) | undulating (6) | imperceptibly (11) |
| primeval (3) | unsubstantial (6) | premonitory (12) |
| transposition (4) | cultist (6) | |
| tentatively (5) | indelible (8) | |

## THE FACTS

1. How old was White when he first went to the lake with his father? How
old was he when he took his own son there?

2. What illusion did White begin to sustain on hearing his own son sneaking out to go down to the boat on the lake?
3. What changes did the author notice in the road leading from the lake to the farmhouse? What did this change say about the passing of time?
4. What difference did the author note between the way guests arrived at the lake in his own boyhood days and their arrival now?
5. What experience precipitated White's realization that time had passed, that he was no longer young, that he was mortal?

## THE STRATEGIES

1. Aside from description, what other mode of development is implicitly part of the structure of this essay?
2. In paragraph 2, White writes that he "was sure that the tarred road would have found it [the lake] out." What is odd about the phrasing of this sentence? What do you think White was trying to achieve in phrasing it that way?
3. Examine the author's boyhood recollections of the lake (paragraph 2). To which of our senses do his detail and images appeal?
4. Examine the description of the fishing boat in paragraph 5. How does White manage to convey such a vivid picture of the boat?
5. In what part of his body did White feel the chill of death? In the context of the essay, why is this such an appropriate place?

## THE ISSUES

1. In paragraph 2, why does White refer to the lake as a "holy spot"? What is the connotation of this term, since the place was not a religious shrine? What, in your life, would be a similar spot? Give reasons for your choice.
2. The author states that he missed the "middle track" of the road leading up to the farmhouse for dinner. Try to imagine yourself in a similar situation forty years hence. What vehicles of transportation, not yet commonly used, might invade your road then?
3. What is the social implication of the words *common* or *nice* in paragraph 8? Have times changed or are these distinctions still made?
4. Not everyone would have reacted the way the author describes himself in the final sentence of the essay. What might be another realistic reaction?
5. What are some clear signs in your life to indicate that you are not immortal? What are your feelings about these signs?

## SUGGESTIONS FOR WRITING

1. Write an essay about any favorite vacation spot or a favorite relative. Be

specific in your description, providing details that evoke the feeling of the place.

2. Write an essay in which you contrast the descriptive styles of "Libido for the Ugly" and "Once More to the Lake." Pinpoint how each author evokes a mood.

James Joyce

## •  HELL  •

*James Joyce (1882–1941) is considered by many to be among the most significant novelists of this century. He was born in Dublin, Ireland, and educated at University College, Dublin. A writer who pushed language to its outer limit of comprehensibility, Joyce wrote poetry, short stories, and novels. His major novels include* A Portrait of the Artist as a Young Man *(1916),* Ulysses *(written between 1914 and 1921 and published in the United States in 1933), and* Finnegans Wake *(1939).*

*Joyce, in this selection from* A Portrait of the Artist as a Young Man, *shows us the wreathing fires of hell and persuades us to smell its stench of brimstone and sin. The description below is so graphic, so detailed, filled with such shuddering imagery, that we almost believe that someone has returned from this dreadful place to tell the tale.*

Hell is a strait and dark and foulsmelling prison, an abode of demons and lost souls, filled with fire and smoke. The straitness of this prisonhouse is expressly designed by God to punish those who refused to be bound by His laws. In earthly prisons the poor captive has at least some liberty of movement, were it only within the four walls of his cell or in the gloomy yard of his prison. Not so in hell. There, by reason of the great number of the damned, the prisoners are heaped together in their awful prison, the walls of which are said to be four thousand miles thick: and the damned are so utterly bound and helpless that, as a blessed saint, saint Anselm, writes in his book on similitudes, they are not even able to remove from the eye a worm that gnaws it.

—They lie in exterior darkness. For, remember, the fire of hell gives forth no light. As, at the command of God, the fire of the Babylonian furnace lost its heat but not its light so, at the command of God, the fire of hell, while retaining the intensity of its heat, burns eternally in darkness. It is a neverending storm of darkness, dark flames and dark smoke of burning brimstone, amid which the bodies are heaped one upon another without even a glimpse of air. Of all the plagues with which the land of the Pharaohs was smitten one plague alone, that of darkness, was called horrible. What name, then, shall we give to the darkness of hell which is to last not for three days alone but for all eternity?

—The horror of this strait and dark prison is increased by its awful   3
stench. All the filth of the world, all the offal and scum of the world, we are told, shall run there as to a vast reeking sewer when the terrible conflagration of the last day has purged the world. The brimstone too which burns there in such prodigious quantity fills all hell with its intolerable stench; and the bodies of the damned themselves exhale such a pestilential odour that as saint Bonaventure says, one of them alone would suffice to infect the whole world. The very air of this world, that pure element, becomes foul and unbreathable when it has been long enclosed. Consider then what must be the foulness of the air of hell. Imagine some foul and putrid corpse that has lain rotting and decomposing in the grave, a jellylike mass of liquid corruption. Imagine such a corpse a prey to flames, devoured by the fire of burning brimstone and giving off dense choking fumes of nauseous loathsome decomposition. And then imagine this sickening stench, multiplied a millionfold and a millionfold again from the millions upon millions of fetid carcasses massed together in the reeking darkness, a huge and rotting human fungus. Imagine all this and you will have some idea of the horror of the stench of hell.

—But this stench is not, horrible though it is, the greatest physical   4
torment to which the damned are subjected. The torment of fire is the greatest torment to which the tyrant has ever subjected his fellowcreatures. Place your finger for a moment in the flame of a candle and you will feel the pain of fire. But our earthly fire was created by God for the benefit of man, to maintain in him the spark of life and to help him in the useful arts whereas the fire of hell is of another quality and was created by God to torture and punish the unrepentant sinner. Our earthly fire also consumes more or less rapidly according as the object which it attacks is more or less combustible so that human ingenuity has even succeeded in inventing chemical preparations to check or frustrate its action. But the sulphurous brimstone which burns in hell is a substance which is specially designed to burn for ever and for ever

with unspeakable fury. Moreover our earthly fire destroys at the same time as it burns so that the more intense it is the shorter is its duration: but the fire of hell has this property that it preserves that which it burns and though it rages with incredible intensity it rages for ever.

—Our earthly fire again, no matter how fierce or widespread it may be, is always of a limited extent: but the lake of fire in hell is boundless, shoreless and bottomless. It is on record that the devil himself, when asked the question by a certain soldier, was obliged to confess that if a whole mountain were thrown into the burning ocean of hell it would be burned up in an instant like a piece of wax. And this terrible fire will not afflict the bodies of the damned only from without but each lost soul will be a hell unto itself, the boundless fire raging in its very vitals. O, how terrible is the lot of those wretched beings! The blood seethes and boils in the veins, the brains are boiling in the skull, the heart in the breast glowing and bursting, the bowels a redhot mass of burning pulp, the tender eyes flaming like molten balls.

—And yet what I have said as to the strength and quality and boundlessness of this fire is as nothing when compared to its intensity, an intensity which it has as being the instrument chosen by divine design for the punishment of soul and body alike. It is a fire which proceeds directly from the ire of God, working not of its own activity but as an instrument of divine vengeance. As the waters of baptism cleanse the soul with the body so do the fires of punishment torture the spirit with the flesh. Every sense of the flesh is tortured and every faculty of the soul therewith: the eyes with impenetrable utter darkness, the nose with noisome odours, the ears with yells and howls and execrations, the taste with foul matter, leprous corruption, nameless suffocating filth, the touch with redhot goads and spikes, with cruel tongues of flame. And through the several torments of the senses the immortal soul is tortured eternally in its very essence amid the leagues upon leagues of glowing fires kindled in the abyss by the offended majesty of the Omnipotent God and fanned into everlasting and ever increasing fury by the breath of the anger of the Godhead.

Consider finally that the torment of this infernal prison is increased by the company of the damned themselves. Evil company on earth is so noxious that even the plants, as if by instinct, withdraw from the company of whatsoever is deadly or hurtful to them. In hell all laws are overturned: there is no thought of family or country, of ties, of relationships. The damned howl and scream at one another, their torture and rage intensified by the presence of beings tortured and raging like themselves. All sense of humanity is forgotten. The yells of the suffering sinners fill the remotest corners of the vast abyss. The mouths of the damned are full of blasphemies against God and of hatred for their fellowsufferers and of curses against those souls which were their accomplices in sin. In olden times it was the custom to punish the parricide, the man who had raised his murderous hand against his father, by casting him into the depths of the sea in a sack in which were placed a cock, a monkey and a serpent. The intention of those lawgivers who framed such a law, which seems cruel in our times, was to punish the criminal by the company of hateful and hurtful beasts. But what is the fury of those dumb beasts compared with the fury of execration which bursts from the parched lips and aching throats of the damned in hell when they behold in their companions in misery those who aided and abetted them in sin, those whose words sowed the first seeds of evil thinking and evil living in their minds, those whose immodest suggestions led them on to sin, those whose eyes tempted and allured them from the path of virtue. They turn upon those accomplices and upbraid them and curse them. But they are helpless and hopeless: it is too late now for repentance.

## VOCABULARY

| | | |
|---|---|---|
| strait (1) | prodigious (3) | parricide (7) |
| similitudes (1) | pestilential (3) | execration (7) |
| offal (3) | fetid (3) | allured (7) |
| conflagration (3) | noisome (6) | upbraid (7) |

## THE FACTS

1. How thick are the walls of hell?
2. What peculiar characteristics does the fire of hell have?
3. What is the greatest physical torment that the damned of hell suffer?
4. What is the source of the fire in hell?
5. How were parricides punished in olden times?

## THE STRATEGIES

1. Examine carefully this description of hell. What is its overall structure? How are its paragraphs deployed?
2. Examine paragraph 4. How is it developed? What is its purpose?

3. What is the purpose of mentioning the "earthly prisons" in paragraph 1?
4. Examine paragraph 5. How is this paragraph structured? What technique does the writer use to make his description so vivid?
5. In the novel *A Portrait of the Artist as a Young Man*, this description of hell is delivered in a sermon. Identify at least one technique that the preacher uses to involve his listeners in the description.

## THE ISSUES

1. Modern minds have, for the most part, rejected the medieval view of a physical hell, where the damned suffer such tortures as heat, cold, foul smell, laceration, and persecution from demons. What, if anything, has replaced this notion of hell?
2. In your view, why do many people believe in paradise and hell? What disadvantage or advantage does the *lack* of belief in these places provide?
3. What effect do you think this sermon on hell might have on young boys listening to it? What is your opinion of the technique used?
4. Is torture as a means of punishment ever justified in a civilized society? Why or why not?
5. A portion of Dante's hell was reserved for those who encouraged others to sin. Where in this excerpt does Joyce express a similar idea? Why do both Dante and Joyce call down a harsh judgment on those who aid and abet evil?

## SUGGESTIONS FOR WRITING

1. Write an essay on hell as it is described here, arguing for or against a belief in its existence.
2. Following the example of this selection, write a brief description of heaven.

### Eudora Welty

# • A WORN PATH •

*Eudora Welty (b. 1909) is an American novelist and short-story writer whose tales about eccentric but charming characters from small Mississippi towns have won her a large audience. The best-known of her stories have been collected in* A Curtain of Green *(1941),* The Wide Net *(1943), and* The Golden Apples *(1949). Among her novels are* Delta Wedding *(1946),* The Ponder Heart *(1954), and* The Optimist's Daughter *(1972). In 1983 she delivered the*

*William E. Massey Sr. Lectures in American Civilization at Harvard, which were published as* One Writer's Beginnings *(1984).*

*In this story, a woman, undaunted by age and hardships, presses on toward her goal—to get the medicine her sick grandchild must have in order to survive.*

It was December—a bright frozen day in the early morning. Far out  1
in the country there was an old Negro woman with her head tied in a
red rag, coming along a path through the pinewoods. Her name was
Phoenix Jackson. She was very old and small and she walked slowly
in the dark pine shadows, moving a little from side to side in her steps,
with the balanced heaviness and lightness of a pendulum in a grandfather clock. She carried a thin, small cane made from an umbrella,
and with this she kept tagging the frozen earth in front of her. This
made a grave and persistent noise in the still air, that seemed meditative, like the chirping of a solitary little bird.

She wore a dark striped dress reaching down to her shoetops, and  2
an equally long apron of bleached sugar sacks, with a full pocket; all
neat and tidy, but every time she took a step she might have fallen over
her shoe-laces, which dragged from her unlaced shoes. She looked
straight ahead. Her eyes were blue with age. Her skin had a pattern
all its own of numberless branching wrinkles and as though a whole
little tree stood in the middle of her forehead, but a golden color ran
underneath, and the two knobs of her cheeks were illuminated by a
yellow burning under the dark. Under the red rag her hair came down
on her neck in the frailest of ringlets, still black, and with an odor like
copper.

Now and then there was a quivering in the thicket. Old Phoenix  3
said, "Out of my way, all you foxes, owls, beetles, jack rabbits, coons,
and wild animals! . . . Keep out from under these feet, little bobwhites. . . . Keep the big wild hogs out of my path. Don't let none of
those come running my direction. I got a long way." Under her small
black-freckled hand her cane, limber as a buggy whip, would switch
at the brush as if to rouse up any hiding things.

On she went. The woods were deep and still. The sun made the  4
pine needles almost too bright to look at, up where the wind rocked.
The cones dropped as light as feathers. Down in the hollow was the
mourning dove—it was not too late for him.

The path ran up a hill. "Seem like there is chains about my feet,  5 time I get this far," she said, in the voice of argument old people keep to use with themselves. "Something always take a hold on this hill— pleads I should stay."

After she got to the top she turned and gave a full, severe look behind where she had come. "Up through pines," she said at length. "Now down through oaks." 6

Her eyes opened their widest and she started down gently. But before she got to the bottom of the hill a bush caught her dress. 7

Her fingers were busy and intent, but her skirts were full and long, so that before she could pull them free in one place they were caught in another. It was not possible to allow the dress to tear. "I in the thorny bush," she said. "Thorns, you doing your appointed work. Never want to let folks past—no sir. Old eyes thought you was a pretty little *green* bush." 8

Finally, trembling all over, she stood free, and after a moment dared to stoop for her cane. 9

"Sun so high!" she cried, leaning back and looking, while the thick tears went over her eyes. "The time getting all gone here." 10

At the foot of this hill was a place where a log was laid across the creek. 11

"Now comes the trial," said Phoenix. 12

Putting her right foot out, she mounted the log and shut her eyes. Lifting her skirt, leveling her cane fiercely before her, like a festival figure in some parade, she began to march across. Then she opened her eyes and she was safe on the other side. 13

"I wasn't as old as I thought," she said. 14

But she sat down to rest. She spread her skirts on the bank around her and folded her hands over her knees. Up above her was a tree in a pearly cloud of mistletoe. She did not dare to close her eyes, and when a little boy brought her a little plate with a slice of marble-cake on it she spoke to him. "That would be acceptable," she said. But when she went to take it there was just her own hand in the air. 15

So she left that tree, and had to go through a barbed-wire fence. There she had to creep and crawl, spreading her knees and stretching her fingers like a baby trying to climb the steps. But she talked loudly to herself: she could not let her dress be torn now, so late in the day, and she could not pay for having her arm or her leg sawed off if she got caught fast where she was. 16

At last she was safe through the fence and risen up out in the  17
clearing. Big dead trees, like black men with one arm, were standing
in the purple stalks of the withered cotton field. There sat a buzzard.

"Who you watching?"  18

In the furrow she made her way along.  19

"Glad this not the season for bulls," she said, looking sideways,  20
"and the good Lord made his snakes to curl up and sleep in the winter.
A pleasure I don't see no two-headed snake coming around that tree,
where it come once. It took a while to get by him, back in the summer."

She passed through the old cotton and went into a field of dead  21
corn. It whispered and shook, and was taller than her head. "Through
the maze now," she said, for there was no path.

Then there was something tall, black, and skinny there, moving  22
before her.

At first she took it for a man. It could have been a man dancing in  23
the field. But she stood still and listened, and it did not make a sound.
It was as silent as a ghost.

"Ghost," she said sharply, "who be you the ghost of? For I have  24
heard of nary death close by."

But there was no answer, only the ragged dancing in the wind.  25

She shut her eyes, reached out her hand, and touched a sleeve. She  26
found a coat and inside that an emptiness, cold as ice.

"You scarecrow," she said. Her face lighted. "I ought to be shut up  27
for good," she said with laughter. "My senses is gone. I too old. I the
oldest people I ever know. Dance, old scarecrow," she said, "while I
dancing with you."

She kicked her foot over the furrow, and with mouth drawn down  28
shook her head once or twice in a little strutting way. Some husks blew
down and whirled in streamers about her skirts.

Then she went on, parting her way from side to side with the cane,  29
through the whispering field. At last she came to the end, to a wagon
track, where the silver grass blew between the red ruts. The quail were
walking around like pullets, seeming all dainty and unseen.

"Walk pretty," she said. "This is the easy place. This is the easy  30
going."

She followed the track, swaying through the quiet bare fields,  31
through the little strings of trees silver in their dead leaves, past cabins
silver from weather, with the doors and windows boarded shut, all

like old women under a spell sitting there. "I walking in their sleep," she said, nodding her head vigorously.

In a ravine she went where a spring was silently flowing through a  32 hollow log. Old Phoenix bent and drank. "Sweetgum makes the water sweet," she said, and drank more. "Nobody know who made this well, for it was here when I was born."

The track crossed a swampy part where the moss hung as white as  33 lace from every limb. "Sleep on, alligators, and blow your bubbles." Then the track went into the road.

Deep, deep the road went down between the high green-colored  34 banks. Overhead the live-oaks met, and it was as dark as a cave.

A black dog with a lolling tongue came up out of the weeds by the  35 ditch. She was meditating, and not ready, and when he came at her she only hit him a little with her cane. Over she went in the ditch, like a little puff of milkweed.

Down there, her senses drifted away. A dream visited her, and she  36 reached her hand up, but nothing reached down and gave her a pull. So she lay there and presently went to talking. "Old woman," she said to herself, "that black dog come up out of the weeds to stall you off, and now there he sitting on his fine tail, smiling at you."

A white man finally came along and found her—a hunter, a young  37 man, with his dog on a chain.

"Well, Granny!" he laughed. "What are you doing there?"  38

"Lying on my back like a June-bug waiting to be turned over, mis-  39 ter," she said, reaching up her hand.

He lifted her up, gave her a swing in the air, and set her down,  40 "Anything broken, Granny?"

"No sir, them old dead weeds is springy enough," said Phoenix,  41 when she had got her breath. "I thank you for your trouble."

"Where do you live, Granny?" he asked, while the two dogs were  42 growling at each other.

"Away back yonder, sir, behind the ridge. You can't even see it from  43 here."

"On your way home?"  44

"No sir, I going to town."  45

"Why, that's too far! That's as far as I walk when I come out myself,  46 and I get something for my trouble." He patted the stuffed bag he carried, and there hung down a little closed claw. It was one of the bobwhites, with its beak hooked bitterly to show it was dead. "Now you go on home, Granny!"

"I bound to go to town, mister," said Phoenix. "The time come around."    47

He gave another laugh, filling the whole landscape. "I know you colored people! Wouldn't miss going to town to see Santa Claus!"    48

But something held Old Phoenix very still. The deep lines in her face went into a fierce and different radiation. Without warning she had seen with her own eyes a flashing nickel fall out of the man's pocket on to the ground.    49

"How old are you, Granny?" he was saying.    50

"There is no telling, mister," she said, "no telling."    51

Then she gave a little cry and clapped her hands, and said, "Git on away from here, dog! Look! Look at that dog!" She laughed as if in admiration. "He ain't scared of nobody. He a big black dog." She whispered, "Sick him!"    52

"Watch me get rid of that cur," said the man. "Sick him, Pete! Sick him!"    53

Phoenix heard the dogs fighting and heard the man running and throwing sticks. She even heard a gunshot. But she was slowly bending forward by that time, further and further forward, the lids stretched down over her eyes, as if she were doing this in her sleep. Her chin was lowered almost to her knees. The yellow palm of her hand came out from the fold of her apron. Her fingers slid down and along the ground under the piece of money with the grace and care they would have in lifting an egg from under a sitting hen. Then she slowly straightened up, she stood erect, and the nickel was in her apron pocket. A bird flew by. Her lips moved. "God watching me the whole time. I come to stealing."    54

The man came back, and his own dog panted about them. "Well, I scared him off that time," he said, and then he laughed and lifted his gun and pointed it at Phoenix.    55

She stood straight and faced him.    56

"Doesn't the gun scare you?" he said, still pointing it.    57

"No sir, I seen plenty go off closer by, in my day, and for less than what I done," she said, holding utterly still.    58

He smiled, and shouldered the gun. "Well, Granny," he said, "you must be a hundred years old, and scared of nothing. I'd give you a    59 dime if I had any money with me. But you take my advice and stay home, and nothing will happen to you."

"I bound to go on my way, mister," said Phoenix. She inclined her head in the red rag. Then they went in different directions, but she could hear the gun shooting again and again over the hill.                      60

She walked on. The shadows hung from the oak trees to the road like curtains. Then she smelled wood-smoke, and smelled the river, and she saw a steeple and the cabins on their steep steps. Dozens of little black children whirled around her. There ahead was Natchez shining. Bells were ringing. She walked on.                      61

In the paved city it was Christmas time. There were red and green electric lights strung and crisscrossed everywhere, and all turned on in the day time. Old Phoenix would have been lost if she had not distrusted her eyesight and depended on her feet to know where to take her.                      62

She paused quietly on the sidewalk, where people were passing by. A lady came along in the crowd, carrying an armful of red-, green-, and silver-wrapped presents; she gave off perfume like the red roses in hot summer, and Phoenix stopped her.                      63

"Please, missy, will you lace up my shoe?" She held up her foot.                      64

"What do you want, Grandma?"                      65

"See my shoe," said Phoenix. "Do all right for out in the country, but wouldn't look right to go in a big building."                      66

"Stand still then, Grandma," said the lady. She put her packages down carefully on the sidewalk beside her and laced and tied both shoes tightly.                      67

"Can't lace 'em with a cane," said Phoenix. "Thank you, missy. I doesn't mind asking a nice lady to tie up my shoes when I gets out on the street."                      68

Moving slowly and from side to side, she went into the stone building and into a tower of steps, where she walked up and around and around until her feet knew to stop.                      69

She entered a door, and there she saw nailed up on the wall the document that had been stamped with the gold seal and framed in the gold frame which matched the dream that was hung up in her head.                      70

"Here I be," she said. There was a fixed and ceremonial stiffness over her body.                      71

"A charity case, I suppose," said an attendant who sat at the desk before her.                      72

But Phoenix only looked above her head. There was sweat on her 73
face; the wrinkles shone like a bright net.

"Speak, up, Grandma," the woman said. "What's your name? We 74
must have your history, you know. Have you been here before? What
seems to be the trouble with you?"

Old Phoenix only gave a twitch to her face as if a fly were bother- 75
ing her.

"Are you deaf?" cried the attendant. 76

But then the nurse came in. 77

"Oh, that's just old Aunt Phoenix," she said. "She doesn't come for 78
herself—she has a little grandson. She makes these trips just as regular
as clockwork. She lives away back off the Old Natchez Trace." She bent
down. "Well, Aunt Phoenix, why don't you just take a seat? We won't
keep you standing after your long trip." She pointed.

The old woman sat down, bolt upright in the chair. 79

"Now how is the boy?" asked the nurse. 80

Old Phoenix did not speak. 81

"I said, how is the boy?" 82

But Phoenix only waited and stared straight ahead, her face very 83
solemn and withdrawn into rigidity.

"Is his throat any better?" asked the nurse. "Aunt Phoenix, don't 84
you hear me? Is your grandson's throat any better since the last time
you came for the medicine?"

With her hand on her knees, the old woman waited, silent, erect 85
and motionless, just as if she were in armor.

"You mustn't take up our time this way, Aunt Phoenix," the nurse 86
said. "Tell us quickly about your grandson, and get it over. He isn't
dead, is he?"

At last there came a flicker and then a flame of comprehension 87
across her face, and she spoke.

"My grandson. It was my memory had left me. There I sat and 88
forgot why I made my long trip."

"Forgot?" The nurse frowned. "After you came so far?" 89

Then Phoenix was like an old woman begging a dignified forgive- 90
ness for waking up frightened in the night. "I never did go to school—
I was too old at the Surrender," she said in a soft voice. "I'm an old
woman without an education. It was my memory fail me. My little
grandson, he is just the same, and I forgot it in the coming."

"Throat never heals, does it?" said the nurse, speaking in a loud, 91 sure voice to Old Phoenix. By now she had a card with something written on it, a little list. "Yes. Swallowed lye. When was it—January—two—three years ago—"

Phoenix spoke unasked now. "No, missy, he not dead, he just the same. Every little while his throat begin to close up again, and he not able to swallow. He not get his breath. He not able to help himself. So the time come around, and I go on another trip for the soothing medicine."   92

"All right. The doctor said as long as you came to get it you could have it," said the nurse. "But it's an obstinate case."   93

"My little grandson, he sit up there in the house all wrapped up, waiting by himself," Phoenix went on. "We is the only two left in the world. He suffer and it don't seem to put him back at all. He got a sweet look. He going to last. He wear a little patch quilt and peep out, holding his mouth open like a little bird. I remembers so plain now. I not going to forget him again, no, the whole enduring time. I could tell him from all the others in creation."   94

"All right." The nurse was trying to hush her now. She brought her a bottle of medicine. "Charity," she said, making a check mark in a book.   95

Old Phoenix held the bottle close to her eyes and then carefully put in into her pocket.   96

"I thank you," she said.   97

"It's Christmas time, Grandma," said the attendant. "Could I give you a few pennies out of my purse?"   98

"Five pennies is a nickel," said Phoenix stiffly.   99

"Here's a nickel," said the attendant.   100

Phoenix rose carefully and held out her hand. She received the nickel and then fished the other nickel out of her pocket and laid it beside the new one. She stared at her palm closely, with her head on one side.   101

Then she gave a tap with her cane on the floor.   102

"This is what come to me to do," she said. "I going to the store and buy my child a little windmill they sells, made out of paper. He going to find it hard to believe there such a thing in the world. I'll march myself back where he waiting, holding it straight up in this hand."   103

She lifted her free hand, gave a little nod, turned round, and walked out of the doctor's office. Then her slow step began on the stairs, going down.   104

## VOCABULARY

meditative (1)  
illuminated (2)  
bobwhites (3)  
limber (3)  
appointed (8)  
furrow (19)

maze (21)  
nary (24)  
strutting (28)  
husks (28)  
pullets (29)  
sweetgum (32)

lolling (35)  
radiation (49)  
ceremonial (71)  
lye (91)

## THE FACTS

1. In paragraph 1, to what piece of antique furniture is Phoenix Jackson's walk compared? What characteristic is Welty trying to get across? Where, later on in the narrative, is the same piece of furniture alluded to again? Why?
2. What is the purpose of the old woman's journey?
3. Essentially this is the story of a courageous woman. What part of the trip is especially difficult for her? How does she manage this obstacle?
4. What details indicate that Phoenix Jackson is slightly senile and therefore not always in touch with reality?
5. What excuse does the old woman offer for not remembering what errand she was on?

## THE STRATEGIES

1. What kind of plot structure is the story based on? What is the conflict in the plot? When is the conflict resolved?
2. Analyze Phoenix's language. What is conveyed through her speech?
3. Point out some specific instances of humor. What kind of humor is it?
4. During what decade would you judge this story to have taken place? What clues to your answer are given in the story?
5. In paragraph 85 we read: "With her hand on her knees, the old woman waited, silent, erect and motionless, just as if she were in armor." What meaning do you attribute to this passage?

## THE ISSUES

1. In Egyptian mythology the phoenix was a bird of great splendor that every five hundred years consumed itself by fire and rose renewed from its own ashes. In what way is Phoenix Jackson like this bird?
2. The narrative abounds in descriptive passages. What is the dominant impression in paragraph 2? Are any details included that do not support this impression? What other descriptive passages can you identify?
3. Why does Phoenix keep talking to herself? What do her monologues add to the total portrait of her?

4. What is the meaning of the episode in which Phoenix steals the nickel? Does the act offend our sense of honesty? Explain your answer.
5. What significance can you attach to the fact that the journey takes place at Christmas time?
6. Phoenix Jackson's journey is in the literary tradition of the mythological quest. What aspects of the story place it in that tradition?

### SUGGESTIONS FOR WRITING

1. Using your imagination, describe Phoenix's journey home. Make your scenes descriptive by selecting details that support a dominant impression.
2. Write an essay comparing and contrasting Phoenix Jackson with the Pigeon Woman in the poem that follows.

**May Swenson**

# • PIGEON WOMAN •

*May Swenson (b. 1919) poet, playwright, and lecturer, was born in Logan, Utah, and educated at Utah State University. She now resides in New York City. She has published a number of collections of poetry including her latest,* New and Selected Things Taking Place *(1978).*

*The meaning of "Pigeon Woman" emerges from the irony contained in a strange old lady's fantasy.*

> Slate, or dirty-marble-colored,
> or rusty-iron-colored, the pigeons
> on the flagstones in front of the
> Public Library make a sharp lake
>
> into which the pigeon woman wades     5
> at exactly 1:30. She wears a
> plastic pink raincoat with a round
> collar (looking like a little
>
> girl, so gay) and flat gym shoes,
> her hair square-cut, orange.     10
> Wide-apart feet carefully enter
> the spinning, crooning waves
>
> (as if she'd just learned how

to walk, each step conscious,
an accomplishment); blue knots in the                15
calves of her bare legs (uglied marble),

age in angled cords of jaw
and neck, her pimento-colored hair,
hanging in thin tassles, is gray
around a balding crown.                              20

The day-old bread drops down
from her veined hand dipping out
of a paper sack. Choppy, shadowy ripples
the pigeons strike around her legs.

Sack empty, she squats and seems to rinse           25
her hands in them—the rainy greens and
oily purples of their necks. Almost
they let her wet her thirsty fingertips—

but drain away in an untouchable tide.
A make-believe trade                                30
she has come to, in her lostness
or illness or age—to treat the motley

city pigeons at 1:30 every day, in all
weathers. It is for them she colors
her own feathers. Ruddy-footed                       35
on the lime-stained paving,

purling to meet her when she comes,
they are a lake of love. Retreating
from her hands as soon as empty,
they are the flints of love.                         40

## VOCABULARY

| crooning | motley | flints |
|----------|--------|--------|
| pimento | purling | |

## THE FACTS

1. What is the dominant impression conveyed by this "pigeon woman"? In terms of her looks, what role could she play in a fairy tale?

2. As the poem develops, how do our feelings change about the woman?
3. What is the fantasy that gives purpose to the woman's life? Describe it.
4. What is the meaning of the final stanza?
5. Is this woman an impossible figment of the poet's imagination, or does she represent a kind of reality? Comment.

## THE STRATEGIES

1. How does the level of language used contribute to the description of the woman?
2. How do you explain the image of the pigeons as a lake?
3. What are the "blue knots in the / calves of her bare legs"? Comment on the effectiveness of this image.
4. What is the meaning of the metaphor "her own feathers" in the next-to-last stanza?
5. Interpret the metaphor "the flints of love" in the final line.

## THE ISSUES

1. Various public, as well as private, agencies have been concerned with the plight of the poor, especially women who have been labeled "bag ladies," "crazy drifters," or "old female transients." What suggestions do you have for dealing with this alienated group of our population? Are we doing enough or should we do more?
2. What is it that keeps this woman from giving up on life? What do you consider the single most important driving force that keeps most people who lead desperate lives from committing suicide?
3. The woman in the poem chooses to feed a flock of pigeons. What other activities could give meaning to such a person's life?
4. How would you describe the male counterpart of the Pigeon Woman? Include the details of his appearance.
5. What measures do you suggest for reducing the number of street vagrants in our major cities?

## SUGGESTIONS FOR WRITING

1. As vividly as possible, describe the relationship between a human being and an animal.
2. Imagine the loneliness that comes from being old and alone. Describe this loneliness in terms of specific, concrete details.

# ══════ •• *ISSUE FOR CRITICAL* •• ══════
# *THINKING*

## *A College Education*

Who should receive a college education? Everyone, or just a small clique of students who are presumed sophisticated and cultured enough to appreciate one? Some argue that pressuring students to attend college accomplishes nothing but resistance and resentment. Others contend that only a liberal education can teach the habit of attention, the art of expression, the ability to see through intellectual poses, the sensitivity to enter into another person's thought, and the courage to think independently, all of which are necessary to save us from decline into barbarism.

The three writers confronting this issue attack the problem from different directions. Father Theodore Hesburgh, a Catholic priest and past president of the University of Notre Dame, argues that a liberal education is the transmitter of values for our society and therefore is indispensable to a country in search of moral authority. David Gardner, president of the University of California, warns of a rising tide of mediocrity in our colleges that, if not stemmed, will allow countries like Japan to surge ahead of the United States technologically, industrially, and intellectually. In an altogether different vein, William Zinsser, a college professor of English, insists that young people who need to find success by following paths other than those leading through college should not be branded as failures or misfits.

### Theodore Hesburgh

# ─────── • HIGHER EDUCATION: • ───────
# WHAT'S THE POINT?

*Theodore Hesburgh (b. 1917) is a prominent American educator. In 1937 he graduated from the University of Notre Dame, and six years later he was ordained as a priest. However, in 1945, when Notre Dame offered him a position as assistant professor of religion, he returned to his alma mater, where he eventually rose to be president. Hesburgh was a member of the U.S. Commission on Civil Rights from 1957 to 1972. He has also been a trustee of the Rockefeller Foundation, the Carnegie Foundation for the Advancement of Teaching, and the Chase Manhattan Bank. The essay that follows is excerpted from Hesburgh's book* The Hesburgh Papers: Higher Values in Higher Education *(1979).*

Somewhere, in that vague morass of rhetoric that has always char-    1
acterized descriptions of liberal education, one always finds a mention
of values. The true purists insist on intellectual values, but there have
always been educators, particularly among founders of small liberal
arts colleges in the nineteenth century, who likewise stressed moral
values as one of the finest fruits of their educational process, especially
if their colleges were inspired by a religious group.

I believe it to be a fairly obvious fact that we have come full circle in    2
our secularized times. Today one hears all too little of intellectual values, and moral values seem to have become a lost cause in the educational process. I know educators of some renown who practically tell
their students, "We don't care what you do around here as long as you
do it quietly, avoid blatant scandal, and don't give the institution a
bad name."

Part of this attitude is an overreaction to *in loco parentis*,* which goes    3
from eschewing responsibility for students' lives to just not caring how
they live. It is assumed that how students live has no relation to their
education, which is, in this view, solely an intellectual process. Those
who espouse this view would not necessarily deny that values are
important in life. They just do not think that values form part of the
higher education endeavor—if, indeed, they can be taught anyway.

Moral abdication or valuelessness seems to have become a sign of    4
the times. One might well describe the illness of modern society and
its schooling as anomie, a rootlessness.

I would like to say right out that I do not consider this to be progress,    5
however modern and stylish it might be. The Greeks (not the fraternities!) were at their best when they insisted that excellence (*arete*) was
at the heart of human activity at its noblest, certainly at the heart of
education at its civilized best. John Gardner wrote a book on the subject which will best be remembered by his trenchant phrase: "Unless
our philosophers and plumbers are committed to excellence, neither
our pipes nor our arguments will hold water."

Do values really count in a liberal education? They have to count if    6
you take the word "liberal" at its face value. To be liberal, an education
must somehow liberate a person actually to be what every person
potentially is: free. Free to be and free to do. What?

Excuse me for making a list, but it is important. The first fruit of a    7

---

*Latin, "in place of a parent."—Ed.

liberal education is to free a person from ignorance, which fundamentally means freedom to think, clearly and logically. Moreover, allied with this release from stupidity—nonthinking or poor thinking—is the freedom to communicate one's thoughts, preferably with clarity, style, and grace, certainly with more than the Neanderthal grunt. A liberal education should also enable a person to judge, which in itself presupposes the ability to evaluate: to prefer this to that, to say this is good and that is bad or, at least, this is better than that. To evaluate is to prefer, to discriminate, to choose, and each of these actions presupposes a sense of values. Liberal education should also enable a person to situate himself or herself within a given culture, religion, race, sex, and to appreciate what is valuable in the given situation, even as simple an evaluation as "black is beautiful." This, too, is a value judgment and a liberation from valuelessness, insecurity, and despair at times. Liberal education, by all of these value-laden processes, should confer a sense of peace, confidence, and assurance on the person thus educated and liberate him or her from the adriftness that characterizes so many in an age of anomie.

Lastly, a liberal education should enable a person to humanize 8 everything that he or she touches in life, which is to say that one is enabled not only to evaluate what one is or does, but that, in addition, one adds value consciously to relationships that might otherwise be banal or superficial or meaningless: relations to God, to one's fellow men, to one's wife or husband or children, to one's associates, one's neighborhood, one's country and world.

In this way, the list of what one expects of liberal education is really 9 a list of the very real values that alone can liberate a person from very real evils or nonvalues—stupidity, meaninglessness, inhumanity.

One might well ask at this juncture, "How are these values attained 10 educationally?" Again, one is almost forced to make a list. Language and mathematics stress clarity, precision, and style if well taught; literature gives an insight into the vast human arena of good and evil, love and hate, peace and violence as real living human options. History gives a vital record of mankind's success and failure, hopes and fears, the heights and the depths of human endeavors pursued with either heroism or depravity—but always depicting real virtue or the lack of it. Music and art purvey a sense of beauty seen or heard, a value to be preferred to ugliness or cacophony. The physical sciences are a symphony of world order, so often unsuccessfully sought by law, but already achieved by creation, a model challenging man's freedom and creativity. The social sciences show man at work, theoretically and practically, creating his world. Too often, social scientists in their quest for a physical scientist's objectivity underrate the influence of freedom—for good or for evil. While a social scientist must remain objective within the givens of his observable data, his best contribution comes when he invokes the values that make the data more meaningful, as Tocqueville does in commenting on the values of democracy in America, Barbara Ward in outlining the value of social justice in a very unjust world, Michael Harrington in commenting on the nonvalue of property. Again, it is the value judgments that ultimately bring the social sciences to life and make them more meaningful in liberating those who study them in the course of a liberal education.

One might ask where the physical sciences liberate, but, even here, the bursting knowledge of the physical sciences is really power to liberate mankind: from hunger, from ignorance and superstition, from grinding poverty and homelessness, all of the conditions that have made millions of persons less than human. But the price of this liberation is value: the value to use the power of science for the humanization rather than the destruction of mankind. 11

Value is simply central to all that is liberalizing in liberal education. Without value, it would be impossible to visualize liberal education as all that is good in both the intellectual and the moral order of human development and liberation. Along the same line of reasoning, President Robben Fleming of Michigan this year asked his faculty why, in the recent student revolution, it was the liberal arts students who so easily reverted to violence, intolerance, and illiberality. Could it not be that their actions demonstrated that liberal education has begun to fail in the most important of its functions: to liberate man from irrationality, valuelessness, and anomie? 12

But, one might legitimately ask, how are these great values transmitted in the process of liberal education? All that I have said thus far would indicate that the values are inherent in the teaching of the various disciplines that comprise a liberal education in the traditional sense. However, one should admit that it is quite possible to study all of these branches of knowledge, including those that explicitly treat of values, philosophy and theology, without emerging as a person who is both imbued with and seized by great liberating and humanizing values. I believe that all that this says is that the key and central factor 13 in liberal education is the teacher-educator, his perception of his role, how he teaches, but particularly, how he lives and exemplifies the values inherent in what he teaches. Values are exemplified better than they are taught, which is to say that they are taught better by exemplification than by words.

I have long believed that a Christian university is worthless in our  14 day unless it conveys to all who study within it a deep sense of the dignity of the human person, his nature and high destiny, his opportunities for seeking justice in a very unjust world, his inherent nobility so needing to be realized, for one's self and for others, whatever the obstacles. I would have to admit, even immodestly, that whatever I have said on this subject has had a miniscule impression on the members of our university compared to what I have tried to do to achieve justice in our times. This really says that while value education is difficult, it is practically impossible unless the word is buttressed by the deed.

If all this is true, it means that all those engaged in education today  15 must look to themselves first, to their moral commitments, to their lives, and to their own values, which, for better or worse, will be reflected in the lives and attitudes of those they seek to educate. There is nothing automatic about the liberal education tradition. It can die if not fostered. And if it does die, the values that sustain an individual and a nation are likely to die with it.

## *VOCABULARY*

| | | |
|---|---|---|
| morass (1) | abdication (4) | purvey (10) |
| blatant (2) | anomie (4) | cacophony (10) |
| eschewing (3) | Neanderthal (7) | exemplification (13) |
| espouse (3) | depravity (10) | buttressed (14) |

## *THE FACTS*

1. What two kinds of values are involved in a liberal education, according to Hesburgh?
2. What is the meaning of John Gardner's quotation, "Unless our philosophers and plumbers are committed to excellence, neither our pipes nor our arguments will hold water"?
3. What is Hesburgh's definition of a liberal education? Where does he state his definition?

4. According to Hesburgh, what is the function of the social and physical sciences in a liberal education? How important are they compared to the humanities?
5. What, in Hesburgh's view, is central to a successful liberal education? How is this transmitted?

## THE STRATEGIES

1. How is this essay organized? List the main topics in order of appearance.
2. What is the relationship between paragraph 6 and paragraphs 7, 8, and 9? Where else in the essay is a similar relationship established?
3. In paragraph 12, what is the purpose of the reference to the University of Michigan?

## THE ISSUES

1. How does Hesburgh's idea of a liberal education compare with your own? Reread Allan Simpson's "Marks of an Educated Man" on pages 211–217) and indicate what ideas Simpson and Hesburgh have in common.
2. How do moral values differ from intellectual values?
3. According to Hesburgh, what is the crucial factor in transmitting values? Do you agree with him? Why or why not?
4. What dangers do you see inherent in college professors imposing their moral values on students? Can this danger be overcome? Why or why not?
5. What teachers in your past have had the strongest influence on you? Why? Describe these teachers as vividly as possible.

## SUGGESTIONS FOR WRITING

1. Write an essay in which you argue for or against a broad base of liberal arts as a requirement for all students graduating from college, regardless of their majors.
2. Do you believe that it is a college professor's duty to teach moral values? Write an essay answering this question.

**David P. Gardner**

## • A NATION AT RISK •

*David P. Gardner (b. 1933) served as president of the University of Utah and is now president of the University of California. In 1981, Ronald Reagan appointed him to head a blue-ribbon commission reporting on the condition of education in*

*America. After eighteen months' work, this task force published a report entitled "A Nation at Risk," from which the following essay is excerpted.*

*"A Nation at Risk" is a call to alarm. In powerful language, this report warns the American people about the worsening state of our educational system and outlines the drastic effects this decline may have unless fundamental reforms are initiated.*

Our Nation is at risk. Our once unchallenged preeminence in com-   1
merce, industry, science, and technological innovation is being over-
taken by competitors throughout the world. This report is concerned
with only one of the many causes and dimensions of the problem, but
it is the one that undergirds American prosperity, security, and civility.
We report to the American people that while we can take justifiable
pride in what our schools and colleges have historically accomplished
and contributed to the United States and the well-being of its people,
the educational foundations of our society are presently being eroded
by a rising tide of mediocrity that threatens our very future as a Nation and a people. What was unimaginable a generation ago has begun to occur—others are watching and surpassing our educational
attainments.

If an unfriendly foreign power had attempted to impose on America   2
the mediocre educational performance that exists today, we might well
have viewed it as an act of war. As it stands, we have allowed this to
happen to ourselves. We have even squandered the gains in student
achievement made in the wake of the Sputnik challenge. Moreover, we
have dismantled essential support systems which helped make those
gains possible. We have, in effect, been committing an act of unthinking, unilateral educational disarmament.

Our society and its educational institutions seem to have lost sight   3
of the basic purposes of schooling, and of the high expectations and
disciplined effort needed to attain them. This report, the result of 18
months of study, seeks to generate reform of our educational system
in fundamental ways to renew the Nation's commitment to schools and
colleges of high quality throughout the length and breadth of our land.

That we have compromised this commitment is, upon reflection,   4
hardly surprising, given the multitude of often conflicting demands
we have placed on our Nation's schools and colleges. They are routinely called on to provide solutions to personal, social, and political
problems that the home and other institutions either will not or cannot

resolve. We must understand that these demands on our schools and colleges often exact an educational cost as well as a financial one.

On the occasion of the Commission's first meeting President Reagan    5
noted the central importance of education in American life when he said: "Certainly there are few areas of American life as important to our society, to our people, and to our families as our schools and colleges." This report, therefore, is as much an open letter to the American people as it is a report to the Secretary of Education. We are confident that the American people, properly informed, will do what is right for their children and for the generations to come.

### THE RISK

History is not kind to idlers. The time is long past when America's    6
destiny was assured simply by an abundance of natural resources and inexhaustible human enthusiasm, and by our relative isolation from the malignant problems of older civilizations. The world is indeed one global village. We live among determined, well-educated, and strongly motivated competitors. We compete with them for international standing and markets, not only with products but also with the ideas of our laboratories and neighborhood workshops. America's position in the world may once have been reasonably secure with only a few exceptionally well-trained men and women. It is no longer.

The risk is not only that the Japanese make automobiles more effi-    7
ciently than Americans and have government subsidies for development and export. It is not just that the South Koreans recently built the world's most efficient steel mill, or that American machine tools, once the pride of the world, are being displaced by German products. It is also that these developments signify a redistribution of trained capability throughout the globe. Knowledge, learning, information, and skilled intelligence are the new raw materials of international commerce and are today spreading throughout the world as vigorously as miracle drugs, synthetic fertilizers, and blue jeans did earlier. If only to keep and improve on the slim competitive edge we still retain in world markets, we must dedicate ourselves to the reform of our educational system for the benefit of all—old and young alike, affluent and poor, majority and minority. Learning is the indispensable investment required for success in the "information age" we are entering.

Our concern, however, goes well beyond matters such as industry    8
and commerce. It also includes the intellectual, moral, and spiritual

strengths of our people which knit together the very fabric of our society. The people of the United States need to know that individuals in our society who do not possess the levels of skill, literacy, and training essential to this new era will be effectively disenfranchised, not simply from the material rewards that accompany competent performance, but also from the chance to participate fully in our national life. A high level of shared education is essential to a free, democratic society and to the fostering of a common culture, especially in a country that prides itself on pluralism and individual freedom.

For our country to function, citizens must be able to reach some    9
common understandings on complex issues, often on short notice and on the basis of conflicting or incomplete evidence. Education helps form these common understandings, a point Thomas Jefferson made long ago in his justly famous dictum:

> I know no safe depository of the ultimate powers of the society but the people themselves; and if we think them not enlightened enough to exercise their control with a wholesome discretion, the remedy is not to take it from them but to inform their discretion.

Part of what is at risk is the promise first made on this continent:    10
All, regardless of race or class or economic status, are entitled to a fair chance and to the tools for developing their individual powers of mind and spirit to the utmost. This promise means that all children by virtue of their own efforts, competently guided, can hope to attain the mature and informed judgment needed to secure gainful employment and to manage their own lives, thereby serving not only their own interests but also the progress of society itself.

## INDICATORS OF THE RISK

The educational dimensions of the risk before us have been amply    11
documented in testimony received by the Commission. For example:

- International comparisons of student achievement, completed a decade ago, reveal that on 19 academic tests American students were never first or second and, in comparison with other industrialized nations, were last seven times.
- Some 23 million American adults are functionally illiterate by the simplest tests of everyday reading, writing, and comprehension.
- About 13 percent of all 17-year-olds in the United States can be

considered functionally illiterate. Functional illiteracy among minority youth may run as high as 40 percent.

- Average achievement of high school students on most standardized tests is now lower than 26 years ago when Sputnik was launched.
- Over half the population of gifted students do not match their tested ability with comparable achievement in school.
- The College Board's Scholastic Aptitude Tests (SAT) demonstrate a virtually unbroken decline from 1963 to 1980. Average verbal scores fell over 50 points and average mathematics scores dropped nearly 40 points.
- College Board achievement tests also reveal consistent declines in recent years in such subjects as physics and English.
- Both the number and proportion of students demonstrating superior achievement on the SATs (i.e., those with scores of 650 or higher) have also dramatically declined.
- Many 17-year-olds do not possess the "higher order" intellectual skills we should expect of them. Nearly 40 percent cannot draw inferences from written material; only one-fifth can write a persuasive essay; and only one-third can solve a mathematics problem requiring several steps.
- There was a steady decline in science achievement scores of U.S. 17-year-olds as measured by national assessments of science in 1969, 1973, and 1977.
- Between 1975 and 1980, remedial mathematics courses in public 4-year colleges increased by 72 percent and now constitute one-quarter of all mathematics courses taught in those institutions.
- Average tested achievement of students graduating from college is also lower.
- Business and military leaders complain that they are required to spend millions of dollars on costly remedial education and training programs in such basic skills as reading, writing, spelling, and computation. The Department of the Navy, for example, reported to the Commission that one-quarter of its recent recruits cannot read at the ninth grade level, the minimum needed simply to understand written safety instructions. Without remedial work they cannot even begin, much less complete, the sophisticated training essential in much of the modern military.

These deficiencies come at a time when the demand for highly  12
skilled workers in new fields is accelerating rapidly. For example:

- Computers and computer-controlled equipment are penetrating
  every aspect of our lives—homes, factories, and offices.
- One estimate indicates that by the turn of the century millions of
  jobs will involve laser technology and robotics.
- Technology is radically transforming a host of other occupations.
  They include health care, medical science, energy production,
  food processing, construction, and the building, repair, and
  maintenance of sophisticated scientific, educational, military, and
  industrial equipment.

Analysts examining these indicators of student performance and the  13
demands for new skills have made some chilling observations. Educational researcher Paul Hurd concluded at the end of a thorough national survey of student achievement that within the context of the
modern scientific revolution, "We are raising a new generation of
Americans that is scientifically and technologically illiterate." In a similar vein, John Slaughter, a former Director of the National Science
Foundation, warned of "a growing chasm between a small scientific
and technological elite and a citizenry ill-informed, indeed uninformed, on issues with a science component."

But the problem does not stop there, nor do all observers see it the  14
same way. Some worry that schools may emphasize such rudiments as
reading and computation at the expense of other essential skills such
as comprehension, analysis, solving problems, and drawing conclusions. Still others are concerned that an over-emphasis on technical
and occupational skills will leave little time for studying the arts and
humanities that so enrich daily life, help maintain civility, and develop
a sense of community. Knowledge of the humanities, they maintain,
must be harnessed to science and technology if the latter are to remain
creative and humane, just as the humanities need to be informed by
science and technology if they are to remain relevant to the human
condition. Another analyst, Paul Copperman, has drawn a sobering
conclusion. Until now, he has noted:

> Each generation of Americans has outstripped its parents in education,
> in literacy, and in economic attainment. For the first time in the history
> of our country, the educational skills of one generation will not surpass,
> will not equal, will not even approach, those of their parents.

It is important, of course, to recognize that *the average citizen* today    15
is better educated and more knowledgeable than the average citizen of
a generation ago—more literate, and exposed to more mathematics,
literature, and science. The positive impact of this fact on the well-
being of our country and the lives of our people cannot be overstated.
Nevertheless, *the average graduate* of our schools and colleges today is
not as well-educated as the average graduate of 25 or 35 years ago,
when a much smaller proportion of our population completed high
school and college. The negative impact of this fact likewise cannot be
overstated.

## HOPE AND FRUSTRATION

Statistics and their interpretation by experts show only the surface    16
dimension of the difficulties we face. Beneath them lies a tension between hope and frustration that characterizes current attitudes about
education at every level.

We have heard the voices of high school and college students, school    17
board members, and teachers; of leaders of industry, minority groups,
and higher education; of parents and State officials. We could hear the
hope evident in their commitment to quality education and in their
descriptions of outstanding programs and schools. We could also hear
the intensity of their frustration, a growing impatience with shoddi-
ness in many walks of American life, and the complaint that this shod-
diness is too often reflected in our schools and colleges. Their
frustration threatens to overwhelm their hope.

What lies behind this emerging national sense of frustration can be    18
described as both a dimming of personal expectations and the fear of
losing a shared vision for America.

On the personal level the student, the parent, and the caring teacher    19
all perceive that a basic promise is not being kept. More and more
young people emerge from high school ready neither for college nor
for work. This predicament becomes more acute as the knowledge
base continues its rapid expansion, the number of traditional jobs
shrinks, and new jobs demand greater sophistication and preparation.

On a broader scale, we sense that this undertone of frustration has    20
significant political implications, for it cuts across ages, generations,
races, and political and economic groups. We have come to understand
that the public will demand that educational and political leaders act
forcefully and effectively on these issues. Indeed, such demands have

already appeared and could well become a unifying national preoccupation. This unity, however, can be achieved only if we avoid the unproductive tendency of some to search for scapegoats among the victims, such as the beleaguered teachers.

On the positive side is the significant movement by political and educational leaders to search for solutions—so far centering largely on the nearly desperate need for increased support for the teaching of mathematics and science. This movement is but a start on what we believe is a larger and more educationally encompassing need to improve teaching and learning in fields such as English, history, geography, economics, and foreign languages. We believe this movement must be broadened and directed toward reform and excellence throughout education.

## EXCELLENCE IN EDUCATION

We define "excellence" to mean several related things. At the level of the *individual learner*, it means performing on the boundary of individual ability in ways that test and push back personal limits, in school and in the workplace. Excellence characterizes a *school or college* that sets high expectations and goals for all learners, then tries in every way possible to help students reach them. Excellence characterizes a *society* that has adopted these policies, for it will then be prepared through the education and skill of its people to respond to the challenges of a rapidly changing world. Our Nation's people and its schools and colleges must be committed to achieving excellence in all these senses.

We do not believe that a public commitment to excellence and educational reform must be made at the expense of a strong public commitment to the equitable treatment of our diverse population. The twin goals of equity and high-quality schooling have profound and practical meaning for our economy and society, and we cannot permit one to yield to the other either in principle or in practice. To do so would deny young people their chance to learn and live according to their aspirations and abilities. It also would lead to a generalized accommodation to mediocrity in our society on the one hand or the creation of an undemocratic elitism on the other.

Our goal must be to develop the talents of all to their fullest. Attaining that goal requires that we expect and assist all students to the limits of their capabilities. We should expect schools to have genuinely high standards rather than minimum ones, and parents to support and encourage their children to make the most of their talents and abilities.

The search for solutions to our educational problems must also include a commitment to life-long learning. The task of rebuilding our system of learning is enormous and must be properly understood and taken seriously: Although a million and a half new workers enter the economy each year from our schools and colleges, the adults working today will still make up about 75 percent of the workforce in the year 2000. These workers, and new entrants into the workforce, will need further education and retraining if they—and we as a Nation—are to thrive and prosper. 25

## THE LEARNING SOCIETY

In a world of ever-accelerating competition and change in the conditions of the workplace, of ever-greater danger, and of ever-larger opportunities for those prepared to meet them, educational reform should focus on the goal of creating a Learning Society. At the heart of such a society is the commitment to a set of values and to a system of education that affords all members the opportunity to stretch their minds to full capacity, from early childhood through adulthood, learning more as the world itself changes. Such a society has as a basic foundation the idea that education is important not only because of what it contributes to one's career goals but also because of the value it adds to the general quality of one's life. Also at the heart of the Learning Society are educational opportunities extending far beyond the traditional institutions of learning, our schools and colleges. They extend into homes and workplaces; into libraries, art galleries, museums, and science centers; indeed, into every place where the individual can develop and mature in work and life. In our view, formal schooling in youth is the essential foundation for learning throughout one's life. But without life-long learning, one's skills will become rapidly dated. 26

In contrast to the ideal of the Learning Society, however, we find that for too many people education means doing the minimum work necessary for the moment, then coasting through life on what may have been learned in its first quarter. But this should not surprise us because we tend to express our educational standards and expectations largely in terms of "minimum requirements." And where there 27 should be a coherent continuum of learning, we have none, but instead an often incoherent, outdated patchwork quilt. Many individual, sometimes heroic, examples of schools and colleges of great merit do exist. Our findings and testimony confirm the vitality of a number of notable schools and programs, but their very distinction stands out against a vast mass shaped by tensions and pressures that inhibit systematic academic and vocational achievement for the majority of students. In some metropolitan areas basic literacy has become the goal rather than the starting point. In some colleges maintaining enrollments is of greater day-to-day concern than maintaining rigorous academic standards. And the ideal of academic excellence as the primary goal of schooling seems to be fading across the board in American education.

Thus, we issue this call to all who care about America and its future:    28
to parents and students; to teachers, administrators, and school board members; to colleges and industry; to union members and military leaders; to governors and State legislators; to the President; to members of Congress and other public officials; to members of learned and scientific societies; to the print and electronic media; to concerned citizens everywhere. America is at risk.

## VOCABULARY

| | | |
|---|---|---|
| preeminence (1) | dictum (9) | beleaguered (20) |
| Sputnik (2) | depository (9) | equitable (23) |
| unilateral (2) | discretion (9) | elitism (23) |
| malignant (6) | inferences (11) | continuum (27) |
| disenfranchised (8) | laser (12) | |
| pluralism (8) | robotics (12) | |

## THE FACTS

1. What, in your own words, is the thesis of the report?
2. What does Gardner mean when he says that "history is not kind to idlers"?
3. What need is implied in paragraph 14?
4. Paragraph 19 states that the number of traditional jobs is shrinking and that many new jobs demand greater sophistication and preparation. What examples of traditional as well as new jobs can you give?
5. How does the essay define the term *excellence*? What purpose does the definition serve?

## THE STRATEGIES

1. From whose point of view is the essay written? How is the point of view stressed?
2. What effect does the quotation from Thomas Jefferson have on the essay? See paragraph 9.
3. In your view, does the commission succeed in proving that America is indeed at risk because of a failing educational system? What, if any, is the strongest proof of the risk?
4. Which section of the essay shows that the entire piece is a persuasive appeal as well as a report?
5. How is elegance of style achieved in the final paragraph?
6. The figure of speech "rising tide of mediocrity," found in the opening paragraph, caught the attention of many political and educational leaders and has been often quoted. Why does this phrase have such an immediate impact?

## THE ISSUES

1. According to paragraph 4, one reason for the decline of our educational system is that we have demanded too much from it, asking it to solve problems that other institutions should solve. What other institutions are implicated? What kinds of problems should these other institutions solve?
2. The essay stresses that a public commitment to excellence must not be made "at the expense of a strong public commitment to the equitable treatment of our diverse population." Do you agree, or do you believe that only a privileged few deserve an excellent education? Defend your view on this question.
3. What specific examples, in addition to those cited in Gardner's report, can you provide to support the aphorism that "history is not kind to idlers"?
4. The report suggests that lifelong learning is necessary in our society, where competition keeps accelerating and conditions of the workplace keep changing. What advantages, if any, other than helping us to compete and to keep up, does lifelong learning provide?
5. Does the essay leave you with a feeling of hope or of despair? Give reasons for your answer.

## SUGGESTIONS FOR WRITING

1. Write a report in which you propose ways that your college can improve its basic skills program. Be specific in your recommendations. You might begin by stating what is wrong with the present system.
2. Write an essay in which you compare and contrast Gardner's report with Hesburgh's essay on pages 419–23. In getting ready for this writing as-

signment, make a list of specific recommendations the two essays share in common and then a list of ideas that seem to differ from one essay to the other.

William Zinsser

————————— • **THE RIGHT TO FAIL** • —————————

*William K. Zinsser (b. 1922), American critic and writer, was born in New York and educated at Princeton. A former columnist for* Look *and* Life, *he has been on the faculty of Yale University since 1970. His books include* Pop Goes America *(1966),* The Lunacy Boom *(1970),* On Writing Well *(1980), and* Writing with a Word Processor *(1983).*

*Zinsser opposes the common view of the college dropout as someone who at best will emerge as a "late bloomer" and at worst will be stuck on the sidelines of success. In fact, he points out, dropping out may be the prelude to greater awareness and more purposeful ambition. It may simply be the sign of a ruggedly individualistic nature.*

I like "dropout" as an addition to the American language because   1
it's brief and it's clear. What I don't like is that we use it almost entirely as a dirty word.

We only apply it to people under twenty-one. Yet an adult who   2
spends his days and nights watching mindless TV programs is more of a dropout than an eighteen-year-old who quits college, with its frequently mindless courses, to become, say, a VISTA volunteer. For the young, dropping out is often a way of dropping in.

To hold this opinion, however, is little short of treason in America.   3
A boy or girl who leaves college is branded a failure—and the right to fail is one of the few freedoms that this country does not grant its citizens. The American dream is a dream of "getting ahead," painted in strokes of gold wherever we look. Our advertisements and TV commercials are a hymn to material success, our magazine articles a toast to people who made it to the top. Smoke the right cigarette or drive the right car—so the ads imply—and girls will be swooning into your deodorized arms or caressing your expensive lapels. Happiness goes to the man who has the sweet smell of achievement. He is our national idol, and everybody else is our national fink.

I want to put in a word for the fink, especially the teen-age fink,   4
because if we give him time to get through his finkdom—if we release
him from the pressure of attaining certain goals by a certain age—he
has a good chance of becoming our national idol, a Jefferson or a
Thoreau, a Buckminster Fuller or an Adlai Stevenson, a man with a
mind of his own. We need mavericks and dissenters and dreamers far
more than we need junior vice-presidents, but we paralyze them by
insisting that every step be a step up to the next rung of the ladder. Yet
in the fluid years of youth, the only way for boys and girls to find their
proper road is often to take a hundred side trips, poking out in different directions, faltering, drawing back, and starting again.

"But what if we fail?" they ask, whispering the dreadful word across   5
the Generation Gap to their parents, who are back home at the Establishment nursing their "middle-class values" and cultivating their
"goal-oriented society." The parents whisper back: "Don't!"

What they should say is "Don't be afraid to fail!" Failure isn't fatal.   6
Countless people have had a bout with it and come out stronger as a
result. Many have even come out famous. History is strewn with eminent dropouts, "loners" who followed their own trail, not worrying
about its odd twists and turns because they had faith in their own
sense of direction. To read their biographies is always exhilarating, not
only because they beat the system, but because their system was better
than the one that they beat.

Luckily, such rebels still turn up often enough to prove that individ-   7
ualism, though badly threatened, is not extinct. Much has been written, for instance, about the fitful scholastic career of Thomas P. F.
Hoving, New York's former Parks Commissioner and now director of
the Metropolitan Museum of Art. Hoving was a dropout's dropout,
entering and leaving schools as if they were motels, often at the request of the management. Still, he must have learned something during those unorthodox years, for he dropped in again at the top of his
profession.

His case reminds me of another boyhood—that of Holden Caulfield   8
in J. D. Salinger's *The Catcher in the Rye*, the most popular literary hero
of the postwar period. There is nothing accidental about the grip that
this dropout continues to hold on the affections of an entire American
generation. Nobody else, real or invented, has made such an engaging
shambles of our "goal-oriented society," so gratified our secret belief
that the "phonies" are in power and the good guys up the creek.

Whether Holden has also reached the top of his chosen field today is one of those speculations that delight fanciers of good fiction. I speculate that he has. Holden Caulfield, incidentally, is now thirty-six.

I'm not urging everyone to go out and fail just for the sheer therapy     9
of it, or to quit college just to coddle some vague discontent. Obviously it's better to succeed than to flop, and in general a long education is more helpful than a short one. (Thanks to my own education, for example, I can tell George Eliot from T. S. Eliot, I can handle the pluperfect tense in French, and I know that Caesar beat the Helvetii because he had enough frumentum.) I only mean that failure isn't bad in itself, or success automatically good.

Fred Zinnemann, who has directed some of Hollywood's most hon-     10
ored movies, was asked by a reporter, when *A Man for All Seasons* won every prize, about his previous film, *Behold a Pale Horse*, which was a box-office disaster. "I don't feel any obligation to be successful," Zinnemann replied. "Success can be dangerous—you feel you know it all. I've learned a great deal from my failures." A similar point was made by Richard Brooks about his ambitious money loser, *Lord Jim*. Recalling the three years of his life that went into it, talking almost with elation about the troubles that befell his unit in Cambodia, Brooks told me that he learned more about his craft from this considerable failure than from his many earlier hits.

It's a point, of course, that applies throughout the arts. Writers,     11
playwrights, painters and composers work in the expectation of periodic defeat, but they wouldn't keep going back into the arena if they thought it was the end of the world. It isn't the end of the world. For an artist—and perhaps for anybody—it is the only way to grow.

Today's younger generation seems to know that this is true, seems     12
willing to take the risks in life that artists take in art. "Society," needless to say, still has the upper hand—it sets the goals and condemns as a failure everybody who won't play. But the dropouts and the hippies are not as afraid of failure as their parents and grandparents. This could mean, as their elders might say, that they are just plumb lazy, secure in the comforts of an affluent state. It could also mean, however, that they just don't buy the old standards of success and are rapidly writing new ones.

Recently it was announced, for instance, that more than two     13
hundred thousand Americans have inquired about service in VISTA (the domestic Peace Corps) and that, according to a Gallup survey,

"more than 3 million American college students would serve VISTA in some capacity if given the opportunity." This is hardly the road to riches or to an executive suite. Yet I have met many of these young volunteers, and they are not pining for traditional success. On the contrary, they appear more fulfilled than the average vice-president with a swimming pool.

Who is to say, then, if there is any right path to the top, or even to 14 say what the top consists of? Obviously the colleges don't have more than a partial answer—otherwise the young would not be so disaffected with an education that they consider vapid. Obviously business does not have the answer—otherwise the young would not be so scornful of its call to be an organization man.

The fact is, nobody has the answer, and the dawning awareness of 15 this fact seems to me one of the best things happening in America today. Success and failure are again becoming individual visions, as they were when the country was younger, not rigid categories. Maybe we are learning again to cherish this right of every person to succeed on his own terms and to fail as often as necessary along the way.

## VOCABULARY

| | | |
|---|---|---|
| VISTA (2) | pluperfect (9) | disaffected (14) |
| unorthodox (7) | frumentum (9) | vapid (14) |

## THE FACTS

1. Which sentence in the opening paragraphs of Zinsser's argument best states his thesis?
2. What two sides of society are pitted against each other in the essay? On whose side is Zinsser?
3. How does Zinsser go about defending a young person's right to fail? What advantage does this method have?
4. In what paragraph does the author explain that he does not consider failure a goal in itself? Why is this qualification necessary?

## THE STRATEGIES

1. What makes Zinsser's title catchy?
2. As he develops his argument, the author often qualifies his meaning and sets limits for interpretation. What purpose do these techniques serve? Point to specific examples as you answer this question.
3. What is the author's purpose in alluding to Holden Caulfield, hero of *Catcher in the Rye* (see paragraph 8)? What is your response to the allusion?

4. What is Zinsser's definition of *dropout*? How does it differ from the Establishment's definition?

## THE ISSUES

1. Do you agree with Zinsser's view that society as a whole distrusts mavericks, loners, or rebels because they do not live up to the rigid standards of success espoused by the Establishment? Or do you believe that history has often chronicled an admiration for such men and women, calling them "rugged individualists" and accepting them as a colorful part of the human heritage? Support your view with examples from history or literature.
2. What advice would you give a friend with high intellect who wanted to drop out of college?
3. What disadvantages can be cited as a warning against dropping out of college?
4. Reread paragraph 9. What list of specific facts, similar to that of the author, can you make thanks to *your* own education?
5. Do you agree with Zinsser that parents and society provide teenagers with rigid standards of success? Give examples to support your view.

## SUGGESTIONS FOR WRITING

1. Write an essay in which you argue either for or against Zinsser's view that some college courses are mindless.
2. Write an essay in which you argue, as does Zinsser, that failure can be a step toward success. Provide appropriate evidence to support your thesis.

# CHAPTER WRITING ASSIGNMENTS

1. Write an essay in which you narrate an incident that proves one of the following:
   a. That people are often bigoted
   b. That having good neighbors is important
   c. That pets are often astoundingly loyal
   d. That difficulties can be stepping stones to success
2. Write a vivid description by following this procedure:
   a. With a notebook in hand, go to the scene of some activity such as an airport, a restaurant, a park, a supermarket, or an employment office.
   b. Observe until you can formulate a general impression of the place.
   c. Take notes that support your general impression. (Leave out the details that do not support that impression.)
   d. Organize your notes and write the description.

# 7
# EXPLAINING

## Illustration and Definition

=========== •• *ADVICE* •• ===========

## HOW TO WRITE WITH EXAMPLES

A writer is under an obligation to support his or her generalizations with examples. Prose that generalizes without examples is tedious and vague. For instance, consider this snippet from an essay in which the writer is trying to define courage:

> Courage is the willingness to take risk when the outcome is uncertain, and when the risk taken may involve harm, loss, or danger to the one taking it. The courageous person fears no one and no thing. He or she is undaunted by danger or peril. He or she will venture boldly into an uncertain situation, hardly giving a thought to the harm or consequences which may result to his or her person.

The writer generalizes throughout the paragraph; one assertion about courage merely sums up and restates another. The paragraph is cloyed with vague, stultifying writing about courage. Without specific examples, twenty volumes of this sort of writing will still not convey to the reader what the writer means by courage. Compare this rewritten version:

> Courage is the willingness to take risk when the outcome is uncertain, and when the risk taken may involve harm, loss or danger to the one taking it. For example, in a Los Angeles suburb, a twelve-year-old girl ran into a burning house to rescue her baby brother, pulled him unconscious out of the burning bedroom, and dragged him down the stairs and outside to safety. This was a rousing display of courage. The girl had been safe outside the flaming house when she remembered her sleeping brother. Disregarding her personal safety, she plunged into the flaming house to save him.

It is easier to understand here what the writer means by courage. First, she generalizes about courage; then she gives an example. The definition of courage is still incomplete—more examples are needed—but at least the writer's meaning is clearer.

The use of examples in writing is necessary because language is ambiguous and circular. Words are defined by other words. The dictionary, for instance, defines courage as "the quality of being fearless or brave; spirit, temper"—in effect, it refers the reader from the one word *courage* to several words: *fearless, brave, spirit, temper*. By giving an example, the writer creates a context specifying more exactly what is meant by *courage* and avoids the circularity inherent in language.

As an instance of how examples are used, consider one of the selections that follows, "Coincidences." The writer opens this essay with a generalization: "There can be extraordinary sarcasms in coincidence." He then proceeds to clarify what he means with three apt examples: within the hour of his coat being stolen he randomly opens the Bible to a passage about watching and keeping one's garments; he is reading a book about a beautiful, cultivated woman who becomes a crook and disbelieving its premise when before his very eyes the lovely Jenny Hansen, queen of the shoplifters, is being transported to the police station; he tries mentally to will the train he is riding to stop, and it comes to a screeching halt because the engineer had suddenly decided that the engine needed water. These examples make abundantly clear what the writer means when he says that there can be extraordinary sarcasms in coincidences.

In another selection, "Mirror, Mirror, on the Wall . . ." by John Leo, the author generalizes that ideas of beauty vary from one era to another. This generalization is then supported with examples from the Stone Age, Greece, Rome, Egypt, Victorian England, and the twentieth century. In this article, moreover, the writer introduces his examples without the use of prefatory transitions such as "my first example is" or "my second example is." Instead, he devotes a separate paragraph to each era and aligns every example with the era to which it belongs. His presentation is logical and smooth, even without the use of mechanical transitions.

The most common accusation made against freshman writing is this: students generalize without giving examples. Movies, a student will write, are wretched things: they distort, they warp, they impose improbable endings on their material. Fine and good. The instructor waits for the examples. Instead, he or she is barraged by more generalities: movies are not only wretched, they are also horrid; they are dishonest; how they end is dictated more by box office probabilities than by dramatic necessities. The result is inconclusive and vague. Only an example could have demonstrated to the instructor what the student meant.

> For instance, in the *Sands of Iwo Jima*, John Wayne . . .

or:

> The movie *China Syndrome* furnishes an example of this . . .

Each should be followed by a discussion of the example.

Our advice therefore is to give many examples of what you mean when you write. Bear in mind that the best writing is specific and concrete; the worst is general and vague.

## 1. Select appropriate examples.

The example you cite must appropriately support your generalization. If you are writing an essay about the dangers of having a handgun in the house, your example must representatively specify this danger. One danger certainly is that someone will accidentally shoot someone else. A more remote danger is that the gun owner's pet orangutan will find the gun and deliberately shoot its master. Since most people do not own pet orangutans, this doleful story would be an unrepresentative example of the dangers of owning a handgun. Far better to cite the typical case of a man whose son thought the gun was unloaded and accidentally shot a friend.

## 2. Make it clear what your examples are illustrating.

Having generalized, most writers will introduce the example with a phrase such as "for example." Other phrases commonly used to introduce examples are:

As an example, consider
For instance
To illustrate
A case in point is
Thus
Hence
An illustration of this

Sometimes a writer will omit the introductory phrase if it is clear from the context of the writing what the example is intended to illustrate. For instance, in Alexander Black's essay "Coincidences" on pages 454–56, the first two examples of extraordinary sarcasms in coincidence are given without any prefacing phrase. However, the third example is linked and introduced with a single connecting word, "Again," to remind the reader that it, too, is cited in support of the generalization about sarcasms in coincidence.

## 3. Do not overuse examples.

Too many examples can be interpreted as padding. If, for instance, a writer declaims against immorality in movies in two sentences, then lists one hundred immoral movies, the instructor will justifiably feel shortchanged. Examples are, after all, subsidiary to generalizations. Essay assignments are intended to give a student practice in original thinking and writing, not in cataloguing. Use examples; but use them judiciously to support a generalization, not to usurp it.

# ══════ •• *EXAMPLES* •• ══════

### Caskie Stinnett

## ────── • FAREWELL, MY UNLOVELY • ──────

*Caskie Stinnett (b. 1911) has been editor in-chief of* Holiday *and* Travel & Leisure *magazines. The author of several books, including* Out of the Red *(1960) and* Back to Abnormal *(1963), Stinnett is a frequent contributor of humorous pieces to the* Atlantic Monthly *and* Reader's Digest.

*In 1976 the author said goodbye to New York because he could no longer stand its indifference. In this farewell essay to the city, he explains what he means by New York's indifference and gives examples of it.*

At noon today I said goodbye to New York forever, thus joining that growing group of people who, for one reason or another, have decided the city is no longer to our liking. This subject—the death of the city of New York—continues to be disinterred with sounds of anger and anguish by those of us who should know better. In reality, of course, New York is not a dying city; the eight million people who huddle together on that tiny rock do so through choice, and while they are aware there is an undiagnosed ailment in the city's bloodstream, they are willing to see it through. It must have been fun to live in New York once; perhaps it will be again. Those of us who are quitting are the impatient ones, the ones who lack the imagination to believe that the bright dream will glow again.

The sad aspect of my departure was that there was so little sadness connected with it, and after ten years it seemed to me that I should have looked back with some slight mistiness in my eyes. Of course, New York and I were never married; we committed a dalliance for ten years, never anything more serious. No vows were ever exchanged, no affection expressed. A lot of literature has been written on this subject—the disenchanted New Yorker—and I've read much of it, but none of the cases seem to fit precisely my feelings about the city. I don't hate New York; there is really nothing there to hate and certainly very little to love. It is a city of indifference, and that's the problem. I found I could only give indifference in return.

Many people find New York an unattractive city to inhabit because  3
of the physical filth, and while, God knows, the city is filthy, I doubt
that that element plays an important role in our decision to leave.
Naples is far dirtier, and so are Bombay and countless other cities, but
a tolerance for dirt seems to grow where some fondness exists. Tan-
giers is one of the dirtiest cities in the world, yet a friend of mine who
possesses flawless taste lives in the casbah there and would live nowhere else. A few days ago in Central Park I saw a man leaning on a
litter can drinking a carton of orange juice, and when he finished he
tossed the container not in the receptacle but on the ground.

I don't understand this, but there is a lot about New York I don't  4
understand. Mainly, I don't understand why the city has no soul, no
detectable heartbeat, why the chief element in the city's emotional
economy is indifference. I think that's what sent me on my way. Vienna
almost suffocates the Viennese with care, Paris manages to imbue her
own with an obsession for their fulfillment, San Francisco exudes a
pride that even gathers to her heart total strangers; but the key to New
York's character is that it doesn't really care about anything. Across the
court from the Manhattan apartment that I have occupied for the past
few years is a dog that quite often hurls insults into the darkness, a
few of which my dog refuses to accept service on and makes a tart
reply. I think I yearn for the people of New York to do somewhat the
same thing; I would like to think they possess a nature that could be
stimulated by something.

A number of New Yorkers have been driven from the city by fear; by  5
the feeling that they are besieged and that if they venture too far from
their neighborhoods they will be mugged or, worse, murdered. I have
never been mugged or physically molested in any way, possibly because my large build does not make me an ideal prospect for a hood-
lum. Yet I recall the lady who was buying a magazine in the Port
Authority Bus Terminal one evening when a stranger walked up and
disemboweled her with a butcher knife. Later arrested, he told police
that he didn't know the lady but "just felt like killing somebody." It's
impossible to protect oneself from such madness, and I think it is the
fool in New York who is not a coward at heart.

I recall, too, the New Year's Eve when, after a dinner party, a friend  6
of mine went down to the street to get a taxicab and the cab veered too
quickly and hit him. His wife and I took him in the cab to Lenox Hill

Hospital, and while we were trying to get emergency treatment for him the cabdriver was screaming at us for his fare. A few weeks ago a fifteen-year-old girl was raped on a subway train. The next day the police expressed the opinion that the girl was partially responsible for the act because she had entered a car in which there were no other passengers. All of these things may happen in other large cities, and undoubtedly do, but they reflect a lack of caring, a sickness of the soul, that I find difficult to accept and impossible to forget.

Crime is widespread and New York's crime statistics are not the    7
worst in the country. Perhaps what troubles me is the kinds of crimes that go on here, the terrible meanness in addition to the offense. I have just read in the paper that three elderly people, sharing an apartment and all confined to wheelchairs because of cerebral palsy, were robbed by intruders. Three Mexican tourists who could speak no English were charged $167 for a taxi ride from Kennedy International Airport to downtown New York. The 217 blind newsdealers of New York recently complained that their customers are stealing coins from their trays, shortchanging them, and frequently mugging them on their way home at night. A savings bank guard who assisted blind customers with their deposit and withdrawal slips was recently charged with forgery and grand larceny after a blind depositor discovered her balance was $169 instead of the $2857 which her Braille accounting indicated should be there. During last year's Central Park Bicycle Race, five of the racers were attacked and had their bikes stolen while the race was in progress. This is something of a handicap in a bicycle race.

I can offer no ready acceptance to the theory that New York's stag-    8
gering size creates meanness in the same proportion. The girls in the shadows of the Madeleine in Paris whisper a soft *"Bon soir"* to their prospective customers, but those in New York seem to feel a need for offensive weapons, as the former finance minister of West Germany discovered when he was accosted by two prostitutes in front of the Plaza Hotel and robbed of $180.

And there is the minor cheating too, so commonplace that it is    9
almost a game with New Yorkers. Some drivers run through traffic lights for five or six seconds after the light has turned red, and it stirs them with pleasure. The cabdriver conveniently neglects to throw his flag upon arrival at your destination, and while you are paying him,

an additional ten cents rings up. It seems to please him more than any other money he has made all day. The hatcheck girl has no change for a dollar. Almost everybody in New York cheats a little.

I had not intended to dwell excessively upon crime in New York, [10] and I have offered these examples to show the nature of the crimes rather than their extent. Nor am I vastly concerned about the politics of the city, since the political structure is almost totally controlled by the labor unions, and the options left open to the mayor and the city council are so slight as to make both of them ceremonial institutions and little more. Russell Baker,* whose satire very often brings him close to the hot fire of truth, once wrote that he was quite familiar with the New York phenomenon called "Strike of the Week," in which the unions take turns at stopping some vital service; he marveled not that these strikes occur but that New Yorkers accept the inconveniences so passively. It is true, of course. The indifference that I can't seem to keep from returning to has often led me to wonder if a point exists at which New Yorkers will say, "Enough. I will tolerate this no longer." I don't think so. During the famous blackout ten years ago, a woman sat in a stalled subway train for eight hours with a cake in her lap. When asked why she hadn't eaten the cake, she replied: "I just didn't care that much." That's real indifference.

I don't want to see children in Central Park playing in unmarked [11] clumps of poison ivy, and I don't want to see any more statues and walls scribbled with spray paint; and I don't want to ride anymore on an obsolete and run-down subway system so poorly marked that even the Transit Authority people find it difficult to give directions. For some reason, I resent the horrid smartness of a city that sends hundreds of people to eat at Elaine's, a celebrity-packed restaurant serving mediocre food, because it's fashionable to be seen there.

New York offers some prizes I shall miss, and I can only hope to find [12] them elsewhere. A few days ago, after a quick rainstorm, I walked across Central Park near the lake and I thought I had never seen a city so lovely. The steel and glass buildings caught the sunlight, and in the clean air they glowed brilliantly. I passed a youth on 74th Street one morning recently and for no reason at all he smiled and said, "Hi."

---

*A syndicated newspaper columnist whose work appears nationally.

In no other city in the whole world are there such beautiful girls; they stride rapidly and with purpose, their faces are filled with vitality, and they seem to meet life eagerly. The tempo of the city itself is exhilarating.

And so I come to the bottom line. I don't want to live in a city where     13
a woman advertises for a lost dog and receives dozens of telephone calls from a variety of people saying they are torturing the animal and will continue to do so unless she pays large sums of money; or in a city where I am told I must always have $10 in my wallet for a possible mugger because without that I will surely be stabbed; or in a city where my mailman leaves a slip in my box at Christmas suggesting the size of the tip he expects. I shall find some of these things wherever I go, and perhaps all of them, but I don't think so. Above all I want to get away from the indifference of New York. I want to care and—it sounds implausibly poignant—be cared about. New York doesn't give a damn. It has seen thousands of us come and go.

## VOCABULARY

| | | |
|---|---|---|
| disinterred (1) | disemboweled (5) | poignant (13) |
| dalliance (2) | exhilarating (12) | |
| imbue (4) | implausibly (13) | |

## THE FACTS

1. What aspect of his departure from New York did Stinnett find so sad?
2. What does Stinnett yearn for the people of New York to do?
3. What about the crime in New York does Stinnett find so troubling?
4. How does Stinnett characterize the political structure of New York?
5. What does Stinnett say he will miss about New York?

## THE STRATEGIES

1. In paragraph 3, what specific examples does Stinnett use to support his contention that the filthiness of New York has little effect on the decision of people to leave it?
2. Paragraph 4 begins with the sentence, "I don't understand this, but there is a lot about New York I don't understand." To what does "this" refer? What is the function of this sentence in the paragraph?
3. Paragraph 4 ends with an implied contrast. What is so ironic about this contrast?

4. How does the author introduce his examples in paragraphs 5 and 6?
5. The examples in paragraph 7 have no introduction but merely follow one after the other. Why is an introduction of these examples unnecessary?

### THE ISSUES

1. If you were to defend New York as a city, what facts might you cite?
2. The author is distressed because, according to him, New York has no soul and "it doesn't really care about anything." How can their inhabitants prevent huge cities like New York from becoming indifferent to the human condition?
3. In paragraph 7, the author reveals how troubled he is about the "terrible meanness" of some crimes committed in New York. As an antidote to his view, what acts of compassion or heroism, performed in a large city, can you cite? Try to cite examples concerning acquaintances of yours.
4. In paragraph 9, the author claims that almost everyone in New York "cheats a little." Do you believe "cheating a little" is a general fact of life? Why or why not? How do you feel about minor infractions of the law?
5. In what large city in the world would you like to live? Give specific reasons and examples to support your answer.

### SUGGESTIONS FOR WRITING

1. What city do you love or hate the most? Write an essay saying why you feel as you do and giving examples of what you love or hate about the city.
2. Write an essay summarizing the messages contained in "Libido for the Ugly" (pages 389–92) and "Farewell, My Unlovely." State what they have in common.

John Leo

# • "MIRROR, MIRROR, • ON THE WALL . . ."

*John Leo (b. 1935), associate editor of* Time, *was born in Hoboken, New Jersey, and educated at the University of Toronto. He has been associated with* Commonweal, The New York Times, *and the* Village Voice.

*In the following brief essay from* Time, *Leo discusses and gives examples of the relativity of beauty.*

The poet may insist that beauty is in the eye of the beholder; the    1
historian might argue that societies create the image of female perfec-

tion that they want. There has always been plenty of evidence to support both views. Martin Luther thought long, beautiful hair was essential. Edmund Burke recommended delicate, fragile women. Goethe insisted on "the proper breadth of the pelvis and the necessary fullness of the breasts." Hottentot men look for sharply projecting buttocks. Rubens favored a full posterior, and Papuans require a big nose. The Mangaians of Polynesia care nothing of fat or thin and never seem to notice face, breasts or buttocks. To the tribesmen, the only standard of sexiness is well-shaped female genitals.

An anthropologized world now knows that notions of what is most attractive do vary with each age and culture. One era's flower is another's frump. Primitive man, understandably concerned with fertility, idealized ample women. One of the earliest surviving sculptures, the Stone Age Venus of Willendorf, depicts a squat woman whose vital statistics—in inches—would amount to 96–89–96. This adipose standard stubbornly recurs in later eras. A 14th-century treatise on beauty calls for "narrow shoulders, small breasts, large belly, broad hips, fat thighs, short legs and a small head." Some Oriental cultures today are turned on by what Simone de Beauvoir calls the "unnecessary, gratuitous blooming" of wrap-around fat.

The Greeks were so concerned with working out precise proportions for beauty that the sculptor Praxiteles insisted that the female navel be exactly midway between the breasts and genitals. The dark-haired Greeks considered fair-haired women exotic, perhaps the start of the notion that blondes have more fun. They also offered early evidence of the rewards that go to magnificent mammaries. When Phryne, Praxiteles' famous model and mistress, was on trial for treason, the orator defending her pulled aside her veil, baring her legendary breasts. The awed judges acquitted her on the spot.

Romans favored more independent, articulate women than the Greeks. Still, there were limits. Juvenal complains of ladies who "discourse on poets and poetry, comparing Vergil with Homer. . . . Wives shouldn't read all the classics—there ought to be some things women don't understand."

In ancient Egypt, women spent hours primping: fixing hair, applying lipstick, eye shadow and fingernail polish, grinding away body and genital hair with pumice stones. It worked: Nefertiti could make the cover of *Vogue* any month she wanted. For Cleopatra, the most famous bombshell of the ancient world, eroticism was plain hard

work. Not a natural beauty, she labored diligently to learn coquettishness and flattery and reportedly polished her amatory techniques by
practicing on slaves.

If Cleopatra had to work so hard at being desirable, can the average    6
woman do less? Apparently not. In the long history of images of
beauty, one staple is the male tendency to spot new flaws in women,
and the female tendency to work and suffer to remedy them. In the
Middle Ages, large women rubbed themselves with cow dung dissolved in wine. When whiter skin was demanded, women applied
leeches to take the red out. Breasts have been strapped down, cantilevered up, pushed together or apart, oiled and siliconed and, in
16th-century Venice, fitted with wool or hair padding for a sexy "duck
breast" look, curving from bodice to groin. In the long run, argues
feminist Elizabeth Gould Davis, flat-chested women are evolutionary
losers. Says she: "The female of the species owes her modern mammary magnificence to male sexual preference."

Still, a well-endowed woman can suddenly find herself out of favor    7
when cultural winds change. The flapper era in America is one example. So is Europe's Romantic Age, which favored the wan, cadaverous
look. In the 1820s, women sometimes drank vinegar or stayed up all
night to look pale and interesting. Fragility was all. Wrote Keats:
"God! she is like a milk-white lamb that bleats / For man's protection."

Victorians took this ideal of the shy, clinging vine, decorously de-    8
sexed it, and assigned it to the wife. According to one well-known
Victorian doctor, it was a "vile aspersion" to suggest that women were
capable of sexual impulses. Inevitably that straitlaced era controlled
women's shapes by severe compression of the waistline, without ac-
centing breasts or hips.

Those womanly curves reasserted themselves at the turn of the    9
century. During the hourglass craze, Lillie Langtry seemed perfection
incarnate at 38–18–38. Since then, the ideal woman in Western culture
has gradually slimmed down. Psyche, the White Rock girl,* was 5 ft.
4 in. tall and weighed in at a hippy 140 lbs. when she first appeared
on beverage bottles in 1893. Now, *sans* cellulite, she is 4 in. taller and
22 lbs. lighter.

In psychological terms, the current slim-hipped look amounts to a    10
rebellion against male domination: waist-trimming corsets are associated with male control of the female body, and narrow hips with a

---

*Psyche has been the emblem of White Rock brand soft drinks and mixes since the nineteenth century.—Ed.

reluctance to bear children. Says Madge Garland, a former editor of British *Vogue:* "The natural shape of the female body has not been revealed and free as it is today for 1,500 years." W. H. Auden once complained that for most of Western history, the sexy beautiful women have seemed "fictionalized," set apart from real life. In the age of the natural look, a beauty now has to seem as though she just strolled in from the beach at Malibu. Like Cheryl Tiegs.

## VOCABULARY

frump (2)               amatory (5)            incarnate (9)
adipose (2)             cantilevered (6)       cellulite (9)
gratuitous (2)          decorously (8)
coquettishness (5)      aspersion (8)

## THE FACTS

1. What kinds of women did primitive man idealize?
2. What was the Greeks' standard of beauty?
3. According to feminist Elizabeth Gould Davis, to what do women owe their "modern mammary magnificence"?
4. What kind of feminine beauty was favored during Europe's Romantic Age?
5. What does the modern, slim-hipped look signify in psychological terms?

## THE STRATEGIES

1. What notion do most of the examples in this essay support? Where is this notion stated?
2. Much of the detail about beauty is given not in full-blown examples, but in sketchy references to the opinions of famous people. What are such references called?
3. In paragraph 3, what does the anecdote about Phryne exemplify?
4. The author quotes Goethe, Simone de Beauvoir, Juvenal, Elizabeth Gould Davis, John Keats, Madge Garland, and W. H. Auden. What effect does all this opinion-sampling have on the tone of the essay?
5. In paragraph 6, the author writes: "In the long history of images of beauty, one staple is the male tendency to spot new flaws in women, and the female tendency to work and suffer to remedy them." How does the author then proceed to support and document this view?

## THE ISSUES

1. Paragraph 2 alludes to an "anthropologized world." How would you define this world? What significance lies in this label?
2. What, for you, constitutes a beautiful female? A beautiful male? Refer to

specific examples from history, the current scene, or from your personal encounters.

3. How do you feel about the present emphasis on an athletic female body? Is it justified, or does it diminish some other innately feminine character-istic? Give reasons for your answer.

4. Even if you agree with the poet that beauty is in the eye of the beholder, argue against this proposition and for an objective standard of beauty in art.

5. In paragraph 8, the author describes the typical Victorian wife as a woman who must never be perceived as having sexual impulses. How would you compare today's American wife with this English woman of the nineteenth-century?

### SUGGESTIONS FOR WRITING

1. Write an essay that specifies your idea of human beauty. Give copious examples to illustrate your point.

2. Follow the instructions above, but make the subject of your essay human ugliness. Be sure to give examples.

### Alexander Black

## •  COINCIDENCES  •

*Alexander Black (1859–1940), American editor and writer, was literary editor of the* Brooklyn Times *and Sunday editor of the* New York World. *Among his books are* The Story of Ohio *(1888) and* Miss Jerry *(1897).*

An essay, no matter how it is developed, must make a point. The point need not be elaborate, and often when the essay is developed by exam-ples it is not. In this essay, the point, announced straight off, is simply that there can be extraordinary sarcasms in coincidence. Frail though it may be, this point is hammered home by examples with such a venge-ance that there is no mistaking the author's meaning.

There can be extraordinary sarcasms in coincidence. One night a    1 thief made off with my overcoat from a restaurant. The restaurant was not of the sort in which one is admonished to be alert. Moreover, I had never been robbed of anything in my life. I was utterly without ad-monitory experience. Naturally, the incident made a rather profound impression. The weather happened to deepen that impression. It was within the hour that I happened to open my Bible to verify the location of the verse from which I took the title of a certain book. And in the verse immediately preceding I read, with an entirely new sense of their significance, these startling words: "Blessed is he that watcheth and keepeth his garments."

On a certain afternoon I was reading a book in a street car. The book   2 was Julian Hawthorne's *The Great Bank Robbery*. Its picture of a beautiful, cultivated, and socially important woman who becomes fascinated by a crook, and under the mesmeric influence of the infatuation actually steals the secret of a safe, set up a lively speculation in my mind. The story was supposed to be founded upon fact—really to transcribe the experiences of a known detective—and the psychology of the thing thus acquired more than merely a speculative interest. All the rest of the story might be true, or be a free transcription of fact, but could this woman be true? I lowered the book in that moment of mental wrestling with skepticism and became conscious that a girl in a greenish-blue dress sat diagonally opposite in the car. It occurred to me that she was very pretty, perhaps even beautiful, and that especially she had about her something exquisite, as a fine breed, that stood out against the profane average of the public huddle. The truth is that I was awed and thrust quite into the mood of a deeper skepticism about the book. Could a girl like *that*, for example, do a coarse, unscrupulous thing, a criminal thing at the behest of any man or any emotion? It was incredible. Hawthorne's fiction began to look tawdry, like a trick to make a melodrama. I should have to say so in my review. Then the car came to a stop. The girl opposite arose. A man on the front platform got off. So did a man on the rear platform who had been standing beside the conductor. Presently I saw that the girl was between them in the street, and when I glanced backward I became aware that the three figures disappeared into the Greene Avenue police station. In a state of disturbed curiosity I went to the conductor. The girl? That was Jenny Hansen. The coppers called her the queen of the shoplifters.

Again: And note that the scene is once more a public conveyance   3 and that once more I am reviewing. Of course a reviewer should be wearing a velvet jacket and be seated in a large place, graciously quiet, and framed against the intrusions of mere life by towering barricades of books. Here, attuned and sheltered, the reviewer should measure the precise degree in which the print in hand synchronizes with Literature. But I was in the cross seat of an elevated train. In that day elevated trains were operated by steam, and this one was bowling along at what seemed to be a hastening rate. My book was Virginia Titcomb's *Mind Cure on a Material Basis,* then a comparatively new subject. I reached a paragraph in which there was speculation upon the ultimate power of thought and will to influence external things. Call it creative imagination, mediumistic projection, or the faith that moves mountains, this power, by whatever name, latent or limited, suggested enormous potentialities. Yet with the most eager cordiality toward the theory one could not avoid bewilderment as to the boundaries. One might influence his own chemistry. This was already admitted. Would it be held that wholly external matter might, as in the Miracles, yield to the white heat of individual wish? Fancy, I said to myself, willing, willing fiercely and with a tremendous concentration, that this train, now midway of two stations, should come to an utter halt, that I, taking the train by the throat, as it were, should screech to it, "Stop!" At that instant (the instant is essential to my drama) the train *did* halt, with so complete a suddenness, with a sharpness so preposterously violent, that I was thrown forward against the seat in front, to the damage of my face. A child fell to the floor of the car. One or two women screamed in fright. For another instant, before there could be room for reason, I had the thrill of an absolutely apocalyptic confirmation, with a twinge that blended chagrin and awe. The world had, at a stroke, acquired a fearful, a prodigious instability. Nothing is too fantastic to last for a second. When I thrust my head out of the window (in company with a dozen others) I discovered that the engineer had quite peremptorily changed his mind and decided to take water at a huge tank which hung about a hundred feet from the point where I had applied the mental brakes.

Others may have had profounder experience. These are my three perfect coincidences.    4

## VOCABULARY

| | | |
|---|---|---|
| admonished (1) | unscrupulous (2) | latent (3) |
| mesmeric (2) | behest (2) | apocalyptic (3) |
| transcribe (2) | tawdry (2) | chagrin (3) |
| skepticism (2) | intrusions (3) | prodigious (3) |
| exquisite (2) | attuned (3) | peremptorily (3) |
| profane (2) | synchronizes (3) | |

## THE FACTS

1. What first coincidence did the author encounter?
2. Who did the beautiful woman in the street car turn out to be?
3. What was the third coincidence?
4. Which of the three coincidences is the best illustration of the proverbial effect of "mind over matter"?

## THE STRATEGIES

1. What is the thesis of this essay? What is unusual about the placement of this thesis?
2. Which of the three examples does the author introduce? How does he introduce it?
3. What transitional expressions does the author use in the first paragraph? What is the function of these expressions?
4. Just before the occurrence of the second and third coincidences, the author was reading a book whose premise he was initially skeptical of. What similar rhetorical device does he use to voice his initial skepticism?
5. Essayists often begin their essays by defining any term crucial to their discussions. Why does the author not define *coincidence* in this essay?

## THE ISSUES

1. What significance, if any, do you attach to the kinds of coincidences narrated by Alexander Black? Give reasons for your answer.
2. What coincidence from literature, history, or your personal life has left a memorable impression on you? Briefly narrate the coincidence.
3. The author claims that some coincidences are laden with "extraordinary sarcasm." What other characteristics could pervade certain coincidences? Give examples.
4. What is the opposite of coincidence? Provide an appropriate example.
5. What lessons can be learned from the fact that coincidences do take place in life? Would you prefer to live in a world free from all coincidences? Why or why not?

## SUGGESTIONS FOR WRITING

1. Write an essay about any perfect coincidence you have had.
2. Write an essay on the adage "appearances are deceiving," in which you offer at least three examples in support of it.

Malcolm Cowley

———————— • **THE VIEW FROM EIGHTY** • ————————

*Malcolm Cowley (b. 1898), American critic and poet, was born in Belsano,
Pennsylvania, and educated at Harvard. After World War I, Cowley lived abroad
for many years among the so-called lost generation of writers, eventually writing
about them in* Exile's Return *(1934) and* Second Flowering *(1973). He was
the literary editor of* The New Republic *from 1930 to 1940 and numbers among
his published works* A Dry Season *(poems, 1942);* Blue Juanita: Collected
Poems *(1964); and, most recently,* The View from Eighty *(1981), from which
this excerpt was taken.*

*The View from Eighty is a heartening and refreshing reminder that old age
does not necessarily entail the loss of literary style, vigor, and wit. Using
examples to show how the aged see the world, Cowley writes with the same
freshness and liveliness that have characterized all his work.*

Even before he or she is 80, the aging person may undergo another     1
identity crisis like that of adolescence. Perhaps there had also been a
middle-aged crisis, the male or the female menopause, but for the rest
of adult life he had taken himself for granted, with his capabilities and
failings. Now, when he looks in the mirror, he asks himself, "Is this
really me?"—or he avoids the mirror out of distress at what it reveals,
those bags and wrinkles. In his new makeup he is called upon to play
a new role in a play that must be improvised. André Gide, that long-
lived man of letters, wrote in his journal, "My heart has remained so
young that I have the continual feeling of playing a part, the part of
the 70-year-old that I certainly am; and the infirmities and weaknesses
that remind me of my age act like a prompter, reminding me of my
lines when I tend to stray. Then, like the good actor I want to be, I go
back into my role, and I pride myself on playing it well."

In his new role the old person will find that he is tempted by new     2
vices, that he receives new compensations (not so widely known), and
that he may possibly achieve new virtues. Chief among these is the
heroic or merely obstinate refusal to surrender in the face of time. One
admires the ships that go down with all flags flying and the captain on
the bridge.

Among the vices of age are avarice, untidiness, and vanity, which     3
last takes the form of a craving to be loved or simply admired. Avarice

is the worst of those three. Why do so many old persons, men and women alike, insist on hoarding money when they have no prospect of using it and even when they have no heirs? They eat the cheapest food, buy no clothes, and live in a single room when they could afford better lodging. It may be that they regard money as a form of power; there is a comfort in watching it accumulate while other powers are dwindling away. How often we read of an old person found dead in a hovel, on a mattress partly stuffed with bankbooks and stock certificates! The bankbook syndrome, we call it in our family, which has never succumbed.

Untidiness we call the Langley Collyer syndrome. To explain, Langley Collyer was a former concert pianist who lived alone with his 70-year-old brother in a brownstone house on upper Fifth Avenue. The once fashionable neighborhood had become part of Harlem. Homer, the brother, had been an admiralty lawyer, but was now blind and partly paralyzed; Langley played for him and fed him on buns and oranges, which he thought would restore Homer's sight. He never threw away a daily paper because Homer, he said, might want to read them all. He saved other things as well and the house became filled with rubbish from roof to basement. The halls were lined on both sides with bundled newspapers, leaving narrow passageways in which Langley had devised booby traps to catch intruders.

On March 21, 1947, some unnamed person telephoned the police to report that there was a dead body in the Collyer house. The police broke down the front door and found the hall impassable, then they hoisted a ladder to a second-story window. Behind it Homer was lying on the floor in a bathrobe; he had starved to death. Langley had disappeared. After some delay, the police broke into the basement, chopped a hole in the roof, and began throwing junk out of the house, top and bottom. It was 18 days before they found Langley's body, gnawed by rats. Caught in one of his own booby traps, he had died in a hallway just outside Homer's door. By that time the police had collected, and the Department of Sanitation had hauled away, 120 tons of rubbish, including besides the newspapers, 14 grand pianos and the parts of a dismantled Model T Ford.

Why do so many old people accumulate junk, not on the scale of Langley Collyer, but still in a dismaying fashion? Their tables are piled high with it, their bureau drawers are stuffed with it, their closet rods bend with the weight of clothes not worn for years. I suppose that the piling up is partly from lethargy and partly from the feeling that everything once useful, including their own bodies, should be preserved. Others, though not so many, have such a fear of becoming Langley Collyers that they strive to be painfully neat. Every tool they own is in its place, though it will never be used again; every scrap of paper is filed away in alphabetical order. At last their immoderate neatness becomes another vice of age, if a milder one.

The vanity of older people is an easier weakness to explain, and to     7
condone. With less to look forward to, they yearn for recognition of what they have been: the reigning beauty, the athlete, the soldier, the scholar. It is the beauties who have the hardest time. A portrait of themselves at twenty hangs on the wall, and they try to resemble it by making an extravagant use of creams, powders, and dyes. Being young at heart, they think they are merely revealing their essential persons. The athletes find shelves for their silver trophies, which are polished once a year. Perhaps a letter sweater lies wrapped in a bureau drawer. I remember one evening when a no-longer athlete had guests for dinner and tried to find his sweater. "Oh, that old thing," his wife said. "The moths got into it and I threw it away." The athlete sulked and his guests went home early.

Often the yearning to be recognized appears in conversation as an     8
innocent boast. Thus, a distinguished physician, retired at 94, remarks casually that a disease was named after him. A former judge bursts into chuckles as he repeats bright things that he said on the bench. Aging scholars complain in letters (or one of them does), "As I approach 70 I'm becoming avid of honors, and such things—medals, honorary degrees, etc.—are only passed around among academics on a *quid pro quo* basis (one hood capping another)." Or they say querulously, "Bill Underwood has ten honorary doctorates and I have only three. Why didn't they elect me to . . . ?" and they mention the name of some learned society. That search for honors is a harmless passion, though it may lead to jealousies and deformations of character, as with Robert Frost in his later years. Still, honors cost little. Why shouldn't the very old have more than their share of them?

To be admired and praised, especially by the young, is an autumnal     9
pleasure enjoyed by the lucky ones (who are not always the most

deserving). "What is more charming," Cicero observes in his famous essay *De Senectute,* "than old age surrounded by the enthusiasm of youth! . . . Attentions which seem trivial and conventional are marks of honor—the morning call, being sought after, precedence, having people rise for you, being escorted to and from the forum. . . . What pleasures of the body can be compared to the prerogatives of influence?" But there are also pleasures of the body, or the mind, that are enjoyed by a greater number of older persons.

Those pleasures include some that younger people find hard to     10 appreciate. One of them is simply sitting still, like a snake on a sun-warmed stone, with a delicious feeling of indolence that was seldom attained in earlier years. A leaf flutters down; a cloud moves by inches across the horizon. At such moments the older person, completely relaxed, has become a part of nature—and a living part, with blood coursing through his veins. The future does not exist for him. He thinks, if he thinks at all, that life for younger persons is still a battle royal of each against each, but that now he has nothing more to win or lose. He is not so much above as outside the battle, as if he had assumed the uniform of some neutral country, perhaps Liechtenstein or Andorra. From a distance he notes that some of the combatants, men or women, are jostling ahead—but why do they fight so hard when the most they can hope for is a longer obituary? He can watch the scrounging and gouging, he can hear the shouts of exultation, the moans of the gravely wounded, and meanwhile he feels secure; nobody will attack him from ambush.

Age has other physical compensations besides the nirvana of dozing     11 in the sun. A few of the simplest needs become a pleasure to satisfy. When an old woman in a nursing home was asked what she really liked to do, she answered in one word: "Eat." She might have been speaking for many of her fellows. Meals in a nursing home, however badly cooked, serve as climactic moments of the day. The physical essence of the pensioners is being renewed at an appointed hour; now they can go back to meditating or to watching TV while looking forward to the next meal. They can also look forward to sleep, which has become a definite pleasure, not the mere interruption it once had been.

Here I am thinking of old persons under nursing care. Others fero-     12 ciously guard their independence, and some of them suffer less than one might expect from being lonely and impoverished. They can be rejoiced by visits and meetings, but they also have company inside their heads. Some of them are busiest when their hands are still. What passes through the minds of many is a stream of persons, images, phrases, and familiar tunes. For some that stream has continued since childhood, but now it is deeper; it is their present and their past combined. At times they conduct silent dialogues with a vanished friend, and these are less tiring—often more rewarding—than spoken conversations. If inner resources are lacking, old persons living alone may seek comfort and a kind of companionship in the bottle. I should judge from the gossip of various neighborhoods that the outer suburbs from Boston to San Diego are full of secretly alcoholic widows. One of those widows, an old friend, was moved from her apartment into a retirement home. She left behind her a closet in which the floor was covered wall to wall with whiskey bottles. "Oh, those empty bottles!" she explained. "They were left by a former tenant."

Not whiskey or cooking sherry but simply giving up is the greatest    13
temptation of age. It is something different from a stoical acceptance of infirmities, which is something to be admired. At 63, when he first recognized that his powers were failing, Emerson wrote one of his best poems, "Terminus":

> It is time to be old,
> To take in sail:—
> The god of bounds,
> Who sets to seas a shore,
> Came to me in his fatal rounds,
> And said: "No more!
> No farther shoot
> Thy broad ambitious branches, and thy root.
> Fancy departs: no more invent;
> Contract thy firmament
> To compass of a tent."

Emerson lived in good health to the age of 79. Within his narrowed    14
firmament, he continued working until his memory failed; then he consented to having younger editors and collaborators. The givers-up see no reason for working. Sometimes they lie in bed all day when moving about would still be possible, if difficult. I had a friend, a distinguished poet, who surrendered in that fashion. The doctors tried to stir him to action, but he refused to leave his room. Another friend,

once a successful artist, stopped painting when his eyes began to fail. His doctor made the mistake of telling him that he suffered from a fatal disease. He then lost interest in everything except the splendid Rolls-Royce, acquired in his prosperous days, that stood in the garage. Daily he wiped the dust from its hood. He couldn't drive it on the road any longer, but he used to sit in the driver's seat, start the motor, then back the Rolls out of the garage and drive it in again, back twenty feet and forward twenty feet; that was his only distraction.

I haven't the right to blame those who surrender, not being able to put myself inside their minds or bodies. Often they must have compelling reasons, physical or moral. Not only do they suffer from a variety of ailments, but also they are made to feel that they no longer have a function in the community. Their families and neighbors don't ask them for advice, don't really listen when they speak, don't call on them for efforts. One notes that there are not a few recoveries from apparent senility when that situation changes. If it doesn't change, old persons may decide that efforts are useless. I sympathize with their problems, but the men and women I envy are those who accept old age as a series of challenges. [15]

For such persons, every new infirmity is an enemy to be outwitted, an obstacle to be overcome by force of will. They enjoy each little victory over themselves, and sometimes they win a major success. Renoir was one of them. He continued painting, and magnificently, for years after he was crippled by arthritis; the brush had to be strapped to his arm. "You don't need your hand to paint," he said. Goya was another of the unvanquished. At 72 he retired as an official painter of the Spanish court and decided to work only for himself. His later years were those of the famous "black paintings" in which he let his imagination run (and also of the lithographs, then a new technique). At 78 he escaped a reign of terror in Spain by fleeing to Bordeaux. He was deaf and his eyes were failing; in order to work he had to wear several pairs of spectacles, one over another, and then use a magnifying glass; but he was producing splendid work in a totally new style. At 80 he drew an ancient man propped on two sticks, with a mass of white hair and beard hiding his face and with the inscription "I am still learning." [16]

Giovanni Papini said when he was nearly blind, "I prefer martyrdom to imbecility." After writing sixty books, including his famous *Life of Christ*, he was at work on two huge projects when he was [17] stricken with a form of muscular atrophy. He lost the use of his left leg, then of his fingers, so that he couldn't hold a pen. The two big books, though never to be finished, moved forward slowly by dictation; that in itself was a triumph. Toward the end, when his voice had become incomprehensible, he spelled out a word, tapping on the table to indicate letters of the alphabet. One hopes never to be faced with the need for such heroic measures.

"Eighty years old!" the great Catholic poet Paul Claudel wrote in    18
his journal. "No eyes left, no ears, no teeth, no legs, no wind! And when all is said and done, how astonishingly well one does without them!"

## VOCABULARY

| | | |
|---|---|---|
| improvised (1) | immoderate (6) | indolence (10) |
| infirmities (1) | condone (7) | exultation (10) |
| avarice (3) | querulously (8) | nirvana (11) |
| succumbed (3) | deformations (8) | climactic (11) |
| lethargy (6) | prerogatives (9) | |

## THE FACTS

1. What kind of crisis does the aging person undergo?
2. What are the virtues of old age? What are its main vices?
3. What is the Langley Collyer syndrome? Why do old people suffer so often from it? What part does society's treatment of the elderly have to play in this syndrome?
4. Why are some old people so vain?
5. What pleasures do the old revel in?

## THE STRATEGIES

1. Aside from examples that illustrate what it is like to be old, what kind of supporting detail does Cowley use? What does its use add to the essay?
2. What is the function of the question in paragraph 6?
3. Old people, says Cowley, suffer chronically from avarice, untidiness, and vanity. He gives extended examples of the second and third of these, but not of the first. How does he support his view that the old are often avaricious? What rhetorical logic lies behind this omission of examples?

4. What extended analogy does Cowley use to describe how the young appear to the old? How effective is this analogy?
5. In this excerpt Cowley gives anecdotes about aging in others, rather than in himself. Do you think this a better tactic than focusing on his own experiences? Why or why not?

## THE ISSUES

1. Has Cowley overlooked any vices or virtues attached to old age? Make a written list of the characteristics of old age you wish to avoid and then a second list of characteristics you wish to develop.
2. What is your answer to the question posed in paragraph 3: "Why do so many old persons, men and women alike, insist on hoarding money when they have no prospect of using it and even when they have no heirs?" Do you agree with Cowley's suggestion that perhaps they regard money as a form of power, or are there other reasons for the avarice?
3. What about old age do you fear most? What do you plan to do in order to alleviate your fear?
4. In "Rabbi Ben Ezra" the famous Victorian poet, Robert Browning, wrote these lines:

> Grow old along with me!
> The best is yet to be,
> The last of life, for which the first was made:
> Our times are in His hand
> Who saith, "A whole I planned,
> Youth shows but half; trust God: see all, nor be afraid."

How do you interpret these lines? Do you agree or disagree with the poet's view? Give reasons for your answer.
5. What kind of person do you imagine yourself to be at age eighty? Describe in detail what kinds of clothes you would wear, how you would spend your time, and what philosophy would guide your existence.

## SUGGESTIONS FOR WRITING

1. Some sociologists have suggested that since women outlive men, marriage laws should be relaxed to allow the elderly to practice polygyny (where a man has more than one wife or mate). Express your views on this issue in an essay in which you use examples to support your thesis.
2. Write an essay giving examples of the way age has affected an elderly friend or relative.

=== •• *ADVICE* •• ===

## HOW TO WRITE A DEFINITION

A definition answers the question "What is it?" Law students must know what a *brief* is before they can compile one; likewise, medical interns rotating through the obstetrics floor of a hospital must know what a *breech* is before they can perform a breech delivery. In the first instance, the law textbook might define *brief* as "a summary of the essential points of a decision." In the second instance, the medical text might tell the interns that "a breech is the lower rear portion of the human trunk" and that a breech birth is, therefore, one in which the buttocks of the baby emerge before its head. No matter what discipline the student is in, no matter what walk of life he or she may eventually choose, the definition will be an indispensable source of information.

Various strategies can be employed to define any word, phrase, or term. How much detail the student must give will vary with how abstract, fuzzy, or controversial the word, phrase, or term is. The following is a thumbnail sketch of how a definition may be constructed.

### 1. Begin with a formal definition.

A formal definition first places a word in a general class and then shows how that word differs from others in the same class. The following definitions illustrate this simple system:

| WORD | GENERAL CLASS | HOW WORD DIFFERS |
|------|---------------|------------------|
| *miracle* | an event or action | that contradicts natural laws |
| *pedant* | a person | who exhibits scholarship ostentatiously |
| *to succor* | to render help | in times of distress |

The formal definition is implicit in most good defining essays. In this section, for example, Gilbert Highet defines *kitsch* by identifying it as a kind of art that is junky; Frank Deford tells us that *cystic fibrosis* is a disease of the lungs. Kitsch is placed in the general class of art, cystic fibrosis in the class of lung diseases. Both are then differentiated from other items in their respective classes—kitsch by its junkiness, cystic fibrosis by its lethal effect on the lungs.

Sometimes it is also useful to define a word by discussing its etymology. In the example below, science writer Isaac Asimov defines *botulism* by referring to its etymology:

Pride of place, however, must be taken by the product of a bacterium which is to be found everywhere and which harms no one—ordinarily. It is Clostridium botulinum. "Clostridium" is Latin for "little spindle," which describes its shape, and "botulinum" is from the Latin word *botulus*, which means "sausage," where it has sometimes been detected.

## 2. Expand the definition by description, example, or comparison/contrast.

In a defining essay more than a simple dictionary definition is required. Further explanation must be given to make the meaning of the term crystal-clear to the reader.

### (a) Description

The meanings of some words may be clarified or elaborated on by a description. In the example below, a student extends her definition of *milksop* with a rather detailed description:

A milksop is a boy or a man who lacks courage and manliness. Usually he is of small stature, with a voice that peeps and squeaks rather than roars. He speaks so timidly that people always ask, "What did you say?" or comment, "I beg your pardon." He is further distinguished by a rather limp and squishy handshake. He merely proffers five appendages dangling uselessly from a wrist. Moreover, the milksop prefers to cock his head and dart his eyes here and there rather than look another in the eye. Wherever you see him, he seems incapable of standing straight, and is either slumping like an understuffed pillow or sagging like a falling doorpost.

### (b) Example

Ambiguous or difficult terms can usually be clarified by examples. In his essay "Kitsch," Gilbert Highet expands on his definition by citing numerous examples of kitsch in art and literature. The following passage, written by a student, extends the definition of *deduction* by supplying an example:

Deduction is the process of drawing conclusions by reasoning from the general to the specific. Consider, for instance, the statement "Johnny cannot read because he was taught by the Montessori method." The reasoning proceeds from a vast generalization:

All children taught by the Montessori method are nonreaders.

Then the reasoning moves to a specific assertion:

Johnny was taught by the Montessori method.

And to a specific conclusion:

Therefore, Johnny cannot read.

The above equation, known as a syllogism, is the most common process of reasoning used in deductions.

### (c) Comparison/Contrast

Sometimes it is useful to define a term by contrasting it with what it is not, or by comparing the term to something similar. For instance, a Spanish poet once defined death as follows: "Death is like a black camel that kneels at the gates of all." This comparison was the poet's way of graphically defining death. But comparisons do not have to be so metaphorical or farfetched. On a plainer level, one might define a pharmacist by comparing/contrasting him or her to a cook. Here is an example of the use of contrast in furthering a definition. The writer, Carl Becker, has just asserted that *democracy* means "government by the people as opposed to government by a tyrant, a dictator, or an absolute monarch." He then proceeds to some contrasting examples:

> Peisistratus, for example, was supported by a majority of the people, but his government was never regarded as a democracy for all that. Caesar's power derived from a popular mandate, conveyed through established republican forms, but that did not make his government any the less a dictatorship. Napoleon called his government a democratic empire, but no one, least of all Napoleon himself, doubted that he had destroyed the last vestiges of the democratic empire. Since the Greeks first used the term, the essential test of democratic government has always been this: the source of political authority must be and remain in the people and not in the ruler.

All the instances cited by Becker help to make clear the definition of democracy by asserting what it is not.

As you write your defining essays, beware of the most common student error—the circular definition. To say that "taxation is the act of imposing taxes" is repetitious. Better to say "Taxation is the principle of levying fees to support basic government services." Examples and detail can then be provided until you have answered the question "What is it?"

## ══════ •• *EXAMPLES* •• ══════

#### John Henry Newman

## ────── • ON LIBERAL KNOWLEDGE • ──────

*John Henry Newman (1801–1890) was an English Catholic prelate and cardinal. His extraordinarily elegant and lucid style earned him a reputation as one of the most talented writers of Victorian England. His best-known works are*

The Idea of a University Defined *(1873) and* Apologia pro Vita Sua *(1864)*,
*his masterpiece.*

*The excerpt below is part of a series of lectures delivered at the Catholic Univer-*
*sity of Dublin in 1852. In this selection Newman gives a definition of liberal*
*knowledge that has influenced modern liberal education.*

Now bear with me, Gentlemen, if what I am about to say, has at first     1
sight a fanciful appearance. Philosophy, then, or Science, is related to
Knowledge in this way:—Knowledge is called by the name of Science
or Philosophy, when it is acted upon, informed, or if I may use a strong
figure, impregnated by Reason. Reason is the principle of that intrinsic
fecundity of Knowledge, which, to those who possess it, is its especial
value, and which dispenses with the necessity of their looking abroad
for any end to rest upon external to itself. Knowledge, indeed, when
thus exalted into a scientific form, is also power; not only is it excellent
in itself, but whatever such excellence may be, it is something more, it
has a result beyond itself. Doubtless; but that is a further consideration, with which I am not concerned. I only say that, prior to its being
a power, it is a good; that it is, not only an instrument, but an end. I
know well it may resolve itself into an art, and terminate in a mechanical process, and in tangible fruit; but it also may fall back upon that
Reason which informs it, and resolve itself into Philosophy. In one case
it is called Useful Knowledge, in the other Liberal. The same person
may cultivate it in both ways at once; but this again is a matter foreign
to my subject; here I do but say that there are two ways of using
Knowledge, and in matter of fact those who use it in one way are not
likely to use it in the other, or at least in a very limited measure. You
see, then, here are two methods of Education; the end of the one is to
be philosophical, of the other to be mechanical; the one rises towards
general ideas, the other is exhausted upon what is particular and external. Let me not be thought to deny the necessity, or to decry the
benefit, of such attention to what is particular and practical, as belongs
to the useful or mechanical arts; life could not go on without them; we
owe our daily welfare to them; their exercise is the duty of the many,
and we owe to the many a debt of gratitude for fulfilling that duty. I
only say that Knowledge, in proportion as it tends more and more to
be particular, ceases to be Knowledge. It is a question whether Knowledge can in any proper sense be predicated of the brute creation;
without pretending to metaphysical exactness of phraseology, which

would be unsuitable to an occasion like this, I say, it seems to me improper to call that passive sensation, or perception of things, which brutes seem to possess, by the name of Knowledge. When I speak of Knowledge, I mean something intellectual, something which grasps what it perceives through the senses; something which takes a view of things; which sees more than the senses convey; which reasons upon what it sees, and while it sees; which invests it with an idea. It expresses itself, not in a mere enunciation, but by an enthymeme:* It is of the nature of science from the first, and in this consists its dignity. The principle of real dignity in Knowledge, its worth, its desirableness, considered irrespectively of its results, is this germ within it of a scientific or a philosophical process. This is how it comes to be an end in itself; this is why it admits of being called Liberal. Not to know the relative disposition of things is the state of slaves or children; to have mapped out the Universe is the boast, or at least the ambition, of Philosophy.

Moreover, such knowledge is not a mere extrinsic or accidental advantage, which is ours to-day and another's to-morrow, which may be got up from a book, and easily forgotten again, which we can command or communicate at our pleasure, which we can borrow for the occasion, carry about in our hand, and take into the market; it is an acquired illumination, it is a habit, a personal possession, and an inward endowment. And this is the reason, why it is more correct, as well as more usual, to speak of a University as a place of education, than of instruction, though, when knowledge is concerned, instruction would at first sight have seemed the more appropriate word. We are instructed, for instance, in manual exercises, in the fine and useful arts, in trades, and in ways of business; for these are methods, which have little or no effect upon the mind itself, are contained in rules committed to memory, to tradition, or to use, and bear upon an end external to themselves. But education is a higher word; it implies an action upon our mental nature, and the formation of a character; it is something individual and permanent, and is commonly spoken of in connexion with religion and virtue. When, then, we speak of the communication of Knowledge as being Education, we thereby really imply that that Knowledge is a state or condition of mind; and since cultivation of mind is surely worth seeking for its own sake, we are thus

2

---

*Truncated syllogism in which one of the premises is understood but not stated.—Ed.

brought once more to the conclusion, which the word "Liberal" and the word "Philosophy" have already suggested, that there is a Knowledge, which is desirable, though nothing come of it, as being of itself a treasure, and a sufficient remuneration of years of labour.

## VOCABULARY

| | | |
|---|---|---|
| fanciful (1) | decry (1) | irrespectively (1) |
| impregnated (1) | predicated (1) | extrinsic (2) |
| intrinsic (1) | metaphysical (1) | illumination (2) |
| fecundity (1) | phraseology (1) | endowment (2) |
| instrument (1) | enunciation (1) | remuneration (2) |

## THE FACTS

1. Newman begins his definition of liberal knowledge (or philosophy) by stating that this kind of knowledge must be impregnated. By what must it be impregnated? Explain this metaphor.
2. Newman helps to define liberal knowledge by stating what it is not. What knowledge does he exclude from liberal knowledge?
3. What is Newman's definition of liberal knowledge? In what way does it differ from the other kind of knowledge described?
4. Name three or four courses offered at your college and classify them under one or the other kind of knowledge.
5. According to Newman, why is it more proper to refer to a university as a place of education than of instruction? Do you agree with his view? Comment.

## THE STRATEGIES

1. Most students consider Newman's style of writing difficult to follow. Can you offer any reasons for this view?
2. What techniques, if any, allow you to follow Newman's train of argument? Point out specific ones if they exist.
3. What is Newman's purpose in alluding to the way animals perceive? Does this allusion break the unity of the paragraph? Explain why or why not.
4. Can you point out parallelism and balance in paragraph 1?

## THE ISSUES

1. What examples from modern life can you give to support Newman's point that "knowledge is power"? Do you believe that having knowledge also requires certain responsibilities? Why or why not?

2. Today, when so much of life depends on what Newman labels "useful knowledge," should a college system still require a certain number of courses in the liberal arts? For instance, should students studying for professions that take years to complete (medicine, engineering, law, architecture, computer science, business management), waste college units on such courses as philosophy, literature, history, or art appreciation? Why or why not?
3. What personal acquaintance of yours would you call truly educated, as defined by Newman? Describe this person. Does this person's lifestyle appeal to you? Why or why not?
5. Newman believes that liberal knowledge is knowledge for knowledge's sake. What would a similar attitude be toward the fine arts?
5. If you were to argue against liberal knowledge for its own sake, what would you say?

### SUGGESTIONS FOR WRITING

1. Write a paragraph in which you define "useful knowledge" according to your own understanding.
2. Write a five-hundred-word essay in which you argue the advantages of a "useful" education over a "liberal" one.

**Gilbert Highet**

## • KITSCH •

*Gilbert Highet (1906–1978) was born in Glasgow, Scotland, educated at the University of Glasgow and at Oxford, and became a naturalized American citizen in 1951. A classicist, Highet was known for his scholarly and critical writing, including* The Classical Tradition *(1949) and* The Anatomy of Satire *(1962).*

*You probably have had some experience with* kitsch *even if you do not know what the word means. You may have friends or relatives whose furniture, curios, or even favorite books are clearly kitschy. Gilbert Highet draws mainly on literary examples to define* kitsch*; but as you shall see, the concept applies to nearly all matters of bad taste.*

If you have ever passed an hour wandering through an antique shop (not looking for anything exactly, but simply looking), you must have noticed how your taste gradually grows numb, and then—if you

1

stay—becomes perverted. You begin to see unsuspected charm in those hideous pictures of plump girls fondling pigeons, you develop a psychopathic desire for spinning wheels and cobblers' benches, you are apt to pay out good money for a bronze statuette of Otto von Bismarck, with a metal hand inside a metal frock coat and metal pouches under his metallic eyes. As soon as you take the things home, you realize that they are revolting. And yet they have a sort of horrible authority; you don't like them; you know how awful they are; but it is a tremendous effort to drop them in the garbage, where they belong.

To walk along a whole street of antique shops—that is an experience    2
which shakes the very soul. Here is a window full of bulbous Chinese deities; here is another littered with Zulu assagais, Indian canoe paddles, and horse pistols which won't fire; the next shopfront is stuffed with gaudy Italian majolica vases, and the next, even worse, with Austrian pottery—tiny ladies and gentlemen sitting on lace cushions and wearing lace ruffles, with every frill, every wrinkle and reticulation translated into porcelain: pink; stiff; but fortunately not unbreakable. The nineteenth century produced an appalling amount of junky art like this, and sometimes I imagine that clandestine underground factories are continuing to pour it out like illicit drugs.

There is a name for such stuff in the trade, a word apparently of    3
Russian origin, kitsch:* it means vulgar showoff, and it is applied to anything that took a lot of trouble to make and is quite hideous.

It is paradoxical stuff, kitsch. It is obviously bad: so bad that you can    4
scarcely understand how any human being would spend days and weeks making it, and how anybody else would buy it and take it home and keep it and dust it and leave it to her heirs. It is terribly ingenious, and terribly ugly, and utterly useless; and yet it has one of the qualities of good art—which is that, once seen, it is not easily forgotten. Of course it is found in all the arts: think of Milan Cathedral, or the statues in Westminster Abbey, or Liszt's settings of Schubert songs. There is a lot of it in the United States—for instance, the architecture of Miami, Florida, and Forest Lawn Cemetery in Los Angeles. Many of Hollywood's most ambitious historical films are superb kitsch. Most Tin Pan Alley love songs are perfect 100 per cent kitsch.

---

*The Russian verb *keetcheetsya* means 'to be haughty and puffed up.'

There is kitsch in the world of books also. I collect it. It is horrible,    5
but I enjoy it.

The gem of my collection is the work of the Irish novelist Mrs.    6
Amanda McKittrick Ros, whose masterpiece, *Delina Delaney*, was published about 1900. It is a stirringly romantic tale, telling how Delina, a
fisherman's daughter from Erin Cottage, was beloved by Lord Gifford,
the heir of Columbia Castle, and—after many trials and even imprisonment—married him. The story is dramatic, not to say impossible;
but it is almost lost to view under the luxuriant style. Here, for example, is a sentence in which Mrs. Ros explains that her heroine used to
earn extra cash by doing needlework.

> She tried hard to assist in keeping herself a stranger to her poor old
> father's slight income by the use of the finest production of steel, whose
> blunt edge eyed the reely covering with marked greed, and offered its
> sharp dart to faultless fabrics of flaxen fineness.

Revolting, but distinctive: what Mr. Polly called 'rockockyo' in manner.
For the baroque vein, here is Lord Gifford saying goodby to his sweetheart:

> My darling virgin! my queen! my Delina! I am just in time to hear the
> toll of a parting bell strike its heavy weight of appalling softness against
> the weakest fibers of a heart of love, arousing and tickling its dormant
> action, thrusting the dart of evident separation deeper into its tubes of
> tenderness, and fanning the flame, already unextinguishable, into vol-
> umes of blaze.

Mrs. Ros had a remarkable command of rhetoric, and could coin an
unforgettable phrase. She described her hero's black eyes as 'glittering
jet revolvers.' When he became ill, she said he fell 'into a state of lofty
fever'—doubtless because commoners have high fever, but lords have
lofty fever. And her reflections on the moral degeneracy of society have
rarely been equaled, in power and penetration:

> Days of humanity, whither hast thou fled? When bows of compulsion,
> smiles for the deceitful, handshakes for the dogmatic, and welcome for
> the tool of power live under your objectionable, unambitious beat, not
> daring to be checked by the tongue of candour because the selfish world
> refuses to dispense with her rotten policies. The legacy of your fore-
> fathers, which involved equity, charity, reason, and godliness, is beyond
> the reach of their frivolous, mushroom offspring—deceit, injustice, mal-

ice and unkindness—and is not likely to be codiciled with traits of harmony so long as these degrading vices of mock ambition fester the
human heart.

Perhaps one reason I enjoy this stuff is because it so closely resembles
a typical undergraduate translation of one of Cicero's finest perora-
tions: sound and fury, signifying nothing. I regret only that I have
never seen Mrs. Ros's poetry. One volume was called *Poems of Puncture*
and another *Bayonets of Bastard Sheen:* alas, jewels now almost unpro-
curable. But at least I know the opening of her lyric written on first
visiting St. Paul's Cathedral:

> Holy Moses, take a look,
> Brain and brawn in every nook!

Such genius is indestructible. Soon, soon now, some earnest re-    7
searcher will be writing a Ph.D. thesis on Mrs. Amanda McKittrick
Ros, and thus (as she herself might put it) conferring upon her dewy
brow the laurels of concrete immortality.

Next to Mrs. Ros in my collection of kitsch is the work of the Scottish    8
poet William McGonagall. This genius was born in 1830, but did not
find his vocation until 1877. Poor and inadequate poets pullulate
in every tongue, but (as the *Times Literary Supplement* observes)
McGonagall 'is the only truly memorable bad poet in our language.' In
his command of platitude and his disregard of melody, he was the true
heir of William Wordsworth as a descriptive poet.

In one way his talents, or at least his aspirations, exceeded those of    9
Wordsworth. He was at his best in describing events he had never
witnessed, such as train disasters, shipwrecks, and sanguinary battles, and in picturing magnificent scenery he had never beheld except with the eye of the imagination. Here is his unforgettable Arctic
landscape:

> Greenland's icy mountains are fascinating and grand,
> And wondrously created by the Almighty's command;
> And the works of the Almighty there's few can understand:
> Who knows but it might be a part of Fairyland?
>
> Because there are churches of ice, and houses glittering like glass,
> And for scenic grandeur there's nothing can it surpass,
> Besides there's monuments and spires, also ruins,
> Which serve for a safe retreat from the wild bruins.

The icy mountains they're higher than a brig's topmast,
And the stranger in amazement stands aghast
As he beholds the water flowing off the melted ice
Adown the mountain sides, that he cries out, Oh! how nice!

McGonagall also had a strong dramatic sense. He loved to tell of    10
agonizing adventures, more drastic perhaps but not less moving than
that related in Wordsworth's 'Vaudracour and Julia.' The happy ending
of one of his 'Gothic' ballads is surely unforgettable:

So thus ends the story of Hanchen, a heroine brave,
That tried hard her master's gold to save,
And for her bravery she got married to the miller's eldest son,
And Hanchen on her marriage night cried Heaven's will be done.

These scanty selections do not do justice to McGonagall's ingenuity    11
as a rhymester. His sound effects show unusual talent. Most poets
would be baffled by the problem of producing rhymes for the proper
names *General Graham* and *Osman Digna,* but McGonagall gets them
into a single stanza, with dazzling effect:

Ye sons of Great Britain, I think no shame
To write in praise of brave General Graham!
Whose name will be handed down to posterity without any stigma,
Because, at the battle of El-Tab, he defeated Osman Digna.

One of McGonagall's most intense personal experiences was his    12
visit to New York. Financially, it was not a success. In one of his vivid
autobiographical sketches, he says, 'I tried occasionally to get an engagement from theatrical proprietors and music-hall proprietors, but
alas! 'twas all in vain, for they all told me they didn't encourage rivalry.'
However, he was deeply impressed by the architecture of Manhattan.
In eloquent verses he expressed what many others have felt, although
without adequate words to voice their emotion:

Oh! Mighty City of New York, you are wonderful to behold,
Your buildings are magnificent, the truth be it told;
They were the only thing that seemed to arrest my eye,
Because many of them are thirteen stories high.

> And the tops of the houses are all flat,
> And in the warm weather the people gather to chat;
> Besides on the house-tops they dry their clothes,
> And also many people all night on the house-tops repose.

Yet McGonagall felt himself a stranger in the United States. And here again his close kinship with Wordsworth appears. The Poet Laureate, in a powerful sonnet written at Calais, once reproached the English Channel for delaying his return by one of those too frequent storms in which (reckless tyrant!) it will indulge itself:    13

> Why cast ye back upon the Gallic shore,
> Ye furious waves! a patriotic Son
> Of England?

In the same vein McGonagall sings with rapture of his return to his 'ain countree':    14

> And with regard to New York, and the sights I did see,
> One street in Dundee is more worth to me,
> And, believe me, the morning I sailed from New York,
> For bonnie Dundee—my heart it felt as light as a cork.

Indeed, New York is a challenging subject for ambitious poets. Here, from the same shelf, is a delicious poem on the same theme, by Ezra Pound:    15

> My City, my beloved
> Thou art a maid with no breasts
> Thou art slender as a silver reed.
> Listen to me, attend me!
> And I will breathe into thee a soul,
> And thou shalt live for ever.

The essence of this kind of trash is incongruity. The kitsch writer is always sincere. He really means to say something important. He feels he has a lofty spiritual message to bring to an unawakened world, or else he has had a powerful experience which he must communicate to the public. But either his message turns out to be a majestic platitude, or else he chooses the wrong form in which to convey it—or, most delightful of all, there is a fundamental discrepancy between the writer and his subject, as when Ezra Pound, born in Idaho, addresses the largest city in the world as a maid with no breasts, and enjoins it to    16 achieve inspiration and immortality by listening to him. This is like climbing Mount Everest in order to carve a head of Mickey Mouse in the east face.

Bad love poetry, bad religious poetry, bad mystical prose, bad novels    17 both autobiographical and historical—one can form a superb collection of kitsch simply by reading with a lively and awakened eye. College songs bristle with it. The works of Father Divine* are full of it—all the more delightful because in him it is usually incomprehensible. One of the Indian mystics, Sri Ramakrishna, charmed connoisseurs by describing the Indian scriptures (in a phrase which almost sets itself to kitsch-music) as

> fried in the butter of knowledge and steeped in the honey of love.

Bad funeral poetry is a rich mine of the stuff. Here, for example, is the opening of a jolly little lament, 'The Funeral' by Stephen Spender, apparently written during his pink period:

> Death is another milestone on their way,
> With laughter on their lips and with winds blowing round them
> They record simply
> How this one excelled all others in making driving belts.

Observe the change from humanism to communism. Spender simply took Browning's 'Grammarian's Funeral,' threw away the humor and the marching rhythm, and substituted wind and the Stakhanovist† speed-up. Such also is a delicious couplet from Archibald MacLeish's elegy on the late Harry Crosby:

> He walks with Ernest in the streets in Saragossa
> They are drunk their mouths are hard they saw *qué cosa*.

From an earlier romantic period, here is a splendid specimen. Col-    18 eridge attempted to express the profound truth that men and animals are neighbors in a hard world; but he made the fundamental mistake of putting it into a monologue address to a donkey:

> Poor Ass! Thy master should have learnt to show
> Pity—best taught by fellowship of Woe!
> Innocent foal! thou poor despised forlorn!
> I hail thee brother. . . .

---

*A black evangelist of New York.—Ed.

†Alexei Stakhanov, a Russian miner who devised a worker incentive system.—Ed.

Once you get the taste for this kind of thing it is possible to find    19
pleasure in hundreds of experiences which you might otherwise have
thought either anesthetic or tedious: bad translations, abstract painting, grand opera . . . Dr. Johnson, with his strong sense of humor,
had a fancy for kitsch, and used to repeat a poem in celebration of
the marriage of the Duke of Leeds, composed by 'an inferiour dome-
stick . . . in such homely rhimes as he could make':

> When the Duke of Leeds shall married be
> To a fine young lady of high quality,
> How happy will that gentlewoman be
> In his Grace of Leed's good company.
>
> She shall have all that's fine and fair,
> And the best of silk and sattin shall wear;
> And ride in a coach to take the air,
> And have a house in St. James's Square.

Folk poetry is full of such jewels. Here is the epitaph on an old    20
gentleman from Vermont who died in a sawmill accident:

> How shocking to the human mind
> The log did him to powder grind.
> God did command his soul away
> His summings we must all obey.

Kitsch is well known in drama, although (except for motion pictures)    21
it does not usually last long. One palmary instance was a play extolling
the virtues of the Boy Scout movement, called *Young England*. It ran for
a matter of years during the 1930's, to audiences almost wholly composed of kitsch-fanciers, who eventually came to know the text quite
as well as the unfortunate actors. I can still remember the opening of
one magnificent episode. Scene: a woodland glade. Enter the hero, a
Scoutmaster, riding a bicycle, and followed by the youthful members
of his troop. They pile bicycles in silence. Then the Scoutmaster raises
his finger, and says (accompanied fortissimo by most of the members
of the audience):

> Fresh water must be our first consideration

In the decorative arts kitsch flourishes, and is particularly wide-    22
spread in sculpture. One of my favorite pieces of bad art is a statue in
Rockefeller Center, New York. It is supposed to represent Atlas, the
Titan condemned to carry the sky on his shoulders. That is an ideal of

somber, massive tragedy: greatness and suffering combined as in Hercules or Prometheus. But this version displays Atlas as a powerful moron, with a tiny little head, rather like the pan-fried young men who appear in the health magazines. Instead of supporting the heavens, he is lifting a spherical metal balloon: it is transparent, and quite empty; yet he is balancing insecurely on one foot like a furniture mover walking upstairs with a beach ball; and he is scowling like a mad baboon. If he ever gets the thing up, he will drop it; or else heave it onto a Fifth Avenue bus. It is a supremely ridiculous statue, and delights me every time I see it.

Perhaps you think this is a depraved taste. But really it is an extension of experience. At one end, Homer. At the other, Amanda McKittrick Ros. At one end, *Hamlet*. At the other, McGonagall, who is best praised in his own inimitable words:    23

> The poetry is moral and sublime
> And in my opinion nothing could be more fine.
> True genius there does shine so bright
> Like unto the stars of night.

## VOCABULARY

| | | |
|---|---|---|
| psychopathic (1) | ingenious (4) | mystical (17) |
| frock coat (1) | luxuriant (6) | incomprehensible (17) |
| bulbous (2) | perorations (6) | connoisseurs (17) |
| Zulu (2) | unprocurable (6) | anesthetic (19) |
| assagais (2) | pullulate (8) | palmary (21) |
| majolica (2) | platitude (8) | extolling (21) |
| reticulation (2) | sanguinary (9) | fortissimo (21) |
| appalling (2) | rapture (14) | spherical (22) |
| illicit (2) | incongruity (16) | depraved (23) |
| paradoxical (4) | enjoins (16) | inimitable (23) |

## THE FACTS

1. Where in his essay does Highet give a succinct definition of *kitsch*? After reading the essay, how would you explain this term to a friend who has never heard it?
2. What examples of kitsch does Highet provide? Name the three that impressed you most. Give reasons for your choice.

3. What metaphor does Mrs. Ros use to describe her hero's black eyes? Provide a metaphor or simile that would not be kitsch.
4. What characteristics of William McGonagall's poetry make it kitsch? Give a brief critique of two or three excerpts reprinted by Highet.
5. What is the essence of *kitsch*, according to the author? In what paragraph is this essence revealed?

## THE STRATEGIES

1. What is the predominant tone of the essay? Supply appropriate examples of this tone.
2. Point out some examples of striking figurative language in the essay. Are they serious or humorous?
3. What mode of development does Highet use more than any other? How does this method help his definition?
4. In the final paragraph, what is the irony of using McGonagall's own words to praise him?

## THE ISSUES

1. Can you think of some well-known examples of kitsch in the United States, not cited by Highet? What makes them kitsch?
2. Highet admits that certain kitsch items delight him. Explain how a person of taste might feel such delight.
3. How do you explain the overwhelming popularity of kitsch?
4. Popular lyrics are always a good source of kitsch. What lines from one of today's well-known songs can you quote as an example of kitsch? Do you still like the song despite the fact that it is kitsch? Give reasons for your answer.
5. Following are excerpts from two different love poems (A and B). Which of them might be considered kitsch? Why?

A.

The time was long and long ago,
　　And we were young, my dear;
The place stands fair in memory's glow,
　　But it is far from here.

The springtimes fade, the summers come,
　　Autumn is here once more;
The voice of ecstasy is dumb,
　　The world goes forth to war.

But though the flowers and birds were dead,
　　And all the hours we knew,
And though a hundred years had fled,
　　I'd still come back to you.

B.

Ah, love, let us be true
To one another! for the world, which seems
To lie before us like a land of dreams,
So various, so beautiful, so new,
Hath really neither joy, nor love, nor light,
Nor certitude, nor peace, nor help for pain;
And we are here as on a darkling plain
Swept with confused alarms of struggle and flight,
Where ignorant armies clash by night.

### SUGGESTIONS FOR WRITING

1. Using Gilbert Highet's definition of *kitsch*, choose one area of popular taste today and show how it fits the definition.
2. Write a paragraph in which you compare or contrast the meaning of *camp* with that of *kitsch*.

**Frank Deford**

———————————— • **CYSTIC FIBROSIS** • ————————————

*Journalist and author Frank Deford (b. 1938) was born in Baltimore and edu-*
*cated at Princeton University. Since 1962 he has been a senior writer for* Sports
Illustrated. *He is also a commentator on sports for radio and television. Among*
*his many published books are* There She Is: The Life and Times of Miss
America *(1971),* The Owner *(1976), and* Alex: The Life of a Child *(1983), a*
*tribute to his daughter who died of cystic fibrosis. Deford is vice-president of the*
*Cystic Fibrosis Foundation.*

*Alexandra Deford, daughter of Frank and Carol Deford, was born in 1971 with*
*the grim genetic inheritance of cystic fibrosis. Eight years later she was dead.*
*This excerpt, taken from her grieving father's loving and moving account of his*
*daughter's brief life, defines this deadly disease by describing its symptoms and*
*showing the brutal and primitive treatment its victims must suffer daily to*
*breathe.*

Cystic fibrosis is, notwithstanding its name, a disease primarily of   1
the lungs. It has nothing to do with cysts. It was not identified as a
distinct clinical entity until the midthirties, and not until some years
later was the full pathology comprehended. Inexplicably, the disease
attacks not only the lungs but other disparate parts of the body: the

pancreas, the major digestive organ; and, in males, the testes. So it undermines breathing, eating, reproduction—all of life itself.

The common agent in all cases is mucus. The cystic fibrosis victim's    2
body manufactures too much mucus, or the mucus is too thick, or both. So baffling is the disease that nobody knows for sure which basic factor is the issue. Whatever, the mucus obstructs the airflow in the lungs and clogs the pancreas and the testes. Adding to the perplexity is the fact that no two patients have the same history, except in the sense that CF is always progressive, always terminal.

The luckiest patients are those born without lung involvement. Oth-    3
ers have such mild cases that they go undetected for years; quite possibly there are even some CF patients who never know they have the disease, but die relatively young of some misunderstood pulmonary involvement. At the other end of the spectrum, some infants are essentially born dead, their tiny bodies so ravaged by the disease that they cannot even begin to draw breath.

As events proved, Alex was toward the worse end of the spectrum.    4
While she died at eight, half of the children now born in the United States with cystic fibrosis who are diagnosed and treated live to the age of eighteen. Be grateful for small favors. Back in the midfifties, when the Cystic Fibrosis Foundation was started, a child with CF could not even expect to live to kindergarten. Regrettably, early steady advances stopped just about the time Alex was born. Until the early seventies almost every passing year saw another year of life expectancy added for a CF kid, but these advances were somewhat illusory. They were largely prophylactic, stemming almost entirely from better maintenance and more powerful antibiotics. The longer life span in no way indicated an approaching cure, nor even a control (as, for example, insulin keeps diabetes under control). In a sense, it isn't accurate to say that we kept Alex alive—we merely postponed her dying.

Alex's day would start with an inhalation treatment that took several    5
minutes. This was a powerful decongestant mist that she drew in from an inhaler to loosen the mucus that had settled in her lungs. Then, for a half hour or more, we would give her postural drainage treatment to accomplish the same ends physically. It is quite primitive, really, but all we had, the most effective weapon against the disease. Alex had to endure eleven different positions, each corresponding to a section of the lung, and Carol or I would pound away at her, thumping her chest, her back, her sides, palms cupped to better "catch" the mucus. Then,

after each position, we would press hard about the lungs with our fingers, rolling them as we pushed on her in ways that were often more uncomfortable than the pounding.

Some positions Alex could do sitting up, others lying flat on our     6
laps. But a full four of the eleven she had to endure nearly upside down, the blood rushing to her head, as I banged away on her little chest, pounding her, rattling her, trying somehow to shake loose that vile mucus that was trying to take her life away. One of her first full sentences was, "No, not the down ones now, Daddy."

Psychologists have found that almost any child with a chronic dis-     7
ease assumes that the illness is a punishment. Soon, the treatment itself blurs with the disease and becomes more punishment. Sick children have highly ambivalent feelings about their doctors, on the one hand hating them for the pain and suffering they inflict, on the other admiring them, wanting to grow up and be doctors. Wendy Braun and Aimee Spengler, Alex's best friends, told me after Alex died that whenever the three of them played doctors and nurses, Alex participated with enthusiasm, but when she played the doctor, it was always cancer she was seeking to cure. She could not bring herself to be a cystic fibrosis doctor. As much as she adored and trusted her specialist, Tom Dolan, she must have associated too much pain with him ever to want to *be* him.

In cystic fibrosis a child must transfer this attitude toward the par-     8
ents, as well, for we were intimately and daily involved in the medical process. Imagine, if you will, that every day of your child's life you forced medicines upon her, although they never seemed to do any good; you required her to participate in uncomfortable regimens, which you supervised; and then, for thirty minutes or more, twice a day, you turned her upside down and pounded on her. And this never seemed to help either. I have been told that parents let their self-conscious resentment of the illness surface during the treatments, and I must face the fact that this was sometimes surely true of me too. In some moments I must have thought that I was also being punished.

And say what you will, explain to me intellectually all you want     9
about how much the postural drainage helped Alex—still, when every day I had to thump my little girl, pound away on her body, sometimes when she was pleading with me, crying out in pain to stop, something came over me, changed me. I guess, over eight years, I did therapy two thousand times, and Carol many more, probably three thousand,

having to manage both times each day when I was traveling. I never understood how she managed. But still, me: Two thousand times I had to beat my sick child, make her hurt and cry and plead—"No, not the down ones, Daddy"—and in the end, for what?

After the therapy was finished, we had to start on the medicines. I    10 recall how exciting it was during one period—Alex was two and a half—when she *only* had to take one antibiotic. How glorious that was, just one antibiotic every day. Usually it was two, and Dr. Dolan had to keep changing them, as Alex's body built up immunities.

She had to take many other medications, too, including, relentlessly,    11 an enzyme preparation named Viokase. The bulk of Viokase is animal enzyme, which Alex needed because her pancreas couldn't produce sufficient enzymes of its own. Relative to the medicines that dealt primarily with her lung problems, Viokase was pretty effective. The minority of CF patients who don't have lung involvement initially can get by with the pancreas problem as long as they diligently take their enzyme substitutes. Alex had to take Viokase every time she ate anything. Of course, considering her lung condition, this seemed like small potatoes. Carol and I didn't even think about it much.

For most of her life, before she learned to swallow pills, Alex took    12 the Viokase as a powder, mixed into apple sauce, which was an inexpensive carrying agent that could transport the drug into the system without its breaking down. And so, before every meal she ever ate, Alex had a plate of apple sauce with the enzyme powder mixed in. It was foul-tasting stuff, a bitter ordeal to endure at every meal. "Oh, my appasaws," she would moan, "my appasaws," always pronouncing it as if it were a cousin to chain saws or buzz saws.

"Come on Alex, eat your Viokase," I would say, and rather impa-    13 tiently, too. After all, she had already been through an inhalation treatment, a half hour of physical therapy, several liquid medications— so what was the big deal with the apple sauce. *Come on, let's go.* Alex had had a great appetite when she was younger, but a few years later she'd just pick at her food. It occurred to me then that if all your life eating was a project, and you couldn't eat a lot of the delicious things everybody else enjoyed, eventually eating would bore you. Imagine having to start off with apple sauce every time you ate anything—and not getting much sympathy for it, either.

Later, doctors and nurses or other people would say, "Alex seems to    14 have lost her appetite," and I would nod gravely, being pretty sure by then that it was psychological. Eating, like everything else for Alex, had become strictly a matter of staying alive.

When she was very young, before she began to comprehend how   15
pointless it all was, Alex was wonderfully accepting of all that was demanded of her. At first, like any baby, she wasn't in any position to quibble; she just seemed to go along, assuming that inhalation, apple sauce, and all that were things all babies endured. When she played with her dolls, she would give them therapy, putting off the down ones if the dolls behaved. After a time Alex began to notice that her brother was not required to endure what she did every day, but that didn't bother her too much either. Since she was the only baby girl around, she simply assumed that therapy was something that all babies and/or all girls must go through.

Only slowly did the recognition come that she was singled out for   16
these things. Then she began to grope for the implications. One spring day when she was four, Alex came into my office and said she had a question. Just one was all she would bother me with. All right, I asked, what was it. And Alex said, "I won't have to do therapy when I'm a lady, will I?"

It was a leading question; she knew exactly where she was tak-   17
ing me.

As directly as I could I said, "No, Alex"—not because I would lie   18
outright about it, but because I knew the score by then. I knew that she would not grow up to be a lady unless a cure was found.

## VOCABULARY

| | | |
|---|---|---|
| disparate (1) | prophylactic (4) | regimens (8) |
| illusory (4) | ambivalent (7) | |

## THE FACTS

1. What is cystic fibrosis? What parts of the organ system does it attack?
2. What is the life expectancy of half the children now born in the United States with cystic fibrosis?
3. What is the attitude of children born with chronic diseases toward the doctors who treat them?
4. What kinds of treatment was Deford's daughter forced to suffer many years before she died in the end at age eight?
5. What question that Alex asked her father indicates that she was searching for the long-term implications of her disease?

## THE STRATEGIES

1. Most definitions place the term to be defined in a certain class and then distinguish it from all others within that class. How and where does Deford use this technique?
2. Examine the first five paragraphs of this excerpt. What logical sequence does Deford follow in his order of topics?
3. What does the description of Alex's daily treatment add to your understanding of *cystic fibrosis*?
4. Deford repeatedly addresses the reader as "you." What effect does this have on you?

## THE ISSUES

1. Do you agree with those who say that babies diagnosed in the womb as suffering from a terminal disease such as cystic fibrosis should be aborted? Why or why not?
2. How should parents treat children who suffer from painful diseases? Should they treat them as they would any other child? Should they give them extra sympathy? Should they be more protective?
3. What personal experience have you had with a young person suffering from some terminal disease or some incurable handicap? Describe the quality of life led by this person.
4. What more, if anything, should be done by our government or society to help families with offspring like the little girl described?
5. Why is it that children tend to think of chronic diseases as punishment?

## SUGGESTIONS FOR WRITING

1. Recently, a child born with Down syndrome was not fed and allowed to die. This famous case of "Baby Doe" raised the issue of whether children born with terminal or incapacitating illnesses should be given any treatment necessary to keep them alive. Write an essay expressing your views on this issue.
2. Write an essay defining the common cold, explaining its effects on you.

### Gordon E. Bigelow

# —— • A PRIMER OF EXISTENTIALISM • ——

*Gordon E. Bigelow (b. 1919) is emeritus professor of American literature at the University of Florida. Among his publications are* Rhetoric and American Poetry of the Early National Period *(1960) and* Frontier Eden: The Literary Career of Majorie Kinnan Rawlings *(1966).*

*Possibly no modern philosophical term is murkier than* existentialism, *which has been applied to authors and thinkers of vastly different stripes. It has been claimed by Christians and atheists, communists and capitalists, optimists and profound pessimists. In many departments of philosophy, existentialism is today as orthodox as any of the "isms" of earlier centuries. But what does it mean? With this lucid exposition, author Bigelow tells us.*

For some years I fought the word by irritably looking the other way    1
whenever I stumbled across it, hoping that like dadaism and some of
the other "isms" of the French *avant garde* it would go away if I ignored
it. But existentialism was apparently more than the picture it evoked
of uncombed beards, smoky basement cafes, and French beatniks re-
galing one another between sips of absinthe with brilliant variations
on the theme of despair. It turned out to be of major importance to
literature and the arts, to philosophy and theology, and of increasing
importance to the social sciences. To learn more about it, I read several
of the self-styled introductions to the subject, with the baffled sensation of a man who reads a critical introduction to a novel only to find
that he must read the novel before he can understand the introduction.
Therefore, I should like to provide here something most discussions of
existentialism take for granted, a simple statement of its basic characteristics. This is a reckless thing to do because there are several kinds
of existentialism and what one says of one kind may not be true of
another, but there is an area of agreement, and it is this common
ground that I should like to set forth here. We should not run into
trouble so long as we understand from the outset that the six major
themes outlined below will apply in varying degrees to particular existentialists. A reader should be able to go from here to the existentialists themselves, to the more specialized critiques of them, or be able to
recognize an existentialist theme or coloration in literature when he
sees it.

A word first about the kinds of existentialism. Like transcendental-    2
ism of the last century, there are almost as many varieties of this *ism*
as there are individual writers to whom the word is applied (not all of
them claim it). But without being facetious we might group them into
two main kinds, the *ungodly* and the *godly*. To take the ungodly or
atheistic first, we would list as the chief spokesmen among many others Jean-Paul Sartre, Albert Camus, and Simone de Beauvoir. Several
of this important group of French writers had rigorous and significant
experience in the Resistance during the Nazi occupation of France in

World War II. Out of the despair which came with the collapse of their nation during those terrible years they found unexpected strength in the single indomitable human spirit, which even under severe torture could maintain the spirit of resistance, the unextinguishable ability to say "No." From this irreducible core in the human spirit, they erected after the war a philosophy which was a twentieth-century variation of the philosophy of Descartes. But instead of saying "I think, therefore I am," they said "I can say No, therefore I exist." As we shall presently see, the use of the word "exist" is of prime significance. This group is chiefly responsible for giving existentialism its status in the popular mind as a literary-philosophical cult.

Of the godly or theistic existentialists we should mention first a mid-nineteenth-century Danish writer, Søren Kierkegaard; two contemporary French Roman Catholics, Gabriel Marcel and Jacques Maritain; two Protestant theologians, Paul Tillich and Nicholas Berdyaev; and Martin Buber, an important contemporary Jewish theologian. Taken together, their writings constitute one of the most significant developments in modern theology. Behind both groups of existentialists stand other important figures, chiefly philosophers, who exert powerful influence upon the movement— Blaise Pascal, Friedrich Nietzsche, Henri Bergson, Martin Heidegger, Karl Jaspers, among others. Several literary figures, notably Tolstoy and Dostoievsky, are frequently cited because existentialist attitudes and themes are prominent in their writings. The eclectic nature of this movement should already be sufficiently clear and the danger of applying too rigidly to any particular figure the general characteristics of the movement which I now make bold to describe:

1. *Existence before essence.* Existentialism gets its name from an insistence that human life is understandable only in terms of an individual man's existence, his particular experience of life. It says that a man *lives* (has existence) rather than *is* (has being or essence), and that every man's experience of life is unique, radically different from everyone else's and can be understood truly only in terms of his involvement in life or commitment to it. It strenuously shuns that view which assumes an ideal of Man or Mankind, a universal of human nature of which each man is only one example. It eschews the question of Greek philosophy, *"What is mankind?"* which suggests that man can be defined if he is ranged in his proper place in the order of nature; it asks instead the question of Job and St. Augustine, *"Who am I?"* with its suggestion

of the uniqueness and mystery of each human life and its emphasis upon the subjective or personal rather than the objective or impersonal. From the outside a man appears to be just another natural creature; from the inside he is an entire universe, the center of infinity. The existentialist insists upon this latter radically subjective view, and from this grows much of the rest of existentialism.

2. *Reason is impotent to deal with the depths of human life.* There are 5 two parts to this proposition—first, that human reason is relatively weak and imperfect, and second, that there are dark places in human life which are "nonreason" and to which reason scarcely penetrates. Since Plato, Western civilization has usually assumed a separation of reason from the rest of the human psyche, and has glorified reason as suited to command the nonrational part. The classic statement of this separation appears in the *Phaedrus*, where Plato describes the psyche in the myth of the chariot which is drawn by the white steeds of the emotions and the black unruly steeds of the appetites. The driver of the chariot is Reason who holds the reins which control the horses and the whip to subdue the surging black steeds of passion. Only the driver, the rational nature, is given human form; the rest of the psyche, the nonrational part, is given a lower, animal form. This separation and exaltation of reason is carried further in the allegory of the cave in the *Republic*. You recall the sombre picture of human life with which the story begins: men are chained in the dark in a cave, with their backs to a flickering firelight, able to see only uncertain shadows moving on the wall before them, able to hear only confused echoes of sounds. One of the men, breaking free from his chains, is able to turn and look upon the objects themselves and the light which casts the shadows; even, at last, he is able to work his way entirely out of the cave into the sunlight beyond. All this he is able to do through his reason; he escapes from the bondage of error, from time and change, from death itself, into the realm of changeless eternal ideas or Truth, and the lower nature which had chained him in darkness is left behind.

Existentialism in our time, and this is one of its most important 6 characteristics, insists upon reuniting the "lower" or irrational parts of the psyche with the "higher." It insists that man must be taken in his wholeness and not in some divided state, that whole man contains not only intellect but also anxiety, guilt, and the will to power—which modify and sometimes overwhelm the reason. A man seen in this light is fundamentally ambiguous, if not mysterious, full of contradictions and tensions which cannot be dissolved simply by taking thought. "Human life," said Berdyaev, "is permeated by underground streams." One is reminded of D. H. Lawrence's outburst against Franklin and his rational attempt to achieve moral perfection: "The Perfectability of Man! . . . The perfectability of which man? I am many men. Which of them are you going to perfect? I am not a mechanical contrivance. . . . It's a queer thing is a man's soul. It is the whole of him. Which means it is the unknown as well as the known. . . . The soul of man is a dark vast forest, with wild life in it." The emphasis in existentialism is not on idea but upon the thinker who has the idea. It accepts not only his power of thought, but his contingency and fallibility, his frailty, his body, blood, and bones, and above all his death. Kierkegaard emphasized the distinction between *subjective* truth (what a person *is*) and *objective* truth (what the person *knows*), and said that we encounter the true self not in the detachment of thought but in the involvement and agony of choice and in the pathos of commitment to our choice. This distrust of rational systems helps to explain why many existential writers in their own expression are paradoxical or prophetic or gnomic, why their works often belong more to literature than to philosophy.

3. *Alienation or estrangement.* One major result of the dissociation of reason from the rest of the psyche has been the growth of science, which has become one of the hallmarks of Western civilization, and an ever-increasing rational ordering of men in society. As the existentialists view them, the main forces of history since the Renaissance have progressively separated man from concrete earthy existence, have forced him to live at ever higher levels of abstraction, have collectivized individual man out of existence, have driven God from the heavens, or what is the same thing, from the hearts of men. They are convinced that modern man lives in a fourfold condition of alienation: from God, from nature, from other men, from his own true self.

The estrangement from God is most shockingly expressed by Nietzsche's anguished cry, "God is dead," a cry which has continuously echoed through the writings of the existentialists, particularly the French. This theme of spiritual barrenness is a commonplace in literature of this century, from Eliot's "Hollow Man" to the novels of

Dos Passos, Hemingway, and Faulkner. It often appears in writers not commonly associated with the existentialists as in this remarkable passage from *A Story-Teller's Story,* where Sherwood Anderson describes his own awakening to his spiritual emptiness. He tells of walking alone late at night along a moonlit road when,

> I had suddenly an odd, and to my own seeming, a ridiculous desire to abase myself before something not human and so stepping into the moonlit road, I knelt in the dust. Having no God, the gods having been taken from me by the life about me, as a personal God has been taken from all modern men by a force within that man himself does not understand but that is called the intellect, I kept smiling at the figure I cut in my own eyes as I knelt in the road. . . .
>
> There was no God in the sky, no God in myself, no conviction in myself that I had the power to believe in a God, and so I merely knelt in the dust in silence and no words came to my lips.

In another passage Anderson wondered if the giving of itself by an entire generation to mechanical things was not really making all men impotent, if the desire for a greater navy, a greater army, taller public buildings, was not a sign of growing impotence. He felt that Puritanism and the industrialism which was its offspring had sterilized modern life, and proposed that men return to a healthful animal vigor by renewed contact with simple things of the earth, among them untrammeled sexual expression. One is reminded of the unkempt and delectable raffishness of Steinbeck's *Cannery Row* or of D. H. Lawrence's quasi-religious doctrine of sex, "blood-consciousness" and the "divine otherness" of animal existence.

Man's estrangement from nature has been a major theme in literature at least since Rousseau and the Romantic movement, and can hardly be said to be the property of existentialists. But this group nevertheless adds its own insistence that one of modern man's most urgent dangers is that he builds ever higher the brick and steel walls of technology which shut him away from a health-giving life according to "nature." Their treatment of this theme is most commonly expressed as part of a broader insistence that modern man needs to shun abstraction and return to "concreteness" or "wholeness." 9

A third estrangement has occurred at the social level and its sign is growing dismay at man's helplessness before the great machine-like colossus of industrialized society. This is another major theme of Western literature, and here again, though they hardly discovered the dan- 10 ger or began the protest, the existentialists in our time renew the protest against any pattern or force which would stifle the unique and spontaneous in individual life. The crowding of men into cities, the subdivision of labor which submerges the man in his economic function, the burgeoning of centralized government, the growth of advertising, propaganda, and mass media of entertainment and communication—all the things which force men into Riesman's "Lonely Crowd"—these same things drive men asunder by destroying their individuality and making them live on the surface of life, content to deal with things rather than people. "Exteriorization," says Berdyaev, "is the source of slavery, whereas freedom is interiorization. Slavery always indicates alienation, the ejection of human nature into the external." This kind of alienation is exemplified by Zero, in Elmer Rice's play "The Adding Machine." Zero's twenty-five years as a bookkeeper in a department store have dried up his humanity, making him incapable of love, of friendship, of any deeply felt, freely expressed emotion. Such estrangement is often given as the reason for man's inhumanity to man, the explanation of injustice in modern society. In Camus' short novel, aptly called *The Stranger,* a young man is convicted by a court of murder. This is a homicide which he has actually committed under extenuating circumstances. But the court never listens to any of the relevant evidence, seems never to hear anything that pertains to the crime itself; it convicts the young man on wholly irrelevant grounds—because he had behaved in an unconventional way at his mother's funeral the day before the homicide. In this book one feels the same dream-like distortion of reality as in the trial scene in *Alice in Wonderland,* a suffocating sense of being enclosed by events which are irrational or absurd but also inexorable. Most disturbing of all is the young man's aloneness, the impermeable membrane of estrangement which surrounds him and prevents anyone else from penetrating to his experience of life or sympathizing with it.

The fourth kind of alienation, man's estrangement from his own true self, especially as his nature is distorted by an exaltation of reason, is another theme having an extensive history as a major part of the Romantic revolt. Of the many writers who treat the theme, Hawthorne comes particularly close to the emphasis of contemporary existentialists. His Ethan Brand, Dr. Rappaccini, and Roger Chillingworth are a recurrrent figure who represents the dislocation in human nature which results when an overdeveloped or misapplied intellect severs "the magnetic chain of human sympathy." Hawthorne is thoroughly existential in his concern for the sanctity of the individual human soul, as well as in his preoccupation with sin and the dark side of human nature, which must be seen in part as his attempt to build back some fullness to the flattened image of man bequeathed to him by the Enlightenment. Whitman was trying to do this when he added flesh and bone and a sexual nature to the spiritualized image of man he inherited from Emerson, though his image remains diffused and attenuated by the same cosmic optimism. Many of the nineteenth-century depictions of man represent him as a figure of power or of potential power, sometimes as daimonic, like Melville's Ahab, but after World War I the power is gone; man is not merely distorted or truncated, he is hollow, powerless, faceless. At the time when his command over natural forces seems to be unlimited, man is pictured as weak, ridden with nameless dread. And this brings us to another of the major themes of existentialism.

4. *"Fear and trembling,"* anxiety. At Stockholm when he accepted the Nobel Prize, William Faulkner said that "Our tragedy today is a general and universal physical fear so long sustained by now that we can even bear it. There are no longer problems of the spirit. There is only one question: When will I be blown up?" The optimistic vision of the Enlightenment which saw man, through reason and its extensions in science, conquering all nature and solving all social and political problems in a continuous upward spiral of Progress, cracked open like a melon on the rock of World War I. The theories which held such high hopes died in that sickening and unimaginable butchery. Here was a concrete fact of human nature and society which the theories could not contain. The Great Depression and World War II deepened the sense of dismay which the loss of these ideals brought, but only with the atomic bomb did this become an unbearable terror, a threat of instant annihilation which confronted all men, even those most insulated by the thick crust of material goods and services. Now the most unthinking person could sense that each advance in mechanical technique carried not only a chromium and plush promise of comfort but a threat as well.

Sartre, following Kierkegaard, speaks of another kind of anxiety which oppresses modern man—"the anguish of Abraham"—the necessity which is laid upon him to make moral choices on his own responsibility. A military officer in wartime knows the agony of choice which forces him to sacrifice part of his army to preserve the rest, as does a man in high political office, who must make decisions affecting the lives of millions. The existentialists claim that each of us might make moral decisions in our own lives which involve the same anguish. Kierkegaard finds that this necessity is one thing which makes each life unique, which makes it impossible to speculate or generalize about human life, because each man's case is irretrievably his own, something in which he is personally and passionately involved. His book *Fear and Trembling* is an elaborate and fascinating commentary on the Old Testament story of Abraham, who was commanded by God to sacrifice his beloved son Isaac. Abraham thus becomes the emblem of man who must make a harrowing choice, in this case between love for his son and love for God, between the universal moral law which says categorically, "thou shalt not kill," and the unique inner demand of his religious faith. Abraham's decision, which is to violate the abstract and collective moral law, has to be made not in arrogance but in fear and trembling, one of the inferences being that sometimes one must make an exception to the general law because he is (existentially) an exception, a concrete being whose existence can never be completely subsumed under any universal.

5. *The encounter with nothingness.* For the man alienated from God, 14 from nature, from his fellow man and from himself, what is left at last but Nothingness? The testimony of the existentialists is that this is where modern man now finds himself, not on the highway of upward Progress toward a radiant Utopia but on the brink of a catastrophic precipice, below which yawns the absolute void, an uncompromised black Nothingness. In one sense this is Eliot's Wasteland inhabited by his Hollow Man who is

> Shape without form, shade without color
> Paralyzed force, gesture without motion.

That is what moves E. A. Robinson's Richard Cory, the man who is everything that might make us wish that we were in his place, to go home one calm summer night and put a bullet through his head.

One of the most convincing statements of the encounter with Nothingness is made by Leo Tolstoy in "My Confession." He tells how in good health, in the prime of life, when he had everything that a man could desire—wealth, fame, aristocratic social position, a beautiful wife and children, a brilliant mind and great artistic talent in the height of their powers, he nevertheless was seized with a growing uneasiness, a nameless discontent which he could not shake or alleviate. His experience was like that of a man who falls sick, with symptoms which he disregards as insignificant; but the symptoms return again and again until they merge into a continuous suffering. And the patient suddenly is confronted with the overwhelming fact that what he took for mere indisposition is more important to him than anything else on earth, that it is death! "I felt the ground on which I stood was crumbling, that there was nothing for me to stand on, that what I had been living for was nothing, that I had no reason for living. . . . To stop was impossible, to go back was impossible; and it was impossible to shut my eyes so as to see that there was nothing before me but suffering and actual death, absolute annihilation." This is the "Sickness Unto Death" of Kierkegaard, the despair in which one wishes to die but cannot. Hemingway's short story, "A Clean, Well-Lighted Place" gives an unforgettable expression of this theme. At the end of the story, the old waiter climbs into bed late at night saying to himself, "What did he fear? It was not fear or dread. It was a nothing which he knew too well. It was all a nothing and a man was nothing too. . . . Nada y pues nada, y nada y pues nada." And then because he has experienced the death of God he goes on to recite the Lord's Prayer in blasphemous despair: "Our Nothing who are in Nothing, nothing be thy nothing. . . ." And then the Ave Maria, "Hail nothing, full of nothing. . . ." This is stark, even for Hemingway, but the old waiter does no more than name the void felt by most people in the early Hemingway novels, a hunger they seek to assuage with alcohol, sex, and violence in an aimless progress from bar to bed to bullring. It goes without saying that much of the despair and pessimism in other contemporary authors springs from a similar sense of the void in modern life.

6. *Freedom.* Sooner or later, as a theme that includes all the others, [16] the existentialist writings bear upon freedom. The themes we have outlined above describe either some loss of man's freedom or some threat to it, and all existentialists of whatever sort are concerned to enlarge the range of human freedom.

For the avowed atheists like Sartre freedom means human auton- [17] omy. In a purposeless universe man is *condemned* to freedom because he is the only creature who is "self-surpassing," who can become something other than he is. Precisely because there is no God to give purpose to the universe, each man must accept individual responsibility for his own becoming, a burden made heavier by the fact that in choosing for himself he chooses for all men "the image of man as he ought to be." A man *is* the sum total of the acts that make up his life— no more, no less—and though the coward has made himself cowardly, it is always possible for him to change and make himself heroic. In Sartre's novel, *The Age of Reason,* one of the least likable of the characters, almost overwhelmed by despair and self-disgust at his homosexual tendencies, is on the point of solving his problem by mutilating himself with a razor, when in an effort of will he throws the instrument down, and we are given to understand that from this moment he will have mastery over his aberrant drive. Thus in the daily course of ordinary life must men shape their becoming in Sartre's world.

The religious existentialists interpret man's freedom differently.    18
They use much the same language as Sartre, develop the same themes concerning the predicament of man, but always include God as a radical factor. They stress the man of faith rather than the man of will. They interpret man's existential condition as a state of alienation from his essential nature which is God-like, the problem of his life being to heal the chasm between the two, that is, to find salvation. The mystery and ambiguity of man's existence they attribute to his being the intersection of two realms. "Man bears within himself," writes Berdyaev, "the image which is both the image of man and the image of God, and is the image of man as far as the image of God is actualized." Tillich describes salvation as "the act in which the cleavage between the essential being and the existential situation is overcome." Freedom here, as for Sartre, involves an acceptance of responsibility for choice and a *commitment* to one's choice. This is the meaning of faith, a faith like Abraham's, the commitment which is an agonizing sacrifice of one's own desire and will and dearest treasure to God's will.

A final word. Just as one should not expect to find in a particular    19
writer all of the characteristics of existentialism as we have described them, he should also be aware that some of the most striking expressions of existentialism in literature and the arts come to us by indirection, often through symbols or through innovations in conventional form. Take the preoccupation of contemporary writers with time. In *The Sound and the Fury,* Faulkner both collapses and expands normal clock time, or by juxtapositions of past and present blurs time into a single amorphous pool. He does this by using various forms of

"stream of consciousness" or other techniques which see life in terms of unique, subjective experience—that is, existentially. The conventional view of externalized life, a rational orderly progression cut into uniform segments by the hands of a clock, he rejects in favor of a view which sees life as opaque, ambiguous, and irrational—that is, as the existentialist sees it. Graham Greene does something like this in *The Power and the Glory.* He creates a scene isolated in time and cut off from the rest of the world, steamy and suffocating as if a bell jar had been placed over it. Through this atmosphere fetid with impending death and human suffering, stumbles the whiskey priest, lonely and confused, pursued by a police lieutenant who has experienced the void and the death of God.

Such expressions in literature do not mean necessarily that the authors are conscious existentialist theorizers, or even that they know the writings of such theorizers. Faulkner may never have read Heidegger—or St. Augustine—both of whom attempt to demonstrate that time is more within a man and subject to his unique experience of it than it is outside him. But it is legitimate to call Faulkner's views of time and life "existential" in this novel because in recent years existentialist theorizers have given such views a local habitation and a name. One of the attractions, and one of the dangers, of existential themes is that they become like Sir Thomas Browne's quincunx: once one begins to look for them, he sees them everywhere. But if one applies restraint and discrimination, he will find that they illuminate much of contemporary literature and sometimes the literature of the past as well. 20

## VOCABULARY

| | | |
|---|---|---|
| dadaism (1) | gnomic (6) | annihilation (12) |
| avant garde (1) | untrammeled (8) | irretrievably (13) |
| transcendentalism (2) | delectable (8) | subsumed (13) |
| facetious (2) | raffishness (8) | alleviate (15) |
| indomitable (2) | quasi-religious (8) | assuage (15) |
| irreducible (2) | colossus (10) | autonomy (17) |
| eclectic (3) | burgeoning (10) | self-surpassing (17) |
| eschews (4) | extenuating (10) | aberrant (17) |
| exaltation (5) | attenuated (11) | amorphous (19) |
| contingency (6) | daimonic (11) | fetid (19) |
| fallibility (6) | truncated (11) | quincunx (20) |

## THE FACTS

1. What are the two main kinds of existentialism? Which of the two do you find more appealing?
2. What experience was crucial in shaping the existentialist philosophy of Sartre, Camus, and Simone de Beauvoir? In what did they find unexpected strength?
3. What six general characteristics does the author find common to most existential philosophies?
4. What is the existential view about the place of reason in human life?
5. According to the existentialist, in what fourfold condition of alienation does mankind live?
6. What is "fear and trembling" anxiety?

## THE STRATEGIES

1. What rhetorical purpose is served by the author's admission of his initial bafflement with existentialism?
2. Some essays have a statement of purpose rather than a thesis. Which of the two does this essay use? Where is it stated, and how does it affect the structure of the essay?
3. What influence do you think the rather abstract content of this essay had on the author's paragraphing?
4. Bigelow numbers the six characteristics of existentialism and then explains them. What rhetorical advantages can you see in a structure consisting of numbered topics? What disadvantages are inherent in such a scheme?
5. In paragraph 1, Bigelow initially refers to himself as "I"; then he abruptly shifts to "we." What is the purpose of this shift?

## THE ISSUES

1. How much does reason influence your life? What other factors have a bearing on your trends and actions?
2. Of the four kinds of alienation mentioned in paragraphs 7–11, which is most prevalent among your close friends? Why?
3. Do you believe that certain principles are absolute and must guide one's life without being questioned, side-stepped, or amended? Why or why not?
4. Do you believe that society is constantly improving, or do you believe it is headed for some monstrous catastrophe? Describe the world the way you think it will be one hundred years from today.
5. What examples can you cite, from literature or from real life, of persons

who were alienated from their own true selves because they exalted reason over other human characteristics? Comment on the source of the alienation.

### SUGGESTIONS FOR WRITING

1. Have you ever experienced the "fear and trembling" over moral choices that this essay describes? Write an essay telling about your experience.
2. The author says that the chief question for the existentialist is "Who am I?" Write an essay defining yourself.

Archibald MacLeish

## • ARS POETICA •

*Archibald MacLeish (1892–1982), poet and playwright, was born in Glencoe, Illinois, and educated at Yale University. Trained as a lawyer, MacLeish served as librarian of Congress and as an adviser to President Franklin D. Roosevelt. A recurrent theme in his poetry was his deep apprehension about the rise of fascism. MacLeish won a Pulitzer Prize for a poetry collection,* Conquistador *(1932), and another for his play* J. B. *(1958).*

*In this famous poem, MacLeish proposes a succinct definition of poetry.*

> A poem should be palpable and mute
> As a globed fruit,
>
> Dumb
> As old medallions to the thumb,
>
> Silent as the sleeve-worn stone 5
> Of casement ledges where the moss has grown—
>
> A poem should be wordless
> As the flight of birds.
>
> A poem should be motionless in time
> As the moon climbs, 10
>
> Leaving, as the moon releases
> Twig by twig the night-entangled trees,
>
> Leaving, as the moon behind the winter leaves,
> Memory by memory the mind—

A poem should be motionless in time                          15
As the moon climbs.

A poem should be equal to:
Not true.

For all the history of grief
An empty doorway and a maple leaf.                           20

For love
The leaning grasses and two lights above the sea—

A poem should not mean
But be.

## VOCABULARY

palpable                    medallions                    casement

## THE FACTS

1. Translated, the poem's Latin title means "the art of poetry." Why is the title in Latin? How does the title relate to the poem?
2. Where does MacLeish give an explicit definition of poetry? How does he convey to the reader what poetry is?
3. In lines 17–18, what does MacLeish mean by the words "equal to: / Not true"?
4. The final stanza contains MacLeish's summarized view of poetry. What is your interpretation of the stanza?

## THE STRATEGIES

1. "Ars Poetica" is developed through a series of paradoxes. Analyze and interpret each.
2. MacLeish suggests that all the history of grief could be summarized by "an empty doorway and a maple leaf." Do you consider this an appropriate image? Can you suggest another equally appropriate image?
3. What image does MacLeish suggest for love? Do you find this appropriate? Explain.
4. What synonyms for *mute* does the poet use? Cite them all.
5. What is the significance of repeating the fifth stanza in the eighth stanza?

## THE ISSUES

1. What are some other definitions of poetry? What is your own definition?

How does it compare or contrast with that of MacLeish?

2. MacLeish states that in a poem all of the history of grief can become "an empty doorway and a maple leaf." What other effective expressions or embodiments of grief can you suggest?

3. What does the author mean when he writes, in stanza 4, that "a poem should be wordless / As the flight of birds"? How does this statement relate to Highet's notion of kitsch? (See Highet's essay on pages 472–480.)

4. Find a short poem that, in your view, perfectly exemplifies MacLeish's view that a poem should "not mean but be." Do you like this poem? Why or why not?

### SUGGESTIONS FOR WRITING

1. Consulting a collection of their works, find a definition of poetry by Wordsworth, Coleridge, Keats, or Shelley. Contrast that definition with "Ars Poetica." State which definition you like best and why.

2. Write a paragraph in which you give a definition of *love,* and support that definition with appropriate images. Then write another paragraph in which you do the same thing for *hate.*

# ═══ •• ISSUE FOR CRITICAL •• ═══
# THINKING

## Crime and Punishment

The execution of convicted murderer Gary Gilmore by the state of Utah on January 17, 1977, sparked a debate that rages still: How should criminals be treated and punished? Some argue that premeditated murder is justifiably punished by execution, while others point to the lack of any evidence that the death penalty deters crime. Some contend that locking up a first-time offender in a prison crammed with hardened and callous criminals does nothing more than school a venal lawbreaker in the art of more sophisticated felony. Others argue that crime deserves punishment, not coddling, and that criminals should pay for their misdeeds by harsh stretches of unpleasant imprisonment. Although most Americans reject the Old Testament's demand for "an eye for an eye, tooth for a tooth" approach to justice, they still want punishment to restore social order, prevent further crime, and rehabilitate the criminal.

Whether or not any system of penal justice can simultaneously punish and rehabilitate a criminal while making restitution to a victim is an imponderable of our time. The three essays that follow try indirectly to answer this implied question. In "The Prisoner's Dilemma," Stephen Chapman points out that the penal system in the United States is just as cruel as that of Islamic countries and wonders why we should feel so smugly self-congratulatory about our own wretched method of punishing criminals. In "A Hanging," George Orwell vents his revulsion to capital punishment in a meticulous and chilling description of a hanging he witnessed. In "In New York: Be Kind to Your Mugger," a victim, Timothy Foote, muses on how he would have reacted had he been armed with a handgun at the time of his mugging. No definitive answers emerge from these essays—the problem is too profoundly complex to admit of any such simplicity. But all of them do well what essays should always do—they start us thinking.

### Stephen Chapman

—————— • **THE PRISONER'S DILEMMA** • ——————

*Stephen Chapman (b. 1907) is associate editor of* The New Republic *magazine, where the article below originally appeared on March 8, 1980.*

*Islamic countries practice a system of justice so vastly different from ours as to arouse horror in most Americans. Punishments prescribed by the Koran range from amputation of a thief's hand to death by stoning of an adulterous couple. Yet, in the view of this author, a contrast between the penal practices of the Western democracies and those of the Islamic countries shows that our system is equally, if not more, barbaric.*

If the punitive laws of Islam were applied for only one year, all the devastating injustices would be uprooted. Misdeeds must be punished by the law of retaliation: cut off the hands of the thief; kill the murderers; flog the adulterous woman or man. Your concerns, your "humanitarian" scruples are more childish than reasonable. Under the terms of Koranic law, any judge fulfilling the seven requirements (that he have reached puberty, be a believer, know the Koranic laws perfectly, be just, and not be affected by amnesia, or be a bastard, or be of the female sex) is qualified to be a judge in any type of case. He can thus judge and dispose of twenty trials in a single day, whereas the Occidental justice might take years to argue them out.

—FROM *SAYINGS OF THE AYATOLLAH KHOMEINI*

One of the amusements of life in the modern West is the opportunity   1
to observe the barbaric rituals of countries that are attached to the customs of the dark ages. Take Pakistan, for example, our newest ally and client state in Asia. Last October President Zia, in harmony with the Islamic fervor that is sweeping his part of the world, revived the traditional Moslem practice of flogging lawbreakers in public. In Pakistan, this qualified as mass entertainment, and no fewer than 10,000 law-abiding Pakistanis turned out to see justice done to 26 convicts. To Western sensibilities the spectacle seemed barbaric—both in the sense of cruel and in the sense of pre-civilized. In keeping with Islamic custom each of the unfortunates—who had been caught in prostitution raids the previous night and summarily convicted and sentenced—was stripped down to a pair of white shorts, which were painted with a red stripe across the buttocks (the target). Then he was shackled against an easel, with pads thoughtfully placed over the kidneys to prevent injury. The floggers were muscular, fierce-looking sorts—convicted murderers, as it happens—who paraded around the flogging platform in colorful loincloths. When the time for the ceremony began, one of the floggers took a running start and brought a five-foot stave down across the first victim's buttocks, eliciting screams from the convict and murmurs from the audience. Each of the 26 received from five to 15 lashes. One had to be carried from the stage unconscious.

Flogging is one of the punishments stipulated by Koranic law, which   2
has made it a popular penological device in several Moslem countries, including Pakistan, Saudi Arabia, and, most recently, the ayatollah's Iran. Flogging, or *ta'zir*, is the general punishment prescribed for offenses that don't carry an explicit Koranic penalty. Some crimes carry automatic *hadd* punishments—stoning or scourging (a severe whipping) for illicit sex, scourging for drinking alcoholic beverages, amputation of the hands for theft. Other crimes—as varied as murder and abandoning Islam—carry the death penalty (usually carried out in public). Colorful practices like these have given the Islamic world an image in the West, as described by historian G. H. Jansen, "of blood dripping from the stumps of amputated hands and from the striped

backs of malefactors, and piles of stones barely concealing the battered bodies of adulterous couples." Jansen, whose book *Militant Islam* is generally effusive in its praise of Islamic practices, grows squeamish when considering devices like flogging, amputation, and stoning. But they are given enthusiastic endorsement by the Koran itself.

Such traditions, we all must agree, are no sign of an advanced 3 civilization. In the West, we have replaced these various punishments (including the death penalty in most cases) with a single device. Our custom is to confine criminals in prison for varying lengths of time. In Illinois, a reasonably typical state, grand theft carries a punishment of three to five years; armed robbery can get you from six to 30. The lowest form of felony theft is punishable by one to three years in prison. Most states impose longer sentences on habitual offenders. In Kentucky, for example, habitual offenders can be sentenced to life in prison. Other states are less brazen, preferring the more genteel sounding "indeterminate sentence," which allows parole boards to keep inmates locked up for as long as life. It was under an indeterminate sentence of one to 14 years that George Jackson served 12 years in California prisons for committing a $70 armed robbery. Under a Texas law imposing an automatic life sentence for a third felony conviction, a man was sent to jail for life last year because of three thefts adding up to less than $300 in property value. Texas also is famous for occasionally imposing extravagantly long sentences, often running into hundreds or thousands of years. This gives Texas a leg up on Maryland, which used to sentence some criminals to life plus a day—a distinctive if superfluous flourish.

The punishment *intended* by Western societies in sending their crim- 4 inals to prison is the loss of freedom. But, as everyone knows, the actual punishment in most American prisons is of a wholly different order. The February 2 [1980] riot at New Mexico's state prison in Santa Fe, one of several bloody prison riots in the nine years since the Attica bloodbath, once again dramatized the conditions of life in an American prison. Four hundred prisoners seized control of the prison before dawn. By sunset the next day 33 inmates had died at the hands of other convicts and another 40 people (including five guards) had been seriously hurt. Macabre stories came out of prisoners being hanged, murdered with blowtorches, decapitated, tortured, and mutilated in a variety of gruesome ways by drug-crazed rioters.

The Santa Fe penitentiary was typical of most maximum-security 5 facilities, with prisoners subject to overcrowding, filthy conditions, and routine violence. It also housed first-time, non-violent offenders, like check forgers and drug dealers, with murderers serving life sentences. In a recent lawsuit, the American Civil Liberties Union called the prison "totally unfit for human habitation." But the ACLU says New Mexico's penitentiary is far from the nation's worst.

That American prisons are a disgrace is taken for granted by experts 6 of every ideological stripe. Conservative James Q. Wilson has criticized our "[c]rowded, antiquated prisons that require men and women to live in fear of one another and to suffer not only deprivation of liberty but a brutalizing regimen." Leftist Jessica Mitford has called our prisons "the ultimate expression of injustice and inhumanity." In 1973 a national commission concluded that "the American correctional system today appears to offer minimum protection to the public and maximum harm to the offender." Federal courts have ruled that confinement in prisons in 16 different states violates the constitutional ban on "cruel and unusual punishment."

What are the advantages of being a convicted criminal in an ad- 7 vanced culture? First there is the overcrowding in prisons. One Tennessee prison, for example, has a capacity of 806, according to accepted space standards, but it houses 2300 inmates. One Louisiana facility has confined four and five prisoners in a single six-foot-by-six-foot cell. Then there is the disease caused by overcrowding, unsanitary conditions, and poor or inadequate medical care. A federal appeals court noted that the Tennessee prison had suffered frequent outbreaks of infectious diseases like hepatitis and tuberculosis. But the most distinctive element of American prison life is its constant violence. In his book *Criminal Violence, Criminal Justice,* Charles Silberman noted that in one Louisiana prison, there were 211 stabbings in only three years, 11 of them fatal. There were 15 slayings in a prison in Massachusetts between 1972 and 1975. According to a federal court, in Alabama's penitentiaries (as in many others), "robbery, rape, extortion, theft and assault are everyday occurrences."

At least in regard to cruelty, it's not at all clear that the system of 8 punishment that has evolved in the West is less barbaric than the grotesque practices of Islam. Skeptical? Ask yourself: would you rather be subjected to a few minutes of intense pain and considerable public humiliation, or be locked away for two or three years in a prison cell crowded with ill-tempered sociopaths? Would you rather lose a hand or spend 10 years or more in a typical state prison? I have taken my own survey on this matter. I have found no one who does not find the Islamic system hideous. And I have found no one who, given the choices mentioned above, would not prefer its penalties to our own.

The great divergence between Western and Islamic fashions in punishment is relatively recent. Until roughly the end of the 18th century, criminals in Western countries rarely were sent to prison. Instead they were subject to an ingenious assortment of penalties. Many perpetrators of a variety of crimes simply were executed, usually by some imaginative and extremely unpleasant method involving prolonged torture, such as breaking on the wheel, burning at the stake, or drawing and quartering. Michel Foucault's book *Discipline and Punish: The Birth of the Prison* notes one form of capital punishment in which the condemned man's "belly was opened up, his entrails quickly ripped out, so that he had time to see them, with his own eyes, being thrown on the fire; in which he was finally decapitated and his body quartered." Some criminals were forced to serve on slave galleys. But in most cases various corporal measures such as pillorying, flogging, and branding sufficed.  9

In time, however, public sentiment recoiled against these measures. They were replaced by imprisonment, which was thought to have two advantages. First, it was considered to be more humane. Second, and more important, prison was supposed to hold out the possibility of rehabilitation—purging the criminal of his criminality—something that less civilized punishments did not even aspire to. An 1854 report by inspectors of the Pennsylvania prison system illustrates the hopes nurtured by humanitarian reformers.  10

> Depraved tendencies, characteristic of the convict, have been restrained by the absence of vicious association, and in the mild teaching of Christianity, the unhappy criminal finds a solace for an involuntary exile from the comforts of social life. If hungry, he is fed; if naked, he is clothed; if destitute of the first rudiments of education, he is taught to read and write; and if he has never been blessed with a means of livelihood, he is schooled in a mechanical art, which in after life may be to him the source of profit and respectability. Employment is not his toil nor labor, weariness. He embraces them with alacrity, as contributing to his moral and mental elevation.

Imprisonment is now the universal method of punishing criminals  11 in the United States. It is thought to perform five functions, each of which has been given a label by criminologists. First, there is simple *retribution:* punishing the lawbreaker to serve society's sense of justice and to satisfy the victims' desire for revenge. Second, there is *specific deterrence:* discouraging the offender from misbehaving in the future. Third, *general deterrence:* using the offender as an example to discourage others from turning to crime. Fourth, *prevention:* at least during the time he is kept off the streets, the criminal cannot victimize other members of society. Finally, and most important, there is *rehabilitation:* reforming the criminal so that when he returns to society he will be inclined to obey the laws and able to make an honest living.

How satisfactorily do American prisons perform by these criteria?   12
Well, of course, they do punish. But on the other scores they don't do so well. Their effect in discouraging future criminality by the prisoner or others is the subject of much debate, but the soaring rates of the last 20 years suggest that prisons are not a dramatically effective deterrent to criminal behavior. Prisons do isolate convicted criminals, but only to divert crime from ordinary citizens to prison guards and fellow inmates. Almost no one contends any more that prisons rehabilitate their inmates. If anything, they probably impede rehabilitation by forcing inmates into prolonged and almost exclusive association with other criminals. And prisons cost a lot of money. Housing a typical prisoner in a typical prison costs far more than a stint at a top university. This cost would be justified if prisons did the job they were intended for. But it is clear to all that prisons fail on the very grounds—humanity and hope of rehabilitation—that caused them to replace earlier, cheaper forms of punishment.

The universal acknowledgment that prisons do not rehabilitate   13
criminals has produced two responses. The first is to retain the hope of rehabilitation but do away with imprisonment as much as possible and replace it with various forms of "alternative treatment," such as psychotherapy, supervised probation, and vocational training. Psychiatrist Karl Menninger, one of the principal critics of American penology, has suggested even more unconventional approaches, such as "a new job opportunity or a vacation trip, a course of reducing exercises, a cosmetic surgical operation or a herniotomy, some night school courses, a wedding in the family (even one for the patient!), an inspiring sermon." This starry-eyed approach naturally has produced a backlash from critics on the right, who think that it's time to abandon

the goal of rehabilitation. They argue that prisons perform an important service just by keeping criminals off the streets, and thus should be used with that purpose alone in mind.

So the debate continues to rage in all the same old ruts. No one, of 14 course, would think of copying the medieval practices of Islamic nations and experimenting with punishments such as flogging and amputation. But let us consider them anyway. How do they compare with our American prison system in achieving the ostensible objectives of punishment? First, do they punish? Obviously they do, and in a uniquely painful and memorable way. Of course any sensible person, given the choice, would prefer suffering these punishments to years of incarceration in a typical American prison. But presumably no Western penologist would criticize Islamic punishments on the grounds that they are not barbaric enough. Do they deter crime? Yes, and probably more effectively than sending convicts off to prison. Now we read about a prison sentence in the newspaper, then think no more about the criminal's payment for his crimes until, perhaps, years later we read a small item reporting his release. By contrast, one can easily imagine the vivid impression it would leave to be wandering through a local shopping center and to stumble onto the scene of some poor wretch being lustily flogged. And the occasional sight of an habitual offender walking around with a bloody stump at the end of his arm no doubt also would serve as a forceful reminder that crime does not pay.

Do flogging and amputation discourage recidivism? No one knows 15 whether the scars on his back would dissuade a criminal from risking another crime, but it is hard to imagine that corporal measures could stimulate a higher rate of recidivism than already exists. Islamic forms of punishment do not serve the favorite new right goal of simply isolating criminals from the rest of society, but they may achieve the same purpose of making further crimes impossible. In the movie *Bonnie and Clyde*, Warren Beatty successfully robs a bank with his arm in a sling, but this must be dismissed as artistic license. It must be extraordinarily difficult, at the very least, to perform much violent crime with only one hand.

Do these medieval forms of punishment rehabilitate the criminal? 16 Plainly not. But long prison terms do not rehabilitate either. And it is just as plain that typical Islamic punishments are no crueler to the convict than incarceration in the typical American state prison.

Of course there are other reasons besides its bizarre forms of pun- 17 ishment that the Islamic system of justice seems uncivilized to the Western mind. One is the absence of due proces. Another is the long list of offenses—such as drinking, adultery, blasphemy, "profiteering," and so on—that can bring on conviction and punishment. A third is all the ritualistic mumbo-jumbo in pronouncements of Islamic law (like that talk about puberty and amnesia in the ayatollah's quotation at the beginning of this article). Even in these matters, however, a little cultural modesty is called for. The vast majority of American criminals are convicted and sentenced as a result of plea bargaining, in which due process plays almost no role. It has been only half a century since a wave of religious fundamentalism stirred this country to outlaw the consumption of alcoholic beverages. Most states also still have laws imposing austere constraints on sexual conduct. Only two weeks ago the *Washington Post* reported that the FBI had spent two and a half years and untold amounts of money to break up a nationwide pornography ring. Flogging the clients of prostitutes, as the Pakistanis did, does seem silly. But only a few months ago Mayor Koch of New York was proposing that clients caught in his own city have their names broadcast by radio stations. We are not so far advanced on such matters as we often like to think. Finally, my lawyer friends assure me that the rules of jurisdiction for American courts contain plenty of petty requirements and bizarre distinctions that would sound silly enough to foreign ears.

Perhaps it sounds barbaric to talk of flogging and amputation, and perhaps it is. But our system of punishment also is barbaric, and probably more so. Only cultural smugness about their system and willful ignorance about our own make it easy to regard the one as cruel and the other as civilized. We inflict our cruelties away from public view, while nations like Pakistan stage them in front of 10,000 onlookers. Their outrages are visible; ours are not. Most Americans can live their lives for years without having their peace of mind disturbed by the knowledge of what goes on in our prisons. To choose imprisonment over flogging and amputation is not to choose human kindness over cruelty, but merely to prefer that our cruelties be kept out of sight, and out of mind.

Public flogging and amputation may be more barbaric forms of punishment than imprisonment, even if they are not more cruel. Society may pay a higher price for them, even if the particular criminal does not. Revulsion against officially sanctioned violence and infliction of pain derives from something deeply ingrained in the Western conscience, and clearly it is something admirable. Grotesque displays of the sort that occur in Islamic countries probably breed a greater tolerance for physical cruelty, for example, which prisons do not do precisely because they conceal their cruelties. In fact it is our admirable intolerance for calculated violence that makes it necessary for us to conceal what we have not been able to do away with. In a way this is a good thing, since it holds out the hope that we may eventually find a way to do away with it. But in another way it is a bad thing, since it permits us to congratulate ourselves on our civilized humanitarianism while violating its norms in this one area of our national life.

## VOCABULARY

punitive (headnote)
devastating (headnote)
adulterous (headnote)
scruples (headnote)
Koranic (headnote)
amnesia (headnote)
Islamic (1)
sensibilities (1)
summarily (1)
shackled (1)
loincloths (1)
penological (2)

malefactors (2)
effusive (2)
superfluous (3)
flourish (3)
macabre (4)
decapitated (4)
ideological (6)
antiquated (6)
deprivation (6)
sociopaths (8)
divergence (9)
ingenious (9)

perpetrators (9)
pillorying (9)
recoiled (10)
depraved (10)
solace (10)
rudiments (10)
alacrity (10)
ostensible (14)
incarceration (14)
recidivism (15)

## THE FACTS

1. Where does Chapman state his thesis? Restate it in your own words.
2. Why does Chapman begin with a detailed description of public flogging in Pakistan?
3. What obvious advantages, according to the author, does the practice of public flogging or public amputation have over the Western convention of sending a criminal to prison?
4. Of the five functions imprisonment should perform (as listed in paragraph 11), which function is completely neglected?
5. Chapman takes the position that our forms of imprisonment are just as barbaric as the punishments of Islam. What are the author's justifications for such a view? (Ask yourself the same questions asked in paragraph 8 and answer them honestly.)

6. What are the main criticisms, in addition to labeling it "bizarre," leveled at the Islamic system of justice? (See paragraph 17.)
7. Does Chapman suggest that the West turn to Islamic forms of punishment? Why or why not?

## THE STRATEGIES

1. Chapman begins with a description of Islamic punishment. In what paragraph does he make his first transition from Islamic punishment to Western punishment? What transitional words does he use?
2. In paragraph 7, how does Chapman maintain coherence as he moves from one point to the next?
3. In contrasting Islamic forms of punishment with those of the West, Chapman spends more time on Western punishment than on Islamic. Why?
4. Which technique for comparison/contrast does the author use primarily—block contrast or point-by-point contrast? (See pp. 526–27.)
5. How does Chapman take care of anticipated opposition to his views?

## THE ISSUES

1. What are some serious problems that the abolition of capital punishment creates?
2. Do you agree with Chapman's point that our system of justice is no more effective than that of the Islamic countries mentioned? Give reasons for your position.
3. What do you feel is the appropriate way to handle the person who commits a rape? A theft? A robbery? A premeditated murder?
4. What aspects, if any, of our prison system bother you the most? Why?
5. What is your solution for the treatment of incorrigible criminals?

## SUGGESTIONS FOR WRITING

1. Henry Schwarzschild, director of the National Coalition Against the Death Penalty, believes that capital punishment has no merits whatsoever. One of the aspects he considers particularly degrading is the "barbarousness of its process (whether by burning at the stake, by hanging from the gallows, by frying in the electric chair, by suffocating in the gas chamber, by shooting at the hands of a firing squad, or by lethal injection with a technology designed to heal and save lives)." Write an essay in which you argue for or against the barbarousness of the process used for capital punishment in most prisons today.
2. Write a critical evaluation of Chapman's argument, focusing on three of his major points.

George Orwell

# • A HANGING •

*George Orwell (1903–1950) was the pseudonym of Eric Arthur Blair. Born in India and educated at Eton, he served with the imperial police in Burma and fought on the republican side in the Spanish civil war. Orwell published two influential novels,* Animal Farm *(1945), and* Nineteen Eighty-four *(1949). He is widely admired for the crisp, lucid prose style of his essays.*

*"A Hanging" illustrates the difficulty of distinguishing between objective and subjective writing. Whereas Orwell only once explicitly states that it is wrong to take a person's life, his narrative nevertheless argues eloquently against the death penalty.*

It was in Burma, a sodden morning of the rains. A sickly light, like    1
yellow tinfoil, was slanting over the high walls into the jail yard. We were waiting outside the condemned cells, a row of sheds fronted with double bars, like small animal cages. Each cell measured about ten feet by ten and was quite bare within except for a plank bed and a pot for drinking water. In some of them brown silent men were squatting at the inner bars, with their blankets draped round them. These were the condemned men, due to be hanged within the next week or two.

One prisoner had been brought out of his cell. He was Hindu, a    2
puny wisp of a man, with a shaven head and vague liquid eyes. He had a thick, sprouting moustache, absurdly too big for his body, rather like the moustache of a comic man on the films. Six tall Indian warders were guarding him and getting him ready for the gallows. Two of them stood by with rifles and fixed bayonets, while the others handcuffed him, passed a chain through his handcuffs and fixed it to their belts, and lashed his arms tight to his sides. They crowded very close about him, with their hands always on him in a careful, caressing grip, as though all the while feeling him to make sure he was there. It was like men handling a fish which is still alive and may jump back into the water. But he stood quite unresisting, yielding his arms limply to the ropes, as though he hardly noticed what was happening.

Eight o'clock struck and a bugle call, desolately thin in the wet air,    3
floated from the distant barracks. The superintendent of the jail, who was standing apart from the rest of us, moodily prodding the gravel with his stick, raised his head at the sound. He was an army doctor, with a grey toothbrush moustache and a gruff voice. "For God's sake

hurry up, Francis," he said irritably. "The man ought to have been dead by this time. Aren't you ready yet?"

Francis, the head jailer, a fat Dravidian in a white drill suit and gold 4 spectacles, waved his black hand. "Yes sir, yes sir," he bubbled. "All iss satisfactorily prepared. The hangman iss waiting. We shall proceed."

"Well, quick march, then. The prisoners can't get their breakfast till 5 this job's over."

We set out for the gallows. Two warders marched on either side of 6 the prisoner, with their rifles at the slope; two others marched close against him, gripping him by arm and shoulder, as though at once pushing and supporting him. The rest of us, magistrates and the like, followed behind. Suddenly, when we had gone ten yards, the procession stopped short without any order or warning. A dreadful thing had happened—a dog, come goodness knows whence, had appeared in the yard. It came bounding among us with a loud volley of barks, and leapt round us wagging its whole body, wild with glee at finding so many human beings together. It was a large woolly dog, half Airedale, half pariah. For a moment it pranced round us, and then, before anyone could stop it, it had made a dash for the prisoner and, jumping up, tried to lick his face. Everyone stood aghast, too taken aback even to grab at the dog.

"Who let that bloody brute in here?" said the superintendent an- 7 grily. "Catch it, someone!"

A warder, detached from the escort, charged clumsily after the dog, 8 but it danced and gambolled just out of his reach, taking everything as part of the game. A young Eurasian jailer picked up a handful of gravel and tried to stone the dog away, but it dodged the stones and came after us again. Its yaps echoed from the jail walls. The prisoner, in the grasp of the two warders, looked on incuriously, as though this was another formality of the hanging. It was several minutes before someone managed to catch the dog. Then we put my handkerchief through its collar and moved off once more, with the dog still straining and whimpering.

It was about forty yards to the gallows. I watched the bare brown 9 back of the prisoner marching in front of me. He walked clumsily with his bound arms, but quite steadily, with that bobbing gait of the Indian who never straightens his knees. At each step his muscles slid neatly into place, the lock of hair on his scalp danced up and down, his feet printed themselves on the wet gravel. And once, in spite of the men who gripped him by each shoulder, he stepped slightly aside to avoid a puddle on the path.

It is curious, but till that moment I had never realized what it means [10] to destroy a healthy, conscious man. When I saw the prisoner step aside to avoid the puddle I saw the mystery, the unspeakable wrongness, of cutting a life short when it is in full tide. This man was not dying, he was alive just as we are alive. All the organs of his body were working—bowels digesting food, skin renewing itself, nails growing, tissues forming—all toiling away in solemn foolery. His nails would still be growing when he stood on the drop, when he was falling through the air with a tenth-of-a-second to live. His eyes saw the yellow gravel and the grey walls, and his brain still remembered, foresaw, reasoned—reasoned even about puddles. He and we were a party of men walking together, seeing, hearing, feeling, understanding the same world; and in two minutes, with a sudden snap, one of us would be gone—one mind less, one world less.

The gallows stood in a small yard, separate from the main grounds [11] of the prison, and overgrown with tall prickly weeds. It was a brick erection like three sides of a shed, with planking on top, and above that two beams and a crossbar with the rope dangling. The hangman, a grey-haired convict in the white uniform of the prison, was waiting beside his machine. He greeted us with a servile crouch as we entered. At a word from Francis the two warders, gripping the prisoner more closely than ever, half led half pushed him to the gallows and helped him clumsily up the ladder. Then the hangman climbed up and fixed the rope round the prisoner's neck.

We stood waiting, five yards away. The warders had formed in a [12] rough circle round the gallows. And then, when the noose was fixed, the prisoner began crying out to his god. It was a high, reiterated cry of "Ram! Ram! Ram! Ram!" not urgent and fearful like a prayer or cry for help, but steady, rhythmical, almost like the tolling of a bell. The dog answered the sound with a whine. The hangman, still standing on the gallows, produced a small cotton bag like a flour bag and drew it down over the prisoner's face. But the sound, muffled by the cloth, still persisted, over and over again: "Ram! Ram! Ram! Ram! Ram!"

The hangman climbed down and stood ready, holding the lever. [13] Minutes seemed to pass. The steady, muffled crying from the prisoner went on and on. "Ram! Ram! Ram!" never faltering for an instant. The superintendent, his head on his chest, was slowly poking the ground with his stick; perhaps he was counting the cries, allowing the prisoner a fixed number—fifty, perhaps, or a hundred. Everyone had changed color. The Indians had gone grey like bad coffee, and one or two of the bayonets were wavering. We looked at the lashed, hooded man on the drop, and listened to his cries—each cry another second of life; the same thought was in all our minds: oh, kill him quickly, get it over, stop that abominable noise!

Suddenly the superintendent made up his mind. Throwing up his head he made a swift motion with his stick. "Chalo!" he shouted almost fiercely. 14

There was a clanking noise, and then dead silence. The prisoner had vanished, and the rope was twisting on itself. I let go of the dog, and it galloped immediately to the back of the gallows; but when it got there it stopped short, barked, and then retreated into a corner of the yard, where it stood among the weeds, looking timorously out at us. We went round the gallows to inspect the prisoner's body. He was dangling with his toes pointed straight downwards, very slowly revolving, as dead as a stone. 15

The superintendent reached out with his stick and poked the bare brown body; it oscillated slightly. "*He's* all right," said the superintendent. He backed out from under the gallows, and blew out a deep breath. The moody look had gone out of his face quite suddenly. He glanced at his wrist-watch. "Eight minutes past eight. Well, that's all for this morning, thank God." 16

The warders unfixed bayonets and marched away. The dog, sobered and conscious of having misbehaved itself, slipped after them. We walked out of the gallows yard, past the condemned cells with their waiting prisoners, into the big central yard of the prison. The convicts, under the command of warders armed with lathis, were already receiving their breakfast. They squatted in long rows, each man holding a tin pannikin, while two warders with buckets marched round ladling out rice; it seemed quite a homely, jolly scene, after the hanging. An enormous relief had come upon us now that the job was done. One felt an impulse to sing, to break into a run, to snigger. All at once every one began chattering gaily. 17

The Eurasian boy walking beside me nodded towards the way we had come, with a knowing smile: "Do you know, sir, our friend (he meant the dead man) when he heard his appeal had been dismissed, he pissed on the floor of his cell. From fright. Kindly take one of my 18 cigarettes, sir. Do you not admire my new silver case, sir? From the boxwalah, two rupees eight annas. Classy European style."

Several people laughed—at what, nobody seemed certain.   19

Francis was walking by the superintendent, talking garrulously:   20 "Well, sir, all hass passed off with the utmost satisfactoriness. It was all finished—flick! like that. It iss not always so—oah, no! I have known cases where the doctor was obliged to go beneath the gallows and pull the prisoner's legs to ensure decease. Most disagreeable!"

"Wriggling about, eh? That's bad," said the superintendent.   21

"Ach, sir, it iss worse when they become refractory! One man, I   22 recall, clung to the bars of hiss cage when we went to take him out. You will scarcely credit, sir, that it took six warders to dislodge him, three pulling at each leg. We reasoned with him. 'My dear fellow,' we said, 'think of all the pain and trouble you are causing to us!' But no, he would not listen! Ach, he wass very troublesome!"

I found that I was laughing quite loudly. Everyone was laughing.   23 Even the superintendent grinned in a tolerant way. "You'd better all come out and have a drink," he said quite genially. "I've got a bottle of whisky in the car. We could do with it."

We went through the big double gates of the prison into the road.   24 "Pulling at his legs!" exclaimed a Burmese magistrate suddenly, and burst into a loud chuckling. We all began laughing again. At that moment Francis' anecdote seemed extraordinarily funny. We all had a drink together, native and European alike, quite amicably. The dead man was a hundred yards away.

### VOCABULARY

| | | |
|---|---|---|
| sodden (1) | taken aback (6) | oscillated (16) |
| wisp (2) | gambolled (8) | pannikin (17) |
| desolately (3) | Eurasian (8) | snigger (17) |
| Dravidian (4) | servile (11) | garrulously (20) |
| magistrates (6) | abominable (13) | refractory (22) |
| aghast (6) | timorously (15) | genially (23) |

### THE FACTS

1. The reporter in this event acts both as observer and as participant. Can you offer a reason for combining these two points of view?
2. Orwell offers few personal opinons on the hanging, but merely shows the

spectacle in full detail. What is the advantage or disadvantage of such a method?

3. In what way does Orwell make clear his special purpose in reporting the hanging?
4. Why does Orwell include the incident about the dog (paragraph 6)?
5. Why does Orwell mention that the victim avoided a puddle (paragraph 10)?
6. We are never told the identity of the prisoner to be hanged nor what crime, if any, he committed. Why did Orwell leave out those details?

## THE STRATEGIES

1. What general mood is created by the opening paragraph? Pick out those words that contribute most to this mood.
2. Analyze the text for freshness of language.
3. In what two paragraphs does the reporter draw attention to himself? What reason is there for these shifts from "we" to "I"?
4. Does Orwell's method—one of showing rather than of telling—prove as convincing as a logical argument against capital punishment? Give the reasoning behind your answer.

## THE ISSUES

1. What is your reaction—emotional as well as intellectual—to the hanging described by Orwell?
2. What political insights, if any, did you glean from this essay?
3. How do you interpret the "enormous relief" mentioned in paragraph 17 and all of the laughing described in paragraphs 18–24? Were these people, including the author, insensitive brutes or is such a relief natural? Explain your answer.
4. If the description had been of a prisoner in a modern prison, strapped in an electric chair or given cyanide, would your reaction be different? Why or why not?
5. What would your reaction be if the essay had revealed that the prisoner had staged an assassination attempt against a minister representing the British government ruling Burma?

## SUGGESTIONS FOR WRITING

1. Following Orwell's model, write an essay in which you describe an event as an objective reporter, but choose only those details that support the general impression you wish to convey.
2. Relate an experience that taught you either that capital punishment is moral or that it is immoral.

Timothy Foote

## ———— • NEW YORK: BE KIND TO • ————
## YOUR MUGGER

*Timothy Foote (b. 1926) is an American newspaper reporter, editor, and author. Born in London and educated at Harvard University, he served as a foreign correspondent for* Life *magazine from 1954 to 1958. He served as associate and senior editor for* Life *from 1958 to 1962. In 1962 he started reviewing books for* Time *magazine and later became its senior editor and book critic. Among Foote's full-length books are* The World of Peter Bruegel *(1968),* The Great Ring-tailed Island Caper *(1979), and* A Sailor's History of the American Revolution *(1980).*

It happened far too late to be a fashionable mugging. Practically    1
everybody the middle-aged householder knew had long since been
assaulted or purse-snatched, or broken and entered in one way or
another. People rarely bothered to talk about muggings at dinner parties any more. Truth to tell, the householder, who often worked late in
the city, had grown a bit smug about being spared so long. He always
walked fast and purposefully. He was in pretty good shape. And he
liked to think that he had acquired from a boyhood in the country
some special alertness, a sharper sense of how to avoid danger than
his acquaintances.

At social gatherings with his wife's suburban friends, he found him-    2
self in a beleaguered minority. He had grown up with guns; still owned
two or three, now never actually used. But he moved in circles where
guests tended to edge away at cocktail parties whenever he admitted
that he wasn't entirely happy with the idea of living unarmed in a state
where only cops and criminals have guns.

He saw the liberals' point, of course. If you overtly distrust the    3
system, in some sort of superstitious way you *are* inviting it not to
work. What was galling was the suspicion that they would forgive all
sorts of antisocial behavior—shoplifting, say, flagrant adultery, embezzlement and, of course, mugging—provided some acceptable frailty of
the psyche or pocketbook could be dredged up to excuse it. Even the
faintest suggestion that an individual might be justified or obliged to
use violence in defending himself touched some deep root of outrage
in his neighbors and his wife.

When the mugging happened, he found himself unready. He was    4 plunging along a shadowy, midtown street well past midnight only a few hundred feet from a hotel where he often stayed when he worked late in the city. Suddenly, he was aware of a dark figure behind and to the left. Then, farther off, exactly abreast of him but ten feet away near the buildings, a second figure appeared. That seemed odd, especially since he now noticed there was not another soul on the street. A taxi's brake lights winked in the distance, though, and the pool of light in front of the hotel reassured him. Just as he reached that welcoming glare, the figure on the left cut in front of him. The other shadow moved up to just behind his shoulder. Hand thrust forward in his jacket pocket, the first figure said, "Gimme your money or I'll cut you."

Except for an instant when his breath came short, the householder  5 did not feel afraid. Or angry. Instead, he even found himself glancing toward the curb where a chauffeur dozed, or maddeningly seemed to doze, at the wheel of a parked limousine. There was still nobody else on the street. He was aware that whatever it was in the thief's pocket might not be a knife. Very likely wasn't. It occurred to him to demand to see the weapon, then dodge toward the hotel. At the same time he felt constrained, in some peculiarly inappropriate way, like an actor walking through a barely rehearsed part. Bits of idiot dialogue ran through his mind: "Show me the blade, and I'll show you the money." Folk wisdom was clear, though: never argue, never resist.

"I'll give you what I have," he said. It wouldn't be much. He didn't  6 own a wallet and never carried more than a few dollars cash. In his pockets he found $17—a ten and seven ones—plus some silver. The boy, for as he handed the money over he saw it was a boy about the age of his youngest son, took the bills and scornfully flung the change into the street.

"Where your wallet, man?"  7

"I don't have a wallet," he said.  8

"You want me to cut you to get your wallet?"  9

Explaining that he had only a folding case full of cards, he fished it  10 out. Grabbing at the case, the boy looked nervous for the first time. After a lightning search, he tossed it toward a green wooden planter near the hotel entryway. In doing so, he let fall a single dollar bill. Caught by a little twist of wind, it skittered an inch or two across the sidewalk.

"You dropped a dollar," the middle-aged householder found him- 11
self saying. He felt the folly of the words as they left his mouth. A
student had lately been killed by a young mugger for saying exactly
the same thing, but in that case, apparently, the suggestion came out
as a kind of derisive irony. His own words, he knew with shame, had
held no irony. They were, in fact, a reflex, an example of sheer, dumb
middle-class helpfulness. He found himself actually blushing at the
thought of having spoken them.

The boy bent to retrieve the lost bill. Then the two thieves loped 12
easily away down the sidewalk. He stood and watched them go. They
wore new jogging shoes and beautiful down jackets of the kind that
after some argument, he had recently bought for his son. They were
good-looking too. Clear-eyed, strong, giving off a kind of energy, like
athletes. It seemed to him that for them the whole thing had been a
sort of game. And there they went, jogging away in step, knees high,
heads up, shoulder to shoulder like some Damon and Pythias of the
inner city. The householder remembered that stride himself. It had
carried him across the playing fields of youth after he had been lucky
enough to score a goal. For that matter, these two, with their fine
jackets and high-stepping pace, looked as carefree as his son and a
friend heading away down a tree-lined street at home.

He found himself astonished. Then, for the first time, he had an 13
urge, as strong as a clenching fist, to kill them. His coat had a special
change pocket cut laterally into the button flap. It was small, but large
enough for a tiny, hammerless handgun he owned and sometimes, to
his wife's horror, threatened to license and carry. In an instant, he
moved his hand, in a theatrical reflex, leveled a pointing finger at the
retreating shapes. With the gun in hand, he knew, *knew*, he would
have fired. Aiming for the legs. But he certainly could have killed them
both for their disdain.

Inside the hotel he got to a phone and gave the police a description. 14
Two boys in ski jackets. Heading south. The time. The place. After he
explained they had taken nothing identifiable, the distant precinct lost
interest. Even if the two were picked up, there was nothing they could
be held for. Besides, he was lucky to be unhurt, to have lost only $17.
All this the bored voice subliminally conveyed to him.

His wife was staying in the hotel. She had come to town for a party, 15
decided to stay in with him, but then gone to bed early. He entered

their darkened room quietly. There was no reason, he realized, to wake her up. Nothing had happened, really. In a sense he hadn't even been mugged. The word seemed to require some actual physical hurt. Or some resistance on his part.

It was only next morning that he told the story. She was shocked, but not deeply so. The tale was too familiar. And there he was, safe and sound. Her natural sympathy, in any case, would go out to the two youths, no doubt driven to crime by circumstances beyond their control. Robert Louis Stevenson, the householder sometimes kiddingly reminded his wife, said that to marry is to domesticate the Recording Angel. But the householder did not really think Stevenson's charge described her. She was generally quite forgetful of details, and rarely accumulated small grievances to hold against any one. [16]

In marrying, though, he often felt he had linked himself to the very archangel of liberalism. His wife would not willingly kill anything, even an invading cockroach. Her grievance against him was that he seemed to her a madman—conservative in some irretrievably dangerous way—simply because he could not wholeheartedly join her belief in progress. Most of all because he kept refusing to agree that poverty is the main cause, and excuse, for crime. His ritual suggestions that most poor kids somehow resist the temptation to cut people up, or snatch purses, always led to deep distress in his wife. [17]

So it was only after some hesitation that he confided to her the unexpected and inappropriate moment when he would gladly have killed the two boys. She would take it as one more sign of his antisocial nature, but his brief, murderous perception was, he felt, the only unusual thing about the whole affair. [18]

"They were rank amateurs," he concluded. "Out for fun. The police can't touch them. Nothing will be done until people fight back. When enough muggers get shot up, word will get around that the work is a losing proposition." [19]

"Oh, no!" his wife exclaimed. For the first time real concern, compassion, urgency, stirred in her voice. "Oh, no! We can't have that," she said. "That would lead to lawlessness." [20]

### VOCABULARY

| | | |
|---|---|---|
| householder (1) | derisive (11) | Robert Louis Stevenson (16) |
| beleaguered (2) | loped (12) | domesticate (16) |

constrained (5)      disdain (13)        irretrievably (17)

skittered (10)       subliminally (14)

### THE FACTS

1. What is meant by "a fashionable mugging" in paragraph 1?
2. What is the liberal's point of view as mentioned in the essay?
3. According to the essay, how does folk wisdom tell you to handle a mugger?
4. Why does the householder inform his mugger that the mugger has dropped one of the dollar bills?
5. What revelation about himself suddenly surprises the householder?
6. How did the householder's wife react when the householder confided his reaction to her?

### THE STRATEGIES

1. The essay never mentions in what city the mugging took place. How, then, is the location clarified?
2. What purpose do paragraphs 2 and 3 serve?
3. What do paragraphs 7, 8, and 9 add to the narration?
4. What is the meaning of the Damon and Pythias allusion? (Look up these names in a good dictionary or encyclopedia.)
5. What is implied in the term "bored voice" of paragraph 11?
6. What purpose, other than narrating a New York mugging, does the essay serve?

### THE ISSUES

1. Do you agree with the wife's exclamation at the end of the essay that we can't shoot up muggers in order to stop their assaults because such violence would merely lead to lawlessness? Explain your answer.
2. How would you have handled this mugging attempt if you had been in the householder's place? Would you have cooperated or resisted? Explain your answer.
3. From your knowledge of sociology, what is the reason for the dramatic increase in street crimes during recent years? What cure do you suggest?
4. Paragraph 11 refers to "sheer, dumb middle-class helpfulness." What other examples of typical middle-class helpfulness can you give? Should we try to abolish this helpfulness in order to avoid unpleasant and dangerous encounters?
5. What punishment, if any, would you suggest for these two muggers if they could have been apprehended by the police?
6. Does the essay take a position on street crime? If it does, what is the position?

## SUGGESTIONS FOR WRITING

1. Write an essay in which you attack the liberal position of being easy on street muggers
2. Write an essay in which you describe how Islamic countries would have dealt with the two muggers in Foote's narration (See "The Prisoner's Dilemma" on pages 503–511). Then evaluate the Islamic attitude.

# CHAPTER WRITING ASSIGNMENTS

1. Write an essay in which you provide illustrations from history, physics, biology, psychology, or literature to prove one of the following maxims:
   a. "Every man is the architect of his own fortune." (Seneca)
   b. "The injury of prodigality leads to this, that he who will not economize will have to agonize." (Confucius)
   c. "The foundation of every state is the education of its youth." (Diogenes)
   d. "The pull of gravity exerts far more influence than one might think." (Anonymous)
   e. "Satire is the guerilla weapon of political warfare." (Horace Greeley)
2. Choose one of the following terms and write an essay in which you first define the term as a dictionary would. Then give an extended definition, using the development most suitable for answering the question, "What is it?"

   a. romance       d. education       g. law
   b. tyranny       e. humility        h. *glasnost*
   c. adolescence   f. prejudice

# 8
# ANALYZING

Comparison/Contrast,
Division/Classification,
and Causal Analysis

### ⚫⚫ *ADVICE* ⚫⚫

## HOW TO WRITE A COMPARISON OR CONTRAST

Comparisons and contrasts clarify a situation by pointing out similarities and differences. *Comparing* means to point out similarities; *contrasting* means to point out differences. Students today are often compared or contrasted with students of yesterday. A Cadillac is contrasted with a Rolls-Royce, or détente with peaceful coexistence. The effects of marijuana are compared with the effects of alcohol. And in a special kind of comparison called *analogy,* conditions are compared that on surface view seem completely unlike: for instance, giving aid to Third World nations is compared to helping ship-wrecked persons into a lifeboat, or the functions of the brain are compared to the functions of an IBM computer. Analogies are useful for illustration but rarely for proving an argument, because sooner or later the analogy breaks down and becomes illogical.

### 1. Clarify the bases of your comparison or contrast.

In writing a comparison/contrast, your first step is to identify the basis of it. Notice, for example, how Emerson's essay "Conservatism and Liberalism" contrasts on the basis of people's attitude toward change and reform. Suzanne Jordan's contrast of fat people and thin people focuses on differences in their personalities, outlooks, and temperaments.

### 2. Organize your comparison or contrast.

Let us assume that you wish to contrast the usefulness of a motorcycle with that of an automobile. First, you must establish the bases on which your contrast will rest—perhaps expense, upkeep, and safety. Once these have been established, you can develop your paragraphs in two ways. One approach is to use the **alternating method**; that is, you write about the difference between a motorcycle and a car insofar as expense is concerned, then move to the difference as far as upkeep is concerned, and finally to the difference as far as safety is concerned. This system would yield the following outline:

   I. Expense
      A. Motorcycle
      B. Automobile
  II. Upkeep
      A. Motorcycle
      B. Automobile

   III. Safety
      A. Motorcycle
      B. Automobile

Another approach is the **block method** of dividing the essay into two parts, one dealing with the motorcycle and its expense, upkeep, and safety, the other dealing similarly with the automobile. This system would be outlined as follows:

   I. Motorcycle
      A. Expense
      B. Upkeep
      C. Safety
   II. Automobile
      A. Expense
      B. Upkeep
      C. Safety

The second system has the advantage of allowing you to deal with one item at a time (the motorcycle, without mentioning the automobile), but has the disadvantage of forcing your reader to wait until the end of the essay to draw a conclusive contrast between the two sides. The first system is more clearly a contrast because it requires the reader to move back and forth between the motorcycle and the automobile, continuously contrasting the two.

### 3. Use verbal indicators to maintain coherence.

A good writer will sprinkle contrast paragraphs with indicators such as "on the other hand," "whereas," "but," "in contrast to," and "unlike." When comparing, the writer will use indicators such as "like," "as," "likewise," "similarly," and "also." These indicators help the coherence of the development.

## ══ •• *EXAMPLES* •• ══

### Ralph Waldo Emerson

## — • *from* CONSERVATISM AND LIBERALISM • —

*Ralph Waldo Emerson (1803–1882), American poet, essayist, and lecturer, was born in Boston and educated at Harvard University. Publication of his essay "Nature" in 1836 established him as a leading spokesman for transcendentalism.*

*This philosophy was based on a belief in the intuitive and spiritual nature of humankind that transcends physical experience. Though he considered himself primarily a poet, Emerson is better known for his essays and lectures.*

*Conservatism and liberalism are nowadays used almost exclusively as political labels. In this essay, however, Emerson contrasts the two philosophies as fundamentally opposing views—not only of politics but of life itself. His essay exemplifies the alternating method of comparing and contrasting.*

The two parties which divide the state, the party of Conservatism and that of Innovation, are very old, and have disputed the possession of the world ever since it was made. This quarrel is the subject of civil history. The conservative party established the reverend hierarchies and monarchies of the most ancient world. The battle of patrician and plebeian, of parent state and colony, of old usage and accommodation to new facts, of the rich and the poor, reappears in all countries and times. The war rages not only in battlefields, in national councils, and ecclesiastical synods, but agitates every man's bosom with opposing advantages every hour. On rolls the old world meantime, and now one, now the other gets the day, and still the fight renews itself as if for the first time, under new names and hot personalities.

Such an irreconcilable antagonism, of course, must have a correspondent depth of seat in the human constitution. It is the opposition of Past and Future, of Memory and Hope, of the Understanding and the Reason. It is the primal antagonism, the appearance in trifles of the two poles of nature. . . .

There is always a certain meanness in the argument of conservatism, joined with a certain superiority in its fact. It affirms because it holds. Its fingers clutch the fact, and it will not open its eyes to see a better fact. The castle, which conservatism is set to defend, is the actual state of things, good and bad. The project of innovation is the best possible state of things. Of course, conservatism always has the worst of the argument, is always apologizing, pleading a necessity, pleading that to change would be to deteriorate; it must saddle itself with the mountainous load of the violence and vice of society, must deny the possibility of good, deny ideas, and suspect and stone the prophet; whilst innovation is always in the right, triumphant, attacking, and sure of final success. Conservatism stands on man's confessed limitations; reform, on his indisputable infinitude; conservatism, on circumstance; liberalism, on power; one goes to make an adroit member of the social frame; the other to postpone all things to the man himself; conservatism is debonair and social; reform is individual and imperious. We are reformers in spring and summer; in autumn and winter we stand by the old; reformers in the morning, conservers at night. Reform is affirmative, conservatism negative; conservatism goes for comfort, reform for truth. Conservatism is more candid to behold another's worth; reform more disposed to maintain and increase its own. Conservatism makes no poetry, breathes no prayer, has no invention; it is all memory. Reform has no gratitude, no prudence, no husbandry. It makes a great difference to your figure and to your thought, whether your foot is advancing or receding. Conservatism never puts the foot forward; in the hour when it does that, it is not establishment, but reform. Conservatism tends to universal seeming and treachery, believes in a negative fate; believes that men's temper governs them; that for me, it avails not to trust in principles; they will fail me; I must bend a little; it distrusts nature; it thinks there is a general law without a particular application,—law for all that does not include any one. Reform in its antagonism inclines to asinine resistance, to kick with hoofs; it runs to egotism and bloated self-conceit; it runs to a bodiless pretension, to unnatural refining and elevation, which ends in hypocrisy and sensual reaction.

And so whilst we do not go beyond general statements, it may be    4
safely affirmed of these two metaphysical antagonists, that each is a good half, but an impossible whole. Each exposes the abuses of the other, but in a true society, in a true man, both must combine. Nature does not give the crown of its approbation, namely, beauty, to any action or emblem or actor, but to one which combines both these elements; not to the rock which resists the waves from age to age, nor to the wave which lashes incessantly the rock, but the superior beauty is with the oak which stands with its hundred arms against the storms of a century, and grows every year like a sapling; or the river which ever flowing, yet is found in the same bed from age to age; or, greatest of all, the man who has subsisted for years amid the changes of nature, yet has distanced himself, so that when you remember what he was, and see what he is, you say, what strides! what a disparity is here!

## *VOCABULARY*

| | | |
|---|---|---|
| hierarchies (1) | ecclesiastical (1) | primal (2) |
| patrician (1) | synods (1) | infinitude (3) |
| plebeian (1) | agitates (1) | debonair (3) |

imperious (3)    sensual (3)    disparity (4)
asinine (3)    approbation (4)

## THE FACTS

1. Emerson writes: "Such an irreconcilable antagonism, of course, must have a correspondent depth of seat in the human constitution" (paragraph 2). What does he mean by that?
2. Which of the two attitudes contrasted has the worst of the argument? Why is the other sure of final success?
3. Emerson says that conservatism is "all memory." What does he mean by that?
4. What are the weaknesses of conservatism? What are the weaknesses of liberalism? Why is it necessary that conservatism and liberalism be combined in a person?
5. Emerson says that either conservatism or liberalism makes a "good half, but an impossible whole." What does he mean by that?

## THE STRATEGIES

1. Reread the final sentence in the first paragraph. Is this the natural wording of this sentence? Why is the sentence worded this way?
2. "The battle of patrician and plebeian, of parent state and colony, of old usage and accommodation to new facts, of the rich and the poor, reappears in all countries and times." What characteristic of style marks the sentence? Which sentences in paragraph 3 show similar construction?
3. "The castle, which conservatism is set to defend, is the actual state of things, good and bad." Does Emerson mean "castle" literally or figuratively? If the latter, what figure of speech is this, and what does "castle" mean?
4. "It makes a great difference to your figure and to your thought, whether your foot is advancing or receding." What figure of speech is this?
5. The contrast between liberalism and conservatism is developed within paragraphs. What technique of sentence construction makes this possible?

## THE ISSUES

1. What issues—political, religious, or social—have recently revealed the antagonism between liberals and conservatives as discussed by Emerson?
2. Most of us are combinations of liberalism and conservatism, being conservative in some matters but liberal in others. Discuss where you stand on the following matters: spending your own money, premarital sex, joining the army, voting for a U.S. president, criminal punishment.

3. Emerson insists that in an ideal person, the two forces of liberalism and conservatism must combine. Do you agree? Why or why not?
4. What important world figure embodies the ideal of combined conservatism and liberalism? Do you admire this person? Why or why not?
5. Emerson uses the symbols of an oak tree and of a river to embody the balance between conservatism and liberalism. Would the following symbols work? Why or why not? Analyze each in turn.

fire

rose

bridge

mountain

## SUGGESTIONS FOR WRITING

1. Contrast your own political beliefs with those of a conservative or a liberal.
2. Analyze and discuss Emerson's characterization of conservatism. What are its most important elements?

### Matthew Arnold

# ———— • HEBRAISM AND HELLENISM • ————

*Matthew Arnold (1822–1888), English poet, lecturer, and critic, was educated at Rugby and Oxford. For most of his life, Arnold held the position of inspector of schools. He is widely known for his poetry,* Empedocles on Etna *(1852) and* New Poems *(1867), and for his works of criticism,* Essays in Criticism *(1865) and* Culture and Anarchy *(1869).*

*This selection compares and contrasts Hebraism (the spirit of the Hebrews) with Hellenism (the spirit of the ancient Greeks).*

Hebraism and Hellenism,—between these two points of influence moves our world. At one time it feels more powerfully the attraction of one of them, at another time of the other; and it ought to be, though it never is, evenly and happily balanced between them.

The final aim of both Hellenism and Hebraism, as of all great spiritual disciplines, is no doubt the same: man's perfection or salvation. The very language which they both of them use in schooling us to reach this aim is often identical. Even when their language indicates by variation,—sometimes a broad variation, often a but slight and subtle variation,—the different courses of thought which are uppermost in each discipline, even then the unity of the final end and aim is still apparent. To employ the actual words of that discipline with which we ourselves are all of us most familiar, and the words of which, therefore, come most home to us, that final end and aim is "that we might be partakers of the divine nature." These are the words of a Hebrew apostle, but of Hellenism and Hebraism alike this is, I say, the aim. When the two are confronted, as they very often are confronted, it is nearly always with what I may call a rhetorical purpose; the speaker's whole design is to exalt and enthrone one of the two, and he uses the other only as a foil and to enable him the better to give effect to his purpose. Obviously, with us, it is usually Hellenism which is thus reduced to minister to the triumph of Hebraism. There is a sermon on Greece and the Greek spirit by a man never to be mentioned without interest and respect, Frederick Robertson,[1] in which this rhetorical use of Greece and the Greek spirit, and the inadequate exhibition of them necessarily consequent upon this, is almost ludicrous, and would be censurable if it were not to be explained by the exigencies of a sermon. On the other hand, Heinrich Heine,[2] and other writers of his sort, give us the spectacle of the table completely turned, and of Hebraism brought in just as a foil and contrast to Hellenism, and to make the superiority of Hellenism more manifest. In both these cases there is injustice and misrepresentation. The aim and end of both Hebraism and Hellenism is, as I have said, one and the same, and this aim and end is august and admirable.

Still, they pursue this aim by very different courses. The uppermost idea with Hellenism is to see things as they really are; the uppermost idea with Hebraism is conduct and obedience. Nothing can do away with this ineffaceable difference. The Greek quarrel with the body and its desires is, that they hinder right thinking; the Hebrew quarrel with them is, that they hinder right acting. "He that keepeth the law, happy is he";[3] "Blessed is the man that feareth the Eternal, that delighteth greatly in his commandments";[4] that is the Hebrew notion of felicity; and, pursued with passion and tenacity, this notion would not let the Hebrew rest till, as is well known, he had at last got

[3]

---

[1]Frederick Robertson (1816–1853), author and well-known clergyman.—Ed.
[2]Heinrich Heine (1797–1856), German poet and critic. Arnold probably got the terms "Hebraism" and "Hellenism" from Heine's writing.—Ed.
[3]He that . . . he: Proverbs 29:18—Ed.
[4]Blessed . . . commandments: Psalms 112:1.—Ed.

out of the law a network of prescriptions to enwrap his whole life, to govern every moment of it, every impulse, every action. The Greek notion of felicity, on the other hand, is perfectly conveyed in these words of a great French moralist: *"C'est le bonheur des hommes,"*[5]— when? when they abhor that which is evil?—no; when they exercise themselves in the law of the Lord day and night?—no; when they die daily?—no; when they walk about the New Jerusalem with palms in their hands?—no; but when they think aright, when their thought hits: *"quand ils pensent juste."* At the bottom of both the Greek and the Hebrew notion is the desire, native in man, for reason and the will of God, the feeling after the universal order,—in a word, the love of God. But, while Hebraism seizes upon certain plain, capital intimations of the universal order, and rivets itself, one may say, with unequalled grandeur of earnestness and intensity on the study and observance of them, the bent of Hellenism is to follow, with flexible activity, the whole play of the universal order, to be apprehensive of missing any part of it, of sacrificing one part to another, to slip away from resting in this or that intimation of it, however capital. An unclouded clearness of mind, an unimpeded play of thought, is what this bent drives at. The governing idea of Hellenism is *spontaneity of consciousness;* that of Hebraism, *strictness of conscience.*

## VOCABULARY

| | | |
|---|---|---|
| Hebraism (title) | censurable (2) | prescriptions (3) |
| Hellenism (title) | exigencies (2) | intimations (3) |
| foil (2) | ineffaceable (3) | |
| ludicrous (2) | felicity (3) | |

## THE FACTS

1. What is the final aim of both Hebraism and Hellenism?
2. According to Arnold, how do speakers generally use the concepts of Hebraism and Hellenism?
3. What is the uppermost idea of Hebraism? What is the uppermost idea of Hellenism?
4. What is the Hebrew notion of felicity? What is the Greek notion?

---

[5]"C'est le bonheur des hommes quand ils pensent juste": It is happiness for men when they think right. Michel Eyquem de Montaigne (1533–1592).—Ed.

## THE STRATEGIES

1. "The Greek quarrel with the body and its desires is, that they hinder right thinking; the Hebrew quarrel with them is, that they hinder right acting." What characteristic does this sentence possess?
2. Where does Arnold use a sentence similar to the one quoted in the preceding question? What does this kind of sentence contribute to the essay?
3. "The Greek notion of felicity, on the other hand, is perfectly conveyed in these words of a great French moralist: 'C'est le bonheur des hommes,'— when? when they abhor that which is evil?—no; when they exercise themselves in the law of the Lord day and night?—no; when they die daily?— no; when they walk about the New Jerusalem with palms in their hands?— no; but when they think aright, when their thought hits: 'quand ils pensent juste.' " What is the purpose of the questions interposed in this sentence?
4. What is the purpose of the French quotation?
5. Elsewhere Arnold quotes the Bible. Why? What is achieved by these quotations, French and biblical alike?

## THE ISSUES

1. Do you agree with Arnold that the Greek and Hebrew ideals both aim at having human beings partake of the divine nature? Do you believe that this aim can be accomplished equally well by using the Greek ideal as by using the Hebrew ideal? Give reasons for your answers.
2. It has been said that the Christian ideals, if taken seriously, would produce slave mentalities as human beings would live in humility, always turning the other cheek, forgiving all enemies, and never fighting back. What difference exists between Arnold's Hebraism and Christianity?
3. What importance do you attach to "right thinking" versus "right acting"?
4. The Greeks were known for their view of humanity as splendid, whereas the Hebrews saw human beings as corrupt. How are these two opposite views reflected in the respective literature of the two cultures?

## SUGGESTIONS FOR WRITING

1. Arnold says that "at the bottom of both the Greek and the Hebrew notion is the desire, native in man, for reason and the will of God, the feeling after the universal order." Analyze and discuss the presence of this desire in yourself, and say whether you draw upon Hebraism or upon Hellenism in fulfilling it.
2. Write an essay in which you use the block method of contrasting Hebraism and Hellenism as defined by Arnold. (See page 527 on how to proceed.)

Suzanne Britt Jordan

# —— • THAT LEAN AND HUNGRY LOOK • ——

*Suzanne Britt Jordan (b. 1946), formerly a university teacher of English, is now a feature writer for the Raleigh, North Carolina, News and Observer.*

*Flying in the face of today's admiration for slimly elegant people, Jordan gives the winning edge to the chubbies, favorably comparing them point by point with "that lean and hungry look" so mistrusted by Shakespeare.*

Caesar was right. Thin people need watching. I've been watching them for most of my adult life, and I don't like what I see. When these narrow fellows spring at me, I quiver to my toes. Thin people come in all personalities, most of them menacing. You've got your "together" thin person, your mechanical thin person, your condescending thin person, your tsk-tsk thin person, your efficiency-expert thin person. All of them are dangerous. 1

In the first place, thin people aren't fun. They don't know how to 2 goof off, at least in the best, fat sense of the word. They've always got to be adoing. Give them a coffee break, and they'll jog around the block. Supply them with a quiet evening at home, and they'll fix the screen door and lick S&H green stamps. They say things like "there aren't enough hours in the day." Fat people never say that. Fat people think the day is too damn long already.

Thin people make me tired. They've got speedy little metabolisms 3 that cause them to bustle briskly. They're forever rubbing their bony hands together and eying new problems to "tackle." I like to surround myself with sluggish, inert, easygoing fat people, the kind who believe that if you clean it up today, it'll just get dirty again tomorrow.

Some people say the business about the jolly fat person is a myth, 4 that all of us chubbies are neurotic, sick, sad people. I disagree. Fat people may not be chortling all day long, but they're a hell of a lot *nicer* than the wizened and shriveled. Thin people turn surly, mean and hard at a young age because they never learn the value of a hot-fudge sundae for easing tension. Thin people don't like gooey soft things because they themselves are neither gooey nor soft. They are crunchy and dull, like carrots. They go straight to the heart of the matter while fat people let things stay all blurry and hazy and vague, the way things actually are. Thin people want to face the truth. Fat people know there is no truth. One of my thin friends is always staring at complex, unsolvable problems and saying, "The key thing is . . ." Fat people never say that. They know there isn't any such thing as the key thing about anything.

Thin people believe in logic. Fat people see all sides. The sides fat    5
people see are rounded blobs, usually gray, always nebulous and truly not worth worrying about. But the thin person persists. "If you consume more calories than you burn," says one of my thin friends, "you will gain weight. It's that simple." Fat people always grin when they hear statements like that. They know better.

Fat people realize that life is illogical and unfair. They know very    6
well that God is not in his heaven and all is not right with the world. If God was up there, fat people could have two doughnuts and a big orange drink anytime they wanted it.

Thin people have a long list of logical things they are always spout-    7
ing off to me. They hold up one finger at a time as they reel off these things, so I won't lose track. They speak slowly as if to a young child. The list is long and full of holes. It contains tidbits like "get a grip on yourself," "cigarettes kill," "cholesterol clogs," "fit as a fiddle," "ducks in a row," "organize" and "sound fiscal management." Phrases like that.

They think these 2,000-point plans lead to happiness. Fat people    8
know happiness is elusive at best and even if they could get the kind thin people talk about, they wouldn't want it. Wisely, fat people see that such programs are too dull, too hard, too off the mark. They are never better than a whole cheesecake.

Fat people know all about the mystery of life. They are the ones    9
acquainted with the night, with luck, with fate, with playing it by ear. One thin person I know once suggested that we arrange all the parts of a jigsaw puzzle into groups according to size, shape and color. He figured this would cut the time needed to complete the puzzle by at least 50 per cent. I said I wouldn't do it. One, I like to muddle through. Two, what good would it do to finish early? Three, the jigsaw puzzle isn't the important thing. The important thing is the fun of four people (one thin person included) sitting around a card table, working a jigsaw puzzle. My thin friend had no use for my list. Instead of joining us, he went outside and mulched the boxwoods. The three remaining fat people finished the puzzle and made chocolate, double-fudged brownies to celebrate.

The main problem with thin people is they oppress. Their good    10
intentions, bony torsos, tight ships, neat corners, cerebral machina-
tions and pat solutions loom like dark clouds over the loose, comfortable, spread-out, soft world of the fat. Long after fat people have
removed their coats and shoes and put their feet up on the coffee table,
thin people are still sitting on the edge of the sofa, looking neat as a
pin, discussing rutabagas. Fat people are heavily into fits of laughter,
slapping their thighs and whooping it up, while thin people are still
politely waiting for the punch line.

Thin people are downers. They like math and morality and reasoned    11
evaluation of the limitations of human beings. They have their skinny
little acts together. They expound, prognose, probe and prick.

Fat people are convivial. They will like you even if you're irregular    12
and have acne. They will come up with a good reason why you never
wrote the great American novel. They will cry in your beer with you.
They will put your name in the pot. They will let you off the hook. Fat
people will gab, giggle, guffaw, gallumph, gyrate and gossip. They are
generous, giving and gallant. They are gluttonous and goodly and
great. What you want when you're down is soft and jiggly, not muscled
and stable. Fat people know this. Fat people have plenty of room. Fat
people will take you in.

## VOCABULARY

| | | |
|---|---|---|
| metabolisms (3) | mulched (9) | guffaw (12) |
| inert (3) | boxwoods (9) | gallumph (12) |
| wizened (4) | machinations (10) | gyrate (12) |
| surly (4) | rutabagas (10) | gluttonous (12) |
| nebulous (5) | prognose (11) | |
| elusive (8) | convivial (12) | |

## THE FACTS

1. In a nutshell, what bothers the author most about thin people?
2. What is your view of the myth about the "jolly fat person" mentioned in
   paragraph 4? What evidence is there for your view?
3. In paragraph 9, what is the "list" objected to by the thin person? What is
   ironic about this objection?
4. The thesis of Jordan's essay is obvious, but what is her underlying purpose?
   Since the essay is humorous, you might say that she simply wants to
   entertain the reader; but what more serious purpose is revealed?

5. In paragraph 10, Jordan claims that thin people "oppress." What evidence does she cite to support this claim?

## THE STRATEGIES

1. The title of the essay is a literary allusion that is echoed in the opening sentence. What is the origin of the allusion? What other allusion can you identify in the essay?
2. What rhetorical organization does the author use to develop her essay? What advantage does her organization present? What other type of organization could be used to contrast thin and fat people?
3. Paragraph 5 and other paragraphs open with short declarative sentences. What is the effect?
4. Here and there throughout the essay, Jordan uses figurative language. Find three examples and label the kind of figure of speech used in each.
5. How does the author achieve humor in her essay? Cite appropriate examples of her techniques.

## THE ISSUES

1. "Thin is in" is irrefutably one of the maxims of today. Why have we placed such emphasis on the slim look?
2. Reread John Leo's essay "Mirror, Mirror, on the Wall . . ." on pages 450–53. What does Leo say about the slim-hipped look of today? Does your answer to question one fit in with his view? Why or why not?
3. Are you convinced by Jordan's logic about the superiority of fat people? How does it strike you? Be specific in your answer.
4. If you were to play devil's advocate, how would you describe the thin person as desirable and the fat person as undesirable? Give specific examples as does Jordan.
5. How much or how little should a person's appearance affect his or her success on the job?

## SUGGESTIONS FOR WRITING

1. Write a five-hundred-word essay in which you prove the superiority of thin people over fat. Follow Suzanne Britt Jordan's style of using vivid details, but remain serious in your approach.
2. Using Jordan's piece as a model, write a five-hundred-word essay in which you contrast tall and short people.

Gilbert Highet

# ——— • DIOGENES AND ALEXANDER • ———

*Gilbert Highet (1906–1978) was born in Glasgow, Scotland, educated at the University of Glasgow and at Oxford, and became a naturalized American citizen in 1951. A classicist, Highet was known for his scholarly and critical writing, including* The Classical Tradition *(1949) and* The Anatomy of Satire *(1962).*

*This essay describes a meeting between two sharply contrasting personalities in Greek history—the Greek Cynic philosopher Diogenes (c. 412–323 B.C.) and Alexander the Great (356–323 B.C.), King of Macedonia. As Highet shows, although the two men occupied strikingly different positions in Greek society, they shared at least one quality that made them unique among the people of their time.*

Lying on the bare earth, shoeless, bearded, half-naked, he looked like a beggar or a lunatic. He was one, but not the other. He had opened his eyes with the sun at dawn, scratched, done his business like a dog at the roadside, washed at the public fountain, begged a piece of breakfast bread and a few olives, eaten them squatting on the ground, and washed them down with a few handfuls of water scooped from the spring. (Long ago he had owned a rough wooden cup, but he threw it away when he saw a boy drinking out of his hollowed hands.) Having no work to go to and no family to provide for, he was free. As the market place filled up with shoppers and merchants and gossipers and sharpers and slaves and foreigners, he had strolled through it for an hour or two. Everybody knew him, or knew of him. They would throw sharp questions at him and get sharper answers. Sometimes they threw jeers, and got jibes; sometimes bits of food, and got scant thanks; sometimes a mischievous pebble, and got a shower of stones and abuse. They were not quite sure whether he was mad or not. He knew they were mad, each in a different way; they amused him. Now he was back at his home. 1

It was not a house, not even a squatter's hut. He thought everybody lived far too elaborately, expensively, anxiously. What good is a house? No one needs privacy; natural acts are not shameful; we all do the same things, and need not hide them. No one needs beds and chairs and such furniture: the animals live healthy lives and sleep on the ground. All we require, since nature did not dress us properly, is one 2 garment to keep us warm, and some shelter from rain and wind. So he had one blanket—to dress him in the daytime and cover him at night—and he slept in a cask. His name was Diogenes. He was the founder of the creed called Cynicism (the word means "doggishness"); he spent much of his life in the rich, lazy, corrupt Greek city of Corinth, mocking and satirizing its people, and occasionally converting one of them.

His home was not a barrel made of wood: too expensive. It was a    3 storage jar made of earthenware, something like a modern fuel tank— no doubt discarded because a break had made it useless. He was not the first to inhabit such a thing: the refugees driven into Athens by the Spartan invasion had been forced to sleep in casks. But he was the first who ever did so by choice, out of principle.

Diogenes was not a degenerate or a maniac. He was a philosopher    4 who wrote plays and poems and essays expounding his doctrine; he talked to those who cared to listen; he had pupils who admired him. But he taught chiefly by example. All should live naturally, he said, for what is natural is normal and cannot possibly be evil or shameful. Live without conventions, which are artificial and false; escape complexities and superfluities and extravagances: only so can you live a free life. The rich man believes he possesses his big house with its many rooms and its elaborate furniture, his pictures and his expensive clothes, his horses and his servants and his bank accounts. He does not. He depends on them, he worries about them, he spends most of his life's energy looking after them; the thought of losing them makes him sick with anxiety. They possess him. He is their slave. In order to procure a quantity of false, perishable goods he has sold the only true, lasting good, his own independence.

There have been many men who grew tired of human society with    5 its complications, and went away to live simply—on a small farm, in a quiet village, in a hermit's cave, or in the darkness of anonymity. Not so Diogenes. He was not a recluse, or a stylite, or a beatnik. He was a missionary. His life's aim was clear to him: it was "to restamp the currency." (He and his father had once been convicted for counterfeiting, long before he turned to philosophy, and this phrase was Diogenes' bold, unembarrassed joke on the subject.) To restamp the currency: to take the clean metal of human life, to erase the old false conventional markings, and to imprint it with its true values.

The other great philosophers of the fourth century before Christ    6 taught mainly their own private pupils. In the shady groves and cool sanctuaries of the Academy, Plato discoursed to a chosen few on the unreality of this contingent existence. Aristotle, among the books and instruments and specimens and archives and research-workers of his Lyceum, pursued investigations and gave lectures that were rightly named *esoteric* "for those within the walls." But for Diogenes, laboratory and specimens and lecture halls and pupils were all to be found in a crowd of ordinary people. Therefore he chose to live in Athens or in the rich city of Corinth, where travelers from all over the Mediterranean world constantly came and went. And, by design, he publicly behaved in such ways as to show people what real life was. He would constantly take up their spiritual coin, ring it on a stone, and laugh at its false superscription.

He thought most people were only half-alive, most men only half-men. At bright noonday he walked through the market place carrying a lighted lamp and inspecting the face of everyone he met. They asked him why. Diogenes answered, "I am trying to find a *man*." 7

To a gentleman whose servant was putting on his shoes for him, Diogenes said, "You won't be really happy until he wipes your nose for you: that will come after you lose the use of your hands." 8

Once there was a war scare so serious that it stirred even the lazy, profit-happy Corinthians. They began to drill, clean their weapons, and rebuild their neglected fortifications. Diogenes took his old cask and began to roll it up and down, back and forward. "When you are all so busy," he said, "I felt I ought to do *something!*" 9

And so he lived—like a dog, some said, because he cared nothing for privacy and other human conventions, and because he showed his teeth and barked at those whom he disliked. Now he was lying in the sunlight, as contented as a dog on the warm ground, happier (he himself used to boast) than the Shah of Persia. Although he knew he was going to have an important visitor, he would not move. 10

The little square began to fill with people. Page boys elegantly dressed, spearmen speaking a rough foreign dialect, discreet secretaries, hard-browed officers, suave diplomats, they all gradually formed a circle centered on Diogenes. He looked them over, as a sober man looks at a crowd of tottering drunks, and shook his head. He knew who they were. They were the attendants of the conqueror of Greece, the servants of Alexander, the Macedonian king, who was visiting his newly subdued realm. 11

Only twenty, Alexander was far older and wiser than his years. Like    12
all Macedonians he loved drinking, but he could usually handle it; and
toward women he was nobly restrained and chivalrous. Like all Macedonians he loved fighting; he was a magnificent commander, but he
was not merely a military automaton. He could think. At thirteen he
had become a pupil of the greatest mind in Greece, Aristotle. No exact
record of his schooling survives. It is clear, though, that Aristotle took
the passionate, half-barbarous boy and gave him the best of Greek
culture. He taught Alexander poetry: the young prince slept with the
*Iliad* under his pillow and longed to emulate Achilles, who brought
the mighty power of Asia to ruin. He taught him philosophy, in particular the shapes and uses of political power: a few years later Alexander
was to create a supranational empire that was not merely a power
system but a vehicle for the exchange of Greek and Middle Eastern
cultures.

Aristotle taught him the principles of scientific research: during his    13
invasion of the Persian domains Alexander took with him a large corps
of scientists, and shipped hundreds of zoological specimens back to
Greece for study. Indeed, it was from Aristotle that Alexander learned
to seek out everything strange which might be instructive. Jugglers
and stunt artists and virtuosos of the absurd he dismissed with a
shrug; but on reaching India he was to spend hours discussing the
problems of life and death with naked Hindu mystics, and later to see
one demonstrate Yoga self-command by burning himself impassively
to death.

Now, Alexander was in Corinth to take command of the League of    14
Greek States which, after conquering them, his father Philip had created as a disguise for the New Macedonian Order. He was welcomed
and honored and flattered. He was the man of the hour, of the century:
he was unanimously appointed commander-in-chief of a new expedi-
tion against old, rich, corrupt Asia. Nearly everyone crowded to Corinth in order to congratulate him, to seek employment with him, even
simply to see him: soldiers and statesmen, artists and merchants,
poets and philosophers. He received their compliments graciously.
Only Diogenes, although he lived in Corinth, did not visit the new
monarch. With that generosity which Aristotle had taught him was a
quality of the truly magnanimous man, Alexander determined to call
upon Diogenes. Surely Dio-genes, the God-born, would acknowledge
the conqueror's power by some gift of hoarded wisdom.

With his handsome face, his fiery glance, his strong supple body,    15
his purple and gold cloak, and his air of destiny, he moved through
the parting crowd, toward the Dog's kennel. When a king approaches,
all rise in respect. Diogenes did not rise, he merely sat up on one elbow.
When a monarch enters a precinct, all greet him with a bow or an
acclamation. Diogenes said nothing.

There was a silence. Some years later Alexander speared his best    16
friend to the wall, for objecting to the exaggerated honors paid to His
Majesty; but now he was still young and civil. He spoke first, with a
kindly greeting. Looking at the poor broken cask, the single ragged
garment, and the rough figure lying on the ground, he said: "Is there
anything I can do for you, Diogenes?"

"Yes," said the Dog, "Stand to one side. You're blocking the    17
sunlight."

There was silence, not the ominous silence preceding a burst of fury,    18
but a hush of amazement. Slowly, Alexander turned away. A titter
broke out from the elegant Greeks, who were already beginning to
make jokes about the Cur that looked at the King. The Macedonian
officers, after deciding that Diogenes was not worth the trouble of
kicking, were starting to guffaw and nudge one another. Alexander
was still silent. To those nearest him he said quietly, "If I were not
Alexander, I should be Diogenes." They took it as a paradox, designed
to close the awkward little scene with a polite curtain line. But Alexander meant it. He understood Cynicism as the others could not. Later
he took one of Diogenes' pupils with him to India as a philosophical
interpreter (it was he who spoke to the naked *saddhus*). He was what
Diogenes called himself, a *cosmopolitēs*, "citizen of the world." Like
Diogenes, he admired the heroic figure of Hercules, the mighty conqueror who labors to help mankind while all others toil and sweat only
for themselves. He knew that of all men then alive in the world only
Alexander the conqueror and Diogenes the beggar were truly free.

## *VOCABULARY*

| | | |
|---|---|---|
| expounding (4) | discoursed (6) | suave (11) |
| conventions (4) | contingent (6) | supranational (12) |
| superfluities (4) | archives (6) | virtuosos (13) |
| stylite (5) | superscription (6) | |

Professor Highet explains the meanings of several words used in the essay. How does he interpret the following?

Cynicism (?)                Dio-genes (14)                cosmopolitēs (18)
esoteric (6)

## THE FACTS

1. What characteristics do Diogenes and Alexander share?
2. In what ways are Diogenes and Alexander different?
3. What is Diogenes's rationale for living so humbly?
4. According to Diogenes, the richer a man is, the more enslaved he becomes. How does he explain this statement?
5. How did the teaching method of Diogenes differ from that of Plato or Aristotle?
6. Paragraph 12 states that Alexander was far older and wiser than his twenty years. How is this maturity indicated?
7. According to the essay, Alexander "understood Cynicism as the others could not." What is Cynicism? Why did Alexander understand it better than others?

## THE STRATEGIES

1. In what paragraph does the focus shift from Diogenes to Alexander?
2. Does Highet draw his contrast by alternating back and forth between Diogenes and Alexander, or does he first draw a full portrait of Diogenes and then a full portrait of Alexander? What does Highet's method require of the reader?
3. How do you explain the paradox "If I were not Alexander, I should be Diogenes"?
4. The opening paragraph contains a sentence characterized by balance and parallelism. What are the opening words of this sentence?
5. What is the literary term for the phrase "to restamp the currency"? What is the meaning?
6. What is the topic sentence for paragraphs 7, 8, and 9? How is it developed?

## THE ISSUES

1. Which of the two men—Alexander or Diogenes—had a better chance for leading a contented life? Give reasons for your answer.
2. Reread the essay "My Wood" by E. M. Forster, pages 206–10. Then make a connection between Alexander's and Diogenes's lives and the essay. Ask yourself which of the two world figures most closely resembles the owner of the wood. Why?
3. Respond to paragraph 2. Do you agree with the idea that man should live

naturally and that we have become far too elaborate? Give reasons for your answer.

4. How important are philosophy, poetry, and the principles of scientific investigation—all subjects taught Alexander by Aristotle—to a modern curriculum? What other subjects, if any, would you add to a balanced curriculum?

5. Which would you prefer being, a person of power or a person of influence? Be specific in describing yourself, later in life, as having achieved either of these characteristics. What job would you be holding? What kind of family life would you lead?

## SUGGESTIONS FOR WRITING

1. Write a five-hundred-word essay in which you state why you admire Alexander more than Diogenes, or vice versa. Base your essay on the portraits of the two men as drawn by Highet.

2. Choosing one of the pairs listed below, write an essay developed by contrast. Begin with a thesis that summarizes the contrast. Keep in mind the basis of your contrast.
   a. jealousy/envy
   b. Thoreau/Gandhi
   c. wisdom/knowledge
   d. statesman/politician
   e. old age/youth

### Bruce Catton

# ——— • GRANT AND LEE: A STUDY • ———
# IN CONTRASTS

*Bruce Catton (1899–1978) is regarded as one of the most outstanding Civil War historians of the twentieth century. His books include* Mr. Lincoln's Army *(1951),* Glory Road *(1952),* A Stillness at Appomattox *(1953, Pulitzer Prize), and* This Hallowed Ground *(1956).*

*The following essay contrasts two famous personalities in American Civil War history: Ulysses S. Grant (1822–1885), commander in chief of the Union army and, later, eighteenth president of the United States (1869–1877); and his principal foe, Robert E. Lee (1807–1870), general in chief of the Confederate armies, who surrendered his forces to Grant in April 1865. The essay illustrates the development of a comparison/contrast between paragraphs, rather than within a paragraph.*

When Ulysses S. Grant and Robert E. Lee met in the parlor of a   1
modest house at Appomattox Court House, Virginia, on April 9, 1865,
to work out the terms for the surrender of Lee's Army of Northern
Virginia, a great chapter in American life came to a close, and a great
new chapter began.

These men were bringing the Civil War to its virtual finish. To be   2
sure, other armies had yet to surrender, and for a few days the fugitive
Confederate government would struggle desperately and vainly,
trying to find some way to go on living now that its chief support was
gone. But in effect it was all over when Grant and Lee signed the
papers. And the little room where they wrote out the terms was the
scene of one of the poignant, dramatic contrasts in American history.

They were two strong men, these oddly different generals, and they   3
represented the strengths of two conflicting currents that, through
them, had come into final collision.

Back of Robert E. Lee was the notion that the old aristocratic concept   4
might somehow survive and be dominant in American life.

Lee was tidewater Virginia, and in his background were family,   5
culture, and tradition . . . the age of chivalry transplanted to a New
World which was making its own legends and its own myths. He
embodied a way of life that had come down through the age of knight-
hood and the English country squire. America was a land that was
beginning all over again, dedicated to nothing much more complicated
than the rather hazy belief that all men had equal rights and should
have an equal chance in the world. In such a land Lee stood for the
feeling that it was somehow of advantage to human society to have a
pronounced inequality in the social structure. There should be a leisure class, backed by ownership of land; in turn, society itself should
be keyed to the land as the chief source of wealth and influence. It
would bring forth (according to this ideal) a class of men with a strong
sense of obligation to the community; men who lived not to gain advantage for themselves, but to meet the solemn obligations which had
been laid on them by the very fact that they were privileged. From
them the country would get its leadership; to them it could look for
the higher values—of thought, of conduct, of personal deportment—
to give it strength and virtue.

Lee embodied the noblest elements of this aristocratic ideal.   6
Through him, the landed nobility justified itself. For four years, the
Southern states had fought a desperate war to uphold the ideals for
which Lee stood. In the end, it almost seemed as if the Confederacy

fought for Lee; as if he himself was the Confederacy . . . the best thing that the way of life for which the Confederacy stood could ever have to offer. He had passed into legend before Appomattox. Thousands of tired, underfed, poorly clothed Confederate soldiers, long since past the simple enthusiasm of the early days of the struggle, somehow considered Lee the symbol of everything for which they had been willing to die. But they could not quite put this feeling into words. If the Lost Cause, sanctified by so much heroism and so many deaths, had a living justification, its justification was General Lee.

Grant, the son of a tanner on the Western frontier, was everything   7
Lee was not. He had come up the hard way and embodied nothing in particular except the eternal toughness and sinewy fiber of the men who grew up beyond the mountains. He was one of a body of men who owed reverence and obeisance to no one, who were self-reliant to a fault, who cared hardly anything for the past but who had a sharp eye for the future.

These frontier men were the precise opposites of the tidewater aris-   8
tocrats. Back of them, in the great surge that had taken people over the Alleghenies and into the opening Western country, there was a deep, implicit dissatisfaction with a past that had settled into grooves. They stood for democracy, not from any reasoned conclusion about the proper ordering of human society, but simply because they had grown up in the middle of democracy and knew how it worked. Their society might have privileges, but they would be privileges each man had won for himself. Forms and patterns meant nothing. No man was born to anything, except perhaps to a chance to show how far he could rise. Life was competition.

Yet along with this feeling had come a deep sense of belonging to a   9
national community. The Westerner who developed a farm, opened a shop, or set up in business as a trader, could hope to prosper only as his own community prospered—and his community ran from the Atlantic to the Pacific and from Canada down to Mexico. If the land was settled, with towns and highways and accessible markets, he could better himself. He saw his fate in terms of the nation's own destiny. As its horizons expanded, so did his. He had, in other words, an acute dollars-and-cents stake in the continued growth and development of his country.

And that, perhaps, is where the contrast between Grant and Lee   10
becomes most striking. The Virginia aristocrat, inevitably, saw himself in relation to his own region. He lived in a static society which could

endure almost anything except change. Instinctively, his first loyalty would go to the locality in which that society existed. He would fight to the limit of endurance to defend it, because in defending it he was defending everything that gave his own life its deepest meaning.

The Westerner, on the other hand, would fight with an equal tenac-   11
ity for the broader concept of society. He fought so because everything he lived by was tied to growth, expansion, and a constantly widening horizon. What he lived by would survive or fall with the nation itself. He could not possibly stand by unmoved in the face of an attempt to destroy the Union. He would combat it with everything he had, because he could only see it as an effort to cut the ground out from under his feet.

So Grant and Lee were in complete contrast, representing two dia-   12
metrically opposed elements in American life. Grant was the modern man emerging; beyond him, ready to come on the stage, was the great age of steel and machinery, of crowded cities and a restless, burgeoning vitality. Lee might have ridden down from the old age of chivalry, lance in hand, silken banner fluttering over his head. Each man was the perfect champion of his cause, drawing both his strengths and his weaknesses from the people he led.

Yet it was not all contrast, after all. Different as they were—in back-   13
ground, in personality, in underlying aspiration—these two great soldiers had much in common. Under everything else, they were marvelous fighters. Furthermore, their fighting qualities were really very much alike.

Each man had, to begin with, the great virtue of utter tenacity and   14
fidelity. Grant fought his way down the Mississippi Valley in spite of acute personal discouragement and profound military handicaps. Lee hung on in the trenches at Petersburg after hope itself had died. In each man there was an indomitable quality . . . the born fighter's refusal to give up as long as he can still remain on his feet and lift his two fists.

Daring and resourcefulness they had, too; the ability to think faster   15
and move faster than the enemy. These were the qualities which gave Lee the dazzling campaigns of Second Manassas and Chancellorsville and won Vicksburg for Grant.

Lastly, and perhaps greatest of all, there was the ability, at the end,   16
to turn quickly from war to peace once the fighting was over. Out of the way these two men behaved at Appomattox came the possibility of a peace of reconciliation. It was a possibility not wholly realized, in the

years to come, but which did, in the end, help the two sections to become one nation again . . . after a war whose bitterness might have seemed to make such a reunion wholly impossible. No part of either man's life became him more than the part he played in their brief meeting in the McLean house at Appomattox. Their behavior there put all succeeding generations of Americans in their debt. Two great Americans, Grant and Lee—very different, yet under everything very much alike. Their encounter at Appomattox was one of the great moments of American history.

## VOCABULARY

| | | |
|---|---|---|
| poignant (2) | sanctified (6) | diametrically (12) |
| deportment (5) | obeisance (7) | burgeoning (12) |
| embodied (6) | tenacity (11) | |

## THE FACTS

1. What was Lee's background? What ideal did he represent?
2. What was Grant's background? What did he represent?
3. What was Grant's view of the past? What was his attitude toward society and democracy?
4. What was the most striking contrast between Grant and Lee?
5. Catton writes that the behavior of Grant and Lee at Appomattox "put all succeeding generations of Americans in their debt." Why?

## THE STRATEGIES

1. Although the article is entitled "Grant and Lee: A Study in Contrasts," Catton begins by examining what Lee represented. Why? What logic is there to his order?
2. What function does paragraph 4 serve? Why is this one sentence set off by itself in a separate paragraph?
3. What common contrast phrase does paragraph 11 use?
4. In paragraph 8 the author writes: "These frontier men were the precise opposites of the tidewater aristocrats." What do these types have to do with a contrast betwen Grant and Lee?
5. What function does paragraph 8 serve?

## THE ISSUES

1. Does an aristocracy still survive in our multicultural United States? If you believe it has survived, describe where and what it is. If you believe it has vanished, then describe what has taken its place.

2. Which kind of citizen do you admire most—the aristocrat or the frontiers-man? Which do you believe is needed most for the betterment of our society today? Give reasons for your answers.
3. The aristocrat believes in form and tradition. How important are these in your view? Which traditions would you be willing to part with? Which would you want to keep?
4. What two women from history present an interesting contrast in two cultures? Describe both women and describe their contrasting cultures.
5. Which U.S. president, besides Ulysses S. Grant, is known for his support of economic growth and expansion? Do you favor continued growth and expansion, or are there other values you cherish more?

## SUGGESTIONS FOR WRITING

1. Examine and analyze the organization of the contrast in this essay. In what various respects are Grant and Lee contrasted? How does Catton order and structure his contrast?
2. Discuss the idea that a society can benefit from the presence of a privileged class.

### Alastair Reid

## • CURIOSITY •

*Alastair Reid (b. 1926) is a contemporary poet. He has translated the works of Jorge L. Borges, Pablo Neruda, and José E. Pacheo.*

*The poem that follows ostensibly draws a contrast between cats and dogs, but careful reading reveals that the animals are symbolic of certain types of people.*

### CURIOSITY

may have killed the cat. More likely,
the cat was just unlucky, or else curious
to see what death was like, having no cause
to go on licking paws, or fathering
litter on litter of kittens, predictably.                                    5

Nevertheless, to be curious
is dangerous enough. To distrust
what is always said, what seems,
to ask odd questions, interfere in dreams,

smell rats, leave home, have hunches,                                    10
does not endear cats to those doggy circles
where well-smelt baskets, suitable wives, good lunches
are the order of things, and where prevails
much wagging of incurious heads and tails.

Face it. Curiosity                                                       15
will not cause us to die—
only lack of it will.
Never to want to see
the other side of the hill
or that improbable country                                              20
where living is an idyll
(although a probable hell)
would kill us all.
Only the curious
have if they live a tale                                                 25
worth telling at all.

Dogs say cats love too much, are irresponsible,
are dangerous, marry too many wives,
desert their children, chill all dinner tables
with tales of their nine lives.                                          30

Well, they are lucky. Let them be
nine-lived and contradictory,
curious enough to change, prepared to pay
the cat-price, which is to die
and die again and again,                                                 35
each time with no less pain.
A cat-minority of one
is all that can be counted on
to tell the truth; and what cats have to tell
on each return from hell                                                 40
is this: that dying is what the living do,
that dying is what the loving do,
and that dead dogs are those who never know
that dying is what, to live, each has to do.

## VOCABULARY

incurious                    idyll

## THE FACTS

1. On the surface this poem is about cats and dogs. What deeper meaning does the poem have?
2. According to the author, what are the advantages of being a cat? What are the disadvantages?
3. Why are cats not loved by the "doggy circles"?
4. Who tells the real truth, cats or dogs?

## THE STRATEGIES

1. The idea of death or dying is used repeatedly throughout the poem. In what different senses are *death*, *die*, and *dying* used?
2. What is the meaning of the parenthetical words in line 22?
3. What do the "doggy circles" of the second stanza symbolize?
4. What kind of person is "nine-lived"?
5. In what way are *living* and *loving* related in the fifth stanza?

## THE ISSUES

1. As portrayed in Reid's poem, which would you rather be, a cat or a dog? Give reasons for your preference.
2. What famous characters from history would you align with cats, which with dogs? Why?
3. In favor of which species, if any, is the poem slanted? How can you tell?
4. Which would you rather be married to, a "cat" or a "dog"? Give reasons for your preference.
5. In an ideal society, what kind of balance or imbalance would you want between the number of "cats" and "dogs"?

## SUGGESTIONS FOR WRITING

1. Using Alastair Reid's poem as a model, write a five-hundred-word essay in which you compare and contrast two kinds of animals symbolic of people. For instance, you could contrast larks and owls, larks being people who rise early and owls people who love to stay up at night.
2. Write a three-hundred-word essay in praise of "dogs" (cautious, conventional people).

**Katherine Mansfield**

# • THE GARDEN PARTY •

*Katherine Mansfield (1888–1923), a British author, grew to master the short story after attaining proficiency as a violincellist. Her first volume of stories,* In a German Pension *(1911), received little attention. But she gained recognition with* Bliss *(1920) and with* The Garden Party *(1922). She has been compared with Anton Chekhov because of the simplicity and the evocativeness of her work. Mansfield suffered from tuberculosis during the last five years of her life and died of this disease at the age of thirty-five.*

And after all the weather was ideal. They could not have had a more 1 perfect day for a garden-party if they had ordered it. Windless, warm, the sky without a cloud. Only the blue was veiled with a haze of light gold, as it is sometimes in early summer. The gardener had been up since dawn, mowing the lawns and sweeping them, until the grass and the dark flat rosettes where the daisy plants had been seemed to shine. As for the roses, you could not help feeling they understood that roses are the only flowers that impress people at garden-parties; the only flowers that everybody is certain of knowing. Hundreds, yes, literally hundreds, had come out in a single night; the green bushes bowed down as though they had been visited by archangels.

Breakfast was not yet over before the men came to put up the 2 marquee.

"Where do you want the marquee put, mother?" 3

"My dear child, it's no use asking me. I'm determined to leave 4 everything to you children this year. Forget I am your mother. Treat me as an honoured guest."

But Meg could not possibly go and supervise the men. She had 5 washed her hair before breakfast, and she sat drinking coffee in a green turban, with a dark wet curl stamped on each cheek. Jose, the butterfly, always came down in a silk petticoat and a kimono jacket.

"You'll have to go, Laura; you're the artistic one." 6

Away Laura flew, still holding her piece of bread-and-butter. It's so 7 delicious to have an excuse for eating out of doors, and besides, she loved having to arrange things; she always felt she could do it so much better than anybody else.

Four men in their shirt-sleeves stood grouped together on the gar- 8 den path. They carried staves covered with rolls of canvas, and they had big tool-bags slung on their backs. They looked impressive. Laura wished now that she had not got the bread-and-butter, but there was nowhere to put it, and she couldn't possibly throw it away. She blushed and tried to look severe and even a little bit short-sighted as she came up to them.

"Good morning," she said, copying her mother's voice. But that 9 sounded so fearfully affected that she was ashamed, and stammered like a little girl, "Oh—er—have you come—is it about the marquee?"

"That's right, miss," said the tallest of the men, a lanky, freckled    10
fellow, and he shifted his tool-bag, knocked back his straw hat and
smiled down at her. "That's about it."

His smile was so easy, so friendly that Laura recovered. What nice    11
eyes he had, small, but such a dark blue! And now she looked at the
others, they were smiling too. "Cheer up, we won't bite," their smiles
seemed to say. How very nice workmen were! And what a beautiful
morning! She mustn't mention the morning; she must be businesslike.
The marquee.

"Well, what about the lily-lawn? Would that do?"    12

And she pointed to the lily-lawn with the hand that didn't hold the    13
bread-and-butter. They turned, they stared in the direction. A little fat
chap thrust out his under-lip, and the tall fellow frowned.

"I don't fancy it," said he. "Not conspicuous enough. You see, with    14
a thing like a marquee," and he turned to Laura in his easy way, "you
want to put it somewhere where it'll give you a bang slap in the eye, if
you follow me."

Laura's upbringing made her wonder for a moment whether it was    15
quite respectful of a workman to talk to her of bangs slap in the eye.
But she did quite follow him.

"A corner of the tennis-court," she suggested. "But the band's going    16
to be in one corner."

"H'm, going to have a band, are you?" said another of the workmen.    17
He was pale. He had a haggard look as his dark eyes scanned the
tennis-court. What was he thinking?

"Only a very small band," said Laura gently. Perhaps he wouldn't    18
mind so much if the band was quite small. But the tall fellow
interrupted.

"Look here, miss, that's the place. Against those trees, over there.    19
That'll do fine."

Against the karakas. Then the karakas-trees would be hidden. And    20
they were so lovely, with their broad, gleaming leaves, and their clusters of yellow fruit. They were like trees you imagined growing on a
desert island, proud, solitary, lifting their leaves and fruits to the sun
in a kind of silent splendour. Must they be hidden by a marquee?

They must. Already the men had shouldered their staves and were    21
making for the place. Only the tall fellow was left. He bent down,
pinched a sprig of lavender, put his thumb and forefinger to his nose
and snuffed up the smell. When Laura saw that gesture she forgot all

about the karakas in her wonder at him caring for things like that—caring for the smell of lavender. How many men that she knew would have done such a thing? Oh, how extraordinarily nice workmen were, she thought. Why couldn't she have workmen for friends rather than the silly boys she danced with and who came to Sunday night supper? She would get on much better with men like these.

It's all the fault, she decided, as the tall fellow drew something on 22 the back of an envelope, something that was to be looped up or left to hand, of these absurd class distinctions. Well, for her part, she didn't feel them. Not a bit, not an atom. . . . And now there came the chock-chock of wooden hammers. Some one whistled, some one sang out, "Are you right there, matey?" "Matey!" The friendliness of it, the—the—Just to prove how happy she was, just to show the tall fellow how at home she felt, and how she despised stupid conventions, Laura took a big bite of her bread-and-butter as she stared at the little draw-ing. She felt just like a work-girl.

"Laura, Laura, where are you? Telephone, Laura!" a voice cried 23 from the house.

"Coming!" Away she skimmed, over the lawn, up the path, up the 24 steps, across the veranda, and into the porch. In the hall her father and Laurie were brushing their hats ready to go to the office.

"I say, Laura," said Laurie very fast, "you might just give a squiz at 25 my coat before this afternoon. See if it wants pressing."

"I will," said she. Suddenly she couldn't stop herself. She ran at 26 Laurie and gave him a small, quick squeeze. "Oh, I do love parties, don't you?" gasped Laura.

"Ra-ther," said Laurie's warm, boyish voice, and he squeezed his 27 sister too, and gave her a gentle push. "Dash off to the telephone, old girl."

The telephone. "Yes, yes; oh yes. Kitty? Good morning, dear. Come 28 to lunch? Do, dear. Delighted of course. It will only be a very scratch meal—just the sandwich crusts and broken meringue-shells and what's left over. Yes, isn't it a perfect morning? Your white? Oh, I certainly should. One moment—hold the line. Mother's calling." And Laura sat back. "What mother? Can't hear."

Mrs. Sheridan's voice floated down the stairs. "Tell her to wear that 29 sweet hat she had on last Sunday."

"Mother says you're to wear that *sweet* hat you had on last Sunday. 30 Good. One o'clock. Bye-bye."

Laura put back the receiver, flung her arms over her head, took a 31 deep breath, stretched and let them fall. "Huh," she sighed, and the moment after the sigh sat up quickly. She was still, listening. All the doors in the house seemed to be open. The house was alive with soft, quick steps and running voices. The green baize door that led to the kitchen regions swung open and shut with a muffled thud. And now there came a long, chuckling absurd sound. It was the heavy piano being moved on its stiff castors. But the air! If you stopped to notice, was the air always like this? Little faint winds were playing chase, in at the tops of the windows, out at the doors. And there were two tiny spots of sun, one on the inkpot, one on a silver photograph frame, playing too. Darling little spots. Especially the one on the inkpot lid. It was quite warm. A warm little silver star. She could have kissed it.

The front door bell pealed, and there sounded the rustle of Sadie's     32 print skirt on the stairs. A man's voice murmured; Sadie answered, careless, "I'm sure I don't know. Wait. I'll ask Mrs. Sheridan."

"What is it, Sadie?" Laura came into the hall.     33

"It's the florist, Miss Laura."     34

It was, indeed. There, just inside the door, stood a wide, shallow     35 tray full of pots of pink lilies. No other kind. Nothing but lilies—canna lilies, big pink flowers, wide open, radiant, almost frighteningly alive on bright crimson stems.

"O-oh, Sadie!" said Laura, and the sound was like a little moan. She     36 crouched down as if to warm herself at that blaze of lilies; she felt they were in her fingers, on her lips, growing in her breast.

"It's some mistake," she said faintly. "Nobody ever ordered so many.     37 Sadie, go and find mother."

But at that moment Mrs. Sheridan joined them.     38

"It's quite right," she said calmly. "Yes, I ordered them. Aren't they     39 lovely?" She pressed Laura's arm. "I was passing the shop yesterday, and I saw them in the window. And I suddenly thought for once in my life I shall have enough canna lilies. The garden-party will be a good excuse."

"But I thought you said you didn't mean to interfere," said Laura.     40 Sadie had gone. The florist's man was still outside at his van. She put her arm round her mother's neck and gently, very gently, she bit her mother's ear.

"My darling child, you wouldn't like a logical mother, would you?     41 Don't do that. Here's the man."

He carried more lilies still, another whole tray.     42

"Bank them up, just inside the door, on both sides of the porch, please," said Mrs. Sheridan. "Don't you agree, Laura?"    43

"Oh, I *do*, mother."    44

In the drawing-room Meg, Jose and good little Hans had at last succeeded in moving the piano.    45

"Now, if we put this chesterfield against the wall and move everything out of the room except the chairs, don't you think?"    46

"Quite."    47

"Hans, move these tables into the smoking-room, and bring a sweeper to take these marks off the carpet and—one moment, Hans—" Jose loved giving orders to the servants, and they loved obeying her. She always made them feel they were taking part in some drama. "Tell mother and Miss Laura to come here at once."    48

"Very good, Miss Jose."    49

She turned to Meg. "I want to hear what the piano sounds like, just in case I'm asked to sing this afternoon. Let's try over 'This Life is Weary.'"    50

*Pom!* Ta-ta-ta *Tee*-ta! The piano burst out so passionately that Jose's face changed. She clasped her hands. She looked mournfully and enigmatically at her mother and Laura as they came in.    51

> This Life is *Wee*-ary,
> A Tear—A Sigh.
> A Love that *Chan*-ges,
>   This Life is *Wee*-ary,
> A Tear—a Sigh.
> A Love that *Chan*-ges,
> And then . . . Good-bye!

But at the word "Good-bye," and although the piano sounded more desperate than ever, her face broke into a brilliant, dreadfully unsympathetic smile.    52

"Aren't I in good voice, mummy?" she beamed.    53

> This Life is *Wee*-ary,
> Hope comes to Die.
> A Dream—a *Wa*-kening.

But now Sadie interrupted them. "What is it, Sadie?"    54

"If you please, m'm, cook says have you got the flags for the sandwiches?"    55

"The flags for the sandwiches, Sadie?" echoed Mrs. Sheridan    56 dreamily. And the children knew by her face that she hadn't got them. "Let me see." And she said to Sadie firmly, "Tell cook I'll let her have them in ten minutes."

Sadie went.    57

"Now, Laura," said her mother quickly. "Come with me into the    58
smoking-room. I've got the names somewhere on the back of an envelope. You'll have to write them out for me. Meg, go upstairs this minute and take that wet thing off your head. Jose, run and finish dressing this instant. Do you hear me, children, or shall I have to tell your father when he comes home to-night? And—and, Jose, pacify cook if you do go into the kitchen, will you? I'm terrified of her this morning."

The envelope was found at last behind the dining-room clock,    59
though how it had got there Mrs. Sheridan could not imagine.

"One of you children must have stolen it out of my bag, because I    60
remember vividly—cream cheese and lemon-curd. Have you done that?"

"Yes."    61

"Egg and—" Mrs. Sheridan held the envelope away from her. "It    62
looks like mice. It can't be mice, can it?"

"Olive, pet," said Laura, looking over her shoulder.    63

"Yes, of course, olive. What a horrible combination it sounds. Egg    64
and olive."

They were finished at last, and Laura took them off to the kitchen.    65
She found Jose there pacifying the cook, who did not look at all terrifying.

"I have never seen such exquisite sandwiches," said Jose's rapturous    66
voice. "How many kinds did you say there were, cook? Fifteen?"

"Fifteen, Miss Jose."    67

"Well, cook, I congratulate you."    68

Cook swept up crusts with the long sandwich knife, and smiled    69
broadly.

"Godber's has come," announced Sadie, issuing out of the pantry.    70
She had seen the man pass the window.

That meant the cream puffs had come. Godber's were famous for    71
their cream puffs. Nobody ever thought of making them at home.

"Bring them in and put them on the table, my girl," ordered cook.    72

Sadie brought them in and went back to the door. Of course Laura    73
and Jose were far too grown-up to really care about such things. All the same, they couldn't help agreeing that the puffs looked very

attractive. Very. Cook began arranging them, shaking off the extra icing sugar.

"Don't they carry one back to all one's parties?" said Laura.    74

"I suppose they do," said practical Jose, who never liked to be carried back. "They look beautifully light and feathery, I must say."    75

"Have one each, my dears," said cook in her comfortable voice. "Yer ma won't know."    76

Oh, impossible. Fancy cream puffs so soon after breakfast. The very idea made one shudder. All the same, two minutes later Jose and Laura were licking their fingers with that absorbed inward look that only comes from whipped cream.    77

"Let's go into the garden, out by the back way," suggested Laura. "I want to see how the men are getting on with the marquee. They're such awfully nice men."    78

But the back door was blocked by cook, Sadie, Godber's man and Hans.    79

Something had happened.    80

"Tuk-tuk-tuk," clucked cook like an agitated hen. Sadie had her hand clapped to her cheek as though she had toothache. Hans's face was screwed up in the effort to understand. Only Godber's man seemed to be enjoying himself; it was his story.    81

"What's the matter? What's happened?"    82

"There's been a horrible accident," said cook. "A man killed."    83

"A man killed! Where? How? When?"    84

But Godber's man wasn't going to have his story snatched from under his very nose.    85

"Know those little cottages just below here, miss?" Know them? Of course, she knew them. "Well, there's a young chap living there, name of Scott, a carter. His horse shied at a traction-engine, corner of Hawke Street this morning, and he was thrown out on the back of his head. Killed."    86

"Dead!" Laura stared at Godber's man.    87

"Dead when they picked him up," said Godber's man with relish. "They were taking the body home as I come up here." And he said to the cook, "He's left a wife and five little ones."    88

"Jose, come here." Laura caught hold of her sister's sleeve and dragged her through the kitchen to the other side of the green baize door. There she paused and leaned against it. "Jose!" she said, horrified, "however are we going to stop everything?"    89

"Stop everything, Laura!" cried Jose in astonishment. "What do    90
you mean?"

"Stop the garden-party, of course." Why did Jose pretend?    91

But Jose was still more amazed. "Stop the garden-party? My dear    92
Laura, don't be so absurd. Of course we can't do anything of the kind.
Nobody expects us to. Don't be so extravagant."

"But we can't possibly have a garden-party with a man dead just    93
outside the front gate."

That really was extravagant, for the little cottages were in a lane to    94
themselves at the very bottom of a steep rise that led up to the house.
A broad road ran between. True, they were far too near. They were the
greatest possible eyesore, and they had no right to be in that neigh-
bourhood at all. They were little mean dwellings painted a chocolate
brown. In the garden patches there was nothing but cabbage stalks,
sick hens and tomato cans. The very smoke coming out of their chimneys was poverty-stricken. Little rags and shreds of smoke, so unlike
the great silvery plumes that uncurled from the Sheridans' chimneys.
Washer-women lived in the lane and sweeps and a cobbler, and a man
whose house-front was studded all over with minute bird-cages. Children swarmed. When the Sheridans were little they were forbidden to
set foot there because of the revolting language and of what they might
catch. But since they were grown up, Laura and Laurie on their prowls
sometimes walked through. It was disgusting and sordid. They came
out with a shudder. But still one must go everywhere; one must see
everything. So through they went.

"And just think of what the band would sound like to that poor    95
woman," said Laura.

"Oh, Laura!" Jose began to be seriously annoyed. "If you're going    96
to stop a band playing every time some one has an accident, you'll lead
a very strenuous life. I'm every bit as sorry about it as you. I feel just
as sympathetic." Her eyes hardened. She looked at her sister just as
she used to when they were little and fighting together. "You won't
bring a drunken workman back to life by being sentimental," she said
softly.

"Drunk! Who said he was drunk?" Laura turned furiously on Jose.    97
She said, just as they had used to say on those occasions, "I'm going
straight up to tell mother."

"Do, dear," cooed Jose.    98

"Mother, can I come into your room?" Laura turned the big glass    99
door-knob.

"Of course, child. Why, what's the matter? What's given you such a    100
colour?" And Mrs. Sheridan turned round from her dressing-table.
She was trying on a new hat.

"Mother, a man's been killed," began Laura.    101

"*Not* in the garden?" interrupted her mother.    102

"No, no!"    103

"Oh, what a fright you gave me!" Mrs. Sheridan sighed with relief,    104
and took off the big hat and held it on her knees.

"But listen, mother," said Laura. Breathless, half-choking, she told    105
the dreadful story. "Of course, we can't have our party, can we?" she
pleaded. "The band and everybody arriving. They'd hear us, mother;
they're nearly neighbours!"

To Laura's astonishment her mother behaved just like Jose; it was    106
harder to bear because she seemed amused. She refused to take Laura
seriously.

"But, my dear child, use your common sense. It's only by accident    107
we've heard of it. If some one had died there normally—and I can't
understand how they keep alive in those poky little holes—we should
still be having our party, shouldn't we?

Laura had to say "yes" to that, but she felt it was all wrong. She sat    108
down on her mother's sofa and pinched the cushion frill.

"Mother, isn't it really terribly heartless of us?" she asked.    109

"Darling!" Mrs. Sheridan got up and came over to her, carrying the    110
hat. Before Laura could stop her she had popped it on. "My child!"
said her mother, "the hat is yours. It's made for you. It's much too
young for me. I have never seen you look such a picture. Look at
yourself!" And she held up her hand-mirror.

"But, mother," Laura began again. She couldn't look at herself; she    111
turned aside.

This time Mrs. Sheridan lost patience just as Jose had done.    112

"You are being very absurd, Laura," she said coldly. "People like    113
that don't expect sacrifices from us. And it's not very sympathetic to
spoil everybody's enjoyment as you're doing now."

"I don't understand," said Laura, and she walked quickly out of the    114
room into her own bedroom. There, quite by chance, the first thing
she saw was this charming girl in the mirror, in her black hat trimmed
with gold daisies, and a long black velvet ribbon. Never had she imagined she could look like that. Is mother right? she thought. And now
she hoped her mother was right. Am I being extravagant? Perhaps it
was extravagant. Just for a moment she had another glimpse of that

poor woman and those little children, and the body being carried into the house. But it all seemed blurred, unreal, like a picture in the news-paper. I'll remember it again after the party's over, she decided. And somehow that seemed quite the best plan. . . .

Lunch was over by half-past one. By half-past two they were all ready for the fray. The green-coated band had arrived and was estab-lished in a corner of the tennis-court.     115

"My dear!" trilled Kitty Maitland, "aren't they too like frogs for words? You ought to have arranged them round the pond with the conductor in the middle on a leaf."     116

Laurie arrived and hailed them on his way to dress. At the sight of him Laura remembered the accident again. She wanted to tell him. If Laurie agreed with the others, then it was bound to be all right. And she followed him into the hall.     117

"Laurie!"     118

"Hallo!" He was half-way upstairs, but when he turned round and saw Laura he suddenly puffed out his cheeks and goggled his eyes at her. "My word, Laura! You do look stunning," said Laurie. "What an absolutely topping hat!"     119

Laura said faintly "Is it?" and smiled up at Laurie, and didn't tell him after all.     120

Soon after that people began coming in streams. The band struck up; the hired waiters ran from the house to the marquee. Wherever you looked there were couples strolling, bending to the flowers, greet-ing, moving on over the lawn. They were like bright birds that had alighted in the Sheridans' garden for this one afternoon, on their way to—where? Ah, what happiness it is to be with people who all are happy, to press hands, press cheeks, smile into eyes.     121

"Darling Laura, how well you look!"     122

"What a becoming hat, child!"     123

"Laura, you look quite Spanish. I've never seen you look so striking."     124

And Laura, glowing, answered softly, "Have you had tea? Won't you have an ice? The passion-fruit ices really are rather special." She ran to her father and begged him. "Daddy darling, can't the band have something to drink?"     125

And the perfect afternoon slowly ripened, slowly faded, slowly its petals closed.     126

"Never a more delightful garden-party . . ." "The greatest suc-cess . . ." "Quite the most . . ."     127

Laura helped her mother with the good-byes. They stood side by side in the porch till it was all over.    128

"All over, all over, thank heaven," said Mrs. Sheridan. "Round up the others, Laura. Let's go and have some fresh coffee. I'm exhausted. Yes, it's been very successful. But oh, these parties, these parties! Why will you children insist on giving parties!" And they all of them sat down in the deserted marquee.    129

"Have a sandwich, daddy dear. I wrote the flag."    130

"Thanks." Mr. Sheridan took a bite and the sandwich was gone. He took another. "I suppose you didn't hear of a beastly accident that happened to-day?" he said.    131

"My dear," said Mrs. Sheridan, holding up her hand, "we did. It nearly ruined the party. Laura insisted we should put it off."    132

"Oh, mother!" Laura didn't want to be teased about it.    133

"It was a horrible affair all the same," said Mr. Sheridan. "The chap was married too. Lived just below in the lane, and leaves a wife and half a dozen kiddies, so they say."    134

An awkward little silence fell. Mrs. Sheridan fidgeted with her cup. Really, it was very tactless of father . . .    135

Suddenly she looked up. There on the table were all those sandwiches, cakes, puffs, all uneaten, all going to be wasted. She had one of her brilliant ideas.    136

"I know," she said. "Let's make up a basket. Let's send that poor creature some of this perfectly good food. At any rate, it will be the greatest treat for the children. Don't you agree? And she's sure to have neighbours calling in and so on. What a point to have it all ready prepared. Laura!" She jumped up. "Get me the big basket out of the stairs cupboard."    137

"But, mother, do you really think it's a good idea?" said Laura.    138

Again, how curious, she seemed to be different from them all. To take scraps from their party. Would the poor woman really like that?    139

"Of course! What's the matter with you to-day? An hour or two ago you were insisting on us being sympathetic, and now—"    140

Oh, well! Laura ran for the basket. It was filled, it was heaped by her mother.    141

"Take it yourself, darling," said she. "Run down just as you are. No, wait, take the arum lilies too. People of that class are so impressed by arum lilies."    142

"The stems will ruin her lace frock," said practical Jose.    143

So they would. Just in time. "Only the basket, then. And, Laura!"—    144

her mother followed her out of the marquee—"don't on any account—"

"What, mother?"    145

No, better not put such ideas into the child's head! "Nothing! Run    146
along."

It was just growing dusky as Laura shut their garden gates. A big    147
dog ran by like a shadow. The road gleamed white, and down below
in the hollow the little cottages were in deep shade. How quiet it
seemed after the afternoon. Here she was going down the hill to somewhere where a man lay dead, and she couldn't realize it. Why couldn't
she? She stopped a minute. And it seemed to her that kisses, voices,
tinkling spoons, laughter, the smell of crushed grass were somehow
inside her. She had no room for anything else. How strange! She
looked up at the pale sky, and all she thought was, "Yes, it was the
most successful party."

Now the broad road was crossed. The lane began, smoky and dark.    148
Women in shawls and men's tweed caps hurried by. Men hung over
the palings; the children played in the doorways. A low hum came
from the mean little cottages. In some of them there was a flicker of
light, and a shadow, crab-like, moved across the window. Laura bent
her head and hurried on. She wished now she had put on a coat. How
her frock shone! And the big hat with the velvet streamer—if only it
was another hat! Were the people looking at her? They must be. It was
a mistake to have come; she knew all along it was a mistake. Should
she go back even now?

No, too late. This was the house. It must be. A dark knot of people    149
stood outside. Beside the gate an old, old woman with a crutch sat in
a chair, watching. She had her feet on a newspaper. The voices stopped
as Laura drew near. The group parted. It was as though she was
expected, as though they had known she as coming here.

Laura was terribly nervous. Tossing the velvet ribbon over her    150
shoulder, she said to a woman standing by, "Is this Mrs. Scott's
house?" and the woman, smiling queerly, said, "It is, my lass."

Oh, to be away from this! She actually said, "Help me, God," as she    151
walked up the tiny path and knocked. To be away from those staring
eyes, or to be covered up in anything, one of those women's shawls
even. I'll just leave the basket and go, she decided. I shan't even wait
for it to be emptied.

Then the door opened. A little woman in black showed in the gloom.    152

Laura said, "Are you Mrs. Scott?" But to her horror the woman    153
answered, "Walk in please, miss," and she was shut in the passage.

"No," said Laura, "I don't want to come in. I only want to leave this    154
basket. Mother sent—"

The little woman in the gloomy passage seemed not to have heard    155
her. "Step this way, please, miss," she said in an oily voice, and Laura
followed her.

She found herself in a wretched little low kitchen, lighted by a    156
smoky lamp. There was a woman sitting before the fire.

"Em," said the little creature who had let her in. "Em! It's a young    157
lady." She turned to Laura. She said meaningly, "I'm 'er sister, miss.
You'll excuse 'er, wont you?"

"Oh, but of course!" said Laura. "Please, please don't disturb her.    158
I—I only want to leave—"

But at that moment the woman at the fire turned round. Her face,    159
puffed up, red, with swollen eyes and swollen lips, looked terrible.
She seemed as though she couldn't understand why Laura was there.
What did it mean? Why was this stranger standing in the kitchen with
a basket? What was it all about? And the poor face puckered up again.

"All right, my dear," said the other. "I'll thenk the young lady."    160

And again she began, "You'll excuse her, miss, I'm sure," and her    161
face, swollen too, tried an oily smile.

Laura only wanted to get out, to get away. She was back in the    162
passage. The door opened. She walked straight through into the bedroom, where the dead man was lying.

"You'd like a look at 'im, wouldn't you?" said Em's sister, and she    163
brushed past Laura over to the bed. "Don't be afraid, my lass—" and
now her voice sounded fond and sly, and fondly she drew down
the sheet—"'e looks a picture. There's nothing to show. Come along,
my dear."

Laura came.    164

There lay a young man, fast asleep—sleeping so soundly, so deeply,    165
that he was far, far away from them both. Oh, so remote, so peaceful.
He was dreaming. Never wake him up again. His head was sunk in
the pillow, his eyes were closed; they were blind under the closed
eyelids. He was given up to his dream. What did garden-parties and
baskets and lace frocks matter to him? He was far from all those things.
He was wonderful, beautiful. While they were laughing and while
the band was playing, this marvel had come to the lane. Happy . . .

happy . . . All is well, said that sleeping face. This is just as it should be. I am content.

But all the same you had to cry, and she couldn't go out of the room 166 without saying something to him. Laura gave a loud childish sob.

"Forgive my hat," she said. 167

And this time she didn't wait for Em's sister. She found her way out 168 of the door, down the path, past all those dark people. At the corner of the lane she met Laurie.

He stepped out of the shadow. "Is that you, Laura?" 169

"Yes." 170

"Mother was getting anxious. Was it all right?" 171

"Yes, quite. Oh, Laurie!" She took his arm, she pressed up against 172 him.

"I say, you're not crying, are you?" asked her brother. 173

Laura shook her head. She was. 174

Laurie put his arm round her shoulder. "Don't cry," he said in his 175 warm, loving voice. "Was it awful?"

"No," sobbed Laura. "It was simply marvellous. But, Laurie—" She 176 stopped, she looked at her brother. "Isn't life," she stammered, "isn't life—" But what life was she couldn't explain. No matter. He quite understood.

"*Isn't* it, darling?" said Laurie. 177

## VOCABULARY

| | | |
|---|---|---|
| rosettes (1) | enigmatically (51) | palings (148) |
| staves (8) | carter (86) | |
| baize (31) | fray (145) | |

## THE FACTS

1. What dominant impression do the details of paragraph 1 convey?
2. What details suggest that the party will cost a great deal of money?
3. What do paragraphs 51–53 indicate?
4. What news do the Godber's delivery man bring? How does it affect the family giving the party?
5. What attitude does the widow and her sister reveal toward Laura when she visits them?

## THE STRATEGIES

1. The entire story is revealed from Laura's point of view. What kind of person is she and how is her character developed?

2. What sharp contrast is drawn in the story? Does the author comment explicitly on this contrast or does she allow her readers to draw their own conclusions? Give reasons for your answer.
3. What sensory impressions dominate paragraph 31? Cite specific examples.
4. In paragraph 22 Laura claims that class distinctions are absurd and that she does not feel any. Is her claim justified? Support your answer with facts from the text.
5. What admonition do you think Laura's mother intended to give in paragraph 144? Finish the admonition.

## THE ISSUES

1. What attitude about the poor is Laura likely to reveal in later life? How do you know?
2. What is the Sheridan family's reaction to the tragedy taking place in the poor laborers' quarters? How does their attitude compare or contrast to a similar situation that might happen today? Support your answer with examples.
3. What archetypal theme is developed toward the end of the story?
4. In your view, how should the Sheridan family have reacted to the laborer's death? Did they do all that was required under the circumstances? What, if anything, should they have done differently or additionally? Be specific in your answers.
5. What ideas do the bird imagery of paragraph 121 and the flower imagery of paragraph 126 contribute to the story?

## SUGGESTIONS FOR WRITING

1. Write an essay arguing for greater awareness and sensitivity on the part of the rich toward the poor.
2. Write an essay listing the advantages of poverty over wealth.
3. Write an essay in which you contrast two present-day nations, one wealthy and one poor. Be sure to clarify the bases of your contrast.

## ══════ •• *ADVICE* •• ══════

## HOW TO WRITE A DIVISION AND CLASSIFICATION

The term *division* refers to any piece of writing that intends to break a subject down into smaller units. For instance, an essay on types of automobiles that analyzes and classifies automobiles according to their sizes is developed by division; similarly, an essay on American types, such as the one anthologized below, is also developed by division.

Division and classification are common to the way we think. We divide and classify the plant and animal kingdoms into phyla, genera, families, and species; we divide the military into the Army, Navy, Air Force, Marines, and Coast Guard. We divide and classify people into kinds and types. When we ask, ''What kind of person is he?'' we are asking for information developed by division and classification. An assignment asking for an essay developed by division is therefore an exercise in this common mode of thinking.

In developing an essay by division, it is useful to make this intent immediately clear. For instance, the essay by William Golding, ''Thinking as a Hobby,'' which is anthologized in this section, makes it clear in the first paragraph what the writer intends to do:

> While I was still a boy, I came to the conclusion that there were three grades of thinking; and since I was later to claim thinking as my hobby, I came to an even stranger conclusion—namely, that I myself could not think at all.

We are therefore prepared for this division of thinking into three types, and for his anecdotes about why he has decided that he cannot think. Likewise, in Max Lerner's essay ''Some American Types,'' the first paragraph (as well as the title) announces the author's intent to divide and classify American personalities:

> Anyone familiar with American literature will know that it contains stock portraits of its own which express social types. I want to use these traditional types as backdrops and stress some of the social roles that are new and still in process of formation.

Having promised a division, both essays deliver it.

## 1. Divide your subject by a single principle.

Once the division is made, stick to it. In the example below, the writer has violated this:

> Mating between man and woman takes place in four stages: the courtship, commitment, marriage, and deciding who will be responsible for household chores.

Courtship, commitment, and marriage are all part of mating; assigning responsibilities for household chores is not. Even if well executed, this essay contains a gross flaw by failing to subdivide its subjects according to the promised single principle—stages of mating.

## 2. Make your categories mutually exclusive.

Obviously, if you are dividing a subject into smaller categories, these must mutually exclude each other. This proposed division fails to develop mutually exclusive categories:

> College students may be divided into three groups: the so-called athletic "jock"; the scholarly "egghead"; and the student working his way through.

Both the "jock" and the "egghead" could also be working their way through college. The categories are therefore not mutually exclusive.

### 3. Make the division complete.

A division is useless if its categories are incomplete. For instance:

> The dialogue and the recitation are the primary ways in which information can be passed from teacher to student.

This division omits the lecture method and is therefore faulty.

Students sometimes wonder why essays are assigned to conform to specific types of development such as division and classification—why a student is not allowed to simply meander over a subject freely. The answer is that writing by strict means of development also trains the student to think. A pattern such as division forces the student to submit his meanderings to the discipline of structure. Moreover, the pattern itself is not only a writing pattern but a thought pattern. Division and classification are a necessary part of logical thinking; assignments on them force a student to think on paper.

Max Lerner

## — • SOME AMERICAN TYPES • —

*Max Lerner (b. 1902), author and lecturer, was born in Minsk, Russia. He attended Yale University and Washington University in St. Louis, and was awarded a Ph.D. from the Robert Brookings Graduate School of Economics and Government in 1927. His works include* Ideas Are Weapons *(1939) and* America as a Civilization *(1957), from which this selection was taken.*

*As its title indicates, this essay comments on our society not by describing individual Americans, but by dividing Americans into certain distinguishable classes or categories.*

Seventeenth-century England produced a number of books on *Characters* depicting English society through the typical personality patterns of the era. Trying something of the same sort for contemporary America, the first fact one encounters is the slighter emphasis on a number of character types than stand out elsewhere in Western society: to be sure, they are to be found in America as well, but they are not characteristically American. One thinks of the scholar, the aesthete, the priest or "parson," the "aristocratic" army officer, the revolutionary student, the civil servant, the male schoolteacher, the marriage broker, the courtesan, the mystic, the saint. Anyone familiar with European literature will recognize these characters as stock literary types and therefore as social types. Each of them represents a point of convergence for character and society. Anyone familiar with American literature will know that it contains stock portraits of its own which express social types. I want to use these traditional types as backdrops and stress some of the social roles that are new and still in process of formation.

Thus there is the *fixer*, who seems an organic product of a society in      2
which the middleman function eats away the productive one. He may be public-relations man or influence peddler; he may get your traffic fine settled, or he may be able—whatever the commodity—to "get it for you wholesale." He is contemptuous of those who take the formal rules seriously; he knows how to cut corners—financial, political, administrative, or moral. At best there is something of the iconoclast in him, an unfooled quality far removed from the European personality types that always obey authority. At worst he becomes what the English call a "spiv" or cultural procurer.

Related to the fixer is the *inside dopester*, as Riesman* has termed      3
him. He is oriented not so much toward getting things fixed as toward being "in the know" and "wised up" about things that innocents take at face value. He is not disillusioned because he has never allowed himself the luxury of illusions. In the 1920s and 1930s he consumed the literature of "debunking"; in the current era he knows everything that takes place in the financial centers of Wall Street, the political centers of Capitol Hill, and the communications centers of Madison Avenue—yet among all the things he knows there is little he believes in. His skepticism is not the wisdom which deflates pretentiousness but that of the rejecting man who knows ahead of time that there is "nothing in it" whatever the "it" may be. In short, he is "hep."

Another link leads to the *neutral* man. He expresses the devaluing      4
tendency in a culture that tries to avoid commitments. Fearful of being caught in the crosscurrents of conflict that may endanger his safety or status, he has a horror of what he calls "controversial figures"—and

---

*David Riesman, American sociologist, wrote *The Lonely Crowd, Faces in the Crowd*, and other works.—Ed.

anyone becomes "controversial" if he is attacked. As the fixer and the inside dopester are the products of a middleman's society, so the neutral man is the product of a technological one. The technician's detachment from everything except effective results becomes—in the realm of character—an ethical vacuum that strips the results of much of their meaning.

From the neutral man to the *conformist* is a short step. Although he is not neutral—in fact, he may be militantly partisan—his partisanship is on the side of the big battalions. He lives in terror of being caught in a minority where his insecurity will be conspicuous. He gains a sense of stature by joining the dominant group, as he gains security by making himself indistinguishable from that group. Anxious to efface any unique traits of his own, he exacts conformity from others. He fears ideas whose newness means they are not yet accepted, but once they are firmly established he fights for them with a courage born of the knowledge that there is no danger in championing them. He hates foreigners and immigrants. When he talks of the "American way," he sees a world in which other cultures have become replicas of his own.

It is often hard to distinguish the conformist from the *routineer*. Essentially he is a man in uniform, sometimes literally, always symbolically. The big public-service corporations—railroads, air lines, public utilities—require their employees to wear uniforms that will imprint a common image of the enterprise as a whole. City employees, such as policemen and firemen, wear uniforms. Gas-station attendants, hotel clerks, bellhops, must similarly keep their appearance within prescribed limits. Even the sales force in big department stores or the typists and stenographers in big corporations tend toward the same uniformity. There are very few young Americans who are likely to escape the uniform of the Armed Services. With the uniform goes an urge toward pride of status and a routineering habit of mind. There is the confidence that comes of belonging to a large organization and sharing symbolically in its bigness and power. There is a sense of security in having grooves with which to move. This is true on every level of corporate business enterprise, from the white-collar employee to "the man in the gray flannel suit," although it stops short of the top executives who create the uniforms instead of wearing them. Even outside the government and corporate bureaus there are signs of American life becoming bureaucratized, in a stress on forms and routines, on "going through channels."

Unlike the conformist or routineer, the *status seeker* may possess a   7
resourceful energy and even originality, but he directs these qualities
toward gaining status. What he wants is a secure niche in a society
whose men are constantly being pulled upward or trodden down.
Scott Fitzgerald has portrayed a heartbreaking case history of this
character type in *The Great Gatsby*, whose charm and energy are in-
vested fruitlessly in an effort to achieve social position. The novels of
J. P. Marquand are embroideries of a similar theme, narrated through
the mind of one who already has status and is confronted by the risk
of losing it. At various social levels the status seeker becomes a
"joiner" of associations which give him symbolic standing.

## VOCABULARY

| | | |
|---|---|---|
| aesthete (1) | iconoclast (2) | battalions (5) |
| courtesan (1) | procurer (2) | replicas (5) |
| mystic (1) | pretentiousness (3) | bureaucratized (6) |
| convergence (1) | hep (3) | niche (7) |
| organic (2) | devaluing (4) | |
| contemptuous (2) | militantly (5) | |

## THE FACTS

1. What stock types exist in Europe that are not so typical of American society—especially as reflected in literature?
2. What do the fixer and inside dopester have in common?
3. Why does the neutral man have a horror of "controversial figures"?
4. Why is it often difficult to distinguish the conformist from the routineer?
5. What does the status seeker want most of all from society?

## THE STRATEGIES

1. What is the purpose of Lerner's introductory paragraph?
2. How does Lerner keep his essay organized and coherent? Point to the
   specific words or passages that help achieve coherence and organization.
3. A good division must divide up an entire group. What entire group does
   Lerner's essay divide up?
4. Lerner describes his types by supplying details that bring each type to life.
   Are some of his descriptions better than others? Why?

## THE ISSUES

1. In describing six types of Americans, has Lerner exhausted all major types?
   If not, which has he left out?

2. In listing his six types, what basic criticism is Lerner leveling at America? Do you agree with his criticism? Why or why not?
3. Have you had any personal dealings with a fixer, an inside dopester, a neutral person, a conformist, a routineer, or a status seeker? Describe this experience and its effect on you.
4. Which of the types Lerner describes do you consider the most harmful to our society? Which is the least harmful? Give reasons for your view.
5. Which of Lerner's types best describes the following people:
   a. The Nazis of World War II
   b. The political lobbyists of Washington, D.C.
   c. Women who buy Gucci shoes, Cartier watches, Yves Saint Laurent dresses, and Giorgio perfume.

## SUGGESTIONS FOR WRITING

1. Divide Americans into recognizable types, using categories that you have created.
2. In paragraph 2, Lerner subdivides the fixer into four more categories: financial, political, administrative, moral. Develop an essay in which these subdivisions are portrayed vividly.

### William Golding

# • THINKING AS A HOBBY •

*English novelist William Golding (b. 1911) was educated at Oxford. Golding once described his hobbies as "thinking, classical Greek, sailing, and archeology." His recent works include* The Pyramid *(1964),* The Scorpion God *(1971), and* Paper Work *(1984), but he is best known for his novel* Lord of the Flies *(1954). In 1983 Golding won the Nobel Prize for Literature.*

*Division and classification is often an exercise in creative thinking in which the essayist tries to find patterns and relationships that are not immediately obvious. In this essay, for example, William Golding concludes that there are three grades of thinking, which he explains with examples and anecdotes. Are there really only three grades of thinking? That is beside the point. The essayist is not a scientific researcher, but an expresser and shaper of opinion. Golding does here what any essayist should do: he makes us think.*

While I was still a boy, I came to the conclusion that there were three grades of thinking; and since I was later to claim thinking as my hobby, I came to an even stranger conclusion—namely, that I myself could not think at all.

I must have been an unsatisfactory child for grownups to deal with. 2
I remember how incomprehensible they appeared to me at first, but
not, of course, how I appeared to them. It was the headmaster of my
grammar school who first brought the subject of thinking before me—
though neither in the way, nor with the result he intended. He had
some statuettes in his study. They stood on a high cupboard behind
his desk. One was a lady wearing nothing but a bath towel. She
seemed frozen in an eternal panic lest the bath towel slip down any
farther, and since she had no arms, she was in an unfortunate position
to pull the towel up again. Next to her, crouched the statuette of a
leopard, ready to spring down at the top drawer of a filing cabinet
labeled A–AH. My innocence interpreted this as the victim's last, despairing cry. Beyond the leopard was a naked, muscular gentleman,
who sat, looking down, with his chin on his fist and his elbow on his
knee. He seemed utterly miserable.

Some time later, I learned about these statuettes. The headmaster 3
had placed them where they would face delinquent children, because
they symbolized to him the whole of life. The naked lady was the
Venus of Milo. She was Love. She was not worried about the towel.
She was just busy being beautiful. The leopard was Nature, and he
was being natural. The naked, muscular gentleman was not miserable.
He was Rodin's Thinker, an image of pure thought. It is easy to buy
small plaster models of what you think life is like.

I had better explain that I was a frequent visitor to the headmaster's 4
study, because of the latest thing I had done or left undone. As we now
say, I was not integrated. I was, if anything, disintegrated; and I was
puzzled. Grownups never made sense. Whenever I found myself in a
penal position before the headmaster's desk, with the statuettes glimmering whitely above him, I would sink my head, clasp my hands
behind my back and writhe one shoe over the other.

The headmaster would look opaquely at me through flashing spec- 5
tacles. "What are we going to do with you?"

Well, what *were* they going to do with me? I would writhe my shoe 6
some more and stare down at the worn rug.

"Look up, boy! Can't you look up?" 7

Then I would look up at the cupboard, where the naked lady was 8
frozen in her panic and the muscular gentleman contemplated the
hindquarters of the leopard in endless gloom. I had nothing to say to
the headmaster. His spectacles caught the light so that you could see

nothing human behind them. There was no possibility of communication.

"Don't you ever think at all?"                                        9

No, I didn't think, wasn't thinking, couldn't think—I was simply     10
waiting in anguish for the interview to stop.

"Then you'd better learn—hadn't you?"                                11

On one occasion the headmaster leaped to his feet, reached up and    12
plonked Rodin's masterpiece on the desk before me.

"That's what a man looks like when he's really thinking."            13

I surveyed the gentleman without interest or comprehension.          14

"Go back to your class."                                             15

Clearly there was something missing in me. Nature had endowed        16
the rest of the human race with a sixth sense and left me out. This
must be so, I mused, on my way back to the class, since whether I had
broken a window, or failed to remember Boyle's Law, or been late
for school, my teachers produced me one, adult answer: "Why can't
you think?"

As I saw the case, I had broken the window because I had tried to    17
hit Jack Arney with a cricket ball and missed him; I could not remember
Boyle's Law because I had never bothered to learn it; and I was late for
school because I preferred looking over the bridge into the river. In
fact, I was wicked. Were my teachers, perhaps, so good that they could
not understand the depths of my depravity? Were they clear, untor-
mented people who could direct their every action by this mysterious
business of thinking? The whole thing was incomprehensible. In my
earlier years, I found even the statuette of the Thinker confusing. I did
not believe any of my teachers were naked, ever. Like someone born
deaf, but bitterly determined to find out about sound, I watched my
teachers to find out about thought.

There was Mr. Houghton. He was always telling me to think. With      18
a modest satisfaction, he would tell me that he had thought a bit
himself. Then why did he spend so much time drinking? Or was there
more sense in drinking than there appeared to be? But if not, and if
drinking were in fact ruinous to health—and Mr. Houghton was ruined, there was no doubt about that—why was he always talking
about the clean life and the virtues of fresh air? He would spread his
arms wide with the action of a man who habitually spent his time
striding along mountain ridges.

"Open air does me good, boys—I know it!"                             19

Sometimes, exalted by his own oratory, he would leap from his desk     20
and hustle us outside into a hideous wind.

"Now, boys! Deep breaths! Feel it right down inside you—huge     21
draughts of God's good air!"

He would stand before us, rejoicing in his perfect health, an open-     22
air man. He would put his hands on his waist and take a tremendous
breath. You could hear the wind, trapped in the cavern of his chest
and struggling with all the unnatural impediments. His body would
reel with shock and his ruined face go white at the unaccustomed
visitation. He would stagger back to his desk and collapse there, useless for the rest of the morning.

Mr. Houghton was given to high-minded monologues about the     23
good life, sexless and full of duty. Yet in the middle of one of these
monologues, if a girl passed the window, tapping along on her neat
little feet, he would interrupt his discourse, his neck would turn of
itself and he would watch her out of sight. In this instance, he seemed
to me ruled not by thought but by an invisible and irresistible spring
in his nape.

His neck was an object of great interest to me. Normally it bulged a     24
bit over his collar. But Mr. Houghton had fought in the First World War
alongside both Americans and French, and had come—by who knows
what illogic?—to a settled detestation of both countries. If either country happened to be prominent in current affairs, no argument could
make Mr. Houghton think well of it. He would bang the desk, his neck
would bulge still further and go red. "You can say what you like," he
would cry, "but I've thought about this—and I know what I think!"

Mr. Houghton thought with his neck.     25

There was Miss Parsons. She assured us that her dearest wish was     26
our welfare, but I knew even then, with the mysterious clairvoyance of
childhood, that what she wanted most was the husband she never got.
There was Mr. Hands—and so on.

I have dealt at length with my teachers because this was my intro-     27
duction to the nature of what is commonly called thought. Through
them I discovered that thought is often full of unconscious prejudice,
ignorance and hypocrisy. It will lecture on disinterested purity while
its neck is being remorselessly twisted toward a skirt. Technically, it is
about as proficient as most businessmen's golf, as honest as most
politicians' intentions, or—to come near my own preoccupation—
as coherent as most books that get written. It is what I came to call

grade-three thinking, though more properly, it is feeling, rather than thought.

True, often there is a kind of innocence in prejudices, but in those 28 days I viewed grade-three thinking with an intolerant contempt and an incautious mockery. I delighted to confront a pious lady who hated the Germans with the proposition that we should love our enemies. She taught me a great truth in dealing with grade-three thinkers; because of her, I no longer dismiss lightly a mental process which for nine-tenths of the population is the nearest they will ever get to thought. They have immense solidarity. We had better respect them, for we are outnumbered and surrounded. A crowd of grade-three thinkers, all shouting the same thing, all warming their hands at the fire of their own prejudices, will not thank you for pointing out the contradictions in their beliefs. Man is a gregarious animal, and enjoys agreement as cows will graze all the same way on the side of a hill.

Grade-two thinking is the detection of contradictions. I reached 29 grade two when I trapped the poor, pious lady. Grade-two thinkers do not stampede easily, though often they fall into the other fault and lag behind. Grade-two thinking is a withdrawal, with eyes and ears open. It became my hobby and brought satisfaction and loneliness in either hand. For grade-two thinking destroys without having the power to create. It set me watching the crowds cheering His Majesty the King and asking myself what all the fuss was about, without giving me anything positive to put in the place of that heady patriotism. But there were compensations. To hear people justify their habit of hunting foxes and tearing them to pieces by claiming that the foxes like it. To hear our Prime Minister talk about the great benefit we conferred on India by jailing people like Pandit Nehru and Gandhi. To hear American politicians talk about peace in one sentence and refuse to join the League of Nations in the next. Yes, there were moments of delight.

But I was growing toward adolescence and had to admit that Mr. 30 Houghton was not the only one with an irresistible spring in his neck. I, too, felt the compulsive hand of nature and began to find that pointing out contradiction could be costly as well as fun. There was Ruth, for example, a serious and attractive girl. I was an atheist at the time. Grade-two thinking is a menace to religion and knocks down sects like skittles. I put myself in a position to be converted by her with an hypocrisy worthy of grade three. She was a Methodist—or at least, her parents were, and Ruth had to follow suit. But, alas, instead of relying on the Holy Spirit to convert me, Ruth was foolish enough to open her pretty mouth in argument. She claimed that the Bible (King James Version) was literally inspired. I countered by saying that the Catholics believed in the literal inspiration of Saint Jerome's *Vulgate*, and the two books were different. Argument flagged.

At last she remarked that there were an awful lot of Methodists, and they couldn't be wrong, could they—not all those millions? That was too easy, said I restively (for the nearer you were to Ruth, the nicer she was to be near to) since there were more Roman Catholics than Methodists anyway; and they couldn't be wrong, could they—not all those hundreds of millions? An awful flicker of doubt appeared in her eyes. I slid my arm round her waist and murmured breathlessly that if we were counting heads, the Buddhists were the boys for my money. But Ruth had *really* wanted to do me good, because I was so nice. She fled. The combination of my arm and those countless Buddhists was too much for her. 31

That night her father visited my father and left, red-cheeked and indignant. I was given the third degree to find out what had happened. It was lucky we were both of us only fourteen. I lost Ruth and gained an undeserved reputation as a potential libertine. 32

So grade-two thinking could be dangerous. It was in this knowledge, at the age of fifteen, that I remember making a comment from the heights of grade two, on the limitations of grade three. One evening I found myself alone in the school hall, preparing it for a party. The door of the headmaster's study was open. I went in. The headmaster had ceased to thump Rodin's Thinker down on the desk as an example to the young. Perhaps he had not found any more candidates, but the statuettes were still there, glimmering and gathering dust on top of the cupboard. I stood on a chair and rearranged them. I stood Venus in her bath towel on the filing cabinet, so that now the top drawer caught its breath in a gasp of sexy excitement. "A-ah!" The portentous Thinker I placed on the edge of the cupboard so that he looked down at the bath towel and waited for it to slip. 33

Grade-two thinking, though it filled life with fun and excitement, did not make for content. To find out the deficiencies of our elders bolsters the young ego but does not make for personal security. I found that grade two was not only the power to point out contradictions. It took the swimmer some distance from the shore and left him there, 34 out of his depth. I decided that Pontius Pilate was a typical grade-two thinker. "What is truth?" he said, a very common grade-two thought, but one that is used always as the end of an argument instead of the beginning. There is a still higher grade of thought which says, "What is truth?" and sets out to find it.

But these grade-one thinkers were few and far between. They did not visit my grammar school in the flesh though they were there in books. I aspired to them, partly because I was ambitious and partly because I now saw my hobby as an unsatisfactory thing if it went no further. If you set out to climb a mountain, however high you climb, you have failed if you cannot reach the top.

I *did* meet an undeniably grade-one thinker in my first year at Oxford. I was looking over a small bridge in Magdalen Deer Park, and a tiny mustached and hatted figure came and stood by my side. He was a German who had just fled from the Nazis to Oxford as a temporary refuge. His name was Einstein.

But Professor Einstein knew no English at that time and I knew only two words of German. I beamed at him, trying wordlessly to convey by my bearing all the affection and respect that the English felt for him. It is possible—and I have to make the admission—that I felt here were two grade-one thinkers standing side by side; yet I doubt if my face conveyed more than a formless awe. I would have given my Greek and Latin and French and a good slice of my English for enough German to communicate. But we were divided; he was as inscrutable as my headmaster. For perhaps five minutes we stood together on the bridge, undeniable grade-one thinker and breathless aspirant. With true greatness, Professor Einstein realized that any contact was better than none. He pointed to a trout wavering in midstream.

He spoke: "Fisch."

My brain reeled. Here I was, mingling with the great, and yet helpless as the veriest grade-three thinker. Desperately I sought for some sign by which I might convey that I, too, revered pure reason. I nodded vehemently. In a brilliant flash I used up half of my German vocabulary. "Fisch. Ja. Ja."

For perhaps another five minutes we stood side by side. Then Professor Einstein, his whole figure still conveying good will and amiability, drifted away out of sight.

I, too, would be a grade-one thinker. I was irreverent at the best of times. Political and religious systems, social customs, loyalties and traditions, they all came tumbling down like so many rotten apples off a tree. This was a fine hobby and a sensible substitute for cricket, since you could play it all the year round. I came up in the end with what must always remain the justification for grade-one thinking, its sign, seal and charter. I devised a coherent system for living. It was a moral system, which was wholly logical. Of course, as I readily admitted, conversion of the world to my way of thinking might be difficult, since my system did away with a number of trifles, such as big business, centralized government, armies, marriage . . .

It was Ruth all over again. I had some very good friends who stood    42
by me, and still do. But my acquaintances vanished, taking the girls with them. Young women seemed oddly contented with the world as it was. They valued the meaningless ceremony with a ring. Young men, while willing to concede the chaining sordidness of marriage, were hesitant about abandoning the organizations which they hoped would give them a career. A young man on the first rung of the Royal Navy, while perfectly agreeable to doing away with big business and marriage, got as red-necked as Mr. Houghton when I proposed a world without any battleships in it.

Had the game gone too far? Was it a game any longer? In those    43
prewar days, I stood to lose a great deal, for the sake of a hobby.

Now you are expecting me to describe how I saw the folly of my    44
ways and came back to the warm nest, where prejudices are so often called loyalties, where pointless actions are hallowed into custom by repetition, where we are content to say we think when all we do is feel.

But you would be wrong. I dropped my hobby and turned pro-    45
fessional.

If I were to go back to the headmaster's study and find the dusty    46
statuettes still there, I would arrange them differently. I would dust Venus and put her aside, for I have come to love her and know her for the fair thing she is. But I would put the Thinker, sunk in his desperate thought, where there were shadows before him—and at his back, I would put the leopard, crouched and ready to spring.

## VOCABULARY

| | | |
|---|---|---|
| incomprehensible (2) | detestation (24) | restively (31) |
| statuettes (2) | clairvoyance (26) | libertine (32) |
| integrated (4) | disinterested (27) | inscrutable (37) |
| penal (4) | proficient (27) | veriest (39) |

opaquely (5)              proposition (28)        revered (39)
ruinous (18)              solidarity (28)         amiability (40)
draughts (21)             Pandit (29)             coherent (41)
impediments (22)          skittles (30)
monologues (23)           flagged (30)

## *THE FACTS*

1. Into what three types does Golding divide all thinking? Describe each type in your own words. Is there a value judgment implied in the division?
2. Why does Golding take up so much time describing some of his grade-school teachers? How are they related to the purpose of the essay?
3. Why is it so difficult to find grade-one thinkers? Describe someone whom you consider a grade-one thinker.
4. How do you interpret Golding's last two paragraphs? Has the author reverted to grade-three or grade-two thinking, or has he become a grade-one thinker? Comment.
5. What does the encounter between Golding and Albert Einstein indicate?

## *THE STRATEGIES*

1. In paragraph 2, the author describes three statuettes on a cupboard behind the headmaster's desk. In what paragraph is each of the statuettes explained? Why is the explanation necessary?
2. Much of the article reflects a young boy's point of view. How is this point of view achieved? Point to some specific passages.
3. Paragraphs 24, 25, and 27 allude to the word *neck* repeatedly. What has the neck come to symbolize in this context?
4. What is the analogy used in paragraph 28 to describe grade-three thinkers? Is the analogy effective? Explain.
5. What is Golding's purpose in alluding to the jailing of Nehru and Gandhi, and to the Americans' refusal to join the League of Nations?

## *THE ISSUES*

1. To be a grade-one thinker, must one do away with big business, centralized government, armies, marriages, and so on? How could one be a grade-one thinker without wanting to destroy these?
2. Golding seems to indicate that his teachers were either conformists, hypocrites, or men of prejudice. Here is a loaded question: What kinds of thinkers do you remember your elementary school teachers to have been? Give examples of their thinking.
3. Grade-three thinkers reveal certain traits. Reread Lerner's essay "Some American Types" on pages 569–72. Which type is a grade-three thinker? Why?

4. What, if anything, is important about grade-two thinking? Does one need to be a grade-two thinker before going on to grade-one?
5. How does nature assist or resist grade-one thinking?

### SUGGESTIONS FOR WRITING

1. Write an essay in which you answer the question, "Does a college education help to get rid of prejudice and hypocrisy?" Support your answer with examples from your own experience.
2. Write an essay in which you divide your acquaintances into types according to the kinds of behavior they project. Be sure that your categories are mutually exclusive and that they take in all your acquaintances.

### John Holt

## • KINDS OF DISCIPLINE •

*John Holt (b. 1923), education theorist, was born in New York. He has taught at Harvard University and at the University of California, Berkeley. His works include* How Children Fail *(1964),* How Children Learn *(1967), and* Freedom and Beyond *(1972), from which this selection was taken.*

*Because* discipline *is an ambiguous and often misunderstood word, the author attempts to give it a clearer meaning by focusing on three specific kinds of discipline.*

A child, in growing up, may meet and learn from three different 1 kinds of disciplines. The first and most important is what we might call the Discipline of Nature or of Reality. When he is trying to do something real, if he does the wrong thing or doesn't do the right one, he doesn't get the result he wants. If he doesn't pile one block right on top of another, or tries to build on a slanting surface, his tower falls down. If he hits the wrong key, he hears the wrong note. If he doesn't hit the nail squarely on the head, it bends, and he has to pull it out and start with another. If he doesn't measure properly what he is trying to build, it won't open, close, fit, stand up, fly, float, whistle, or do whatever he wants it to do. If he closes his eyes when he swings, he doesn't hit the ball. A child meets this kind of discipline every time he tries to *do* something, which is why it is so important in school to give children more chances to do things, instead of just reading or listening to someone talk (or pretending to). This discipline is a great teacher. The learner never has to wait long for his answer; it usually comes quickly, often instantly. Also it is clear, and very often points toward the needed correction; from what happened he can not only see that what he did was wrong, but also why, and what he needs to do instead. Finally, and most important, the giver of the answer, call it Nature, is impersonal, impartial, and indifferent. She does not give opinions, or make judgments; she cannot be wheedled, bullied, or fooled; she does not get angry or disappointed; she does not praise or blame; she does not remember past failures or hold grudges; with her one always gets a fresh start, this time is the one that counts.

The next discipline we might call the Discipline of Culture, of Society, of What People Really Do. Man is a social, a cultural animal. Children sense around them this culture, this network of agreements, customs, habits, and rules binding the adults together. They want to understand it and be a part of it. They watch very carefully what people around them are doing and want to do the same. They want to do right, unless they become convinced they can't do right. Thus children rarely misbehave seriously in church, but sit as quietly as they can. The example of all those grownups is contagious. Some mysterious ritual is going on, and children, who like rituals, want to be part of it. In the same way, the little children that I see at concerts or operas, though they may fidget a little, or perhaps take a nap now and then, rarely make any disturbance. With all those grownups sitting there, neither moving nor talking, it is the most natural thing in the world to imitate them. Children who live among adults who are habitually courteous to each other, and to them, will soon learn to be courteous. Children who live surrounded by people who speak a certain way will speak that way, however much we may try to tell them that speaking that way is bad or wrong.

The third discipline is the one most people mean when they speak of discipline—the Discipline of Superior Force, of sergeant to private, of "you do what I tell you or I'll make you wish you had." There is bound to be some of this in a child's life. Living as we do surrounded by things that can hurt children, or that children can hurt, we cannot avoid it. We can't afford to let a small child find out from experience the danger of playing in a busy street, or of fooling with the pots on the top of a stove, or of eating up the pills in the medicine cabinet. So, along with other precautions, we say to him, "Don't play in the street, or touch things on the stove, or go into the medicine cabinet, or I'll punish you." Between him and the danger too great for him to imagine we put a lesser danger, but one he can imagine and maybe therefore wants to avoid. He can have no idea of what it would be like to be hit by a car, but he can imagine being shouted at, or spanked, or sent to his room. He avoids these substitutes for the greater danger until he can understand it and avoid it for its own sake. But we ought to use this discipline only when it is necessary to protect the life, health, safety, or well-being of people or other living creatures, or to prevent destruction of things that people care about. We ought not to assume too long, as we usually do, that a child cannot understand the real nature of the danger from which we want to protect him. The sooner he avoids the danger, not to escape our punishment, but as a matter of good sense, the better. He can learn that faster than we think. In Mexico, for example, where people drive their cars with a good deal of spirit, I saw many children no older than five or four walking unattended on the streets. They understood about cars, they knew what to do. A child whose life is full of the threat and fear of punishment is locked into babyhood. There is no way for him to grow up, to learn to take responsibility for his life and acts. Most important of all, we should not assume that having to yield to the threat of our superior force is good for the child's character. It is never good for *anyone's* character. To bow to superior force makes us feel impotent and cowardly for not having had the strength or courage to resist. Worse, it makes us resentful and vengeful. We can hardly wait to make someone pay for our humiliation, yield to us as we were once made to yield. No, if we cannot always avoid using the Discipline of Superior Force, we should at least use it as seldom as we can.

There are places where all three disciplines overlap. Any very de- 4 manding human activity combines in it the disciplines of Superior Force, of Culture, and of Nature. The novice will be told, "Do it this way, never mind asking why, just do it that way, that is the way we always do it." But it probably *is* just the way they always do it, and usually for the very good reason that it is a way that has been found to work. Think, for example, of ballet training. The student in a class is told to do this exercise, or that; to stand so; to do this or that with his head, arms, shoulders, abdomen, hips, legs, feet. He is constantly corrected. There is no argument. But behind these seemingly autocratic demands by the teacher lie many decades of custom and tradition, and behind that, the necessities of dancing itself. You cannot make the moves of classical ballet unless over many years you have acquired, and renewed every day, the needed strength and suppleness in scores of muscles and joints. Nor can you do the difficult motions, making them look easy, unless you have learned hundreds of easier ones first. Dance teachers may not always agree on all the details of teaching these strengths and skills. But no novice could learn them all by himself. You could not go for a night or two to watch the ballet and then, without any other knowledge at all, teach yourself how to do it. In the same way, you would be unlikely to learn any complicated and difficult human activity without drawing heavily on the experience of those who know it better. But the point is that the authority of these experts or teachers stems from, grows out of their greater competence and experience, the fact that what they do *works*, not the fact that they happen to be the teacher and as such have the power to kick a student out of the class. And the further point is that children are always and everywhere attracted to that competence, and ready and eager to submit themselves to a discipline that grows out of it. We hear constantly that children will never do anything unless compelled to by bribes or threats. But in their private lives, or in extracurricular activities in school, in sports, music, drama, art, running a newspaper, and so on, they often submit themselves willingly and wholeheartedly to very intense disciplines, simply because they want to learn to do a given thing well. Our Little-Napoleon football coaches, of whom we have too many and hear far too much, blind us to the fact that millions of children work hard every year getting better at sports and games without coaches barking and yelling at them.

## VOCABULARY

| | | |
|---|---|---|
| wheedled (1) | impotent (3) | autocratic (4) |
| ritual (2) | novice (4) | |

## THE FACTS

1. What principle or basis of division does Holt use?
2. How does Holt clarify for the reader what he means by "Discipline of Nature or of Reality"? Is this method of clarification effective? Why?
3. What are the advantages of learning from nature or reality?
4. What additional examples can you supply of the ways in which children submit to the discipline of culture or society?
5. According to the author, when should the discipline of superior force be used? Do you agree?
6. At the end of his essay Holt identifies the most successful motivation for discipline. What is it?

## THE STRATEGIES

1. In the last sentence of paragraph 1, the author uses the feminine pronouns *she* and *her* in referring to nature. What is his purpose?
2. What transitional guideposts does the author use in order to gain coherence and organization?
3. What is the effect of labeling certain football coaches "Little Napoleons"?

## THE ISSUES

1. What additional examples can you supply of the ways in which children submit to the discipline of culture or society?
2. What tips can you provide for someone who has no discipline in studying college courses? What method has worked best for you personally?
3. Holt warns adults that the use of superior force in order to punish children is never good for the children's characters (see paragraph 3) and should therefore be used as little as possible. What, in your opinion, is the result of never using this superior force in the training of children? Give examples to support your point.
4. Our society is witnessing the self-destruction of many young people due to chemical abuse of one kind or another. How is this abuse tied to Holt's idea of discipline?
5. How important is discipline in your life? Do you choose friends who are strongly disciplined, or do you prefer those who are more "laid back" and like to "hang loose"? Give reasons for your answers.

## SUGGESTIONS FOR WRITING

1. Write a five-hundred-word essay in which you divide discipline according to the kinds of effects it produces. Example: discipline that results in strong study habits.
2. Develop the following topic sentence into a three-paragraph essay: "To be successful, a person must have three kinds of discipline: of the intellect, of the emotions, and of the body." Use Holt's essay as a model for your organization.

### Francis Bacon

## • THE IDOLS •

*Francis Bacon (1561–1626) was born in London and educated at Trinity College, Cambridge, and at Gray's Inn. Bacon is generally credited with applying the inductive method of logic to scientific investigation. His essays, which are notable for their aphoristic style, are his best-known works.*

*This excerpt comes from* Novum Organum *(1620), possibly Bacon's most famous work. Bacon was struggling against the traditions of medieval scholasticism, which assumed a given and unchangeable set of premises from which, by deductive logic, one could infer truths about the world. Our way of thinking today, especially in science, is just the opposite, thanks in part to Bacon. We begin not with givens but with questions. We proceed by gathering data and using induction to draw conclusions. (See the discussion of logic in Chapter 9.) This method of thinking does not completely safeguard us from Bacon's* Idols, *but it does help keep them at bay.*

The *Idols* and false notions which have already preoccupied the human understanding, and are deeply rooted in it, not only so beset men's minds, that they become difficult to access, but even when access is obtained, will again meet and trouble us in the instauration of the sciences, unless mankind, when forewarned, guard themselves with all possible care against them. 1

Four species of *Idols* beset the human mind: to which (for distinction's sake) we have assigned names: calling the first *Idols of the Tribe*; the second *Idols of the Den*; the third *Idols of the Market*; the fourth *Idols of the Theater*. 2

The formation of notions and axioms on the foundations of true *induction*, is the only fitting remedy, by which we can ward off and expel these *Idols*. It is however of great service to point them out. For the doctrine of *Idols* bears the same relation to the *interpretation of nature*, as that of the confutation of sophisms does to common logic. 3

The *Idols of the Tribe* are inherent in human nature, and the very tribe or race of man. For man's sense is falsely asserted to be the standard of things. On the contrary, all the perceptions, both of the senses and the mind, bear reference to man, and not to the universe, and the human mind resembles those uneven mirrors, which impart their own properties to different objects, from which rays are emitted, and distort and disfigure them. 4

The *Idols of the Den* are those of each individual. For every body (in addition to the errors common to the race of man) has his own individual den or cavern, which intercepts and corrupts the light of nature; either from his own peculiar and singular disposition, or from his education and intercourse with others, or from his reading, and the authority acquired by those whom he reverences and admires, or from a different impression produced on the mind, as it happens to be preoccupied and predisposed, or equable and tranquil, and the like: so that the spirit of man (according to its several dispositions) is vari- 5 able, confused, and as it were actuated by chance; and Heraclitus* said well that men search for knowledge in lesser worlds and not in the greater or common world.

There are also *Idols* formed by the reciprocal intercourse and society  6 of man with man, which we call *Idols of the Market*, from the commerce and association of men with each other. For men converse by means of language; but words are formed at the will of the generality; and there arises from a bad and unapt formation of words a wonderful obstruction to the mind. Nor can the definitions and explanations, with which learned men are wont to guard and protect themselves in some instances, afford a complete remedy: words still manifestly force the understanding, throw everything into confusion, and lead mankind into vain and innumerable controversies and fallacies.

Lastly there are *Idols* which have crept into men's minds from the  7 various dogmas of peculiar systems of philosophy, and also from the perverted rules of demonstration, and these we denominate *Idols of the Theater*. For we regard all the systems of philosophy hitherto received or imagined, as so many plays brought out and performed, creating fictitious and theatrical worlds. Nor do we speak only of the present systems, or of the philosophy and sects of the ancients, since numerous other plays of a similar nature can be still composed and made to agree with each other, the causes of the most opposite errors being generally the same. Nor, again, do we allude merely to the general systems, but also to many elements and axioms of sciences, which have become inveterate by tradition, implicit credence and neglect. We must, however, discuss each species of *Idols* more fully and distinctly in order to guard the human understanding against them.

## VOCABULARY

| | | |
|---|---|---|
| beset (1) | inherent (4) | denominate (7) |
| instauration (1) | predisposed (5) | sects (7) |
| axioms (3) | equable (5) | inveterate (7) |
| induction (3) | reciprocal (6) | implicit (7) |
| confutation (3) | wont (6) | credence (7) |
| sophisms (3) | dogmas (7) | |

---

*Greek philosopher of the sixth century B.C.—Ed.

## THE FACTS

1. Exactly what is being divided in this essay? Why does Bacon use the term *idols*?
2. Using your own words, describe each idol in the order listed by Bacon. Supply an example for each from your own experience.
3. According to Bacon, what is the remedy for all these idols? How will this remedy work?

## THE STRATEGIES

1. What connection is there between Bacon's thought and his style?
2. Point out specific words or phrases to show that Bacon's style is archaic.
3. What method of thinking does Bacon use in order to conclude that idols preoccupy the human understanding? Trace his use of the method in the essay.
4. What is the analogy used to illustrate the last idol? Explain how this analogy helps clarify the idol.

## THE ISSUES

1. Compare Bacon's division with some more contemporary ideas on the same subject. Is his essay still valid, or is it out of date? Give reasons for your answer.
2. What specific examples can you cite to illuminate Bacon's "idols of the tribe"?
3. How dangerous to present society are "idols of the market"? Give reasons for your opinion.
4. What examples can you cite from your own upbringing to indicate that you have bowed to "idols of the den"?
5. In your view, what ideas marketed publicly today are dangerous but highly seductive—especially for the naïve?

## SUGGESTIONS FOR WRITING

1. Write an essay in which you divide your bad habits into three or four categories. Make sure that these categories are mutually exclusive and that they include the entire range of your bad habits.
2. Write a brief report on Francis Bacon's major contributions to society. In the report, organize these contributions into separate divisions.

Sylvia Plath

## ——————— • DEATH & CO. • ———————

*Sylvia Plath (1932–1963) was born in Boston and educated at Smith College and at Cambridge. She was a precocious child whose early poems won many prizes and awards. She published several volumes of poetry, including* Colossus and Other Poems *(1962) and* Ariel *(1968), and one partly autobiographical novel,* The Bell Jar *(1971). She died by her own hand in London.*

*This poem by Plath exposes the personal fear and horrors haunting a human being.*

Two, of course there are two.
It seems perfectly natural now—
The one who never looks up, whose eyes are lidded
And balled, like Blake's,*
Who exhibits                                                                           5

The birthmarks that are his trademark—
The scald scar of water,
The nude
Verdigris of the condor.
I am red meat. His beak                                                                 10

Claps sidewise: I am not his yet.
He tells me how badly I photograph.
He tells me how sweet
The babies look in their hospital
Icebox, a simple                                                                        15

Frill at the neck,
Then the flutings of their Ionian†
Death-gowns,
Then two little feet.
He does not smile or smoke.                                                             20

The other does that,
His hair long and plausive.
Bastard

---

*William Blake (1757–1827), English poet of the pre-Romantic period.—Ed.
†Anything pertaining to the Ionians, a Hellenic people who settled in Attica about 1100 B.C.—Ed.

Masturbating a glitter,
He wants to be loved.    25

I do not stir.
The frost makes a flower.
The dew makes a star,
The dead bell,
The dead bell.    30

Somebody's done for.

## VOCABULARY

verdigris                    condor                    plausive

## THE FACTS

1. What is the meaning of the title and how does it relate to the purpose of the poem?
2. Who are the "two" mentioned in the opening line of the poem? Who is the speaker? What is the context of the words spoken?
3. What are the characteristics of "the one who never looks up"? Support your answer with examples from the poem.
4. What are the characteristics of "the other"? Support your answer with examples from the poem.
5. What is the speaker's reaction to "Death & Co."? How do you interpret the reaction?

## THE STRATEGIES

1. Where does the first description end and the second begin? What word forms the connecting link between the two?
2. What is the cumulative effect of "balled" eyes, "scald scar," "verdigris of the condor," and "his beak claps sidewise"?
3. How do you interpret the lines "The frost makes a flower" and "The dew makes a star"?

## THE ISSUES

1. Is the contemplation of death useful to a life well lived? Or is it best to concentrate on living by avoiding thoughts about death? Explain your answer thoroughly.
2. Plath seems to be attracted as well as compelled by death. Is her attitude typical or atypical of the people you know? Explain your answer by giving examples.

3. What is your view of death? Who in your past has helped shape this view?
4. What facets does life, as opposed to death, reveal to you? What metaphors or similes can you create to represent these facets?
5. Reread the essay "Diogenes and Alexander" on pages 539–43. How do you think these two men would view death? Explain your opinions.

## SUGGESTIONS FOR WRITING

1. Write a paragraph in which you describe the kind of person who wrote "Death & Co." Do not judge her, but try to express how she feels.
2. Paraphrase Plath's poem by using concrete prose to describe the two subjects presented by her. Use imagery of your own choice to make your subjects come to life.

=======•• *ADVICE* ••=======

## HOW TO WRITE A CAUSAL ANALYSIS

Some essays have as their dominant purpose the analysis of cause or effect. *Cause* refers to events that have occurred in the past; *effect* refers to consequences that will occur in the future. An essay on why some students get poor grades, which points to the failure to study, is analyzing cause. However, an essay on the consequences of failing to study for a test is analyzing effect. Both essays are said to be rhetorically developed by causal analysis, even though one focuses on cause and the other on effect. Generally, the essay asking for the analysis of cause or for the prediction of effect requires the most abstract thinking and gives students the most trouble. Causes do not parade around wearing identity tags. Moreover, even simple effects can be said to be produced by a complex of multiple causes, which the student must sift out and analyze.

Take, for instance, the straightforward enough incident of a student getting a poor grade on a test. Why did the student get a poor grade? Possibly, because he failed to study. On the other hand, perhaps the student failed to study because he thought he was doomed to failure anyway, and didn't see any point in a meaningless exertion. Why did he feel that way? Possibly, because the instructor impressed upon the class how high her standards were, and how impossible it was for anyone to pass. The instructor, in turn, may have been reacting to pressure brought by the Regents against her and her department, for having in the past given out too many high grades. The Regents, on the other hand, may have been set upon by the community because of a newspaper article that accused the university of wasting taxpayers' money by giving out cheap grades. The possibilities are virtually endless. Every cause, if traced back patiently enough, will lead through infinite regression to the Creator.

It is useful, therefore, to bear in mind that there are three kinds of causes: necessary, contributory, and sufficient. A necessary cause is one that *must* be present for an effect to occur, but by itself cannot cause the occurrence of the effect. For instance, irrigation is necessary for a good crop of corn, but irrigation alone will not result in a good crop. Other factors such as adequate sunshine, good soil, and correct planting must also be present.

A contributory cause is one that *may* produce an effect, but cannot produce the effect by itself. For instance, good training may help a fighter win a bout, but that alone is not enough. The fighter also has to have sharper reflexes, more skill, and more strength than his opponent.

A sufficient cause is one that *can* produce an effect by itself. For instance, a heart attack alone can kill, even though the person may have other problems such as an ulcer, a toothache, or a weak back.

Most causes are not sufficient; they are either contributory or necessary. Bearing this in mind will restrain you from dogmatizing about cause. For instance, the following assertions mistake a contributory cause for a sufficient one:

> Crime in America is caused by a breakdown of discipline in the family structure. In the farming days, both the father and the mother were around to supervise the upbringing and disciplining of the children. Nowadays, however, the father is away working, as is the mother, and the children are left to the schools for rearing. This breakdown of the family structure is the cause of crime.

The fragmentation of the family is probably a contributory cause of crime, but it is hardly a sufficient one. Many children reared in families where both parents work have not succumbed to crime. Simplistic thinking and writing about cause usually come from mistaking a contributory for a sufficient cause.

## 1. Make your purpose initially clear.

For example, the article by Roger Rosenblatt, "Why the Justice System Fails," asks this simple question in the second paragraph: "Why does the system fail?" It then proceeds to answer it in unsparing detail. This sort of definiteness in the early going adds a guiding focus to your essay.

## 2. Be modest in your choice of a subject.

It is difficult enough to analyze the causes of simple effects without compounding your problem through the choice of a monstrously large subject. The student who takes it upon herself to write an essay on the causes of war is already in deep trouble. Such a complex phenomenon bristles with thousands of causes. Selecting a more manageable subject for causal analysis will make your task a lot easier.

## 3. Concentrate on proximate, as opposed to remote, causes.

As we pointed out earlier, it is easy in analysis of cause to become entangled in the infinite. In a series of causations, the proximate cause is the nearest cause. For instance, in the case of the student who received poor grades, the proximate cause for the poor grade was failure to study. The remote cause was the dissatisfaction of the community with the university. Common sense should guide you in this sort of analysis; but since infinity can be unraveled out of the reason why someone purchases a popsicle, it is, as a rule of thumb, safer to stay with the proximate cause and ignore the remote.

## 4. Do not dogmatize about cause.

Institutions of learning rigorously demand that students analyze cause with caution and prudence. The reasoning is simple enough: colleges and universities are quite determined to impress their students with the complexity of the world. It is advisable, therefore, that you be modest in your claims of causation. You can easily temper a dogmatic statement by interjecting qualifiers into your claims. Instead of

> The divorce rate in America is caused by the sexual revolution, with its promiscuity and ideas on free love.

you could more prudently write:

> The divorce rate in America is probably influenced by the sexual revolution, with its promiscuity and ideas on free love.

This paragraph, for instance, had it been written by a student, would no doubt draw criticism from his instructor:

> This brings me to the major cause of unhappiness, which is that most people in America act not on impulse but on some principle, and that principles upon which people act are usually based upon a false psychology and a false ethic. There is a general theory as to what makes for happiness and this theory is false. Life is conceived as a competitive struggle in which felicity consists in getting ahead of your neighbor. The joys which are not competitive are forgotten.

Yet this paragraph is from a Bertrand Russell article, "The Unhappy American Way," which we will read with much sagacious head-nodding. Bertrand Russell was a Nobel laureate, a mathematician, and a noted philosopher when he wrote this. No doubt it is unfair, but his obvious accomplishments gain for him a temporary suspension of the rules against dogmatizing. Students,

however, are not readily granted such license. For the time being, anyway, we
advise that you generalize about cause prudently.

## •• *EXAMPLES* ••

### Roger Rosenblatt

## — • WHY THE JUSTICE SYSTEM FAILS • —

*Roger Rosenblatt (b. 1940) is a graduate of Harvard University, where he earned
a Ph.D. and briefly taught English. He is now a writer and editor at* Time
*magazine. Rosenblatt has been featured on television reading his eloquent* Time
*essays.*

*In the following essay, which served as a 1981* Time *cover story, the author
offers some straightforward opinions on the shortcomings of our criminal justice
system. In developing his thesis, Rosenblatt cites statistics, case histories, and
testimony from experts.*

Anyone who claims it is impossible to get rid of the random violence    1
of today's mean streets may be telling the truth, but is also missing the
point. Street crime may be normal in the U.S., but it is not inevitable
at such advanced levels, and the fact is that there are specific reasons
for the nation's incapacity to keep its street crime down. Almost all
these reasons can be traced to the American criminal justice system. It
is not that there are no mechanisms in place to deal with American
crime, merely that the existing ones are impractical, inefficient, anach-
ronistic, uncooperative, and often lead to as much civic destruction as
they are meant to curtail.

Why does the system fail? For one thing, the majority of criminals    2
go untouched by it. The police learn about one-quarter of the thefts
committed each year, and about less than half the robberies, burglaries
and rapes. Either victims are afraid or ashamed to report crimes, or
they may conclude gloomily that nothing will be done if they do.
Murder is the crime the police do hear about, but only 73% of the
nation's murders lead to arrest. The arrest rates for lesser crimes are
astonishingly low—59% for aggravated assault in 1979, 48% for rape,
25% for robbery, 15% for burglary.

Even when a suspect is apprehended, the chances of his getting    3
punished are mighty slim. In New York State each year there are some
130,000 felony arrests; approximately 8,000 people go to prison. There
are 94,000 felony arrests in New York City; 5,000 to 6,000 serve time. A
1974 study of the District of Columbia came up with a similar picture.
Of those arrested for armed robbery, less than one-quarter went to
prison. More than 6,000 aggravated assaults were reported; 116 people
were put away. A 1977 study of such cities as Detroit, Indianapolis and
New Orleans produced slightly better numbers, but nothing to counteract the exasperation of New York Police Commissioner Robert
McGuire: "The criminal justice system almost creates incentives for
street criminals."

It is hard to pinpoint any one stage of the system that is more    4
culpable than any other. Start with the relationship between police and
prosecutors. Logic would suggest that these groups work together like
the gears of a watch since, theoretically, they have the same priorities:
to arrest and convict. But prosecutors have enormous caseloads, and
too often they simply focus on lightening them. Or they work too fast
and lose a case; or they plea-bargain and diminish justice. The police
also work too fast too often, are concerned with "clearing" arrests, for
which they get credit. They receive no credit for convictions. Their
work gets sloppy—misinformation recorded, witnesses lost, no fol-
low-up. That 1974 study of the District of Columbia indicated that fully
one-third of the police making arrests failed to process a single conviction. A study released this week of 2,418 police in seven cities showed
that 15% were credited with half the convictions; 31% had no convictions whatever.

The criminal justice system is also debased by plea bargaining. At    5
present nine out of ten convictions occur because of a guilty plea
arrived at through a deal between the state and defendant, in which
the defendant forgoes his right to trial. Of course, plea bargaining
keeps the courts less crowded and doubtless sends to jail, albeit for a
shorter stretch, some felons who might have got off if judged by their
peers. And many feel that a bargain results in a truer level of justice,
since prosecutors tend to hike up the charge in the first place in antic-
ipation of the defendant's copping a plea. Still, there are tricks like
"swallowing the gun"—reducing the charge of armed robbery to unarmed robbery—that are performed for expediency, not for justice.

"Justice delayed is justice denied," is a root principle of common    6
law, but nowadays the right to a speedy trial is so regularly denied that

the thought seems antique. Last Aug. 1, a witness was prepared to testify that Cornelius Wright, 18, shot him five times in the chest, stomach and legs. Because of a series of mishaps and continuances, Wright has been stewing in the Cook County jail for more than eight months. In fact, Wright's delay is the norm; eight months is the average time between arrest and trial. Continuances have so clogged Chicago's courts that the city's Crime Commission issues a monthly "Ten Most Wanted Dispositions" list in an effort to prod the system.

Detroit Deputy Police Chief James Bannon believes that trial delays    7
work against the victim. "The judge doesn't see the hysterical, distraught victim. He sees a person who comes into court after several months or years who is totally different. He sees a defendant that bears no relationship to what he appeared to be at the time of the crime. He sits there in a nice three-piece suit and keeps his mouth shut. And the judge doesn't see the shouting, raging animal the victim saw when she was being raped, for example. Both the defendant and victim have lawyers, and that's what the court hears: law. It doesn't hear the guts of the crime."

Procedural concerns can cause delays, and in rare cases defendants'    8
rights can be carried to absurd extremes. California Attorney General George Deukmejian* tells of Willie Edward Level, who was convicted of beating a Bakersfield College woman student to death with a table leg. Level was informed of his right to remain silent and/or have an attorney present (the *Miranda* ruling). He waived these rights and confessed the murder. Yet the California Court of Appeals threw out the conviction because Level had asked to speak to his mother at the time of his arrest and had not been permitted to; had he been able to do so, it was argued, he might not have made his confession.

"There's nothing in *Miranda* that says a defendant has the right to    9
talk with his mother or a friend," says Deukmejian. "It says he can talk to a lawyer or not at all. It's so much of this kind of thing that makes a mockery of the system. And every time you have one of these rulings it has the effect of dragging out the length of cases, which builds in more and more delays. We've got a murder case in Sacramento that's been in the pretrial state for four years."

Add to this the fact that witnesses are discouraged and lost by trial    10
delays. In New York the average number of appearances a witness has

---

*Later governor of California.—Ed.

to make in a given disposition is 17. Few people have the time or stamina to see a case through.

Then there is the matter of bail. In a recent speech before the American Bar Association, Chief Justice Warren Burger argued for tightening the standards for releasing defendants on bail, which seems justifiable. But the subject is complicated. Technically, judges are supposed to base their decisions about bail strictly on the likelihood of a defendant's appearing for trial. In practice, however, this is mere guesswork, and a great many serious crimes are committed by people out on bail or by bail jumpers, who are often given bail when rearrested. One sound reason for a bail system is to avoid locking up anyone before he is proved guilty. But it is simply unrealistic to disregard the criterion of likely dangerousness, even though it raises serious constitutional questions. It has probably resulted in more tragedies than a different standard would result in denials of civil liberties.    11

Judges blame the cops, and cops blame the judges. Patrick F. Healy, executive director of the Chicago Crime Commission, says judges are plain lazy. "Last year we did a spot check, and the judges' day on the bench totaled 3 hours 49 minutes." The judges will not concede laziness, but several of the nation's best, like Marvin Frankel, former federal judge in the District Court of Manhattan, admit to a "remarkable lack of consistency" in the judiciary. Judge Lois Forer, a most respected criminal-court justice in Philadelphia, contends that it "simply isn't true" that defendants get off on technicalities. It is just that "the system is overloaded." She also emphasizes the problem of sloppy preparations: "It's truly painful when there's someone you're pretty sure committed a crime, and they [police, prosecutors] don't bring in the evidence."    12

Almost every critic of the system cites the lack of prison space. Despite the enormously high operating costs ($4 billion annually for all U.S. penal institutions), more prison space is an absolute necessity. New York State has between 22,000 and 24,000 jail cells. All are filled, some beyond proper capacity. Twice this year local officials in Missouri were asked not to send any more inmates to the state penitentiary. As a result the St. Louis county jail had to retain seven prisoners who ought to have been in the state pen, even though it meant holding eleven more inmates than the jail was intended to hold. Florida, which already has a higher proportion of its citizenry under lock and key than any other state, may need to spend $83 million on new prison    13 construction and staff. This month 223 supposedly nonviolent inmates of Illinois' 13 prisons were given early release to make room for 223 newcomers. New York Police Inspector Richard Dillon, one of the nation's most thoughtful law officers, cites lack of prison space as the primary cause of city crime—the ultimate reason for inappropriate plea bargains, premature paroles, careless bail and too brief sentences.

Finally, the criminal justice system fails at its most sensitive level, that of juvenile crime. Until recently few juvenile courts admitted there was such a thing as a bad boy, restricting their vision of youthful offenders to memories of Father Flanagan's Boys Town or to Judge Tom Clark's quaint view that "every boy, in his heart, would rather steal second base than an automobile." In fact, there are several boys these days who would prefer to kill the umpire, and who have done so, only to receive light sentences or none at all. A study by Marvin Wolfgang at the University of Pennsylvania traced the criminal careers of 10,000 males born in 1948. By the age of 16, 35% had one arrest, but then almost all stopped committing crimes. A small group, however, did not: 627 had five arrests by the time they were adults. They accounted for two-thirds of all the violent crime attributed to the group and almost all the homicides. "This is the group that society is afraid of, and rightly so," says Wolfgang. He is now studying a new group, born in 1958, which is "even nastier and more violent. We should concentrate on them and capture them as soon as possible."

Of course, there is no place to put this hard core, and that is part of the problem. The main difficulty, however, is a Pollyannish, outdated vision of youth, one that results in treating a child not as a potentially responsible human being but rather as some vague romantic entity, capable of continuous regeneration. An underage murderer may be put away for a few months or not at all. As Harvard's James Q. Wilson says, "The adult system is harsh, but before that it's a free ride." The ride is not only free, but clean. At the age of 18, juvenile criminals in many states start all over with unblemished records no matter how many crimes they have committed earlier.

In short, the criminal justice system is not really a system—at least not one in which the individual parts work well on their own or mesh effectively with each other. Few of the participants deny this, and while there is a natural tendency for each stratum—police, lawyers, prosecutors, judges, prison officials—to lay the blame for the system's failures on one another, nobody is happy with the current situation. Reforming the system, however, is a tricky business, especially when reforms are likely to tend toward severity. "For my part," said Oliver Wendell Holmes in *Olmstead* vs. *U.S.*, "I think it a less evil that some criminals should escape than that the Government should play an ignoble part." Whatever reforms are contemplated, Justice Holmes will preside.

## VOCABULARY

| | | |
|---|---|---|
| anachronistic (1) | albeit (5) | penal (13) |
| apprehended (3) | distraught (7) | regeneration (15) |
| exasperation (3) | stamina (10) | stratum (16) |
| culpable (4) | criterion (11) | ignoble (16) |

## THE FACTS

1. What is the author's exact thesis? Where is it stated? What key words control the thesis?
2. How many causes does Rosenblatt cite for the failure of our justice system? List each cause separately.
3. What is the meaning of the principle that "justice delayed is justice denied"? How is this principle related to an individual's constitutional rights?
4. Why is the matter of bail a difficult problem?
5. How do judges and police officers contribute to the problem of injustice?
6. What is the meaning of Rosenblatt's final sentence?

## THE STRATEGIES

1. Paragraph 1 introduces the author's thesis. What is the purpose of paragraphs 2 and 3? Comment on the effectiveness of these paragraphs.
2. What is the subject developed in paragraphs 6–10? Why does the author take several paragraphs to develop this subject?
3. Rosenblatt uses several quotations in his essay. How do these strengthen his causal analysis?
4. How do you interpret the allusions to *Miranda* (paragraph 8), Father Flanagan (paragraph 14), and Pollyanna (paragraph 15)? What do they have in common?
5. The following legal terms are explained in context. What is the meaning of each?
   a. plea bargaining
   b. copping a plea
   c. continuances
   d. dispositions
   e. procedural delays
   f. pretrial

## THE ISSUES

1. Has the author exhausted all of the causes leading to the failure of our justice system? Can you think of some additional causes? If so, what are they and how can they be rectified? Give specific examples.
2. Do you think it is better to have a few guilty criminals go free than to appoint courts who rule with greater severity toward criminals than is evident now? Give reasons for your answer.
3. Do you agree with the author's view that society has a Pollyannish vision of youth (see paragraphs 14 and 15)? Or, do you think it is realistic to treat all young people as if they were basically good? What would happen if adolescent criminals were given the same punishments as adults?
4. Building more prisons in order to avoid overcrowding means higher taxes. Would you be willing to bear a tax increase in order to build more prisons? Why or why not?
5. If you were assigned the task of supporting the system of plea bargaining, what would you say?

## SUGGESTIONS FOR WRITING

1. Write a five-hundred-word essay in which you analyze the causes for one of the following situations:
   a. The unwillingness of witnesses to get involved in a crime they have observed.
   b. This decade's extraordinary rise in divorce rates.
   c. The growing number of women entering lifelong professions.
   d. The rise in the street population—that is, men and women who actually live and sleep in the streets of our major cities.
   Begin with a thesis that states the general cause or causes; then develop your essay through the use of facts and personal experience. Use expert testimony if it makes your analysis more effective.
2. Write a five-hundred-word essay in which you offer reasons why plea bargaining is either good or bad for a justice system. Begin with a clear thesis and supply examples to illustrate your views.

### George Gilder

## • WHY MEN MARRY •

*George F. Gilder (b. 1943) is program director of the International Center for Economic Policy Studies and chairman of the Economic Roundtable at the Lehrman Institute. He is also a social commentator, contributing to the* Wall Street

Journal, Harper's Magazine, *and many other publications. Gilder's books include* Sexual Suicide *(1973) and* Naked Nomads: Unmarried Men in America *(1974), from which the following essay is reprinted. It provides a thoroughly fresh and illuminating view of our society's bachelors.*

Men marry for love. But what does this mean beyond what they got ₁ in their lives as single men: the flash of a new face, new flesh across a room. The glimpse of breasts shifting softly in a silken blouse. The open sesame of a missing ring. The excited pursuit, the misunderstood meanings, the charged meetings. The telling touch of hands. The eyes welling open to the gaze. The scent of surrender. The pillowed splash of unbound hair. The ecstatic slipping between new sheets. The race. The winning. The chase and the conquest . . . and back on the road. Definitely back on the road. Free again. Strong again. For new women, new pursuit. What more is there in life—in love—than this?

Marriage means giving it all up. Giving up love? That is how it ₂ seems to the single man, and that is why he fears it. He must give up his hunter's heart, forgo the getaway Honda growl, shear off his shaggy hair, restrict his random eye, hang up his handgun, bow down and enter the cage. At bottom, what he is is hunter. No way he will be hubby.

And yet, he will. For years he lunges at women's surfaces, but as ₃ time passes he learns of a deeper promise. For years he may not know the reasons or believe them or care. The heart, it is said, has its reasons. They spring from the primal predicament of man throughout the history of the race: the need to choose a particular woman and stay by her and provide for her if he is to know his children and they are to love him and call him father.

In procreative love, both partners consciously or unconsciously ₄ glimpse a future infant—precarious in the womb, vulnerable in the world, and in need of nurture and protection. In the swelter of their bodies together, in the shape and softnesses of the woman, in the protective support of the man, the couple senses the outlines of a realm that can endure and perpetuate their union: a pattern of differences and complements that goes beyond the momentary pleasures of reciprocal sex.

Marriage asks men to give up their essential sexuality only as part ₅ of a clear scheme for replacing it with new, far more important, and ultimately far more sexual roles: husband and father. Without these roles, a woman can bear a child, but the man is able only to screw. He can do it a lot, but after his first years it will only get him unthreaded, and in the end he is disconnected and alone. In his shallow heats and frustrations, he all too often becomes a menace to himself and his community.

There are millions of single men, unlinked to any promising reality, dissipating their lives by the years, moving from job to job, woman to woman, illusion to embitterment. Yet they are not hopeless. Many more millions have passed through the same sloughs, incurred the same boozy dreams, marijuana highs, cocaine crashes, sex diseases, job vapors, legal scrapes, wanderings. They follow the entire syndrome and then break out of it. Normally they do not escape through psychiatrists' offices, sex-education courses, VISTA or Peace Corps programs, reformatories, or guidance-counseling uplift. What happens, most of the time—the only effective thing that happens, the only process that reaches the sources of motivation and character—is falling in love.

Love is effective because it works at a deeper, more instinctual level than the other modes of education and change. Love does not teach or persuade. It possesses and transforms. . . .

It is not just an intelligent appraisal of his circumstances that transforms the single man. It is not merely a desire for companionship or "growth." It is a deeper alchemy of change, flowing from a primal source. It seeps slowly into the flesh, the memory, the spirit; it rises through a life, until it can ignite. It is a perilous process, full of chances for misfire and mistake—or for an ever more mildewed middle age. It is not entirely understood. But we have seen it work, and so have we seen love. Love infuses reason and experience with the power to change a man caught in a morbid present into a man passionately engaged with the future.

The change that leads to love often comes slowly. Many of the girls a man finds will not help. They tend to go along with him and affirm his single life. But one morning he turns to the stranger sleeping next to him, who came to him as easily as a whiskey too many, and left him as heavy-headed, and decides he must seek a better way to live. One day he looks across the room over a pile of dirty dishes and cigarette butts and beer cans and sex magazines and bills and filthy laundry, and he does not see the evidence of happy carousing and bachelor freedom; he sees a trap closing in upon him more grimly than any marriage. One day while joking with friends about the latest of his acquaintances to be caught and caged, he silently wonders, for a moment, whether he really wishes it were he.

Suddenly he has a new glimpse of himself. His body is beginning 10 to decline, grow weaker and slower, even if he keeps it fit. His body, which once measured out his few advantages over females, is beginning to intimate its terrible plan to become as weak as an older woman's. His aggressiveness, which burst in fitful storms throughout his young life but never seemed to cleanse him—his aggression for which he could so rarely find the adequate battle, the harmonious chase—is souring now. His job, so below his measure as a man, so out of tune with his body and his inspiration, now stretches ahead without joy or relief.

His sex, the force that drove the flower of his youth, drives still, 11 drives again and again the same hard bargain—for which there are fewer and fewer takers, in a sexual arena with no final achievement for the single man, in which sex itself becomes work that is never done.

The single man is caught on a reef and the tide is running out. He is 12 being biologically stranded and he has a hopeless dream. Studs Terkel's book *Working* registers again and again men's desire to be remembered. Yet who in this world is much remembered for his job?

Stuck with what he may sense as a choice between being trapped 13 and being stranded, he still may respond by trying one more fling. The biological predicament can be warded off for a time, like Hemingway's hyena. Death often appears in the guise of eternal youth, at the ever-infatuating fountains: alcohol, drugs, hallucinogenic sex. For a while he may believe in the disguise. But the hyena returns and there is mortality in the air—diseases, accidents, concealed suicides, the whole range of the single man's aggression, turned at last against himself.

But where there is death, there is hope. For the man who is in touch 14 with his mortality, but not in the grips of it, is also in touch with the sources of his love. He is in contact with the elements—the natural fires and storms so often used as metaphors for his passions. He is a man who can be deeply and effectively changed. He can find his age, his relation to the world, his maturity, his future. He can burn his signature into the covenant of a specific life.

The man has found a vital energy and a possibility of durable 15 change. It has assumed the shape of a woman. It is the same form that has caught his eye and roiled his body all these years. But now there will be depths below the pleasing surfaces, meanings beyond the momentary ruttings. There will be a sense that this vessel contains the secrets of new life, that the womb and breasts bear a message of immortality. There will be a knowledge that to treat this treasure as an object—mere flesh like his own, a mere matrix of his pleasure—is to defile life itself. It is this recognition that she offers a higher possibility—it is this consciousness that he has to struggle to be worthy of her—that finally issues the spark. And then arises the fire that purges and changes him as it consumes his own death. His children . . . they will remember. It is the only hope.

The man's love begins in a knowledge of inferiority, but it offers a     16
promise of dignity and purpose. For he then has to create, by dint of his own effort, and without the miracle of a womb, a life that a woman could choose. Thus are released and formed the energies of civilized society. He provides, and he does it for a lifetime, for a life.

## VOCABULARY

| | | |
|---|---|---|
| sesame (1) | syndrome (6) | intimate (10) |
| procreative (4) | alchemy (8) | metaphors (14) |
| perpetuate (4) | primal (8) | covenant (14) |
| reciprocal (4) | ignite (8) | ruttings (15) |
| dissipating (6) | perilous (8) | matrix (15) |
| sloughs (6) | infuses (8) | |

## THE FACTS

1. What does the single man seem to be giving up when he gets married?
2. What urge ultimately causes a bachelor to settle down and get married?
3. Why is the power of marriage to change a man referred to as "alchemy"?
4. Who or what is the "hyena" referred to in paragraph 13?
5. By creating a life that a woman could choose, what energies are released and to what purpose?

## THE STRATEGIES

1. How does the author capture the reader's attention in paragraph one?
2. What are the connotations of the phrase "the getaway Honda growl" in paragraph 2? Why is this phrase appropriate?
3. How does the author achieve harmony and coherence in paragraph 4?
4. What is the effect of "screw" in paragraph 5? Why do you think the author used this word?

5. What metaphor is used in paragraph 9 to indicate what carousing has become for the bachelor? Why is this an apt figure of speech? What other figures of speech can you point out in the essay?

## THE ISSUES

1. If you were to summarize the author's thesis in one sentence, what would it state?
2. What advice would you give a young man on how to avoid feeling trapped by marriage?
3. What advantages, if any, does the single life have?
4. Is it essential to marry for love? Or would it be just as good for society to marry for convenience? Bolster your answer with supportive evidence.
5. The last paragraph states that "the man's love begins in a knowledge of inferiority, but it offers a promise of dignity and purpose." What is the meaning of this statement? Do you agree or disagree? Why or why not?

## SUGGESTIONS FOR WRITING

1. Using Gilder's essay as a model, write a causal analysis of why women marry.
2. Explain the main causes of why most modern marriages fail.

### Henry David Thoreau

# ———— • WHY I WENT TO THE WOODS • ————

*Henry David Thoreau (1817–1862), essayist, lecturer, and moralist, was born in Concord, Massachusetts, and educated at Harvard University. He is regarded as one of the seminal influences on American thought and literature. His most famous work is* Walden *(1854), which grew out of the journal recording his solitary existence in a cabin beside Walden Pond, near Concord. His essay, "Civil Disobedience" (1849), has been enormously influential since it was first published and has affected the actions and thoughts of such men as Mahatma Gandhi and Martin Luther King, Jr.*

*In this excerpt from* Walden, *Thoreau explains why he went to the woods to live by himself. Unlike many of the writers in this section, Thoreau writes in a voice rich with metaphors, allusions, and images.*

I went to the woods because I wished to live deliberately, to front    1
only the essential facts of life, and see if I could not learn what it had
to teach, and not, when I came to die, discover that I had not lived. I

did not wish to live what was not life, living is so dear; nor did I wish to practise resignation, unless it was quite necessary. I wanted to live deep and suck out all the marrow of life, to live so sturdily and Spartan-like as to put to rout all that was not life, to cut a broad swath and shave close, to drive life into a corner, and reduce it to its lowest terms, and, if it proved to be mean, why then to get the whole and genuine meanness of it, and publish its meanness to the world; or if it were sublime, to know it by experience, and be able to give a true account of it in my next excursion. For most men, it appears to me, are in a strange uncertainty about it, whether it is of the devil or of God, and have *somewhat hastily* concluded that it is the chief end of man here to "glorify God and enjoy him forever."

Still we live meanly, like ants; though the fable tells us that we were    2
long ago changed into men; like pygmies we fight with cranes; it is error upon error, and clout upon clout, and our best virtue has for its occasion a superfluous and evitable wretchedness. Our life is frittered away by detail. An honest man has hardly need to count more than his ten fingers, or in extreme cases he may add his ten toes, and lump the rest. Simplicity, simplicity, simplicity! I say, let your affairs be as two or three, and not a hundred or a thousand; instead of a million count half a dozen, and keep your accounts on your thumb-nail. In the midst of this chopping sea of civilized life, such are the clouds and storms and quicksands and thousand-and-one items to be allowed for, that a man has to live, if he would not founder and go to the bottom and not make his port at all, by dead reckoning, and he must be a great calculator indeed who succeeds. Simplify, simplify. Instead of three meals a day, if it be necessary eat but one; instead of a hundred dishes, five; and reduce other things in proportion. Our life is like a German Confederacy, made up of petty states, with its boundary forever fluctuating, so that even a German cannot tell you how it is bounded at any moment. The nation itself, with all its so-called internal improvements, which, by the way are all external and superficial, is just such an unwieldy and overgrown establishment, cluttered with furniture and tripped up by its own traps, ruined by luxury and heedless expense, by want of calculation and a worthy aim, as the million households in the lands; and the only cure for it, as for them, is in a rigid economy, a stern and more than Spartan simplicity of life and elevation of purpose. It lives too fast. Men think that it is essential that the *Nation* have commerce, and export ice, and talk through a telegraph, and ride thirty miles an hour, without a doubt, whether *they* do or not; but

whether we should live like baboons or like men, is a little uncertain. If we do not get our sleepers, and forge rails, and devote days and nights to the work, but go to tinkering upon our *lives* to improve *them*, who will build railroads? And if railroads are not built, how shall we get to heaven in season? But if we stay at home and mind our business, who will want railroads? We do not ride on the railroad; it rides upon us. Did you ever think what those sleepers* are that underlie the railroad? Each one is a man, an Irishman, or a Yankee man. The rails are laid on them, and they are covered with sand, and the cars run smoothly over them. They are sound sleepers, I assure you. And every few years a new lot is laid down and run over; so that, if some have the pleasure of riding on a rail, others have the misfortune to be ridden upon. And when they run over a man that is walking in his sleep, a supernumerary sleeper in the wrong position, and wake him up, they suddenly stop the cars, and make a hue and cry about it, as if this were an exception. I am glad to know that it takes a gang of men for every five miles to keep the sleepers down and level in their beds as it is, for this is a sign that they may sometimes get up again.

Why should we live with such hurry and waste of life? We are    3 determined to be starved before we are hungry. Men say that a stitch in time saves nine, and so they take a thousand stitches to-day to save nine to-morrow. As for *work*, we haven't any of any consequence. We have the Saint Vitus' dance, and cannot possibly keep our heads still. If I should only give a few pulls at the parish bell-rope, as for a fire, that is, without setting the bell, there is hardly a man on his farm in the outskirts of Concord, notwithstanding that press of engagements which was his excuse so many times this morning, nor a boy, nor a woman, I might almost say, but would foresake all and follow that sound, not mainly to save property from the flames, but, if we will confess the truth, much more to see it burn, since burn it must, and we, be it known, did not set it on fire,—or to see it put out, and have a hand in it, if that is done as handsomely; yes, even if it were the parish church itself. Hardly a man takes a half-hour's nap after dinner, but when he wakes he holds up his head and asks, "What's the news?" as if the rest of mankind had stood his sentinels. Some give directions to be waked every half-hour, doubtless for no other purpose; and then, to pay for it, they tell what they have dreamed. After a night's sleep the news is as indispensable as the breakfast. "Pray tell me anything

---

*Crossties. Thoreau is playing on the word.—Ed.

new that has happened to a man anywhere on this globe,"—and he reads it over his coffee and rolls, that a man has had his eyes gouged out this morning on the Wachito River; never dreaming the while that he lives in the dark unfathomed mammoth cave of this world, and has but the rudiment of an eye himself.

For my part, I could easily do without the post-office. I think that 4 there are very few important communications made through it. To speak critically, I never received more than one or two letters in my life—I wrote this some years ago—that were worth the postage. The penny-post is, commonly, an institution through which you seriously offer a man that penny for his thoughts which is so often safely offered in jest. And I am sure that I never read any memorable news in a newspaper. If we read of one man robbed, or murdered, or killed by accident, or one house burned, or one vessel wrecked, or one steamboat blown up, or one cow run over on the Western Railroad, or one mad dog killed, or one lot of grasshoppers in the winter,—we never need read of another. One is enough. If you are acquainted with the principle, what do you care for a myriad instances and applications? To a philosopher all *news*, as it is called, is gossip, and they who edit and read it are old women over their tea. Yet not a few are greedy after this gossip. There was such a rush, as I hear, the other day at one of the offices to learn the foreign news by the last arrival, that several large squares of plate glass belonging to the establishment were broken by the pressure,—news which I seriously think a ready wit might write a twelvemonth, or twelve years, beforehand with sufficient accuracy. As for Spain, for instance, if you know how to throw in Don Carlos and the Infanta, and Don Pedro and Seville and Granada, from time to time in the right proportions,—they may have changed the names a little since I saw the papers,—and serve up a bullfight when other entertainments fail, it will be true to the letter, and give us as good an idea of the exact state or ruin of things in Spain as the most succinct and lucid reports under this head in the newspapers: and as for England, almost the last significant scrap of news from that quarter was the revolution of 1649; and if you have learned the history of her crops for an average year, you never need attend to that thing again, unless your speculations are of a merely pecuniary character. If one may judge who rarely looks into the newspapers, nothing new does ever happen in foreign parts, a French revolution not excepted.

What news! how much more important to know what that is which 5 was never old! "Kieou-he-yu (great dignitary of the state of Wei) sent a man to Khoung-tseu to know his news. Khoung-tseu caused the messenger to be seated near him, and questioned him in these terms: What is your master doing? The messenger answered with respect: My master desires to diminish the number of his faults, but he cannot come to the end of them. The messenger being gone, the philosopher remarked: What a worthy messenger! What a worthy messenger!" The preacher, instead of vexing the ears of drowsy farmers on their day of rest at the end of the week,—for Sunday is the fit conclusion of an ill-spent week, and not the fresh and brave beginning of a new one,—with this one other draggle-tail of a sermon, should shout with thundering voice, "Pause! Avast! Why so seeming fast, but deadly slow?"

Shams and delusions are esteemed for soundless truths, while reality is fabulous. If men would steadily observe realities only, and not allow themselves to be deluded, life, to compare it with such things as we know, would be like a fairy tale and the Arabian Nights' Entertainments. If we respected only what is inevitable and has a right to be, music and poetry would resound along the streets. When we are unhurried and wise, we perceive that only great and worthy things have any permanent and absolute existence, that petty fears and petty pleasures are but the shadow of the reality. This is always exhilarating and sublime. By closing the eyes and slumbering, and consenting to be deceived by shows, men establish and confirm their daily life of routine and habit everywhere, which still is built on purely illusory foundations. Children, who play life, discern its true law and relations more clearly than men, who fail to live it worthily, but who think that they are wiser by experience, that is, by failure. I have read in a Hindoo book, that "there was a king's son, who, being expelled in infancy from his native city, was brought up by a forester, and, growing up to maturity in that state, imagined himself to belong to the barbarous race with which he lived. One of his father's ministers having discovered him, revealed to him what he was, and the misconception of his character was removed, and he knew himself to be a prince. So soul," continues the Hindoo philosopher, "from the circumstances in which it is placed, mistakes its own character, until the truth is revealed to it by some holy teacher, and then it knows itself to be *Brahme*." I perceive that we inhabitants of New England live this mean life that we do because our vision does not penetrate the surface of things. We think that that *is* which *appears* to be. If a man should walk through this town and see only the reality, where, think you, would the "Mill-dam" go to? If he should give us an account of the realities he beheld there, we should not recognize the place in his description. Look at the meeting-house, or a court-house, or a jail, or a shop, or a dwelling-house, and say what that thing really is before a true gaze, and they would all go to pieces in your account of them. Men esteem truth remote, in the outskirts of the system, behind the farthest star, before Adam and after the last man. In eternity there is indeed something true and sublime. But all these times and places and occasions are now and here. God himself culminates in the present moment, and will never be more divine in the lapse of all the ages. And we are enabled to apprehend at all what is sublime and noble only by the perpetual instilling and drenching of the reality that surrounds us. The universe constantly and obediently answers to our conceptions; whether we travel fast or slow, the track is laid for us. Let us spend our lives in conceiving then. The poet or the artist never yet had so fair and noble a design but some of his posterity at least could accomplish it.

Let us spend one day as deliberately as Nature, and not be thrown off the track by every nutshell and mosquito's wing that falls on the rails. Let us rise early and fast, or breakfast, gently and without perturbation; let company come and let company go, let the bells ring and the children cry,—determined to make a day of it. Why should we knock under and go with the stream? Let us not be upset and overwhelmed in that terrible rapid and whirlpool called a dinner, situated in the meridian shallows. Weather this danger and you are safe, for the rest of the way is down hill. With unrelaxed nerves, with morning vigor, sail by it, looking another way, tied to the mast like Ulysses.* If the engine whistles, let it whistle till it is hoarse for its pains. If the bell rings, why should we run? We will consider what kind of music they are like. Let us settle ourselves, and work and wedge our feet downward through the mud and slush of opinion, and prejudice, and tradition, and delusion, and appearance, that alluvion which covers the globe, through Paris and London, through New York and Boston and Concord, through Church and State, through poetry and philosophy and religion, till we come to a hard bottom and rocks in place, which we can call *reality*, and say, This is, and no mistake; and then begin, having a *point d'appui*,† below freshet and frost and fire, a place where you might found a wall or a state, or set a lamp-post safely, or perhaps

7

---

*tied . . . Ulysses: In Homer's *Odyssey*, Ulysses had himself tied to the mast of his boat so that he could listen, but not respond, to the irresistible songs of the Sirens, who were believed to lure ships to their doom.—Ed.
†*point d'appui*: point of stability.—Ed.

a gauge, not a Nilometer, but a Realometer, that future ages might know how deep a freshet of shams and appearances had gathered from time to time. If you stand right fronting and face to face to a fact, you will see the sun glimmer on both its surfaces, as if it were a cimeter, and feel its sweet edge dividing you through the heart and marrow, and so you will happily conclude your mortal career. Be it life or death, we crave only reality. If we are really dying, let us hear the rattle in our throats and feel cold in the extremities; if we are alive, let us go about our business.

Time is but the stream I go a-fishing in. I drink at it; but while I drink I see the sandy bottom and detect how shallow it is. Its thin current slides away, but eternity remains. I would drink deeper; fish in the sky, whose bottom is pebbly with stars. I cannot count one. I know not the first letter of the alphabet. I have always been regretting that I was not as wise as the day I was born. The intellect is a cleaver; it discerns and rifts its way into the secret of things. I do not wish to be any more busy with my hands than is necessary. My head is hands and feet. I feel all my best faculties concentrated on it. My instinct tells me that my head is an organ for burrowing, as some creatures use their snout and fore paws, and with it I would mine and burrow my way through these hills. I think that the richest vein is somewhere hereabouts; so by the divining-rod and thin rising vapors, I judge; and here I will begin to mine.

## *VOCABULARY*

| | | |
|---|---|---|
| superfluous (2) | succinct (4) | freshet (7) |
| evitable (2) | pecuniary (4) | meridian (7) |
| supernumerary (2) | posterity (6) | alluvion (7) |
| rudiment (3) | culminates (6) | |
| myriad (4) | perturbation (7) | |

## *THE FACTS*

1. Why did Thoreau go to the woods? What, in his opinion, is wrong with the nation?
2. Thoreau writes: "We do not ride on the railroad; it rides upon us." What does he mean?
3. What is Thoreau's definition of "news"? What is his definition of gossip? According to Thoreau, how does news differ from gossip?

4. What does Thoreau mean when he says that the "universe constantly and obediently answers to our conceptions"? How, then, is truth possible?
5. Where, according to Thoreau, is truth to be found? What prevents us from finding it?

## THE STRATEGIES

1. Reread the final sentence of paragraph 1. What tone is Thoreau using?
2. Thoreau uses two anecdotes in this excerpt (paragraphs 5 and 6). What do these have in common? What do they indicate about the writer's philosophy?
3. "We have the Saint Vitus' dance, and cannot possibly keep our heads still" (paragraph 3). What figure of speech is this? Can you find other examples of this same figure of speech in the text? What effect do they have on Thoreau's writing?
4. "Our life is like a German Confederacy, made up of petty states, with its boundary forever fluctuating, so that even a German cannot tell you how it is bounded at any moment" (paragraph 2). What figure of speech is this? How does it differ from the example in the preceding question?
5. An allusion is a figure of speech in which some famous historical or literary figure or event is casually mentioned. Can you find an allusion in Thoreau's text? (Hint: examine paragraph 7.) What effect does the allusion have on the writer's style?

## THE ISSUES

1. Reread the essay "Diogenes and Alexander," on pages 539–43. What views about society do Diogenes and Thoreau share? Do you agree with these views? Why or why not?
2. Thoreau witnessed the creation of the railroad and felt that it was an intrusion on life. In paragraph 2 he states, "We do not ride on the railroad; it rides upon us." What new industrial creation of your time might evoke a similar statement from some social commentator like Thoreau?
3. Do you agree with Thoreau that few important communications reach you through the post office? Why or why not?
4. In paragraph 6, Thoreau follows in Plato's footsteps when he tells us that only great and worthy things have absolute existence, but that petty things are a mere shadow of reality. Imagine yourself to be like Thoreau, living alone out in the woods. What would be essential to your life? What would seem petty? Give examples.
5. What memorable experience, if any, have you had of being alone in nature? How did this experience affect you? What did you learn from it?

## SUGGESTIONS FOR WRITING

1. Write an essay describing the clutter of petty affairs in an average person's life. Suggest some ways of simplifying life.
2. Pretend that you are Thoreau and that you have just been brought back to life and introduced to twentieth-century America. Write a diary putting down your first impressions.

## TERM PAPER SUGGESTION

Thoreau was once sent to jail for refusing to pay his taxes. Research this episode and write about it.

### H. L. Mencken

## ———— • THE SATISFACTION OF LIFE • ————

*Henry Louis Mencken (1880–1956) was an editor, author, and critic. He began his journalism career on the* Baltimore Morning Herald *and later became editor of the* Baltimore Evening Herald. *From 1906 until his death he was on the staff of the* Baltimore Sun *(or Evening Sun). In 1924, with George Jean Nathan, Mencken founded the* American Mercury, *and served as its editor from 1925 to 1933. Mencken's writing was chiefly devoted to lambasting the smug, conventional attitudes of the middle class. Among his numerous works is* The American Language, *Mencken's monumental study of the American idiom, first published in 1919.*

*In 1932, noted historian Will Durant asked numerous famous people to tell him what gave their lives purpose. Among the answers he received was the following laconic statement by H. L. Mencken.*

You ask me, in brief, what satisfaction I get out of life, and why I go on working. I go on working for the same reason that a hen goes on laying eggs. There is in every living creature an obscure but powerful impulse to active functioning. Life demands to be lived. Inaction, save as a measure of recuperation between bursts of activity, is painful and dangerous to the healthy organism—in fact, it is almost impossible. Only the dying can be really idle.

The precise form of an individual's activity is determined, of course, by the equipment with which he came into the world. In other words, it is determined by his heredity. I do not lay eggs, as a hen does, because I was born without any equipment for it. For the same reason

I do not get myself elected to Congress, or play the violoncello, or teach metaphysics in a college, or work in a steel mill. What I do is simply what lies easiest to my hand. It happens that I was born with an intense and insatiable interest in ideas, and thus like to play with them. It happens also that I was born with rather more than the average facility for putting them into words. In consequence, I am a writer and editor, which is to say, a dealer in them and concocter of them.

There is very little conscious volition in all this. What I do was ordained by the inscrutable fates, not chosen by me. In my boyhood, yielding to a powerful but still subordinate interest in exact facts, I wanted to be a chemist, and at the same time my poor father tried to make me a business man. At other times, like any other relatively poor man, I have longed to make a lot of money by some easy swindle. But I became a writer all the same, and shall remain one until the end of the chapter, just as a cow goes on giving milk all her life, even though what appears to be her self-interest urges her to give gin.

I am far luckier than most men, for I have been able since boyhood to make a good living doing precisely what I have wanted to do—what I would have done for nothing, and very gladly, if there had been no reward for it. Not many men, I believe, are so fortunate. Millions of them have to make their livings at tasks which really do not interest them. As for me, I have had an extraordinarily pleasant life, despite the fact that I have had the usual share of woes. For in the midst of those woes I still enjoyed the immense satisfaction which goes with free activity. I have done, in the main, exactly what I wanted to do. Its possible effects upon other people have interested me very little. I have not written and published to please other people, but to satisfy myself, just as a cow gives milk, not to profit the dairyman, but to satisfy herself. I like to think that most of my ideas have been sound ones, but I really don't care. The world may take them or leave them. I have had my fun hatching them.

Next to agreeable work as a means of attaining happiness I put what Huxley called the domestic affections—the day to day intercourse with family and friends. My home has seen bitter sorrow, but it has never seen any serious disputes, and it has never seen poverty. I was completely happy with my mother and sister, and I am completely happy with my wife. Most of the men I commonly associate with are friends of very old standing. I have known some of them for more than thirty years. I seldom see anyone, intimately, whom I have known for less than ten years. These friends delight me. I turn to them when work is done with unfailing eagerness. We have the same general tastes, and see the world much alike. Most of them are interested in music, as I am. It has given me more pleasure in this life than any other external thing. I love it more every year.

As for religion, I am quite devoid of it. Never in my adult life have I     6 experienced anything that could be plausibly called a religious impulse. My father and grandfather were agnostics before me, and though I was sent to Sunday-school as a boy and exposed to the Christian theology I was never taught to believe it. My father thought that I should learn what it was, but it apparently never occurred to him that I would accept it. He was a good psychologist. What I got in Sunday-school—besides a wide acquaintance with Christian hymnology—was simply a firm conviction that the Christian faith was full of palpable absurdities, and the Christian God preposterous. Since that time I have read a great deal in theology—perhaps much more than the average clergyman—but I have never discovered any reason to change my mind.

The act of worship, as carried on by Christians, seems to me to be     7 debasing rather than ennobling. It involves grovelling before a Being who, if He really exists, deserves to be denounced instead of respected. I see little evidence in this world of the so-called goodness of God. On the contrary, it seems to me that, on the strength of His daily acts, He must be set down a most stupid, cruel and villainous fellow. I can say this with a clear conscience, for He has treated me very well—in fact, with vast politeness. But I can't help thinking of His barbaric torture of most of the rest of humanity. I simply can't imagine revering the God of war and politics, theology and cancer.

I do not believe in immortality, and have no desire for it. The belief     8 in it issues from the puerile egos of inferior men. In its Christian form it is little more than a device for getting revenge upon those who are having a better time on this earth. What the meaning of human life may be I don't know: I incline to suspect that it has none. All I know about it is that, to me at least, it is very amusing while it lasts. Even its troubles, indeed, can be amusing. Moreover, they tend to foster the human qualities that I admire most—courage and its analogues. The noblest man, I think, is that one who fights God, and triumphs over Him. I have had little of this to do. When I die I shall be content to vanish into nothingness. No show, however good, could conceivably be good forever.

## VOCABULARY

violoncello (2)

metaphysics (2)

insatiable (2)

volition (3)

plausibly (6)

hymnology (6)

palpable (6)

preposterous (6)

villainous (6)

barbaric (7)

revering (7)

puerile (8)

analogues (8)

## THE FACTS

1. This essay suggests some reasons why Mencken goes on living. What is his main reason? What analogies does he use to clarify this reason?
2. What is Mencken's general evaluation of his life? Has it been good or bad? Cite passages to support your answer.
3. How does Mencken feel about critical acceptance of his literary work?
4. How would you summarize Mencken's attitude toward religion? Compare or contrast your view with his.
5. In his conclusion, Mencken states that when he dies, he will be content to vanish into nothingness. What is the cause for this attitude? Is his a common view?

## THE STRATEGIES

1. What tone does the author maintain throughout his essay?
2. What is the author's definition of a writer? See paragraph 2.
3. What are several examples of parallelism in paragraph 2?
4. What pronoun ties paragraph 3 to the preceding paragraphs?
5. In his final paragraph, what symbol does the author choose to represent his life? Is this an appropriate symbol? Why or why not?

## THE ISSUES

1. Mencken tells us that he does not believe in immortality and that he has no desire for it (see paragraph 8). How does his belief compare with your own or that of the persons you most respect?
2. Argue against Mencken's view of God as described in paragraph 7. What are some evidences of "the so-called goodness of God"?
3. How does Mencken keep from being depressed or morose about his existential view of life?

4. Mencken states that music has given him more pleasure in this life than any other external thing. What external thing has given *you* the most pleasure in life? Why?

5. Reword paragraph 5 to fit your circumstances at home. How does your situation compare or contrast with that of Mencken?

## SUGGESTIONS FOR WRITING

1. Write a companion piece for Mencken's essay. Entitle it "The Meaning of Death" and begin by saying, "You ask me, in brief, how I handle the question of death. . . ." Like Mencken, include some specific examples.

2. In his opening paragraph Mencken states "Life demands to be lived" and "Only the dying can be really idle." Develop an essay that will clarify Mencken's meaning.

Katherine Anne Porter

### • FLOWERING JUDAS •

*Katherine Anne Porter (1890–1980) was a master of the short story and a highly accomplished stylist. She published collections of short stories including* Flowering Judas *(1930), collections of essays and miscellaneous pieces including* The Day Before *(1952), and a novel,* Ship of Fools *(1962).*

*Fiction often focuses on the causes for a character's behavior. This story draws heavily on symbolism to explain the behavior of its main character, Laura.*

Braggioni sits heaped upon the edge of a straight-backed chair much too small for him, and sings to Laura in a furry, mournful voice. Laura has begun to find reasons for avoiding her own house until the latest possible moment, for Braggioni is there almost every night. No matter how late she is, he will be sitting there with a surly, waiting expression, pulling at his kinky yellow hair, thumbing the strings of his guitar, snarling a tune under his breath. Lupe the Indian maid meets Laura at the door, and says with a flicker of a glance towards the upper room, "He waits." 1

Laura wishes to lie down, she is tired of her hairpins and the feel of her long tight sleeves, but she says to him, "Have you a new song for me this evening?" If he says yes, she asks him to sing it. If he says no, she remembers his favorite one, and asks him to sing it again. Lupe brings her a cup of chocolate and plate of rice, and Laura eats at the 2 small table under the lamp, first inviting Braggioni, whose answer is always the same: "I have eaten, and besides, chocolate thickens the voice."

Laura says, "Sing, then," and Braggioni heaves himself into song. He scratches the guitar familiarly as though it were a pet animal, and sings passionately off key, taking the high notes in a prolonged painful squeal. Laura, who haunts the markets listening to the ballad singers, and stops every day to hear the blind boy playing his reed-flute in Sixteenth of September Street, listens to Braggioni with pitiless courtesy, because she dares not smile at his miserable performance. Nobody dares to smile at him. Braggioni is cruel to everyone, with a kind of specialized insolence, but he is so vain of his talents, and so sensitive to slights, it would require a cruelty and vanity greater than his own to lay a finger on the vast cureless wound of his self-esteem. It would require courage, too, for it is dangerous to offend him, and nobody has this courage.

Braggioni loves himself with such tenderness and amplitude and eternal charity that his followers—for he is a leader of men, a skilled revolutionist, and his skin has been punctured in honorable warfare— warm themselves in the reflected glow, and say to each other: "He has a real nobility, a love of humanity raised above mere personal affections." The excess of this self-love has flowed out, inconveniently for her, over Laura, who, with so many others, owes her comfortable situation and her salary to him. When he is in a very good humor, he tells her, "I am tempted to forgive you for being a *gringa. Gringita!*"* and Laura, burning, imagines herself leaning forward suddenly, and with a sound back-handed slap wiping the suety smile from his face. If he notices her eyes at these moments he gives no sign.

She knows what Braggioni would offer her, and she must resist tenaciously without appearing to resist, and if she could avoid it she would not admit even to herself the slow drift of his intention. During these long evenings which have spoiled a long month for her, she sits in her deep chair with an open book on her knees, resting her eyes on the consoling rigidity of the printed page when the sight and sound of Braggioni singing threaten to identify themselves with all her remembered afflictions and to add their weight to her uneasy premonitions

---

*Gringa:* the feminine of *gringo*, a disparaging term used by Spanish Americans in referring to foreigners, especially Americans and the English. However, *gringita* is the diminutive form and is therefore not disparaging.—Ed.

of the future. The gluttonous bulk of Braggioni has become a symbol of her many disillusions, for a revolutionist should be lean, animated by heroic faith, a vessel of abstract virtues. This is nonsense, she knows it now and is ashamed of it. Revolution must have leaders, and leadership is a career for energetic men. She is, her comrades tell her, full of romantic error, for what she defines as cynicism in them is merely "a developed sense of reality." She is almost too willing to say, "I am wrong, I suppose I don't really understand the principles," and afterward she makes a secret truce with herself, determined not to surrender her will to such expedient logic. But she cannot help feeling that she has been betrayed irreparably by the disunion between her way of living and her feeling of what life should be, and at times she is almost contented to rest in this sense of grievance as a private store of consolation. Sometimes she wishes to run away, but she stays. Now she longs to fly out of this room, down the narrow stairs, and into the street where the houses lean together like conspirators under a single mottled lamp, and leave Braggioni singing to himself.

Instead she looks at Braggioni, frankly and clearly, like a good child 6 who understands the rules of behavior. Her knees cling together under sound blue serge, and her round white collar is not purposely nun-like. She wears the uniform of an idea, and has renounced vanities. She was born Roman Catholic, and in spite of her fear of being seen by someone who might make a scandal of it, she slips now and again into some crumbling little church, kneels on the chilly stone, and says a Hail Mary on the gold rosary she bought in Tehuantepec. It is no good and she ends by examining the altar with its tinsel flowers and ragged brocades, and feels tender about the battered doll-shape of some male saint whose white, lace-trimmed drawers hang limply around his ankles below the hieratic dignity of his velvet robe. She has encased herself in a set of principles derived from her early training, leaving no detail of gesture or of personal taste untouched, and for this reason she will not wear lace made on machines. This is her private heresy, for in her special group the machine is sacred, and will be the salvation of the workers. She loves fine lace, and there is a tiny edge of fluted cobweb on this collar, which is one of twenty precisely alike, folded in blue tissue paper in the upper drawer of her clothes chest.

Braggioni catches her glance solidly as if he had been waiting for it, 7 leans forward, balancing his paunch between his spread knees, and sings with tremendous emphasis, weighing his words. He has, the song relates, no father and no mother, nor even a friend to console him; lonely as a wave of the sea he comes and goes, lonely as a wave. His mouth opens round and yearns sideways, his balloon cheeks grow oily with the labor of song. He bulges marvelously in his expensive garments. Over his lavender collar, crushed upon a purple necktie, held by a diamond hoop: over his ammunition belt of tooled leather worked in silver, buckled cruelly around his gasping middle: over the tops of his glossy yellow shoes Braggioni swells with ominous ripeness, his mauve silk hose stretched taut, his ankles bound with the stout leather thongs of his shoes.

When he stretches his eyelids at Laura she notes that his eyes are   8 the true tawny yellow cat's eyes. He is rich, not in money, he tells her, but in power, and his power brings with it the blameless ownership of things, and the right to indulge his love of small luxuries. "I have a taste for the elegant refinements," he said once, flourishing a yellow handkerchief before her nose. "Smell that? It is Jockey Club, imported from New York." Nonetheless he is wounded by life. He will say so presently. "It is true everything turns to dust in the hand, to gall on the tongue." He sighs and his leather belt creaks like a saddle girth. "I am disappointed in everything as it comes. Everything." He shakes his head. "You, poor thing, you will be disappointed too. You are born for it. We are more alike than you realize in some things. Wait and see. Some day you will remember what I have told you, you will know that Braggioni was your friend."

Laura feels a slow chill, a purely physical sense of danger, a warning   9 in her blood that violence, mutilation, a shocking death, waits for her with lessening patience. She has translated this fear into something homely, immediate, and sometimes hesitates before crossing the street. "My personal fate is nothing, except as the testimony of a mental attitude," she reminds herself, quoting from some forgotten philosophic primer, and is sensible enough to add, "Anyhow, I shall not be killed by an automobile if I can help it."

"It may be true I am as corrupt, in another way, as Braggioni," she   10 thinks in spite of herself, "as callous, as incomplete," and if this is so, any kind of death seems preferable. Still she sits quietly, she does not run. Where could she go? Uninvited she has promised herself to this place; she can no longer imagine herself as living in another country, and there is no pleasure in remembering her life before she came here.

Precisely what is the nature of this devotion, its true motives, and   11 what are its obligations? Laura cannot say. She spends part of her days in Xochimilco, near by, teaching Indian children to say in English,

"The cat on the mat." When she appears in the classroom they crowd about her with smiles on their wise, innocent, clay-colored faces, crying, "Good morning, my titcher!" in immaculate voices, and they make of her desk a fresh garden of flowers every day.

During her leisure she goes to union meetings and listens to busy important voices quarreling over tactics, methods, internal politics. She visits prisoners of her own political faith in their cells, where they entertain themselves with counting cockroaches, repenting of their indiscretions, composing their memoirs, writing out manifestoes and plans for their comrades who are still walking about free, hands in pockets, sniffing fresh air. Laura brings them food and cigarettes and a little money, and she brings messages disguised in equivocal phrases from the men outside who dare not set foot in the prison for fear of disappearing into the cells kept empty for them. If the prisoners confuse night and day, and complain, "Dear little Laura, time doesn't pass in this infernal hole, and I won't know when it is time to sleep unless I have a reminder," she brings them their favorite narcotics, and says in a tone that does not wound them with pity, "Tonight will really be night for you," and though her Spanish amuses them, they find her comforting, useful. If they lose patience and faith, and curse the slowness of their friends in coming to their rescue with money and influence, they trust her not to repeat everything, and if she inquires, "Where do you think we can find money, or influence?" they are certain to answer, "Well, there is Braggioni, why doesn't he do something?"

She smuggles letters from headquarters to men hiding from firing squads in back streets in mildewed houses, where they sit in tumbled beds and talk bitterly as if all Mexico were at their heels, when Laura knows positively they might appear at the band concert in the Alameda on Sunday morning, and no one would notice them. But Braggioni says, "Let them sweat a little. The next time they may be careful. It is very restful to have them out of the way for a while." She is not afraid to knock on any door in any street after midnight, and enter in the darkness, and say to one of these men who is really in danger: "They will be looking for you—seriously—tomorrow morning after six. Here is some money from Vicente. Go to Vera Cruz and wait."

She borrows the money from the Roumanian agitator to give to his bitter enemy the Polish agitator. The favor of Braggioni is their disputed territory, and Braggioni holds the balance nicely, for he can use them both. The Polish agitator talks love to her over café tables, hoping to exploit what he believes is her secret sentimental preference for him, and he gives her misinformation which he begs her to repeat as the solemn truth to certain persons. The Roumanian is more adroit. He is generous with his money in all good causes, and lies to her with an air of ingenuous candor, as if he were her good friend and confidant. She never repeats anything they may say. Braggioni never asks questions. He has other ways to discover all that he wishes to know about them.

Nobody touches her, but all praise her gray eyes, and the soft, round   15
under lip which promises gayety, yet is always grave, nearly always firmly closed: and they cannot understand why she is in Mexico. She walks back and forth on her errands, with puzzled eyebrows, carrying her little folder of drawings and music and school papers. No dancer dances more beautifully than Laura walks, and she inspires some amusing, unexpected ardors, which cause little gossip, because nothing comes of them. A young captain who had been a soldier in Zapata's army attempted, during a horseback ride near Cuernavaca, to express his desire for her with the noble simplicity befitting a rude folk-hero: but gently, because he was gentle. This gentleness was his defeat, for when he alighted, and removed her foot from the stirrup, and essayed to draw her down into his arms, her horse, ordinarily a tame one, shied fiercely, reared and plunged away. The young hero's horse careered blindly after his stable-mate, and the hero did not return to the hotel until rather late that evening. At breakfast he came to her table in full charro dress, gray buckskin jacket and trousers with strings of silver buttons down the legs, and he was in a humorous, careless mood. "May I sit with you?" and "You are a wonderful rider. I was terrified that you might be thrown and dragged. I should never have forgiven myself. But I cannot admire you enough for your riding!"

"I learned to ride in Arizona," said Laura.   16

"If you will ride with me again this morning, I promise you a horse   17
that will not shy with you," he said. But Laura remembered that she must return to Mexico City at noon.

Next morning the children made a celebration and spent their play-   18
time writing on the blackboard. "We lov ar ticher," and with tinted chalks they drew wreaths of flowers around the words. The young hero wrote her a letter: "I am a very foolish, wasteful, impulsive man. I should have first said I love you, and then you would not have run

away. But you shall see me again." Laura thought, "I must send him a box of colored crayons," but she was trying to forgive herself for having spurred her horse at the wrong moment.

A brown, shock-haired youth came and stood in her patio one night 19 and sang like a lost soul for two hours, but Laura could think of nothing to do about it. The moonlight spread a wash of gauzy silver over the clear spaces of the garden, and the shadows were cobalt blue. The scarlet blossoms of the Judas tree were dull purple, and the names of the colors repeated themselves automatically in her mind, while she watched not the boy, but his shadow, fallen like a dark garment across the fountain rim, trailing in the water. Lupe came silently and whispered expert counsel in her ear: "If you throw him one little flower, he will sing another song or two and go away." Laura threw the flower, and he sang a last song and went away with the flower tucked in the band of his hat. Lupe said, "He is one of the organizers of the Typographers Union, and before that he sold corridos in the Merced market, and before that, he came from Guanajuato, where I was born. I would not trust any man, but I trust least those from Guanajuato."

She did not tell Laura that he would be back again the next night, 20 and the next, nor that he would follow her at a certain fixed distance around the Merced market, through the Zócolo, up Francisco I. Madero Avenue, and so along the Paseo de la Reforma to Chapultepec Park, and into the Philosopher's Footpath, still with that flower withering in his hat, and an indivisible attention in his eyes.

Now Laura is accustomed to him, it means nothing except that he is 21 nineteen years old and is observing a convention with all propriety, as though it were founded on a law of nature, which in the end it might well prove to be. He is beginning to write poems which he prints on a wooden press, and he leaves them stuck like handbills in her door. She is pleasantly disturbed by the abstract, unhurried watchfulness of his black eyes which will in time turn easily towards another object. She tells herself that throwing the flower was a mistake, for she is twenty-two years old and knows better; but she refuses to regret it, and persuades herself that her negation of all external events as they occur is a sign that she is gradually perfecting herself in the stoicism she strives to cultivate against that disaster she fears, though she cannot name it.

She is not at home in the world. Every day she teaches children who 22 remain strangers to her, though she loves their tender round hands and their charming opportunist savagery. She knocks at unfamiliar doors not knowing whether a friend or a stranger shall answer, and even if a known face emerges from the sour gloom of that unknown interior, still it is the face of a stranger. No matter what this stranger says to her, nor what her message to him, the very cells of her flesh reject knowledge and kinship in one monotonous word. No. No. No. She draws her strength from this one holy talismanic word which does not suffer her to be led into evil. Denying everything, she may walk anywhere in safety, she looks at everything without amazement.

No, repeats this firm unchanging voice of her blood; and she looks    23
at Braggioni without amazement. He is a great man, he wishes to impress this simple girl who covers her great round breasts with thick dark cloth, and who hides long, invaluably beautiful legs under a heavy skirt. She is almost thin except for the incomprehensible fullness of her breasts, like a nursing mother's, and Braggioni, who considers himself a judge of women, speculates again on the puzzle of her notorious virginity, and takes the liberty of speech which she permits without a sign of modesty, indeed, without any sort of sign, which is disconcerting.

"You think you are so cold, *gringita!* wait and see. You will surprise    24
yourself some day! May I be there to advise you!" He stretches his eyelids at her, and his ill-humored cat's eyes waver in a separate glance for the two points of light marking the opposite ends of a smoothly drawn path between the swollen curve of her breasts. He is not put off by that blue serge, nor by her resolutely fixed gaze. There is all the time in the world. His cheeks are bellying with the wind of song. "Oh girl with the dark eyes," he sings, and reconsiders. "But yours are not dark. I can change all that. O girl with the green eyes, you have stolen my heart away!" then his mind wanders to the song, and Laura feels the weight of his attention being shifted elsewhere. Singing thus, he seems harmless, he is quite harmless, there is nothing to do but sit patiently and say "No," when the moment comes. She draws a full breath, and her mind wanders also, but not far. She dares not wander too far.

Not for nothing has Braggioni taken pains to be a good revolutionist    25
and a professional lover of humanity. He will never die of it. He has the malice, the cleverness, the wickedness, the sharpness of wit, the hardness of heart, stipulated for loving the world profitably. *He will never die of it*. He will live to see himself kicked out from his feeding trough by other hungry world-saviors. Traditionally he must sing in

spite of his life which drives him to bloodshed, he tells Laura, for his father was a Tuscany peasant who drifted to Yucatan and married a Maya woman: a woman of race, an aristocrat. They gave him the love and knowledge of music, thus: and under the rip of his thumbnail, the strings of the instrument complain like exposed nerves.

Once he was called Delgadito by all the girls and married women who ran after him; he was so scrawny all his bones showed under his thin cotton clothing, and he could squeeze his emptiness to the very backbone with his two hands. He was a poet and the revolution was only a dream then; too many women loved him and sapped away his youth, and he could never find enough to eat anywhere, anywhere! Now he is a leader of men, crafty men who whisper in his ear, hungry men who wait for hours outside his office for a word with him, emaciated men with wild faces who waylay him at the street gate with a timid, "Comrade, let me tell you . . ." and they blow the foul breath from their empty stomachs in his face.    26

He is always sympathetic. He gives them handfuls of small coins from his own pocket, he promises them work, there will be demonstrations, they must join the unions and attend meetings, above all they must be on the watch for spies. They are closer to him than his own brothers, without them he can do nothing—until tomorrow, comrade!    27

Until tomorrow. "They are stupid, they are lazy, they are treacherous, they would cut my throat for nothing," he says to Laura. He has good food and abundant drink, he hires an automobile and drives in the Paseo on Sunday morning, and enjoys plenty of sleep in a soft bed beside a wife who dares not disturb him; and he sits pampering his bones in easy billows of fat, singing to Laura, who knows and thinks these things about him. When he was fifteen, he tried to drown himself because he loved a girl, his first love, and she laughed at him. "A thousand women have paid for that," and his tight little mouth turns down at the corners. Now he perfumes his hair with Jockey Club, and confides to Laura: "One woman is really as good as another for me, in the dark. I prefer them all."    28

His wife organizes unions among the girls in the cigarette factories, and walks in picket lines, and even speaks at meetings in the evening. But she cannot be brought to acknowledge the benefits of true liberty. "I tell her I must have my freedom, net. She does not understand my point of view." Laura has heard this many times. Braggioni scratches    29 the guitar and meditates. "She is an instinctively virtuous woman, pure gold, no doubt of that. If she were not, I should lock her up, and she knows it."

His wife, who works so hard for the good of the factory girls, employs part of her leisure lying on the floor weeping because there are so many women in the world, and only one husband for her, and she never knows where nor when to look for him. He told her; "Unless you can learn to cry when I am not here, I must go away for good." That day he went away and took a room at the Hotel Madrid.

It is this month of separation for the sake of higher principles that has been spoiled not only for Mrs. Braggioni, whose sense of reality is beyond criticism, but for Laura, who feels herself bogged in a nightmare. Tonight Laura envies Mrs. Braggioni, who is alone, and free to weep as much as she pleases about a concrete wrong. Laura has just come from a visit to the prison, and she is waiting for tomorrow with a bitter anxiety as if tomorrow may not come, but time may be caught immovably in this hour, with herself transfixed, Braggioni singing on forever, and Eugenio's body not yet discovered by the guard.

Braggioni says: "Are you going to sleep?" Almost before she can shake her head, he begins telling her about the May-day disturbances coming on in Morelia, for the Catholics hold a festival in honor of the Blessed Virgin, and the Socialists celebrate their martyrs on that day. "There will be two independent processions, starting from either end of town, and they will march until they meet, and the rest depends . . ." He asks her to oil and load his pistols. Standing up, he unbuckles his ammunition belt, and spreads it laden across her knees. Laura sits with the shells slipping through the cleaning cloth dipped in oil, and he says again he cannot understand why she works so hard for the revolutionary idea unless she loves some man who is in it. "Are you not in love with someone?" "No," says Laura. "And no one is in love with you?" "No." "Then it is your own fault. No woman need go begging. Why, what is the matter with you? The legless beggar woman in the Alameda has a perfectly faithful lover. Did you know that?"

Laura peers down the pistol barrel and says nothing, but a long, slow faintness rises and subsides in her; Braggioni curves his swollen fingers around the throat of the guitar and softly smothers the music out of it, and when she hears him again he seems to have forgotten her, and is speaking in the hypnotic voice he uses when talking in small rooms to a listening, close-gathered crowd. Some day this world, now seemingly so composed and eternal, to the edges of every sea shall be merely a tangle of gaping trenches, or crashing walls and broken bodies. Everything must be torn from its accustomed place where it has rotted for centuries, hurled skyward and distributed, cast down again clean as rain, without separate identity. Nothing shall survive that the stiffened hands of poverty have created for the rich and no one shall be left alive except the elect spirits destined to procreate a new world cleansed of cruelty and injustice, ruled by benevolent anarchy: "Pistols are good, I love them, cannon are even better, but in the end I pin my faith to good dynamite," he concludes, and strokes the pistol lying in her hands. "Once I dreamed of destroying this city, in case it offered resistance to General Ortíz, but it fell into his hands like an overripe pear."

He is made restless by his own words, rises and stands waiting. 34 Laura holds up the belt to him: "Put that on and go kill somebody in Morelia, and you will be happier," she says softly. The presence of death in the room makes her bold. "Today, I found Eugenio going into a stupor. He refused to allow me to call the prison doctor. He had taken all the tablets I brought him yesterday. He said he took them because he was bored."

"He is a fool, and his death is his own business," says Braggioni, 35 fastening his belt carefully.

"I told him if he had waited only a little while longer, you would 36 have got him set free," said Laura. "He said he did not want to wait."

"He is a fool and we are well rid of him," says Braggioni, reaching 37 for his hat.

He goes away. Laura knows his mood has changed, she will not see 38 him any more for a while. He will send word when he needs her to go on errands into strange streets, to speak to the strange faces that will appear, like clay masks with the power of human speech, to mutter their thanks to Braggioni for his help. Now she is free, and she thinks, I must run while there is time. But she does not go.

Braggioni enters his own house where for a month his wife has 39 spent many hours every night weeping and tangling her hair upon her pillow. She is weeping now, and she weeps more at the sight of him, the cause of all her sorrows. He looks about the room. Nothing is changed, the smells are good and familiar, he is well acquainted with the woman who comes toward him with no reproach except grief on her face. He says to her tenderly: "You are so good, please don't cry any more, you dear good creature." She says, "Are you tired, my angel? Sit here and I will wash your feet." She brings a bowl of water, and kneeling, unlaces his shoes, and when from her knees she raises her sad eyes under her blackened lids, he is sorry for everything, and bursts into tears. "Ah, yes, I am hungry, I am tired, let us eat something together," he says, between sobs. His wife leans her head on his arm and says, "Forgive me!" and this time he is refreshed by the solemn, endless rain of her tears.

Laura takes off her serge dress and puts on a white linen nightgown    40 and goes to bed. She turns her head a little to one side, and lying still, reminds herself that it is time to sleep. Numbers tick in her brain like little clocks, soundless doors close of themselves around her. If you would sleep, you must not remember anything, the children will say tomorrow, good morning, my teacher, the poor prisoners who come every day bringing flowers to their jailor. 1–2–3–4–5—it is monstrous to confuse love with revolution, night with day, life with death—ah, Eugenio!

The tolling of the midnight bell is a signal, but what does it mean?    41 Get up, Laura, and follow me: come out of your sleep, out of your bed, out of this strange house. What are you doing in this house? Without a word, without fear she rose and reached for Eugenio's hand, but he eluded her with a sharp, sly smile and drifted away. This is not all, you shall see—Murderer, he said, follow me, I will show you a new country, but it is far away and we must hurry. No, said Laura, not unless you take my hand, no; and she clung first to the stair rail, and then to the topmost branch of the Judas tree that bent down slowly and set her upon the earth, and then to the rocky ledge of a cliff, and then to the jagged wave of a sea that was not water but a desert of crumbling stone. Where are you taking me, she asked in wonder but without fear. To death, and it is a long way off, and we must hurry, said Eugenio. No, said Laura, not unless you take my hand. Then eat these flowers, poor prisoner, said Eugenio in a voice of pity, take and eat: and from the Judas tree he stripped the warm bleeding flowers, and held them to her lips. She saw that his hand was fleshless, a cluster of small white petrified branches, and his eye sockets were without light, but she ate the flowers greedily for they satisfied both hunger and thirst. Murderer! said Eugenio, and Cannibal! This is my body and my blood. Laura cried No! and at the sound of her own voice, she awoke trembling, and was afraid to sleep again.

## VOCABULARY

suety (4)

premonitions (5)

vessel (5)

mottled (5)

hieratic (6)

equivocal (12)

adroit (14)

ingenuous (14)

stoicism (21)

opportunist (22)

talismanic (22)

disconcerting (23)

emaciated (26)

transfixed (31)

procreate (33)

anarchy (33)

## THE FACTS

1. What is Laura like? Why is she in Mexico?
2. What is Braggioni like? How does he feel about the revolution?
3. In paragraph 5 Porter writes: "The gluttonous bulk of Braggioni has become a symbol of her many disillusions, for a revolutionist should be lean, animated by heroic faith, a vessel of abstract virtues." What does this reveal about Laura? What does it reveal about Braggioni?
4. What is Laura's attitude toward men? What is Braggioni's attitude toward women?
5. What is the significance of the dream at the end of the story? Notice certain images related to Christ's Last Supper. Remember also that dreams can reveal a person's unconscious feelings.

## THE STRATEGIES

1. Examine the descriptions of Braggioni (paragraphs 1, 3, 7, 8). What animal is he associated with in these descriptions? What is the significance of this association?
2. "Braggioni loves himself with such tenderness and amplitude and eternal charity that his followers—for he is a leader of men, a skilled revolutionist, and his skin has been punctured in honorable warfare—warm themselves in the reflected glow, and say to each other: 'He has a real nobility, a love of humanity raised above mere personal affections.'" What tone is Porter using here? Explain.
3. Reread paragraph 20. Why does Porter use so many place names in it? What do they contribute to the story?
4. Braggioni's wife washes his feet with water. What is the significance of this act? How does it relate to the rest of the story?
5. How is the Judas tree in the dream related to Roman Catholic ritual?

## THE ISSUES

1. How does Braggioni compare or contrast with one of the following modern revolutionary leaders?

a. Ayatollah Khomeini of Iran
b. Fidel Castro of Cuba
c. Muammar Qadhafi of Libya

2. According to paragraph 26, Braggioni was once young and idealistic. What do you think made him change into the manipulator revealed in the story?
3. What do you think the future holds for Laura? Speculate on how the next few years will unravel for her. Will she survive? Where? Will she ever fall in love?
4. What is your reaction to Braggioni's prophecy of the world, as stated in paragraph 33? Is his view realistic? Why or why not?
5. According to the story, Laura envies Mrs. Braggioni (see paragraph 31). How do you explain this envy?

### *SUGGESTIONS FOR WRITING*

1. Analyze and discuss the use of religious symbolism in this story.
2. Analyze and discuss Laura's motive for living in Mexico and associating herself with the revolution.
3. Write a causal analysis of Laura's character. Why is she paralyzed and seemingly aloof?

Robert Frost

# • DESIGN •

*Robert Frost (1874–1963) was a lecturer, poet, and teacher. When he was nine-teen and working in a mill in Lawrence, Massachussetts, the* Independent *accepted and published "My Butterfly, an Elegy"—the poem that began Frost's career as one of America's great poets. Rugged New England farm life was the inspiration for many of his poems.*

*Like much of Frost's poetry, "Design" appears on the surface to be simple and plain. But a closer study will reveal subtleties and depth. The speaker observes nature with a philosophic mind.*

> I found a dimpled spider, fat and white,
> On a white heal-all, holding up a moth
> Like a white piece of rigid satin cloth—
> Assorted characters of death and blight
> Mixed ready to begin the morning right,
> Like the ingredients of a witches' broth—

5

A snow-drop spider, a flower like a froth,
And dead wings carried like a paper kite.

What had that flower to do with being white,
The wayside blue and innocent heal-all?                                    10
What brought the kindred spider to that height,
Then steered the white moth thither in the night?
What but design of darkness to appall?—
If design govern in a thing so small.

## VOCABULARY

characters                    kindred                              appall
blight

## THE FACTS

1. The heal-all is a wildflower, usually blue or violet, but occasionally white, commonly found blooming along footpaths and roads. The name derives from the belief that this flower possessed healing qualities. As described in the first stanza, what do the spider, the heal-all, and the moth have in common?
2. Three questions are asked in the second stanza. How can these be condensed into one question? And what answer is implied in the poem?
3. The "argument from design" was a well-known eighteenth-century argument for the existence of God. It proposed a broad view of history and the cosmos, which revealed that some divine intelligence fashioned and then sustained existence. What twist does Frost give this argument?
4. Is the poem probing a sufficient, a necessary, or a contributory cause?

## THE STRATEGIES

1. What five examples of figurative language are used in the first stanza? Tell what effect each has.
2. In the second stanza, why does the poet use the adjective *kindred* in connection with the spider?
3. In the second stanza, what synonyms does the poet use to repeat the concept of design?

## THE ISSUES

1. The problem of whether or not our destinies are controlled by some higher intelligence concerns most thinking persons. Why do you suppose human beings wrestle so often with this problem?

2. Reread Mencken's essay "The Satisfaction of Life" (pages 614–17). Which paragraph expresses the same thought as Frost's line "What but design of darkness to appall?"
3. How would you argue against Frost's theme? Use an example from nature to take the opposite viewpoint.
4. Judging from past experience, which of your intimate acquaintances are better able to cope with life, those with a strong belief in a God who controls human destiny, or those with the belief that existence is simply experience and that no god controls any aspect of the universe?

### SUGGESTIONS FOR WRITING

1. Using an example from nature, write a brief essay showing how an incontrovertible harmony seems to regulate the activities of the world as a whole.
2. Write a brief essay in which you explain what in the poem causes you to like or dislike it.

# ══ •• *ISSUE FOR CRITICAL* •• ══
# *THINKING*

## The Treatment of Animals

Animal experimentation is the use of living nonhuman creatures in the laboratory for medical, psychological, or other scientific testing. The scope of this testing is enormous and varied. Animals are used in surgical experiments to test new procedures and assess experimental surgical techniques. They are used to gauge the effectiveness as well as the side-effects of new drugs. They are used to evaluate cancer therapies and to measure the effects of stress. Every year, millions of animals (one author places the figure at sixty-four million) lose their lives in these experiments.

In all but a few rare cases, the beneficiaries of this experimentation are humans and not the animal species on which the experiment was performed. We use animals because the same tests and procedures might injure or kill humans. Medical ethics permit experimentation on human subjects only in extraordinary cases, where traditional methods and knowledge are helpless to save the life of the patient.

It is unquestionably true that humans have benefited greatly from animal experiments. Insulin was first isolated by Sir Frederick Banting, a Canadian physician, who made his finding by surgically removing the pancreases of dogs and recording the effects that the loss of this gland had on their systems. Banting destroyed hundreds of dogs, but his work saved the lives of millions of human diabetics. Tumors are commonly induced in animals by experimenters seeking a cure for cancer. The artificial heart was first tried out in calves before one was implanted in the body of Barney Clark.

In spite of these benefits to the human race, animal-rights groups have mounted a serious lobbying effort for the abolition of animal experimentation. One such group even succeeded in bringing the issue to a vote in a committee of the California legislature, where the abolitionists were rebuffed.

This issue seems to come down to this: Is the benefit humans derive from this experimentation worth the cost in the lives of animals? The case against animal experiments is made by Patricia Curtis, a freelance writer and editor who wonders whether an alien race superior to humans would be morally entitled to experiment on *us*. Then a minister, Arthur Tennies, contends that hunting and killing animals is in line with nature. Finally, a short narrative by James Herriot, a writer and a veterinarian, poses the question, "Do animals have souls?"

Patricia Curtis

# • THE ARGUMENT AGAINST • ANIMAL EXPERIMENTATION

*Patricia Curtis (b. 1924) is a writer and editor whose main interests are feminism and the humane treatment of animals. She was educated at the University of Missouri, earning her B.A. degree in 1945, and has worked as an assistant managing editor and editor for various national publications. Her published books include* The Breakfast and Brunch Book *(1972) and* Animal Doctors *(1977).*

The professor was late leaving the medical school because he'd had     1
to review papers by his third-year students in experimental surgery. It was well after 11 when he wearily drove his car into the garage. The house was dark except for a hall light left on for him. His wife and youngsters were already asleep, he realized, and the professor suddenly felt lonely as he fit his key in the lock. But even as he pushed

open the door, Sabrina was there to welcome him. She was always waiting for him, lying on the rug just inside the door.

The little dog leaped up ecstatically, wagging her tail and licking the professor's hand. The professor stroked her affectionately. She flopped on her back and grinned at him as he tickled her chest and belly; then she jumped to her feet and danced around his legs as he walked into the kitchen to get something to eat. Sabrina's exuberant joy at his return never failed to cheer him.

Early next morning, the professor drove back to the medical school and entered the laboratory. He noticed that a dog on which one of his students had operated the previous afternoon still had an endotracheal tube in its throat and obviously had not received pain medication. He must be more strict in his orders, he thought to himself. Another dog had bled through its bandages and lay silently in a pool of blood. Sloppy work, the professor thought—must speak to that student. None of the dogs made any sounds, because new arrivals at the laboratory were always subjected to an operation called a ventriculocordectomy that destroyed their vocal cords so that no barks or howls disturbed people in the medical school and surrounding buildings.

The professor looked over the animals that would be used that day by his surgery students. He came across a new female dog that had just been delivered by the dealer. Badly frightened, she whined and wagged her tail ingratiatingly as he paused in front of her cage. The professor felt a stab. The small dog bore an amazing resemblance to Sabrina. Quickly he walked away. Nevertheless, he made a note to remind himself to give orders for her vocal cords to be destroyed and for her to be conditioned for experimental surgery.

American researchers sacrifice approximately 64 million animals annually. Some 400,000 dogs, 200,000 cats, 33,000 apes and monkeys, thousands of horses, ponies, calves, sheep, goats and pigs, and millions of rabbits, hamsters, guinea pigs, birds, rats and mice are used every year in experiments that often involve intense suffering. The research establishment has generally insisted that live animals provide the only reliable tests for drugs, chemicals and cosmetics that will be used by people. Researchers also believe that animal experiments are necessary in the search for cures for human illnesses and defects. There is no question that many important medical discoveries, from polio vaccine to the physiology of the stress response, have indeed been made through the use of animals. Thus universities, medical and scientific institutions, pharmaceutical companies, cosmetics manufacturers and the military have always taken for granted their right to use animals in almost any way they see fit.

But increasing numbers of scientists are beginning to ask themselves some hard ethical questions and to re-evaluate their routine use of painful testing tools such as electric shock, stomach tubes, hot plates, restraining boxes and radiation devices. A new debate has arisen over whether all such experiments are worth the suffering they entail. 6

Strongly opposing curtailment of animal experimentation are groups such as the National Society for Medical Research, which insists that any such reduction would jeopardize public safety and scientific progress. The N.S.M.R. was formed to resist what it considers the threat of Government regulation of animal research and to refute the charges of humane societies. Many scientists, however, although they firmly believe that some animal research is necessary, no longer endorse such an absolutist approach to the issue. 7

"Some knowledge can be obtained at too high a price," writes British physiologist Dr. D. H. Smyth in his recent book *Alternatives to Animal Experiments*. 8

"The lives and suffering of animals must surely count for something," says Jeremy J. Stone, director of the Washington-based Federation of American Scientists, which has devoted an entire newsletter to a discussion of the rights of animals. 9

According to physiologist Dr. F. Barbara Orlans of the National Institutes of Health, "Within the scientific community there's a growing concern for animals that has not yet had a forum." Dr. Orlans is president of the newly formed Scientists' Center for Animal Welfare, which hopes to raise the level of awareness on the part of fellow scientists and the public about avoidable suffering inflicted on lab animals, wildlife, and animals raised for meat. "We will try to be a voice of reason. We can perhaps be a link between scientists and the humane organizations," Dr. Orlans explains. "We hope also to provide solid factual data on which animal-protection decisions can be based." 10

Another link between researchers and humane organizations is a new committee comprising more than 400 doctors and scientists that has been formed by Friends of Animals, a national animal-welfare group. Headed by eight M.D.'s, the committee is making a survey of 11

Federally funded animal-research projects. Friends of Animals hopes that the study will expose not only needless atrocities performed on animals, but also boondoggles involving taxpayers' money.

One reason scientists are no longer so indifferent to the suffering    12
they inflict on animals is the discoveries that science itself has made. We now know that many animals feel, think, reason, communicate, have sophisticated social systems, and even, on occasion, behave altruistically toward each other. Communication by sign language with higher primates, demonstrations of the intelligence of dolphins and whales, observations of the complex societies of wolves and other animals, and many other investigations have narrowed the gap between ourselves and the rest of the animal kingdom, making it more difficult to rationalize inhumane experiments. Dr. Dallas Pratt, author of *Painful Experiments on Animals*, points out that "among the rats and mice, the computers and oscilloscopes, there is Koko"—referring to the young gorilla whom a California primatologist has taught a working vocabulary of 375 words and concepts in sign language and who has even learned to take snapshots with a Polaroid camera. It's hard not to feel squeamish about subjecting animals to inhumane experiments when they possess almost-human intelligence.

The thinking of researchers is also beginning to be affected by the    13
growing movement for animal rights. The rising concern for the welfare of animals is seen by some people as a natural extension of contemporary movements promoting civil rights, women's rights, homosexual rights, human rights, and children's rights. Public interest in preserving endangered species is based first on an increasing awareness of the complexity and fragility of ecosystems, and second on the notion, still much debated, that any species of plant or animal, from the lowly snail darter to the blue whale, has the right to continue to exist. From here it is only a short logical step to the belief that animals have the right to exist without suffering unnecessarily.

Near the top of the list of animal-welfare activists' causes is putting    14
an end to inhumane experiments on laboratory animals. In Great Britain, where a vigorous antivivisection movement has existed for more than a century, a clandestine group called the Animal Liberation Front conducts commando-style raids on laboratories, liberating animals and sabotaging research equipment. A.L.F. members have also been known to slash tires and pour sugar in the gas tanks of trucks used by animal dealers who supply labs. To be sure, this group of zealots hasn't

made much of a dent in England's vast research community, but it does appeal to a gut reaction on the part of many Britons against animal research.

Animal-rights activists are not merely sentimental do-gooders and   15
pet-lovers. They have mounted a philosophical attack on the traditional Western attitude toward animals, branding it as "speciesist" (like racist or sexist), a term derived from the word "speciesism," coined by psychologist and author Dr. Richard Ryder. The Australian philosopher Peter Singer, in his influential 1975 book *Animal Liberation*, argued that the "speciesist" rationalization, "Human beings come first," is usually used by people who do nothing for either human or nonhuman animals. And he pointed out the parallels between the oppression of blacks, women, and animals: Such oppression is usually rationalized on the grounds that the oppressed group is inferior.

In 1977, when outraged antivivisectionists heard about some highly   16
unpleasant electric-shock and burn experiments conducted on young pigs in Denmark, they wasted no time in pointing out the irony that the tests were being conducted by Amnesty International, the human-rights organization. Amnesty International was attempting to prove that human prisoners could be tortured without leaving any marks, and pigs were used because of the similarity of their skin to ours. (The tests were subsequently discontinued.)

Paradoxically, the public tends to be "speciesist" in its reaction to   17
animal experimentation: For many people, a test is permissible when it inflicts pain on a "lower" animal like a hamster, but not when the victim is a dog. When it was discovered in the summer of 1976 that the American Museum of Natural History was damaging the brains of cats and running painful sex experiments on them, hundreds of people picketed in protest. The museum's Animal Behavior Department defended itself on the grounds that the research was intended to gain a better understanding of human sexual responses. Animal-rights groups, scientists among them, were not convinced of the necessity of the tests, which came to an end only when the chief researcher retired. But the protesters made no stir about the pigeons, doves, and rats that suffered in the same laboratory.

If United States Army researchers had used guinea pigs instead of   18
beagles when they tried out a poison gas, they probably would not have provoked the public outcry that resulted in the curtailment of their funding in 1974. When a few Avon saleswomen quit their jobs last

spring after reading about painful eye-makeup tests the company conducts on rabbits, they did not complain about the thousands of guinea pigs and rats Avon routinely puts to death in acute-toxicity tests.

It is not known whether any single vertebrate species is more or less    19
immune to pain than another. A neat line cannot be drawn across the evolutionary scale dividing the sensitive from the insensitive. Yet the suffering of laboratory rats and mice is regarded as trivial by scientists and the public alike. These rodents have the dubious honor of being our No. 1 experimental animals, composing possibly 75 percent of America's total lab-animal population. As Russell Baker once wrote, "This is no time to be a mouse."

Rats and mice are specifically excluded from a Federal law designed    20
to give some protection to laboratory animals. The Animal Welfare Act, passed in 1966 and amended in 1970, is administered by the Department of Agriculture and covers only about 4 percent of laboratory animals. Animal advocates worked hard for the bill, which sets some standards for the housing of animals in laboratories and at the dealers' facilities from which many of them are obtained. But the law places no restrictions on the kinds of experiments to which animals may be subjected. It does indicate that pain-relieving drugs should be used on the few types of animals it covers—but it includes a loophole so as not to inhibit researchers unduly. If a scientist claims that pain is a necessary part of an experiment, anesthetics or analgesics may be withheld.

One standard test conducted on rats by drug companies is called    21
the "writhing test" because of the agonized way the animals react to irritants injected into their abdomens. Paradoxically, this test assesses the efficacy of pain-killers, which are administered only after the rats show signs of acute suffering.

Equally common are psychological experiments in "learned help-    22
lessness" that have been conducted on rats, dogs, and other kinds of animals. In some of these tests, caged animals are given painful electric shocks until they learn certain maneuvers to obtain their food. As they become adept at avoiding the shocks, the researchers keep changing the rules so that the animals have to keep learning more and more ways to avoid shocks. Ultimately no way remains to escape, and the animals simply give up and lie on the floors of their cages, passively receiving shock after shock. Researchers have attempted to draw parallels between "learned helplessness" and depression in human

beings, but some critics have difficulty perceiving their necessity. "What more are we going to learn about human depression by continuing to produce immobility in animals?" asks former animal experimenter Dr. Roger Ulrich, now a research professor of psychology at Western Michigan University.

Electric shock is widely used on many different kinds of animals in    23
various types of research. In one experiment typical of a series that has been under way since 1966 at the Armed Forces Radiobiology Research Institute in Bethesda, Md., 10 rhesus monkeys were starved for 18 hours and then "encouraged" with electric prods to run rapidly on treadmills. This went on for several weeks before the monkeys were subjected to 4,600 rads of gamma-neutron radiation. Then they were retested on the treadmills for six hours, and subsequently for two hours each day until they died. Mean survival time for the vomiting, incapacitated monkeys was recorded in A.F.R.R.I.'s report as 37 hours. Dogs have been used in similar experiments, whose purpose is to get an idea of the effects of radiation on human endurance.

Now A.F.R.R.I. and other American research facilities are having to    24
look for new sources of monkeys. In March 1978, the Government of India banned further export of rhesus monkeys to the United States. The native population was dwindling and Prime Minister Morarji R. Desai cited violations of a previous agreement that restricted the use of rhesus monkeys to medical research under humane conditions. "There is no difference between cruelty to animals and cruelty to human beings," the ascetic Prime Minister stated. The International Primate Protection League, a four-year-old watchdog group whose members include many scientists and especially primatologists (Jane Goodall, for one), had spread word in the Indian press that American scientists were using rhesus monkeys in grisly trauma experiments. According to the Primate Protection League, these tests included dipping monkeys in boiling water at the University of Kansas, shooting them in the face with high-powered rifles at the University of Chicago, and slamming them in the stomach with a cannon-impactor traveling at a speed of 70 miles per hour at the University of Michigan.

"I feel justified in stating that fully 80 percent of the experiments    25
involving rhesus monkeys are either unnecessary, represent useless duplication of previous work, or could utilize nonanimal alternatives," wrote Illinois Wesleyan University biologist Dr. John E. McArdle, a specialist in primate functional anatomy, in a letter to Prime Minister

Desai, who so far has held firm despite pressure from the American scientific community to rescind the ban. In the meantime, researchers are making do with non-Indian rhesus monkeys and a close relative, the crab-eating macaque.

One of the arguments in favor of animal tests is that under the controlled circumstances of the experimental laboratory they are likely to be objective and consistent. But the results of the same tests conducted on the same kinds of animals often differ from one laboratory to the next. When 25 cooperating companies, including Avon, Revlon, and American Cyanamid, conducted a comprehensive study of eye- and skin-irritation tests using rabbits, the results varied widely. The study concluded that these tests "should not be recommended as standard procedures in any new regulations" because they yielded "unreliable results." 26

One of these tests, the Draize Ophthalmic Irritancy Test, is used to evaluate the effect upon the eyes of household and aerosol products, shampoos, and eye makeup. Rabbits are used because their eyes do not have effective tear glands and thus cannot easily flush away or dissolve irritants. The animals are pinioned in stocks and their eyes are exposed to a substance until inflammation, ulceration, or gross damage occurs. 27

Many investigators concede that the data provided by such experiments are often inconsistent and that the stresses caused by crowded cages, callous treatment, pain, and fear can affect animals' metabolisms and thus confuse test results. "Since there is hardly a single organ or biochemical system in the body that is not affected by stress," says Dr. Harold Hillman, a British physiologist, "it is almost certainly the main reason for the wide variation reported among animals on whom painful experiments have been done." 28

Very often, different species respond differently to substances or situations. The rationale for many animal tests is that they predict human reactions, but thalidomide, for example, did not produce deformities in the fetuses of dogs, cats, monkeys, and hamsters. On the other hand, insulin has been proved harmful to rabbits and mice although it saves human lives. 29

Researchers are becoming increasingly dubious about the efficacy of the LD/50, a test for acute toxicity that consists of force-feeding a group of animals a specific substance until half of them die, ostensibly providing a quantitative measure of how poisonous the substance is. 30

In *Painful Experiments on Animals*, Dr. Pratt asks what we learn from forcing hair dye or face powder into a dog or rat through a stomach tube until its internal organs rupture.

One small victory for animal-welfare activists that was hailed by many American scientists was the 1975 Canadian ban on the use of vertebrate animals by students participating in science fairs. Children had been awarded prizes for attempting heart-transplant surgery on unanesthetized rabbits, amputating the feet of lizards, performing Caesarean operations on pregnant mice, bleeding dogs into a state of shock and blinding pigeons. Remarking that such "experiments" were a distortion of the spirit of research, science-fair officials ruled out all such projects except observations of the normal living patterns of wild or domestic animals. 31

In this country, the search for adequate substitutes for laboratory animals was officially launched last summer when the year-old American Fund for Alternatives to Animal Research made its first grant— $12,500 to a biology professor at Whitman College in Walla Walla, Wash. The award to Dr. Earl William Fleck will help finance his development of a test substituting one-celled organisms called tetrahymena for animals in screening substances for teratogens, agents that can cause birth defects. It is expected that the test, if and when perfected, will be cheaper, quicker, more accurate, and certainly more humane than putting thousands of pregnant animals to death. 32

According to veterinarian Thurman Grafton, executive director of the National Society for Medical Research, people who talk about alternatives to animals are creating false hopes. "These new technologies can only be adjuncts to the use of animals," he claims. "While they serve a purpose in furnishing clues as to what direction a type of research might take, you will always ultimately need an intact animal with all its living complications and interchanging biochemical functions to properly assay a drug." 33

"Not so," says Ethel Thurston, administrator of the American Fund for Alternatives. "Enough progress has already been made to indicate that certain techniques can completely replace animals." 34

Several of these techniques have been developed over the last five years in Great Britain, where the Lord Dowding Fund for Humane Research has given grants totaling more than $400,000 to dozens of scientists engaged in research aimed at finding experimental substitutes for animals. Dowding is currently financing several develop- 35 mental studies of the Ames Test, a promising technique invented by a Berkeley biochemistry professor, Dr. Bruce Ames, that uses salmonella bacteria rather than animals to determine the carcinogenic properties of chemicals. (It was the Ames Test that recently revealed the possible carcinogenic dangers of certain hair dyes.) Another Dowding Fund recipient, research physician Dr. John C. Petricciani, now with the Food and Drug Administration, has devised a method of assessing how tumors grow by inoculating the tumor cells into skin from 9-day-old chicken embryos instead of into living animals.

Animal tests are frequently replaced by other methods discovered    36 and developed by scientists like Dr. Ames who are not trying to avoid the use of animals per se but are simply searching for simpler and more cost-efficient ways to achieve their goals. Dr. Hans Stich, a Canadian cancer researcher, for example, has devised a new test for detecting carcinogenicity in chemicals; it uses human cells, takes one week and costs only about $260. The traditional method, using rats and mice, takes three years and costs approximately $150,000.

In addition to egg embryos, bacteria, and simple organisms, possi-    37 ble substitutes for animals include tissue cultures, human and other mammal cells grown in test tubes, and organ banks. Preserved human corneas, for instance, might be used to spare rabbits the agony of the Draize test. Computers could also play a role if researchers used them fully to analyze experimental data, predict the properties of new drugs, and test theoretical data. Computers can even be programmed to simulate living processes. Mechanical models and audio-visual aids can and do substitute for animals as teaching instruments. Simulated human models could provide valid information in car-crash tests.

Last winter, Representative Robert F. Drinan, Democrat of Massa-    38 chusetts, introduced a bill authorizing the Department of Health, Education and Welfare to fund projects aimed at discovering research methods that would reduce both the numbers of animals used in laboratories and the suffering to which they are subjected.

Meanwhile, medical and military research and an unending stream    39 of new pharmaceutical, cosmetic, and household products are resulting in an ever-increasing use of animals in the laboratory.

The most recent and thorough exploration of alternatives is Dr. D.    40 H. Smyth's book *Alternatives to Animal Experiments*, which examines every option and weighs its pros and cons. He concludes that there is certainly reason to hope that the numbers of laboratory animals can be drastically reduced, but also warns that it is unlikely a complete phasing out of animal experimentation will happen soon. "By the time we can produce complete alternatives to living tissue," Dr. Smyth writes, "we will not need those alternatives because we will already understand how living tissues work."

Still, Dr. Smyth asks, "Does this mean we can perpetrate any cruelty    41 on animals to satisfy scientific curiosity in the hope that it will one day be useful? To me it certainly does not. . . . Everyone has a right to decide that certain procedures are unacceptable."

Richard Ryder calls animal experimenters to task for trying to have    42 it both ways: Researchers defend their work scientifically on the basis of the *similarities* between human beings and animals, but defend it morally on the basis of the *differences*.

And there's the rub: The differences aren't as reassuringly clear-cut    43 as they once were. We now know that some animals have a more highly developed intelligence than some human beings—infants, for example, or the retarded and the senile. Dr. Ryder asks, "If we were to be discovered by some more intelligent creatures in the universe, would they be justified in experimenting on us?"

## VOCABULARY

| | | |
|---|---|---|
| exuberant (2) | clandestine (14) | ostensibly (30) |
| ingratiatingly (4) | zealots (14) | adjuncts (33) |
| boondoggles (11) | incapacitated (23) | carcinogenicity (36) |
| altruistically (12) | ascetic (24) | simulated (37) |
| squeamish (12) | rescind (25) | |
| ecosystems (13) | pinioned (27) | |

## THE FACTS

1. To what surgical procedure were new animals at the laboratory always subjected? What was the purpose of this procedure?
2. According to the author, what absolutist approach to animal experimentation do many scientists now reject?
3. What new knowledge about animals has led many scientists to reexamine how laboratory animals are treated?
4. What connection does Curtis see between the movement for animal rights and the various human rights movements?
5. What does the author mean by the terms *speciesist* and *speciesism*? To whom are these terms applied?

6. Which animals were specifically excluded from the Animal Welfare Act of 1966? What justification lay behind its exclusion?
7. What are experiments in "learned helplessness"? What are these experiments supposed to discover?
8. What possible substitutes to the use of laboratory animals does the author mention?

## THE STRATEGIES

1. Curtis opens her article by describing the behavior of a professor toward his own pet and toward the animals in his laboratory. What is the purpose of this dramatized beginning? How effective is it?
2. The author concedes that important medical discoveries have been made through the use of animals in experiments. How does she then counter this weakness in her own argument?
3. How does the author support her argument that some experiments are needlessly cruel to animals?
4. A standard tactic taught in argumentation is to state an opponent's case and then refute it. Where, and to what effect, does Curtis use this tactic?
5. What part does authority testimony play in the author's argument?
6. Curtis seems to favor the use of bacteria and unicellular organisms in place of animals in experiments. Is she guilty of "speciesism" in this choice?

## THE ISSUES

1. Why do you think animal welfare activists are so fervent about their desire to protect animals from scientific experimentation? How do you compare or contrast your own views with theirs?
2. What do you think of the analogy drawn in paragraph 15 between the oppression of animals and the oppression of blacks and women? Is this an appropriate, fair analogy? Give reasons for your answer.
3. If the experimentation on animals would result in a cure for AIDS, would you consider it requisite even if animals had to suffer great pain? Explain your answer.
4. The essay ends with this question: "'If we were to be discovered by some more intelligent creatures in the universe, would they be justified in experimenting on us?'" How would you answer this question? Give reasons for your answer.
5. Even if you are in harmony with the major thesis of Curtis's essay, what opposing arguments can you present?

## SUGGESTIONS FOR WRITING

1. What moral obligations, if any, do we have toward animals? Write an essay giving your views on this question.

2. Write an essay refuting Curtis's argument. Use expert testimony and examples to strengthen your case.

Arthur C. Tennies

—— • IN DEFENSE OF DEER HUNTING • ——
AND KILLING

*Arthur C. Tennies (b. 1931) is a Presbyterian minister and writer. He began his clerical career as the pastor of United Presbyterian churches of Vermont. Since 1967 he has worked for the state council of churches in Syracuse, New York.*

*Tennies has contributed to several magazines and church publications. He has written a book,* A Church for Sinners, Seekers, and Sunday Non-Saints *(1974).*

"You hunt deer?" When I nodded, my shocked colleague went on    1
to say, "Why my whole image of you has been shattered. How can you kill such beautiful creatures?"

And so would many others who view the deliberate killing of deer    2
as brutal and senseless. Such people look upon the hunter as a barbaric hangover from the distant past of the human race. To my colleague, the incongruity between the barbarism of hunting and normal civilized conduct was made more intense because I was a minister. How could I as a minister do such a thing?

I thought about that as I drove through the early morning darkness    3
toward the southeastern part of Chenango County. It was a little after 5 A.M. I had gotten up at 4, something I do only in the case of an emergency or when I am going deer hunting. It was cold, the temperature in the 20s. With the ground frozen, it would be too noisy for still hunting until the sun had had a chance to thaw the frost. So it would be wait and freeze. My first thoughts about why I would hunt deer had nothing to do with the supposed barbarism of it. I thought of the foolishness of it. Wait hour after hour in the cold, feet numb, hands numb, and small chance of getting a deer.

I was going to hunt on Schlafer Hill on the farm of Pershing Schlafer.    4
My choice of a place to hunt had been determined by the party permit that three of us had, which allowed us to kill one other deer of either sex besides the three bucks that we were allowed.

I thought about the party system in New York, the way the state   5
controlled the size of the deer herd. The state is divided into about 40
deer-management areas. The state biologists know how many deer
each area can handle, how many deer can feed on the browse available
without destroying it. If there are too many deer, they will kill the
plants and bushes upon which they depend. The next step is starvation for large numbers. Since the deer's natural predators were wiped
out by the first settlers, the only control over their numbers now is
starvation or hunting. Thus, so many deer must be killed in a deer-
management area. A certain number will be killed by motor vehicles.
The biologists can estimate how many will be killed on the hihgways
and also the number of bucks that will be killed. The surplus is taken
care of by issuing a set number of party permits.

I have often marveled at the state biologists, their skill and knowl-   6
edge in managing the deer herd. As I have pondered the problems of
people—poverty, starvation, injustice, and all the others—and our
frantic and often futile efforts to solve these problems, I have thought,
"If only we could manage the problems of people as well as we can
manage a deer herd."

Then I realize the great difference between the two. People are not   7
for being managed. We manage people only by robbing them of the
right to choose—and the most brutal attempts to manage are ultimately frustrated by the obstinacy of human nature, its refusal to be
managed. A handful of biologists may manage a deer herd and a
handful of scientists may be able to put a man on the moon, but no
handful of planners will ever manage the human race. And so I
thought again, as the car rushed through the dark, that all of our
modern management techniques would fail to come up with quick and
perfect solutions to the problems of people.

While the darkness was still on the land, I reached the bottom of the   8
hill. I parked the car, put on my hunting shirts, took my gun, and
began the long climb up the hill. For a few minutes, I could hardly see
the old road. Slowly my eyes adjusted to the dark. The trees in the
woods on my right took shape and the road became clearly visible. I
walked with greater confidence. As I climbed, the sun climbed toward
the horizon to drive away the night. By the time I reached the top of
the hill, the half-light of dawn had arrived.

Off to my left in the valley were lights and people, but on the hill I   9
was alone. It had not always been that way. Once long ago the hilltop

had been filled with people. Following the Revolution, white settlers came into Chenango County, and some had chosen that hilltop. I stopped and tried to picture in my mind their struggles to turn the forest into farms. I looked at the stone fence off to my right and wondered how many days it had taken to clear the stones from the fields and pile them into a fence. The fence ran into the woods. Woods again where there had been fields or pasture.

I looked on down the road. I could not see the old barn down farther $\quad$ 10 on the left, the only structure from the past still standing. All of the others were gone. I had seen before the crumbling stone foundations where once houses had stood. A half century or more ago, if I had stood there, I could have seen a half-dozen houses. Smoke would have been rolling out of chimneys as fires were started to chase away the cold. Men and boys would have been outside and in the barns getting the chores done. Women and girls would have been busy in the kitchen getting breakfast. The hill would have been full of people and empty of deer. Now it was empty of people and full of deer.

On that hill and on many others, like Bucktooth Run, is a story of $\quad$ 11 the hand of a man upon the land. Before the settlers came, only a few deer lived on that hill, far fewer than there are now, because the forests provided little food for the deer. The few were soon killed off. While the disappearance of the deer was the fault of the early hunters, there was more to it than that. There was no room for deer on the hill. As my Dad, who was born on Bucktooth Run, has pointed out:

*These farms were worked over morning and evening by the farmers and* $\quad$ 12 *their sons and their dogs going after the cattle. The wood lots were worked over during the winter for wood. The larger tracts of woodland were worked over by the lumbermen.*

*Then came World War I and the years following. Large areas of land were* $\quad$ 13 *abandoned. Where once the woods resounded to the call of "Come, boss!" and in the winter the woods echoed the ring of the ax and whine of the saw, the sylvan stillness, for months on end, was unbroken by the human voice. Where once the deer had no place to rest from the constant activity of the busy farmer and lumberman, there was now a chance for the deer to carry on its life in solitude.*

*In 1900 there were no deer in much of New York. The state did some stocking* $\quad$ 14 *shortly after that, and deer came across the border from Pennsylvania. The abandoned land provided a perfect setting for the deer and there were no natural enemies to stay their march. By the late 1930s, most of the state had a deer season.*

So as the farmers retreated from the hill, the deer returned. Now 15 the hill is perfect for deer . . . some fields used by farmers, like Pershing, for pasture and hay, good feed for deer for most of the year . . . brush for browse during the winter . . . woods, old and new, mixed with evergreen for cover. And most of the year, except during the hunting season, only a few people make their way to the top of the hill.

Let nature have her way and in another century nature's hospitality 16 to the deer will be withdrawn as large trees again cover the hill as they did before the first white settlers came.

I started to walk again and felt like I had left one world, the world of 17 technology, and entered another one, the world of nature. The rush to get things done had to give way to waiting and patience, for nature does not live at our frantic pace. The noise had to give way to quietness, for only in silence can one get close to a deer.

But the ground crunched beneath my feet, so I walked to a likely 18 spot and waited. Two hours and nothing, except a few small birds. Finally the cold forced me to move. I walked and found some fresh tracks in the snow. I followed them for an hour, trying to get close enough to the deer wandering in the woods ahead of me. But I was too noisy. All I saw was the flash of brown bodies and white tails too far ahead. I waited some more. No luck. I walked to another spot where deer cross.

I waited another hour. It was warmer now. Finally a deer appeared, 19 a head above a rise. It started to come nearer. Then it stopped. Something was wrong. It decided to leave. As I turned, my gun came up and I shot. It lurched sideways, kicking and thrashing, disappearing under a pine tree. I walked to the spot. No deer. I went around the tree and there it lay. In a second it was dead.

I looked down at the deer, a button buck, and I thought: This is 20 the way of nature, one creature feeding on another. Thousands of years ago our forebears survived in just this way. They killed, gutted, butchered, and ate. Now we buy in a supermarket or order in a restaurant.

The first task was to gut the deer, kind of a messy process. I got my 21 knife out, turned the deer on his back, and slit him open. I spilled the guts out on the ground. I saved the liver and heart, even though the heart had been mangled by the bullet. I cut through the diaphragm and pulled the lungs out.

Then I was ready to pull the deer back to the car. It was 3 P.M. when 22

I got to the car. Time yet to hunt for a buck, so I dumped the deer into the trunk. Back up the hill, but no luck. As night came on, I got back to the car. I tied the deer on the top of the trunk and started for home.

As I drove toward home, I had a sense of satisfaction. I had fitted    23
myself to nature's way and had been successful. For a few short hours, I had marched to the beat of nature's drum, not that of our modern world. At least for me, the barrier that we had built between nature and us could still be breached.

Back in suburbia, I parked the car in the driveway and went into the    24
house. Jan and the kids were eating supper.

"Any luck?" Jan asked.    25

"Not much."    26

"Did you get a deer?" one of the kids asked.    27

"Yup, a button buck."    28

Then the excited rush to see the deer, and the thrill of shared suc-    29
cess.

After that there was the tedious job of butchering. I hung the deer    30
in the garage. Then I began the task of skinning it. Once skinned, I cut the deer in half, then in quarters. Jan washed the blood and hair off of each quarter. I then cut the quarters into smaller pieces, and then Jan sliced it up into roasts, steaks, and stew meat.

"Can you get the brains out?" Jan wanted to know.    31

"I can try, but why the brains?"    32

"We always had brains when we butchered."    33

So I went to work to cut the skull open and get the brains out.    34

When I got back into the kitchen, Jan had a skillet on.    35

"Let's have some venison," she said.    36

"At this hour?"    37

"Sure."    38

So she had some brains and I had some liver. As I sat there weary,    39
eating the liver, I thought, "This meal is on the table because I put it there." By our efforts, and ours alone, it had gone from field to table.

"Don't you want some brains?" Jan asked.    40

"No."    41

"But they are a delicacy."    42

"That may be, but I'll stick to the liver."    43

As I went to sleep that night I thought: "I suppose that no matter    44
what I say, a lot of people will still never understand why I hunt deer. Well, they don't have to, but let only vegetarians condemn me."

## VOCABULARY

delicacy (4)             futile (6)             venison (36)
frantic (6)              lurched (19)

## THE FACTS

1. How, according to Tennies, do some people regard the killing of deer? How do they regard the hunter?
2. Why do you think Tennies mentions that he is a minister?
3. What is the purpose of paragraph 5? Why does Tennies describe deer management in such detail?
4. Why does the author reminisce about the people who used to live on the land? What does the reminiscence have to do with his argument in favor of deer hunting?
5. Where did the deer in New York come from? How did they get there?
6. In paragraph 19, Tennies describes how he shot and killed a deer. What does his description contribute to his defense of deer hunting?

## THE STRATEGIES

1. The first two paragraphs contain three questions. What purpose do these questions serve?
2. What analogy does the author draw in paragraphs 6 and 7? Why does the analogy break down?
3. Why are paragraphs 12 and 13 printed in italics?
4. How does Tennies achieve pacing in paragraphs 17 to 19?
5. What figure of speech is used in paragraph 23? What does it mean?

## THE ISSUES

1. What arguments would someone opposed to deer hunting put forward as a rebuttal to Tennies's essay? Imagine yourself in that person's frame of mind.
2. What aspects of deer hunting would *not* appeal to you? Try to describe them in unappealing terms.
3. What is your response to Tennies's view that the world of nature is a world of quiet and patience whereas the world of technology is a world of noise and frantic activity?
4. What is your opinion of the author's final statement—"let only vegetarians condemn me." What does he mean? Is he justified in making this statement?
5. What is your opinion of bullfighting? How do you compare it to deer hunting?

## *SUGGESTIONS FOR WRITING*

1. Write an essay in which you compare the way our forebears nourished themselves with the way we eat today. State the advantages and disadvantages of each system.
2. Choosing one particular animal, write an essay either in defense or in opposition to hunting or capturing it.

**James Herriot**

## • DO ANIMALS HAVE SOULS? •

*James Herriot (b. 1916) is a veterinarian who has used his experiences in caring for animals as the topics of many stories that have won him popularity with a worldwide audience. Born James Alfred Wight in Scotland, he graduated from Glasgow Veterinary College. The next forty years were spent practicing veterinary medicine in a Yorkshire village whose many characters became the focal points of his writing. His enormously successful books—none of them written until Herriot was over fifty—include* All Creatures Great and Small *(1972),* All Things Bright and Beautiful *(1974),* All Things Wise and Wonderful *(1977), and* The Lord God Made Them All *(1981).*

The card dangled above the old lady's bed. It read "God is Near" but it wasn't like the usual religious text. It didn't have a frame or ornate printing. It was just a strip of cardboard about eight inches long with plain lettering which might have said "No smoking" or "Exit" and it was looped carelessly over an old gas bracket so that Miss Stubbs from where she lay could look up at it and read "God is Near" in square black capitals. 1

There wasn't much more Miss Stubbs could see; perhaps a few feet of privet hedge through the frayed curtains but mainly it was just the cluttered little room which had been her world for so many years. 2

The room was on the ground floor and in the front of the cottage, and as I came up through the wilderness which had once been a garden I could see the dogs watching me from where they had jumped on to the old lady's bed. And when I knocked on the door the place almost erupted with their barking. It was always like this. I had been visiting regularly for over a year and the pattern never changed; the furious barking, then Mrs. Broadwith who looked after Miss Stubbs would push all the animals but my patient into the back kitchen and 3 open the door and I would go in and see Miss Stubbs in the corner in her bed with the card hanging over it.

She had been there for a long time and would never get up again. But she never mentioned her illness and pain to me; all her concern was for her three dogs and two cats.

Today it was old Prince and I was worried about him. It was his heart—just about the most spectacular valvular incompetence I had ever heard. He was waiting for me as I came in, pleased as ever to see me, his long, fringed tail waving gently.

The sight of that tail used to make me think there must be a lot of Irish Setter in Prince, but I was inclined to change my mind as I worked my way forward over the bulging black and white body to the shaggy head and upstanding Alsatian ears. Miss Stubbs often used to call him "Mr. Heinz," and though he may not have had 57 varieties in him his hybrid vigour had stood him in good stead. With his heart he should have been dead long ago.

"I thought I'd best give you a ring, Mr. Herriot," Mrs. Broadwith said. She was a comfortable, elderly widow with a square, ruddy face contrasting sharply with the pinched features on the pillow. "He's been coughing right bad this week and this morning he was a bit staggery. Still eats well, though."

"I bet he does." I ran my hands over the rolls of fat on the ribs. "It would take something really drastic to put old Prince off his grub."

Miss Stubbs laughed from the bed and the old dog, his mouth wide, eyes dancing, seemed to be joining in the joke. I put my stethoscope over his heart and listened, knowing well what I was going to hear. They say the heart is supposed to go "lub-dup, lub-dup," but Prince's went "swish-swoosh, swish-swoosh." There seemed to be nearly as much blood leaking back as was being pumped into the circulatory system. And another thing, the "swish-swoosh" was a good bit faster than last time; he was on oral digitalis but it wasn't quite doing its job.

Gloomily I moved the stethoscope over the rest of the chest. Like all old dogs with a chronic heart weakness he had an ever-present bronchitis and I listened without enthusiasm to the symphony of whistles, rales, squeaks and bubbles which signalled the workings of Prince's lungs. The old dog stood very erect and proud, his tail still waving slowly. He always took it as a tremendous compliment when I examined him and there was no doubt he was enjoying himself now. Fortunately his was not a very painful ailment.

Straightening up, I patted his head and he responded immediately    11
by trying to put his paws on my chest. He didn't quite make it and
even that slight exertion started his ribs heaving and his tongue lolling.
I gave him an intramuscular injection of digitalin and another of mor-
phine hydrochloride which he accepted with apparent pleasure as part
of the game.

"I hope that will steady his heart and breathing, Miss Stubbs. You'll    12
find he'll be a bit dopey for the rest of the day and that will help, too.
Carry on with the tablets, and I'm going to leave you some more
medicine for his bronchitis." I handed over a bottle of my old standby
mixture of ipecacuanha and ammonium acetate.

The next stage of the visit began now as Mrs. Broadwith brought in    13
a cup of tea and the rest of the animals were let out of the kitchen.
There were Ben, a Sealyham, and Sally, a Cocker Spaniel, and they
started a deafening barking contest with Prince. They were closely
followed by the cats, Arthur and Susie, who stalked in gracefully and
began to rub themselves against my trouser legs.

It was the usual scenario for the many cups of tea I had drunk with    14
Miss Stubbs under the little card which dangled above her bed.

"How are you today?" I asked.    15

"Oh, much better," she replied and immediately, as always, changed    16
the subject.

Mostly she liked to talk about her pets and the ones she had known    17
right back to her girlhood. She spoke a lot, too, about the days when
her family were alive. She loved to describe the escapades of her three
brothers and today she showed me a photograph which Mrs. Broadwith had found at the bottom of a drawer.

I took it from her and three young men in the knee breeches and    18
little round caps of the nineties smiled up at me from the yellowed old
print; they all held long church warden pipes and the impish humour
in their expressions came down undimmed over the years.

"My word, they look really bright lads, Miss Stubbs," I said.    19

"Oh, they were young rips!" she exclaimed. She threw back her    20
head and laughed, and for a moment her face was radiant, trans-
figured by her memories.

The things I had heard in the village came back to me; about the    21
prosperous father and his family who lived in the big house many
years ago. Then the foreign investments which crashed and the sud-

den change in circumstances. "When t'owd feller died he was about skint," one old man had said. "There's not much brass there now."

Probably just enough brass to keep Miss Stubbs and her animals alive and to pay Mrs. Broadwith. Not enough to keep the garden dug or the house painted or for any of the normal little luxuries.    22

And, sitting there, drinking my tea, with the dogs in a row by the bedside and the cats making themselves comfortable on the bed itself, I felt as I had often felt before—a bit afraid of the responsibility I had. The one thing which brought some light into the life of the brave old woman was the transparent devotion of this shaggy bunch whose eyes were never far from her face. And the snag was that they were all elderly.    23

There had, in fact, been four dogs originally, but one of them, a truly ancient Golden Labrador, had died a few months previously. And now I had the rest of them to look after and none of them less than ten years old.    24

They were perky enough but all showing some of the signs of old age; Prince with his heart, Sally beginning to drink a lot of water which made me wonder if she was starting with a pyometra, Ben growing steadily thinner with his nephritis. I couldn't give him new kidneys and I hadn't much faith in the hexamine tablets I had prescribed. Another peculiar thing about Ben was that I was always having to clip his claws; they grew at an extraordinary rate.    25

The cats were better, though Susie was a bit scraggy and I kept up a morbid kneading of her furry abdomen for signs of lymphosarcoma. Arthur was the best of the bunch; he never seemed to ail anything beyond a tendency for his teeth to tartar up.    26

This must have been in Miss Stubb's mind because, when I had finished my tea, she asked me to look at him. I hauled him across the bedspread and opened his mouth.    27

"Yes, there's a bit of the old trouble there. Might as well fix it while I'm here."    28

Arthur was a huge, grey, neutered tom, a living denial of all those theories that cats are cold-natured, selfish and the rest. His fine eyes, framed in the widest cat face I have ever seen, looked out on the world with an all-embracing benevolence and tolerance. His every movement was marked by immense dignity.    29

As I started to scrape his teeth his chest echoed with a booming    30 purr like a distant outboard motor. There was no need for anybody to hold him; he sat there placidly and moved only once—when I was using forceps to crack off a tough piece of tartar from a back tooth and accidentally nicked his gum. He casually raised a massive paw as if to say "Have a care, chum," but his claws were sheathed.

My next visit was less than a month later and was in response to an 31 urgent summons from Mrs. Broadwith at six o'clock in the evening. Ben had collapsed. I jumped straight into my car and in less than ten minutes was threading my way through the overgrown grass in the front garden with the animals watching from their window. The barking broke out as I knocked, but Ben's was absent. As I went into the little room I saw the old dog lying on his side, very still, by the bed.

D.O.A. is what we write in the day book. Dead on arrival. Just three 32 words but they covered all kinds of situations—the end of milk fever cows, bloated bullocks, calves in fits. And tonight they meant that I wouldn't be clipping old Ben's claws any more.

It wasn't often these nephritis cases went off so suddenly but his 33 urine albumen had been building up dangerously lately.

"Well, it was quick, Miss Stubbs. I'm sure the old chap didn't suffer 34 at all." My words sounded lame and ineffectual.

The old lady was in full command of herself. No tears, only a fixity 35 of expression as she looked down from the bed at her companion for so many years. My idea was to get him out of the place as quickly as possible and I pulled a blanket under him and lifted him up. As I was moving away, Miss Stubbs said, "Wait a moment." With an effort she turned on to her side and gazed at Ben. Still without changing expression, she reached out and touched his head lightly. Then she lay back calmly as I hurried from the room.

In the back kitchen I had a whispered conference with Mrs. Broad- 36 with. "I'll run down t'village and get Fred Manners to come and bury him," she said. "And if you've got time could you stay with the old lady while I'm gone. Talk to her, like, it'll do her good."

I went back and sat down by the bed. Miss Stubbs looked out of the 37 window for a few moments then turned to me. "You know, Mr. Herriot," she said casually, "it will be my turn next."

"What do you mean?"                                                 38

"Well, tonight Ben has gone and I'm going to be the next one. I just 39 know it."

"Oh, nonsense! You're feeling a bit low, that's all. We all do when something like this happens." But I was disturbed. I had never heard her even hint at such a thing before. 40

"I'm not afraid," she said. "I know there's something better waiting for me. I've never had any doubts." There was silence between us as she lay calmly looking up at the card on the gas bracket. 41

Then the head on the pillow turned to me again. "I have only one fear." Her expression changed with startling suddenness as if a mask had dropped. The brave face was almost unrecognisable. A kind of terror flickered in her eyes and she quickly grasped my hand. 42

"It's my dogs and cats, Mr. Herriot. I'm afraid I might never see them when I'm gone and it worries me so. You see, I know I'll be reunited with my parents and my brothers but . . . but . . ." 43

"Well, why not with your animals?" 44

"That's just it." She rocked her head on the pillow and for the first time I saw tears on her cheeks. "They say animals have no souls." 45

"Who says?" 46

"Oh, I've read it and I know a lot of religious people believe it." 47

"Well I don't believe it." I patted the hand which still grasped mine. "If having a soul means being able to feel love and loyalty and gratitude, then animals are better off than a lot of humans. You've nothing to worry about there." 48

"Oh, I hope you're right. Sometimes I lie at night thinking about it." 49

"I know I'm right, Miss Stubbs, and don't you argue with me. They teach us vets all about animals' souls." 50

The tension left her face and she laughed with a return of her old spirit. "I'm sorry to bore you with this and I'm not going to talk about it again. But before you go, I want you to be absolutely honest with me. I don't want reassurance from you—just the truth. I know you are very young but please tell me—what are your beliefs? Will my animals go with me?" 51

She stared intently into my eyes. I shifted in my chair and swallowed once or twice. 52

"Miss Stubbs, I'm afraid I'm a bit foggy about all this," I said. "But I'm absolutely certain of one thing. Wherever you are going, they are going too." 53

She still stared at me but her face was calm again. 54

"Thank you, Mr. Herriot. I know you are being honest with me. 55

That is what you really believe, isn't it?"

"I do believe it," I said. "With all my heart I believe it." 56

It must have been about a month later and it was entirely by accident 57
that I learned I had seen Miss Stubbs for the last time. When a lonely,
penniless old woman dies people don't rush up to you in the street to
tell you. I was on my rounds and a farmer happened to mention that
the cottage in Corby village was up for sale.

"But what about Miss Stubbs?" I asked. 58

"Oh, went off sudden about three weeks ago. House is in a bad 59
state, they say—nowt been done at it for years."

"Mrs. Broadwith isn't staying on, then?" 60

"Nay, I hear she's staying at t'other end of village." 60

"Do you know what's happened to the dogs and cats?" 61

"What dogs and cats?" 62

I cut my visit short. And I didn't go straight home though it was 63
nearly lunch time. Instead I urged my complaining little car at top
speed to Corby and asked the first person I saw where Mrs. Broadwith
was living. It was a tiny house but attractive and Mrs. Broadwith
answered my knock herself.

"Oh, come in, Mr. Herriot. It's right good of you to call." I went 64
inside and we sat facing each other across a scrubbed table top.

"Well, it was sad about the old lady," she said. 65

"Yes, I've only just heard." 66

"Any road, she had a peaceful end. Just slept away at finish." 67

"I'm glad to hear that." 68

Mrs. Broadwith looked round the room. "I was real lucky to get this 69
place—it's just what I've always wanted."

I could contain myself no longer. "What's happened to the ani- 70
mals?" I blurted out.

"Oh, they're in t'garden," she said calmly. "I've got a grand big 71
stretch at back." She got up and opened the door and with a surge of
relief I watched my old friends pour in.

Arthur was on my knee in a flash, arching himself ecstatically 72
against my arm while his outboard motor roared softly above the
barking of the dogs. Prince, wheezy as ever, tail fanning the air,
laughed up at me delightedly between barks.

"They look great, Mrs. Broadwith. How long are they going to 73
be here?"

"They're here for good. I think just as much about them as t'old lady   74
ever did and I couldn't be parted from them. They'll have a good home
with me as long as they live."

I looked at the typical Yorkshire country face, at the heavy cheeks   75
with their grim lines belied by the kindly eyes. "This is wonderful," I
said. "But won't you find it just a bit . . . er . . . expensive to feed
them?"

"Nay, you don't have to worry about that. I 'ave a bit put away."   76

"Well fine, fine, and I'll be looking in now and then to see how they   77
are. I'm through the village every few days." I got up and started for
the door.

Mrs. Broadwith held up her hand. "There's just one thing I'd like   78
you to do before they start selling off the things at the cottage. Would
you please pop in and collect what's left of your medicines. They're in
t'front room."

I took the key and drove along to the other end of the village. As I   79
pushed open the rickety gate and began to walk through the tangled
grass the front of the cottage looked strangely lifeless without the faces
of the dogs at the window; and when the door creaked open and I
went inside the silence was like a heavy pall.

Nothing had been moved. The bed with its rumpled blankets was   80
still in the corner. I moved around, picking up half-empty bottles, a jar
of ointment, the cardboard box with old Ben's tablets—a lot of good
they had done him.

When I had got everything I looked slowly round the little room. I   81
wouldn't be coming here any more and at the door I paused and read
for the last time the card which hung over the empty bed.

Old people and their attachment to their beloved animals. It shone   82
with a quiet radiance in the case of Miss Stubbs. Her courage and faith
were inspiring. So many people write to me voicing the same worry as
Miss Stubbs: "Do dogs have souls?" I can say that I am as sure now as
I was then that her pets have gone where she has gone. Another thing
which worries old people is what will happen to their pets when they
die. Who will look after them? Will they be treated kindly? I know
from my experiences in practice that some of these old folk are less
concerned about their own welfare than with the unbearable thought
that their animals might be neglected after they are gone. This is a
dread which will continue to haunt people, but I have found that it is

very often groundless. We live in a compassionate country and there are a lot of Mrs. Broadwiths about.

## VOCABULARY

| | | |
|---|---|---|
| privet (2) | lolling (11) | transfigured (20) |
| valvular (5) | intramuscular (11) | tartar (26) |
| Alsatian (6) | scenario (14) | sheathed (30) |
| circulatory (9) | breeches (18) | belied (75) |
| oral (9) | rips (20) | pall (79) |

### THE FACTS

1. What does the card hanging over Miss Stubbs's bed indicate about this woman?
2. What gives social meaning to Miss Stubbs's life despite her long illness?
3. What is revealed about Miss Stubbs's past?
4. What is Miss Stubbs's major concern about dying? Why does she have this concern? How does the narrator reassure her?
5. What happens to the animals after Miss Stubbs's death? According to the author, what does this indicate?

### THE STRATEGIES

1. What does the narrator's point of view add to the story?
2. What do paragraphs 17 to 22 add to the story?
3. Which of the animals seems most human? Why?
4. What tone does Herriot use in paragraphs 50 to 55? How important is the tone?
5. How does the narrator convey that the characters in the story are from Yorkshire?

### THE ISSUES

1. Compare Miss Stubbs's situation with that of a typical welfare case in our society. What differences do you see? How important do you consider these differences? Explain your answer.
2. As you consider Miss Stubbs's condition, what is its most tragic aspect? How important is this in your hierarchy of requirements for personal happiness?
3. What is your view of the theological discussion, between the narrator and Miss Stubbs, about whether or not animals have souls?
4. After reading this story, how do you feel about animal experimentation in scientific laboratories?

5. New Delhi, India, is presently experiencing a serious problem with gangs of monkeys roaming the city and stealing food or attacking citizens. Ten years ago, the situation was kept in ecological balance because large numbers of monkeys were sent overseas for laboratory experiments in medical research. However, recent laws passed in India have outlawed selling these monkeys to foreign nations. Complicating the matter is the Hindu religion, stating that monkeys are descendants of the god Hanuman, who long ago helped Rama defeat demon armies. If you were asked to solve the monkey problem in India, how would you proceed?

## SUGGESTIONS FOR WRITING

1. Write an essay in which you propose a plan to help the lonely elderly in your community by providing them with animal pets. Describe your plan and state its advantages clearly.
2. Write an essay in which you argue either for or against animals having souls. Take into consideration recent scientific reports on the ability of animals to feel and to communicate.

# CHAPTER WRITING ASSIGNMENTS

1. Choose one of the following subjects and develop an essay by dividing the subject into categories:
   a. anxieties
   b. colleges
   c. humor
   d. values
   e. violence
   f. fashions
   g. children
   h. books
   i. movies
   j. painting styles
   k. political systems
2. Write an essay in which you contrast one of the following pairs of concepts:
   a. jealousy–envy
   b. liberty–license
   c. servant–slave
   d. democracy–demagoguery
   e. art–craft
   f. politician–statesman
   g. talent–ability

3. Write a causal analysis for one of the following conditions:
   a. The poor writing habits of today's students
   b. The lack of popular financial support for museums, concerts, and other art forms
   c. The fall of the U.S. dollar overseas
   d. The need for prison reform
   e. The worldwide popularity of rock music
   f. The rise in child pornography
   g. The failure of the rapid transit system in most large cities
   h. The need to conserve our beaches
   i. Our tendency to buy throwaway items
   j. Homelessness

# 9
# ARGUMENTATION

## INTRODUCTION TO ARGUMENTATION

**Argumentation** is a term of rhetorical intent, not of form. It refers to any essay or speech whose aim is to sway or persuade a reader. Because writers resort to many techniques and devices to achieve this aim, the argumentation essay tends to be a mixture of rhetorical forms; that is, you are likely to find the writer defining, describing, narrating, or even dividing during the course of the argument. The tone of the essay can vary from the savage sarcasm of Jonathan Swift's "A Modest Proposal" to the offhand flippancy of Mike Royko's "Farewell to Fitness." And the subject matter can include any topic from the nearly infinite spectrum of issues about which people are likely to argue.

What elements are most likely to sway us in an argumentative essay, to make us change our minds and believe a writer's arguments? It is difficult to give a blanket answer to this question, but research suggests some clues. First, there is our perception of the writer's credentials to hold an opinion on the subject. If we think the writer competent and qualified on the subject—a medical doctor writing on a medical topic, for example—we are more likely to believe the advocated opinion. Should you hold a particular qualification to write on the subject, then mentioning it will probably help your case. You do not have to blare out your credentials with an obnoxious trumpeting, but can do it subtly. Here are two examples, taken from the debate over nuclear weapons (pages 113–40). First, Roger Fisher tells us in passing about his contact with NATO officers:

> Last spring I gave the officers at the NATO Defense College in Rome a hypothetical war in Europe, and asked them to work out NATO's war aims. The "war" was presumed to have grown out of a general strike in East Germany, with Soviet and West German tanks fighting on both sides of the border. Deterrence had failed. I told the officers: "You are in charge of the hotline message to Moscow. What is the purpose of this war? What are you trying to do?"

Notice the roundabout point being made: The writer teaches NATO officers at their defense college. Surely, we think, this experience qualifies him as an expert on nuclear strategy.

The second example comes from Fisher's debate opponent, Charlton Heston. At the outset we are tempted to ask what an actor can possibly know about nuclear weapons. Anticipating our doubt, Heston begins by tantalizing us with a hint:

> I was in Los Alamos a few weeks ago, doing a minor chore for the Atomic Testing Laboratory the University of California maintains there. As I was leaving, they presented me with a sample of a rare mineral . . . trinitite. It was formed instantaneously, thirty-eight years ago, from the sand of the New Mexican desert in the atomic test, code-named "Trinity," that validated the atomic bombs that ended World War II.

We do not know what the "minor chore" was, but the fact that Heston was asked to do it in the first place and then rewarded for doing it with a piece of trinitite cannot hurt his case. Later, Heston also name-drops about his contact with high-level brass:

> Lastly, our satellites are vulnerable in ways I will not specify to attacks from an increasingly effective Soviet anti-satellite technology. I've attended classified briefings in recent weeks, both by the Strategic Air Command and at Los Alamos.

Again, he is making clear his credentials for claiming to know something about the subject.

Another element that inclines us to believe an argumentative essay is the quality of its reasoning. If the writer's logic is sound, if the facts and supporting details strike us as reasonable and strong, then we are likely to be swayed by the conclusions. This is not as self-evident a proposition as it sounds. People who ardently believe one side of an issue frequently persuade themselves that the facts supporting the other are wrong. But presenting your facts in all their glory, while making the links between the propositions of your argument instantly clear, will make it harder for anyone to easily dismiss your conclusions. For example, in her essay "How the Superwoman Myth Puts Women Down," Sylvia Rabiner draws a valid logical connection between the media's glamorization of high-level professional women and the feeling of inferiority this "hype" instills in women destined to low-level careers. She bolsters her argument with appropriate examples and facts from the workplace.

Finally, arguments are persuasive if they appeal to our self-interests. We are more likely to believe an argument if we think there is something in it for us. This insight explains why arguers of all stripes always huff and puff to portray themselves and their views as if they agreed exactly with our self-interests, even if the correspondence is frequently far-fetched. The underlying appeal of Jonathan Swift's ironic proposal, for instance, is to the self-interests of Irish citizens who Swift thinks would be better off in a unified Ireland free from British exploitation.

The essays in this chapter both teach and exemplify argumentation. Richard Altick, in "Obstacles to Clear Thinking," acquaints us with argumentative trickery; John Sherwood, in "Introduction to Logic," shares with us the legitimate sources of belief. Swift savagely attacks the policy of the eighteenth-century English towards a destitute and starving Ireland, while Royko tries to persuade us that indolence and early death are preferable to exercise, asceticism, and long life. Rabiner reasons with us about feminist stereotypes, and James Michie, in "Dooley Is a Traitor," creates a poetic persona who beguiles us with antiwar arguments. The Issues section focuses on belief in

God—discouraged as a dinner party topic by polite hosts and hostesses, but taken on here with style and wit. The efforts of all of these writers to persuade us teaches argumentation in the best possible way—by good example.

Richard D. Altick

——— • **OBSTACLES TO CLEAR THINKING** • ———

*Richard Daniel Altick (b. 1915), American literary historian and biographer, has been a professor of English at Ohio State University since 1968. His works include* The Scholar Adventurers *(1959);* The English Common Reader: A Social History of the Mass Reading Public, 1800–1900 *(1957); and* Preface to Critical Reading *(1969), from which this selection is excerpted.*

*This article identifies some of the common types of logical errors that you are likely to encounter in political debate, in the media, and even in everyday argument. Learning the formal names of these errors is unimportant; what is important is being able to recognize these common logical slips well enough to avoid them in your own reasoning.*

In addition to the many pitfalls awaiting the unwary in formal inductive and deductive thinking, there are a number of common errors which perhaps can be called "abuses of logic" only by courtesy; some of them, at least, may best be described as sheer avoidances of logic. 1

1. Among them, an important class involves the *introduction of irrelevant and irrational evidence*. In the chapter on connotation, we have met a number of examples of such errors. There they were termed "name-calling" and "glittering generalities." Here we shall give them the labels they have in the books on clear thinking. But it is far less important to remember their names than it is to be able to recognize instances of them when we meet them—and to react to them as intelligent readers should react. 2

(a) The *argumentum ad hominem*. Here the writer or speaker departs from his task of proving the point at issue to prejudice his audience against his opponent. In American politics, this argument (which is too dignified a word for it!) is called "mud slinging." If, for example, in attacking his opponent's position on the reduction of the national debt, a candidate refers to Mr. X's intimate connection with certain well-known gamblers, he ceases to argue his case on its objective 3 merits and casts doubt upon his opponent's personal character. His object is not primarily to hurt Mr. X's feelings, but to arouse bias against Mr. X in his hearer's mind. Every critical reader or listener must train himself to detect and reject these irrelevant aspersions. It may be, indeed, that Mr. X *has* shady connections with the underworld. But that has nothing to do with the abstract rights or wrongs of his position on a national issue. Although, as the history of American politics shows, it is a hard thing to do, issues should be discussed apart from character and motives. The latter are also important, since obviously they bear upon a candidate's fitness for public office, but they call for a separate discussion.

(b) The *argumentum ad populum*. This too involves an appeal to the feelings, passions, and prejudices, rather than the reason, of the group addressed; but whereas the preceding argument is directed specifically against one's opponent, the *ad populum* argument has a wider range. The writer uses emotionally weighted words to bias his audience in favor of or against a person (not necessarily his opponent), an idea, a political party, a class, a nation. The monotonously repeated phrases of Communist propaganda against Americans—"Wall Street monopolists," "rich gangsters," "capitalistic warmongers"—are the most familiar recent examples of the negative, or name-calling, aspect of this argument. But just as common is the other aspect—that of the glittering generality, by which a writer attempts to sway his readers to enthusiasm for something or someone. The twin language-devices of the *argumentum ad populum*, then, are the stenchbomb and the perfume atomizer. The constant task of the critical reader is to ignore the odor with which an idea has been sprayed and to concentrate on the idea itself.

The "transfer" device is a particular favorite of those who find it to their advantage to use the *argumentum ad populum*. Like the use of name-calling and the glittering generality, it depends for its effectiveness upon the reader's or hearer's willingness to associate one idea with another, even though the two are not logically connected. Essentially, it represents an attempt to clothe one's pet policy or principle in borrowed raiment which will lend it a strength and dignity it does not possess by itself.

A common example of transfer is the habit which political orators have of working into their speeches quotations from Scripture or from the secular "sacred writings" (the Declaration of Independence, the

Preamble to the Constitution, the Gettysburg Address). Such quotations are depended upon to arouse favorable emotions in the breasts of the auditors, emotions which are then transferred to the orator's pet policy. Much of William Jennings Bryan's success as a public figure was due to the way in which he transformed an ordinary political campaign into a quasi-religious crusade by his "Cross of Gold" speech: "You shall not press down upon the brow of labor this crown of thorns; you shall not crucify mankind upon a cross of gold!" Actually, although the underlying idea, that the national monetary policy at the end of the nineteenth century worked to the serious disadvantage of the "common man," was entirely valid, the metaphor in which it was expressed was not. There is no connection between economics and the passion and crucifixion of Jesus. But the metaphor succeeded admirably in rallying to Bryan's ranks millions of Americans to whom Biblical quotation and allusion had the most powerful of connotations. It is noteworthy that as the influence of the Bible upon men's emotional habits declines, knowing politicians make less use of Biblical references; but such standard emotion-rousers as mention of Valley Forge, the Founding Fathers, and Abraham Lincoln are still found sprinkled through much propaganda. Whether they have any logical connection with the issues discussed is, to the speaker and (he hopes) to his audience, irrelevant; what they do is shed their own emotional effulgence upon ideas and pleas which might not otherwise be so acceptable.

The advertiser employs the transfer device just as commonly. Perhaps the most familiar instance of it is the use of the picture of a beautiful girl, not merely to attract attention to the advertisement but also to place the reader in a receptive frame of mind. Whether the girl has anything to do with the subject of the advertisement does not matter—so long as the reader is pleasantly affected. At certain periods when patriotic sentiment runs high, as during a war, commercial advertisers use the emotional symbols of patriotism for their own needs. Not only do they use the national colors and pictures of, or references to, the fighting men; their text often is designed to arouse fervent patriotic emotions which can then be transferred to a particular product. The following advertisement, dominated by a large drawing of the eagle on the United States seal, once appeared in eastern newspapers:

PRIDE IN THE AMERICAN WAY

The way of life that is American, that expounds democracy, is a proud
way of life. It is a manner of living so fine, so high in ideals and purpose

that it stands over and above all others. The Grabosky Family, makers of Royalist cigars, are proud to be members of The American Family, proud to present a cigar so fine in quality that it stands above all others. Over 50 years of superb cigar-making experience lies behind Royalist . . . a proud name in a proud America.[1]

(c) The *argumentum ad verecundiam*. This is a special instance of the more general "transfer" device. Here it is not a matter of borrowing prestige from one institution, such as religion or a nation, to adorn something else; instead, the prestige is specifically that of a great name, an "authority," which is expected to have weight with the public. On the general matter of authority we shall have more to say in a little while. At this point, we need only stress the importance of critically analyzing any appeal which uses quotations from men and women who have achieved fame in one field or another. One crucial question is: Is the question appropriate here? Does it have real relevance to the point at issue? It is all very well to quote Jefferson or Lincoln or Franklin Roosevelt in support of one's political stand—but it must be remembered that circumstances have changed immensely since these quotations were first uttered, and their applicability to a new situation is open to question. The implication is, This man, who we all agree *was* great and wise, said certain things which prove the justice of my own stand; therefore it behooves you to believe I am right. But to have a valid argument, the writer must prove that the word of the authorities whom he cites has a logical bearing on the present issue. If that is true, then he is borrowing not so much their popular prestige as their wisdom—which is perfectly permissible.

In essence, what the writer who invokes august authority for his point of view does is to imply that if the great men of the past were living today, they would write testimonials in behalf of his position. The familiar testimonials of present-day advertising are another instance of the transfer device. In some cases, the authority who testifies has some connection with the type of product advertised. The problem to settle here is, when we decide which brand of cigarette is best, how much weight may we reasonably attach to the enthusiastic statements of tobacco buyers, warehousemen, and auctioneers? In other cases, the testifying authority may have no formal, professional connection with the product advertised. An actor, who may very well be a master

---

[1]Note that the brand name of the cigar is not conspicuously in harmony with the sentiments expressed in the advertisement itself, yet it probably sells cigars. Why?

of his particular art, praises a whiskey, an after-shaving lotion, or a new convertible. He likes it, he says: but, we may ask, does the fact that he is a successful actor make him any better qualified than anyone who is *not* an actor to judge a whiskey, a lotion, or a car? Competence in one field does not necessarily imply competence in another.

Furthermore, in recent times it has been increasingly the custom for advertisers to borrow the prestige of science and medicine to enhance the reputation of their products. The American people have come to feel for the laboratory scientist and the physician an awe once reserved for bishops and statesmen. The alleged approval of such men thus carries great weight when it is a question of selling something, or (which is the same thing) inducing someone to believe something. Phrases such as "leading medical authorities say . . ." or "independent laboratory tests show . . ." are designed simply to transfer the prestige of science, which presumably is incapable of either error or corruption, to a toothpaste or a cereal. Seldom if ever are the precise "medical authorities" or "independent laboratories" named. But the mere phrases have vast weight with the uncritical. Similarly too the honorific "Dr." or "professor" implies that the person quoted speaks with all the authority of which learned men are capable—when as a matter of fact "doctorates" can be bought from mail-order colleges. Whenever, therefore, an attempt is made to convince by appeal to the prestige that surrounds the learned, the reader should demand full credentials. Just *what* medical authorities say this? Can they be trusted? *What* independent laboratories made the test—and what, actually, did the test reveal? Who is this man that speaks as a qualified educator or psychologist or economist? Regardless of the fact that he is called "doctor," does he know what he is talking about?

In all cases where the persuasive power of reputation and authority is invoked in behalf of a policy or a product, it is profitable to remember that before he can testify in a court of law, a man about to provide specialized evidence, which may have an important bearing on the jury's decision, must establish his competence in his field. A pathologist, a psychiatrist, an engineer, is asked briefly to outline the nature of his special training and experience. It would not hurt if, when we encounter the appeal to authority in any type of persuasive writing, we adopted the strategy of the opposing lawyer and probed more deeply into the witness' genuine competence to speak on the particular issue that is before us. A few pages later on, we shall suggest some pertinent questions in this respect.

2. *Begging the question*. Here the statement which is ostensibly of- 12
fered as a proposition to be proved actually assumes the proposition
as already proven. "This ordinance will certainly reduce juvenile delinquency, because it provides for steps which will prevent crimes on the
part of teen-agers." In other words, A is good because A is good. "The
reason why Sally is so mischievous is that she has just a little of
the devil in her." "I would trust him with any of my personal affairs
because he is certainly a reliable lawyer."

Every instance of name-calling or of the glittering generality in- 13
volves question-begging. When a writer or speaker brands someone a
"dangerous radical" or acclaims a policy as "the only way to escape
national disaster" he is using words the truth of which he never questions—nor expects his audience to question. Yet all such words and
phrases, weighted as they are with emotion and charged with controversy, stand very much in need of proof. And even if, when stripped
of their irrelevant emotional wording, the ideas can be established as
true, the argument remains sterile. Since its premise is identical with
its conclusion, nobody who does not already accept the conclusion
will accept the premise, and hence it convinces nobody.

3. *False analogy*. This fallacy consists of presenting a situation which 14
is acknowledged to be true, and then, on the basis of it, commenting
on another situation which is said to be similar. It is usually employed
in an attempt to simplify and make more vivid a complex issue. Newspaper political cartoons are often nothing more than pictorial analogies. Often, of course, such analogies serve admirably to point up,
dramatically and colorfully, the crux of a problem. The analogy of a
governmental agency in the role of the legendary Dutch boy, trying
desperately to stop a leak in the dike ("national economy") while the
waves of the sea ("inflation") are already spilling over the top of the
dike, is plainly very useful. But the ever-present danger is that the
analogy will assume a vital resemblance between the two objects of
comparison, where none really exists. "Don't change horses in the
middle of a stream" is a familiar cry in political campaigns when,
pleading a national emergency, the partisans of the incumbent in office
declare he cannot be superseded without grave danger to the country.
There is, of course, a superficial similarity between the two situations:
changing horses in the middle of a swift stream is dangerous, and so
too may be changing public officials at certain junctures in national
affairs. But riding horseback is not much like being president of the
United States, and while there may be only one or two reasons why

one should or should not change horses, there may be very many
reasons, none of them having anything to do with horseback riding,
why one man should be elected president and not another. Equally
dangerous is any attempt to prove a point which is based on the fancy
that the nations of the world are like school children, and that when
one nation does not have its way it goes into a corner and sulks; or that
two opponents, labor and capital, for example, may be likened to two
prize-fighters squaring off in the ring, with some government official
or agency as referee. Such analogies are, we repeat, useful in drama-
tizing a situation; but it is always perilous to maintain that because two
situations are ''alike'' in one or two respects, what is true of one is
necessarily true of the other.

4. *Oversimplification*. False analogy may well be considered a partic-    15
ular type of oversimplification—than which there is no more common
error. When we discussed in the beginning of this chapter the method
of reasoning by hypothesis, we stressed the fact that no hypothesis
can be considered sound unless we have taken into account all the
factors that are related to it. Unfortunately, with our natural human
indolence, to say nothing of our intellectual limitations, we are always
eager to view questions in their simplest terms and to make our decisions on the basis of only a few of the many aspects which the problem
involves. If that is true of problems of a practical nature, such as those
we used to illustrate the use of the hypothesis, how much more true it
is of those involving a problem of human conduct, or a grave decision
facing the voters or the statesmen of a nation! Few of the decisions
which we are called upon to make are so simple that we can say with
confidence that one choice is completely right and the other is completely wrong. The problem of the so-called minority groups in America, for instance, is not simply one of abstract justice, as many would
like to think it; it involves deeply complex questions of economics,
sociology, and politics. Nor can we say with easy assurance: ''The
federal government should guarantee every farmer a decent income,
even if the money comes from the pocketbooks of the citizens who are
the farmer's own customers''—or ''It is the obligation of every educational institution to purge its faculty of everyone who holds leftist
sympathies.'' Perhaps each of these propositions is sound, perhaps
neither is; but before he adopts it as a settled conviction, the intelligent
man or woman must canvass its full implications, just as he should do
with any hypothesis. After the implications have been explored, it may

be found that there is more evidence telling against the proposition than there is supporting it; in which case it should be abandoned. In any event, no one can call himself a conscientious citizen who fails to explore, so far as he is humanly able, the honest pros and cons of any issue he is called upon to help decide—and then to adopt the position he feels is best justified by the evidence he has surveyed.

Countless false generalizations concerning parties, races, religions,    16
and nations—to say nothing of individuals—are the result of the deep-seated human desire to reduce a complex idea to its simplest terms. Democrats tend naturally to think all Republicans as progress-obstructing conservatives, when in fact many Republicans are more "liberal" than many Democrats. Many Protestants regard Catholics as bigoted and superstitious, even though the views they regard as "bigoted" and the practices they regard as "superstitious" may have their roots deep in the philosophical grounds of the Catholic religion. Similarly many Catholics regard Protestants as infidels or atheists, although there may be as much philosophical justification for Protestant doctrine as there is for Catholic. It is easier to condemn than to understand. But every man and woman has a pressing moral, as well as intellectual obligation to examine the basis of every judgment he or she makes: "Am I examining every aspect of the issue that needs to be examined—do I understand the pros and cons of the problem sufficiently to be able to make a fair decision—or am I taking the easiest way out?"

5. The innate intellectual laziness of human beings invites one fur-    17
ther, crowning device of deception: the *distortion or the actual suppression of the truth*. If men will not actively demand the truth, why should persuaders provide them with it, when doing so would hurt their chances of success? And so it is usual in all forms of persuasion to prevent considerations which would damage the cause from reaching the minds of those who are to be persuaded.

(a) One such device—there are many—is *card stacking* (also called    18
"smoke screen"[2]), which is used by a group, a political party for instance, to divert attention from certain issues which it does not care to have discussed. Card stacking consists of laying heavy and insistent

---

[2]Although their purposes are the same, card stacking and the smoke screen have slightly different techniques. The first is usually prepared in advance; the second is impromptu, being devised to meet exigencies as they occur in the course of an argument.

emphasis upon certain selected topics, discussion of which can probably do the party no harm. The party then hopes that the public, its attention centered on these topics, will not bother about the less attractive side of the party's record or program. A state administration, running for re-election, may devote all its propaganda to boasting about the reduction in taxes which it has effected in an "economy program"—and it will assiduously fail to mention the way in which state services have deteriorated as a result of the "slashed budget." This same practice is evident in virtually every advertisement one reads. The attractive points of a product are dwelt upon unceasingly; the less attractive ones, never. An automobile may be streamlined and easy-riding, it may have fast pickup in traffic, it may have a wealth of gadgets—these facts will be proclaimed from every newspaper, magazine, and billboard; but that the car eats up gasoline and oil, has a poorly made engine block, and costs $200 more than other cars in the same price-class—these facts are religiously suppressed. But, as you will no doubt agree, they are worth knowing about.

(b) Another closely related means by which attention is drawn from    19
the whole truth is one dear to every practical politician: the *red herring*. The red herring is an irrelevant issue which is drawn across the path of an argument when one side or the other is becoming embarrassed and wishes to change the subject. In a campaign for the mayoralty of a large city, for example, Party A (which is in office) may find itself in serious trouble because Party B has successfully given evidence of its waste of public funds. Four days before the election, therefore, Party A suddenly "discovers" that Party B's candidate has been seen in night clubs with a lady who is not his wife. Party A hopes that the injection into the contest of another, more appealing, topic of discussion will allow the public to forget the serious accusations that have been leveled against it. Whether or not Party A is able to prove that the B candidate's private frailties (if they do exist) disqualify him from holding public office, the red herring will have served its purpose if it ends the embarrassing talk about Party A's own shortcomings.

(c) A third such device is that of *wrenching from context*. A sentence    20
or a phrase can easily mean one thing when it is quoted alone, and a quite different thing if it is read against the background of the whole discussion to which it belongs. An extreme example is a sentence from a newspaper review of a new movie: "For about five minutes 'Fruits of Desire' is a top-notch show, brilliantly acted and magnificently photo-

graphed. After that it degenerates into a dismal spectacle of Hollywood hokum." It would not be surprising to see the subsequent advertisements of the movie flaunting this headline: "'A top-notch show, brilliantly acted and magnificently photographed . . . a spectacle'—Smith, *Daily News.*" The familiar "avoid foreign entanglements" advice in Washington's farewell address, when read in full context, means something very different from what it means when quoted separately. And probably no public figure whose statements are quoted in the newspapers or on the radio has ever escaped the chagrin that comes from seeing prominence given to one or two paragraphs of his latest speech which, thus isolated, completely distort his total argument. Such quotations must always be read with the greatest caution. The only way to be sure that they fairly represent the author's viewpoint is to read the complete text of his speech as printed in, for instance, *The New York Times.*

## VOCABULARY

| | | |
|---|---|---|
| aspersions (3) | ostensibly (12) | indolence (15) |
| raiment (5) | acclaims (13) | impromptu (footnote 2) |
| effulgence (6) | fallacy (14) | assiduously (18) |
| behooves (8) | partisans (14) | chagrin (20) |
| august (9) | superseded (14) | |
| invoked (11) | junctures (14) | |

# •• DISCUSSION ••

### John C. Sherwood

# • INTRODUCTION TO LOGIC •

*John C. Sherwood (b. 1918) was born in Hempstead, New York, and educated at Yale University. Since 1961, he has taught at the University of Oregon. The following selection comes from his* Discourse of Reason *(1964).*

*Sherwood discusses the relationship between belief, values, and logic. He defines the difference between induction and deduction, between generalizations and judgments, and discusses the use of each in everyday reasoning.*

Even for the most skeptical, belief is an absolute necessity for prac-     1
tical experience. At the very least, we have to have faith that the material world will continue in its accustomed ways, that tomorrow as
today iron will be hard and clay soft, that objects will continue to fall
toward the earth instead of flying off into the sky. Even in the less
certain and less easily analyzed realm of human character, we constantly act on beliefs—that a soft answer turneth away wrath, that a
veteran soldier will fight bravely, that a mother will love and protect
her children, that the mailman will deliver the mail instead of stealing
it. Without belief, action would be paralyzed; we should never know
what to do in a given situation. What really distinguishes the rational
from the irrational thinker is not the presence or absence of belief, but
the grounds on which belief is accepted.

There are some sources of belief which are either absolutely un-     2
sound or to be resorted to only when all other methods fail. A "hunch"
is not an absolutely useless guide, because it may be based on knowledge which has temporarily slipped our minds, but we would be foolish to trust a hunch when objective evidence was available. Our casual
impression of a prospective employee may be useful, but full knowledge of his previous record is more valuable. Tradition may be a proper
guide in some areas of life, but we cannot accept witchcraft or even the
Newtonian physics because our forefathers did. All too often we believe simply because we want to believe. It is comforting to think that
"there is always room at the top" or that "there are no atheists in
foxholes" or that "football makes good citizens." But such beliefs are
the most treacherous of all beliefs, because we tend to protect them by
ignoring contrary evidence until at some crisis the brute facts force
themselves on our attention. An unfounded belief is not merely wrong
morally; it is an unsafe guide to conduct.

What then are the legitimate sources of belief? In a scientific age we     3
instinctively answer, evidence or investigation. We believe that a
worker is reliable because we have seen him at work frequently over a
considerable period of time; we believe that a certain remedy will cure
a certain disease because trained observers have watched its operation
in a large number of cases (here, as often, we have to trust the reports
of others' investigations); we believe that haste makes waste because
we have seen it happen so many times. In effect, we infer from a
certain number of instances of a thing that a characteristic of the thing
we have observed in those instances will also appear in other in-

stances. This is the process of *induction*. Somewhat less often (unless we are very much given to theoretical reasoning) we use *deduction*. Where induction puts facts together to get ideas or *generalizations*, deduction puts ideas together to discover what other ideas can be inferred from them. If John is the son of David who is the son of William, then John must be the grandson of William—we know this without asking. If a student must pass composition to graduate, and Mr. X has not yet passed it, then Mr. X cannot yet graduate. In each case, given the first two ideas or *premises*, we know that the third—the *conclusion*—must be true: no further investigation is needed. (If the conclusion proved not to be true, then we would assume that one of the premises was wrong; perhaps a student must take composition unless excused.)

In every mind there will be a few beliefs which cannot be proved    4
either by induction or deduction: basic standards of value, ultimate articles of faith, matters of inner conviction which we would be hard put to prove but without which we could scarcely think or act. Religious principles might be thought of as the most obvious example, but philosophy and even science illustrate the same necessity. In plane geometry we must begin with axioms and postulates from which the rest of the system is deduced. It is an article of faith that "things equal to the same thing are equal to each other"; we must believe it or give up plane geometry. Virtually all induction, and hence all scientific conclusions and practically all action depend on a faith in the uniformity of nature—that the laws of matter will be the same tomorrow as today. It seems only common sense to assume that water will continue to freeze at 32° Fahrenheit hereafter, but there is no way of proving the assumption theoretically.

Induction and deduction are not merely the tools of the philosopher    5
and the scientist, but in rough-and-ready half-conscious forms are part of the everyday thought processes of all sane human beings, however limited their education. It is not infrequently argued that logic in the more formal sense is neither necessary nor useful for human life, since "common" or "horse" sense can serve us far better in practical affairs. All this involves a half-truth. In the first place, we might question whether logic and common sense are really so opposed. If common sense has any value, it is because it is based on "experience"; in other words, having generalized from a series of seemingly like instances observed in the past, we apply the generalization to a further instance

that has just come to our attention. What really distinguishes common sense from logic is that it tends to take shortcuts: it seldom bothers to work out all the steps in the argument. Certain processes work in our brains, and we acquire a sudden conviction that something is true. It is fortunate that we have common sense and "intuition" to depend on, for time does not always allow us to work things out logically or go hunting for evidence. It is certainly better to investigate a prospective employee thoroughly, but if we have to fill the job on the spot, we shall have to trust our impressions of his character. Very rarely (if we are wise) we may even trust our common sense in preference to what seems to be scientific evidence. Many a parent or teacher has finally nerved himself to go against the "scientific findings" of a child psychologist or educator. (But perhaps here what is wrong is not really science but its interpretation by self-appointed prophets.) Whole areas of human decision lie outside of the range of logic and sometimes even of common sense. One may be able to prove by critical principle that a book has every virtue that belongs to a masterpiece, and the book may in fact be quite unreadable. Science has not conquered all areas of human life. It is useless to tell a young man that a certain girl has all the qualifications of an ideal wife if he happens to hate her. Nevertheless, to scorn logic and hold to "horse sense" is a dangerous business. An appeal to common sense—or worst yet, intuition—all too often represents an attempt to evade the responsibility of looking at evidence or working out the problem rationally. Common sense sometimes tells people peculiar things about such matters as family life and racial and economic problems. If by common sense we mean a kind of informal, everyday logic, then it is an absolute necessity of rational existence; but if by it we mean a defiance of logic, it ought not to exist at all, and it is unhappily true that most of us use logic too little rather than too much.* To come down to the practical problem of communication—which after all is our basic concern here—our personal intuitions are probably of very little interest to our readers or listeners, who may even not be much impressed by our common sense, however much they may value their own. What they expect from us is logic and evidence.

---

*Perhaps we should distinguish common sense, which does involve some conscious reasoning on evidence, from intuition, which involves no reasoning at all, but only a "feeling" that something is so. Intuition certainly ought to be a last resort, but sometimes there is nothing else to follow. Often, if the intuition is sound, one can find evidence or construct an argument to confirm it. One ought to be able to defend it rationally, however irrational its origins.

By its very nature, logic deals in statements or *propositions*; they are   6
the materials of deductive reasoning and the products of inductive
reasoning. By a proposition we mean a group of words which can be
affirmed or denied—of which it can be said it is either true or false.
(Even if it is false, it is still a proposition.) Not all sentences are propositions. A question or command is not a proposition; we cannot say
that "Who is there?" is true or that "Do your homework!" is false. A
proposition is roughly equivalent to the grammarian's *declarative sentence*, though not exactly equivalent, since a declarative sentence might
contain several different propositions ("The sky is blue, and the grass
is green") or express what is really a question or command ("The
audience will leave quietly").

Another important distinction is that between a proposition which   7
is merely factual and one which implies a *judgment*. "He served at
Valley Forge" and "He was a loyal soldier" are both statements, but
not of the same kind. The first is a matter of fact: either he served or
he did not, and there is the possibility at least of proving the matter
one way or another to the satisfaction of all. The second is a little
different; it passes a judgment since the word "loyal" implies praise
for something the speaker approves of or judges good. Another
speaker, fully apprised of the same facts, might differ because of a
differing conception of what constitutes loyalty, and absolute proof
one way or another is impossible, since an element of personal feeling
will always enter in. We should not confuse this distinction between
*fact* and *judgment* with the distinction between *established truth* and
*mere opinion*. Fact here means "piece of verifiable information"; what
makes it a fact is the concrete quality which makes conclusive proof at
least theoretically possible. "Columbus died in 1491" and "Martians
have six legs" are in this sense factual, though the one statement is
known to be false and the other is at present impossible of verification.
"George Washington was loyal" still involves a judgment, however
much the statement is confirmed by evidence and however universally
it is believed. A British writer in 1776 might plausibly have called
Washington disloyal, and while we could find plenty of arguments to
challenge the writer with, it is very possible that we should never come
to an agreement with him. Unhappily for logic, the distinction between fact and judgment is far from clear-cut. The statement "He is
intelligent" certainly contains an element of judgment; yet it is susceptible of confirmation by means of standard tests and might approach
the status of a fact. It may be especially hard to distinguish between

judgments and generalizations derived from a number of facts. Generalizations, like statements of single facts, differ from judgments in not necessarily implying any approval or disapproval. "A 1.5 concentration of alcohol in the blood usually impairs reactions" is a generalization; "It is wrong to drive in such a state" is a judgment.

Needless to say, judgments are not to be condemned; they are 8 merely to be recognized for what they are. It may not always be easy to do this. When the educator says "The learner cannot be considered aside from his environment," he seems to be stating a generalization. But a little reflection reminds us that, rightly or wrongly, pupils are often judged without reference to their environment, and that to make sense the sentence must read "The learner *ought not* to be considered aside from his environment"—a form which clearly identifies it as a judgment. "Good children brush their teeth" has the form of a generalization and might actually represent the result of investigation on the dental habits of children known to be "good." Probably, however, it is a judgment, telling how the speaker thinks children ought to behave, and in a certain context the sentence might amount to a command. What is important is to make our meaning clear in the first place, and to show our readers that our evaluations have been rational. Judgments may be supported by evidence and argument; they need not be mere emotional reactions. The statement "He was loyal" can be supported by a definition of loyalty and instances of loyal conduct.

It goes without saying that one cannot work logically with a state- 9 ment which does not have a clear-cut, ascertainable meaning. Puritanical logicians sometimes deny cognitive meaning to any statement which cannot be proved true or false (or at least shown to be probable or improbable) by reference to material facts. Since such an assumption would throw out much philosophy and theology, we should hardly wish to go so far, but we should at least try to avoid those statements, all too common in controversy, which do nothing more than express feeling or prejudice. The following is technically a valid argument: X is a no-good rat; No-good rats should be hung; X should be hung. But we should hope that no jury would follow such reasoning. . . . One cannot deduce anything from a feeling.

## VOCABULARY

| | | |
|---|---|---|
| prospective (2) | postulates (4) | impairs (7) |
| infer (3) | intuition (5) | ascertainable (9) |

| | | |
|---|---|---|
| induction (3) | propositions (6) | puritanical (9) |
| deduction (3) | apprised (7) | cognitive (9) |
| premises (3) | plausibly (7) | |
| axioms (4) | susceptible (7) | |

## THE FACTS

1. What is the difference between a rational and an irrational thinker?
2. What are legitimate sources of belief?
3. What is induction? What is deduction? How do they differ?
4. The author says scientific induction depends on an act of faith. Faith in what?
5. What is the difference between "common sense" and "logic"?
6. What is a proposition? Where do propositions come from? What is the difference between a proposition and an axiom?
7. What is the difference between a fact and a judgment? Between a generalization and a judgment?

## THE STRATEGIES

1. Examine the opening sentences of the first four paragraphs. What key word is repeated in each sentence? What effect does this repetition have on these paragraphs?
2. The author readily supports his generalizations with examples. What does this contribute to the selection?
3. What method of logic does this article most heavily rely on—induction or deduction?
4. In paragraph 3 the author uses the pronoun *we*. Whom does this *we* refer to? What effect does its use have on the examples?
5. In paragraph 2 the author gives three examples of unfounded beliefs: (a) "there is always room at the top"; (b) "there are no atheists in foxholes"; (c) "football makes good citizens." By what other name are these and similar beliefs known?

## THE ISSUES

1. List five statements of fact that apply to your own life; then rephrase them as statements of judgment. How do they differ?
2. Discuss at least one instance in history when it was appropriate to abandon a belief because of contrary logic or when it was appropriate to abandon logic because of a contrary belief.
3. How important do you consider common sense in the daily affairs of society?
4. It has been said that pollsters have replaced the ancient prophets and

oracles. How effective do you consider opinion polls in predicting the future?

5. When is it necessary to be skeptical about an assertion presented to you?

### SUGGESTIONS FOR WRITING

1. Write an essay in which you clarify the difference between a *fact* and a *judgment*. Use examples to make the distinction precise.
2. Discuss at least one instance in your life where you either abandoned a belief because of contrary logic or abandoned logic because of a contrary belief.

Jonathan Swift

## • A MODEST PROPOSAL •

### For Preventing the Children of Poor People From Being a Burthen to Their Parents or the Country and for Making Them Beneficial to the Public

*Considered one of the greatest satirists in the English language, Jonathan Swift (1667–1745) was born in Dublin and educated at Trinity College. His satirical masterpiece,* Gulliver's Travels, *was published in 1726, by which time Swift was already regarded by the Irish as a national hero for his* Drapier's Letters *(1724). Originally published as a pamphlet, ''A Modest Proposal'' first appeared in 1729.*

*In this famous satire, Swift, assuming the role of a concerned and logical citizen, turns society's indifference to the value of human life into an outraged attack against poverty in Ireland.*

It is a melancholy object to those who walk through this great town,    1
or travel in the country, when they see the streets, the roads, and cabin doors crowded with beggars of the female sex followed by three, four, or six children, all in rags and importuning every passenger for an alms. These mothers, instead of being able to work for their honest livelihood, are forced to employ all their time in strolling, to beg sustenance for their helpless infants, who, as they grow up, either turn thieves for want of work or leave their dear native country to fight for the Pretender in Spain or sell themselves to the Barbadoes.*

---

*Swift refers to the exiled Stuart claimant of the English throne, and to the custom of poor emigrants to commit themselves to work for a number of years to pay off their transportation to a colony.—Ed.

I think it is agreed by all parties that this prodigious number of   2
children, in the arms or on the backs or at the heels of their mothers
and frequently of their fathers, is in the present deplorable state of the
kingdom a very great additional grievance, and therefore whoever
could find out a fair, cheap, and easy method of making these children
sound and useful members of the commonwealth would deserve
so well of the public as to have his statue set up for a preserver of
the nation.

But my intention is very far from being confined to provide only for   3
the children of professed beggars; it is of a much greater extent, and
shall take in the whole number of infants at a certain age who are born
of parents in effect as little able to support them as those who demand
our charity in the streets.

As to my own part, having turned my thoughts for many years upon   4
this important subject and maturely weighed the several schemes of
other projectors, I have always found them grossly mistaken in their
computation. It is true, a child just dropped from its dam may be
supported by her milk for a solar year, with little other nourishment,
at the most not above the value of two shillings, which the mother may
certainly get, or the value in scraps, by her lawful occupation of begging; and it is exactly at one year old that I propose to provide for them
in such a manner as, instead of being a charge upon their parents or
the parish or wanting food and raiment for the rest of their lives, they
shall on the contrary contribute to the feeding, and partly to the clothing, of many thousands.

There is likewise another great advantage in my scheme, that it will   5
prevent those voluntary abortions and that horrid practice of women
murdering their bastard children, alas! too frequent among us, sacrificing the poor innocent babes, I doubt more to avoid the expense than
the shame, which would move tears and pity in the most savage and
inhuman breast.

The number of souls in this kingdom being usually reckoned one   6
million and a half, of these I calculate there may be about two hundred
thousand couple whose wives are breeders, from which number I
subtract thirty thousand couple who are able to maintain their own
children (although I apprehend there cannot be so many, under the
present distresses of the kingdom); but this being granted, there will
remain a hundred and seventy thousand breeders. I again subtract
fifty thousand for those women who miscarry or whose children die
by accident or disease within the year. There only remain a hundred

and twenty thousand children of poor parents annually born. The question therefore is how this number shall be reared and provided for, which, as I have already said, under the present situation of affairs is utterly impossible by all the methods hitherto proposed. For we can neither employ them in handicraft or agriculture; we neither build houses (I mean in the country) nor cultivate land; they can very seldom pick up a livelihood by stealing, till they arrive at six years old, except where they are of towardly parts, although I confess they learn the rudiments much earlier, during which time they can, however, be properly looked upon only as *probationers*; as I have been informed by a principal gentleman in the County of Cavan who protested to me that he never knew above one or two instances under the age of six, even in a part of the kingdom so renowned for the quickest proficiency in that art.

I am assured by our merchants that a boy or a girl before twelve    7
years old is no saleable commodity, and even when they come to this age they will not yield above three pounds or three pounds and a half a crown at most on the exchange, which cannot turn to account either to the parents or the kingdom, the charge of nutriment and rags having been at least four times that value.

I shall now, therefore, humbly propose my own thoughts, which I    8
hope will not be liable to the least objection.

I have been assured by a very knowing American of my acquain-    9
tance in London that a young, healthy child well nursed is, at a year old, a most delicious, nourishing, and wholesome food, whether stewed, roasted, baked, or boiled; and I make no doubt that it will equally serve in a fricassee or a ragout.

I do therefore humbly offer it to public consideration that of the    10
hundred and twenty thousand children already computed, twenty thousand may be reserved for breed, whereof only one fourth part to be males, which is more than we allow to sheep, black cattle, or swine; and my reason is that these children are seldom the fruits of marriage, a circumstance not much regarded by our savages; therefore one male will be sufficient to serve four females. That the remaining hundred thousand may, at a year old, be offered in sale to the persons of quality and fortune through the kingdom, always advising the mother to let them suck plentifully in the last month, so as to render them plump and fat for a good table. A child will make two dishes at an entertainment for friends; and when the family dines alone, the fore- or hindquarter will make a reasonable dish, and seasoned with a little pepper

or salt, will be very good boiled on the fourth day, especially in winter. I have reckoned, upon a medium, that a child just born will weigh twelve pounds, and in a solar year, if tolerably nursed, will increase to twenty-eight pounds.

I grant this food will be somewhat dear, and therefore very proper   11
for the landlords, who, as they have already devoured most of the parents, seem to have the best title to the children.

Infant's flesh will be in season throughout the year, but more plen-   12
tifully in March and a little before and after; for we are told by a grave author, an eminent French physician, that fish being a prolific diet, there are more children born in Roman Catholic countries about nine months after Lent than at any other season; therefore, reckoning a year after Lent, the markets will be more glutted than usual, because the number of Popish infants is at least three to one in this kingdom; and therefore it will have one other collateral advantage, by lessening the number of Papists among us. I have already computed the charge of nursing a beggar's child (in which list I reckon all cottagers, laborers, and four fifths of the farmers) to be about two shillings per annum, rags included; and I believe no gentleman would repine to give ten shillings for the carcass of a good fat child, which, as I have said, will make four dishes for excellent nutritive meat, when he has only some particular friend or his own family to dine with him. Thus the squire will learn to be a good landlord and grow popular among his tenants; the mother will have eight shillings net profit and be fit for work till she produces another child.

Those who are more thrifty (as I must confess the times require)   13
may flay the carcass, the skin of which, artificially dressed, will make admirable gloves for ladies and summer boots for fine gentlemen.

As to our city of Dublin, shambles* may be appointed for this pur-   14
pose in the most convenient parts of it; and butchers, we may be assured, will not be wanting, although I rather recommend buying the children alive than dressing them hot from the knife as we do roasting pigs.

A very worthy person, a true lover of his country, and whose virtues   15
I highly esteem, was lately pleased in discoursing on this matter to offer a refinement upon my scheme. He said that many gentlemen of his kingdom having of late destroyed their deer, he conceived that the want of venison might be well supplied by the bodies of young lads

---

*Slaughterhouses.—Ed.

and maidens, not exceeding fourteen years of age nor under twelve, so great a number of both sexes in every country being now ready to starve for want of work and service; and these to be disposed of by their parents if alive, or otherwise by their nearest relations. But with due deference to so excellent a friend and so deserving a patriot, I cannot be altogether in his sentiments; for as to the males, my American acquaintance assured me, from frequent experience, that their flesh was generally tough and lean, like that of our school-boys, by continual exercise, and their taste disagreeable; and to fatten them would not answer the charge. Then as to the females, it would, I think, with humble submission, be a loss to the public, because they would soon become breeders themselves, and besides, it is not improbable that some scrupulous people might be apt to censure such a practice (although indeed very unjustly) as a little bordering upon cruelty, which, I confess, has always been with me the strongest objection against any project, however so well intended.

But in order to justify my friend, he confessed that this expedient 16 was put into his head by the famous Psalmanazar, a native of the island Formosa, who came from thence to London above twenty years ago and in conversation told my friend that in his country, when any young person happened to be put to death, the executioner sold the carcass to persons of quality as a prime dainty and that in his time the body of a plump girl of fifteen, who was crucified for an attempt to poison the emperor, was sold to his imperial Majesty's prime minister of state and other great mandarins of the court in joints from the gibbet at four hundred crowns. Neither, indeed, can I deny that if the same use were made of several plump young girls in this town who, without one single groat to their fortunes, cannot stir abroad without a chair, and appear at playhouse and assemblies in foreign fineries which they never will pay for, the kingdom would not be the worse.

Some persons of a desponding spirit are in great concern about that 17 vast number of poor people who are aged, diseased, or maimed, and I have been desired to employ my thoughts what course may be taken to ease the nation of so grievous an encumbrance. But I am not in the least pain upon the matter, because it is very well known that they are every day dying and rotting by cold, and famine, and filth, and vermin, as fast as can be reasonably expected. And as to the young laborers, they are now in almost as hopeful a condition; they cannot get work and consequently pine away for want of nourishment to a degree that if at any time they are accidentally hired to common labor, they have not strength to perform it; and thus the country and themselves are happily delivered from the evils to come.

I have too long digressed and therefore shall return to my subject. 18 I think the advantages by the proposal which I have made are obvious and many, as well as of the highest importance.

For first, as I have already observed, it would greatly lessen the 19 number of Papists, with whom we are yearly overrun, being the principal breeders of the nation as well as our most dangerous enemies, and who stay at home on purpose to deliver the kingdom to the Pretender, hoping to take their advantage by the absence of so many good Protestants, who have chosen rather to leave their country than stay at home and pay tithes, against their conscience, to an Episcopal curate.

Secondly, the poorer tenants will have something valuable of their 20 own which by law may be made liable to distress and help to pay their landlord's rent, their corn and cattle being already seized and money a thing unknown.

Thirdly, whereas the maintenance of a hundred thousand children 21 from two years old and upward cannot be computed at less than ten shillings apiece per annum, the nation's stock will thereby be increased fifty thousand pounds per annum, beside the profit of a new dish introduced to the tables of all gentlemen of fortune in the kingdom who have any refinement in taste. And the money will circulate among ourselves, the goods being entirely of our own growth and manufacture.

Fourthly, the constant breeders, beside the gain of eight shillings 22 sterling per annum by the sale of their children, will be rid of the charge of maintaining them after the first year.

Fifthly, this food would likewise bring great custom to taverns, 23 where the vintners will certainly be so prudent as to procure the best receipts for dressing it to perfection and consequently have their houses frequented by all the fine gentlemen who justly value themselves upon their knowledge in good eating; and a skillful cook who understands how to oblige his guests will contrive to make it as expensive as they please.

Sixthly, this would be a great inducement to marriage, which all 24 wise nations have either encouraged by rewards or enforced by laws and penalties. It would increase the care and tenderness of mothers toward their children when they were sure of a settlement for life to the poor babes, provided in some sort by the public, to their annual profit or expense. We could see an honest emulation among the married women, which of them could bring the fattest child to the market. Men would become as fond of their wives during the time of their pregnancy as they are now of their mares in foal, their cows in calf, or sows when they are ready to farrow, nor offer to beat or kick them (as is too frequent a practice) for fear of a miscarriage.

Many other advantages might be enumerated. For instance, the 25 addition of some thousand carcasses in our exportation of barreled beef; the propagation of swine's flesh and improvement in the art of making good bacon, so much wanted among us by the great destruction of pigs, too frequent at our table, which are no way comparable in taste or magnificence to a well-grown fat yearling child, which, roasted whole, will make a considerable figure at a lord mayor's feast or any other public entertainment. But this and many others I omit, being studious of brevity.

Supposing that one thousand families in this city would be constant 26 customers for infant's flesh, beside others who might have it at merry-meetings, particularly at weddings and christenings, I compute that Dublin would take off annually about twenty thousand carcasses and the rest of the kingdom (where probably they will be sold somewhat cheaper) the remaining eighty thousand.

I can think of no one objection that will possibly be raised against 27 this proposal unless it should be urged that the number of people will be thereby much lessened in the kingdom. This I freely own, and it was indeed one principal design in offering it to the world. I desire the reader will observe that I calculate my remedy for this one individual kingdom of Ireland and for no other that ever was, is, or I think ever can be, upon earth. Therefore let no man talk to me of other expedients; of taxing our absentees at five shillings a pound; of using neither clothes nor household furniture except what is of our own growth and manufacture; of utterly rejecting the materials and instruments that promote foreign luxury; of curing the expensiveness of pride, vanity, idleness, and gaming in our women; of introducing a vein of parsimony, prudence, and temperance; of learning to love our country, in the want of which we differ even from Laplanders and the inhabitants of Tupinamba; of quitting our animosities and factions, nor acting any longer like the Jews, who were murdering one another at the very moment their city was taken; of being a little cautious not to sell our country and conscience for nothing; of teaching landlords to have at least one degree of mercy toward their tenants; lastly, of putting a spirit of honesty, industry, and skill into our shop-keepers, who, if a resolution could now be taken to buy only our native goods, would immediately unite to cheat and exact upon us in the price, the measure, and the goodness, nor could ever yet be brought to make one fair proposal of just dealing, though often and earnestly invited to it.

Therefore, I repeat, let no man talk to me of these and the like 28 expedients till he has at least some glimpse of hope that there will be ever some hearty and sincere attempt to put them in practice.

But as to myself, having been wearied out for many years with 29 offering vain, idle, visionary thoughts and at length utterly despairing of success, I fortunately fell upon this proposal, which, as it is wholly new, so it has something solid and real, of no expense and little trouble, full in our own power, and whereby we can incur no danger in disobliging England. For this kind of commodity will not bear exportation, the flesh being of too tender a consistence to admit a long continuance in salt, although perhaps I could name a country which would be glad to eat up our whole nation without it.

After all, I am not so violently bent upon my own opinion as to 30 reject any offer proposed by wise men which shall be found equally innocent, cheap, easy, and effectual. But before some thing of that kind shall be advanced in contradiction to my scheme and offering a better, I desire the author or authors will be pleased maturely to consider two points: first, as things now stand, how they will be able to find food and raiment for a hundred thousand useless mouths and backs; and secondly, there being a round million of creatures in human figure throughout this kingdom whose whole subsistence, put into a common stock, would leave them in debt two millions of pounds sterling, adding those who are beggars by profession to the bulk of farmers, cottagers, and laborers, with the wives and children who are beggars in effect, I desire those politicians who dislike my overture, and may perhaps be so bold as to attempt an answer, that they will first ask the parents of these mortals whether they would not at this day think it a great happiness to have been sold for food at a year old in the manner I prescribe, and thereby have avoided such a perpetual scene of misfortunes as they have since gone through by the oppression of landlords, the impossibility of paying rent without money or trade, the want of common sustenance, with neither house nor clothes to cover them from the inclemencies of the weather, and the most inevitable prospect of entailing the like of greater miseries upon their breed forever.

I profess in the sincerity of my heart that I have not the least personal   31 interest in endeavoring to promote this necessary work, having no other motive than the public good of my country, by advancing our trade, providing for infants, relieving the poor, and giving some pleasure to the rich. I have no children by which I can propose to get a single penny, the youngest being nine years old and my wife past childbearing.

## VOCABULARY

| | | |
|---|---|---|
| importuning (1) | censure (15) | parsimony (27) |
| sustenance (1) | gibbet (16) | overture (30) |
| prodigious (2) | encumbrance (17) | inclemencies (30) |
| proficiency (6) | digressed (18) | |
| collateral (12) | propagation (25) | |

## THE FACTS

1. What premise is "A Modest Proposal" based on? What is the chief assumption of its argument?
2. Reread paragraph 11. Why do the landlords have "the best title to the children"?
3. Swift's satire redefines children in economic terms. What does this say about his view of the society he lived in?
4. What does the satire imply about religious feelings in Ireland during Swift's time?
5. Given the state of affairs as the author describes them, is his argument logical? Explain.

## THE STRATEGIES

1. What is the effect of the word *modest* in the title?
2. Swift describes people with words like *breeder, dam, carcass, yearling child.* What effect do these words have?
3. Satire usually hints at the true state of things as it proposes its own alternatives. How does Swift hint at the true state of things? Give examples.
4. How would you characterize the tone of this piece?
5. Reread the final paragraph. What is its purpose?

## THE ISSUES

1. Do you consider satire an effective way to call attention to social ills? Why or why not?
2. Which paragraphs reveal Swift's real suggestions for improving the economic condition of the Irish? How do these paragraphs fit into the general scheme of Swift's essay?
3. What condition existing in our country today would make an excellent subject for the kind of satire used by Swift? What satirical proposal can you suggest?
4. How persuasive do you consider this essay? Would a more straightforward essay be more effective? Why or why not?
5. Is Swift's essay simply a literary masterpiece, to be studied within its context, or does it have a message for us today?

## SUGGESTIONS FOR WRITING

1. Infer from "A Modest Proposal" the state of life in Ireland during Swift's time. Make specific references to the article to justify your inferences.
2. Discuss the relationship implied in "A Modest Proposal" between society and the individual.

Mike Royko

## ———— • FAREWELL TO FITNESS • ————

*Mike Royko (b. 1932), a columnist for the Chicago* Sun Times, *was born in Chicago and attended Wright Junior College. In 1972 he won the Pulitzer prize for distinguished commentary. His books include* Up Against It *(1967) and* Boss: Richard J. Daley of Chicago *(1971).*

At least once a week, the office jock will stop me in the hall, bounce on the balls of his feet, plant his hands on his hips, flex his pectoral muscles and say: "How about it? I'll reserve a racquetball court. You can start working off some of that. . . ." And he'll jab a finger deep into my midsection.   1

It's been going on for months, but I've always had an excuse: "Next week, I've got a cold." "Next week, my back is sore." "Next week, I've got a pulled hamstring." "Next week, after the holidays."   2

But this is it. No more excuses. I made one New Year's resolution,   3 which is that I will tell him the truth. And the truth is that I don't want to play racquetball or handball or tennis, or jog, or pump Nautilus machines, or do push-ups or sit-ups or isometrics, or ride a stationary bicycle, or pull on a rowing machine, or hit a softball, or run up a flight of steps, or engage in any other form of exercise more strenuous than rolling out of bed.

This may be unpatriotic, and it is surely out of step with our muscle-flexing times, but I am renouncing the physical-fitness craze.     4

Oh, I was part of it. Maybe not as fanatically as some. But about 15     5 years ago, when I was 32, someone talked me into taking up handball, the most punishing court game there is.

From then on it was four or five times a week—up at 6 a.m., on the     6 handball court at 7, run, grunt, sweat, pant until 8:30, then in the office at 9. And I'd go around bouncing on the balls of my feet, flexing my pectoral muscles, poking friends in their soft guts, saying: "How about working some of that off? I'll reserve a court," and being obnoxious.

This went on for years. And for what? I'll tell you what it led to: I     7 stopped eating pork shanks, that's what. It was inevitable. When you join the physical-fitness craze, you have to stop eating wonderful things like pork shanks because they are full of cholesterol. And you have to give up eggs benedict, smoked liverwurst, Italian sausage, butter-pecan ice cream, Polish sausage, goose-liver paté, Sara Lee cheesecake, Twinkies, potato chips, salami-and-Swiss-cheese sand-wiches, double cheeseburgers with fries, Christian Brothers brandy with a Beck's chaser, and everything else that tastes good.

Instead, I ate broiled skinless chicken, broiled whitefish, grapefruit,     8 steamed broccoli, steamed spinach, unbuttered toast, yogurt, egg-plant, an apple for dessert and Perrier water to wash it down. Blahhhhh!

You do this for years, and what is your reward for panting and     9 sweating around a handball-racquetball court, and eating yogurt and the skinned flesh of a dead chicken?

—You can take your pulse and find that it is slow. So what? Am     10 I a clock?

—You buy pants with a narrower waistline. Big deal. The pants     11 don't cost less than the ones with a big waistline.

—You get to admire yourself in the bathroom mirror for about 10     12 seconds a day after taking a shower. It takes five seconds to look at your flat stomach from the front, and five more seconds to look at your flat stomach from the side. If you're a real creep of a narcissist, you can add another 10 seconds for looking at your small behind with a mirror.

That's it.                                                                                      13

Wait, I forgot something. You will live longer. I know that because   14
my doctor told me so every time I took a physical. My fitness-conscious doctor was very slender—especially the last time I saw him, which was at his wake.

But I still believe him. Running around a handball court or jogging   15
five miles a day, eating yogurt and guzzling Perrier will make you live longer.

So you live longer. Have you been in a typical nursing home lately?   16
Have you walked around the low-rent neighborhoods where the gee-zers try to survive on Social Security?

If you think living longer is rough now, wait until the 1990s, when   17
today's Me Generation potheads and coke sniffers begin taking care of the elderly (today's middle-aged joggers). It'll be: "Just take this little happy pill, gramps, and you'll wake up in heaven."

It's not worth giving up pork shanks and Sara Lee cheesecake.   18

Nor is it the way to age gracefully. Look around at all those middle-   19
aged jogging chicken-eaters. Half of them tape hairpieces to their heads. That's what comes from having a flat stomach. You start think-ing that you should also have hair. And after that comes a facelift. And that leads to jumping around a disco floor, pinching an airline steward-ess and other bizarre behavior.

I prefer to age gracefully, the way men did when I was a boy. The   20
only time a man over 40 ran was when the cops caught him burglariz-ing a warehouse. The idea of exercise was to walk to and from the corner tavern, mostly to. A well-rounded health-food diet included pork shanks, dumplings, Jim Beam and a beer chaser.

Anyone who was skinny was suspected of having TB or an ulcer. A   21
fine figure of a man was one who could look down and not see his knees, his feet or anything else in that vicinity. What do you have to look for, anyway? You ought to know if anything is missing.

A few years ago I was in Bavaria, and I went to a German beer hall.   22
It was a beautiful sight. Everybody was popping sausages and pork shanks and draining quart-sized steins of thick beer. Every so often they'd thump their magnificent bellies and smile happily at the boom-ing sound that they made.

Compare that to the finish line of a marathon, with all those ema-   23 ciated runners sprawled on the grass, tongues hanging out, wheezing, moaning, writhing, throwing up.

If that is the way to happiness and a long life, pass me the  24 cheesecake.

May you get a hernia, Arnold Schwarzenegger. And here's to you,  25 Orson Welles.

## VOCABULARY

| | | |
|---|---|---|
| pectoral (1) | paté (7) | bizarre (19) |
| hamstring (2) | narcissist (12) | emaciated (23) |
| isometrics (3) | wake (14) | |
| cholesterol (7) | geezers (16) | |

## THE FACTS

1. Why is this essay appealing? What literary characteristics enhance its charm?
2. What aspect of the thin craze seems to disgust Royko most? Do you share his attitude? Give reasons to support your answer.
3. What is the meaning of the question "Am I a clock?" (see paragraph 10)? What answer is expected from the reader?
4. What does Royko like about his past? Why? What is your reaction to his description?
5. How were thin people viewed when Royko was growing up? Do you think he is telling the truth or just testing you?

## THE STRATEGIES

1. How does the author establish intimacy with his reader?
2. How would you characterize the humor in paragraph 14? Is it offensive or not? Give reasons for your answer.
3. What is the implication of the two questions asked in paragraph 16?
4. What contrast is developed in paragraphs 22 and 23?
5. What is the meaning of the references to Arnold Schwarzenegger and Orson Welles?

## THE ISSUES

1. If you were a lover of aerobic exercise, how would you counter Royko's essay?
2. Do you believe the present emphasis on exercise is merely a phase we are

going through, like changing our style of clothing, or do you think exercise will become a natural and permanent part of preventive medicine, with most of the public participating? Give reasons for your answer.

3. What is your response to Royko's view, expressed in paragraph 16? Do you agree or disagree? Why or why not?

4. Is there some truth to Royko's cynical view of how the Me Generation will take care of the elderly in the 1990s? Explain your answer.

5. From your newspaper reading, does all scientific research support the fact that jogging and other aerobic exercises are always beneficial?

### SUGGESTIONS FOR WRITING

1. Write a five-hundred-word essay in which you create your own argument either for or against regular physical exercise. Include facts, experience, and expert testimony.

2. Write a persuasive argument to support the following thesis: "Strong evidence exists to support the notion that exercise can be detrimental to a person's health."

### Sylvia Rabiner

—————— • HOW THE SUPERWOMAN • ——————
MYTH PUTS WOMEN DOWN

*Sylvia Rabiner (b. 1939), freelance writer and teacher, was born in New York and educated at Hunter College and New York University. Her articles have appeared in* Mademoiselle, Working Mother, *and* The New Republic.

*Any reader of popular magazines is familiar with the superwoman of whom the author writes. She is extolled as having everything: brains, brawn, children, career, husband, respect, fame, and money. She moves from boardroom to kitchen to nursery with equal ease. But is she real? Or is she merely a fantasy created by advertisers trying to profit from the feminist movement? This essay takes a long, hard, and discontented look at her.*

Sunday afternoon. I'm making my usual desultory way through the Sunday Times when I come upon Linda Kanner. Ms. Kanner is prominently on display in The National Economic Survey, where she is referred to as a woman "in the vanguard of women taking routes to the executive suite that were formerly traveled by men." A quick runthrough of the article reveals that she is a marketing consultant with an M.B.A. degree from Harvard and a degree from The Simmons School of Social Work. She is married to a physician who has an M.B.A., too. Somewhere along the way she has managed to find time to produce two sons, and all this glory is hers at age 31.

Well, there goes my Sunday afternoon. After reading about Ms. Kanner, I will be in a muddy slump until nightfall at least. Every time I come across one of these proliferating articles about the successful woman of today, I am beset by feelings of self-contempt, loathing, and failure. Moreover, I hate Ms. Kanner, too, and if she were in my living room at the moment, I would set fire to her M.B.A. I am a six-year-old child once again, listening while my mother compares me to one of my flawless cousins.

Let me tell you, it's getting harder all the time to be a successful woman. In the old days, a woman was usually judged by the man she had ensnared. If he was a good provider and she kept the house clean, was a good cook, and raised a few decent children, she was well regarded by her peers and most likely by herself as well. Now the mainstream Women's Movement has thrust forth a new role model: the capitalist feminist. The career woman with a twist, she's not your old-time spinster who sacrificed marriage and motherhood for professional advancement, but a new, trickier model who has it all—a terrific career, a husband with a terrific career, and a couple of children as well.

We have Isabel Van Devanter Sawhill, successful economist, wife of New York University president John, and mother; or Letty Cottin Pogrebin, successful author, editor, activist, wife of lawyer Bert, and mother. A recent article in Newsweek investigated the life-styles of working couples with children. Their random democratic sampling included Kathy Cosgrove, vice-president of a public relations firm, wife of Mark, an advertising executive; Consuelo Marshall, Superior Court commissioner, wife of George, Columbia Pictures executive; Charlotte Curtis, associate editor of the New York Times, wife of William Hunt, neurosurgeon; and Patricia Schroeder, congresswoman, wife of lawyer Jim. Patricia, the article gushed, managed at 35 to "gracefully combine career, marriage, and family." The article was capped by a description of Carla Hills, Secretary of Housing and Urban Development, presidential possibility for the supreme court, wife of Roderick, chairman of the Securities and Exchange Commission, and mother of four. There was a photograph of Mrs. Hills presiding over her impeccable family at the dinner table. The article was swingy and upbeat. If they can do it, how about you? . . . Another afternoon ruined.

I turned for instruction to Letty Cottin Pogrebin, embodiment of the  5
success game. Letty is now an editor at *Ms.* and author of two books— "How to Make It in a Man's World" and "Getting Yours." Those titles reveal Letty's commitment to self-advancement. She doesn't hesitate to tell her readers that she is a woman to emulate. Letty was an executive at 21. She married a man whom she adores and has three "happy, well-behaved, bright, and spirited kids." I gleaned all this from Letty's first book. Since Letty was also gracefully combining career, marriage, and family, I thought I might get some pointers from her.

Letty Cottin arrived at Bernard Geis in 1960. After six months she  6
was promoted to the position of director of publicity, advertising, and subsidiary rights. She met her husband at a party and married him a couple of months later. She proceeded to have her first children (twins) as planned "early in marriage but after one full year as unencumbered newlyweds." Their next baby fit in perfectly after the three-year space between children which they deemed most desirable. She sums up: "It's better to be working than not working; it's better to be married than single; it's better to be a mommy as well as a Mrs. But it's best to be all four at once!"

Now, where does that leave me? My thumbnail autobiography fol-  7
lows: I am a child of my times, definitely more the rule than the exception to it. Raised in the '40s and '50s, the words *career* and *goal* were not spoken when I was in the room. I got the standard New York City College Jewish Parental Advice to Daughters. "Take a few education courses. Then if . . . God forbid . . . anything should happen, you can always take care of yourself." Nora Ephron said that she always knew she wanted to write (Dorothy Parker was her idol). When her less motivated college friends went off after graduation and got married, Nora went off and wrote. A few remarkable women like Nora and Letty undoubtedly knew at the age of 18 or younger what profession they wanted to pursue, but most of us at Hunter College, as I recall, were thundering off in a herd to stand under the marriage canopy. A bunch of simpletons, you say? Not so. We had produced the school plays, edited the school newspapers, put together the creative publications, belonged to Arista, and frequently had our names on the honor roll. What was happening, then? Well, let's call it econom-

ics. We were the children of immigrant or near immigrant parents. Hard-working, uneducated or self-educated, they didn't know how to guide their bright daughters. The depression had been deeply felt and was well remembered. Their watchword was security. Dorothy Parker was my idol, too, but to my parents, writing was not a job. With encouragement from neither parents nor teachers, most of us sought security in marriage or teaching.

Now, I married neither wisely nor well, which to judge by current   8 divorce statistics, proves me to be obstinately average. I worked to put my husband through graduate school, traveled where his career dictated, had two children as a matter of course and in the fall of 1969, although I had felt suffocated by my marriage, I protestingly and hysterically suffered its demise. My child support settlement would have done nicely to keep me in a cozy little tenement on Avenue C and 5th Street. I wanted to remain part of the middle class so I had to work: I had two children under the age of five and couldn't possibly pay a housekeeper. And I didn't really want a day-care center or babysitter with my boys eight or nine hours a day while I was at work. I wanted to be with them, so I found a job teaching night classes, and I tended home and sons during the day. A divorced woman with kids has a lot of things to think about. She is usually racing around trying to pay bills, do her job reasonably well, have some kind of social life, and be a loving mother too.

After 1969 I noticed that I never walked down a street, I ran. I ate   9 standing up. I screamed at my sons a lot. The astute reader will detect here the subtle differences between Letty's life and mine. I admit I was failing in being a successful woman, I didn't have a terrific career, and I didn't have a husband with a terrific career. Where were all those dynamic, achieving wonderful men that the women in the news stories found and married? Not in the playgrounds and supermarkets where I spent my days, not in the classrooms where I spent my evenings, and not in any of the other places I checked out with varying degrees of enthusiasm on the weekends when I had a babysitter. As for my long-range career goals—well, to tell the truth, I was grateful to have my teaching contract renewed each semester. My concession to getting ahead was to return to graduate school to earn my M.A. degree. I was able to indulge in this luxury only because the university at which I taught offered me free tuition. At $91 a credit, graduate school is hardly a priority of the divorced working mother. It appears that in addition to all my other errors in judgment, I've made the mistake of living in New York City during a recession. Last June I lost the teaching job that was supposed to be my security in case . . . God forbid . . . anything happened. After collecting unemployment insurance for five months, I am now typing, filing, and serving my boss his coffee four times a day.

Now, I ask you—do I need to read about the triumphant lives of    10 Helen Gurley Brown or Mary Wells Lawrence? Statistics currently indicate that there are 7.2 million families headed by women. Most of us are clerks, secretaries, waitresses, salesgirls, social workers, nurses, and—if lucky enough to still be working—teachers. For us, the superwoman who knits marriage, career, and motherhood into a satisfying life without dropping a stitch is as oppressive a role model as the airbrushed Bunny in the Playboy centerfold, or That Cosmopolitan Girl. While I struggle to keep my boat afloat in rough waters with prevailing high winds, I am not encouraged to row on by media hypes of ladies who run companies, serve elegant dinners for 30, play tennis with their husbands, earn advanced degrees, and wear a perfect size eight. They exist, I know, a privileged, talented minority, but to encourage me by lauding their achievements is like holding Sammy Davis, Jr., up as a model to a junior high school class in Bed.-Stuy. What does it really have to do with them?

Women are self-critical creatures. We can always find reasons to hate    11 ourselves. Single women believe they are failing if they don't have a loving, permanent relationship; working mothers are conflicted about leaving their children; divorced women experience guilt over the break-up of their marriages; housewives feel inadequate because they don't have careers; career women are wretched if they aren't advancing, and everyone is convinced she is too fat!

It is ironic that feminism, finally respectable, has been made to    12 backfire in this way. The superwoman image is a symbol of the corruption of feminist politics. It places emphasis on a false ideal of individual success. We are led to believe that if we play our cards right, we'll get to the top, but in the present system it won't work; there just isn't that much room up there. And in our class society, those at the top probably were more than halfway up to start with. The superwoman image ignores the reality of the average working woman or housewife. It elevates an elite of upper-class women executives. The media loves it because it is glamorous and false. In the end it threatens nothing in the system. In fact, all it does is give women like me a sense of inferiority.

## VOCABULARY

| | | |
|---|---|---|
| desultory (1) | embodiment (5) | astute (9) |
| vanguard (1) | emulate (5) | concession (9) |
| proliferating (2) | unencumbered (6) | indulge (9) |
| impeccable (4) | demise (8) | |

## THE FACTS

1. By what measure does Rabiner feel a woman was judged a success or failure in the old days? How is she judged today?
2. What new role model has the feminist movement thrust on women?
3. According to Rabiner, why did most of the women of her generation pursue goals of marriage and motherhood rather than try to develop careers?
4. Why does Rabiner think the superwoman myth is so unfair to the vast majority of working women?
5. What does Rabiner find is so ironic about the image of the superwoman?

## THE STRATEGIES

1. The article is tightly organized around a clear central idea. Where is this central idea stated?
2. What do paragraphs 4, 5, and 6 contribute to Rabiner's argument?
3. In paragraphs 7, 8, and 9 Rabiner gives a thumbnail sketch of her own life as a working mother. What implied relationship exists between these paragraphs and the three that preceded them?
4. This article is organized into four parts. What are they and what does each part do?
5. What specific details does Rabiner use in paragraph 11 to support her assertion that women are self-critical creatures?

## THE ISSUES

1. Do you believe the picture is as bad as Rabiner portrays it? Explain your answer.
2. Do you agree with Rabiner's statement that feminism is finally respectable? When, if ever, was it *not* respectable?
3. What advantages can you cite for combining a career with marriage and family? What disadvantages?
4. What advice would you give your daughter about seeking a profession such as medicine or law?

5. How would you feel about going back to the standards of success described in paragraph 6? Explain your answer.

### SUGGESTIONS FOR WRITING

1. Write an essay examining the pros and cons of the feminist movement, saying whether you think it has improved the lot of women, not affected it, or made it worse.
2. What is your idea of success in life? Write an essay specifying what you would have to do or become in order to consider yourself a success.

### James Michie

# • DOOLEY IS A TRAITOR •

*James Michie (b. 1927), British poet and translator, is director of The Bodley Head Ltd. publishers, London, and a former lecturer at London University. His works include* Possible Laughter *(1959),* The Odes of Horace *(trans. 1964), and* The Epigrams of Martial *(trans. 1973).*

*In this humorous poem a murderer makes a spirited defense against being compelled to fight a war not of his own making.*

"So then you won't fight?"
"Yes, your Honour," I said, "that's right."
"Now is it that you simply aren't willing,
Or have you a fundamental moral objection to killing?"
Says the judge, blowing his nose                                              5
And making his words stand to attention in long rows.
I stand to attention too, but with half a grin
(In my time I've done a good many in).
"No objection at all, sir," I said
"There's a deal of the world I'd rather see dead—                             10
Such as Johnny Stubbs or Fred Settle or my last landlord, Mr. Syme.
Give me a gun and your blessing, your Honour, and I'll be killing
      them all the time.
But my conscience says a clear no
To killing a crowd of gentlemen I don't know.                                 15
Why, I'd as soon think of killing a worshipful judge,
High-court, like yourself (against whom, God knows, I've got no
      grudge—

So far), as murder a heap of foreign folk.
If you've got no grudge, you've got no joke                                          20
To laugh at after."
                        Now the words never come flowing
Proper for me till I get the old pipe going.
And just as I was poking
Down baccy, the judge looks up sharp with "No smoking,                              25
Mr. Dooley. We're not fighting this war for fun.
And we want a clearer reason why you refuse to carry a gun.
This war is not a personal feud, it's a fight
Against wrong ideas on behalf of the Right.
Mr. Dooley, won't you help to destroy evil ideas?"                                   30
"Ah, your Honour, here's
The tragedy," I said. "I'm not a man of the mind.
I couldn't find it in my heart to be unkind
To an idea. I wouldn't know one if I saw one. I haven't one of my own.
So I'd best be leaving other people's alone."                                        35
"Indeed," he sneers at me, "this defence is
Curious for someone with convictions in two senses.
A criminal invokes conscience to his aid
To support an individual withdrawal from a communal crusade
Sanctioned by God, led by the Church, against a godless, churchless            40
    nation!"
I asked his Honour for a translation.
"You talk of conscience," he said. "What do you know of the
    Christian creed?"
"Nothing, sir, except what I can read,                                               45
That's the most you can hope for from us jail-birds.
I just open the Book here and there and look at the words.
And I find when the Lord himself misliked an evil notion
He turned it into a pig and drove it squealing over a cliff into
    the ocean,                                                                       50
And the loony ran away
And lived to think another day.
There was a clean job done and no blood shed!
Everybody happy and forty wicked thoughts drowned dead.
A neat and Christian murder. None of your mad slaughter                              55
Throwing away the brains with the blood and the baby with the
    bathwater.

Now I look at the war as a sportsman. It's a matter of choosing
The decentest way of losing.
Heads or tails, losers or winners,                                        60
We all lose, we're all damned sinners.
And I'd rather be with the poor cold people at the wall that's shot
Than the bloody guilty devils in the firing-line, in Hell and
    keeping hot."
"But what right, Dooley, what right," he cried,                          65
"Have you to say the Lord is on your side?"
"That's a dirty crooked question," back I roared.
"I said not the Lord was on my side, but I was on the side of
    the Lord."
Then he was up at me and shouting,                                       70
But by and by he calms: "Now we're not doubting
Your sincerity, Dooley, only your arguments,
Which don't make sense."
('Hullo,' I thought, 'that's the wrong way round.
I may be skylarking a bit, but my brainpan's sound.')                   75
Then biting his nail and sugaring his words sweet:
"Keep your head, Mr. Dooley. Religion is clearly not up your street.
But let me ask you as a plain patriotic fellow
Whether you'd stand there so smug and yellow
If the foe were attacking your own dear sister."                        80
"I'd knock their brains out, mister,
On the floor," I said. "There," he says kindly, "I knew you were no
    pacifist.
It's your straight duty as a man to enlist.
The enemy is at the door." You could have downed                        85
Me with a feather. "Where?" I gasp, looking round.
"Not this door," he says angered. "Don't play the clown.
But they're two thousand miles away planning to do us down.
Why, the news is full of the deeds of those murderers and rapers."
"Your Eminence," I said, "my father told me never to believe            90
    the papers
But to go by my eyes,
And at two thousand miles the poor things can't tell truth from lies."
His fearful spectacles glittered like the moon: "For the last time
    what right                                                          95
Has a man like you to refuse to fight?"

"More right," I said, "than you.
You've never murdered a man, so you don't know what it is I
    won't do
I've done it in good hot blood, so haven't I the right to make bold          100
To declare that I shan't do it in cold?"
Then the judge rises in a great rage
And writes DOOLEY IS A TRAITOR in black upon a page
And tells me I must die.
"What, me?" says I.                                                         105
"If you still won't fight."
"Well, yes, your Honour," I said, "that's right."


## THE FACTS

1. Dooley is an admitted murderer, yet he still refuses to fight. Why? What is his primary objection to war?
2. How many arguments does the judge use in trying to persuade Dooley? What are they and in what order are they used?
3. Are the judge's arguments logical? Do they appeal to reason and evidence, or to emotion?


## THE STRATEGIES

1. The poem is written in rhyming couplets. What does the rhyme contribute to the poem's tone?
2. How is Dooley characterized? What techniques are used?
3. How is the judge characterized? What techniques are used?


## THE ISSUES

1. Evaluate critically the saying "All's fair in love and war." Has this attitude prevailed throughout history? Is it morally valid?
2. What is the poet's point in reflecting a pacifist view through a criminal rather than, say, a minister or a respected private citizen?
3. Do you perceive a difference between killing a rapist attacking your sister and killing an unknown enemy during war? Explain your answer.


## SUGGESTIONS FOR WRITING

1. Analyze the logic in the exchanges between Dooley and the judge. Pinpoint the difference between their respective ways of thinking.

2. Assume that you are in Dooley's position and must argue against your participation in a war. Formulate an argument in your defense.

# ══ •• *ISSUE FOR CRITICAL* •• ══
# *THINKING*
## *The Existence of God*

The decision to believe or disbelieve in God is primal to every human being.    1
It affects all our aspirations, values, and attitudes. On one end of the belief–disbelief continuum is the believer, who sees a cosmic plan in everything and feels that God gives meaning to every human life. On the other end is the dogmatic disbeliever, the atheist, who refuses even to admit the possibility that a divine being exists and who ascribes mechanical causation to every phenomenon and event in the universe. Between these two stands the agnostic, whose creed is doubt. The agnostic sees nothing in the external world to encourage belief in a God, but is unwilling to subscribe to the dogmatic disbelief of the atheist.

The three essays that follow represent varying attitudes about the existence    2
of God. Clarence Darrow says that he is an agnostic, that he doubts, but he argues with an atheist's logic. The beginning of the universe, says Darrow, is unknown to us and never can be known. The soul is a myth. Where can it come from, and where does it go after the death of the body?

On the side of belief is Bishop Gerald Kennedy, who argues that God is a    3
necessity, not a choice. He uses familiar arguments to reinforce his faith: We cannot look at a sunset, at the marvels of nature, without gasping at the intelligence behind it. The implicit moral law that pervades the universe and all its creatures must have a source, says Kennedy, and that source is God.

In describing three aspects of nature, Annie Dillard simply suggests that    4
we look at the larger picture so that we can at least hurl the right question into the philosophical darkness.

All three writers are no doubt sincere, but it is unlikely that any of them    5
will sway any firm adherent of the opposite camp. If God exists, all of us will eventually find out the truth. If God does not exist, none of us will ever know it. That, in a nutshell, is the paradox underlying this ultimate controversy.

Gerald Kennedy

# ———————— • I BELIEVE IN GOD • ————————

*Gerald Kennedy (1907–1980) made news when he was elected bishop of the United Methodist Church at the early age of forty-one. He was nationally known for the eloquence of his sermons and as the author of many books, among them* I Believe *(1958), from which the following excerpt was taken.*

I never met an atheist. I have met a few people who claimed they    1
were atheists. But when we talked it over, it always seemed to me they were objecting to someone else's idea of God rather than insisting that there was no God. There is a story about a man at a convention of atheists who became annoyed because he thought the other delegates were backing down from their atheism. He made a speech against this compromising attitude and ended by saying, "I am a real atheist, thank God!"

## *We cannot live without God*

There are people who will insist they are atheists. For them the    2
words of Tolstoy* are to the point. He said that God is he without whom we cannot live. If some people insist there is no God and yet go on living, how shall we explain it? Let us say they go on living because they act as if they had not said it. Tolsoy was right. If a man really did not believe in God, he could not go on living as a man. We have to live as if we believe there is something in this universe that gives our life meaning. And when we face this basic fact in living as men, God has found us.

I do not see how anyone in a day like ours can doubt that God is    3
real. We have been trying to get along without him for some time, and look at the sorry shape our world is in. We have felt that we ourselves could solve all our problems. We have set ourselves up high and wor-shiped gods made by our own hands—gods named Science, Progress, Money, Power, Prosperity, Pleasure, Reason, Education, Success. For a while these gods seemed to take the place of the God of our fathers well enough. But they have proved to be false gods. Worshiping them is superstition and not religion. Sometimes they turn their worshipers

---

*Leo Tolstoy (1828–1910), Russian author of *War and Peace* (1866) and other novels.—Ed.

into monsters, madmen, or dull robots. If we follow them farther, we plunge into the abyss. God is he without whom men cannot live.

The point is that God is not a matter of choice; he is a matter of necessity. We cannot do as we please, cannot take him or leave him. When we go our own way, we go wrong. When we try to build a life or a society without coming to terms with him, we build on the sand. A civilization is always built on a religion. Once men begin to doubt their faith in God, they are on the way down. Experience shows that God is the reality on which life is built. Let a man doubt that he himself is real if he must, but never let him doubt that God is real.

It takes less effort to believe the most difficult doctrines of Christianity than it does to believe the universe began by chance. Men who accept that idea show more willingness to believe the unlikely than the most conservative of Christians. To put blind force in place of God calls for more blind credulity than a thinking man can muster. We turn from such nonsense to the opening words of Genesis, "In the beginning God . . ." The simple words shine in their own light and speak with conviction.

### How shall we describe God?

I cannot undertake a profound, philosophical, exhaustive discussion of the nature of God. I am simply writing as a witness, telling what I believe about God. To the lazy, indifferent Christian people of our time I would like to say: "Why don't you take the time to find out what Christianity says about God? You would be ashamed to know as little about how your car operates as you know about what the great Christian thinkers have said about God." Christian people should not be content to take their ideas about God from experts in other fields— who mean well but do not know what the Church has been teaching.

Surely God has left enough signs of his presence to show plain men some things about his nature. For one thing, God is an artist who has given us beauty on every side. Painters, poets, and musicians know we can live in a world that is beyond the world our minds can grasp. It is the world of beauty. Sometimes we need help to see and hear, but you and I have enough appreciation in us to respond to the wonder of God's presence in Nature.

We remember autumn woods, mountains at sunrise, sunsets by the sea, forest groves at noontime, valleys by moonlight. Every place and every season has its special beauty for us. We cannot be a part of it without feeling our hearts rise up in worship. Admiral Byrd* in his book *Alone* described his feelings as he watched a day die at the South Pole. He wrote: "The conviction came that that rhythm was too orderly, too harmonious, too perfect to be a product of blind chance—that, therefore, there must be purpose in the whole and that man was part of that whole and not an accidental offshoot."

### *God is mind*

We cannot look at the wonders of the natural world without seeing    9
a great Mind at work. Whether we think of the miracle of the atom or try vainly to understand what billions of light years mean, we cannot escape this conviction: the world reveals a Mind that makes our own minds count for something only as they can recognize this greater Mind. We do not create; we only discover. Most of our thinking is seeing and appreciating the marvels that prove a vast Intelligence at work. The glory of science is that it can reveal this truth. The weakness of science is its pride that assumes these marvels of nature are no longer God's because men have understood them. Nature's laws were not set up by men. They were operating a long time before man appeared.

The greatest scientists recognize how little their minds are beside    10
the Mind revealed in the world of nature. They speak of "thinking the thoughts of God after him." They speak of standing on the ocean shore with a few shells in their hands while the great mystery of God stretches out before them. They speak of the universe as being not a great machine but a great thought. Men are growing dissatisfied with the nineteenth-century theory that nature is a substitute for God. They are driven at last to confess that nature is clear proof of a mighty Mind at work. In the words of Shakespeare, man increasingly

> Finds tongues in trees, books in the running brooks,
> Sermons in stones.

### *God is righteousness*

Beside the laws of nature there is the moral law. This would seem to    11
say that God is the champion of the right. He has established an order

---

*Richard Evelyn Byrd (1888–1957), American polar explorer.—Ed.

that holds up good and tears down evil. Any man who is not an idiot knows that the sense of right and wrong is real.

The court of last appeal is the sense of "I ought." Against this we 12 cannot argue, nor can we explain it apart from God. Some people have tried to make conscience out as merely social custom, but for his conscience' sake many a man defies social custom and goes against public opinion. Some people would say conscience is only a matter of education and home training. But every man recognizes the demands of conscience and sees them much alike no matter what his home training or cultural background has been. Every man has a conscience, and every man's conscience tells him he should do what is right and not do what is wrong.

Where does conscience come from? It comes from the God who 13 created the world and men. We have a sense of owing something to the one who made us. Even when no man knows of our fault and there is no chance that any man will ever find it out, still we are guilty in our own eyes. We are guilty because we know there is Another who also knows all about it. How often a sensitive man who shrinks from an unpleasant duty says to himself: "If only God would leave me alone! If only he would let me be comfortable!" But God will not let us alone. When it comes to putting his demands upon us, God neither slumbers nor sleeps.

The moral law shows in the history of nations and societies. The 14 children of Israel discovered it early. In Deborah's song of joy over the fall of an oppressor she says:

> From heaven fought the stars,
>> from their courses they fought against Sisera.
>> —Judg. 5:20

She knew that the universe itself is against wrong. Israel's prophets saw this so clearly that God became real to them in every event of history. He was the deciding force in battles, in social life, in politics. We can be sure of one thing: no nation founded on injustice can long endure. When men or nations do wrong, they will be punished. In the words of the Old Testament:

> Righteousness exalteth a nation;
>> But sin is a reproach to any people.
>> —Prov. 14:34

None of this makes sense if we have a blind machine for a world. It makes sense only when we see that back of all our affairs there is God, who protects the good and destroys the evil.

### God is a person

The Christian truth that takes first place and includes all I have been saying is this: God is a person. This troubles a good many people. They suppose Christians are childish folks who think of God as if he were only a man. Such people prefer to talk about God as a "principle," or an "idea."    15

Let me make clear what I am *not* saying. I am not making God an old man with a long white beard. The Gospel of John saves us from that mistake by insisting that "God is a Spirit."    16

But I am saying God is a person. By this I mean he has will, mind, purpose, freedom, self-consciousness. The highest creation we know in the world is a person. The climax of the whole process of creation is a personality. Persons tower over nature and the animal kingdom. We must say God is at least a person, or we would be making him something of less value than a man. Principles and ideas do not mean as much as persons. God may be more than personal; but since we do not know anything that is more, we shall go as high as we know.    17

### God faces men

All of this becomes clear in the Christian experience of being found by God. When God finds a man, that man meets a Divine Person who faces him with personal claims. The man has to do much more than heed a moral principle or adjust his life to the law of right and wrong. He has to go through a personal experience. It is like David's experience when Nathan pointed to him and said, "Thou art the man." It is like Jesus' experience when he heard a voice from out the heavens say, "Thou art my beloved Son."    18

Until a man finds God and is found by God, he begins at no beginning and he works to no end. In other words, God is not one of the elective courses in the school of life; he is the one required course. Without this course we cannot pass our final examinations. There is nothing to take the place of God. Everything goes wrong without him. Nothing fits into place until a man has put God at the center of his thought and action.    19

Life has no purpose without God, and no generation should under-    20 stand that better than ours. For we have most of the things we thought we wanted. We can travel swiftly; we can send messages over vast distances; we can produce more comforts of life than our fathers could imagine. Today the poor can enjoy things which would have been luxuries to the ancient kings. Yet something has gone wrong. We are no longer thrilled to think we will soon produce still more goods, more comforts. All our trinkets have not brought us peace of mind. In spite of our heroic conquests over nature, the feeling haunts us that we spend our time on toys and trivialities, and we are moved by no mighty purposes.

Only God can keep our sense of values straight. William Temple,    21
late Archbishop of Canterbury, once said that the world is like a shop window where some prankster has gone in and changed all the price tags. On the expensive articles he has put the low prices, and on the cheap articles he has put the high prices. We pay more than we should for what does not satisfy us, and we neglect the things we really need. Isaiah's question is for us: "Wherefore do ye spend money for that which is not bread? and your labor for that which satisfieth not?" (Isa. 55:2). People who forget God also forget what is worth striving for.

Without God we cannot have human brotherhood, which is the    22
recognition of each man's worth. If you can rob men of their belief that they are the sons of God, you pave the way for tyranny. This is not just somebody's opinion. This is history. We have only one bulwark against the cheapening of human life. It is to maintain at all costs the Christian belief that God created each man and made him a son of God. Like coins, men have value, not in themselves, but because they bear the stamp of the King.

We can find freedom only in God. God's demands often seem se-    23
vere, yet they free us more than anything we know. When we try to get away from his demands, we end up as slaves to ourselves or to other men. But when we decide we must obey God rather than men, we feel we have been set free. It is like escaping from a prison. In God's service we find perfect freedom.

All the things that make us men have their roots in God. He is like    24
the air we breathe and the water we drink. Eddie Rickenbacker, the famous flyer, drifted around on a life raft for twenty-one days, hopelessly lost in the Pacific. A friend later asked him what lesson he had learned. "The biggest lesson I learned from that experience," he said, "was that if you have all the fresh water you want to drink and all the

food you want to eat, you ought never to complain about anything."
So it is with the man who has lost God. He comes to know that God is
man's one necessary possession.

I believe in God because he has faced me and laid his claims upon    25
me. Just as a man knows it when he falls in love, or knows it when he
thrills to the beauty of nature, so he knows it when God places his
demand upon him. Maybe he cannot be as precise as John Wesley*
and say that it happened about a quarter of nine. But he knows that
once he was lost and now he is found, and all his life is changed. The
experience makes him humble. He may have learned enough about
God to live by, but he now finds the ruling passion of his life is to learn
*more* about him.

That is the hope of every Christian. It is the worthiest goal for any    26
man's life. When we have gone far enough to be able to say, "I believe
in God," we stand at the beginning of life's great adventure.

## *VOCABULARY*

| | | |
|---|---|---|
| atheist (1) | harmonious (8) | trinkets (20) |
| superstition (3) | champion (11) | trivialities (20) |
| credulity (5) | oppressor (14) | bulwark (22) |
| exhaustive (6) | elective (19) | |

## *THE FACTS*

1. Why does Bishop Kennedy say there are no real atheists?
2. According to Kennedy, in what three areas does God reveal himself?
3. What Christian truth, according to Kennedy, precedes all other truths?
   Why does this truth trouble some people?
4. According to Kennedy, what happens when God finds a human being?
   What results if the human response is not there?
5. Why, according to Kennedy, is human brotherhood impossible without
   God?
6. What is the paradox of paragraph 23? Explain it in your own words.

## *THE STRATEGIES*

1. What characteristics of this essay indicate that it is not a theological treatise
   or a piece of careful research?

---

*John Wesley (1703–1791), British theologian and founder of Methodism—Ed.

2. How does paragraph 10 maintain syntactical coherence and balance?
3. What is the purpose of the quotation in paragraph 6? How effective is this technique?
4. What analogy is used in paragraph 19 to clarify what God is and what God is not? How effective do you find this analogy?
5. What similies do you find in paragraphs 22–24? Explain each one.
6. What is the purpose of the quotation "I believe in God" in the final paragraph?

### THE ISSUES

1. How do you think an atheist would answer Kennedy's claim that there are no atheists?
2. Of the three areas in which, according to Kennedy, God reveals himself, do you consider one more important than the others? If so, which one and why? If not, why not? Do a critical analysis of each of the three areas.
3. What is your philosophical response to the Christian idea that God is a person? Does the idea make God a demigod like many classical Greek heroes? Or does God transcend origin?
4. Do you agree with Kennedy's claim that without God, life has no purpose? Why or why not?
5. What is your reaction to someone who claims to have experienced God?

### SUGGESTIONS FOR WRITING

1. Choosing one of the following theses, support it with examples from nature:
   a. God's presence is clearly revealed in the wonders of nature.
   b. Many natural phenomena are incompatible with the idea of a benevolent creator.
2. In five hundred words, argue for or against the idea that conscience is merely a product of social custom or home training.
3. Write a five-hundred-word essay in which you support the idea that obedience to some law—human or divine—is the only guarantee of individual freedom.

### Clarence Darrow

## ——————— • WHY I AM AN AGNOSTIC • ———————

*Clarence Darrow (1857–1938), American trial lawyer, was born in Kinsman, Ohio, and practiced law first in Ohio and later in Chicago. Darrow bitterly opposed the death penalty and defended more than one hundred accused murderers, none of whom was ever executed. He wrote a novel entitled* Farmington *(1904) and an analysis of the treatment of criminals called* Crime: Its Cause and Treatment *(1922).*

An agnostic is a doubter. The word is generally applied to those who    1
doubt the verity of accepted religious creeds or faiths. Everyone is an agnostic as to the beliefs or creeds they do not accept. Catholics are agnostic to the Protestant creeds, and the Protestants are agnostic to the Catholic creed. Anyone who thinks is an agnostic about something, otherwise he must believe that he is possessed of all knowledge. And the proper place for such a person is in the madhouse or the home for the feeble-minded. In a popular way, in the western world, an agnostic is one who doubts or disbelieves the main tenets of the Christian faith.

I would say that belief in at least three tenets is necessary to the faith    2
of a Christian: a belief in God, a belief in immortality, and a belief in a supernatural book. Various Christian sects require much more, but it is difficult to imagine that one could be a Christian, under any intelligent meaning of the word, with less. Yet there are some people who claim to be Christians who do not accept the literal interpretation of all the Bible, and who give more credence to some portions of the book than to others.

I am an agnostic as to the question of God. I think that it is impos-    3
sible for the human mind to believe in an object or thing unless it can form a mental picture of such object or thing. Since man ceased to worship openly an anthropomorphic God and talked vaguely and not intelligently about some force in the universe, higher than man, that is responsible for the existence of man and the universe, he cannot be said to believe in God. One cannot believe in a force excepting as a force that pervades matter and is not an individual entity. To believe in a thing, an image of the thing must be stamped on the mind. If one is asked if he believes in such an animal as a camel, there immediately arises in his mind an image of the camel. This image has come from experience or knowledge of the animal gathered in some way or other. No such image comes, or can come, with the idea of a God who is described as a force.

Man has always speculated upon the origin of the universe, includ-    4
ing himself. I feel, with Herbert Spencer, that whether the universe

had an origin—and if it had—what the origin is will never be known by man. The Christian says that the universe could not make itself; that there must have been some higher power to call it into being. Christians have been obsessed for many years by Paley's argument that if a person passing through a desert should find a watch and examine its spring, its hands, its case and its crystal, he would at once be satisfied that some intelligent being capable of design had made the watch. No doubt this is true. No civilized man would question that someone made the watch. The reason he would not doubt it is because he is familiar with watches and other appliances made by man. The savage was once unfamiliar with a watch and would have had no idea upon the subject. There are plenty of crystals and rocks of natural formation that are as intricate as a watch, but even to intelligent man they carry no implication that some intelligent power must have made them. They carry no such implication because no one has any knowledge or experience of someone having made these natural objects which everywhere abound.

To say that God made the universe gives us no explanation of the beginnings of things. If we are told that God made the universe, the question imediately arises: Who made God? Did he always exist, or was there some power back of that? Did he create matter out of nothing, or is his existence coextensive with matter? The problem is still there. What is the origin of it all? If, on the other hand, one says that the universe was not made by God, that it always existed, he has the same difficulty to confront. To say that the universe was here last year, or millions of years ago, does not explain its origin. This is still a mystery. As to the question of the origin of things, man can only wonder and doubt and guess.

As to the existence of the soul, all people may either believe or disbelieve. Everyone knows the origin of the human being. They know that it came from a single cell in the body of the mother, and that the cell was one out of ten thousand in the mother's body. Before gestation the cell must have been fertilized by a spermatozoön from the body of the father. This was one out of perhaps a billion spermatozoa that was the capacity of the father. When the cell is fertilized a chemical process begins. The cell divides and multiplies and increases into millions of cells, and finally a child is born. Cells die and are born during the life of the individual until they finally drop apart, and this is death.

If there is a soul, what is it, and where did it come from, and where does it go? Can anyone who is guided by his reason possibly imagine a soul independent of a body, or the place of its residence, or the character of it, or anything concerning it? If man is justified in any belief or disbelief on any subject, he is warranted in the disbelief in a soul. Not one scrap of evidence exists to prove any such impossible thing.

Many Christians base the belief of a soul and God upon the Bible.    8
Strictly speaking, there is no such book. To make the Bible, sixty-six books are bound into one volume. These books are written by many people at different times, and no one knows the time or the identity of any author. Some of the books were written by several authors at various times. These books contain all sorts of contradictory concepts of life and morals and the origin of things. Between the first and the last nearly a thousand years intervened, a longer time than has passed since the discovery of America by Columbus.

When I was a boy the theologians used to assert that the proof of    9
the divine inspiration of the Bible rested on miracles and prophecies. But a miracle means a violation of a natural law, and there can be no proof imagined that could be sufficient to show the violation of a natural law; even though proof seemed to show violation, it would only show that we were not acquainted with all natural laws. One believes in the truthfulness of a man because of his long experience with the man, and because the man has always told a consistent story. But no man has told so consistent a story as nature.

If one should say that the sun did not rise, to use the ordinary    10
expression, on the day before, his hearer would not believe it, even though he had slept all day and knew that his informant was a man of the strictest veracity. He would not believe it because the story is inconsistent with the conduct of the sun in all the ages past.

Primitive and even civilized people have grown so accustomed to    11
believing in miracles that they often attribute the simplest manifestations of nature to agencies of which they know nothing. They do this when the belief is utterly inconsistent with knowledge and logic. They believe in old miracles and new ones. Preachers pray for rain, knowing full well that no such prayer was ever answered. When a politician is sick, they pray for God to cure him, and the politician almost invariably dies. The modern clergyman who prays for rain and for the health of the politician is no more intelligent in this matter than the primitive man who saw a separate miracle in the rising and setting of the sun,

in the birth of an individual, in the growth of a plant, in the stroke of
lightning, in the flood, in every manifestation of nature and life.

As to prophecies, intelligent writers gave them up long ago. In all    12
prophecies facts are made to suit the prophecy, or the prophecy was
made after the facts, or the events have no relation to the prophecy.
Weird and strange and unreasonable interpretations are used to explain simple statements, that a prophecy may be claimed.

Can any rational person believe that the Bible is anything but a    13
human document? We now know pretty well where the various books
came from, and about when they were written. We know that they
were written by human beings who had no knowledge of science, little
knowledge of life, and were influenced by the barbarous morality of
primitive times, and were grossly ignorant of most things that men
know today. For instance, Genesis says that God made the earth, and
he made the sun to light the day and the moon to light the night, and
in one clause disposes of the stars by saying that "he made the stars
also." This was plainly written by someone who had no conception of
the stars. Man, by the aid of his telescope, has looked out into the
heavens and found stars whose diameter is as great as the distance
between the earth and the sun. We know that the universe is filled
with stars and suns and planets and systems. Every new telescope
looking further into the heavens only discovers more and more worlds
and suns and systems in the endless reaches of space. The men who
wrote Genesis believed, of course, that this tiny speck of mud that we
call the earth was the center of the universe, the only world in space,
and made for man, who was the only being worth considering. These
men believed that the stars were only a little way above the earth, and
were set in the firmament for man to look at, and for nothing else.
Everyone today knows that this conception is not true.

The origin of the human race is not as blind a subject as it once was.    14
Let alone God creating Adam out of hand, from the dust of the earth,
does anyone believe that Eve was made from Adam's rib—that the
snake walked and spoke in the Garden of Eden—that he tempted Eve
to persuade Adam to eat an apple, and that it is on that account that
the whole human race was doomed to hell—that for four thousand
years there was no chance for any human to be saved, though none of
them had anything whatever to do with the temptation; and that finally men were saved only through God's son dying for them, and that
unless human beings believed this silly, impossible and wicked story

they were doomed to hell? Can anyone with intelligence really believe that a child born today should be doomed because the snake tempted Eve and Eve tempted Adam? To believe that is not God-worship, it is devil-worship.

Can anyone call this scheme of creation and damnation moral? It    15 defies every principle of morality, as man conceives morality. Can anyone believe today that the whole world was destroyed by flood, save only Noah and his family and a male and female of each species of animal that entered the Ark? There are almost a million species of insects alone. How did Noah match these up and make sure of getting male and female to reproduce life in the world after the flood had spent its force? And why should all the lower animals have been destroyed? Were they included in the sinning of man? This is a story which could not beguile a fairly bright child of five years of age today.

Do intelligent people believe that the various languages spoken by    16 man on earth came from the confusion of tongues at the Tower of Babel, some four thousand years ago? Human languages were dispersed all over the face of the earth long before that time. Evidences of civilizations are in existence now that were old long before the date that romancers fix for the building of the Tower, and even before the date claimed for the flood.

Do Christians believe that Joshua made the sun stand still, so that    17 the day could be lengthened, that a battle might be finished? What kind of person wrote that story, and what did he know about astronomy? It is perfectly plain that the author thought that the earth was the center of the universe and stood still in the heavens, and that the sun either went around it or was pulled across its path each day, and that the stopping of the sun would lengthen the day. We know now that had the sun stopped when Joshua commanded it, and had it stood still until now, it would not have lengthened the day. We know that the day is determined by the rotation of the earth upon its axis, and not by the movement of the sun. Everyone knows that this story simply is not true, and not many even pretend to believe the childish fable.

What of the tale of Balaam's ass speaking to him, probably in He-    18 brew? Is it true, or is it a fable? Many asses have spoken, and doubtless some in Hebrew, but they have not been that breed of asses. Is salvation to depend on a belief in a monstrosity like this?

Above all the rest, would any human being today believe that a child    19 was born without a father? Yet this story was not at all unreasonable

in the ancient world; at least three or four miraculous births are recorded in the Bible, including John the Baptist and Samson. Immaculate conceptions were common in the Roman world at the time and at
the place where Christianity really had its nativity. Women were taken
to the temples to be inoculated of God so that their sons might be
heroes, which meant, generally, wholesale butchers. Julius Caesar was
a miraculous conception—indeed, they were common all over the
world. How many miraculous-birth stories is a Christian now expected
to believe?

In the days of the formation of the Christian religion, disease meant    20
the possession of human beings by devils. Christ cured a sick man by
casting out the devils, who ran into the swine, and the swine ran into
the sea. Is there any question but what that was simply the attitude
and belief of a primitive people? Does anyone believe that sickness
means the possession of the body by devils, and that the devils must
be cast out of the human being that he may be cured? Does anyone
believe that a dead person can come to life? The miracles recorded in
the Bible are not the only instances of dead men coming to life. All
over the world one finds testimony of such miracles: miracles which
no person is expected to believe, unless it is his kind of a miracle. Still
at Lourdes today, and all over the present world, from New York to Los
Angeles and up and down the lands, people believe in miraculous
occurrences, and even in the return of the dead. Superstition is everywhere prevalent in the world. It has been so from the beginning, and
most likely will be so unto the end.

The reasons for agnosticism are abundant and compelling. Fantastic    21
and foolish and impossible consequences are freely claimed for the
belief in religion. All the civilization of any period is put down as a
result of religion. All the cruelty and error and ignorance of the period
has no relation to religion. The truth is that the origin of what we call
civilization is not due to religion but to skepticism. So long as men
accepted miracles without question, so long as they believed in original sin and the road to salvation, so long as they believed in a hell
where man would be kept for eternity on account of Eve, there was no
reason whatever for civilization: life was short, and eternity was long,
and the business of life was preparation for eternity.

When every event was a miracle, when there was no order or system    22
or law, there was no occasion for studying any subject, or being interested in anything excepting a religion which took care of the soul. As

man doubted the primitive conceptions about religion, and no longer accepted the literal, miraculous teachings of ancient books, he set himself to understand nature. We no longer cure disease by casting out devils. Since that time, men have studied the human body, have built hospitals and treated illness in a scientific way. Science is responsible for the building of railroads and bridges, of steamships, of telegraph lines, of cities, towns, large buildings and small, plumbing and sanitation, of the food supply, and the countless thousands of useful things that we now deem necessary to life. Without skepticism and doubt, none of these things could have been given to the world.

The fear of God is not the beginning of wisdom. The fear of God is    23
the death of wisdom. Skepticism and doubt lead to study and investigation, and investigation is the beginning of wisdom.

The modern world is the child of doubt and inquiry, as the ancient    24
world was the child of fear and faith.

## VOCABULARY

| | | |
|---|---|---|
| agnostic (1) | anthropomorphic (3) | beguile (15) |
| verity (1) | pervades (3) | skepticism (21) |
| tenets (1) | coextensive (5) | |
| credence (2) | veracity (10) | |

## THE FACTS

1. What three minimum beliefs of Christianity does Darrow cite?
2. Darrow rejects the idea of miracles. What is the basis of his argument? Is it logical?
3. Darrow writes: "As to prophecies, intelligent writers gave them up long ago." How would you characterize that statement? Is it logical? illogical? alogical?
4. According to Darrow, what has been religion's influence on civilization?
5. How does Darrow characterize the thinking behind religion? By implication, what kind of thinking does he suggest in its place?

## THE STRATEGIES

1. How does Darrow marshal his argument against religion? Does he rely heavily on a single technique?
2. What evidence does Darrow present to support his argument?
3. Is this argument primarily inductive or deductive?

4. Reread paragraph 10. What technique does Darrow use to present his argument?
5. In paragraph 18 Darrow writes: "Many asses have spoken, and doubtless some in Hebrew, but they have not been that breed of asses." How would you characterize his tone?
6. Darrow writes: "When I was a boy the theologians used to assert that the proof of the divine inspiration of the Bible rested on miracles and prophecies. But a miracle means a violation of a natural law, and there can be no proof imagined that could be sufficient to show the violation of a natural law; even though the proof seemed to show violation, it would only show that we were not acquainted with all natural laws." How would you characterize this reasoning?

### THE ISSUES

1. What is your reaction to the persona from whose point of view this essay is written? Analyze his tone, his voice, and his style.
2. How do you think Bishop Kennedy answers Darrow's claim that no one can prove the existence of God?
3. Which case do you find easier to argue logically—the case for the existence of God, or the case against the existence of God? Explain your answer.
4. How strong is your desire to know how the universe began? Why?
5. What is your definition of a miracle? Have you ever witnessed one? If so, describe it.

### SUGGESTIONS FOR WRITING

1. Write an essay in which you contrast Darrow's view of God with that of Bishop Kennedy.
2. State your own religious beliefs and attempt to justify them logically.

**Annie Dillard**

# • HEAVEN AND EARTH IN JEST •

*Annie Dillard (b. 1945) is a writer known best for her collections of essays and poems about nature and God. Born in Pittsburgh, Pennsylvania, she attended the Ellis School and Hollins College in Virginia, from which she received an M.A. in literature. In 1974 her* Tickets for a Prayer Wheel, *a book of poems, was published. But her best-known works are two collections of essays:* Teaching a Stone to Talk *(1982) and* Pilgrim at Tinker Creek *(1974), the latter for which she received the Pulitzer Prize and from which the following essay is excerpted.*

I used to have a cat, an old fighting tom, who would jump through     1
the open window by my bed in the middle of the night and land on
my chest. I'd half-awaken. He'd stick his skull under my nose and
purr, stinking of urine and blood. Some nights he kneaded my bare
chest with his front paws, powerfully, arching his back, as if sharpen-
ing his claws, or pummeling a mother for milk. And some mornings
I'd wake in daylight to find my body covered with paw prints in blood;
I looked as though I'd been painted with roses.

It was hot, so hot the mirror felt warm. I washed before the mirror     2
in a daze, my twisted summer sleep still hung about me like sea kelp.
What blood was this, and what roses? It could have been the rose of
union, the blood of murder, or the rose of beauty bare and the blood
of some unspeakable sacrifice or birth. The sign on my body could
have been an emblem or a stain, the keys to the kingdom or the mark
of Cain. I never knew. I never knew as I washed, and the blood
streaked, faded, and finally disappeared, whether I'd purified myself
or ruined the blood sign of the passover. We wake, if we ever wake at
all, to mystery, rumors of death, beauty, violence. . . . "Seem like
we're just set down here," a woman said to me recently, "and don't
nobody know why."

These are morning matters, pictures you dream as the final wave     3
heaves you up on the sand to the bright light and drying air. You
remember pressure, and a curved sleep you rested against, soft, like a
scallop in its shell. But the air hardens your skin; you stand; you leave
the lighted shore to explore some dim headland, and soon you're lost
in the leafy interior, intent, remembering nothing.

I still think of that old tomcat, mornings, when I wake. Things are     4
tamer now; I sleep with the window shut. The cat and our rites are
gone and my life is changed, but the memory remains of something
powerful playing over me. I wake expectant, hoping to see a new
thing. If I'm lucky I might be jogged awake by a strange birdcall. I

dress in a hurry, imagining the yard flapping with auks, or flamingos. This morning it was a wood duck, down at the creek. It flew away.

I live by a creek, Tinker Creek, in a valley in Virginia's Blue Ridge.    5 An anchorite's hermitage is called an anchor-hold; some anchor-holds were simple sheds clamped to the side of a church like a barnacle to a rock. I think of this house clamped to the side of Tinker Creek as an anchor-hold. It holds me at anchor to the rock bottom of the creek itself and it keeps me steadied in the current, as a sea anchor does, facing the stream of light pouring down. It's a good place to live; there's a lot to think about. The creeks—Tinker and Carvin's—are an active mystery, fresh every minute. Theirs is the mystery of the continuous creation and all that providence implies: the uncertainty of vision, the horror of the fixed, the dissolution of the present, the intricacy of beauty, the pressure of fecundity, the elusiveness of the free, and the flawed nature of perfection. The mountains—Tinker and Brushy, McAfee's Knob and Dead Man—are a passive mystery, the oldest of all. Theirs is the one simple mystery of creation from nothing, of matter itself, anything at all, the given. Mountains are giant, restful, absorbent. You can heave your spirit into a mountain and the mountain will keep it, folded, and not throw it back as some creeks will. The creeks are the world with all its stimulus and beauty; I live there. But the mountains are home.

The wood duck flew away. I caught only a glimpse of something like    6 a bright torpedo that blasted the leaves where it flew. Back at the house I ate a bowl of oatmeal; much later in the day came the long slant of light that means good walking.

If the day is fine, any walk will do; it all looks good. Water in partic-    7 ular looks its best, reflecting blue sky in the flat, and chopping it into graveled shallows and white chute and foam in the riffles. On a dark day, or a hazy one, everything's washed-out and lack-luster but the water. It carries its own lights. I set out for the railroad tracks, for the hill the flocks fly over, for the woods where the white mare lives. But I go to the water.

Today is one of those excellent January partly cloudies in which light    8 chooses an unexpected part of the landscape to trick out in gilt, and then shadow sweeps it away. You know you're alive. You take huge steps, trying to feel the planet's roundness arc between your feet.

Kazantzakis says that when he was young he had a canary and a globe. When he freed the canary, it would perch on the globe and sing. All his life, wandering the earth, he felt as though he had a canary on top of his mind, singing.

West of the house, Tinker Creek makes a sharp loop, so that the creek is both in back of the house, south of me, and also on the other side of the road, north of me. I like to go north. There the afternoon sun hits the creek just right, deepening the reflected blue and lighting the sides of trees on the banks. Steers from the pasture across the creek come down to drink; I always flush a rabbit or two there; I sit on a fallen trunk in the shade and watch the squirrels in the sun. There are two separated wooden fences suspended from cables that cross the creek just upstream from my tree-trunk bench. They keep the steers from escaping up or down the creek when they come to drink. Squirrels, the neighborhood children, and I use the downstream fence as a swaying bridge across the creek. But the steers are there today.  9

I sit on the downed tree and watch the black steers slip on the creek bottom. They are all bred beef: beef heart, beef hide, beef hocks. They're a human product like rayon. They're like a field of shoes. They have cast-iron shanks and tongues like foam insoles. You can't see through to their brains as you can with other animals; they have beef fat behind their eyes, beef stew.  10

I cross the fence six feet above the water, walking my hands down the rusty cable and tightroping my feet along the narrow edge of the planks. When I hit the other bank and terra firma,* some steers are bunched in a knot between me and the barbed-wire fence I want to cross. So I suddenly rush at them in an enthusiastic sprint, flailing my arms and hollering, "Lightning! Copperhead! Swedish meatballs!" They flee, still in a knot, stumbling across the flat pasture. I stand with the wind on my face.  11

When I slide under a barbed-wire fence, cross a field, and run over a sycamore trunk felled across the water, I'm on a little island shaped like a tear in the middle of Tinker Creek. On one side of the creek is a steep forested bank; the water is swift and deep on that side of the island. On the other side is the level field I walked through next to the steers' pasture; the water between the field and the island is shallow and sluggish. In summer's low water, flags and bulrushes grow along  12

---

*From Latin for "firm earth."—Ed.

a series of shallow pools cooled by the lazy current. Water striders patrol the surface film, crayfish hump along the silt bottom eating filth, frogs shout and glare, and shiners and small bream hide among roots from the sulky green heron's eye. I come to this island every month of the year. I walk around it, stopping and staring, or I straddle the sycamore log over the creek, curling my legs out of the water in winter, trying to read. Today I sit on dry grass at the end of the island by the slower side of the creek. I'm drawn to this spot. I come to it as to an oracle; I return to it as a man years later will seek out the battlefield where he lost a leg or an arm.

A couple of summers ago I was walking along the edge of the island 13 to see what I could see in the water, and mainly to scare frogs. Frogs have an inelegant way of taking off from invisible positions on the bank just ahead of your feet, in dire panic, emitting a froggy "Yike!" and splashing into the water. Incredibly, this amused me, and, incredibly, it amuses me still. As I walked along the grassy edge of the island, I got better and better at seeing frogs both in and out of the water. I learned to recognize, slowing down, the difference in texture of the light reflected from mudbank, water, grass, or frog. Frogs were flying all around me. At the end of the island I noticed a small green frog. He was exactly half in and half out of the water, looking like a schematic diagram of an amphibian, and he didn't jump.

He didn't jump; I crept closer. At last I knelt on the island's winter- 14 killed grass, lost, dumbstruck, staring at the frog in the creek just four feet away. He was a very small frog with wide, dull eyes. And just as I looked at him, he slowly crumpled and began to sag. The spirit vanished from his eyes as if snuffed. His skin emptied and drooped; his very skull seemed to collapse and settle like a kicked tent. He was shrinking before my eyes like a deflating football. I watched the taut, glistening skin on his shoulders ruck, and rumple, and fall. Soon, part of his skin, formless as a pricked balloon, lay in floating folds like bright scum on top of the water: it was a monstrous and terrifying thing. I gaped bewildered, appalled. An oval shadow hung in the water behind the drained frog; then the shadow glided away. The frog skin bag started to sink.

I had read about the giant water bug, but never seen one. "Giant 15 water bug" is really the name of the creature, which is an enormous, heavy-bodied, brown insect. It eats other insects, tadpoles, fish, and frogs. Its grasping forelegs are mighty and hooked inward. It seizes a victim with these legs, hugs it tight, and paralyzes it with enzymes injected during a vicious bite. That one bite is the only bite it ever takes. Through the puncture shoot the poisons that dissolve the victim's muscles and bones and organs—all but the skin—and through it the giant water bug sucks out the victim's body, reduced to a juice. This event is quite common in warm fresh water. The frog I saw was being sucked by a giant water bug. I had been kneeling on the island grass; when the unrecognizable flap of frog skin settled on the creek bottom, swaying, I stood up and brushed the knees of my pants. I couldn't catch my breath.

Of course, many carnivorous animals devour their prey alive. The usual method seems to be to subdue the victim by downing or grasping it so it can't flee, then eating it whole or in a series of bloody bites. Frogs eat everything whole, stuffing prey into their mouths with their thumbs. People have seen frogs with their wide jaws so full of live dragonflies they couldn't close them. Ants don't even have to catch their prey: in the spring they swarm over newly hatched, featherless birds in the nest and eat them tiny bite by bite. 16

That it's rough out there and chancy is no surprise. Every live thing is a survivor on a kind of extended emergency bivouac. But at the same time we are also created. In the Koran, Allah asks, "The heaven and the earth and all in between, thinkest thou I made them *in jest*?" It's a good question. What do we think of the created universe, spanning an unthinkable void with an unthinkable profusion of forms? Or what do we think of nothingness, those sickening reaches of time in either direction? If the giant water bug was not made in jest, was it then made in earnest? Pascal* uses a nice term to describe the notion of the creator's, once having called forth the universe, turning his back to it: *Deus Absconditus*.† Is this what we think happened? Was the sense of it there, and God absconded with it, ate it, like a wolf who disappears round the edge of the house with the Thanksgiving turkey? "God is subtle," Einstein said, "but not malicious." Again, Einstein said that "nature conceals her mystery by means of her essential grandeur, not by her cunning." It could be that God has not absconded but spread, as our vision and understanding of the universe have spread, to a 17

---

*Blaise Pascal (1623–1662) French philosopher and mathematician.—Ed.
†From Latin for "the vanished God."—Ed.

fabric of spirit and sense so grand and subtle, so powerful in a new way, that we can only feel blindly of its hem. In making the thick darkness a swaddling band for the sea, God "set bars and doors" and said, "Hitherto shalt thou come, but no further." But have we come even that far? Have we rowed out to the thick darkness, or are we all playing pinochle in the bottom of the boat?

Cruelty is a mystery, and the waste of pain. But if we describe a world to compass these things, a world that is a long, brute game, then we bump against another mystery: the inrush of power and light, the canary that sings on the skull. Unless all ages and races of men have been deluded by the same mass hypnotist (who?), there seems to be such a thing as beauty, a grace wholly gratuitous. About five years ago I saw a mockingbird make a straight vertical descent from the roof gutter of a four-story building. It was an act as careless and spontaneous as the curl of a stem or the kindling of a star. 18

The mockingbird took a single step into the air and dropped. His wings were still folded against his sides as though he were singing from a limb and not falling, accelerating thirty-two feet per second per second, through empty air. Just a breath before he would have been dashed to the ground, he unfurled his wings with exact, deliberate care, revealing the broad bars of white, spread his elegant, white-banded tail, and so floated onto the grass. I had just rounded a corner when his insouciant step caught my eye; there was no one else in sight. The fact of his free fall was like the old philosophical conundrum about the tree that falls in the forest. The answer must be, I think, that beauty and grace are performed whether or not we will or sense them. The least we can do is try to be there. 19

Another time I saw another wonder: sharks off the Atlantic coast of Florida. There is a way a wave rises above the ocean horizon, a triangular wedge against the sky. If you stand where the ocean breaks on a shallow beach, you see the raised water in a wave is translucent, shot with lights. One late afternoon at low tide a hundred big sharks passed the beach near the mouth of a tidal river in a feeding frenzy. As each green wave rose from the churning water, it illuminated within itself the six- or eight-foot-long bodies of twisting sharks. The sharks disappeared as each wave rolled toward me; then a new wave would swell above the horizon, containing in it, like scorpions in amber, sharks that roiled and heaved. The sight held awesome wonders: power and beauty, grace tangled in a rapture with violence. 20

We don't know what's going on here. If these tremendous events are   21
random combinations of matter run amok, the yield of millions of
monkeys at millions of typewriters, then what is it in us, hammered
out of those same typewriters, that they ignite? We don't know. Our
life is a faint tracing on the surface of mystery, like the idle, curved
tunnels of leaf miners on the face of a leaf. We must somehow take a
wider view, look at the whole landscape, really see it, and describe
what's going on here. Then we can at least wail the right question
into the swaddling band of darkness, or, if it comes to that, choir the
proper praise.

## VOCABULARY

| | | |
|---|---|---|
| emblem (2) | stimulus (5) | carnivorous (16) |
| headland (3) | chute (7) | bivouac (17) |
| anchorite (5) | riffles (7) | pinochle (17) |
| hermitage (5) | oracle (12) | gratuitous (18) |
| providence (5) | schematic (13) | insouciant (19) |
| dissolution (5) | amphibian (13) | translucent (20) |
| fecundity (5) | ruck (14) | illuminated (20) |
| elusiveness (5) | enzymes (15) | |

## THE FACTS

1. What was it that left an emblem of blood on Dillard?
2. What symbolic difference does Dillard make between the creeks and the mountains she sees from her dwelling in Tinker Creek?
3. What aspect of nature does each of the following encounters represent: the frog devoured by a giant waterbug, the mockingbird gracefully falling toward earth, and the sharks engaging in a feeding frenzy?
4. What is meant by Dillard's comment, "We don't know what's going on here"? (paragraph 21)
5. What suggestion is given as the first step to a better understanding of creation? What would this step achieve?

## THE STRATEGIES

1. Most critics praise Dillard for her poetic style. What makes her style poetic? Support your answer with specific examples.
2. In paragraph 2, why does Dillard choose to quote a woman whose language is ungrammatical?
3. What is the reference for "These" at the beginning of paragraph 3? Why does Dillard neglect to supply the reference?

4. What is the purpose of so many questions in paragraph 17? Does Dillard answer these questions?
5. What is the reference to "millions of monkeys at millions of typewriters" in paragraph 21?

### THE ISSUES

1. What is the most beautiful scene of nature you can conjure up from memory? Describe it in detail. Conversely, what is the ugliest? How did these scenes affect you intellectually or emotionally?
2. What is your explanation for so much seemingly random cruelty in nature?
3. What symbolic meaning would you attribute to the following phenomena in nature: an oak tree, a snowflake, an apple seed, rose thorns, a whirlpool, the moon, an ant hill, sea kelp? Add symbols of your own and interpret them.
4. Should our government get involved in preserving the ecobalance of nature so that industry will not destroy it? If so, in what circumstances?
5. Try to answer any of the questions posed in paragraph 17.

## CHAPTER WRITING ASSIGNMENTS

1. Write an essay discussing the idea that religion is a conditioned reflex.
2. Analyze the logic in "Dooley Is a Traitor."
3. Construct an argument for or against competitiveness in business.
4. Should a belief in creation be taught along with Darwin's theory of evolution? Write an essay arguing for or against this question.

### TERM PAPER SUGGESTIONS

Investigate the major arguments related to any one of the following subjects:

a. The influence of the church in our country today
b. Animal experimentation
c. Better care for the poor
d. Increased emphasis on physical fitness
e. Careful monitoring of the ecosystems on our planet
f. Equal rights for women (or another minority) in our country

# 10
# THE MEANING OF WORDS

## INTRODUCTION TO THE MEANING OF WORDS

In his autobiography, *Good-bye to All That*, the poet and translator Robert Graves tells of a professor who shunned conversational English in favor of words and phrases usually found only in books. Graves reports the following exchange between this pedantic soul and T. E. Lawrence, the well-known "Lawrence of Arabia," who was then in residence at Oxford. "Was it very caliginous in the metropolis?" asked the professor. "Somewhat caliginous, but not altogether inspissated," replied Lawrence tongue-in-cheek.

Its inanity aside, this exchange demonstrates not only the wonderful versatility of language that makes it possible for us to say simple things in complex ways, but also the awful ways in which some of us use words. Ideally, we should use words to make ourselves clear, to express ourselves honestly, to say truly what we feel and think. Unhappily, many of us use words to puff ourselves up, to hide our thoughts or feelings, and to impress our fellows. Language is essentially a plastic medium capable of being bent and twisted in the minds of speakers and writers. People will use words in their own peculiar ways, and not even the combined outrage of dictionaries and public opinion is likely to stop them.

Although we do not side with those purists who use no word until it has been branded with the imprimatur of a standard dictionary, we still think the abuse of words a pity. Language should be a living bridge between minds otherwise cut off from one another. It should not be a blur, a deliberate screen thrown up for reasons of vanity or deceit. You should write what you think and as well as you can think it. You should not write what you do not think, even if you write it well.

Something like the above is said or hinted at by several of the writers in this section. Richard Redfern, in "A Brief Lexicon of Jargon," humors us with a lesson in how to write wordily. George Orwell, in "Politics and the English Language," warns us that linguistic deceit is a close ally of political shenanigans. *Time* magazine's "Baffle-Gab Thesaurus" provides us with a chart that allows the creation of meaningless jaw-busting phrases. Later we get a semantic parable from S. I. Hayakawa, an amusing lesson in how culture affects words and beliefs from anthropologist Laura Bohannon, and a Chekhov play about language and courtship. The chapter ends with a discussion in the Issues section of sexist language, which voices feminists' opposition to the use of *he* and *him* as generalized pronouns.

We do not know whether using *he* or *him* when a *she* or *her* could very well be meant is as warping to gender fairness as some have alleged. In fact, much about the power and effect of language remains a mystery. These articles give us a glimpse into that mystery and can help conscientious writers build a bridge between their intentions and the expectations of their readers.

# ══ •• *ADVICE* •• ══

Richard K. Redfern

# ── • A BRIEF LEXICON OF JARGON • ──

## For Those Who Want to Speak and Write Verbosely and Vaguely

*Richard K. Redfern (b. 1916) was born in Dixon, Illinois. He received his Ph.D. in English from Cornell University in 1950. Between 1968 and 1981, he was professor of English at Clarion State College, Pennsylvania.*

*Through verbal irony this "Lexicon" tells how to avoid the vagueness and verbosity in much of today's bureaucratic language.*

## AREA

The first rule about using *area* is simple. Put *area* at the start or end 1
of hundreds of words and phrases. *The area of* is often useful when you
want to add three words to a sentence without changing its meaning.

| INSTEAD OF | SAY OR WRITE | |
|---|---|---|
| civil rights | the area of civil rights | 2 |
| in spelling and pronunciation | in the area of spelling and pronunciation | |
| problems, topics | problem areas, topic areas | |
| major subjects | major subject (*or* subject-matter) areas | |

Second, particularly in speech, use *area* as an all-purpose synonym. 3
After mentioning scheduled improvements in classrooms and offices,
use *area* for later references to this idea. A few minutes later, in talking
about the courses to be offered next term, use *area* to refer to required
courses, to electives, and to both required and elective courses. Soon
you can keep three or four *area's* going and thus keep your audience
alert by making them guess which idea you have in mind, especially if
you insert, once or twice, a neatly disguised geographical use of *area*:
"Graduate student response in this area is gratifying."

## FIELD

If the temptation arises to say "clothing executive," "publishing ex- 4
ecutive," and the like, resist it firmly. Say and write "executive in the

clothing field" and "executive in the field of publishing." Note that *the field of* (like *the area of*) qualifies as jargon because it adds length, usually without changing the meaning, as in "from the field of literature as a whole" and "prowess in the field of academic achievement" (which is five words longer than the "academic prowess" of plain English). With practice you can combine *field* with *area*, *level*, and other standbys:

> In the sportswear field, this is one area which is growing. (Translation from context: Ski sweaters are selling well.)
>
> [The magazine is] a valuable source of continuing information for educators at all levels and for everyone concerned with this field. (Plain English: The magazine is a valuable source of information for anyone interested in education.)

A master of jargon can produce a sentence so vague that it can be   5
dropped into dozens of other articles and books: "At what levels is coverage of the field important?" Even in context (a scholarly book about the teaching of English), it is hard to attach meaning to *that* sentence!

## IN TERMS OF

A sure sign of the ability to speak and write jargon is the redundant   6
use of *in terms of*. If you are a beginner, use the phrase instead of prepositions such as *in* ("The faculty has been divided in terms of opinions and attitudes") and *of* ("We think in terms of elementary, secondary, and higher education"). Then move on to sentences in which you waste more than two words:

| INSTEAD OF | SAY OR WRITE |   7 |
|---|---|---|
| The Campus School expects to have three fourth grades. | In terms of the future, the Campus School expects to have three fourth grades. (5 extra words) | |
| I'm glad that we got the response we wanted. | I'm glad that there was a response to that in terms of what we wanted. (6 extra words) | |

Emulate the masters of jargon. They have the courage to abandon   8
the effort to shape a thought clearly:

A field trip should be defined in terms of where you are.

They are trying to get underway some small and large construction in terms of unemployment.

When we think in terms of muscles, we don't always think in terms of eyes.

## LEVEL

Although *level* should be well known through overuse, the unobser- 9 vant young instructors may need a review of some of its uses, especially if they are anxious to speak and write *on the level of* jargon. (Note the redundancy of the italicized words.)

| INSTEAD OF | SAY OR WRITE | 10 |
|---|---|---|
| She teaches fifth grade. | She teaches on the fifth grade level. (3 extra words) | |
| Readers will find more than one meaning. | It can be read on more than one level of meaning. (4 extra words) | |
| My students | The writers on my level of concern (5 extra words) | |

## LONG FORMS

When the shorter of two similar forms is adequate, choose the 11 longer; e.g., say *analyzation* for *analysis*), *orientate* (for *orient*), *origination* (for *origin*), *summarization* (for *summary*). Besides using an unnecessary syllable or two, the long form can make your audience peevish when they know the word has not won acceptance or, at least, uneasy ("Is that a new word that I ought to know?"). If someone asks why you use *notate* instead of *note* (as in "Please notate in the space below your preference . . ."), fabricate an elaborate distinction. Not having a dictionary in his pocket, your questioner will be too polite to argue.

With practice, you will have the confidence to enter unfamiliar ter- 12 ritory. Instead of the standard forms (*confirm, interpret, penalty, register,* and *scrutiny*), try *confirmate, interpretate, penalization, registrate,* and *scrutinization.*

You have little chance of making a name for yourself as a user of 13 jargon unless you sprinkle your speech and writing with vogue words and phrases, both the older fashions (e.g., *aspect, background, field, level, situation*) and the new (e.g., *escalate, relate to, share with; facility, involvement; limited, minimal*). An old favorite adds the aroma of the cliché, while a newly fashionable term proves that you are up-to-date. Another advantage of vogue words is that some of them are euphemisms. By using *limited,* for example, you show your disdain for the directness and clarity of *small,* as in "a man with a limited education" and "a limited enrollment in a very large room."

Unfortunately, some vogue expressions are shorter than standard English, but their obscurity does much to offset the defect of brevity. 14

| INSTEAD OF | SAY OR WRITE | 15 |
|---|---|---|
| The children live in a camp and have both classes and recreation outdoors. | The children live in a camp-type situation. | |
| She reads, writes, and speaks German and has had four years of Latin. | She has a good foreign-language background. | |
| Many hospitals now let a man stay with his wife during labor. | The trend is to let the father have more involvement. | |

A final word to novices: dozens of words and phrases have been 16 omitted from this brief lexicon, but try to spot them yourselves. Practice steadily, always keeping in mind that the fundamentals of jargon—verbosity and needless vagueness—are best adorned by pretentiousness. Soon, if you feel the impulse to say, for example, that an office has one secretary and some part-time help, you will write "Administrative clerical aids implement the organizational function." Eventually you can produce sentences which mean anything or possibly nothing: "We should leave this aspect of the definition relatively operational" or "This condition is similar in regard to other instances also."

### *VOCABULARY*

| | | |
|---|---|---|
| lexicon (title) | peevish (11) | novices (16) |
| jargon (title) | escalate (13) | verbosity (16) |
| redundant (6) | cliché (13) | |
| emulate (8) | euphemism (13) | |

# ══ •• *DISCUSSION* •• ══

### George Orwell

# • POLITICS AND THE •
# ENGLISH LANGUAGE

*George Orwell (1903–1950) was the pseudonym of Eric Arthur Blair. Born in India and educated at Eton, he served with the imperial police in Burma and fought on the republican side in the Spanish civil war. Orwell published two influential novels,* Animal Farm *(1945) and* Nineteen Eighty-four *(1949). He is widely admired for the crisp, lucid prose style of his essays.*

*The Sapir-Whorf hypothesis (see "Of Girls and Chicks," in the upcoming Issues section, pages 791–98) argues that the way we use language influences the way we think. Orwell hews closely to this theory in the essay that follows. Thought corrupts language, he writes, and language corrupts thought. Write in an inane and stilted style and we will end up thinking in an inane and stilted way. If Orwell is right—if style is the underpinning of thinking—then we are all obliged to be at our best every time we pick up a pen or open our mouths.*

Most people who bother with the matter at all would admit that the    1
English language is in a bad way, but it is generally assumed that we cannot by conscious action do anything about it. Our civilization is decadent and our language—so the argument runs—must inevitably share in the general collapse. It follows that any struggle against the abuse of language is a sentimental archaism, like preferring candles to electric light or hansom cabs to aeroplanes. Underneath this lies the half-conscious belief that language is a natural growth and not an instrument which we shape for our own purposes.

Now, it is clear that the decline of a language must ultimately have    2
political and economic causes: it is not due simply to the bad influence of this or that individual writer. But an effect can become a cause, reinforcing the original cause and producing the same effect in an intensified form, and so on indefinitely. A man may take to drink because he feels himself to be a failure, and then fail all the more completely because he drinks. It is rather the same thing that is happening to the English language. It becomes ugly and inaccurate because our thoughts are foolish, but the slovenliness of our language

makes it easier for us to have foolish thoughts. The point is that the process is reversible. Modern English, especially written English, is full of bad habits which spread by imitation and which can be avoided if one is willing to take the necessary trouble. If one gets rid of these habits one can think more clearly, and to think clearly is a necessary first step towards political regeneration: so that the fight against bad English is not frivolous and is not the exclusive concern of professional writers. I will come back to this presently, and I hope that by that time the meaning of what I have said here will have become clearer. Meanwhile, here are five specimens of the English language as it is now habitually written.

These five passages have not been picked out because they are es-   3 pecially bad—I could have quoted far worse if I had chosen—but because they illustrate various of the mental vices from which we now suffer. They are a little below the average, but are fairly representative samples. I number them so that I can refer back to them when necessary:

(1)  I am not, indeed, sure whether it is not true to say that the Milton who once seemed not unlike a seventeenth-century Shelley had not become, out of an experience ever more bitter in each year, more alien [sic] to the founder of that Jesuit sect which nothing could induce him to tolerate.

Professor Harold Laski<br>(Essay in Freedom of Expression)

(2)  Above all, we cannot play ducks and drakes with a native battery of idioms which prescribes such egregious collocations of vocables as the Basic put up with for tolerate or put at a loss for bewilder.

Professor Lancelot Hogben (Interglossa)

(3)  On the one side we have the free personality: by definition it is not neurotic, for it has neither conflict nor dream. Its desires, such as they are, are transparent, for they are just what institutional approval keeps in the forefront of consciousness; another institutional pattern would alter their number and intensity; there is little in them that is natural, irreducible, or culturally dangerous. But on the other side, the social bond itself is nothing but the mutual reflection of these self-secure integrities. Recall the definition of love. Is not this the very picture of a small academic? Where is there a place in this hall of mirrors for either personality or fraternity?

Essay on psychology in Politics (New York)

(4) All the "best people" from the gentlemen's clubs, and all the frantic fascist captains, united in common hatred of Socialism and bestial horror of the rising tide of the mass revolutionary movement, have turned to acts of provocation, to foul incendiarism, to medieval legends of poisoned wells, to legalize their own destruction of proletarian organizations, and rouse the agitated petty-bourgeoisie to chauvinistic fervour on behalf of the fight against the revolutionary way out of the crisis.

*Communist pamphlet*

(5) If a new spirit *is* to be infused into this old country, there is one thorny and contentious reform which must be tackled, and that is the humanization and galvanization of the B.B.C. Timidity here will bespeak canker and atrophy of the soul. The heart of Britain may be sound and of strong beat, for instance, but the British lion's roar at present is like that of Bottom in Shakespeare's *Midsummer Night's Dream*—as gentle as any sucking dove. A virile new Britain cannot continue indefinitely to be traduced in the eyes or rather ears, of the world by the effete languors of Langham Place, brazenly masquerading as "standard English." When the Voice of Britain is heard at nine o'clock, better far and infinitely less ludicrous to hear aitches honestly dropped than the present priggish, inflated, inhibited, school-ma'amish arch braying of blameless bashful mewing maidens!

*Letter in* Tribune

Each of these passages has faults of its own, but, quite apart from   4
avoidable ugliness, two qualities are common to all of them. The first is staleness of imagery; the other is lack of precision. The writer either has a meaning and cannot express it, or he inadvertently says something else, or he is almost indifferent as to whether his words mean anything or not. This mixture of vagueness and sheer incompetence is the most marked characteristic of modern English prose, and especially of any kind of political writing. As soon as certain topics are raised, the concrete melts into the abstract and no one seems able to think of turns of speech that are not hackneyed: prose consists less and less of *words* chosen for the sake of their meaning, and more and more of *phrases* tacked together like the sections of a prefabricated henhouse. I list below, with notes and examples, various of the tricks by means of which the work of prose-construction is habitually dodged:

*Dying metaphors.* A newly invented metaphor assists thought by   5
evoking a visual image, while on the other hand a metaphor which is

technically "dead" (e.g., *iron resolution*) has in effect reverted to being an ordinary word and can generally be used without loss of vividness. But in between these two classes there is a huge dump of worn-out metaphors which have lost all evocative power and are merely used because they save people the trouble of inventing phrases for themselves. Examples are: *Ring the changes on, take up the cudgels for, toe the line, ride roughshod over, stand shoulder to shoulder with, play into the hands of, no axe to grind, grist to the mill, fishing in troubled waters, on the order of the day, Achilles' heel, swan song, hotbed.* Many of these are used without knowledge of their meaning (what is a "rift," for instance?), and incompatible metaphors are frequently mixed, a sure sign that the writer is not interested in what he is saying. Some metaphors now current have been twisted out of their original meaning without those who use them even being aware of the fact. For example, *toe the line* is sometimes written *tow the line*. Another example is *the hammer and the anvil*, now always used with the implication that the anvil gets the worst of it. In real life it is always the anvil that breaks the hammer, never the other way about: a writer who stopped to think what he was saying would be aware of this, and would avoid perverting the original phrase.

*Operators* or *verbal false limbs.* These save the trouble of picking out appropriate verbs and nouns, and at the same time pad each sentence with extra syllables which give it an appearance of symmetry. Characteristic phrases are *render inoperative, militate against, make contact with, be subjected to, give rise to, give grounds for, have the effect of, play a leading part (role) in, making itself felt, take effect, exhibit a tendency to, serve the purpose of,* etc., etc. The keynote is the elimination of simple verbs. Instead of being a single word, such as *break, stop, spoil, mend, kill,* a verb becomes a *phrase,* made up of a noun or adjective tacked on to some general-purpose verb such as *prove, serve, form, play, render.* In addition, the passive voice is wherever possible used in preference to the active, and noun constructions are used instead of gerunds (*by examination of* instead of *by examining*). The range of verbs is further cut down by means of the *-ize* and *de-* formations, and the banal statements are given in appearance of profundity by means of the *not un-* formation. Simple conjunctions and prepositions are replaced by such phrases as *with respect to, having regard to, the fact that, by dint of, in view of, in the interests of, on the hypothesis that;* and the ends of sentences are saved from anticlimax by such resounding common-places as *greatly to be desired, cannot be left out of account, a development to be expected in the near future, deserving of serious consideration, brought to a satisfactory conclusion,* and so on and so forth.

*Pretentious diction.* Words like *phenomenon, element, individual* (as noun), *objective, categorical, effective, virtual, basic, primary, promote, constitute, exhibit, exploit, utilize, eliminate, liquidate,* are used to dress up simple statements and give an air of scientific impartiality to biased judgments. Adjectives like *epoch-making, epic, historic, unforgettable, triumphant, age-old, inevitable, inexorable, veritable,* are used to dignify the sordid processes of international politics, while writing that aims at glorifying war usually takes on an archaic colour, its characteristic words being: *realm, throne, chariot, mailed fist, trident, sword, shield, buckler, banner, jackboot, clarion.* Foreign words and expressions such as *cul de sac, ancien régime, deus ex machina, mutatis mutandis, status quo, gleichshaltung, weltanschauung,* are used to give an air of culture and elegance. Except for the useful abbreviations *i.e., e.g.,* and *etc.,* there is no real need for any of the hundreds of foreign phrases now current in English. Bad writers, and especially scientific, political and sociological writers, are nearly always haunted by the notion that Latin or Greek words are grander than Saxon ones, and unnecessary words like *expedite, ameliorate, predict, extraneous, deracinated, clandestine, subaqueous* and hundreds of others constantly gain ground from their Anglo-Saxon opposite numbers.* The jargon peculiar to Marxist writing (*hyena, hangman, cannibal, petty bourgeois, these gentry, lacquey, flunkey, mad dog, White Guard,* etc.) consists largely of words and phrases translated from Russian, German or French; but the normal way of coining a new word is to use a Latin or Greek root with the appropriate affix and, where necessary, the size formation. It is often easier to make up words of this kind (*deregionalize, impermissible, extramarital, nonfragmentary,* and so forth) than to think up the English words that will cover one's meaning. The result, in general, is an increase in slovenliness and vagueness.

7

---

*An interesting illustration of this is the way in which the English flower names which were in use till very recently are being ousted by Greek ones, *snapdragon* becoming *antirrhinum, forget-me-not* becoming *myosotis,* etc. It is hard to see any practical reason for this change of fashion: it is probably due to an instinctive turning-away from the more homely word and a vague feeling that the Greek word is scientific.

*Meaningless words.* In certain kinds of writing, particularly in art    8
criticism and literary criticism, it is normal to come across long passages which are almost completely lacking in meaning.* Words like
*romantic, plastic, values, human, dead, sentimental, natural, vitality,* as
used in art criticism, are strictly meaningless, in the sense that they
not only do not point to any discoverable object, but are hardly ever
expected to do so by the reader. When one critic writes, "The outstanding feature of Mr. X's work is its living quality," while another writes,
"The immediately striking thing about Mr. X's work is its peculiar
deadness," the reader accepts this as a simple difference of opinion. If
words like *black* and *white* were involved, instead of the jargon words
*dead* and *living,* he would see at once that language was being used in
an improper way. Many political words are similarly abused. The word
*Fascism* has now no meaning except in so far as it signifies "something
not desirable." The words *democracy, socialism, freedom, patriotic, realistic, justice,* have each of them several different meanings which cannot
be reconciled with one another. In the case of a word like *democracy,*
not only is there no agreed definition, but the attempt to make one is
resisted from all sides. It is almost universally felt that when we call a
country democratic we are praising it: consequently the defenders of
every kind of régime claim that it is a democracy, and fear that they
might have to stop using the word if it were tied down to any one
meaning. Words of this kind are often used in a consciously dishonest
way. That is, the person who uses them has his own private definition,
but allows his hearer to think he means something quite different.
Statements like *Marshal Pétain was a true patriot, The Soviet Press is the
freest in the world, The Catholic Church is opposed to persecution,* are almost
always made with intent to deceive. Other words used in variable
meanings, in most cases more or less dishonestly, are: *class, totalitarian,
science, progressive, reactionary, bourgeois, equality.*

Now that I have made this catalogue of swindles and perversions,    9
let me give another example of the kind of writing that they lead to.
This time it must of its nature be an imaginary one. I am going to

---

*Example: "Comfort's catholicity of perception and image, strangely Whitmanesque in range, almost the exact
opposite in aesthetic compulsion, continues to evoke that trembling atmospheric accumulative hinting at a
cruel, an inexorably serene timelessness. . . . Wrey Gardiner scores by aiming at simple bull's-eyes with
precision. Only they are not so simple, and through this contented sadness runs more than the surface bitter-
sweet of resignation." (*Poetry Quarterly.*)

translate a passage of good English into modern English of the worst sort. Here is a well-known verse from *Ecclesiastes:*

> I returned and saw under the sun, that the race is not to the swift, nor the battle to the strong, neither yet bread to the wise, nor yet riches to men of understanding, nor yet favor to men of skill; but time and chance happeneth to them all.

Here it is in modern English:                                                    10

> Objective consideration of contemporary phenomena compels the con-clusion that success or failure in competitive activities exhibits no tend-ency to be commensurate with innate capacity, but that a considerable element of the unpredictable must invariably be taken into account.

This is a parody, but not a very gross one. Exhibit (3), above, for    11 instance, contains several patches of the same kind of English. It will be seen that I have not made a full translation. The beginning and ending of the sentence follow the original meaning fairly closely, but in the middle the concrete illustrations—race, battle, bread—dissolve into the vague phrase "success or failure in competitive activities." This had to be so, because no modern writer of the kind I am discussing—no one capable of using phrases like "objective consideration of contemporary phenomena"—would ever tabulate his thoughts in that precise and detailed way. The whole tendency of modern prose is away from concreteness. Now analyse these two sentences a little more closely. The first contains forty-nine words but only sixty syllables, and all its words are those of everyday life. The second contains thirty-eight words of ninety syllables: eighteen of its words are from Latin roots, and one from Greek. The first sentence contains six vivid im-ages, and only one phrase ("time and chance") that could be called vague. The second contains not a single fresh, arresting phrase, and in spite of its ninety syllables it gives only a shortened version of the meaning contained in the first. Yet without a doubt it is the second kind of sentence that is gaining ground in modern English. I do not want to exaggerate. This kind of writing is not yet universal, and outcrops of simplicity will occur here and there in the worst-written page. Still, if you or I were told to write a few lines on the uncertainty of human fortunes, we should probably come much nearer to my imaginary sentence than to the one from *Ecclesiastes.*

As I have tried to show, modern writing at its worst does not consist    12
in picking out words for the sake of their meaning and inventing images in order to make the meaning clearer. It consists in gumming
together long strips of words which have already been set in order by
someone else, and making the results presentable by sheer humbug.
The attraction of this way of writing is that it is easy. It is easier—even
quicker, once you have the habit—to say *In my opinion it is not an
unjustifiable assumption that* than to say *I think*. If you use ready-made
phrases, you not only don't have to hunt for words; you also don't have
to bother with the rhythms of your sentences, since these phrases are
generally so arranged as to be more or less euphonious. When you are
composing in a hurry—when you are dictating to a stenographer, for
instance, or making a public speech—it is natural to fall into a pretentious, Latinized style. Tags like *a consideration which we should do well to
bear in mind* or *a conclusion to which all of us would readily assent* will save
many a sentence from coming down with a bump. By using stale
metaphors, similes and idioms, you save much mental effort, at the
cost of leaving your meaning vague, not only for your reader but for
yourself. This is the significance of mixed metaphors. The sole aim of
a metaphor is to call up a visual image. When these images clash—as
in *The Fascist octopus has sung its swan song, the jackboot is thrown into the
melting pot*—it can be taken as certain that the writer is not seeing a
mental image of the objects he is naming; in other words he is not
really thinking. Look again at the examples I gave at the beginning of
this essay. Professor Laski (1) uses five negatives in fifty-three words.
One of these is superfluous, making nonsense of the whole passage,
and in addition there is the slip *alien* for *akin*, making further nonsense,
and several avoidable pieces of clumsiness which increase the general
vagueness. Professor Hogben (2) plays ducks and drakes with a battery which is able to write prescriptions, and, while disapproving of
the every day phrase *put up with*, is unwilling to look *egregious* up in
the dictionary and see what it means; (3), if one takes an uncharitable
attitude towards it, is simply meaningless: probably one could work
out its intended meaning by reading the whole of the article in which
it occurs. In (4), the writer knows more or less what he wants to say,
but an accumulation of stale phrases chokes him like tea leaves blocking a sink. In (5), words and meaning have almost parted company.
People who write in this manner usually have a general emotional
meaning—they dislike one thing and want to express solidarity with

another—but they are not interested in the detail of what they are saying. A scrupulous writer, in every sentence that he writes, will ask himself at least four questions, thus: What am I trying to say? What words will express it? What image or idiom will make it clearer? Is this image fresh enough to have an effect? And he will probably ask himself two more: Could I put it more shortly? Have I said anything that is avoidably ugly? But you are not obliged to go to all this trouble. You can shirk it by simply throwing your mind open and letting the ready-made phrases come crowding in. They will construct your sentences for you—even think your thoughts for you, to a certain extent—and at need they will perform the important service of partially concealing your meaning even from yourself. It is at this point that the special connection between politics and the debasement of language becomes clear.

In our time it is broadly true that political writing is bad writing.  13 Where it is not true, it will generally be found that the writer is some kind of rebel, expressing his private opinions and not a "party line." Orthodoxy, of whatever colour, seems to demand a lifeless, imitative style. The political dialects to be found in pamphlets, leading articles, manifestos, White Papers and the speeches of under-secretaries do, of course, vary from party to party, but they are all alike in that one almost never finds in them a fresh, vivid, home-made turn of speech. When one watches some tired hack on the platform mechanically repeating the familiar phrase—*bestial atrocities, iron heel, bloodstained tyranny, free peoples of the world, stand shoulder to shoulder*—one often has a curious feeling that one is not watching a live human being but some kind of dummy: a feeling which suddenly becomes stronger at moments when the light catches the speaker's spectacles and turns them into blank discs which seem to have no eyes behind them. And this is not altogether fanciful. A speaker who uses that kind of phraseology has gone some distance towards turning himself into a machine. The appropriate noises are coming out of his larynx, but his brain is not involved as it would be if he were choosing his words for himself. If the speech he is making is one that he is accustomed to make over and over again, he may be almost unconscious of what he is saying, as one is when one utters the responses in church. And this reduced state of consciousness, if not indispensable, is at any rate favorable to political conformity.

In our time, political speech and writing are largely the defence of  14 the indefensible. Things like the continuance of British rule in India, the Russian purges and deportations, the dropping of the atom bombs on Japan, can indeed be defended, but only by arguments which are too brutal for most people to face, and which do not square with the professed aims of political parties. Thus political language has to consist largely of euphemism, question-begging and sheer cloudy vagueness. Defenceless villages are bombarded from the air, the inhabitants driven out into the countryside, the cattle machine-gunned, the huts set on fire with incendiary bullets: this is called *pacification*. Missions of peasants are robbed of their farms and set trudging along the roads with no more than they can carry: this is called *transfer of population* or *rectification of frontiers*. People are imprisoned for years without trial, or shot in the back of the neck or sent to die of scurvy in Arctic lumber camps: this is called *elimination of unreliable elements*. Such phraseology is needed if one wants to name things without calling up mental pictures of them. Consider for instance some comfortable English professor defending Russian totalitarianism. He cannot say outright, "I believe in killing off your opponents when you can get good results by doing so." Probably, therefore, he will say something like this:

> While freely conceding that the Soviet régime exhibits certain features which the humanitarian may be inclined to deplore, we must, I think, agree that a certain curtailment of the right to political opposition is an unavoidable concomitant of transitional periods, and that the rigours which the Russian people have been called upon to undergo have been amply justified in the sphere of concrete achievement.

The inflated style is itself a kind of euphemism. A mass of Latin 15 words falls upon the facts like soft snow, blurring the outlines and covering up all the details. The great enemy of clear language is insincerity. When there is a gap between one's real and one's declared aims, one turns as it were instinctively to long words and exhausted idioms, like a cuttlefish squirting out ink. In our age there is no such thing as "keeping out of politics." All issues are political issues, and politics itself is a mass of lies, evasions, folly, hatred and schizophrenia. When the general atmosphere is bad, language must suffer. I should expect to find—this is a guess which I have not sufficient knowledge to verify—that the German, Russian and Italian languages have all deteriorated in the last ten or fifteen years, as a result of dictatorship.

But if thought corrupts language, language can also corrupt 16 thought. A bad usage can spread by tradition and imitation, even among people who should and do know better. The debased language that I have been discussing is in some ways very convenient. Phrases like *a not unjustifiable assumption, leaves much to be desired, would serve no good purpose, a consideration which we should do well to bear in mind*, are a continuous temptation, a packet of aspirins always at one's elbow. Look back through this essay, and for certain you will find that I have again and again committed the very faults I am protesting against. By this morning's post I have received a pamphlet dealing with conditions in Germany. The author tells me that he "felt impelled" to write it. I open it at random, and here is almost the first sentence that I see: "[The Allies] have an opportunity not only of achieving a radical trans- formation of Germany's social and political structure in such a way as to avoid a nationalistic reaction in Germany itself, but at the same time of laying the foundations of a co-operative and unified Europe." You see, he "feels impelled" to write—feels, presumably, that he has some- thing new to say—and yet his words, like cavalry horses answering the bugle, group themselves automatically into the familiar dreary pattern. This invasion of one's mind by ready-made phrases *(lay the foundations, achieve a radical transformation)* can only be prevented if one is constantly on guard against them, and every such phrase anaesthe- tizes a portion of one's brain.

I said earlier that the decadence of our language is probably curable.    17 Those who deny this would argue, if they produced an argument at all, that language merely reflects existing social conditions, and that we cannot influence its development by any direct tinkering with words and constructions. So far as the general tone or spirit of a lan- guage goes, this may be true, but it is not true in detail. Silly words and expressions have often disappeared, not through any evolutionary process but owing to the conscious action of a minority. Two recent examples were *explore every avenue* and *leave no stone unturned*, which were killed by the jeers of a few journalists. There is a long list of flyblown metaphors which could similarly be got rid of if enough people would interest themselves in the job; and it should also be possible to laugh the *not un-* formation out of existence,* to reduce the amount of Latin and Greek in the average sentence, to drive out for- eign phrases and strayed scientific words, and, in general, to make pretentiousness unfashionable. But all these are minor points. The

---

*One can cure oneself of the *not un-* formation by memorizing this sentence: *A not unblack dog was chasing a not unsmall rabbit across a not ungreen field*.

defence of the English language implies more than this, and perhaps it is best to start by saying what it does *not* imply.

To begin with it has nothing to do with archaism, with the salvaging [18] of obsolete words and turns of speech, or with the setting up of a "standard English" which must never be departed from. On the contrary, it is especially concerned with the scrapping of every word or idiom which has outworn its usefulness. It has nothing to do with correct grammar and syntax, which are of no importance so long as one makes one's meaning clear, or with the avoidance of Americanisms, or with having what is called a "good prose style." On the other hand it is not concerned with fake simplicity and the attempt to make written English colloquial. Nor does it even imply in every case preferring the Saxon word to the Latin one, though it does imply using the fewest and shortest words that will cover one's meaning. What is above all needed is to let the meaning choose the word, and not the other way about. In prose, the worst thing one can do with words is to surrender to them. When you think of a concrete object, you think wordlessly, and then, if you want to describe the thing you have been visualizing you probably hunt about till you find the exact words that seem to fit it. When you think of something abstract you are more inclined to use words from the start, and unless you make a conscious effort to prevent it, the existing dialect will come rushing in and do the job for you, at the expense of blurring or even changing your meaning. Probably it is better to put off using words as long as possible and get one's meaning as clear as one can through pictures or sensations. Afterwards one can choose—not simply *accept*—the phrase that will best cover the meaning, and then switch round and decide what impression one's words are likely to make on another person. This last effort of the mind cuts out all stale or mixed images, all prefabricated phrases, needless repetitions, and humbug and vagueness generally. But one can often be in doubt about the effect of a word or a phrase, and one needs rules that one can rely on when instinct fails. I think the following rules will cover most cases:

(i)   Never use a metaphor, simile or other figure of speech which you are used to seeing in print.
(ii)  Never use a long word where a short one will do.
(iii) If it is possible to cut a word out, always cut it out.
(iv)  Never use the passive when you can use the active.

(v) Never use a foreign phrase, a scientific word or a jargon word if you can think of an everyday English equivalent.

(vi) Break any of these rules sooner than say anything outright barbarous.

These rules sound elementary, and so they are, but they demand a deep change of attitude in anyone who has grown used to writing in the style now fashionable. One could keep all of them and still write bad English, but one could not write the kind of stuff that I quoted in those five specimens at the beginning of this article.

I have not here been considering the literary use of language, but merely language as an instrument for expressing and not for concealing or preventing thought. Stuart Chase and others have come near to claiming that all abstract words are meaningless, and have used this as a pretext for advocating a kind of political quietism. Since you don't know what Fascism is, how can you struggle against Fascism? One need not swallow such absurdities as this, but one ought to recognize that the present political chaos is connected with the decay of language, and that one can probably bring about some improvement by starting at the verbal end. If you simplify your English, you are freed from the worst follies of orthodoxy. You cannot speak any of the necessary dialects, and when you make a stupid remark its stupidity will be obvious, even to yourself. Political language—and with variations this is true of all political parties, from Conservatives to Anarchists—is designed to make lies sound truthful and murder respectable, and to give an appearance of solidity to pure wind. One cannot change this all in a moment, but one can at least change one's own habits, and from time to time one can even, if one jeers loudly enough, send some worn-out and useless phrase—some *jackboot, Achilles' heel, hotbed, melting pot, acid test, veritable inferno* or other lump of verbal refuse—into the dustbin where it belongs.

19

### VOCABULARY

| | | |
|---|---|---|
| decadent (1) | banal (6) | scrupulous (12) |
| archaism (1) | pretentious (7) | debasement (12) |
| slovenliness (2) | régime (8) | orthodoxy (13) |
| inadvertently (4) | parody (11) | incendiary (14) |
| hackneyed (4) | arresting (11) | schizophrenia (15) |
| metaphor (5) | euphonious (12) | barbarous (18) |
| evocative (5) | solidarity (12) | quietism (19) |

## THE FACTS

1. What connections does the author make between politics and the English language?
2. In paragraph 3 Orwell cites five examples of bad writing. What two faults do all of the examples share?
3. According to Orwell, why do people use hackneyed imagery and prefabricated phrases?
4. Many people use big words and foreign words in order to sound educated. According to Orwell, what do such words do to a piece of writing?
5. What does Orwell mean when he states that "in our time, political speech and writing are largely the defence of the indefensible" (paragraph 14)?
6. Orwell states, "In prose, the worst thing one can do with words is to surrender to them" (paragraph 18). Give an example of what he means by this surrender.
7. Enumerate Orwell's six elementary rules concerning the choice of words and phrases. If, in your opinion, he has left out any major rule, state it.

## THE STRATEGIES

1. Orwell deplores the use of stale imagery. Identify at least three examples of fresh imagery that he uses in his essay.
2. What is the analogy used for illustration in paragraph 2?
3. Which paragraph is developed first by contrast and then by example?
4. In what paragraph does Orwell make the transition from poor writing in general to poor writing in politics? Point out the transitional sentence.
5. What is the topic sentence for paragraph 14? What is the chief method of development?

## THE ISSUES

1. Do you agree with Orwell's opening statement that English is in a bad way? If you had to, how would you refute this statement?
2. What are some examples from the current political, psychological, or economic scene that indicate how foolish thought is reflected in writing?
3. What are some dead metaphors used by most students nowadays? What fresher image or metaphor do you suggest for each?
4. What kind of writing do you consider truly bad? Bring an example to class for discussion.
5. What rules, if followed, would most improve your own writing? List at least three. How do you plan to implement these rules?

## SUGGESTIONS FOR WRITING

1. Using Orwell's standards, analyze a speech or article written by some contemporary politician.

2. In a brief essay, attack or defend Orwell's statement: "If you simplify your English, you are freed from the worst follies of orthodoxy."

──────── • **BAFFLE-GAB THESAURUS** • ────────

*We present the "Baffle-Gab Thesaurus" as an amusing exercise. Try writing a letter of complaint to an imaginary firm, flooding your content with combinations from this obfuscating word guide. (And if you do not already know the word* obfuscating, *look it up.) (From* Time, *September 13, 1968.)*

As any self-respecting bureaucrat knows, it is bad form indeed to use a single, simple word when six or seven obfuscating ones will do.

But where is the Washington phrasemaker to turn if he is hung up for what Horace called "words a foot and a half long"? Simple. Just glance at the Systematic Buzz Phrase Projector, or s.b.p.p.

The s.b.p.p. has aptly obscure origins but appears to come from a Royal Canadian Air Force listing of fuzzy phrases. It was popularized in Washington by Philip Broughton, a U.S. Public Health Service official, who circulated it among civil servants and businessmen. A sort of mini-thesaurus of baffle-gab, it consists of a three-column list of 30 overused but appropriately portentous words. Whenever a GS-14 or deputy assistant secretary needs an opaque phrase, he need only think of a three digit number—any one will do as well as the next—and select the corresponding "buzz words" from the three columns. For example, 257 produces "systematized logistical projection," which has the ring of absolute authority and means absolutely nothing.

Broughton's baffle-gab guide:

| A | B | C |
|---|---|---|
| 0) Integrated | Management | Options |
| 1) Total | Organizational | Flexibility |
| 2) Systematized | Monitored | Capability |
| 3) Parallel | Reciprocal | Mobility |
| 4) Functional | Digital | Programming |
| 5) Responsive | Logistical | Concept |
| 6) Optional | Transitional | Time-Phase |
| 7) Synchronized | Incremental | Projection |
| 8) Compatible | Third-Generation | Hardware |
| 9) Balanced | Policy | Contingency |

# •• *EXAMPLES* ••

### S. I. Hayakawa

## • A SEMANTIC PARABLE •

*Samuel Ichiye Hayakawa (b. 1906) was born in Vancouver, British Columbia, and educated at the University of Wisconsin. He was president of San Francisco State College from 1969 to 1973 and U.S. senator from California from 1977 to 1983. His works include* Language in Action *(1939) and* Language in Thought and Action *(1978), from which this selection was taken.*

*In "A Semantic Parable," S. I. Hayakawa suggests what can result when people feel labeled. He also shows how words inevitably lead to quarrels when each of the arguing parties bestows a different meaning on the words used in the argument.*

Once upon a time (said the Professor), there were two small communities, spiritually as well as geographically situated at a considerable distance from each other. They had, however, these problems in common: Both were hard hit by a depression, so that in each of the towns there were about one hundred heads of families unemployed. There was, to be sure, enough food, enough clothing, enough materials for housing, but these families simply did not have money to procure these necessities.

The city fathers of A-town, the first community, were substantial businessmen, moderately well educated, good to their families, kindhearted, and sound-thinking. The unemployed tried hard, as unemployed people usually do, to find jobs; but the situation did not improve. The city fathers, as well as the unemployed themselves, had been brought up to believe that there is always enough work for everyone, if you only look for it hard enough. Comforting themselves with this doctrine, the city fathers could have shrugged their shoulders and turned their backs on the problem, except for the fact that they were genuinely kindhearted men. They could not bear to see the unemployed men and their wives and children starving. In order to prevent starvation, they felt that they had to provide these people with some means of sustenance. Their principles told them, nevertheless, that if people were given something for nothing, it would demoralize their character. Naturally this made the city fathers even more unhappy, because they were faced with the horrible choice of (1) letting the unemployed starve, or (2) destroying their moral character.

The solution they finally hit upon, after much debate and soul- 3 searching, was this. They decided to give the unemployed families relief of fifty dollars a month; but to insure against the pauperization of the recipients, they decided that this fifty dollars was to be accompanied by a moral lesson, to wit: the obtaining of the assistance would be made so difficult, humiliating, and disagreeable that there would be no temptation for anyone to go through the process unless it was absolutely necessary; the moral disapproval of the community would be turned upon the recipients of the money at all times in such a way that they would try hard to get off relief and regain their self-respect. Some even proposed that people on relief be denied the vote, so that the moral lesson would be more deeply impressed upon them. Others suggested that their names be published at regular intervals in the newspapers, so that there would be a strong incentive to get off relief. The city fathers had enough faith in the goodness of human nature to expect that the recipients would be grateful, since they were getting something for nothing, something which they hadn't worked for.

When the plan was put into operation, however, the recipients of 4 the relief checks proved to be an ungrateful, ugly bunch. They seemed to resent the cross-examinations and inspections at the hands of the relief investigators, who, they said, took advantage of a man's misery to snoop into every detail of his private life. In spite of uplifting editorials in A-town *Tribune* telling how grateful they ought to be, the recipients of the relief refused to learn any moral lessons, declaring that they were "just as good as anybody else." When, for example, they permitted themselves the rare luxury of a movie or an evening of bingo, their neighbors looked at them sourly as if to say, "I work hard and pay my taxes just in order to support loafers like you in idleness and pleasure." This attitude, which was fairly characteristic of those members of the community who still had jobs, further embittered the relief recipients, so that they showed even less gratitude as time went on and were constantly on the lookout for insults, real or imaginary, from people who might think that they weren't as good as anybody else. A number of them took to moping all day long, to thinking that their lives had been failures; one or two even committed suicide. Others found that it was hard to look their wives and kiddies in the face, because they had failed to provide. They all found it difficult to maintain their club and fraternal relationships, since they could not help feeling that their fellow citizens despised them for having sunk so low. Their wives, too, were unhappy for the same reasons and gave up their social activities. Children whose parents were on relief felt inferior to classmates whose parents were not public charges. Some of these children developed inferiority complexes which affected not only their grades at school, but their careers after graduation. Several other relief recipients, finally, felt they could stand their loss of self-respect no longer and decided, after many efforts to gain honest jobs, to earn money by their own efforts, even if they had to go in for robbery. They did so and were caught and sent to the state penitentiary.

The depression, therefore, hit A-town very hard. The relief policy 5 had averted starvation, no doubt, but suicide, personal quarrels, unhappy homes, the weakening of social organizations, the maladjustment of children, and, finally, crime, had resulted. The town was divided in two, the "haves" and the "have-nots," so that there was class hatred. People shook their heads sadly and declared that it all went to prove over again what they had known from the beginning, that giving people something for nothing inevitably demoralizes their character. The citizens of A-town gloomily waited for prosperity to return, with less and less hope as time went on.

The story of the other community, B-ville, was entirely different. 6 B-ville was a relatively isolated town, too far out of the way to be reached by Rotary Club speakers and university extension services. One of the aldermen, however, who was something of an economist, explained to his fellow aldermen that unemployment, like sickness, accident, fire, tornado, or death, hits unexpectedly in modern society, irrespective of the victim's merits or deserts. He went on to say that B-ville's homes, parks, streets, industries, and everything else B-ville was proud of had been built in part by the work of these same people who were now unemployed. He then proposed to apply a principle of insurance: If the work these unemployed people had previously done for the community could be regarded as a form of premium paid to the community against a time of misfortune, payments now made to them to prevent their starvation could be regarded as insurance claims. He therefore proposed that all men of good repute who had worked in the community in whatever line of useful endeavor, whether as machinists, clerks, or bank managers, be regarded as citizen policyholders, having claims against the city in the case of unemployment for fifty dollars a month until such time as they might again be employed. Naturally, he had to talk very slowly and patiently, since the idea was entirely new to his fellow aldermen. But he described his plan as a "straight business proposition," and finally they were persuaded. They worked out the details as to the conditions under which citizens should be regarded as policyholders in the city's social insurance plan to everybody's satisfaction and decided to give checks for fifty dollars a month to the heads of each of B-ville's indigent families.

B-ville's claim adjusters, whose duty it was to investigate the claims of the citizen policyholders, had a much better time than A-town's relief investigators. While the latter had been resentfully regarded as snoopers, the former, having no moral lesson to teach but simply a business transaction to carry out, treated their clients with business-like courtesy and got the same amount of information as the relief investigators with considerably less difficulty. There were no hard feelings. It further happened, fortunately, that news of B-ville's plans reached a liberal newspaper editor in the big city at the other end of the state. This writer described the plan in a leading feature story headed "B-VILLE LOOKS AHEAD. Great Adventure in Social Pioneering Launched by Upper Valley Community." As a result of this publicity, inquiries about the plan began to come to the city hall even before the first checks were mailed out. This led, naturally, to a considerable feeling of pride on the part of the aldermen, who, being boosters, felt that this was a wonderful opportunity to put B-ville on the map.

Accordingly, the aldermen decided that instead of simply mailing out the checks as they had originally intended, they would publicly present the first checks at a monster civic ceremony. They invited the governor of the state, who was glad to come to bolster his none-too-enthusiastic support in that locality, the president of the state university, the senator from their district, and other functionaries. They decorated the National Guard armory with flags and got out the American Legion Fife and Drum Corps, the Boy Scouts, and other civic organizations. At the big celebration, each family to receive a social insurance check was marched up to the platform to receive it, and the governor and the mayor shook hands with each of them as they came trooping up in their best clothes. Fine speeches were made; there was much cheering and shouting; pictures of the event showing the recipients of the checks shaking hands with the mayor, and the governor patting the heads of the children, were published not only in the local papers but also in several metropolitan picture sections.

Every recipient of these insurance checks had a feeling, therefore,    9
that he had been personally honored, that he lived in a wonderful little town, and that he could face his unemployment with greater courage and assurance, since his community was back of him. The men and women found themselves being kidded in a friendly way by their acquaintances for having been "up there with the big shots," shaking hands with the governor, and so on. The children at school found themselves envied for having had their pictures in the papers. All in all, B-ville's unemployed did not commit suicide, were not haunted by a sense of failure, did not turn to crime, did not get personal maladjustments, did not develop class hatred, as the result of their fifty dollars a month. . . .

At the conclusion of the Professor's story, the discussion began:    10

"That just goes to show," said the Advertising Man, who was    11
known among his friends as a realistic thinker, "what good promotional work can do. B-ville's city council had real advertising sense, and that civic ceremony was a masterpiece . . . made everyone happy . . . put over the scheme in a big way. Reminds me of the way we do things in our business: as soon as we called horse-mackerel tuna-fish, we developed a big market for it. I suppose if you called relief 'insurance,' you could actually get people to like it, couldn't you?"

"What do you mean, 'calling' it insurance?" asked the Social    12
Worker. "B-ville's scheme wasn't relief at all. It *was* insurance. That's what all such payments should be. What gets me is the stupidity of A-town's city council and all people like them in not realizing that what they call 'relief' is simply the payment of just claims which those unemployed have on a community in a complex interdependent industrial society."

"Good grief, man! Do you realize what you're saying?" cried the    13
Advertising Man in surprise. "Are you implying that those people had any *right* to that money? All I said was that it's a good idea to *disguise* relief as insurance if it's going to make people any happier. But it's still relief, no matter what you *call* it. It's all right to kid the public along to reduce discontent, but we don't need to kid ourselves as well!"

"But they *do* have a right to that money! They're not getting some-    14

thing for nothing. It's insurance. They did something for the community, and that's their prem—"

"Say, are you crazy?"    15

"Who's crazy?"    16

"You're crazy. Relief is relief, isn't it? If you'd only call things by their    17
right names . . ."

"But, confound it, insurance is insurance, isn't it?"    18

(Since the gentlemen are obviously losing their tempers, it will be    19
best to leave them. The Professor has already sneaked out. When last
heard of, not only had the quarrelers stopped speaking to each other,
but so had their wives—and the Advertising Man was threatening to
disinherit his son if he didn't break off his engagement with the Social
Worker's daughter.)

This story has been told not to advance arguments in favor of "social    20
insurance" or "relief" or for any other political and economic arrangement, but simply to show a fairly characteristic sample of language in
action. Do the words we use make as much difference in our lives as
the story of A-town and B-ville seems to indicate? We often talk about
"choosing the right words to express our thoughts," as if thinking
were a process entirely independent of the words we think in. But is
thinking such an independent process? Do the words we utter arise as
a result of the thoughts we have, or are the thoughts we have determined by the linguistic systems we happen to have been taught? The
Advertising Man and the Social Worker seem to be agreed that the
results of B-ville's program were good, so that we can assume that
their notions of what is socially desirable are similar. Nevertheless,
they *cannot agree*.

Alfred Korzybski, in his preface to *Science and Sanity*, . . . asks the    21
reader to imagine what the state of technology would be if all lubri-
cants contained emery dust, the presence of which had never been
detected. Machines would be short-lived and expensive; the machine
age would be a dream of the distant future. If, however, someone were
to discover the presence of the emery, we should at once know *in what
direction to proceed* in order to release the potentialities of machine
power.

Why do people disagree? It isn't a matter of education or intelli-    22
gence, because quarreling, bitterness, conflict, and breakdown are just
as common among the educated as the uneducated, among the clever
as the stupid. Human relations are no better among the privileged
than the underprivileged. Indeed, well-educated people are often the

cleverest in proving that insurance is *really* insurance and that relief is *really* relief—and being well educated they often have such high principles that nothing will make them modify their position in the slightest. Are disagreements then the inevitable results of the nature of human problems and the nature of man? Possibly so—but if we give this answer, we are confessing to being licked before we have even started our investigations.

The student of language observes, however, that it is an extremely   23
rare quarrel that does not involve some kind of *talking*. Almost invariably, before noses are punched or shooting begins, *words are exchanged*—sometimes only a few, sometimes millions. We shall, therefore, look for the "previously undetected emery dust" (or whatever it is that heats up and stops our intellectual machinery) in *language*— that is to say, *our linguistic habits* (how we talk and think and listen) and *our unconscious attitudes toward language*. If we are even partially successful in our search, we may get an inkling of the *direction in which to proceed* in order to release the now imperfectly realized potentialities of human co-operation.

P.S. Those who have concluded that the point of the story is that the   24
Social Worker and the Advertising Man were "only arguing about different names for the same thing," are asked to reread the story and explain what they mean by (1) "only" and (2) "the same thing."

## VOCABULARY

| | | |
|---|---|---|
| semantic (title) | incentive (3) | functionaries (8) |
| parable (title) | averted (5) | interdependent (12) |
| procure (1) | aldermen (6) | lubricants (21) |
| demoralize (2) | indigent (6) | |

## THE FACTS

1. The story is called a "parable." What specifically makes it such?
2. What is the dilemma of A-town? Can you suggest any group or groups in our society today who might have suffered a similar experience?
3. With which paragraph does the crux of the story begin?
4. According to Hayakawa, what is the reason for disagreements? To what extent do education and intelligence prevent them? Explain.
5. Where, according to Hayakawa, shall we find the answer to the problem of proper communication?
6. What does Hayakawa mean by "our linguistic habits"?

## THE STRATEGIES

1. Why does Hayakawa use a professor to tell the story of A-town and B-ville?
2. What is the purpose of the direct quotations in paragraph 4?
3. What kind of image does B-ville reflect? Cite the details that create this image.
4. In paragraph 21, Hayakawa alludes to an analogy drawn by Alfred Korzybski. How would you explain this analogy in your own words?
5. What is the function of the "P.S." in the story? What is the implied expectancy of the author?

## THE ISSUES

1. Does how we label certain situations make a difference? For instance, does it matter whether we call a person "crippled," "disabled," or "handicapped"? Explain your answer.
2. What words, if any, in our language should be stark so that the impact on the listener is not softened? Give examples.
3. What suggestions do you have for helping the poor or otherwise disadvantaged in your city without warping their self-respect?
4. When our government attempts a diplomatic resolution of some problem with the Chinese or Russians, an expert translator is always present. How does this fact relate to Hayakawa's essay?
5. What example from your own experience can you cite to support Hayakawa's view that most quarrels begin with *talking*?

## SUGGESTIONS FOR WRITING

1. Choose a group within our society that you consider to have been labeled in some way. Describe the results of this labeling. Be specific in your use of examples and details. Here are some possibilities: police, migrant workers, garbage collectors.
2. Look through some recent newspapers to find words that have the potential for being misunderstood unless they are given a specific meaning. Explain why you think these words are potentially dangerous.

Laura Bohannan

# • SHAKESPEARE IN THE BUSH •

*Laura Bohannan (b. 1922) is a cultural anthropologist who was born in New York and educated at the University of Arizona and at Oxford. Since 1969, she has been teaching at the University of Illinois.*

*Cultural anthropologists are all concerned with* meaning, *with the difficult task of translation from one language to another. In this classic of anthropology, Laura Bohannan shows the difficulty of translating the meaning of* Hamlet *to the Tiv in West Africa. The article forcefully demonstrates that different cultures live in separate worlds of meaning.*

Just before I left Oxford for the Tiv in West Africa, conversation turned to the season at Stratford. "You Americans," said a friend, "often have difficulty with Shakespeare. He was, after all, a very English poet, and one can easily misinterpret the universal by misunderstanding the particular." 1

I protested that human nature is pretty much the same the whole world over; at least the general plot and motivation of the greater tragedies would always be clear—everywhere—although some details of custom might have to be explained and difficulties of translation might produce other slight changes. To end an argument we could not conclude, my friend gave me a copy of *Hamlet* to study in the African bush: it would, he hoped, lift my mind above its primitive surroundings, and possibly I might, by prolonged meditation, achieve the grace of correct interpretation. 2

It was my second field trip to that African tribe, and I thought myself ready to live in one of its remote sections—an area difficult to cross even on foot. I eventually settled on the hillock of a very knowledgeable old man, the head of a homestead of some hundred and forty people, all of whom were either his close relatives or his wives and children. Like the other elders of the vicinity, the old man spent most of his time performing ceremonies seldom seen these days in the more accessible parts of the tribe. I was delighted. Soon there would be three months of enforced isolation and leisure, between the harvest that takes place just before the rising of the swamps and the clearing of new farms when the water goes down. Then, I thought, they would have even more time to perform ceremonies and explain them to me. 3

I was quite mistaken. Most of the ceremonies demanded the presence of elders from several homesteads. As the swamps rose, the old men found it too difficult to walk from one homestead to the next, and the ceremonies gradually ceased. As the swamps rose even higher, all activities but one came to an end. The women brewed beer from maize and millet. Men, women, and children sat on their hillocks and drank it. 4

People began to drink by dawn. By midmorning the whole homestead was singing, dancing, and drumming. When it rained, people 5 had to sit inside their huts: there they drank and sang or they drank and told stories. In any case, by noon or before, I either had to join the party or retire to my own hut and my books. "One does not discuss serious matters when there is beer. Come drink with us." Since I lacked their capacity for the thick native beer, I spent more and more time with *Hamlet*. Before the end of the second month, grace descended on me. I was quite sure that *Hamlet* had only one possible interpretation, and that one universally obvious.

Early every morning, in the hope of having some serious talk before    6
the beer party, I used to call on the old man at his reception hut—a circle of posts supporting a thatched roof above a low mud wall to keep out wind and rain. One day I crawled through the low doorway and found most of the men of the homestead sitting huddled in their ragged cloths on stools, low plank beds, and reclining chairs, warming themselves against the chill of the rain around a smoky fire. In the center were three pots of beer. The party had started.

The old man greeted me cordially. "Sit down and drink." I accepted    7
a large calabash full of beer, poured some into a small drinking gourd, and tossed it down. Then I poured some more into the same gourd for the man second in seniority to my host before I handed my calabash over to a young man for further distribution. Important people shouldn't ladle beer themselves.

"It is better like this," the old man said, looking at me approvingly    8
and plucking at the thatch that had caught in my hair. "You should sit and drink with us more often. Your servants tell me that when you are not with us, you sit inside your hut looking at a paper."

The old man was acquainted with four kinds of "papers": tax re-    9
ceipts, bride price receipts, court fee receipts, and letters. The messenger who brought him letters from the chief used them mainly as a badge of office, for he always knew what was in them and told the old man. Personal letters from the few who had relatives in the government or mission stations were kept until someone went to a large market where there was a letter writer and reader. Since my arrival, letters were brought to me to be read. A few men also brought me bride price receipts, privately, with requests to change the figures to a higher sum. I found moral arguments were of no avail, since in-laws are fair game, and the technical hazards of forgery difficult to explain to an illiterate people. I did not wish them to think me silly enough to look at any such papers for days on end, and I hastily explained that my "paper" was one of the "things of long ago" of my country.

"Ah," said the old man. "Tell us." 10

I protested that I was not a storyteller. Storytelling is a skilled art 11
among them; their standards are high, and the audiences critical—and
vocal in their criticism. I protested in vain. This morning they wanted
to hear a story while they drank. They threatened to tell me no more
stories until I told them one of mine. Finally, the old man promised
that no one would criticize my style "for we know you are struggling
with our language." "But," put in one of the elders, "you must explain
what we do not understand, as we do when we tell you our stories."
Realizing that here was my chance to prove *Hamlet* universally intelli-
gible, I agreed.

The old man handed me some more beer to help me on with my 12
story-telling. Men filled their long wooden pipes and knocked coals
from the fire to place in the pipe bowls; then, puffing contentedly, they
sat back to listen. I began in the proper style, "Not yesterday, not
yesterday, but long ago, a thing occurred. One night three men were
keeping watch outside the homestead of the great chief, when suddenly they saw the former chief approach them."

"Why was he no longer their chief?" 13

"He was dead," I explained. "That is why they were troubled and 14
afraid when they saw him."

"Impossible," began one of the elders, handing his pipe on to his 15
neighbor, who interrupted, "Of course it wasn't the dead chief. It was
an omen sent by a witch. Go on."

Slightly shaken, I continued. "One of these three was a man who 16
knew things"—the closest translation of scholar, but unfortunately it
also meant witch. The second elder looked triumphantly at the first.
"So he spoke to the dead chief saying, 'Tell us what we must do so you
may rest in your grave,' but the dead chief did not answer. He vanished, and they could see him no more. Then the man who knew
things—his name was Horatio—said this event was the affair of the
dead chief's son, Hamlet."

There was a general shaking of heads round the circle. "Had the 17
dead chief no living brothers? Or was this son the chief?"

"No," I replied, "That is, he had one living brother who became the 18
chief when the elder brother died."

The old men muttered: such omens were matters for chiefs and 19
elders, not for youngsters; no good could come of going behind a
chief's back; clearly Horatio was not a man who knew things.

"Yes, he was," I insisted, shooing a chicken away from my beer. "In   20
our country the son is next to the father. The dead chief's younger
brother had become the great chief. He had also married his elder
brother's widow only about a month after the funeral."

"He did well," the old man beamed and announced to the others,   21
"I told you that if we knew more about Europeans, we would find they
really were very like us. In our country also," he added to me, "the
younger brother marries the elder brother's widow and becomes the
father of his children. Now, if your uncle, who married your widowed
mother, is your father's full brother, then he will be a real father to you.
Did Hamlet's father and uncle have one mother?"

His question barely penetrated my mind; I was too upset and   22
thrown too far off balance by having one of the most important elements of *Hamlet* knocked straight out of the picture. Rather uncertainly
I said that I thought they had the same mother, but I wasn't sure—the
story didn't say. The old man told me severely that these genealogical
details made all the difference and that when I got home I must ask
the elders about it. He shouted out the door to one of his younger
wives to bring his goatskin bag.

Determined to save what I could of the mother motif, I took a deep   23
breath and began again. "The son Hamlet was very sad because his
mother had married again so quickly. There was no need for her to do
so, and it is our custom for a widow not to go to her next husband
until she has mourned for two years."

"Two years is too long," objected the wife, who had appeared with   24
the old man's battered goatskin bag. "Who will hoe your farms for you
while you have no husband?"

"Hamlet," I retorted without thinking, "was old enough to hoe his   25
mother's farms himself. There was no need for her to remarry." No one
looked convinced. I gave up. "His mother and the great chief told
Hamlet not to be sad, for the great chief himself would be a father to
Hamlet. Furthermore, Hamlet would be the next chief: therefore he
must stay to learn the things of a chief. Hamlet agreed to remain, and
all the rest went off to drink beer."

While I paused, perplexed at how to render Hamlet's disgusted   26
soliloquy to an audience convinced that Claudius and Gertrude had
behaved in the best possible manner, one of the younger men asked
me who had married the other wives of the dead chief.

"He had no other wives," I told him.   27

"But a chief must have many wives! How else can he brew beer and     28
prepare food for all his guests?"

I said firmly that in our country even chiefs had only one wife, that     29
they had servants to do their work, and that they paid them from tax
money.

It was better, they returned, for a chief to have many wives and sons     30
who would help him hoe his farms and feed his people; then everyone
loved the chief who gave much and took nothing—taxes were a bad
thing.

I agreed with the last comment, but for the rest fell back on their     31
favorite way of fobbing off my questions: "That is the way it is done,
so that is how we do it."

I decided to skip the soliloquy. Even if Claudius was here thought     32
quite right to marry his brother's widow, there remained the poison
motif, and I knew they would disapprove of fratricide. More hopefully
I resumed, "That night Hamlet kept watch with the three who had
seen his dead father. The dead chief again appeared, and although the
others were afraid, Hamlet followed his dead father off to one side.
When they were alone, Hamlet's dead father spoke."

"Omens can't talk!" The old man was emphatic.     33

"Hamlet's dead father wasn't an omen. Seeing him might have been     34
an omen, but he was not." My audience looked as confused as I
sounded. "It *was* Hamlet's dead father. It was a thing we call a 'ghost.'"
I had to use the English word, for unlike many of the neighboring
tribes, these people didn't believe in the survival after death of any
individuating part of the personality.

"What is a 'ghost'? An omen?"     35

"No, a 'ghost' is someone who is dead but who walks around and     36
can talk, and people can hear him and see him but not touch him."

They objected. "One can touch zombis."     37

"No, no! It was not a dead body the witches had animated to sacri-     38
fice and eat. No one else made Hamlet's dead father walk. He did it
himself."

"Dead men can't walk," protested my audience as one man.     39

I was quite willing to compromise. "A 'ghost' is the dead man's     40
shadow."

But again they objected. "Dead men cast no shadows."     41

"They do in my country," I snapped.     42

The old man quelled the babble of disbelief that arose immediately    43
and told me with that insincere, but courteous, agreement one extends
to the fancies of the young, ignorant, and superstitious, "No doubt in
your country the dead can also walk without being zombis." From the
depths of his bag he produced a withered fragment of kola nut, bit off
one end to show it wasn't poisoned, and handed me the rest as a peace
offering.

"Anyhow," I resumed, "Hamlet's dead father said that his own    44
brother, the one who became chief, had poisoned him. He wanted
Hamlet to avenge him. Hamlet believed this in his heart, for he did not
like his father's brother." I took another swallow of beer. "In the country of the great chief, living in the same homestead, for it was a very
large one, was an important elder who was often with the chief to
advise and help him. His name was Polonius. Hamlet was courting
his daughter, but her father and her brother . . . [I cast hastily about
for some tribal analogy] warned her not to let Hamlet visit her when
she was alone on her farm, for he would be a great chief and so could not
marry her."

"Why not?" asked the wife, who had settled down on the edge of    45
the old man's chair. He frowned at her for asking stupid questions and
growled, "They lived in the same homestead."

"That was not the reason," I informed him. "Polonius was a    46
stranger who lived in the homestead because he helped the chief, not
because he was a relative."

"Then why couldn't Hamlet marry her?"    47

"He could have," I explained, "but Polonius didn't think he would.    48
After all, Hamlet was a man of great importance who ought to marry
a chief's daughter, for in his country a man could have only one wife.
Polonius was afraid that if Hamlet made love to his daughter, then no
one else would give a high price for her."

"That might be true," remarked one of the shrewder elders, "but a    49
chief's son would give his mistress's father enough presents and pa-
tronage to more than make up the difference. Polonius sounds like a
fool to me."

"Many people think he was," I agreed. "Meanwhile Polonius sent    50
his son Laertes off to Paris to learn the things of that country, for it was
the homestead of a very great chief indeed. Because he was afraid that
Laertes might waste a lot of money on beer and women and gambling,

or get into trouble by fighting, he sent one of his servants to Paris secretly, to spy out what Laertes was doing. One day Hamlet came upon Polonius's daughter Ophelia. He behaved so oddly he frightened her. Indeed"—I was fumbling for words to express the dubious quality of Hamlet's madness—"the chief and many others had also noticed that when Hamlet talked one could understand the words but not what they meant. Many people thought that he had become mad." My audience suddenly became much more attentive. "The great chief wanted to know what was wrong with Hamlet, so he sent for two of Hamlet's age mates [school friends would have taken long explanation] to talk to Hamlet and find out what troubled his heart. Hamlet, seeing that they had been bribed by the chief to betray him, told them nothing. Polonius, however, insisted that Hamlet was mad because he had been forbidden to see Ophelia, whom he loved."

"Why," inquired a bewildered voice, "should anyone bewitch Hamlet on that account?"   51

"Bewitch him?"   52

"Yes, only witchcraft can make anyone mad, unless, of course, one sees the beings that lurk in the forest."   53

I stopped being a storyteller, took out my notebook and demanded to be told more about these two causes of madness. Even while they spoke and I jotted notes, I tried to calculate the effect of this new factor on the plot. Hamlet had not been exposed to the beings that lurk in the forest. Only his relatives in the male line could bewitch him. Barring relatives not mentioned by Shakespeare, it had to be Claudius who was attempting to harm him. And, of course, it was.   54

For the moment I staved off questions by saying that the great chief also refused to believe that Hamlet was mad for the love of Ophelia and nothing else. "He was sure that something much more important was troubling Hamlet's heart."   55

"Now Hamlet's age mates," I continued, "had brought with them a famous storyteller. Hamlet decided to have this man tell the chief and all his homestead a story about a man who had poisoned his brother because he desired his brother's wife and wished to be chief himself. Hamlet was sure the great chief could not hear the story without making a sign if he was indeed guilty, and then he would discover whether his dead father had told him the truth."   56

The old man interrupted, with deep cunning, "Why should a father lie to his son?" he asked.   57

I hedged: "Hamlet wasn't sure that it really was his dead father." It 58
was impossible to say anything, in that language, about devil-inspired
visions.

"You mean," he said, "it actually was an omen, and he knew witches 59
sometimes send false ones. Hamlet was a fool not to go to one skilled
in reading omens and divining the truth in the first place. A man-who-
sees-the-truth could have told him how his father died, if he really had
been poisoned, and if there was witchcraft in it; then Hamlet could
have called the elders to settle the matter."

The shrewd elder ventured to disagree. "Because his father's brother 60
was a great chief, one-who-sees-the-truth might therefore have been
afraid to tell it. I think it was for that reason that a friend of Hamlet's
father—a witch and an elder—sent an omen so his friend's son would
know. Was the omen true?"

"Yes," I said, abandoning ghosts and the devil; a witch-sent omen it 61
would have to be. "It was true, for when the storyteller was telling his
tale before all the homestead, the great chief rose in fear. Afraid that
Hamlet knew his secret, he planned to have him killed."

The stage set of the next bit presented some difficulties of transla- 62
tion. I began cautiously. "The great chief told Hamlet's mother to find
out from her son what he knew. But because a woman's children are
always first in her heart, he had important elder Polonius hide behind
a cloth that hung against the wall of Hamlet's mother's sleeping hut.
Hamlet started to scold his mother for what she had done."

There was a shocked murmur from everyone. A man should never 63
scold his mother.

"She called out in fear, and Polonius moved behind the cloth. Shout- 64
ing, 'A rat!' Hamlet took his machete and slashed through the cloth." I
paused for dramatic effect. "He had killed Polonius!"

The old men looked at each other in supreme disgust. "That Polo- 65
nius truly was a fool and a man who knew nothing! What child would
not know enough to shout, 'It's me!'" With a pang, I remembered that
these people are ardent hunters, always armed with bow, arrow, and
machete; at the first rustle in the grass an arrow is aimed and ready,
and the hunter shouts "Game!" If no human voice answers immediately, the arrow speeds on its way. Like a good hunter Hamlet had
shouted, "A rat!"

I rushed in to save Polonius's reputation. "Polonius did speak. 66
Hamlet heard him. But he thought it was the chief and wished to

kill him to avenge his father. He had meant to kill him earlier that evening . . ." I broke down, unable to describe to these pagans, who had no belief in individual afterlife, the difference between dying at one's prayers and dying "unhousell'd, disappointed, unaneled."

This time I had shocked my audience seriously. "For a man to raise  67
his hand against his father's brother and the one who has become his father—that is a terrible thing. The elders ought to let such a man be bewitched."

I nibbled at my kola nut in some perplexity, then pointed out that  68
after all the man had killed Hamlet's father.

"No," pronounced the old man, speaking less to me than to the  69
young men sitting behind the elders. "If your father's brother has killed your father, you must appeal to your father's age mates; *they* may avenge him. No man may use violence against his senior relatives." Another thought struck him. "But if his father's brother had indeed been wicked enough to bewitch Hamlet and make him mad that would be a good story indeed, for it would be his fault that Hamlet, being mad, no longer had any sense and thus was ready to kill his father's brother."

There was a murmur of applause. *Hamlet* was again a good story to  70
them, but it no longer seemed quite the same story to me. As I thought over the coming complications of plot and motive, I lost courage and decided to skim over dangerous ground quickly.

"The great chief," I went on, "was not sorry that Hamlet had killed  71
Polonius. It gave him a reason to send Hamlet away, with his two treacherous age mates, with letters to a chief of a far country, saying that Hamlet should be killed. But Hamlet changed the writing on their papers, so that the chief killed his age mates instead." I encountered a reproachful glare from one of the men whom I had told undetectable forgery was not merely immoral but beyond human skill. I looked the other way.

"Before Hamlet could return, Laertes came back for his father's  72
funeral. The great chief told him Hamlet had killed Polonius. Laertes swore to kill Hamlet because of this, and because his sister, Ophelia, hearing her father had been killed by the man she loved, went mad and drowned in the river."

"Have you already forgotten what we told you?" The old man was  73
reproachful. "One cannot take vengeance on a madman; Hamlet killed Polonius in his madness. As for the girl, she not only went mad, she

was drowned. Only witches can make people drown. Water itself can't hurt anything. It is merely something one drinks and bathes in."

I began to get cross. "If you don't like the story, I'll stop." 74

The old man made soothing noises and himself poured me some 75 more beer. "You tell the story well, and we are listening. But it is clear that the elders of your country have never told you what the story really means. No, don't interrupt! We believe you when you say your marriage customs are different, or your clothes and weapons. But people are the same everywhere; therefore, there are always witches and it is we, the elders, who know how witches work. We told you it was the great chief who wished to kill Hamlet, and now your own words have proved us right. Who were Ophelia's male relatives?"

"There were only her father and her brother." Hamlet was clearly 76 out of my hands.

"There must have been many more; this also you must ask of your 77 elders when you get back to your country. From what you tell us, since Polonius was dead, it must have been Laertes who killed Ophelia, although I do not see the reason for it."

We had emptied one pot of beer, and the old men argued the point 78 with slightly tipsy interest. Finally one of them demanded of me, "What did the servant of Polonius say on his return?"

With difficulty I recollected Reynaldo and his mission. "I don't think 79 he did return before Polonius was killed."

"Listen," said the elder, "and I will tell you how it was and how your 80 story will go, then you may tell me if I am right. Polonius knew his son would get into trouble, and so he did. He had many fines to pay for fighting, and debts from gambling. But he had only two ways of getting money quickly. One was to marry off his sister at once, but it is difficult to find a man who will marry a woman desired by the son of a chief. For if the chief's heir commits adultery with your wife, what can you do? Only a fool calls a case against a man who will someday be his judge. Therefore Laertes had to take the second way: he killed his sister by witchcraft, drowning her so he could secretly sell her body to the witches."

I raised an objection. "They found her body and buried it. Indeed 81 Laertes jumped into the grave to see his sister once more—so, you see, the body was truly there. Hamlet, who had just come back, jumped in after him."

"What did I tell you?" The elder appealed to the others. "Laertes 82 was up to no good with his sister's body. Hamlet prevented him, because the chief's heir, like a chief, does not wish any other man to grow rich and powerful. Laertes would be angry, because he would have killed his sister without benefit to himself. In our country he would try to kill Hamlet for that reason. Is this not what happened?"

"More or less," I admitted. "When the great chief found Hamlet was 83 still alive, he encouraged Laertes to try to kill Hamlet and arranged a fight with machetes between them. In the fight both the young men were wounded to death. Hamlet's mother drank the poisoned beer that the chief meant for Hamlet in case he won the fight. When he saw his mother die of poison, Hamlet, dying, managed to kill his father's brother with his machete."

"You see, I was right!" exclaimed the elder. 84

"That was a very good story," added the old man, "and you told it 85 with very few mistakes. There was just one more error, at the very end. The poison Hamlet's mother drank was obviously meant for the survivor of the fight, whichever it was. If Laertes had won, the great chief would have poisoned him, for no one would know that he arranged Hamlet's death. Then, too, he need not fear Laertes' witchcraft; it takes a strong heart to kill one's only sister by witchcraft.

"Sometime," concluded the old man, gathering his ragged toga 86 about him, "you must tell us some more stories of your country. We, who are elders, will instruct you in their true meaning, so that when you return to your own land your elders will see that you have not been sitting in the bush, but among those who know things and who have taught you wisdom."

## VOCABULARY

| | | |
|---|---|---|
| hillock (3) | motif (23) | patronage (49) |
| accessible (3) | retorted (25) | unhousell'd (66) |
| calabash (7) | soliloquy (26) | unaneled (66) |
| hazards (9) | fratricide (32) | toga (86) |
| genealogical (22) | zombis (37) | |

## THE FACTS

1. In relating her experience with a primitive tribe in West Africa, what point does Bohannan make about language and culture?

2. While the author tells her story, we learn a great deal about the customs and beliefs of the Tiv. What are some of these customs and beliefs?
3. What is the proper style of beginning a story among the Tiv? What is our equivalent?
4. What causes the repeated breakdown in communicating the Hamlet story?
5. What desire on the part of the elders is revealed in the final paragraph?

## THE STRATEGIES

1. What is the purpose for such a long introductory description of the homestead where the Hamlet story is told?
2. The story consists largely of narrative development. What other technique is used? What is its purpose?
3. Why is there no accurate Tiv translation for the word *scholar*?
4. If you had to translate the word *restaurant* for primitive people, what might you say?
5. What is the implied meaning of the final sentence in the selection?
6. Laura Bohannan is an anthropologist. Toward what level of education in her audience does she aim?

## THE ISSUES

1. How could the Hamlet story be made comprehensible to a tribe like the Tiv?
2. Do you agree with the Englishman of the first paragraph or with Bohannon about whether or not the general plot of great stories can be understood by all people, human nature being what it is? Give reasons for your answer.
3. What advantages accrue from a culture with an oral tradition of story telling? Explain your answer.
4. How would you explain a ghost to a child? Be specific.
5. Which of the following stories would you choose to tell a group of primitive people so that they could understand it? Give reasons for your choice:
   a. Little Red Riding Hood
   b. The Scarlet Letter
   c. David and Goliath
   d. Romeo and Juliet

## SUGGESTIONS FOR WRITING

1. Summarize the plot of *Othello* or some other famous play or story so that someone who does not understand English well can understand it.
2. Using all the details gathered from your reading of this essay, write a vivid description of the Tiv tribe.

**Anton Chekhov**

Translated by Eric Bentley

———————— • **THE BRUTE** • ————————

*Anton Pavlovich Chekhov (1860–1904) was a Russian physician turned short-story writer and dramatist. The son of a grocer and grandson of a serf, Chekhov earned international acclaim for his stories and plays, which realistically portrayed Russian life. Among his theatrical masterpieces are* The Seagull *(1896),* Uncle Vanya *(1899),* The Three Sisters *(1901), and* The Cherry Orchard *(1904). His best stories are collected in* At Twilight *(1887) and* Stories *(1888).*

*In the play that follows, Chekhov demonstrates with great humor how two people can say one thing but in reality mean quite the opposite.*

## Characters

MRS. POPOV, *widow and landowner, small, with dimpled cheeks.*
MR. GRIGORY S. SMIRNOV, *gentleman farmer, middle-aged.*
LUKA, *Mrs. Popov's footman, an old man.*
GARDENER
COACHMAN
HIRED MEN

*The drawing room of a country house.* MRS. POPOV, *in deep mourning, is staring hard at a photograph.* LUKA *is with her.*

LUKA.    It's not right, ma'am, you're killing yourself. The cook has    1
gone off with the maid to pick berries. The cat's having a high old time in the yard catching birds. Every living thing is happy. But you stay moping here in the house like it was a convent, taking no pleasure in nothing. I mean it, ma'am! It must be a full year since you set foot out of doors.

MRS. POPOV.    I must never set foot out of doors again, Luka. Never! I    2
have nothing to set foot out of doors *for*. My life is done. *He* is in his grave. I have buried myself alive in this house. We are *both* in our graves.

LUKA.    You're off again, ma'am. I just won't listen to you no more.    3
Mr. Popov is dead, but what can we do about that? It's God's
doing. God's will be done. You've cried over him, you've done
your share of mourning, haven't you? There's a limit to everything. You can't go on weeping and wailing forever. My old lady
died, for that matter, and I wept and wailed over her a whole
month long. Well, that was it. I couldn't weep and wail all my life,
she just wasn't worth it. (He sighs.) As for the neighbours, you've
forgotten all about them, ma'am. You don't visit them and you
don't let them visit you. You and I are like a pair of spiders, we
never see the light of day. And it isn't like there was no nice people
around either. The whole county's swarming with 'em. There's a
regiment quartered at Riblov, and the officers are so good-
looking! The girls can't take their eyes off them—There's a ball at
the camp every Friday—The military band plays most every day
of the week—What do you say, ma'am? You're young, you're
pretty, you could enjoy yourself! Ten years from now you may
want to strut and show your feathers to the officers, and it'll be
too late.

MRS. POPOV (firmly).    You must never bring this subject up again,    4
Luka. Since Popov died, life has been an empty dream to me, you
know that. *You* may think I am alive. Poor ignorant Luka! You are
wrong. I am dead. I'm in my grave. Never more shall I see the
light of day, never strip from my body this . . . raiment of death!
Are you listening, Luka? Let his ghost learn how I love him! Yes,
*I* know, and *you* know, he was often unfair to me, he was cruel to
me, and he was unfaithful to me. What of it? *I* shall be faithful to
*him*, that's all. I will show him how *I* can love. Hereafter, in a
better world than this, he will welcome me back, the same loyal
girl I always was—

LUKA.    Instead of carrying on this way, ma'am, you should go out in    5
the garden and take a bit of a walk, ma'am. Or why not harness
Toby and take a drive? Call on a couple of the neighbours, ma'am?

MRS. POPOV (breaking down).    Oh, Luka!    6

LUKA.    Yes, ma'am? What have I said, ma'am? Oh dear!    7

MRS. POPOV.    Toby! You said Toby! He adored that horse. When he    8
drove me out to the Korchagins and the Vlasovs, it was always
with Toby! He was a wonderful driver, do you remember, Luka?

So graceful! So strong! I can see him now, pulling at those reins with all his might and main! Toby! Luka, tell them to give Toby an extra portion of oats today.

LUKA.    Yes, ma'am.    9
*(A bell rings.)*

MRS. POPOV.    Who is that? Tell them I'm not at home.    10

LUKA.    Very good, ma'am. *(Exit.)*    11

MRS. POPOV *(gazing again at the photograph).*    You shall see, my Popov,    12
how a wife can love and forgive. Till death do us part. Longer than that. Till death re-unite us forever! *(Suddenly a titter breaks through her tears.)* Aren't you ashamed of yourself, Popov? Here's your little wife, being good, being faithful, so faithful she's locked up here waiting for her own funeral, while you—doesn't it make you ashamed, you naughty boy? You were terrible, you know. You were unfaithful, and you made those awful scenes about it, you stormed out and left me alone for weeks—
*(Enter LUKA.)*

LUKA *(upset).*    There's someone asking for you, ma'am. Says he    13
must—

MRS. POPOV.    I suppose you told him that since my husband's death I    14
see no one?

LUKA.    Yes, ma'am. I did, ma'am. But he wouldn't listen, ma'am. He    15
says it's urgent.

MRS. POPOV *(shrilly).*    I see no one!!    16

LUKA.    He won't take no for an answer, ma'am. He just curses and    17
swears and comes in anyway. He's a perfect monster, ma'am. He's in the dining room right now.

MRS. POPOV.    In the dining room, is he? I'll give him his comeup-    18
pance. Bring him in here this minute.
*(Exit LUKA.)*
*(Suddenly sad again.)* Why do they do this to me? Why? Insulting my grief, intruding on my solitude? *(She sighs.)* I'm afraid I'll have to enter a convent. I will, I *must* enter a convent!
*(Enter MR. SMIRNOV and LUKA.)*

SMIRNOV *(to LUKA).*    Dolt! Idiot! You talk too much! *(Seeing MRS. PO-*    19

POV. *With dignity*.) May I have the honour of introducing myself, madam? Grigory S. Smirnov, landowner and lieutenant of artillery, retired. Forgive me, madam, if I disturb your peace and quiet, but my business is both urgent and weighty.

MRS. POPOV *(declining to offer him her hand)*.   What is it you wish, sir?   20

SMIRNOV.   At the time of his death, your late husband—with whom   21
I had the honour to be acquainted ma'am—was in my debt to the tune of twelve hundred rubles. I have two notes to prove it. Tomorrow, ma'am, I must pay the interest on a bank loan. I have therefore no alternative, ma'am, but to ask you to pay me the money today.

MRS. POPOV.   Twelve hundred rubles? But what did my husband owe   22
it to you for?

SMIRNOV.   He used to buy his oats from me, madam.   23

MRS. POPOV *(to LUKA, with a sigh)*.   Remember what I said, Luka: tell   24
them to give Toby an extra portion of oats today!
(*Exit LUKA.*)
My dear Mr.—what was the name again?

SMIRNOV.   Smirnov, ma'am.   25

MRS. POPOV.   My dear Mr. Smirnov, if Mr. Popov owed you money,   26
you shall be paid—to the last ruble, to the last kopeck. But today—you must excuse me, Mr.—what was it?

SMIRNOV.   Smirnov, ma'am.   27

MRS. POPOV.   Today, Mr. Smirnov, I have no ready cash in the house.   28
(*SMIRNOV starts to speak.*)
Tomorrow, Mr. Smirnov, no, the day after tomorrow, all will be well. My steward will be back from town. I shall see that he pays what is owing. Today, no. In any case, today is exactly seven months from Mr. Popov's death. On such a day you will understand that I am in no mood to think of money.

SMIRNOV.   Madam, if you don't pay up now, you can carry me out   29
feet foremost. They'll seize my estate.

MRS. POPOV.   You can have your money.   30
(*He starts to thank her.*)
Tomorrow.

*(He again starts to speak.)*
That is: the day after tomorrow.

SMIRNOV.    I don't need the money the day after tomorrow. I need it    31
today.

MRS. POPOV.    I'm sorry, Mr.—    32

SMIRNOV *(shouting)*.    Smirnov!    33

MRS. POPOV *(sweetly)*.    Yes, of course. But you can't have it today.    34

SMIRNOV.    But I can't wait for it any longer!    35

MRS. POPOV.    Be sensible, Mr. Smirnov. How can I pay you if I don't    36
have it?

SMIRNOV.    You don't have it?    37

MRS. POPOV.    I don't have it.    38

SMIRNOV.    Sure?    39

MRS. POPOV.    Positive.    40

SMIRNOV.    Very well. I'll make a note to that effect. *(Shrugging.)* And    41
then they want me to keep cool. I meet the tax commissioner on
the street, and he says, ''Why are you always in such a bad humour, Smirnov?'' Bad humour! How can I help it, in God's name?
I need money, I need it desperately. Take yesterday: I leave home
at the crack of dawn, I call on all my debtors. Not a one of them
pays up. Footsore and weary, I creep at midnight into some little
dive, and try to snatch a few winks of sleep on the floor by the
vodka barrel. Then today, I come here, fifty miles from home,
saying to myself, ''At last, at last, I can be sure of something,'' and
you're not in the mood! You give me a mood! Christ, how can I
help getting all worked up?

MRS. POPOV.    I thought I'd made it clear, Mr. Smirnov, that you'll get    42
your money the minute my steward is back from town?

SMIRNOV.    What the hell do I care about your steward? Pardon the    43
expression, ma'am. But it was you I came to see.

MRS. POPOV.    What language! What a tone to take to a lady! I refuse    44
to hear another word. *(Quickly, exit.)*

SMIRNOV.    Not in the mood, huh? ''Exactly seven month since    45
Popov's death,'' huh? How about me? *(Shouting after her.)* Is there

this interest to pay, or isn't there? I'm asking you a question: is there this interest to pay, or isn't there? So your husband died, and you're not in the mood, and your steward's gone off some place, and so forth and so on, but what can I do about all that, huh? What do *you* think I should do? Take a running jump and shove my head through the wall? Take off in a balloon? You don't know my *other* debtors. I call on Gruzdeff. Not at home. I look for Yaroshevitch. He's hiding out. I find Kooritsin. He kicks up a row, and I have to throw him through the window. I work my way right down the list. Not a kopeck. Then I come to you, and God damn it to hell, if you'll pardon the expression, you're not in the mood! *(Quietly, as he realizes he's talking to air.)* I've spoiled them all, that's what, I've let them play me for a sucker. Well, I'll show them, I'll show this one. I'll stay right here till she pays up. Ugh! *(He shudders with rage.)* I'm in a rage! I'm in a positively towering rage! Every nerve in my body is trembling at forty to the dozen! I can't breathe, I feel ill, I think I'm going to faint, hey, you there! *(Enter* LUKA.*)*

LUKA.   Yes, sir? Is there anything you wish, sir?                    46

SMIRNOV.   Water! Water! No, make it vodka.                          47
*(Exit* LUKA.*)*
Consider the logic of it. A fellow creature is desperately in need of cash, so desperately in need that he has to seriously contemplate hanging himself, and this woman, this mere chit of a girl, won't pay up, and why not? Because, forsooth, she isn't in the mood! Oh, the logic of women! Come to that, I never have liked them, I could do without the whole sex. Talk to a woman? I'd rather sit on a barrel of dynamite, the very thought gives me gooseflesh. Women! Creatures of poetry and romance! Just to see one in the distance gets me mad. My legs start twitching with rage. I feel like yelling for help.
*(Enter* LUKA, *handing* SMIRNOV *a glass of water.)*

LUKA.   Mrs. Popov is indisposed, sir. She is seeing no one.        48

SMIRNOV.   Get out.                                                  49
*(Exit* LUKA.*)*
Indisposed, is she? Seeing no one, huh? Well, she can see me or not, but I'll be here. I'll be right here till she pays up. If you're sick

for a week, I'll be here for a week. If you're sick for a year, I'll be here for a year. You won't get around *me* with your widow's weeds and your schoolgirl dimples. I know all about dimples. *(Shouting through the window.)* Semyon, let the horses out of those shafts, we're not leaving, we're staying, and tell them to give the horses some oats, yes, oats, you fool, what do you think? *(Walking away from the window.)* What a mess, what an unholy mess! I didn't sleep last night, the heat is terrific today, not a damn one of 'em has paid up, and here's this—this skirt in mourning that's not in the mood! My head aches, where's that—*(He drinks from the glass.)* Water, ugh! You there!
*(Enter* LUKA.*)*

LUKA.    Yes, sir. You wish for something, sir?                                50

SMIRNOV.    Where's that confounded vodka I asked for?                        51
*(Exit* LUKA.*)*
*(*SMIRNOV *sits and looks himself over.)* Oof! A fine figure of a man I am! Unwashed, uncombed, unshaven, straw on my vest, dust all over me. The little woman must've taken me for a highwayman. *(Yawns.)* I suppose it wouldn't be considered polite to barge into a drawing room in this state, but who cares? I'm not a visitor, I'm a creditor—most unwelcome of guests, second only to Death.
*(Enter* LUKA.*)*

LUKA *(handing him the vodka).*    If I may say so, sir, you take too many    52
liberties, sir.

SMIRNOV.    What?!                                                           53

LUKA.    Oh, nothing, sir, nothing.                                          54

SMIRNOV.    Who in hell do you think you're talking to? Shut your            55
mouth!

LUKA *(aside).*    There's an evil spirit abroad. The Devil must have sent    56
him. Oh! *(Exit* LUKA.*)*

SMIRNOV.    What a rage I'm in! I'll grind the whole world to powder.        57
Oh, I feel ill again. You there!
*(Enter* MRS. POPOV.*)*

MRS. POPOV *(looking at the floor).*    In the solitude of my rural retreat,   58
Mr. Smirnov, I've long since grown unaccustomed to the sound of the human voice. Above all, I cannot bear shouting. I must beg you not to break the silence.

SMIRNOV.    Very well. Pay me my money and I'll go.    59

MRS. POPOV.    I told you before, and I tell you again. Mr. Smirnov. I    60
have no cash, you'll have to wait till the day after tomorrow. Can
I express myself more plainly?

SMIRNOV.    And *I* told *you* before, and *I* tell *you* again, that I need the    61
money today, that the day after tomorrow is too late, and that if
you don't pay, and pay now, I'll have to hang myself in the morning!

MRS. POPOV.    But I have no cash. This is quite a puzzle.    62

SMIRNOV.    You won't pay, huh?    63

MRS. POPOV.    I *can't* pay, Mr. Smirnov.    64

SMIRNOV.    In that case, I'm going to sit here and wait. *(Sits down.)*    65
You'll pay up the day after tomorrow? Very good. Till the day after
tomorrow, here I sit. *(Pause. He jumps up.)* Now look, do I have to
pay that interest tomorrow, or don't I? Or do you think I'm joking?

MRS. POPOV.    I must ask you not to raise your voice, Mr. Smirnov. This    66
is not a stable.

SMIRNOV.    Who said it was? Do I have to pay the interest tomorrow    67
or not?

MRS. POPOV.    Mr. Smirnov, do you know how to behave in the pres-    68
ence of a lady?

SMIRNOV.    No, madam, I do not know how to behave in the presence    69
of a lady.

MRS. POPOV.    Just what I thought. I look at you, and I say: ugh! I hear    70
you talk, and I say to myself: "That man doesn't know how to talk
to a lady."

SMIRNOV.    You'd like me to come simpering to you in French, I sup-    71
pose. "*Enchanté, madame! Merci beaucoup* for not paying zee
money, *madame! Pardonnez-moi* if I 'ave disturbed you, *madame!*
How *charmante* you look in mourning, *madame!*"

MRS. POPOV.    Now you're being silly, Mr. Smirnov.    72

SMIRNOV *(mimicking).*    "Now you're being silly, Mr. Smirnov." "You    73
don't know how to talk to a lady, Mr. Smirnov." Look here, Mrs.
Popov, I've known more women than you've known pussy cats.
I've fought three duels on their account. I've jilted twelve, and

been jilted by nine others. Oh, yes, Mrs. Popov, I've played the fool in my time, whispered sweet nothings, bowed and scraped and endeavoured to please. Don't tell me I don't know what it is to love, to pine away with longing, to have the blues, to melt like butter, to be weak as water. I was full of tender emotion. I was carried away with passion. I squandered half my fortune on the sex. I chattered about women's emancipation. But there's an end to everything, dear madam. Burning eyes, dark eyelashes, ripe, red lips, dimpled cheeks, heaving bosoms, soft whisperings, the moon above, the lake below—I don't give a rap for that sort of nonsense any more, Mrs. Popov. I've found out about women. Present company excepted, they're liars. Their behaviour is mere play acting; their conversation is sheer gossip. Yes, dear lady, women, young or old, are false, petty, vain, cruel, malicious, unreasonable. As for intelligence, any sparrow could give them points. Appearances, I admit, can be deceptive. In appearance, a woman may be all poetry and romance, goddess and angel, muslin and fluff. To look at her exterior is to be transported to heaven. But I have looked at her interior, Mrs. Popov, and what did I find there—in her very soul? A crocodile. *(He has gripped the back of the chair so firmly that it snaps.)* And, what is more revolting, a crocodile with an illusion, a crocodile that imagines tender sentiments are its own special province, a crocodile that thinks itself queen of the realm of love! Whereas, in sober fact, dear madam, if a woman can love anything except a lapdog you can hang me by the feet on that nail. For a man, love is suffering, love is sacrifice. A woman just swishes her train around and tightens her grip on your nose. Now, you're a woman, aren't you, Mrs. Popov? You must be an expert on some of this. Tell me, quite frankly, did you ever know a woman to be—faithful, for instance? Or even sincere? Only old hags, huh? Though some women are old hags from birth. But as for the others? You're right: a faithful woman is a freak of nature—like a cat with horns.

MRS. POPOV.    Who is faithful, then? Who *have* you cast for the faithful    74
lover? Not man?

SMIRNOV.    Right first time, Mrs. Popov: man.    75

MRS. POPOV *(going off into a peal of bitter laughter)*.    Man! Man is faith-    76
ful! that's a new one! *(Fiercely.)* What right do you have to say this,

Mr. Smirnov? Men faithful? Let me tell you something. Of all the men I have ever known my late husband Popov was the best. I loved him, and there are women who know how to love, Mr. Smirnov. I gave him my youth, my happiness, my life, my fortune. I worshipped the ground he trod on—and what happened? The best of men was unfaithful to me, Mr. Smirnov. Not once in a while. All the time. After he died, I found his desk drawer full of love letters. While he was alive, he was always going away for the week-end. He squandered my money. He made love to other women before my very eyes. But, in spite of all, Mr. Smirnov, *I* was faithful, Mr. Smirnov! Unto death. And beyond. I am *still* faithful, Mr. Smirnov! Buried alive in this house, I shall wear mourning till the day I, too, am called to my eternal rest.

SMIRNOV *(laughing scornfully).*   Expect me to believe that? As if I   77
couldn't see through all this hocus-pocus. Buried alive! Till you're called to your eternal rest! Till when? Till some little poet—or some little subaltern with his first moustache—comes riding by and asks: "Can that be the house of the mysterious Tamara who for love of her late husband has buried herself alive, vowing to see no man?" Ha!

MRS. POPOV *(flaring up).*   How dare you? How dare you insinuate—?   78

SMIRNOV.   You may have buried yourself alive, Mrs. Popov, but you   79
haven't forgotten to powder your nose.

MRS. POPOV *(incoherent).*   How dare you? How—?   80

SMIRNOV.   Who's raising his voice now? Just because I call a spade a   81
spade. Because I shoot straight from the shoulder. Well, don't shout at me, I'm not your steward.

MRS. POPOV.   I'm not shouting, you're shouting! Oh, leave me alone!   82

SMIRNOV.   Pay me the money, and I will.   83

MRS. POPOV.   You'll get no money out of me!   84

SMIRNOV.   Oh, so that's it!   85

MRS. POPOV.   Not a ruble, not a kopeck. Get out! Leave me alone!   86

SMIRNOV.   Not being your husband, I must ask you not to make   87
scenes with me. *(He sits.)* I don't like scenes.

MRS. POPOV *(choking with rage).*   You're sitting down?   88

SMIRNOV.    Correct, I'm sitting down.    89

MRS. POPOV.    I asked you to leave!    90

SMIRNOV.    Then give me the money. *(Aside.)* Oh, what a rage I'm in,    91
what a rage!

MRS. POPOV.    The impudence of the man! I won't talk to you a moment    92
longer. Get out. *(Pause.)* Are you going?

SMIRNOV.    No.    93

MRS. POPOV.    No?!    94

SMIRNOV.    No.    95

MRS. POPOV.    On your head be it. Luka!    96
*(Enter* LUKA.*)*
Show the gentleman out, Luka.

LUKA *(approaching).*    I'm afraid, sir, I'll have to ask you, um, to leave,    97
sir, now, um—

SMIRNOV *(jumping up).*    Shut your mouth, you old idiot! Who do you    98
think you're talking to? I'll make mincemeat of you.

LUKA *(clutching his heart).*    Mercy on us! Holy saints above! *(He falls*    99
*into an armchair.)* I'm taken sick! I can't breathe!!

MRS. POPOV.    Then where's Dasha? Dasha! Dasha! Come here at once!    100
*(She rings.)*

LUKA.    They've gone picking berries, ma'am, I'm alone here—Water,    101
water, I'm taken sick!

MRS. POPOV *(to* SMIRNOV*).*    Get out, you!    102

SMIRNOV.    Can't you even be polite with me, Mrs. Popov?    103

MRS. POPOV *(clenching her fists and stamping her feet).*    With you? You're    104
a wild animal, you were never house-broken!

SMIRNOV.    What? What did you say?    105

MRS. POPOV.    I said you were a wild animal, you were never house-    106
broken.

SMIRNOV *(advancing upon her).*    And what right do you have to talk to    107
me like that?

MRS. POPOV.    Like what?    108

SMIRNOV.    You have insulted me, madam.    109

MRS. POPOV.   What of it? Do you think I'm scared of you?   110

SMIRNOV.   So you think you can get away with it because you're a   111
woman. A creature of poetry and romance, huh? Well, it doesn't
go down with me. I hereby challenge you to a duel.

LUKA.   Mercy on us! Holy saints alive! Water!   112

SMIRNOV.   I propose we shoot it out.   113

MRS. POPOV.   Trying to scare me again? Just because you have big fists   114
and a voice like a bull? You're a brute.

SMIRNOV.   No one insults Grigory S. Smirnov with impunity! And I   115
don't care if you *are* a female.

MRS. POPOV (*trying to outshout him*).   Brute, brute, brute!   116

SMIRNOV.   The sexes are equal, are they? Fine: then it's just prejudice   117
to expect men alone to pay for insults. I hereby challenge—

MRS. POPOV (*screaming*).   All right! You want to shoot it out? All right!   118
Let's shoot it out!

SMIRNOV.   And let it be here and now!   119

MRS. POPOV.   Here and now! All right! I'll have Popov's pistols here in   120
one minute! (*Walks away, then turns.*) Putting one of Popov's bullets through your silly head will be a pleasure! Au revoir. (*Exit.*)

SMIRNOV.   I'll bring her down like a duck, a sitting duck. I'm not one   121
of your little poets, I'm no little subaltern with his first moustache. No, sir, there's no weaker sex where I'm concerned!

LUKA.   Sir! Master! (*He goes down on his knees.*) Take pity on a poor old   122
man, and do me a favour: go away. It was bad enough before, you
nearly scared me to death. But a duel—!

SMIRNOV (*ignoring him*).   A duel! That's equality of the sexes for you!   123
That's women's emancipation! Just as a matter of principle I'll
bring her down like a duck. But what a woman! "Putting one of
Popov's bullets through your silly head . . ." Her cheeks were
flushed, her eyes were gleaming! And by God, she's accepted the
challenge! I never knew a woman like this before!

LUKA.   Sir! Master! Please go away! I'll always pray for you!   124

SMIRNOV (*again ignoring him*).   What a woman! Phew!! *She's* no sour   125
puss, *she's* no cry baby. She's fire and brimstone. She's a human
cannon ball. What a shame I have to kill her!

LUKA *(weeping).*    Please, kind sir, please, go away!    126

SMIRNOV *(as before).*    I like her, isn't that funny? With those dimples    127
and all? I like her. I'm even prepared to consider letting her off
that debt. And where's my rage? It's gone. I never knew a woman
like this before.
*(Enter* MRS. POPOV *with pistols.)*

MRS. POPOV *(boldly).*    Pistols, Mr. Smirnov! *(Matter of fact.)* But before    128
we start, you'd better show me how it's done. I'm not too familiar
with these things. In fact I never gave a pistol a second look.

LUKA.    Lord, have mercy on us, I must go hunt up the gardener and    129
the coachman. Why has this catastrophe fallen upon us, O Lord?
*(Exit.)*

SMIRNOV *(examining the pistols).*    Well, it's like this. There are several    130
makes: one is the Mortimer, with capsules, especially constructed
for duelling. What you have here are Smith and Wesson triple-
action revolvers, with extractor, first-rate job, worth ninety rubles
at the very least. You hold it this way. *(Aside.)* My God, what eyes
she has! They're setting me on fire.

MRS. POPOV.    This way?    131

SMIRNOV.    Yes, that's right. You cock the trigger, take aim like this,    132
head up, arm out like this. Then you just press with this finger
here, and it's all over. The main thing is, keep cool, take slow aim,
and don't let your arm jump.

MRS. POPOV.    I see. And if it's inconvenient to do the job here, we can    133
go out in the garden.

SMIRNOV.    Very good. Of course, I should warn you: I'll be firing in    134
the air.

MRS. POPOV.    What? This is the end. Why?    135

SMIRNOV.    Oh, well—because—for private reasons.    136

MRS. POPOV.    Scared, huh? *(She laughs heartily.)* Now don't you try to    137
get out of it, Mr. Smirnov. My blood is up. I won't be happy till
I've drilled a hole through that skull of yours. Follow me. What's
the matter? Scared?

SMIRNOV.    That's right. I'm scared.    138

MRS. POPOV.    Oh, come on, what's the matter with you?    139

SMIRNOV.    Well, um, Mrs. Popov, I, um, I like you.    140

MRS. POPOV *(laughing bitterly).*    Good God! He like me, does he? The    141
gall of the man. *(Showing him the door.)* You may leave, Mr.
Smirnov.

SMIRNOV *(quietly puts the gun down, takes his hat, and walks to the door.*    142
*Then he stops and the pair look at each other without a word. Then,*
*approaching gingerly).*    Listen, Mrs. Popov. Are you still mad at
me? I'm in the devil of a temper myself, of course. But then, you
see—what I mean is—it's this way—the fact is—(*Roaring.)* Well,
is it my fault, damn it, if I like you? *(Clutches the back of a chair. It*
*breaks.)* Christ, what fragile furniture you have here. I like you.
Know what I mean? I could fall in love with you.

MRS. POPOV.    I hate you. Get out!    143

SMIRNOV.    What a woman! I never saw anything like it. Oh, I'm lost,    144
I'm done for, I'm a mouse in a trap.

MRS. POPOV.    Leave this house, or I shoot!    145

SMIRNOV.    Shoot away! What bliss to die of a shot that was fired by    146
that little velvet hand! To die gazing into those enchanting eyes.
I'm out of my mind. I know: you must decide at once. Think for
one second, then decide. Because if I leave now, I'll never be back.
Decide! I'm a pretty decent chap. Landed gentleman, I should
say. Ten thousand a year. Good stable. Throw a kopeck up in the
air, and I'll put a bullet through it. Will you marry me?

MRS. POPOV *(indignant, brandishing the gun).*    We'll shoot it out! Get    147
going! Take your pistol!

SMIRNOV.    I'm out of my mind. I don't understand anything any    148
more. *(Shouting.)* You there! That vodka!

MRS. POPOV.    No excuses! No delays! We'll shoot it out!    149

SMIRNOV.    I'm out of my mind. I'm falling in love. I *have* fallen in love.    150
*(He takes her hand vigorously; she squeals.)* I love you. *(He goes down*
*on his knees.)* I love you as I've never loved before. I jilted twelve,
and was jilted by nine others. But I didn't love a one of them as I
love you. I'm full of tender emotion. I'm melting like butter. I'm
weak as water. I'm on my knees like a fool, and I offer you my
hand. It's a shame, it's a disgrace. I haven't been in love in five
years. I took a vow against it. And now, all of a sudden, to be

swept off my feet, it's a scandal. I offer you my hand, dear lady. Will you or won't you? You won't? Then don't. *(He rises and walks toward the door.)*

MRS. POPOV.    I didn't say anything.    151

SMIRNOV *(stopping).*    What?    152

MRS. POPOV.    Oh, nothing, you can go. Well, no, just a minute. No, you can go. Go! I detest you! But, just a moment. Oh, if you knew how furious I feel! *(Throws the gun on the table.)* My fingers have gone to sleep holding that horrid thing. *(She is tearing her hand-kerchief to shreds.)* And what are you standing around for? Get out of here!    153

SMIRNOV.    Goodbye.    154

MRS. POPOV.    Go, go, go! *(Shouting.)* Where are you going? Wait a minute! No, no, it's all right, just go. I'm fighting mad. Don't come near me, don't come near me!    155

SMIRNOV *(who is coming near her).*    I'm pretty disgusted with myself— falling in love like a kid, going down on my knees like some moongazing whippersnapper, the very thought gives me goose-flesh. *(Rudely).* I love you. But it doesn't make sense. Tomorrow, I have to pay that interest, and we've already started mowing. *(He puts his arm about her waist.)* I shall never forgive myself for this.    156

MRS. POPOV.    Take your hands off me, I hate you! Let's shoot it out!    157
*(A long kiss. Enter* LUKA *with an axe, the* GARDENER *with a rake, the* COACHMAN *with a pitchfork,* HIRED MEN *with sticks.)*

LUKA *(seeing the kiss).*    Mercy on us! Holy saints alive!    158

MRS. POPOV *(dropping her eyes).*    Luka, tell them in the stable that Toby    159
is *not* to have any oats today.

## *VOCABULARY*

| | | |
|---|---|---|
| regiment (3) | confounded (51) | subaltern (77) |
| rubles (21) | highwayman (51) | insinuate (78) |
| kopeck (26) | rural (58) | impudence (92) |
| commissioner (41) | simpering (71) | impunity (115) |
| indisposed (48) | endeavoured (73) | enchanting (146) |
| shafts (49) | emancipation (73) | brandishing (147) |

## THE FACTS

1. What is Chekhov trying to prove in this play? Do you agree with him? Why or why not?
2. In what aspects do Mrs. Popov and Mr. Smirnov resemble each other?
3. What are Mrs. Popov's *stated* reasons for remaining faithful to her husband's memory? What are her *real* reasons?
4. What is Luka's role in the play?
5. Which words are the turning point of the play?
6. Does either Mrs. Popov or Mr. Smirnov really change character in the play? Give reasons for your answer.
7. What is the meaning of the allusion to Toby in Mrs. Popov's final comment? Explain.

## THE STRATEGIES

1. At the start of the play, Mrs. Popov laces her speeches with figurative imagery emphasizing her vision of life as terribly tragic. What are some of these figures of speech? In which paragraph do they occur?
2. Mr. Smirnov uses highly connotative language to indicate his contempt for women. For instance, he draws a sharp contrast between a woman's exterior and her interior. What images does he associate with a woman's exterior? What images with her interior?
3. Much of the language Mr. Smirnov uses to describe his dislike of women is hyperbolic (so exaggerated that we can't possibly take him literally). What are some specific examples of hyperbole?
4. In paragraph 73, Mr. Smirnov implies that faithful women are to be found only among "hags." Look up this word in the dictionary to trace its etymology. What did it originally mean? What does it mean today?
5. In paragraph 150, Mr. Smirnov suddenly uses figurative language to indicate that he is falling in love. He compares himself to several things (such comparisons are labeled *similes*). What are some of the comparisons?
6. What are some trite expressions used by Mrs. Popov in paragraph 76? What effect do they have?
7. What image is evoked by the term "subaltern with his first moustache"? (See paragraph 121.)
8. Whose language is more exaggerated—Mr. Smirnov's or Mrs. Popov's? Consequently, who in the end has to make the greater reversal?

## THE ISSUES

1. What do you think of Mrs. Popov's attitude that, although while alive her husband was flagrantly cruel and unfaithful to her, she will be loving and

faithful to his memory so that in a better world she can reap the rewards of a faithful, loving wife?

2. What is the meaning of paragraph 71? Why does Smirnov use French?

3. Is there any point in debating who is more faithful—men or women? Give reasons for your answer.

4. What is it that attracts Mr. Smirnov to Mrs. Popov? Is this attraction realistic? Give reasons for your answer.

5. What are the advantages of marriage to a person like Mrs. Popov? What are the disadvantages? Which kind of spouse would you prefer—a spirited, fiery person, or a soft-spoken, gentle one?

## SUGGESTIONS FOR WRITING

1. Write a three-hundred-word essay in which you satirize male infidelity. Use connotative or exaggerated language and some figures of speech to heighten the humor.

2. Write a brief essay describing either the male or female in language of high praise. Use connotative words and figures of speech to enhance the essay.

**Carl Sandburg**

—————————— • **THREES** • ——————————

*Carl Sandburg (1878–1967), American poet and biographer, was born in Galesburg, Illinois, to poor Swedish immigrants. He won a Pulitzer Prize for his* Complete Poems *(1950) and also for his ambitious multivolume biography of* Abraham Lincoln *(1926–1939).*

*This poem touches on the ideals that humans live by and are prepared to die for.*

I was a boy when I heard three red words
a thousand Frenchmen died in the streets
for: Liberty, Equality, Fraternity—I asked
why men die for words.

I was older; men with mustaches, sideburns,          5
lilacs, told me the high golden words are:
Mother, Home, and Heaven—other older men with
face decorations said: God, Duty, Immortality
—they sang these threes slow from deep lungs.

Years ticked off their say-so on the great clocks          10

of doom and damnation, soup and nuts: meteors flashed
their say-so: and out of great Russia came three
dusky syllables workmen took guns and went out to die
for: Bread, Peace, Land.

And I met a marine of the U.S.A., a leatherneck with          15
a girl on his knee for a memory in ports circling the
earth and he said: Tell me how to say three things
and I always get by—gimme a plate of ham and eggs—
how much?—and, do you love me, kid?

## THE FACTS

1. What is the theme of this poem?
2. At this stage in your life, on which of the word-clusters mentioned do you place *highest* value? Why?
3. What values are implied by each word-cluster?
4. What kind of person does the marine of the last stanza appear to be?

## THE STRATEGIES

1. Who is the speaker in the poem? What does he represent?
2. What is the connotation of "mustaches, sideburns, / lilacs" in the second stanza?
3. What is the effect of juxtaposing such words as "doom and damnation" with "soup and nuts"?
4. Why does the poet allude to Russia in the third stanza?
5. How does the poet indicate the passing of time?

## THE ISSUES

1. What is the association of Frenchmen with the words *Liberty, Equality, Fraternity*?
2. As people age, do they tend to become more idealistic or more cynical? Give reasons for your answer.
3. Are the syllables alluded to in the third stanza still "dusky" today?
4. How does this poem relate to the chapter we are studying?

## SUGGESTIONS FOR WRITING

1. Write an analysis of the meaning of this poem.
2. Write an essay on the three most important words in your life and explain why they are so important to you.

# ═══ •• *ISSUE FOR CRITICAL* •• ═══ *THINKING*

## *Sexist Language*

Language reflects the prejudices of society. We tend to judge people by the way they speak, and to misjudge those who do not speak the way we do. Some members of minority groups acknowledge the power of hidden language snobbery by expending enormous energy in trying to imitate the speech of those who hold power, while those who hold power often disparage the speech of those groups who do not. And even though most people with liberated views may not explicitly admit such attitudes, many still secretly hold them.

In the last ten years, the feminist movement has drawn attention to the sexist elements in our language that reflect, to an overwhelming extent, the values of a male-dominated world. In its wake feminism has led women to wonder why they have to change their surnames when they marry; why female doctors are called "lady doctor" while their male counterpart is simply referred to as "doctor"; why men often patronizingly addressed their female staff members as "girls," "honey," or "sweetie." Feminist scholars point with dismay at the astounding number of words ending in "man" which are descriptive of roles that can be played by either sex: "chairman," "congressman," "policeman," and so forth. They wonder why a woman sculptor is called a "sculptress," a woman actor an "actress," and a woman poet a "poetess" when sex designation is utterly irrelevant to the occupation. And they see no valid reason for using the generic "he," "his," and "him" unless the antecedent subject is obviously male.

Discovery of these biases in the language has led many feminist scholars to propose reform. Some have suggested sex-neutral generic pronouns; others have proposed sex-neutral nouns to replace those whose suffixes specify the male sex. Others have proposed making drastic changes in even liturgical wording if it reflects a male bias. But this kind of conscious linguistic reform is not without its opponents. Many linguistic experts on the other side of the fence argue that reforms upset grammatical rules, thwart tradition, and make the language sound awkward, as in "every student must use his or her own workbook" instead of "every student must use his own workbook." To them, terms like "freshperson" instead of "freshman" sound clumsy and pretentious, to say the least. The middle attitude argues that sexist language is a reflection of a sexist attitude, not its cause, and that as women take on a more powerful role in society, the language will naturally reflect this change.

In the meantime, lively debates continue on how much our language should be manipulated to avoid male bias. The first essay in this Issue section, "Of Girls and Chicks," is by Francine Frank and Frank Anshen, whose little book *Language and the Sexes* has influenced many college classes. These authors demonstrate through examples how women are put down by certain nouns, verbs, and adjectives in our language. In "Mom and Pop Forgive Them," on the other hand, John Garvey analyzes the changes in sexist language proposed for a modern liturgical reader and finds them highly inappropriate. Finally, a university professor, Robin Lakoff, demonstrates in "You Are What You Say" how women's language is often more dainty than men's. These essays encourage the reader to think about whether or not we are unconsciously perpetuating sexism in our society.

Francine Frank and Frank Anshen

# ———— • OF GIRLS AND CHICKS • ————

*Francine Frank (b. 1931) is Director of Linguistics at the State University of New York, Albany. She earned her Ph.D. from the University of Illinois, Urbana, in 1955, and has contributed numerous articles to professional journals. She also teaches in the Women's Studies program at the Albany campus of SUNY. Frank Anshen (b. 1942) is an associate professor of linguistics at the State University of New York, Stonybrook. He is the author of* Statistics and Language *and the founder of the New York Council on Linguistics.*

*The editorial policies of most major publishers explicitly ban sex stereotyping. This means not only that writers cannot imply a gender bias in roles or jobs (even if the implication is accurate), but also that they cannot use* he *as the generalized third-person pronoun ("If a student thinks this course will be a snap,* he *is in for a rude awakening.") Most of these reforms were adopted by publishers in the 1970s in response to the criticism of feminists that gender-biased pronouns elevated men while demeaning women. But apparently, as this excerpt from the book* Language and the Sexes *(1983) shows with numerous examples, sex stereotyping in English is more widespread than commonly thought. Unanswered is the question of whether the stereotyping merely mirrors reality or is in some way responsible for creating it.*

English is a sexist language! Angry women have often been driven  1
to make such a statement. But is it accurate? Can we really label some

languages as more sexist than others? In a recent movie, a rather obnoxious adolescent described his favorite pastime as "cruising chicks."
If the adolescent had been female, she would not have had a parallel
term to refer to finding boys. This asymmetry in vocabulary is a linguistic reflection of sexism in our society.

One of the more intriguing and controversial hypotheses of modern    2
linguistics is the idea that the grammatical structure of a language may
influence the thought processes of speakers of that language. Regardless of the truth of that idea, known among linguists as the Sapir-
Whorf hypothesis, it seems clear that we can gain insights into the
culture and attitudes of a group by examining the language of that
group. Eskimos live in an environment in which the condition of snow
is vital to survival, and they therefore have a large number of distinct
words for different kinds of snow. Most Hindi speakers live in areas of
India where it does not snow and, as a result, Hindi has only a single
word equivalent to the two English words *snow* and *ice*. In Modern
English, the plethora of words such as *road, avenue, freeway, highway,
boulevard, street, turnpike, expressway, parkway, lane*, and *interstate*, might
lead one to conclude that automobiles are very important to Americans, while the relative scarcity of words for various types of kinfolk
would suggest that extended familial relationships are not very important to Americans. (We do not, for example, have separate words for
our mother's brother and our father's brother.) In this chapter, we will
look at the linguistic treatment of women in English for clues to the
attitudes towards women held by speakers of English.

First let us consider what the last members of the following groups    3
have in common: Jack and Jill, Romeo and Juliet, Adam and Eve, Peter,
Paul and Mary, Hansel and Gretel, Roy Rogers and Dale Evans, Tristan
and Isolde, Guys and Dolls, Abelard and Heloise, man and wife, Dick
and Jane, Burns and Allen, Anthony and Cleopatra, Sonny and Cher,
Fibber Magee and Molly, Ferdinand and Isabella, Samson and Delilah,
and Stiller and Meara. That's right, it is a group of women who have
been put in their place. Not that women must always come last: Snow
White gets to precede all seven of the dwarfs, Fran may follow Kukla,
but she comes before Ollie, Anna preceded the King of Siam, although
it must be noted that, as colonialism waned, she was thrust to the rear
of the billing in "The King and I." Women with guns are also able to
command top billing, as in Frankie and Johnny, and Bonnie and Clyde.
The moral is clear: a woman who wants precedence in our society
should either hang around with dwarfs or dragons, or shoot some-

body. "Women and children first" may apply on sinking ships, but it clearly doesn't apply in the English language.

Not only are women put off, they are also put down, numerically and otherwise. In the real world, women slightly outnumber men. But the world created for American schoolchildren presents a different picture. In an article describing the preparation of a dictionary for schoolchildren, Alma Graham recounts the imbalance discovered in schoolbooks in all subjects in use in the early 1970s. A computer analysis of five million words in context revealed many subtle and not-so-subtle clues to the status of women in American society. The numbers alone tell us a lot: men outnumber women seven to one, boys outnumber girls two to one; girls are even in the minority in home economics books, where masculine pronouns outnumber feminine ones two to one. In general, the pronouns *he, him,* and *his* outnumber *she, her,* and *hers,* by a ratio of four to one.

When the linguistic context of the above pronouns was analyzed to see if they were generics, referring to people regardless of sex, it was found that of 940 examples, almost eighty percent clearly referred to male human beings; next came references to male animals, to persons such as sailors and farmers, who were assumed to be male, and only thirty-two pronouns were true generics. In another set of words, we do find more women; mothers outnumber fathers, and wives appear three times as often as husbands. However, children are usually labelled by referring to a male parent (Jim's son rather than Betty's son), most mothers have sons rather than daughters, and so do most fathers. There are twice as many uncles as aunts and every first-born child is a son. It is not altogether clear from all this how the race reproduces itself without dying out in a few generations. Notice further that, although the word *wife* is more frequent, expressions like *the farmer's wife, pioneers and their wives,* etc., indicate that the main characters are male.

Consider now another area of our language. English has a large number of nouns which appear to be neutral with regard to sex, but actually are covertly masculine. Although the dictionary may define *poet* as one who writes poetry, a woman who writes poetry appears so anomalous or threatening to some, that they use the special term *poetess* to refer to her. There is no corresponding term to call attention to the sex of a man who writes poetry, but then we find nothing remarkable in the fact that poetry is written by men. Of course, if a woman is sufficiently meritorious, we may forgive her her sex and refer to her as a poet after all, or, wishing to keep the important fact of her sex in our consciousness, we may call her a *woman poet*. However, to balance the possible reward of having her sex overlooked, there remains the possibility of more extreme punishment; we may judge her work so harshly that she will be labelled a *lady poet*. Once again, the moral is clear: people who write poetry are assumed to be men until proven otherwise, and people identified as women who write poetry are assumed to be less competent than sexually unidentified (i.e., presumably male) people who write poetry.

If the phenomenon we have been discussing were limited to poetry,    7 we might not regard it as very significant; after all, our society tends to regard poets as somewhat odd anyway. But, in fact, it is widespread in the language. There is a general tendency to label the exception, which in most cases turns out to be women. Many words with feminine suffixes, such as *farmerette, authoress,* and *aviatrix,* have such a clear trivializing effect, that there has been a trend away from their use and a preference for *woman author* and the like. The feminines of many ethnic terms, such as *Negress* and *Jewess,* are considered particularly objectionable. Other words, such as *actress* and *waitress,* seem to have escaped the negative connotations and remain in use. However, we note that waiters often work in more expensive establishments than do waitresses, that actresses belong to "Actor's Equity," and that women participants in theatrical groups have begun to refer to themselves as "actors." On rare occasions, this presumption of maleness in terms which should be sexually neutral, works to women's advantage. If someone is called a *bastard*, either as a general term of abuse, or as a statement of the lack of legal marital ties between that person's parents, we assume that person is a male. While an illegitimate child may be of either sex, only men are bastards in common usage. Although the dictionary seems to regard this as a sex-neutral term, a recent dictionary of slang gives the term *bastarda* as a "female bastard/law, Black/."

Sometimes the feminine member of a pair of words has a meaning    8 which is not only inferior to the masculine one, but also different from it. Compare, for instance, a *governor* with a *governess* or a *major* with a *majorette*. Ella Grasso was the governor of Connecticut, and a high ranking woman in the U.S. Army would certainly not be a majorette. In a large number of cases, the supposed feminine form does not even exist to refer to a woman occupying a "male" position. Women, for example, may be United States Senators, but there is no such thing as a *Senatress*. Often, where the feminine noun does exist, it will acquire sexual overtones not found in the original: compare a *mistress* with a *master*.

The last effect even spills over to adjectives applied to the two sexes. A *virtuous* man may be patriotic or charitable or exhibit any one of a number of other admirable traits; a *virtuous* woman is chaste. (The word *virtue* is, itself, derived from the Latin word for *man*.) Similarly, consider Robin Lakoff's example of the different implications involved in saying *He is a professional* versus *She is a professional*. Although adjectives also may come in seemingly equivalent pairs like *handsome* and *pretty*, they prove not to be equivalent in practice; it is a compliment to call a woman *handsome* and an insult to call a man *pretty*. In other cases, where pairs of adjectives exist, one term covers both sexes and the other one tends to refer only to one sex, usually females. So, members of both sexes may be *small*, but only women seem to be *petite*; both boys and girls may have a *lively* personality, but when did you meet a *vivacious* boy?

In addition to this use of certain adjectives almost exclusively to refer to women, descriptions of women typically include more adjectives and expressions referring to physical appearance than do descriptions of men. The media clearly reflect this tendency; a report on an interview with a well-known woman rarely fails to mention that she is *attractive* or *stylish*, or to say something about her clothes or the color of her hair or eyes, even if the context is a serious one like politics or economics, where such details have no importance. Readers are also likely to be informed of the number and ages of her children. Men are not treated in a parallel fashion.

Verbs turn out to be sex-differentiated also. Prominent among such verbs are those which refer to women's linguistic behavior and reflect some of the stereotypes discussed in an earlier chapter. Women, for example, may *shriek* and *scream*, while men may *bellow*. Women and children (girls?) hold a virtual monopoly on *giggling*, and it seems that men rarely *gossip* or *scold*. There are also a large number of sex-marked verbs which refer to sexual intercourse. In their article, "Sex-marked Predicates in English," Julia P. Stanley and Susan W. Robbins note the abundance of terms which describe the male role in sexual intercourse, and the lack of parallel terms for women's role. Women are thus assigned a passive role in sex by our language.

Another set of words which are presumably sex-neutral are the ones    12
that end in *-man*. This suffix, which is pronounced with a different
vowel from the one in the word *man*, supposedly indicates a person of
either sex. It is commonly found in words designating professions—
*salesman, postman, congressman,* for example—and in some other
expressions such as *chairman* and *freshman*. However, the very fact that
there exist female counterparts for many of these words, such as *chair-
woman* and *congresswoman,* indicates that they are thought of as typically male and, as in the case of poets, when a woman is referred to,
her sex must be clearly indicated. In the case of *salesman,* there are a
variety of feminine forms: *saleswoman, saleslady,* and *salesgirl.* Although
they appear to be synonymous, they convey significant social distinctions; someone referred to as a *saleslady* or a *salesgirl* probably works
in a retail establishment such as a department store or a variety store.
A woman who sells mainframe computers to large corporations would
be called a *saleswoman,* or even a *salesman.* The more important the
position, the less likely it is to be held by a *-girl* or a *-lady,* and the more
likely it is to be the responsibility of a *-man.*

If speakers of English often have a choice of using separate words    13
for men and women, of pretending that a single word with a male
marker like *chairman* refers to both sexes, or of using a truly sex-neutral
term like *chairperson* or *chair,* speakers of some other languages do not
enjoy such freedom. They are constrained by the grammar of their
languages to classify the nouns they use according to something called
gender. Grammatical gender is a feature of most European languages
and of many others as well. Depending on the language, nouns may
be classified according to whether they are animate or inanimate, human or non-human, male or female, or, in the case of inanimate objects, the class may depend on shape or some other characteristic. In
some languages, meaning plays little part in determining noun class
or gender; it may be predictable from the phonetic shape of the words,
or it may be completely arbitrary. In the European tradition, genders
are labeled *masculine* and *feminine* and, if there is a third noun class,
*neuter.* This is in spite of the fact that most words included in all three
of these classes represent inanimate objects like *tables and doors,* abstract concepts like *freedom,* or body parts like *head, toe, nose,* etc. Some
of us English speakers may begin to wonder about the strange world
view of speakers of languages which classify books as masculine and
tables as feminine, especially when we notice that the word for nose is
feminine in Spanish, but masculine in French and Italian. It turns out,

however, that they are not following some animistic practice whereby inanimate objects are thought of as having sexual attributes; in the modern European languages at least, grammatical gender is, for most nouns, a purely arbitrary classification, often the result of linguistic tradition and of a number of historical accidents. The labels come from the fact that most nouns referring to males belong to one class and most nouns referring to females belong to another class and, following the human practice of classifying everything in terms of ourselves, we extend the distinguishing labels to all nouns. There are, not surprisingly, exceptions to this prevalent mode of classification, which lead to the oddity of such words as the French *sentinelle*, 'guard', being grammatically feminine, although most guards are men, while two German words for 'young woman', *Fraulein* and *Mädchen*, are grammatically neuter.

Are speakers of languages with grammatical gender completely straitjacketed by their grammar and forced to be sexist? We will return to this question in the final chapter. For now, we note that in these languages, the masculine forms usually serve as generics and are considered the general forms, in much the same way as the *-man* words are in English. Just as there are often alternatives to these masculine words in English, other languages also have many words that are potentially neutral and can belong to either gender, depending on the sex of the person referred to—French *poète* and Spanish *poeta* are examples, despite the dictionaries' classification of them as masculine. Yet speakers often insist on signalling the sex of women poets by adding suffixes parallel to the English *-ess*, *poétesse* and *poetisa* being the French and Spanish equivalents, or by tacking on the word for woman, as in *médecin femme*, one term for "woman doctor" in French.

Although it is true that the masculine forms serve as the unmarked or neutral terms in many languages, this does not seem to be a universal feature of human languages, as some have claimed. Iroquoian languages use feminine nouns as unmarked or generic terms; however, in the case of Iroquoian occupational terms, which are composed of a pronoun and a verb (literally translated as "she cooks" or "he cooks"), the sex-typing of the job determines whether the masculine or feminine pronoun is used. In Modern Standard Arabic many nouns switch to the feminine gender when they are pluralized. In many European languages, abstract nouns are predominantly in the feminine gender.

English nouns no longer exhibit grammatical gender, but the language does have a large number of words that refer to members of one sex only. In addition, when we do not know the sex of the person referred to by a noun such as *writer* or *student*, the choice of the pronoun will, as in Iroquois, often depend on culturally defined sex roles. *Teacher*, therefore, is usually *she*, while *professor*, *doctor*, and *priest* usually go with *he*. This brings us to the question of the "generic" use of *he* and the word *man*.

In the case of the word *man*, as in *Man is a primate*, it has been argued 17 that this usage is independent of sex, that it refers to all members of the species, and that it is just an etymological coincidence that the form for the species is the same as that for the male members of the species. Certainly, using the same form for the entire species and for half the species creates the possibility of confusion, as those colonial women discovered who rashly thought that the word *man* in the sentence "All men are created equal" included them. More confusion may come about when we use phrases like *early man*. Although this presumably refers to the species, notice how easy it is to use expressions like *early man and his wife* and how hard it is to say things like *man is the only animal that menstruates* or even *early woman and her husband*. As with the poetical examples discussed earlier, the common theme running through these last examples is that the male is taken as the normal, that masculine forms refer both to the sex and the species, while women are the exception, usually absorbed by the masculine, but needing special terms when they become noticeable.

If the above examples have not convinced you that *man* as a generic 18 is at best ambiguous, consider the following quote from Alma Graham:

> If a woman is swept off a ship into the water, the cry is "Man overboard!" If she is killed by a hit-and-run driver, the charge is "manslaughter." If she is injured on the job, the coverage is "workmen's compensation." But if she arrives at a threshold marked "Men Only," she knows the admonition is not intended to bar animals or plants or inanimate objects. It is meant for her.

## *VOCABULARY*

| | | |
|---|---|---|
| asymmetry (1) | covertly (6) | phonetic (13) |
| plethora (2) | anomalous (6) | animistic (13) |
| precedence (3) | meritorious (6) | etymological (17) |
| generics (5) | connotations (7) | |

## THE FACTS

1. What is the Sapir-Whorf hypothesis?
2. How does the world presented in American schoolbooks differ from the real one in which schoolchildren live? What does this indicate?
3. In what way are verbs sex-differentiated?
4. Why does it seem unsuitable to call a female seller of mainframe computers a *saleslady*? What would you call a female who sells cosmetic products door-to-door?
5. What effect do suffixes like *-ette,-ess,* or *-trix* have?

## THE STRATEGIES

1. What is the authors' definition of *sexism*? How do they support it?
2. In paragraph 2, the authors give three examples to support their thesis that "we can gain insights into the culture and attitudes of a group by examining the language of that group." With what prefacing word or phrase or other technique are these examples introduced?
3. What is the moral of the examples listed in paragraph 3? What tone are the authors using in presenting that moral?
4. What connotative distinctions exist between the meanings of *poetess, woman poet,* and *lady poet*? How clear or unclear are these distinctions to you?
5. Would it make any difference in the credibility of the authors' arguments if the male author were given first listing rather than second? Why would it or why wouldn't it make a difference?

## THE ISSUES

1. What effect on the English language in our country do you think the feminist movement is likely to produce in the next decade?
2. How do you think language evolved with as many sex biases as the authors say it has? Do you agree with the experts in linguistics who are trying to manipulate the language so as to rectify the bias? Why or why not?
3. Do you believe that women should retain their maiden names once they get married? Why or why not?
4. Review paragraph 9. What other adjectives seem to separate males and females?
5. What, if anything, do you plan to change in your own writing in order to avoid sex bias? If you do not plan to make any changes, state why.

## SUGGESTIONS FOR WRITING

1. Is sexism in language a reflection of, or the cause of, sex bias in society? Write an essay arguing either position on that question.

2. Do the differences between men and women justify the use of different words to refer to them and their behavior? Argue for or against this view in an essay.

John Garvey

———— • **MOM AND POP FORGIVE THEM** • ————

*John Garvey (b. 1944), a graduate of Notre Dame University, is a teacher, author, and editor. He is a regular contributor to* Commonweal *magazine, from which the following essay has been excerpted.*

There are a number of things to be said about the new readings    1
offered for liturgical use by the National Council of Churches, all but one of them negative. That single thing is that the intention was a decent one. According to the *New York Times*, members of the committee which produced the readings felt that "the use of sexually inclusive language in public worship will undergird other efforts for equality between men and women." This fine aim is not advanced by a tin-eared, antihistorical approach to Scripture. Here are some of the versions (it would not be at all accurate to call them translations; they are revisions) offered by the committee:

> *And because you are children, God has sent the Spirit of the Child into our hearts, crying, "God! my Mother and Father!"* . . . (Gal. 4:6)
> *For God so loved the world that God gave God's only Child, that whoever believes in that Child should not perish, but have eternal life.* (John 3:16)

In an article in *The Lutheran*, Bishop James R. Crumley, Jr., of the    2
Lutheran Church in America, said of the above version of John's language, "Attempting to avoid pronouns simply illustrates the need for them in the first place." Bishop Crumley also worried that speaking of God as Mother and Father would not show God's asexuality so much as it might imply God's bisexuality. The Lutheran Church in America will not recommend the use of the new lectionary to its churches. Archbishop Iakovos of the Greek Orthodox Archdiocese of North and South America said that these versions do not "reflect the traditions and reverence of the Holy Scriptures."

I have learned (when arguing against usages like "If anyone wants    3
to reserve a seat, they should see the ticket manager") that the issue of gender in languages arouses passionate responses. Let me argue

against what has been done in this lectionary by moving to another field, one which matters very much to me. I believe that nonviolence is essential to being Christian. Not everyone agrees with that, just as many would not call the feminist cause essential to Christianity. But if any particular moral focus—justice towards women, nonviolence, the needs of the poor—is allowed to force the revision of Scripture or the partial censoring of literature we will lose the kind of memory that matters to poetry and to a deeper understanding of the symbols which move at levels deeper than rationality and ideology.

Gandhi (hardly a violent sort) was inspired by the *Bhagavad-Gita*.    4
Battle is the metaphor which moves that poem, both literal battle—the protagonist wonders whether it is right for him to engage in it—and spiritual struggle. The poem begins,

> *On the field of Truth, on the battle-field of life, what came to pass, Sanjaya, when my sons and their warriors faced those of my brother Pandu? (The Bhaga-vad Gita.* Tr. Juan Mascaró. Penguin 1962*)*

Despite my firm belief in nonviolence I am not sure that this could    5
be better rendered,

> *In the office of Truth, at the committee meeting of life, what came to pass*
> (etc.)

I don't mean this to be as flippant as the above might make it seem,    6
but some attempts to deal with real problems are so insensitive to other questions, and to the limitations of our own age's understanding, that if taken seriously they will lead us into a set of problems at least as thorny as the ones we are trying to solve. To take one example, gutting the Old Testament of its most violent scenes, or bowdlerizing them to make them less violent, has resonances which move more deeply than the question we hope to address when we move in with the editor's pencil. Moses lifts his arms at God's command for victory, and when he lowers them in weariness his army begins to lose; when they are raised again, propped up by his companions, the army begins to win. At its most superficial level this is an important metaphor about prayer, and it goes even deeper than that.

I kneel in churches, when kneeling is called for, and in social circum-    7
stances find myself shaking hands. Both of these rather common symbols have their roots in war. Kneeling puts you in a physically vulnerable position before a superior who can kill you, now that you aren't on your feet and able to maneuver. A handshake means putting

your sword hand into the hand of another, whose sword hand is held by yours: you keep one another from striking. This is at once a sign of peace, in its most negative and limited form, and of peace's vulnerability. It is not at all a sign of peace's fullness, but is rooted in the fragility of wordly peace. It comes to us from the ancient history of the West, and in all its limitation is full of peaceful meaning.

The language of Scripture is in some ways comparable. No one I    8
know imagines that God is physically male. But is that all that the language of Scripture means in referring to God as Father? Is another primitive and complicated level of metaphor at work in symbols which involve sex? We speak of "mother earth," and mean a recurrent fertility which happens naturally and rhythmically.

The mother was a symbol of fertility, oasis-like, and the womb and    9
the navel were signs of our return to that source. Fatherhood did not have that necessity or earthiness about it. Without entering into the complicated question of which symbol is the better one for expressing our relationship to the divine (my feeling is that we need both, as Julian of Norwich knew when she referred to divine motherhood), it could be that God seen as Father is necessary in moving symbolically towards the idea of creation from nothing, a creation which *did not need to be*. Symbols are not simply reduced, and they are dealt with simply only by high-school English teachers and those ideologically inclined folk—I really don't care what their causes are, how good or how bad or how silly—who think that we can make the world over with mind and force, as if we were ruled primarily by reason and that tiny part of the imagination we are aware of. There are vaginal and phallic symbols all over the mythical landscape, especially the Hindu part. The magician's wand is phallic, and so is the Easter candle plunged into the waters of the baptismal font, which is plainly womblike. To reduce sexual symbols to tokens which we trade in crude exchanges about power and economic equality is to miss much that symbols have to tell us. I wouldn't for a moment claim that those symbols have nothing at all to do with power and equality, or that their evolution wasn't influenced by some very ugly factors.

But the *more* which is involved where there is more to it than that is    10
very important—even of the essence. The weirdness involved in being human is that we are at once ape and angel. We are gifted and cursed with teeth and claws and instincts which pull at us from where we have been and push us towards what we will be. It would not be a human improvement to file down our canine teeth because of what

they imply about what we have come from. To deny or forget that origin is dangerous. It is also not only dangerous but foolish to see it as simply bad, bad as it may often have been. A religion which has become an anti-idolatrous form of monotheism (what a dreadful way to talk about the living God, but here we are, impaled on a language) does in fact have patriarchal origins. Like the handshake, or the grin which reveals the canine tooth, the language of Scripture tells us what we have come from and points the way to what we will be. It is part of incarnation, of being flesh and having a long history. It should not be rewritten to prop up a less carnal, and therefore less historical and finally less real, picture of ourselves.

## VOCABULARY

| | | |
|---|---|---|
| liturgical (1) | bowdlerizing (6) | phallic (9) |
| undergird (1) | resonances (6) | evolution (9) |
| feminist (3) | maneuver (7) | anti-idolatrous (10) |
| censoring (3) | vulnerability (7) | monotheism (10) |
| ideology (3) | fragility (7) | impaled (10) |
| protagonist (4) | oasis-like (9) | |
| flippant (6) | vaginal (9) | |

## THE FACTS

1. How would you summarize Garvey's argument in a single sentence? Comment on the validity of his proposition.
2. In Garvey's opinion, what is the only good point about the new lectionary offered by the National Council of Churches? Do you see other good aspects? If so, what are they?
3. According to Bishop Crumley, what danger is there in using language that portrays God's sexuality?
4. According to the author, what common customs of our society originate from war?
5. Why, according to Garvey, is it inappropriate to tamper with the symbolism implicit in a male God?
6. What is the symbolic meaning of the human canine tooth? Why must we not obliterate this meaning?

## THE STRATEGIES

1. What is the meaning of the essay's title? Explain the title's origin. What purpose does such a title serve?

2. In paragraph 4, why is Gandhi referred to? Since he is Hindu and not Christian, why should his person be used as support for the thesis?
3. In paragraph 8, the symbol of "Mother Earth" is explained. How would you explain the following symbols: a *cross*, a *forked road*, an *eagle*, a *weeping willow tree*, a *little lamb*, a *red rose*?
4. What words in Garvey's conclusion reveal the purpose of his essay?

### THE ISSUES

1. What is your view of God's sexuality? Is it masculine? Feminine? Both? Neither? Explain your answer.
2. How do you feel about the attempt on the part of certain religious organizations to get rid of sexist language in the Bible, especially in references to the deity?
3. How would it change your view of God if she were portrayed as a woman?
4. What would be lost or gained if we were to refer to Father Earth rather than Mother Earth?
5. Why are symbols not easily reduced to logic?

### SUGGESTIONS FOR WRITING

1. Write an essay in which you cite male sex biases in the English language. Argue for a change in certain words. Consider, for instance, such terms as *statesman, manful, mankind,* or *manslaughter.*
2. In five hundred words or less, reveal what you believe are female characteristics of Jesus as he is described by many contemporary preachers or moralists.
3. Write a five-hundred-word argument for or against desexing the Bible. Use facts, experience, and expert testimony to support your position.

### Robin Lakoff

───────── • **YOU ARE WHAT YOU SAY** • ─────────

*Robin Lakoff (b. 1942) is a professor of linguistics at the University of California, Berkeley. She has been particularly recognized for her work on linguistic stereotypes and on the language associated with sex roles. Among her books is* Language and Woman's Place *(1975). The essay below first appeared in the July 1974 issue of* Ms.

"Women's language" is that pleasant (dainty?), euphemistic, never-    1
aggressive way of talking we learned as little girls. Cultural bias was

built into the language we were allowed to speak, the subjects we were allowed to speak about, and the ways we were spoken of. Having learned our linguistic lesson well, we go out in the world, only to discover that we are communicative cripples—damned if we do, and damned if we don't.

If we refuse to talk "like a lady," we are ridiculed and criticized for being unfeminine. ("She thinks like a man" is, at best, a left-handed compliment.) If we do learn all the fuzzy-headed, unassertive language of our sex, we are ridiculed for being unable to think clearly, unable to take part in a serious discussion, and therefore unfit to hold a position of power.

It doesn't take much of this for a woman to begin feeling she deserves such treatment because of inadequacies in her own intelligence and education.

"Women's language" shows up in all levels of English. For example, women are encouraged and allowed to make far more precise discriminations in naming colors than men do. Words like *mauve, beige, ecru, aquamarine, lavender,* and so on, are unremarkable in a woman's active vocabulary, but largely absent from that of most men. I know of no evidence suggesting that women actually *see* a wider range of colors than men do. It is simply that fine discriminations of this sort are relevant to women's vocabularies, but not to men's; to men, who control most of the interesting affairs of the world, such distinctions are trivial—irrelevant.

In the area of syntax, we find similar gender-related peculiarities of speech. There is one construction, in particular, that women use conversationally far more than men: the tag-question. A tag is midway between an outright statement and a yes-no question; it is less assertive than the former, but more confident than the latter.

A *flat statement* indicates confidence in the speaker's knowledge and is fairly certain to be believed; a *question* indicates a lack of knowledge on some point and implies that the gap in the speaker's knowledge can and will be remedied by an answer. For example, if, at a Little League game, I have had my glasses off, I can legitimately ask someone else: "Was the player out at third?" A *tag question*, being intermediate between statement and question, is used when the speaker is stating a claim, but lacks full confidence in the truth of that claim. So if I say, "Is Joan here?" I will probably not be surprised if my respondent answers "no"; but if I say, "Joan is here, isn't she?" instead, chances are I am already biased in favor of a positive answer, wanting only confirmation. I still want a response, but I have enough knowledge (or think I have) to predict that response. A tag question, then, might be thought of as a statement that doesn't demand to be believed by anyone but the speaker, a way of giving leeway, of not forcing the addressee to go along with the views of the speaker.

Another common use of the tag-question is in small talk when the speaker is trying to elicit conversation: "Sure is hot here, isn't it?"    7

But in discussing personal feelings or opinions, only the speaker normally has any way of knowing the correct answer. Sentences such as "I have a headache, don't I?" are clearly ridiculous. But there are other examples where it is the speaker's opinions, rather than perceptions, for which corroboration is sought, as in "The situation in Southeast Asia is terrible, isn't it?"    8

While there are, of course, other possible interpretations of a sentence like this, one possibility is that the speaker has a particular answer in mind—"yes" or "no"—but is reluctant to state it baldly. This sort of tag question is much more apt to be used by women than by men in conversation. Why is this the case?    9

The tag question allows a speaker to avoid commitment, and thereby avoid conflict with the addressee. The problem is that, by so doing, speakers may also give the impression of not really being sure of themselves, or looking to the addressee for confirmation of their views. This uncertainty is reinforced in more subliminal ways, too. There is a peculiar sentence intonation-pattern, used almost exclusively by women, as far as I know, which changes a declarative answer into a question. The effect of using the rising inflection typical of a yes-no question is to imply that the speaker is seeking confirmation, even though the speaker is clearly the only one who has the requisite information, which is why the question was put to her in the first place:    10

(Q) When will dinner be ready?

(A) Oh . . . around six o'clock . . . ?

It is as though the second speaker were saying, "Six o'clock—if that's okay with you, if you agree." The person being addressed is put in the position of having to provide confirmation. One likely consequence of this sort of speech-pattern in a woman is that, often unbeknownst to herself, the speaker builds a reputation of tentativeness, and others will refrain from taking her seriously or trusting her with any real responsibilities, since she "can't make up her mind," and "isn't sure of herself."

Such idiosyncrasies may explain why women's language sounds    11
much more "polite" than men's. It is polite to leave a decision open,
not impose your mind, or views, or claims, on anyone else. So a tag-
question is a kind of polite statement, in that it does not force agreement or belief on the addressee. In the same way a request is a polite
command, in that it does not force obedience on the addressee, but
rather suggests something be done as a favor to the speaker. A clearly
stated order implies a threat of certain consequences if it is not followed, and—even more impolite—implies that the speaker is in a
superior position and able to enforce the order. By couching wishes in
the form of a request, on the other hand, a speaker implies that if the
request is not carried out, only the speaker will suffer; noncompliance
cannot harm the addressee. So the decision is really left up to the
addressee. The distinction becomes clear in these examples:

Close the door.                                                12
Please close the door.                                         13
Will you close the door?                                       14
Will you please close the door?                                15
Won't you close the door?                                      16

In the same ways as words and speech patterns used *by* women    17
undermine her image, those used *to describe* women make matters even
worse. Often a word may be used of both men and women (and perhaps of things as well); but when it is applied to women, it assumes a
special meaning that, by implication rather than outright assertion, is
derogatory to women as a group.

The use of euphemisms has this effect. A euphemism is a substitute    18
for a word that has acquired a bad connotation by association with
something unpleasant or embarrassing. But almost as soon as the new
word comes into common usage, it takes on the same old bad connotations, since feelings about the things or people referred to are not
altered by a change of name; thus new euphemisms must be constantly found.

There is one euphemism for *woman* still very much alive. The word,    19
of course is *lady*. *Lady* has a masculine counterpart, namely *gentleman*,
occasionally shortened to *gent*. But for some reason *lady* is very much
commoner than *gent(leman)*.

The decision to use *lady* rather than *woman*, or vice versa, may    20
considerably alter the sense of a sentence, as the following examples
show:

(a) A woman (lady) I know is a dean at Berkeley.

(b) A woman (lady) I know makes amazing things out of shoelaces and old boxes.

The use of *lady* in (a) imparts a frivolous, or nonserious, tone to the    21
sentence: the matter under discussion is not one of great moment. Similarly, in (b), using *lady* here would suggest that the speaker considered the "amazing things" not to be serious art, but merely a hobby or an aberration. If *woman* is used, she might be a serious sculptor. To say *lady doctor* is very condescending, since no one ever says *gentleman doctor* or even *man doctor*. For example, mention in the San Francisco *Chronicle* of January 31, 1972, of Madalyn Murray O'Hair as the *lady atheist* reduces her position to that of scatterbrained eccentric. Even *woman atheist* is scarcely defensible: sex is irrelevant to her philosophical position.

Many women argue that, on the other hand, *lady* carries with it    22
overtones recalling the age of chivalry: conferring exalted stature on the person so referred to. This makes the term seem polite at first, but we must also remember that these implications are perilous: they suggest that a "lady" is helpless, and cannot do things by herself.

*Lady* can also be used to infer frivolousness, as in titles of organiza-    23
tions. Those that have a serious purpose (not merely that of enabling "the ladies" to spend time with one another) cannot use the word *lady* in their titles, but less serious ones may. Compare the *Ladies' Auxiliary* of a men's group, or the *Thursday Evening Ladies' Browning and Garden Society* with *Ladies' Liberation* or *Ladies' Strike for Peace*.

What is curious about this split is that *lady* is in origin a euphe-    24
mism—a substitute that puts a better face on something people find uncomfortable—for *woman*. What kind of euphemism is it that subtly denigrates the people to whom it refers? Perhaps *lady* functions as a euphemism for *woman* because it does not contain the sexual implications present in *woman*: it is not "embarrassing" in that way. If this is so, we may expect that, in the future, *lady* will replace woman as the primary word for the human female, since *woman* will have become too blatantly sexual. That this distinction is already made in some contexts at least is shown in the following examples, where you can try replacing *woman* with *lady*:

(a) She's only twelve, but she's already a woman.
(b) After ten years in jail, Harry wanted to find a woman.
(c) She's my woman, see, so don't mess around with her.

Another common substitute for *woman* is *girl*. One seldom hears a    25 man past the age of adolescence referred to as a boy, save in expressions like "going out with the boys," which are meant to suggest an air of adolescent frivolity and irresponsibility. But women of all ages are "girls": one can have a man—not a boy—Friday, but only a girl—never a woman or even a lady—Friday; women have girlfriends, but men do not—in a nonsexual sense—have boyfriends. It may be that this use of *girl* is euphemistic in the same way the use of *lady* is: in stressing the idea of immaturity, it removes the sexual connotations lurking in *woman*. *Girl* brings to mind irresponsibility: you don't send a girl to do a woman's errand (or even, for that matter, a boy's errand). She is a person who is both too immature and too far from real life to be entrusted with responsibilities or with decisions of any serious or important nature.

Now let's take a pair of words which, in terms of the possible relationships in an earlier society, were simple male-female equivalents, analogous to *bull : cow*. Suppose we find that, for independent reasons, society has changed in such a way that the original meanings now are irrelevant. Yet the words have not been discarded, but have acquired new meanings, metaphorically related to their original senses. But suppose these new metaphorical uses are no longer parallel to each other. By seeing where the parallelism breaks down, we discover something about the different roles played by men and women in this culture. One good example of such a divergence through time is found in the pair, *master : mistress*. Once used with reference to one's power over servants, these words have become unusable today in their original master-servant sense as the relationship has become less prevalent in our society. But the words are still common.    26

Unless used with reference to animals, *master* now generally refers to a man who has acquired consummate ability in some field, normally nonsexual. But its feminine counterpart cannot be used this way. It is practically restricted to its sexual sense of "paramour." We start out with two terms, both roughly paraphrasable as "one who has power over another." But the masculine form, once one person is no longer able to have absolute power over another, becomes usable metaphorically in the sense of "having power over *something*." *Master* requires as its object only the name of some activity, something inanimate and abstract. But *mistress* requires a masculine noun in the possessive to precede it. One cannot say: "Rhonda is a mistress." One must be *someone's* mistress. A man is defined by what he does, a woman by her    27 sexuality, that is, in terms of one particular aspect of her relationship to men. It is one thing to be an *old master* like Hans Holbein, and another to be an *old mistress*.

The same is true of the words *spinster* and *bachelor*—gender words      28
for "one who is not married." The resemblance ends with the definition. While *bachelor* is a neuter term, often used as a compliment, *spinster* normally is used pejoratively, with connotations of prissiness, fussiness, and so on. To be a bachelor implies that one has the choice of marrying or not, and this is what makes the idea of a bachelor existence attractive, in the popular literature. He has been pursued and has successfully eluded his pursuers. But a spinster is one who has not been pursued, or at least not seriously. She is old, unwanted goods. The metaphorical connotations of *bachelor* generally suggest sexual freedom; of *spinster*, puritanism or celibacy.

These examples could be multiplied. It is generally considered a *faux*      29
*pas*, in society, to congratulate a woman on her engagement, while it is correct to congratulate her fiancé. Why is this? The reason seems to be that it is impolite to remind people of things that may be uncomfortable to them. To congratulate a woman on her engagement is really to say, "Thank goodness! You had a close call!" For the man, on the other hand, there was no such danger. His choosing to marry is viewed as a good thing, but not something essential.

The linguistic double standard holds throughout the life of the rela-      30
tionship. After marriage, bachelor and spinster become man and wife, not man and woman. The woman whose husband dies remaind "John's widow"; John, however, is never "Mary's widower."

Finally, why is it that salesclerks and others are so quick to call      31
women customers "dear," "honey," and other terms of endearment they really have no business using? A male customer would never put up with it. But women, like children, are supposed to enjoy these endearments, rather than be offended by them.

In more ways than one, it's time to speak up.      32

## VOCABULARY

| | | |
|---|---|---|
| euphemistic (1) | tentativeness (10) | analogous (26) |
| discriminations (4) | idiosyncrasies (11) | metaphorical (26) |
| syntax (5) | derogatory (17) | paraphrasable (27) |
| baldly (9) | connotation (18) | pejoratively (28) |

addressee (10)        aberration (21)       eluded (28)
subliminal (10)       eccentric (21)        puritanism (28)
intonation (10)       perilous (22)         celibacy (28)
declarative (10)      infer (23)            *faux pas* (29)
inflection (10)       denigrates (24)

## THE FACTS

1. How does the author define "women's language"? Why are women damned if they do and damned if they don't?
2. What is a tag question? What effect does it have?
3. Why does women's language sound more polite than men's?
4. When associated with a profession, an organization, or a title, what does the word *lady* imply?
5. What has happened to the words *master* and *mistress* as time has passed? How have their meanings changed?

## THE STRATEGIES

1. What relationship exists between the title of the essay and its content?
2. Which rhetorical mode is used in paragraph 4? Is this mode used elsewhere in the essay?
3. How is the transition made from paragraph 9 to paragraph 10?
4. What function does the opening sentence of paragraph 11 serve?
5. What is the purpose of paragraph 18? Is the purpose important? Why or why not?

## THE ISSUES

1. Do you believe that women should speak the same way as men or do you believe that they must maintain a certain feminine style? Explain your answer.
2. What is your opinion of the following women in terms of their femininity? How does their style either attract or repel you? Be specific in your comments:
   a. Germaine Greer
   b. Nancy Reagan
   c. Sandra Day O'Connor
   d. Margaret Thatcher
   e. Jeane Kirkpatrick
   f. Shirley MacLaine
3. What other colors can you add to the list mentioned in paragraph 4 as being used typically by women, but not men?
4. What is your opinion of the social value of tag questions?

5. Do you agree with the author's conclusion, "It's time to speak up"? (see final paragraph.) Explain your answer.

## SUGGESTIONS FOR WRITING

1. Write an essay comparing Lakoff's views with those of Frank and Anshen.
2. Write an essay in which you argue either for or against changing the language in order to promote the cause of feminism.

# CHAPTER WRITING ASSIGNMENTS

1. Analyze Alan Simpson's "Marks of an Educated Man" (pages 211–17) in terms of sexist language.
2. Write an essay indicating how a study of semantics can prevent quarrels between persons as well as governments. Use specific examples to strengthen your points.
3. Using all of the information gleaned from this chapter, write an essay in which you demonstrate how a knowledge of semantics can help improve writing.

## TERM PAPER SUGGESTION

Write a research paper on S. I. Hayakawa's contribution to semantics as a linguistic science.

# APPENDIX OF OPTIONAL ASSIGNMENTS

# •• *ASSIGNMENT 1:* ••
# *THE RESEARCH PAPER*

## WHY ENGLISH INSTRUCTORS ASSIGN RESEARCH PAPERS

The research paper is rarely greeted with joy by students, but it still remains one of the most important of all college assignments. Writing one entails thinking critically about a subject, tracking down and evaluating facts for relevance and truth, organizing materials in support of a thesis, and cultivating a readable style. Success in college depends largely on the acquisition of these skills, which are also essential for accomplishment in business, the major professions, and even in private life. Salespeople often research a market and analyze it for trends; lawyers track down facts and organize them in preparing briefs and contracts; journalists depend on investigative research to gather material for stories. Engineers, nurses, secretaries, actors, architects, insurance agents—virtually all the professions rely on and use the research techniques exemplified in this chapter.

## HOW TO CHOOSE YOUR TOPIC

Typically, English instructors grant students the freedom to choose their own research topics, thus promoting exploration and self-discovery. If such a choice is indeed available to you, we recommend some preliminary browsing through the library until you come across a subject that arouses your curiosity—be it primitive Indians, the reign of the last empress of China, some influential sports figure, the complexities of the New York stock exchange, children's psychological problems, or the fiction or poetry of a modern writer. Here are some tips on finding a suitable topic:

1. Try working with a familiar subject. For instance, you may have been fascinated by historical attempts of the super-rich to manipulate the U.S. economy such as the Gould–Fisk scheme to corner gold in 1869, with the consequent Black Friday market panic. Now you must find out more about Jay Gould, who became symbolic of autocratic business practices and was hated by most American businesspeople. Research will supply the necessary information.
2. If familiarity fails, try an entirely new area. Perhaps you have always wanted to learn about Lenin's philosophy of government, genetic engineering, evolution in the Paleozoic era, the Roman empress Galla Placidia, the causes of earthquakes, pre-Columbian art, or the historical

causes for the political unrest in Ireland. A research paper finally gives you the opportunity.

3. Use books and magazines to suggest possible topics. The library is a gold mine of hidden information. Browse through book stacks and magazine racks. Some topic of interest is bound to leap out at you.

On the other hand, avoid topics for which a single source can provide all the needed information; those that require no development but end as soon as started; those so popular that everything about them has already been written and said; those so controversial that you have only fresh fuel to add to the already raging fire; or those decidedly unsuited to your audience, as for example, a paper advocating violent overthrow of the U.S. Constitution and written for a teacher who is a conservative Republican.

## HOW TO NARROW YOUR SUBJECT

Good research papers deal with topics of modest and workable proportions. To attempt a paper on the galaxies of the universe or on World War II is to attempt the impossible. A simple but practical way to narrow your subject is to subdivide it into progressively smaller units until you reach a topic specific enough for a paper. The following diagram on the sport of fencing illustrates what we mean:

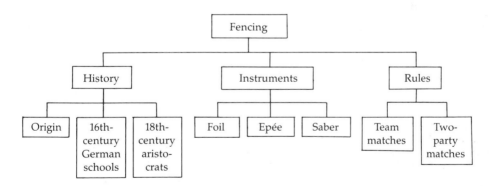

Any of the entries found on the lowest subdivision is a properly narrowed subject. For instance, you could write a useful paper on the sixteenth-century German schools that taught fencing to European gentlemen, or on the use of the saber in fencing, or on the rules of modern team fencing. But a paper just on fencing would be overly ambitious and tricky to write.

Another point to bear in mind is that unlike the typical class-written paper, in which you must first formulate a thesis and then write the text, the research paper completely reverses this process: you first gather evidence, study it, and only then deduce a thesis. The assembled facts, statistics, graphs, schematics, arguments, expert testimony, and so on will suggest a conclusion that will be your thesis. What you learn in this process of writing the research paper is not only how to write, but also how to infer a reasonable conclusion from a body of evidence.

## THE PROCESS OF WRITING THE PAPER

You have narrowed your subject. You do not yet have a thesis or a definite topic, but you have a likely subject area to explore. You can do it in these simple steps:

### 1. Find and evaluate sources.

To do this you must spend time in a library, which is not a jumble of sources but rather a systematized retrieval network. Materials for your subject will be listed in the card catalog, in appropriate indexes, in reference works, on shelves, in files, and—in a modernized library—on a computer screen. Evaluate each source by scanning titles, tables of contents, chapter headings, or article summaries. Check the date of publication to make sure that the information in the source is still valid. Ask the reference librarian for help. As you work, list each possible source on its own bibliography card, providing the information necessary for easy retrieval. Here is an example:

---

813.409
Sch.                                    College Library

Schneider, Robert W.  Five Novelists
    of the Progressive Era.
    New York: Columbia University
    Press, 1965
Chapter 5 evaluates the novels of
Winston Churchill, stating why they
were loved by contemporaries but
scorned by succeeding generations.

---

## 2. Take notes.

Using your pile of bibliography cards, retrieve the books, magazines, pamphlets, and other identified sources and place them in front of you. Skim the source to get the drift of its content. Decide if it contains material relevant enough to warrant a more detailed reading. Once you have skimmed your sources, you can start taking four basic kinds of notes: (1) summary, in which you record the gist of a passage; (2) paraphrase, in which you restate in your own words what the source says; (3) direct quotation, in which you copy the exact words of a source; and (4) personal comments, in which you express your own views on the subject or source.

Write down your notes on cards, which can be easily shuffled or discarded when you get down to the business of writing the paper. For easier reorganization of your notes, restrict each card to a single idea. To guard against unintentional plagiarism, copy down only exact quotations from your sources while digesting and expressing all other ideas in your own words. At some point at this stage (it varies from paper to paper), a thesis will occur to you. When it does, jot it down on a card for permanent reference. This will be the starting point of your paper.

## 3. Write the first draft.

With a jumble of notes strewn on your desk, you may feel bewildered about what to include or exclude as you tackle your first draft. This may well be the time for an outline, which can either be adjusted later to fit your paper or your paper subsequently adjusted to fit your outline. In any case, by now you should have become something of an expert on your subject. As you write, you will be backing up your own opinions and views with source material uncovered by your research and recorded in your notes.

## 4. Use proper documentation.

Except for statements that are common knowledge ("Abraham Lincoln was shot by Wilkes Booth"), all information taken from your sources—whether quoted, paraphrased, or summarized—must be accompanied by a source citation given in parentheses and conforming to the proper format. We provide two sample papers in this chapter—one in the Modern Language Association (MLA) format, the other in the American Psychological Association (APA) format. Use the MLA author-work format if your instructor tells you to, or if your paper is on a subject in the liberal arts, such as literature, philosophy, history, religion, or fine arts. For a paper in a more scientific field, such as psychology, sociology, or anthropology, the APA author-date format should be used. In any event, check with your instructor about the documentation format that is expected and appropriate.

Both the MLA and APA documentary styles are represented in this appendix by two carefully annotated student papers serving as general models and illustrating most of the documenting problems you are likely to encounter. For more complex citations, we recommend that you consult a style sheet or a research paper handbook. Both MLA and APA have gone to a system of parenthetical documentation, which gives brief but specific information about the sources within the text itself. The MLA style cites the author's surname or the title of a work, followed by a page number; the APA style cites the author's surname, followed by a date and a page number. In both styles, the author's name, work, and date can be omitted from the parentheses if they have already been supplied within the text. The rule of thumb is this: If the citation cannot be smoothly worked into the text, it should be supplied within parentheses. This kind of parenthetical documentation is obviously easier and simpler than either footnotes or endnotes because the citation can be given as the paper is being written and is not tediously repeated in three places: the text, the note, and the bibliography. Moreover, the writer does not have to contend with typing in superscript notes (always a chore) or keeping track of a note sequence.

Flexibility in citations is a characteristic shared by both the MLA and APA styles. For example, you might choose to cite the author's name in the text while putting the page (MLA) or year and page (APA) in parentheses:

*MLA example:*
In her *Autobiography,* Agatha Christie admits that often she felt the physical presence of Hercule Poirot (263).
*APA example:*
According to *800-Cocaine* by Mark S. Gold (1985, p. 21), cocaine has exploded into a full-blown business with brand names.

Or you might choose to include most of the citation in the parentheses:

*MLA example:*
The author began to realize how much she liked Poirot and how much a part of her life he had become (Christie, *Autobiography* 421).
*APA example:*
During the airing of ABC's *Good Morning, America* (Ross & Bronkowski, 1986), case histories were analyzed in an extremely serious tone.

In any case, the overriding aim should be to cite the necessary information without interrupting the flow of the text. What cannot elegantly be worked into the text is cited within parentheses.

## 5. Prepare "Works Cited" or "References."

The sources cited in your text must be alphabetically listed in full at the end of your paper. Under the MLA style of documentation, the list is entitled

"Works Cited"; under the APA style, it is entitled "References." Both styles require the same general information but differ slightly in details of capitalization and order. MLA entries, for example, begin with a surname, followed by a full Christian name; on the other hand, APA requires a surname, followed only by initials. In MLA entries the author's name is followed by the title of the work, whereas in APA entries the author's name is followed by the date. Other differences are also minor: MLA requires titles of books or periodicals to be underlined, articles or chapters to be placed within quotation marks, and all words of a title to be capitalized. On the other hand, APA underlines the titles of books and magazines but uses no quotation marks around the titles of chapters or articles within these longer works. APA capitalizes only the first word of a book or article title and the first word of a subtitle (if there is one) while typing all other words in lowercase. See the sample student papers for specific examples of how to handle various bibliographical matters.

## 6. Write the final copy.

Revising and editing your paper is the final step. Do not be easy on yourself; pretend, instead, that the paper is someone else's and badly in need of work. Check for logical progression, completeness of development, and mechanical correctness. The task of rewriting and revising can be simplified if you know how to use a word processor, which will spare you the tedious chore of retyping every page that needs changing. Still, the only way to produce an excellent paper is to pore over it paragraph by paragraph for weaknesses or faults. After careful review and editing, type the final copy using one of the formats exemplified by the two student papers. If you are following the APA format, you will need to write an abstract summarizing your findings (see student sample, page 859). Remember that the appearance of a paper can add to or detract from its quality. Here are some important tips on manuscript appearance:

1. Use 8½ x 11 (20 pound), white nonerasable bond. Double space throughout the paper, except where indicated otherwise on the student sample.
2. Except for page numbers, use one-inch margins at the top, bottom, and sides of the paper. (For page numbers, see item 6.)
3. Use a clean typewriter ribbon and type only on one side of the paper. Avoid fancy typefaces such as script.
4. Place a balanced and uncluttered outline before the text of the paper. Double-space throughout the outline. (See item 6 for paginating the outline.)
5. Do not use a title page unless your instructor specifies otherwise. Instead, type your name, the instructor's name, course number, and date on the first page of the outline, repeating this information in the upper

left-hand corner on the first page of the text. The title should be centered and double-spaced below the date. (See sample papers.)

6. Number pages consecutively throughout the paper in the upper right-hand corner. Do not follow page numbers by hyphens, parentheses, periods, or other characters. Number the outline with lowercase Roman numerals (*i, ii, iii,* and so on). Number the first page of the paper itself, beginning with an Arabic *1* and on throughout the entire paper, including "Works Cited" or "References."

7. Double-check the appropriate format (MLA or APA) for citing and documentation.

## SAMPLE STUDENT PAPERS

Following are facsimiles of two student papers, the first in the Modern Language Association (MLA) style, the second in the American Psychological Association (APA) style. Both papers are complete with sentence outline, text, and final bibliographic listings. Both papers have been annotated to draw your attention to variations in style, content, and format.

# ANNOTATED STUDENT RESEARCH PAPER: MODERN LANGUAGE ASSOCIATION (MLA) STYLE

1.* The first page seen by your teacher is the outline of your paper. Paginate the outline with small roman numerals. Write your name in the top left-hand margin, followed by the course title and number, your teacher's name, and the date when the paper is due.

2. Center the title of your paper and quadruple space before the thesis. A good title should tell the reader what the paper is about. Double space throughout the outline.

3. The thesis consists of a single declarative sentence preceded by the word *Thesis*. The rest of the outline follows the rules for correct sentence outlining. (See sample outline of E. M. Forster's "My Wood," pp. 206–17; the "Introduction" and "Conclusion" entries in the Forster outline are optional.) Some instructors allow topic outlines, which consist of phrases rather than full sentences. Do not make the outline too long. A rule of thumb is that for every five pages of writing you have one page of outline. The outline leaves out the details of the paper, mentioning only major points.

---

*The arabic numerals in the margins of the research paper correspond to the comments that follow.

i

1    Elynor Baughman

English 101

Professor McCuen

May 21, 1987

2            The Bilingually Handicapped Child


3    Thesis:  Early compensatory educational pro—

grams give the bilingual child a head

start that will better prepare the

child for handling schoolwork.

    I.  Empirical evidence indicates that bi—

lingualism obstructs a child's speech

development.

        A.  There are varying degrees of bi—

linguals.

            1.  Coordinate bilinguals speak two

languages independently of one

another.

            2.  Compound bilinguals tend to

mix the words of their two

languages.

        B.  Bilinguals have difficulty with

tests involving vocabulary and

concepts.

ii

II.  Unlike children of many European coun-
     tries, a child in a bilingual community
     in the United States is under a double
     strain.

    A.  The language and values expected at
         school are different from those ex-
         pected at home.

        1.  A "heritage of conflict" sepa-
             rates the bilinguals from the
             rest of the community.

        2.  The bilinguals have limited con-
             tact with English.

    B.  Every individual needs some degree
         of proficiency in the dominant
         language.

    C.  The parents' role is important in
         helping children master a language.

III.  There are several programs of early com-
      pensatory education for the bilingual
      child.

    A.  English as a Second Language pro-
         grams exist for the bilingual.

        1.  Such programs do not address the
             problem of biculturalism, which

iii

makes translation difficult.

2.  Shifts from one language to another often confuse the child.

B.  The University of Michigan is experimenting with a bilingual program
based on both cultures and
languages.

C.  Preschool education programs provide
formal training for bilingual children that enhance their chances of
success.

D.  Bicultural, bilingual television
programs for Hispanic-American
children have been started.

E.  Early compensatory language education seems to be the best approach
and should be given the highest
priority.

**4.**    College papers require no title page. Simply write your name in the top left-hand margin of the first page, followed by the course title and number, your teacher's name, and the date the paper is due—all of this information double spaced, each entry on a separate line. Then double space again, center the title (capitalizing only the first, last, and principal words and without underlining), and quadruple space. Then begin the introduction of the paper. Double space throughout the body of the paper. A 1" margin is required on all sides. Start numbering the body of the paper with "1" typed in the upper right-hand corner of the first page. Beginning with page 2, type your last name before the page number (so that misplaced pages can be easily found). When you hand in the paper, do not staple it or place it in a folder; just use a large paper clip.

**5.**    The first paragraph captures the reader's interest by drawing attention to the difficult plight of children handicapped at school because they don't handle the English language adequately. The last sentence of this opening paragraph is the thesis. It is placed in the classical position at the end of the opening paragraph, where it can control the rest of the essay. Since the student author is taking a stand on the issue of training bilingual students, her paper results in an argumentative paper rather than a report. The parenthetical citations refer the reader to a bibliographical "Works Cited" list at the end of the paper. Integrating documentary sources into the flow of the paper takes considerable skill. Sometimes you may wish to mention the full name of an author in your text. If so, only the page numbers of the citation need be mentioned within parentheses. Usually it is best to introduce the full name of an author the first time a source is used; then subsequent citations will mention (within parentheses) only the page numbers, or the title followed by the page numbers. Notice that the final period follows the final parenthesis of the citation except in case of a long quotation set off from the main text (see annotation 7). Study the parenthetical documentation of this paper to see the various possibilities for handling source citations.

1

4       Elynor Baughman

        English 101

        Professor McCuen

        May 21, 1987

                The Bilingually Handicapped Child

5           Children who cannot communicate in En-

        glish are unlikely to do well in school.  Ac-

        cording to sociologist Joyce Hertzler, if a

        child has to use one language at home and an-

        other at school, he must be able to express

        himself adequately in both or face censure

        (432-33).  A recent study entitled "Bilin-

        gual Education" indicates that approximately

        five million children in the United States

        attend public schools and speak a language

        other than English in their homes and commu-

        nities (<u>School and Society</u> 290).  Many of

        these children are handicapped in communica-

        tion and thought processes and have to repeat

        the early grades in school several times.

        Coming from a different cultural and language

        background that renders them unable to con-

        ceptualize in English, bilingual children

6.  The second paragraph introduces the author's first major subidea, that bilingualism obstructs a child's speech development. This subidea is preceded by a statement that serves as transition from the thesis to the first major subidea. Such transitions are important for smooth and coherent development. Without them, the paper would hop and skip abruptly.

7.  The author observes research convention by introducing the source of a long or important quotation, especially when referring to the source for the first time. Such an introduction adds not only coherence but also a note of authority. Typical introductions are as follows:

As Dr. Leonard Smith states . . .
According to research analyst Rose Darkwood . . .
Anthropologist Margaret Mead observes that . . .
Gilbert Highet explains . . .

Any quotation longer than three lines should be indented ten spaces (left-hand margin only) and should *not* be enclosed in quotation marks. Do *not* single space long quotations. The parenthetical citation follows the final period of the quotation. When a work has been authored by two people, both last names are cited.

8.  Notice that in this paragraph and in other paragraphs that follow the quoted material is brief and so well integrated into the grammatical structure of the writer's text that no formal introduction is necessary.

Baughman 2

consequently tend to lag behind their monolingual peers.    Early compensatory educational programs give the bilingual child a
head start that will better prepare the child
for handling schoolwork.

6         The acquisition of skill in two languages often imposes a considerable burden
upon a child.    Having to keep up their mother
tongue while also learning a new language obstructs the speech development of many children.    In 1969, behaviorist Catherine

7    Landreth made the following observation:

If two languages are spoken in the
home, or if the child is forced to
learn a foreign language while he is
still learning his mother tongue,
he gets confused and his skill in
both languages is retarded. (Morgan
and King 66)

8         A study of bilingual Chinese children in
Hawaii and monolingual children on the main-
land found that in either language, "the bilingual group was below the average of
monolinguals of the same age" (Landreth 194).

Baughman 3

Only "the superior bilingual child," who is
more adept at concept formation and has a
greater mental flexibility, is capable of
performing as well as or better than the monolingual child (Landreth 194).

A bilingual person is usually one who is
able to understand and speak two languages
with native-like control.  Donald Dugas suggests that there are varying degrees of bilingualism.  The "coordinate bilingual" has
two distinct and separate sets of speech habits.  He speaks the two languages independently of one another.  The "compound
bilingual" tends to mix the words or constructions of one language within another
(294).  Many American immigrants are compound
bilinguals.  They gave up the use of their
native language and learned English imperfectly, and therefore speak neither language
well.  A "bilingual experience," according to
Leonard Kosinski, is a situation in which
children who speak English at school hear a
foreign language spoken in the home (14T).

Children who come from homes where lit-

**9.** The second major subidea is introduced. First the writer indicates how children may handle a foreign language in Europe; then she shows how the situation in the United States differs from that of Europe. The contrast is accentuated by the word *but*. Other useful contrast words include *however, on the other hand, whereas,* and *unlike.*

Baughman 4

tle or no English is spoken have considerable
difficulty with test items that involve vocabulary.   When children have to function in
two incompatible language systems, their bilingualism must be taken into account in the
evaluation of their test results (Landreth
195).

9         In many European countries, children
master several languages with ease, but there
is no marked cultural discrimination involved
and the several languages are used with seemingly equal facility in the community.   Faye
Bumpass, a teacher of English as a Second Language, believes that acquiring native-like
control of several languages without great
social or psychic strain is not difficult if
the conditions for learning them are consistent (4).   But, if the language and values
expected at school are different from those
expected at home, the child is under a double
strain.   These dual values seem to be detrimental to success.   Thomas P. Carter, who
studied the language problems of Mexican-
American students, states that Americaniza-

**10.**   Since part of her thesis focuses on the importance of "early" compensatory help for the bilingual child, the author now brings in the issue of how parents can help give the child a head start. The author's reference to a study of Los Angeles schools gives the paper strong support: these schools continue to train a huge number of immigrant students and are thus familiar with the problem of bilingualism.

Baughman 5

tion has been much easier for non–English–
speaking people who have not resisted accul–
turation (1).

A division of communities into contrast–
ing groups leads to a lack of understanding
and to the development of prejudicial atti–
tudes.   In the Southwest, where these groups
have had a "heritage of conflict," cultural
differences tend to keep them apart, with the
result that one group may have limited contact
with the English language.   If a child has
inadequate stimulation in the language he is
being taught at school, there will be definite
deficiencies in his speech development (Man–
uel 12).

Proficiency in the dominant language is
important for the welfare of both the indi–
vidual and the community.   Every individual
must not only prepare to earn a living in the
society in which he lives, but must be able to
communicate in the dominant language if he is
to obtain a job and function effectively.

10          Parents are a major influence in shaping
the language facility of their children.

**11.**   The paragraph introduces the third and final major subidea, namely that there are several programs of early compensatory education for the bilingual child. This section of the paper is the longest because it is the bedrock support for the thesis.

They can strongly encourage their children to
master the language taught in school and can
address them in English some of the time.
Limited early contact with English and inadequate stimulation results in deficiencies in
the language.   If there is insufficient verbal interaction in English between the parents and the child, the child will hesitate to
use the language.   If two languages are spoken in a home, it is better for the child to
hear one language exclusively from one of the
parents.   The importance of children hearing
English in the home was determined in a Los
Angeles school study in 1968.   The study revealed that "the exclusive use of English
contributes consistently and positively for
Mexican-American pupils at all grade levels"
(Carter 19).

11      There are several early compensatory
programs designed to help the bilingually
handicapped child.   Many of these programs
are funded by the federal government. Most of
the compensatory programs teach the bilingual

**12.**   This page and the next consist mostly of paraphrasing, which means that the student has assimilated the information of some important source and has rewritten it in her own writing style, using her own words instead of the author's. Following each paraphrase, she provides proper documentation to credit the source for the information used. Using someone else's ideas without providing proper documentation is considered plagiarism, a serious wrong in scholarship.

Baughman 7

child English as a second language.   In En-

glish as a Second Language programs, the

child's first language is used primarily un-

til his ability in English permits the use of

both languages.   At this stage translation is

important.

12     Although much of the new language may du-

plicate words and concepts the child already

knows in his first language, there will be

many words and concepts that do not carry the

same cultural meaning (Carter 109).   Some

translations then will be like mutations that

go off in different directions.   For in-

stance, some Spanish words, such as <u>simpa-</u>

<u>tico</u>, have no literal translation in English.

Bilingualism is consequently often accom-

panied by biculturalism, which makes transla-

tion from one language to another difficult,

if not impossible (Hertzler 428).   Shifting

from one language to another in school may

also confuse a child and make him slower in

acquiring facility in the new language (Man-

uel 128).   The child's tendency is to trans-

late from one language to the other rather

**13.**  Although most of the material on this page reflects the ideas of outside sources, important commentary is nevertheless provided by the student author following the parenthetical citations. It is this commentary that gives the paper its point of view and argumentative edge. As is proper in a formal research paper, the author expresses her opinions without using the personal pronouns *I, me,* and *my.*

Baughman 8

than to think in the new language.    Encourag-

ing the use of English as soon as possible

benefits the bilingual child because constant

practice in the new language makes fluency

attainable sooner.

With federal funding, the University of

Michigan has been experimenting with a bilin-

gual education program that teaches the cur-

riculum in two languages (Dugas 294).    The

theory is that drawing the curriculum from

American and foreign cultures, and having

both English- and non-English-speaking stu-

13    dents attend, may result in a more complete

liberal education.    Perhaps bilingual pro-

grams such as this one will widen the bilin-

gual's horizons culturally as well as

linguistically and help to reduce the social

hostility against the bilingual child.

Preschool education programs for bilin-

guals provide formal school opportunities

prior to entrance into the first grade. A

close relationship exists between oral lan-

guage ability and the successful development

of reading skills.    There is some evidence

**14.** Because of the importance of the study involved, the student quotes Carter rather than paraphrasing him.

Baughman 9

that preschool programs enhance the bilin-

gual's potential for success in the first grade.

> A study in nine New Mexico towns
>
> found that first and second graders
>
> with a year of preschool language
>
> instruction achieved much better
>
> than the control group that had no
>
> such experience. (Carter 152)

14

Preschool programs develop the bilin-

gual's speaking vocabulary, his interest in

books, and his communication and listening

skills.

The first national bilingual, bicultural

Spanish-English educational television pro-

gram started in the fall of 1973.  According

to an editorial in the <u>Los Angeles Times</u> writ-

ten by Bella Stumbo, the program was geared to

children from preschool up to eight years of

age.  The theory was that television program-

ming can provide a stimulating linguistic

environment that offers good language models.

Children have very flexible speech habits in

their early years and can be taught to produce

sounds by imitation.  With television, more-

**15.**   When referring to a newspaper article, cite the section (or edition) as well as the page number—for easier retrieval.

**16.**   The student uses ellipsis points, consisting of three spaced periods (people . . .) to indicate that she has left out a passage from the quotation. The material was eliminated because it was irrelevant to the point being made. If the student had left out an entire sentence, the ellipsis would follow a regular period (people. . . .).

**17.**   When a work has been authored by three people, list all three last names within parentheses following the citation. For works authored by more than three people, use "et al." (Smith et al.).

Baughman 10

over, the child has the advantage of seeing

the instructor's mouth and facial movements

15    when words are being pronounced (pt. 1:4).

Television has an enormous potential for

helping children learn a foreign language

without making it a chore.   The hope is that

the television medium will eventually present

good educational programs that will help the

bilingually handicapped child.

16        According to Leonard Bloomfield, "the

bilingual acquires his second language in

early childhood--after early childhood few

people . . . reach perfection in a foreign

language" (56).   Young children have keen au-

ditory perception, few inhibitions, and ea-

gerness, which enable them to learn a new

language easily.   The first impact of any

language on a child always comes by way of a

conversational approach.   By the age of five

most children have mastered the fundamental

rules of grammar without any direct training

17    (Mussen, Conger, and Kagan 202).   A child's

progress in language during the preschool

years is astounding, and for this reason early

**18.**   The final paragraph neatly wraps up the paper's argument by reasserting its thesis in forceful and straightforward language.

Baughman 11

compensatory education for the bilingually

handicapped should be given a very high

priority.   Introducing a new language before

speech habits are formed has many psychologi-

cal advantages and will enable the child to

speak without an accent (Manuel 123).

18        Although many studies have treated the

linguistic development of children from the

point of view of bilingualism, much of what

has been written about any phase of bilin-

gualism seems to be based on speculative

thinking, and it is doubtful whether all of

the assumptions are sound.   Most of the pro-

grams offered to aid the bilingually handi-

capped are at first- and second-grade levels

and may already be too late to help the child.

Early compensatory education, offered at the

preschool level, would bring bilingually

handicapped children up to a level where they

would be reached by existing educational

practices. If the oral phase of learning a

language can be mastered before a child starts

school, the other related phases (reading and

writing) should follow with relative ease.

**19.** The heading "Works Cited" is centered on the page two inches from the top, followed by quadruple spacing. The entire page is double spaced, within as well as between bibliographic entries. Bibliographic entries differ from note entries not so much in content as in form. See explanation 21 for typical bibliographic form. The second and subsequent lines of each bibliography entry are indented five spaces. The entries appear in alphabetical order according to the first letter of the entry. Left and right margins are one inch.

**20.** Typical entry for an unsigned magazine article. Notice that the year is followed by a colon and then the page number(s).

**21.** Typical entry for a book with one author. Notice that the last name of the author appears first, followed by a comma and his first name. Periods followed by two spaces separate the major components of the entry (name. title. facts of publication.). No page reference is supplied. Names of well-known publishers are abbreviated ("Holt" for "Holt, Rinehart, and Winston").

**22.** Typical entry for a signed article in a periodical issued quarterly. Notice that for all articles appearing in periodicals, magazines, or newspapers, the pages of the *entire* article must be given, not just the page(s) referred to in the research paper. Since the periodical is issued quarterly, the volume number precedes the publication date (within parentheses) and a colon separates the publication date from the page numbers.

Baughman 12

**19**                  Works Cited

**20**   "The Argument for Bilingual Education."

Saturday Review 29 Apr. 1972: 54.

"Bilingual Education." School and Society

100 (Summer 1972): 290–95.

**21**   Bloomfield, Leonard. Language. New York:

Holt, 1961.

Bumpass, Faye L. Teaching Young Students En-

glish as a Foreign Language. New York:

American Book, 1963.

Carter, Thomas P. Mexican-Americans in

School: A History of Educational Ne-

glect. New York: College Entrance Exam-

ination Board, 1970.

**22**   Dugas, Donald. "Bilingualism and Language

Learning." School and Society 95 (Sum-

mer 1967): 294–96.

Hertzler, Joyce O. A Sociology of Language.

New York: Random, 1965.

Kosinski, Leonard V. "New Look at the Bilin-

gual Student." Senior Scholastic 4 Oct.

1963: 14T.

**23.**   Typical entry for a book with two authors. Notice the name of the second author appears in its normal order with the Christian name first, preceded by a comma and the word *and*. If a book is by more than three authors, use the name of the first author (last name first), followed by "et al." (Witt, Charles B., et al.)

**24.**   Typical entry for a book in an edition other than the first. Notice that the edition is preceded as well as followed by a period (*Child Development and Personality*. 5th ed.).

**25.**   Typical entry for a newspaper article. Notice that the section of the paper is cited as well as the page.

Baughman 13

Landreth, Catherine.   Early Childhood Behav-

    ior and Learning.   New York: Knopf,

    1969.

Manuel, Herschel T.   Spanish-Speaking Chil-

    dren of the Southwest.   Austin, Texas:

    University of Texas Press, 1965.

23   Morgan, Clifford T., and Richard A. King.

    Introduction to Psychology.   New York:

    McGraw, 1966.

24   Mussen, Paul Henry, John Janeway Conger, and

    Jerome Kagan.   Child Development and

    Personality.   5th ed.   New York:

    Harper, 1979.

25   Stumbo, Bella.   "Nueva Programa for Children

    of Two Cultures."   Los Angeles Times

    24 Nov. 1972, pt. 4:1.

ANNOTATED STUDENT RESEARCH PAPER
AMERICAN PSYCHOLOGICAL ASSOCIATION (APA) STYLE

1.   A running head—an abbreviated version of the title—is placed at the top right-hand side of each page. Do not use more than 50 characters (including spaces) for the running head.

2.   The page number is placed one double-spaced line below the running head.

3.   The first page of the paper is the title page. It includes the title of the paper, the name of the student, the name of the class, the name of the institution, and the date.

**1**                                          Dian Fossey

**2**                                                    1




**3**                          Dian Fossey: A Scientist

                   Who Stopped Caring About Science

                              Margie Vickers

                               English 101

                      Glendale Community College

                          December 14, 1987

**4.**   Following the title page is the **abstract**, a brief summary of the paper's major ideas. The heading *Abstract* is centered at the top of the page.

**5.**   The abstract itself is written in coherent paragraph form but leaves out the details of the research.

Dian Fossey

2

4        Abstract

5        Dian Fossey, an occupational therapist
turned anthropologist, was dedicated to sin-
gle-handedly preserving the mountain gorilla
of Africa, an obsession that may have led to
her brutal, unsolved murder.

With anthropologist Louis Leakey as her
mentor, Fossey overcame linguistic as well as
political barriers to follow her anthropolog-
ical goals of preserving gorillas as a species
and studying them in their natural habitat.
Much of Fossey's success has been attributed
to her ability to anthropomorphize the gorilla and, in some respects, to act like a gorilla herself, keeping low to the ground and
imitating the gorillas' vocalizations.  Her
mysterious and brutal murder on December 17,
1985, led to international speculation about
the motive for such an act.  Some colleagues
blamed her soured human relationships, accusing her of having a split personality.  Others believed she was killed by angry poachers

Dian Fossey

3

whose hunting of gorillas she had thwarted.

But the Rwandan government's tribunal accused

her student researcher, Wayne McGuire, who

had escaped to the United States and thus

avoided standing trial.   To this day, Fos-

sey's murder remains unsolved.   In the end,

this dedicated researcher sacrificed her life

for the well-being of the African mountain

gorilla.

**6.** The body of the paper begins on page 4. The full title of the page is centered at the top of the page.

**7.** The introductory paragraph contains no documentation, as it is the student's own conclusion. The final sentence is the thesis of the paper. Notice that it is worded slightly differently from the thesis in the outline, but the idea is the same.

**8.** The citation refers to specific pages in two separate authors' works. Since both sources agree on Fossey's yearly income and on her $8,000 loan, both are mentioned.

Dian Fossey

4

6        Dian Fossey: A Scientist Who

Stopped Caring About Science

7        Dian Fossey was a controversial, many-

faceted loner.  She never endeared herself to

human society, nor did she try to be accepted

by it.  Her life had only two purposes: to

map scientifically the lives of gorillas, and

to conserve their existence and habitat.

This woman's obsessive, single-handed dedica-

tion to the mountain gorilla may have led to

her brutal, unsolved murder.

At the age of 31, it occurred to Dian

Fossey that half her life had passed unevent-

fully.  After reading George Shaller's book

on the mountain gorilla, she decided to fly to

Africa.  To finance the trip, she took out an

$8,000 loan against her $5,200 yearly income

as an occupational therapist (Hayes, 1986, p.

8        65, and Smith, 1986, p. 35).  Virginia Morell

(1986), a journalist interested in Fossey's

work, called her "a lover of animals since

childhood" who had traveled to East Africa

"simply to see vast herds of wildlife and

9.   Since the author and year are given earlier, only the page is cited here.

10.   This is a typical full parenthetical citation for a magazine article. The order is as follows: author, year, page. Notice that the sentence period follows the final parenthesis.

Dian Fossey

5

visit the Leakeys' well—known digs at Olduvai
Gorge" (p. 20).   From this trip and conversa—
tions with Leakey, a seed was planted in Fos—
sey's mind to return someday to study the
gorillas (Morell, 1986, p. 20).

Louis Leakey, East Africa's resident ex—
pert on the origins of early man and a key
figure in launching long—term primate stud—
ies, appreciated women who appreciated ani—
mals (Hayes, 1986, p. 65).   Since his success
with Jane Goodall and her chimpanzees, he had
been looking for a woman to observe gorillas.
Leakey was of the belief that women were bet—
ter suited than men to observing apes because
he saw them as more perceptive about social
bonds, more patient, and less threatening to
male leaders of primate groups (Morell, 1986,
p. 21).   After a reacquaintance with Leakey
at a lecture in 1966, Fossey was immediately
hired, and eight months later sent on her way
to Africa. Before her departure, Leakey
tested the sincerity of her resolution by
asking her to have her appendix removed as a

**11.**   The subject of the research paper is always referred to by her surname without title ("Fossey") or by her full name ("Dian Fossey"), but never merely by her first name ("Dian").

**12.**   Numbers that can be written out in two words or less may be spelled out; otherwise they must be expressed as numerals. Any passage with many numbers should have them expressed as numerals.

Dian Fossey

6

precaution against developing appendicitis
and needing surgery out in the jungle (Mc-
Guire, 1987, p. 36).    Fossey, who was engaged
to be married to the scion of a British family
with extensive holdings in Rhodesia, immediately broke off her engagement to accept
Leakey's challenge (Brower, 1986, p. 53).

11          From every standpoint, Fossey was ill-
prepared for Africa.    She had no training in
the science of animal behavior, spoke no African languages, and knew nothing about camp-
ing.    She was totally dependent on Leakey's
guidance.    Yet Leakey provided her only with
a two-day course in field observation, given
by Jane Goodall, and a Land Rover to take her
from Nairobi six hundred miles into the Congo
(Hayes, 1986, p. 65).

12          The trek to camp Karisoke, where her
field work was to proceed, was extremely arduous.    Just to reach the trailhead to Karisoke required a four-hour bus ride.    Then
followed a 2,000-feet climb through sometimes
impenetrable vegetation.    At this altitude of

13.   Words in a foreign language must be underlined.

Dian Fossey

7

10,000 feet, the weather was often wet, misty, and bone chilling (McGuire, 1987, p. 30)—typical conditions Fossey would experience while observing gorillas.    The camp, located in Rwanda's Parc National des Volcans, was narrowly limited to a stretch 25 miles in length and from 6 to 12 miles in width (Hayes, 1986, p. 65).    It was here that Fossey set up housekeeping.    But she had barely settled in when, six months after arriving, the Congo was in a state of revolution (Hayes, p. 65).    On July 19, 1966, Fossey was escorted down to the military post of Rumangabo and placed under house arrest.    She was held for two weeks, in which time she was beaten and raped.    Acquaintances later claimed that this trauma had a profound affect on Fossey's future attitude toward all Africans (Hayes, p. 65).    Other difficulties prevailed.    For instance, in Rwanda Fossey found signs of sumu or witchcraft.    These signs included crossed sticks leading to poacher traps that signified death to any who tampered, buried animal ribs that

**14.**   Since the "1981" date was supplied earlier in the same paragraph, only the author and page are cited here.

Dian Fossey

8

reputedly could kill meddlers, and poisons
that her African staff said could make them
waste away (Morell, 1986, p. 20).    Despite
all of these obstacles, Fossey began her work.

While the mountain gorilla was officially protected, the Rwandan government felt
that the people needed more land for agriculture and more meat for food to feed the over-
populated area (Fossey, 1981, p. 514).    This
emphasis resulted in less area for the gorilla
to live and more encroachment of poachers
hunting for antelope.    Tradition and circumstances complicated the poachers' motivation
in gorilla killing.    Sometimes young gorillas
were caught in traps meant for antelopes.
Other times, hunters under the influence of
hashish just killed for the thrill of killing
(Fossey, p. 515).    The promise of money in
exchange for capturing young gorillas, to be
sent to zoos or European pet shops, lured a
number of natives.    The black market offered
$1,200 for a gorilla head and $600 for a hand
(McBee, 1986, p. 74).    Before long, the go-

Dian Fossey

9

rilla perched dangerously on the edge of extinction, a problem Fossey faced and tried to
head off.

In her early research, Fossey discovered
that the powerful but shy gorillas responded
to her attentions when she herself acted like
a gorilla.  She learned to imitate gorilla
vocalizations (hoots, grunts, belches), to
munch the foliage they ate, and to keep low to
the ground (Fossey, 1981, p. 515).  Fossey's
ability to act like a gorilla became a primary
cause for her success as an anthropologist.
It was also her downfall.  A dominant factor
in Fossey's becoming obsessed with gorillas
was her succumbing to anthropomorphism--that
is, humanizing the gorilla.  This natural,
irresistible urge is dangerous in science,
particularly in the behavioral sciences; it
is anti-science.  The researcher loses the
ability to differentiate between the object
observed and the person observing it.  With
women researchers who are childless, this is

**15.**   This is a quotation within a work. David Watts is mentioned to let the reader know that he is *not* the author of the work in which the quotation appears. Morell is the author. "Fossey" appears in brackets to clarify the "she" pronoun. Brackets indicate editorial addition.

**16.**   Quotation by subject of paper within another author's work.

**17.**   Quotation by subject within her own work.

Dian Fossey

10

15    particularly true.   David Watts, a research
assistant at the University of Michigan, drew
the following conclusion about Fossey:
"Everyone who studies the gorillas falls in
love with them.   I think she [Fossey] took
this to an extreme.   She used gorillas as re-
placements for the human relationships she
didn't have" (Morell, 1986, p. 21).   Fossey's
favorite gorilla, Digit, was killed by poachers on December 31, 1977.   He was buried be-

16    hind her cabin.   Fossey was said to have la-
mented, "From that moment on, I came to live
within an insulated part of myself" (Hayes,

17    1986, p. 68).   On another occasion Fossey
said, "Digit was a favorite among the habit-
uated gorillas I was studying; in fact, I was
unashamed to call him 'my beloved Digit'"
(Fossey, 1981, p. 501).

Fossey shared her work with many students, but their relationships with her
soured because she was perceived as a task-
master with field research standards so high
that they could not be kept.   According to

**18.**   Example of placing the date immediately following the author's name. This convention is popular with scientific papers.

**19.**   Author and page have been cited earlier; thus, only the page is needed.

**20.**   This section contains several quotations attempting to shed light on the subject's personality. Notice that all of the quotations are smoothly and grammatically integrated into text. They are properly documented.

Dian Fossey

11

18    Goodall (1986), Fossey's definition of field

work was: "You simply drive yourself to ex—

haustion and drive others in the same manner"

19    (p. 132).    Her courage to refuse to give way

to threats from native poachers, who resented

her protection of the gorillas, and her stam—

ina in facing the charge of an angry silver—

back, were legendary (Goodall, p. 132).    In

brief, her co-workers simultaneously admired

and resented her.

20          Wayne McGuire, a student researcher who

for five months lived at the camp with Fossey,

stated, "A lot of people get strange up here.

It's the loneliness that is hardest to cope

with.    You forget how to speak English, for—

get how to interact with humans" (Brower,

1986, p. 53).    Dian's hermitlike lifestyle

was evident when she admitted, "I have no

friends.    The more you learn about the dig—

nity of the gorilla, the more you want to

avoid people" (Smith, 1986, p. 35).    Research

assistants Amy Vedder and Bill Weber believed

**21.**   Since this information refers to the same author, work, and year as the citation immediately preceding, only the page is given.

Dian Fossey

12

there were two sides to Fossey's personality:
"She could be charming and she could be hateful."   They also felt that she was an alcoholic and suffered from insomnia (Hayes,
1986, p. 70).   Fellow researcher Goodall
(1986) described her as "a complex person with
startling abruptness as she swung from one
mood to another" (p. 132).

In her fierce determination to find and
stop poachers, Fossey routinely combed the
gorillas' favorite feeding grounds and cut
animal traps almost as fast as they were set
up (Fosscy, 1981, p. 518).   She found evidence in 64 gorilla skeletal specimens, collected throughout the Virunga mountains, that
poachers were responsible for at least two-
thirds of the total gorilla deaths (p. 511).
Fossey was so intent on saving the gorillas
that she even exploited the natives' super-
stitions by terrorizing them with Halloween
masks (Goodall, 1986, p. 134).   She bought
beads to use as well as firecrackers (Morell,

21

**22.**   Mention is made in the text that the citation comes from *Discover* magazine. Wayne McGuire is mentioned because he plays a leading role in the final days of Dian Fossey. Notice that all of the references are smoothly integrated into the text.

Dian Fossey

13

1986, p. 21).   In an article on Fossey, pub-

**22**   lished in <u>Discover</u> magazine, Wayne McGuire is

quoted as saying that he got "a feeling of

eeriness here, a feeling of black magic.   She

[Fossey] believed in it, I think, and she had

a local reputation for being a witch" (Brower,

1987, p. 48).   Fossey used harsh methods of

interrogation when dealing with poachers.

She burned houses, commanded unauthorized pa-

trols to cut traps, and bribed the govern-

ment's own park guards to bring her captured

poachers for interrogation (Brower, p. 53).

It was said that she pistol-whipped poachers

(McBee, 1986, p. 74).   She was even accused

of "nettle lashing."   Her men would "whip the

culprits with virulent nettles that sting on

contact with the skin, like an electric shock"

(Hayes, 1986, p. 68).   On two occasions she

held hostage the children of poachers.   Cer-

tain graduate students who were not accepted

by her spread stories that she administered

mind-altering drugs (Hayes, p. 68).

Dian Fossey

14

Using vigilante tactics against poachers eventually put Fossey at odds with the Rwanda government.   She came to believe that park officials were in collusion with poachers.   A consortium, called the Mountain Gorilla Project, was formed with the help of the President of Rwanda.   Fossey did not feel that this group was necessary.   Moreover, she opposed its setting up of tourist groups who would come into "her domain" (Hayes, 1986, p. 68). The hostility on the government side was evident when the director of tourism, Laurent Habiyaremye, forced Fossey, who suffered from emphysema, to trek down the mountain every other month to renew her visa (McGuire, 1987, p. 30).   Her most acrimonious encounter with Habiyaremye took place at a 60th anniversary celebration for the park in which her camp was located.   She was not invited.   Habiyaremye acknowledged everyone and everything, but never mentioned Fossey.   After the ceremony, some government officials indicated some regret about this obvious snub, and the Presi-

**23.**   The opening sentence of the paragraph is short and shockingly emphatic. Quotations are used when providing important aspects of the murder.

Dian Fossey

15

dent of Rwanda expressed his annoyance with

Habiyaremye.    And a few weeks later, some ar-

ticles came out in the newspaper openly crit-

icizing Habiyaremye's behavior (McGuire,

p. 40).

**23**          Shortly after 6:00 A.M. on December 17,

1985, Dian Fossey was found brutally murdered

in her cabin at the Karisoke Research Center.

A sheet of corrugated metal had been torn off

her bedroom wall in order to get to her (Mc-

Guire, 1987, p. 28).    "A brutal gash ran di-

agonally across her forehead (McGuire, p.

29).    Virginia Morell, a fellow researcher,

said, "No one who knew Fossey

well . . . was surprised by her violent end"

(Hayes, 1986, p. 70).    The fact that Fossey

had so many enemies was clearly the reason why

those who knew her in Nairobi considered her

murder predictable, if not inevitable (Hayes,

p. 70).    Her fellow worker, Wayne McGuire

(1987), whose relationship with Fossey is

darkened by mysterious shadows, claimed that

Fossey was ill.    He stated that before her

Dian Fossey

16

murder, her weakened physical condition due to emphysema (she was a heavy smoker), along with her inability to sleep, left her gaunt and frail.   She was unable to physically search out gorillas, and she became a virtual prisoner in the camp (McGuire, 1987, p. 31).

Colleagues and acquaintances suspected that poachers had murdered Fossey, but the Rwandan government had different ideas.   In August of 1986 an arrest warrant was issued for Wayne McGuire.   He was regarded as the principal author of the murder, and five accomplices (workers at the camp) were also charged.   McGuire was accused of murdering Fossey in order to acquire her notes.   Of the five Rwandans arrested, four were let go, and one committed suicide.   The Rwandans, in looking for evidence associated with the murder, were very sloppy.   They picked up everything in Fossey's room so no fingerprints could be found; they failed to follow or look into barefoot tracks leading from the scene; and they did not dust the murder weapon for

**24.**    Since McGuire was accused by the Rwandan government of murdering Fossey, his comments here are significant.

**25.**    Notice how an accumulation of quotations is worked into the text.

Dian Fossey

17

**24**    fingerprints (McGuire, 1987, p. 44).    On December 18, 1986, a Rwandan tribunal convicted
Wayne McGuire in absentia of Dian Fossey's
murder and sentenced him to death by a firing
squad.    However, he had escaped to the United
States (McGuire, p. 28).    Ian Redmond, a biologist who spent two years at Karisoke, insisted, "The charge is nonsense.    They've
concentrated on trying to find someone who is
not a Rwandan" (Smith, 1986, p. 35).    Others
questioned why, if he were guilty, McGuire
remained at the camp for some time after
Fossey's murder and wondered what he could
have gained from stealing her notes since he
had constant access to them during his stay
there (Smith, p. 35).

**25**        The Reverend Elton Wallace, a Seventh-
day Adventist minister, spoke these words at
Fossey's funeral: "Dian Fossey was born to a
home of comfort and privilege, which she left
by choice to live among a race facing extinction (Hayes, 1986, p. 70).    Goodall (1986)
wrote, "She spent her last months where she

**26.**   The student does not offer an opinion as to who murdered Fossey but prefers to leave the issue open-ended. The unsolved mystery adds an element of suspense to the paper.

Dian Fossey

18

wanted to be, near the magnificent animals to
whom she had devoted her life (p. 134)."
Harold Hayes (1986), editor of <u>California</u>
magazine, wrote this about her death: "In defense of these animals, Fossey was herself
beaten, robbed, raped, and ultimately murdered" (p. 70).   Susanna McBee (1986) proclaimed that Fossey's death "has reunited
conservation groups and galvanized Rwanda's
government to take protective action" in behalf of Africa's wildlife (p. 74).

26      It must be stated that Dian Fossey was a
dedicated researcher, who overcame enormous
obstacles in order to pursue what she deemed
important for the preservation of the mountain gorillas.   In the end, she sacrificed
her life for their well being. Her tragic murder remains unsolved, with accusing fingers
pointing in different directions.

27.    The reference list follows the APA rules for listing sources:

- The title "References" appears centered on the page.
- The reference list is double-spaced throughout.
- Each unit of the citation ends with a period.
- Only those works actually cited in the paper appear in the reference list.
- The sources are listed in alphabetical order by the surname of the author. The surname is followed by initial(s) only, not full Christian names.
- The date of publication is enclosed in parentheses. For magazines, a comma follows the year, followed by the month—written out in full—and the date.
- Only the first word of a book or article title (and the first word of a subtitle, if there is one) is capitalized; the remaining words are typed entirely in lowercase letters. However, each word in the title of a periodical is capitalized.
- The titles of books and periodicals are underlined. No quotation marks are placed around the title of articles within these longer works.

The following items do not appear in the student research paper sample, but since they are common, we provide the appropriate format:

**Book with a single author**
Jones, E. (1931).    On the nightmare.    London: Hogarth.

**Book with two or more authors**
Terman, L. M., & Merrill, M. A. (1937).    Measuring intelligence.    Cambridge, Mass.: The Riverside Press.

**Edited book**
Friedman, R. J., & Katz, M. M. (Eds.). (1974).    The psychology of depression: Contemporary theory and research.    New York: Wiley.

**Article or chapter in an edited book**
Waxer, P. (1979).    Therapist training in nonverbal behavior.    In A. Wolfgang (Ed.), Nonverbal behavior: Applications and cultural implications (pp. 221–240).    New York: Academic Press.

**Journal article, paginated anew in each issue**
Rosenthal, G. A. (1983).    A seed-eating beetle's adaptations to poisonous seed.    Scientific American, 249(6), 56–67.

**Journal article, paginated throughout the annual volume**
Rodney, J., Hollender, B., & Campbell, P. (1983).    Hypnotizability and phobic behavior.    Journal of Abnormal Psychology, 92, 386–389.

**Newspaper article**
Goodman, E. (1983, December 123).    Bouvia case crosses the "rights" line.    Los Angeles Times, Part 2, p. 5.

Dian Fossey

19

27                   References


Brower, M. (1986, February 17).   The strange

    death of Dian Fossey. A People Weekly,

    pp. 46–54.

Fossey, D. (1981, April).   The imperiled

    mountain gorilla. National Geographic,

    pp. 511–16, 518–22.

Goodall, J. (1986, May).   Mountain warrior.

    Omni, pp. 132, 134.

Hayes, H. (1986, November).   The dark romance

    of Dian Fossey. Life, pp. 64–66, 68, 70.

McBee, S. (1986, June 9).   Great apes get new

    lease on life.   U.S. News and World Re-

    port, p. 74.

McGuire, W. (1986, April).   I didn't kill

    Dian.   She was my friend.   Discover,

    pp. 28–32, 34, 36–37, 40, 44–48.

Morell, V. (1986, April).   Dian Fossey: Field

    science and death in Africa.   Science,

    pp. 17, 20–21.

Smith, W. E. (1986, September 1).   Case of

    the gorilla lady murder.   Time, p. 35.

# •• *ASSIGNMENT 2:* ••
# *THE LITERARY PAPER*

## HOW TO WRITE A PAPER ABOUT LITERATURE

Literature is a difficult subject to write about. First, it is a subject about which there is no shortage of opinions. A famous play such as *Hamlet* has been so thoroughly studied and interpreted that it would take a tome or two to collect everything that has been written about it. Beginning writers must therefore always live in dread that what they have to say about a work may be blasphemously contrary to established opinion.

Second, the beginning writer is often unaware of the tradition or era into which a piece of literature falls. Yet to write intelligently about a piece of literature, a student must be able to distinguish the qualities of its literary tradition from the properties singular to the particular work. It is nearly impossible, for instance, to write comprehensibly about the work of a Romantic poet unless one knows something about the disposition of Romanticism.

But the beginning student is rarely called upon to perform any such feat of interpretation. Instead, what an instructor generally wishes to evoke from a student-writer is simply an intelligent exploration of a work's meaning, along with a straightforward discussion of one or two of its techniques. The student might therefore be asked to analyze the meaning of a sonnet and to comment briefly on its prosody; or to discuss the theme of a short story and to examine the actions and attitudes of a principal character; or to explain the social customs upon which a certain play is based.

Even so, there are numerous pitfalls awaiting the beginning commentator on literature. The first of these is a tendency to emote over a literary favorite. Students who have fallen victim to this trait will mistake sentimentality for judgment, and write enthusiastically about how much they like a particular work. But this is not what the teacher is generally looking for in a student's essay. What is desired is not an outpouring of affection, but the careful expression of critical judgment.

A second mistake beginning students of literature often make is assuming that one opinion about a literary piece is as valid and as good as another. It is only in literature classes that one finds such extreme democracy. Geologists do not assume that one opinion about a rock is the same as another; neither do chemists nor astronomers blithely accept every theory about chemicals and planets. This fallacious view of criticism has its origin in the mistaken belief that one's primary reaction toward literature is emotional. But the emotional response evoked by the literary work is not what a writing assignment is designed to draw out of a student. Instead, what the instructor is looking for is reasoned opinion based on a close reading of the text. Disagreements in interpretation can then be referred back to the text, and evidence can be gathered to support one view over another. It is very much like two lawyers getting together to interpret the fine print on a contract. It is not at all like two people trying to reconcile their differing reactions to anchovy pizza. Interpretations that cannot be supported by the text may be judged farfetched or simply wrong; those that can be supported may be judged *more* right.

But perhaps the most common mistake of the student-critic is a tendency to serve up inconsistent, unproven, and fanciful interpretations of the literary work. Often, these take the guise of rather exotic meanings that the student has inferred, for which scanty (if any) evidence exists. In its most extreme form, this tendency leads to rampant symbol-hunting, where the writer finds complex and knotty meanings bristling behind the most innocent statements. The only known cure for this is the insistence that all interpretations be grounded in material taken from the text itself. If you have devised an ingenious explanation or reading of a work, be certain that you can point to specific passages from it that support your interpretations, and always make sure that other passages do not contradict your thesis.

## The In-Class Essay on Literature

Often students are asked to analyze and interpret literature in class-written essays. The literary work may consist of a poem, of a passage from a novel being read by the class, of a short story, or of a play. Depending on how the assignment is worded, the student may be required to find and express the theme, analyze an action, interpret a symbol, or comment on form.

## Finding and Expressing a Theme

The theme of a literary work is its central or dominant idea, its comment on life. Finding and expressing this idea involves a form of literary algebra that requires students to think logically from cause to effect. Of course, writers say more than any summary theme can possibly express; nor should finding a theme involve smothering a writer's work under a crude and simplistic summary. Instead, in the summary you should compress what you interpret as the emphasis of the work into a few brief sentences.

Consider the poem "Design" (page 631). A moth has been found dead in a spider's web spun on a heal-all flower. The poet wonders what could have brought the moth to this particular flower, where a web was spun and a spider was waiting. Why didn't the moth go to another, safer flower? This apparently trivial discovery leads the poem to speculate that destiny operates in random and mysterious ways, which is more or less the central emphasis or theme of the poem.

This theme can, of course, be stated in several different ways. So, for that matter, can the theme of any poem or other literary work. What you must do, after you have deciphered the theme of the work, is to make a statement and prove it. Proof can be supplied by quoting lines and passages from the work. The instructor can then reconstruct the process of thinking behind your conclusion. If you have misinterpreted the work, the proof allows the instructor to see how your misreading occurred.

## Analyzing Character and Action

Fictional characters behave according to the same hopes, fears, hates, and loves that motivate real people. But the characters of fiction are found in exotic dilemmas real people hardly ever encounter. Consequently, fiction provides us with an opportunity to ponder how common people might react in uncommon situations; we can then draw moral lessons, psychological principles, and philosophical insights from their behavior. Without fiction, we would remain hemmed in by the narrow horizons of reality and experience.

By asking you to write an essay explaining why a certain character performed a certain action, your instructor is fostering valuable skills of social analysis. If you can understand the rage and jealousy of Othello or the isolated pride of Hester Prynne, you are better equipped to understand these emotions in yourself or in your acquaintances.

When you state that a certain character behaves a certain way, the burden of proof is on you. It is not enough to say that Hamlet was indecisive or weak, or that Lear was overweening and arrogant, or that Laura in "Flowering Judas" (page 618) betrayed her friends by being emotionally detached. In every instance, you must quote passages that prove your interpretation.

## Interpreting Symbols

In its most literal sense, a symbol is a thing that stands for something beyond itself. The dove is a symbol of peace; the flag is the symbol of a country. In literature, a symbol is created when an author invests an object, an idea, or an action with a significance far beyond itself. A person may also be treated in such a way as to symbolize a class or a group of people.

Most of the time, symbolism is implicit in literature. The reader is left to unravel the meaning of the symbol. Indeed, the effect of a symbol would otherwise be ruined by preachiness. But occasionally an author will come out and say what a certain symbol means. For instance, at the end of "Flowering Judas," the following exchange takes place between Laura and Eugenio:

> Where are you taking me, she asked in wonder but with fear. To death, and it is a long way off, and we must hurry, said Eugenio. No, said Laura, not unless you take my hand. Then eat these flowers, poor prisoner, said Eugenio, in a voice of pity, take and eat: and from the Judas tree he stripped the warm bleeding

flowers, and held them to her lips. She saw that his hand was fleshless, a cluster of white petrified branches, and his eye sockets were without light, but she ate the flowers greedily for they satisfied both hunger and thirst. Murderer! said Eugenio, and Cannibal! This is my body and blood. Laura cried No! and at the sound of her own voice, she awoke trembling, and was afraid to sleep again.

This is a complex and difficult piece of writing that can be read in many different ways. But notice that the author has chosen to be explicit about the symbol of the flowers, making crystal-clear the themes of sacrifice and betrayal in Laura's dream.

In the interpretation of symbols, it is less a matter of who is right or wrong than of who has proven a point and who has not. Symbols rarely have cut-and-dried, unarguable meanings. Considerable variation in the interpretation of symbols is not only possible, but extremely likely. Whatever your interpretation, however, it must be supported by material quoted from the text.

## Commenting on Form

For the most part, this type of assignment applies to poetry, where the student has numerous opportunities to express a knowledge of the terms and concepts of prosody. (Fiction and drama contain fewer nameable techniques.) In writing about a poem, you may be asked to describe its verse form or its meter, or to label and identify various tropes and figures of speech.

Wherever possible, use the formal names of any techniques present in a work. If you know that the poem you are analyzing is an Italian sonnet, it does no harm to say so. If you know that a certain action in a play occurs in its *denouement*, you should not be bashful about using that term. If a story begins *in media res* and then proceeds in *flashbacks*, you should say so. Your use of such labels will show an instructor that you have not only mastered the meaning of the work, but have also grasped its form.

In summary, when writing about literature, you should do more than simply ascribe a certain interpretation to the literary work. Your prime purpose should be to prove that your reading of the work is reasonable and logical. Passages from the work should be liberally quoted to support your paper's interpretation of it. Above all, never assume that any reading of a work, no matter how unsupported or farfetched, will do.

Bear one thing in mind before you begin to write your paper: Famous literary works, especially works regarded as classics, have been thoroughly studied to the point where prevailing opinion on them has assumed the character of orthodoxy. What may seem to you a brilliant insight may, in fact, be nothing more than what critics have been saying about the writer and his or her works for years. Saying that Hemingway's male characters suffer from *machismo* is a little like the anthropology student opining that humans are bipedal. Both remarks are undoubtedly true, but they are neither original nor insightful. You should, therefore, check out the prevailing critical opinions on a writer before attempting to dogmatize on your own.

## SUGGESTIONS FOR WRITING

1. Following the style advocated by your instructor, write a five- to eight-page research paper on one of the following psychological problems:
   a. Anorexia nervosa among teenage girls
   b. Loneliness and alienation among the elderly
   c. The effects of divorce on children under the age of ten
   d. Alcoholism among high school students
   Be sure to document any significant statement not your own.
2. Write a paper on the relationship between art and social class. Focus your research on the following queries:
   a. Does art reflect a class bias?
   b. Do different classes hold to different standards for judging art?
   c. Are these standards related to the ways different classes perceive the world?
   d. Is there a sociology of art?
3. Choosing any poem or short story in this book, write a literary analysis focusing on theme, character, action, or form.

## APPENDIX WRITING ASSIGNMENTS

Write a research paper, following the format suggested by your instructor. Above all, choose a topic in which you have a genuine interest. The following titles and restricted theses are presented to stimulate your own investigation:

| TITLE | THESIS |
|---|---|
| "A Look at Thomas Wolfe" | The inconsistencies in Thomas Wolfe's writing can be directly attributed to constant family conflicts, to his doubts concerning his country's economic stability, and to his fear of not being accepted by his reading public. |
| "American Architectural Development" | The development of American architecture was greatly attenuated until the eighteenth century because of the lack of adequate transportation and manufacturing facilities, and the fact that city life had not formed prior to that century. |

| TITLE (cont'd.) | THESIS (cont'd.) |
|---|---|
| "Wordsworth and Coleridge: Their Diverse Philosophies" | Although Wordsworth and Coleridge were both Romantic poets, they believed in two completely different philosophies of nature. |
| "Why Jazz Was What We Wanted" | This paper deals with the various trends that led to the rise, development, and recognition of jazz as an important part of American musical culture during the nineteenth and twentieth centuries. |
| "The Influence of Imagism on Twentieth-Century Poetry" | Imagism, a self-restricted movement, has greatly influenced twentieth-century poetry. |
| "Automation and Employment" | The current fear of humans' being displaced by machines, or what alarmists term the "automation hysteria," seems to be based on insubstantial reports. |
| "Needed: A New Definition of Insanity" | Our courts need a better definition of insanity because neither the M'Naghten Rule nor the psychological definition is adequate. |
| "The Proud Sioux" | In this paper I shall prove that the Sioux Indians, although confined to a shabby reservation, still fought on peacefully against their captors—the white man and his hard-to-accept peace terms. |
| "Women's Fashions After the World Wars" | The First World War and the Second World War had significant effects on women's fashions in America. |
| "Charlie Chaplin" | This paper deals with the various factors that made Charlie Chaplin the master of silent movies. |
| "The Funnies" | Today's funnies reflect a change in America's attitude toward violence, ethnic minorities, and ecology. |
| "The Decline of the Mayans" | The four most popular theories that have been advanced to explain the abrupt end of the Mayan civilization are: the effects of natural disaster, physical weaknesses, detrimental social changes, and foreign influence. |

| TITLE (*cont'd.*) | THESIS (*cont'd.*) |
|---|---|
| "Relief Paintings in Egyptian Mastabas" | The relief paintings found in the mastabas depict the everyday life of the Egyptian people. |
| "Athena" | The goddess Athena bestowed her favors not on those who worshipped her, but on those who fought for their beliefs. |
| "Goldfish" | Originally from China, goldfish have been bred into one of the most beautiful and marketable species of fish. |

## THE LITERARY PAPER

The following literary paper is one student's response to the following assignment: "Write a 500-word critical analysis of Eudora Welty's 'A Worn Path,' (see pp. 406–14) focusing on character, action, mood, setting, and literary techniques such as diction, figurative language, and symbolism. Choose those strategies that best illumine the theme of the narrative."

1.*   The introductory paragraph captures the reader's attention by creating a "jewel" metaphor. It also presents the reviewer's unqualified literary judgment—that "A Worn Path" is an excellent, moving story.

---

*The arabic numerals in the margins of the literary paper correspond to the comments that follow.

1

Douglas B. Inman

English 102

Professor McCuen

March 15, 1988

A Worn, But Lightly Traveled Path

1          In this day when mediocrity is praised as
inspiration and chaos as art, it is refreshing
to find among the literary dung heaps a jewel,
shining and glittering and making one forget,
for the moment, the overwhelming stench and
filth that threatens to suffocate, and
squeeze the very life from one's literary
soul.    Eudora Welty's "A Worn Path" is such a
rare jewel.    Here is a story that exudes
craftsmanship from every pore.    It is filled
with finely turned phrases, distinctly vivid
imagery, and carefully constructed moods;
but, more importantly, it tells its story
well, communicating on many different levels.
Ms. Welty demonstrates a firm command of the
art of storytelling, and the way she weaves
this particular tapestry of words will con-

**2.**   Paragraph two provides a summary of the story's literal level, allowing even the uninitiated reader to comprehend the reviewer's coming comments and interpretations.

**3.**   Paragraph three begins the most important part of this critical review. The student has chosen to focus on the symbolic level of the story. For him, the importance of the narrative lies in its relationship to the history of black freedom in America.

Inman 2

vince the reader that here is a lady who could
turn a sow's ear into silk.

2      "A Worn Path" is the portrait of Phoenix
Jackson, an old Negro woman, seen making a
trip to town to retrieve badly needed medicine
for her ailing grandchild.   Burdened by age
and faced with obstacles, she nevertheless
presses on, stoically pursuing her goal.   On
the most obvious level, this is the story of
an eccentric but delightful woman whose
spirit belies her advanced years.   She makes
the long and arduous trip to town despite the
great distance, the many obstacles she encounters, and an encroaching senility that
gently touches the soul of the reader.   She
climbs hills, crosses a creek by way of a suspended log, crawls under a barbed wire fence,
marches through fields, confronts a stray
dog, and comes to grips with exhaustion, hallucinations, and a failing memory.   And
throughout these ordeals, the author reveals
a character filled with pride and dignity.

3      But there is another story here, one
played out on a much deeper level.   It is the

4.   Here, as in several other passages, the reviewer carefully quotes from the story in order to bolster his argument—that the plight of Phoenix Jackson is also the history of blacks in America. Notice that each quotation is smoothly integrated into the main text of the essay.

5.   The reviewer is straightforward in his explication of the thorn bush as a significant individual symbol within the total allegorical framework.

Inman 3

story of black people in America, and their
struggle for freedom and equality.   The path
Phoenix follows is the road of life for her
people, and the obstacles she encounters on
the way become the challenges of being black.
For instance, she comes to a hill.   "Seems

4       like there is chains about my feet, time I get
this far," she says, and we know that it is
the hill out of slavery that she must climb.
And she does it, although "something," white
people perhaps, "pleads I should stay."   And
when she gets to the top, she turns and gives
a "full, severe look behind her where she had
come."   Doubtless this action represents the
black race scrutinizing in retrospect some
especially difficult scene in the drama of
their freedom.   Phoenix encounters opposition to her newfound freedom in the form of a

5       thorny bush, and here her dress is a symbol of
that freedom, as she struggles to free herself
from the thorns without tearing her garment.
But she maintains her dignity, showing no
spite for the thorns, saying "you doing your
appointed work.   Never want to let folks

**6, 7.** Two more symbols—the marble cake and the scarecrow—are interpreted.

**8.** The reviewer alludes to Egyptian mythology in order to draw attention to the special significance of the heroine's name.

Inman 4

past—." And finally, trembling from the experience, "she stood free."

6        But freedom for blacks is an illusive
thing, as the reader understands when a small
boy seems to bring Phoenix a slice of marble-
cake, "but when she went to take it there was
just her own hand in the air." Like the
cake, freedom for the blacks has historically
often been a seductive picture that seemed
real; yet, when the blacks tried to claim it,
it dissolved back into fantasy.

7        Phoenix passes through the childhood of
her race when she traverses fields of "withered cotton" and "dead corn." She encounters
"something tall, black, and skinny," and it is
both a scarecrow and the image of slavery
past. "Who be you the ghost of?" she asks,
but there is only silence and the scarecrow
dancing in the wind. And here Phoenix is the
Negro of the past giving way to the future, as
she intones, "Dance, old scarecrow, while I
dancing with you."

8        In this story, birds are used repeatedly
to symbolize freedom. The character's very

**9.**  The reviewer points out other bird symbols and interprets them. Even the little grandson is seen as a bird symbol. Again, quotations from the story are used as primary sources to support the reviewer's claims.

Inman 5

name, Phoenix, is an illustration of this

strategy, for the phoenix was a bird in Egyp-

tian mythology which, every five hundred

years, would consume itself in fire and then

rise renewed from the ashes, as blacks rose

9        from slavery after the Civil War.   Other bird

symbols occur.   For instance, Phoenix comes

to a place where quail are walking about, and

she tells them, as she would young Negroes,

"Walk pretty.   This is the easy place.   This

is the easy going," referring to the new time

of freedom after the Civil War.   And when she

encounters a white hunter, she sees in his

sack a bobwhite, "with its beak hooked bit-

terly to show it was dead," indicating that

even though slavery has been abolished,

whites still managed to oppress blacks, and

the struggle for black freedom is not yet

complete.

Phoenix's grandson represents the new

generation of blacks who never knew slavery,

but still feel its impact, and he too is por-

trayed as a bird of freedom.   "He suffer and

it don't seem to put him back at all.   He got

**10.**   The reviewer begins to summarize by focusing on the mood of the story, calling it "optimistic." In other words, the summary appraisal is that this is a story of hope and triumph, not of bitterness and despair.

Inman 6

a sweet look.   He going to last.   He wear a
little patch quilt and peep out, holding his
mouth open like a little bird," she tells a
nurse in town.

10        Overall, the story is an optimistic outlook on the black experience.   Though much of
the action focuses on earlier hardship, it
ends with hope for the future, as can be seen
when Phoenix finally reaches town.   There, it
is Christmas time, while during her journey it
is simply a cold December day.   In town, dozens of black children whirl around her in the
street, bells are ringing, and colorful
lights abound.   "Here I be," she says, indicating the end of the journey, the attaining
of freedom and new life.   And already the
past is being forgotten; all the slavery, the
fight for freedom, the long and painful road
to happiness is but a dim memory.   "It was my
memory had left me," she says near the end,
"There I sat and forgot why I made my long
trip."

        "Forgot?" asks the nurse.   "After you
came so far?"

**11.**   The final paragraph makes the point that it is Phoenix Jackson, the heroine and major character of the story, who gives the story its meaning and beauty. The concluding sentence brings the analysis full circle by using the same jewel/gem metaphor used in the introduction.

Inman 7

11        This is the story of a courageous and
dignified old woman on a long journey, but it
is also the story of a courageous and dignified race, and their long struggle for freedom
and equality.   With wonderful artistry, Eudora Welty takes the reader along, to travel
this worn path of struggle that has been
trudged by so many peoples over the ages.
She shows the dignity in the struggle and the
hope of a new generation.   And she does so
with the craftsmanship of a fine watchmaker.
One cannot help but be changed in some way by
this beautiful story.   "A Worn Path" is truly
a gem.

# •• *ASSIGNMENT 3:* ••
# *A SAMPLING OF STUDENT ESSAYS*

Narration
Description
Example
Definition
Comparison/contrast
Division and classification
Causal analysis
Argument

# NARRATION

ANT KINGDOMS

The narrative be-
gins in the middle
of an action. No
background mate-
rial is provided.
Instead, the
reader is involved
immediately in a
situation.

One day when I was twelve, I remember    1
calmly sitting atop a large dirt hill in a
vacant lot.    This vacant lot happened to be
in a residential neighborhood of some suburban community or such, but that was not important.    The heat of the day was important.
It must have been summertime because it was
immeasurably hot and I was dying of thirst.

From where I sat everything appeared to    2
be brown, except for the sky which was pale
blue and without clouds.    The dirt hill itself was composed of light brown, powdery,
dry earth.    There was no scent connected
with the dirt hill, save an occasional wind-
borne essence of wild sage and sumac trees.

The introduction
is followed by a
meticulous, de-
tailed description
of an ant hill as
seen from up
close.

As I began to investigate my dirt hill    3
more closely, I discovered a little ant hill
near my left foot.    I had never really examined an ant hill before, so I scooted myself
nearer to it.

My first observation was that the ants    4
were in perpetual motion, and I was immedi-

ately fascinated by their enterprise.    The
ants seemed to have a passion for hard work,
and all were involved in some activity.
Some built tunnels, some built hills, and
every individual ant seemed to be doing
something constructive for the society.
Indeed, after close inspection for about
three minutes or hours, I was greatly impressed by what I took to be their puritanic
work ethic.    And I decided to study them
with care.    "Here," it occurred to me, "is
an ant kingdom."

This paragraph is a flashback to an earlier time.

Before I came across this ant kingdom, T    5
had held a rather poor opinion of ants.    I
had regarded them as selfish, stupid creatures.    If they weren't falling into half-
full jars of honey or discarded bottles of
soda-pop, they could certainly be found
swarming over half-eaten apples and dirty
fragments of candy bars.    They had struck
me as useless, disgusting insects.

The author's view of ants is changing. He returns to the present and continues to scrutinize the ants.

But now I realized that there were some    6
ants who worked together to build and maintain an orderly ant kingdom in a dirt hill on
a vacant lot.    I was quite pleased with my-

self for seeing this different side of ants.
Although I did not fully understand my new
relationship with ants, I knew that I had met
up with something awesome and purposeful in
the insect kingdom.   And so I immersed myself in the pleasant scrutiny of this treasure.

    I shifted from my sitting position and          7
got down on my hands and knees.   I wanted a
closer look, so I lowered my right eye and
subjected the ants to the most grueling of
inspections.   I observed some ants carrying
huge boulders, pinched in between their
mighty jaws, for miles and miles.   They carried them from one end of the ant kingdom to
the other, dropped them, and returned for
more.   Some other ants stood guard at entrance holes.   Still other ants speedily ran
about, from one ant to another to yet another, stopping momentarily to rub antennae,
and then scurrying off in no particular direction or course.

    I thought that I had seen enough, so I          8
jumped up and stood next to the ants.
Brushing the dust off the deteriorating

knees of my jeans, I placed grimy hands on my hips. I tossed my head gently, without taking my eyes off the ant kingdom, and broke into an innocent burst of laughter. I thought of walking away, but an odd curiosity restrained me. I bent over slightly and again assaulted the ant kingdom with my utmost attention and interest. It was still very hot . . . and I was still dying of thirst, but somehow the importance of the ant kingdom seemed to overshadow my predicament.

Time is passing. The same ant hill is now described from a distance. Notice the change in perspective.

I now looked down on the entire ant kingdom. My mouth opened and I began breathing more rapidly. I now saw the kingdom from an altitude of five feet. This perspective actually made the ant kingdom seem silly and purposeless.

9

Another flashback to a time when the narrator used to watch his father work.

Suddenly, the scene bore no semblance of order or reason. It brought to memory another scene: I remembered watching my father as he was working on some wood furniture. He was sanding down a tabletop. He was using an electric sander which scraped and vibrated the veneer off the wood. The very

10

fine powdery sawdust, which was the product of this sanding process, fluidly danced on the tabletop as my father continued his work.    And this, I thought, was what the ant kingdom now looked like: nothing more significant than the discarded shavings of a carpenter's tools.

I felt deceived and stupid for fantasizing about ants and their kingdoms as if they were anything more than mere, insignificant insects.    The ants oozed from the ant holes . . . millions of ants perhaps . . . all over the dirt hill.    It was a scene of frenzy and panic.    There were ants crawling and scurrying over the hill as far as the eye could see; ants exploding in purposeless commotion, scrounging around for crumbs, decaying vegetable and animal matter; ants dancing and swaying to a mysterious, inaudible rhythm of their own.

Somehow, I was enraged by the scene of random, purposeless scurrying.    I wanted to put an end to this stupid burst of ant activity.    It then occurred to me that I <u>could</u> put an end to it.    At first, I was shocked

**11**

**12**

and frightened by this idea, but I continued
to explore its possibilities.

The theme of the narration is: Often man has the opportunity to play God. The question: How will man comport himself? Will he be benign, malevolent, or indifferent?

I realized that I, just a young boy dying
of thirst on a hot summer day, could——on a
whim——crush the ant kingdom with my feet and
scatter it all over the hill.   And I could
do this simply by grinding my heels into the
dirt.   I could disrupt and destroy millions
of frenzied, hyperactive lives.

13

A separate, brief paragraph is used for emphasis.

And, on the other hand, I could leave the
ants alone.

14

I felt immediately guilty for having
thought first of destroying the ants.   But
more than that, I was amazed (almost beyond
belief) that I had a choice in this matter.
I was in control and could destroy or preserve millions of tiny living creatures.
And I could act out of my affection, pity,
hatred, or lack of something better to do!

15

Dazed and awe-struck by this sudden sense
of responsibility, I walked away from the
hill to slake my thirst, leaving behind millions of ants to live out their lives in
peace, and feeling as though I had just made
a significant moral choice.

16

# DESCRIPTION

GONE WITH THE WIND

The opening sentence states the dominant impression: "The town I grew up in is gone." The rest of the essay simply supports this dominant impression by supplying appropriate and specific details. No irrelevancies weaken the central notion of a vanished place.

The town I grew up in is gone.  Now don't
get me wrong, there is a town in the same
geographical location, and it's still called
Pismo Beach, but it's not the one I grew up
in.  My home town didn't disappear in a
blinding flash, as did whole villages in the
cataclysm at Hiroshima; rather, it slowly
withdrew from existence under the double on-
slaught of time and masses of humanity.

1

Note the personification of the pier by having it "shake" and "shudder." Note, too, the personification of the swells as monsters. "Cottonball clouds" is an effective metaphor. The seagulls "wheel" and "soar"; they don't just "fly."

A few remnants of my old home town still
exist.  For instance, the public pier is
still there, but it's a new, rebuilt pier.
It doesn't shake and shudder like the old one
did when the monster swells came rolling in
from Hawaii and beyond.

2

The foothills still slope gently--grass
green in springtime--and the far hills are
still painted purple by the shadows of the
cotton-ball clouds.  The blue Pacific is
still blue and seagulls still wheel and soar
over the beaches, but most of the pelicans
are gone and the clumps of driftwood on the

3

beaches have been replaced by bottles and cans and white plastic jugs.

Progress is personified as a god with bulldozer body and steam shovel arms.

The bottom land just south of Pismo has fallen to the great god Progress.  His bulldozer body and steam shovel arm have ravished it.  This is where I used to hunt cottontails and jacks and ground squirrels with my first .22.  Now the place is a shopping center and a mobile home park, and the rabbits are mostly fading stains on the nearby concrete freeway.

Note how delicately the writer handles the rabbits being killed by cars.

On the west side of Highway One, just south of the town, a hobo camp used to lie hidden among the eucalyptus trees, leaving traces and hints of a special kind of rakishly free life, limited to hobos only.  But the hobos had to find a new place to live because most of the trees have been replaced by campgrounds and gas stations and weekend people.  Here also the dune buggies are grinding down the sand dunes faster than the wind off the ocean builds them up, and the unmuffled roar of internal combustion obliterates the crashing of the surf.

4

5

The use of "perch" is appropriate since the restaurants and motels have replaced birds.

Just north of town, expensive motels and restaurants now perch atop the cliffs where once sea birds made their nests and where a kid could go fishing on a blue and green summer day.

6

The ending summarizes the nostalgic mood of the essay.

I suppose children are still being born and raised in this new Pismo Beach, but they're not growing up in my home town.

7

## EXAMPLE

### HANDSOME IS AS HANDSOME DOES

The opening sentence is the author's thesis: inner beauty is more important than outward appearance. Then she announces that she plans to present three people from history or literature who were outwardly ugly but inwardly beautiful. These examples will help to prove her thesis.

Inner beauty is more important than outward appearance.  Some of the ugliest people in fiction and history have had immense charm and great beauty of soul.  After all, what is the good of an Adonis appearance when it hides a shallow, evil character?  Three famous men come to mind who were outwardly unattractive but inwardly beautiful.

1

Quasimodo, the hunchback of

My first example is Quasimodo, the hunchback of Notre Dame, with his monstrous grimace, square nose, and horseshoe mouth.  He had only one eye because his right eye was

2

Notre Dame, a famous fictional character, serves as the first example. Notice how coherence is maintained by using the transitional phrase "my first example." Such details as Quasimodo's "monstrous grimace," his "horseshoe mouth," his right eye "buried by an enormous wart," and his ill-proportioned body make this example vivid. Effective figurative language completes the picture: teeth "like the tusk of an elephant," the look of "a great giant that had been broken into pieces and ill-soldered together."

completely buried by an enormous wart.   His mouth was full of irregular and jagged teeth, with a horny lip over which one of those teeth protruded like the tusk of an elephant.   His chin was forked in such a way that he appeared devilish.   Red bristles covered his enormous head; between his shoulders rose an enormous hump counterbalanced by a projecting chest in front, thus he was called "the Hunchback of Notre Dame." Carrying this massive bulk were two crooked legs, with immense feet.   His hands were huge.   He looked like a great giant that had been broken into pieces and ill-soldered together.   Despite all his deformities, this heroic man had a formidable inner strength, agility, and courage.   Even though all Quasimodo had ever seen directed towards him was hatred and disgust, he was able to love and show fierce loyalty.   He was a most gentle creature covered by a monstrous exterior.

Paragraph 3 introduces the second example, Cyrano de Bergerac. The

My second example is Cyrano de Bergerac, with his enormous nose that made him look ri-

3

phrase "My second example" provides coherence and continuity. Numerous details support the impression that Cyrano's nose is what ruins his appearance. A clear contrast between his absurd looks and his noble wit is established. The words "although" and "however" stress the contrast.

diculously ugly.    Although Cyrano accepted the fact that he had a huge nose, his sense of personal honor and pride would never allow anyone to poke fun at his nose.    The grotesqueness of his nose contrasted sharply with his ability to write and speak lovely poetry.    He was utterly witty, romantic, and dashing.    His behavior revealed aristocracy as well as nobility.    He had convinced himself that because of his looks he was incapable of ever winning a lady's love.    However, in the end, his brave and tender heart, his brilliant mind, and his poetic declarations won him the lover he so much desired, the lovely Roxanne.

Paragraph 4 begins with "Still another example." Here again the author takes great pains to include details that flesh out the portrait of a man who looks gangling but is much loved and admired.

Still another example is Abraham Lincoln, one of our great forefathers.    Looking at portraits of "Abe," one would never call him handsome.    Mr. Lincoln had a lanky frame, large feet, and powerful hands.    His arms and legs were long, strikingly out of proportion with his slender torso and small head.    His sallow and sunken cheeks stood out like those of a cadaver laid out.    But, with all his exterior ugliness, inside there

4

was a man with great intellect, admirable
shrewdness, good judgment, and common sense.
He was vigorous and strong.   His humility
and sensitivity made him a loved figure.   He
was a down-to-earth individual, totally devoid of pomposity or vanity.   His great human kindness and gentle spirit were well
known.   By most standards of beauty he was
ugly; yet, he was one of our most admired
presidents.   The world remembers him with
deep love.

The essay con-
cludes with a re-
wording of the
age-old "Don't
judge-a-book-by-
its-cover" admon-
ishment.

One must not judge by appearances alone.
Inside a battered trunk, one may discover a
beautiful treasure.

5

# DEFINITION

The essay opens
with a lexical defi-
nition of *credibil-
ity*. Then the
writer announces
that he will look at
three contexts in
which the word is
commonly used.

### WHAT IS CREDIBILITY?

<u>Credibility</u> is the quality of being wor-
thy of belief and trust.   This word is most
often used in three contexts—the private,
the political, and the collective.   An
analysis of its applications in each context
will serve to broaden the scope of the defi-

1

nition and will enable us to have a fuller understanding of the word itself.

The writer deals with the first context, private credibility.

Private credibility has to do with belief in a lone figure.  When we claim that so-and-so has credibility, we are saying that this individual is trustworthy and that his pursuit of truth is unaffected by opportunism, greed, ambition, or any other self-promoting vice.  When a person commands this degree of credibility, it is likely that his persuasions may be taken as a standard by which other men are judged.  Therefore the label "credible" is an accolade not to be accorded lightly.  The lack of credibility

The writer defines *credibility* by stating what it is not.

also plays a part here.  In this instance the person is distrusted and is not to be relied on for espousals or information.  When a person has no credibility, he is shunned like a bad stench or a rampant disease.  Furthermore, private credibility spans the gamut of varied relationships, from the brief and cursory to the profound and inti-

The writer uses a specific example of a brief relationship and of a profound relationship.

mate.  For example, the credibility of an insurance salesman may be of great concern, as will be the credibility of a wife.  In

2

either case, the credible person is one who can be trusted.  He or she will not turn traitor or turncoat.

The writer deals with the second context, political credibility.

3

Political credibility is often explored by journalists and by citizens concerned with the ethics of our government.  Politics is the context in which today the word credibility is most often used.  In this context it usually means that a given political leader acts candidly, following a straight course in the interest of our country.  In belief, he is politically incorruptible.  Unfortunately, sometimes his integrity is limited to the field of politics.  At home or among friends he may be quite villainous.  Nevertheless, we place great value on political credibility.  Did Brezhnev have credibility when he talked détente with Kissinger?  Did Chairman Mao have credibility when he claimed that all China wanted was to maintain her independence?  Do the dozens of politicians running for office have credibility when they promise us Utopia if we elect them?  These questions we ask in order to assess political credibility.  Of

Specific examples are used to help clarify the definition.

course, many times a politician falls far short of ideal political credibility. Indeed, the word is more often used in the negative than in the positive sense, as when we ask, "Does he vacillate in his stand?" "Does he rob the poor to satisfy the rich?" "Does he say one thing but do another?" These questions attempt to assess a politician's credibility negatively. Political integrity has been of special concern to Americans in the last decade. Intense public scrutiny of political figures has been a feature of the sixties and is still now of concern in the seventies. Earlier this concern was not so deeply felt. As late as the fifties, the masses generally viewed all politicians as statesmen who were basically trustworthy and admirable. But today popular opinion is more apprehensive and critical. A proper understanding of the word credibility as applied to politics is therefore of great importance.

The writer deals with the third context, collective credibility.

Collective credibility refers to the trustworthiness of a group. What is basically involved is whether or not the operat-

4

ing procedures of the group are reliable as well as truthful. If they are, then the group will have collective credibility. It will be judged to act out its roles as an honest, believable organization. Most of us look for this kind of credibility when we choose a garage, a department store, or a cleaning establishment. We require this

Again specific examples help to clarify the definition.

kind of credibility whenever money or service is involved. We depend on it in our daily business transactions. Truth and reliability are the crux of collective credibility.

The writer has achieved his purpose because he has answered the question, "What is *credibility*?"

I have tried to indicate that <u>credibility</u>    5
has differing meanings. The context of any given usage is vital to the meaning of the word. It is nowadays an important term, a "relevant" term. All people should be able to use it competently and with a proper understanding of its various contexts. If this essay has helped at all in this respect, it has served its purpose.

# COMPARISON/CONTRAST

THE DARLING AND THE DESPOT

The opening paragraph presents a thesis that not only predicts a contrast between two famous people, but also neatly controls the essay by limiting the contrast to three areas—manner, purpose, and influence.

The first half of paragraph 2 describes the manner of one of the members to be contrasted; the second half describes the manner of the other member. The opening phrase "On the one hand" anticipates the opposing half, which must then begin with "On the other hand," and it does.

1    Pope John Paul II and the Ayatollah Khomeini, two of the world's most charismatic religious leaders, present a sharp contrast in manner, purpose, and influence.

2    On the one hand, we have the Ayatollah Ruhollah Khomeini, who is eighty years old. He wears a black turban on his head and a forbidding glare under his beetle brows. He is stern and white-bearded, and speaks rude, peasant-like Persian. His manner is aloof and unyielding. He does not care to chat about ordinary matters, and after he makes a decision, he leaves the room. Experts on Iran have described him as arrogant and pious, stubborn and vengeful, humorless and inflexible. On the other hand, we have Pope John Paul II (Karol Wojtyla), who is now sixty-one years old. His twinkling blue eyes and dimples are set off by a hearty laugh and an infectious sense of humor. He has a compassionate, far-seeing gaze, and he loves to sing. As cardinal, he earned a

reputation for courageous calm in carrying out his teaching assignments in Krakow, under Soviet rule.  His style is confident and crusading rather than hand-wringing and finger-wagging.

Paragraph 3 contrasts the Ayatollah with the Pope in the areas of purpose. The move from one character to the other is made with the phrase "Far different from . . .," which gives coherence and balance to the paragraph.

3

Khomeini has proclaimed that he will get all of the Muslims in the world to carry the revolutionary Islamic policy to final victory.  He talks of "liberating the whole Middle East from exploitation."  But, if he is permitted to carry out his purpose, he will set all of Islam back to the seventh century by strict adherence to the Koran. Iran's new constitution is an Islamic version of Plato's Republic, with Khomeini as philosopher-king.  By interpreting the Koran literally, Khomeini will encourage such barbaric practices as public floggings for minor offenses, oppression of women, and imprisonment without trial for anyone who opposes the Islamic religion.  Far different from the Ayatollah, Pope John Paul II has impressed both supporters and detractors with his eagerness to tackle some of the most divisive issues confronting the 724 million

Catholics and others around the globe.    His

intentions are clear—to renow Christianity

and make it a vital force in a world torn by

conflict and despair.    He pleads with man-

kind to feed the starving and comfort the

wounded all over the world.    He wants unity

and peace among nations.

Paragraph 4 intro-
duces the area of
influence as the
basis for contrast-
ing the Ayatollah
and the Pope.
This time the shift
from one member
to the other is
made by the use
of the phrase "In
complete contrast
to. . . ." Notice
that in each area
of contrast, the
author describes
the Ayatollah first
and the Pope sec-
ond. This kind of
consistency helps
the reader to fol-
low the contrast
without confu-
sion.

    The sphere of influence of these two men        4

is incalculable.    Everything they do has a

considerable effect on our world today, and

each believes he speaks for God.    In his own

mind, the Ayatollah receives directions from

God on how to apply the principles of the Ko-

ran and the Shari'a (Islamic Law) to life and

politics.    He has the ability to rouse his

35.2 million subjects to both adulation and

fury.    He has turned Iranian against Iranian

while inspiring hatred and fear of other re-

ligions.    He is a fervent anti-Semite and

abhors everything about the Western world.

At this very moment people of the B'Hai faith

are being executed by the hundreds on his or-

der.    In complete contrast to the Ayatollah,

Pope John Paul II has revitalized the Church

and reestablished its waning influence.   He has done so with remarkable showmanship, easy informality, and popular appeal. Since he grew up the hard way, under Naziism and Communism, he was able to help bring about détente between Church and State in Poland.   The recent attempt on his life has endeared him to millions not necessarily of his own faith, and his subsequent recovery has strengthened their hope for peace in the world.

In the final paragraph, the author offers her resolute opinion about the superiority of the Pope over the Ayatollah. Her final sentence sounds smooth and polished due to its parallelism and balance.

We have here two religious leaders, but what a tremendous contrast! Khomeini holds power over his countrymen, but it is a negative power--the power to imprison, to dismember, to execute.   It is the power of veto.   Pope John Paul II, however, emissary to "the Light of the World," goes on spreading love, promoting understanding along with better morals, and establishing a measure of peace in a turbulent world.   Two religious leaders have made an impact on our world— the one signifying all that is harsh and evil; the other, all that is gentle and good.

5

# DIVISION AND CLASSIFICATION

The opening sentence is also the thesis. Quickly and directly the author gets to her point by announcing that her literary tastes so far have been revealed in five categories of books.

Paragraph 2 introduces the first category, books containing nonsensical phrases and concepts. Several examples are cited.

BOOKS THAT CHANGED MY WORLD

In reviewing my literary tastes from pre-school age to the present, I have found that the progression of my reading interests can be divided into five eras, each era representing a phase of my character. Clearly, the books included in each era were the major influences that helped to mold my personality and add enjoyment to my life.

The first era was characterized by an infatuation with repeated nonsensical phrases and concepts. An example was the classic line in Wanda Gag's Nothing at All: "I'm busy getting dizzy; I'm busy getting dizzy," which supposedly had the effect of solidifying an invisible dog. Fascinated by the rhyme scheme and meter, I would endlessly repeat the phrase until my mother, driven to distraction, attempted to lure me away from those lyrical chants by introducing another book, Barnaby and Mr. O'Malley, a series of sophisticated cartoons by Crookett Johnson. Flatly ignoring the sophistication, I became

1

2

obsessed with Mr. O'Malley's favorite epi-
thet, "Cushlsmochree!" and it soon replaced
"I'm busy getting dizzy" as a source of irritation to my parents and teachers.   But with
the advent of Barnaby and Mr. O'Malley, I
also became aware, perhaps for the first
time, of character traits.   Mr. O'Malley, an
egotistical, cigar-smoking fairy godfather,
immediately caught my fancy and became my
early childhood hero.   Similarly, Yertle
the Turtle, Cat in the Hat, and other Dr.
Seussian creations, fascinated me not so
much because of the unlikely names of the
protagonists, but because of their exploits
and personalities.

<table>
<tr><td>

Paragraph 3 intro-
duces the second
category, books
with an abun-
dance of plot and
characters. Again,
examples are pro-
vided to clarify
the category.

</td><td>

Once I was able to analyze plots and ex-
plore characters, I reached for books that
had an abundance of both.   Consequently,
from approximately the third to the sixth
grade, I passed through an interlude of in-
nocent compassion, empathizing strongly with
each major character.   From the mixture of
animal stories, biographies, and sports fic-
tion that I read, three totally unrelated
books emerged as the leading influence in

</td><td>

3

</td></tr>
</table>

this period.     First on the list was Charlotte's Web by E. B. White, which brought out
my pity for the plight of four-legged animals and, in this case, eight-legged insects.     In The Story of Helen Keller by
Lorena Hickok, I was immediately attracted
to the courage and persistence of this blind
and deaf humanitarian; she became the subject of many of my book reports and poems.
Then there were also Sholom Aleichem's stories.     They radiated warmth and humanity,
despite the irony and subtle humor this author used to describe his family and the situations in which they found themselves.

Paragraph 4 intro-
duces the third
category, books
that engaged the
author's imagina-
tion. Two authors,
along with some
of their works, are
cited as exam-
ples—Rod Serling
and James
Thurber.

Following my graduation from elementary     4
school, and lasting until the eighth grade,
the development of my imagination took precedence over any other personality trait.     I
spent hours creating tragic, romantic, and
exciting fantasies about ghosts, witches,
and charmed princesses.     I toyed briefly
with science-fiction, but found it for the
most part dull.     A notable exception,
though, was Rod Serling's Stories from the

<u>Twilight Zone</u>. Perhaps it was Serling's re-
alism that appealed to me, or else his imaginative plots.   Whatever the reason, he
became, in my brief period of examining the
"far out," a favorite author.   But it was
the humorous fantasy of James Thurber's
<u>Thirteen Clocks</u> and <u>The Wonderful O</u> that
stands out as the major influence during
those marvelously open days. Thurber ex-
pertly combined all of the traits in previous books that had appealed to me.   He
employed nonsense syllables, evoked deep
compassion for his oftentimes bumbling
heroes, and mingled science-fiction with
fantasy in appropriate proportions.

Paragraph 5 intro-
duces the fourth
category, books
that created in the
author a social
and political
awareness. As be-
fore, examples are
provided.

My preoccupation with fantasy was short-
lived, however.   The 1964 elections and two
books that were sent to me by a book club introduced a new period of social and political awareness.   <u>Inherit the Wind</u> by Lawrence
and Lee and <u>Seven Days in May</u> by Knebel and
Bailey jolted me out of my world of Thurber-
esque capers into the harsh realities of social conflicts.   That mindless bigotry,

5

such as pictured in <u>Inherit the Wind</u>, could exist shocked mo, but that the U.S. government could actually make mistakes destroyed my naive faith in Washington, D.C., as the Rock of Gibraltar.  For the first time in my life, I began to view politics with cynicism and mistrust.

Paragraph 6 introduces the final category, books that were chosen for the influence on the author's personal philosophy. Inadvertently, however, this category also influenced the author's own style of writing.

6

Having developed a social conscience, I began to confine my literary choices to provocative books that might influence my personal philosophy, which was then and is now nebulous and open to occasional revisions. I sought books with subtle character portrayal and obscure meanings.  Two of these books, <u>Nine Stories</u> by J. D. Salinger and <u>The Ginger Man</u> by J. P. Donleavy, inadvertently had greater effects on my style of writing than on my philosophy.  <u>Nine Stories</u> is a conglomeration of short essays, unique for their realism, concern with lack of communication, and droll humor.  <u>The Ginger Man</u>, a vivid description of an Irishman's totally hedonistic, erotic existence, uses a stream-of-consciousness style characterized by an abundance of four-letter Anglo-Saxon words.

For several months, I tried to copy the style of these two authors, thinking how modern and avant garde I was being.

The final paragraph serves as a conclusive statement, in which the author indicates that her tastes today have come full circle since she loves books combining some of the same characteristics she loved as a child.

Today, from a few years' distance, I find it interesting to realize how my literary tastes metamorphosed with maturity.  As I contemplate which books give me most pleasure now, I seem to reach back into childhood to reclaim some of the same elements I loved in books then: a love of nonsense phrases, a feeling of compassion, and flights of fantasy.

7

## CAUSAL ANALYSIS

WHY DO AMERICAN MEN LIKE TO WATCH
FOOTBALL ON TELEVISION?

The introduction lets the reader know that the tone of the essay is satirical.

My qualifications for tackling this question are immense. I have spent uncountable numbers of hours watching football on television and have seen every double or triple-header ever shown.  One autumn weekend I watched so much football that I passed into a coma which gave rise to a secondary, rare illness known to neurological faddists as

1

synaptic disjunction--which simply means
that I have a marked tendency to go bananas,

The thesis is intro-
duced in the last
sentence of the
first paragraph.

especially when I write compositions.   But,
to return to the topic on hand--why American
men like to watch television football--the
answer is plainly this: we like to watch
football because we have an inherited love
of gore and mayhem.

Humorous defini-
tion of *gore*; exam-
ples illustrate the
definition.

    In papers of this kind, the writer is

2

expected to define all unfamiliar terms.
Gore, however, does not need to be defined,
for it is very familiar.   Gore means blood.
Blood means a sanguineous discharge from the
circulatory system of a human.   No matter
how enchantingly spilled, the blood of any
other species is merely blood, but never
gore.   I will give an example.   If an en-
terprising promoter garnered every speckle-
breasted sparrow in North America, placed
every bird in the Los Angeles Coliseum las-
soed to individual stakes tied across the
muzzles of a million cannons, and, at a given
signal, to the accompaniment of any kind of
background music, fired each cannon, blowing

off the respective head of each bird, the
display would still not qualify as gore.
Nor would it matter if the promoter showed a
thousand instant replays of each bird having
its head blown off, showed the replays in Ci-
nerama or even in slow motion.   For gore, as
its minimum requirement, or what legal experts refer to as its sine qua non, requires
that human blood be spilled.

I will furnish an illustration of bona                3
fide gore in football.   One Sunday I watched
the New York Jets play the Pittsburgh Steelers.   Mean Joe Greene, weighing about 280
lbs. and playing defensive end for the
Steelers, beat one blocker and hurled over
the startled, drooping mouth of another.
Directly in the path of his freefall stood
an unsuspecting Joe Namath.   For a milli-
second the two were petrified in a pre-gore
pose--Mean Joe Greene obeying the law of
gravity and hurtling on a collision trajec-
tory, Namath with one leg extended like the
statue of an Egyptian Pharaoh, his arm
cocked to release the ball, his teeth flash-

ing a winsome smile.   Mean Joe Greene then landed on Joe Namath's patolla (an unfortunate weakness of Namath——no matter to which end of his body a blow is directed, it always somehow strikes his knees) with a resounding crack that snapped through the airwaves of America.   The gore was lovely and vast.   As Namath was borne away on a khaki stretcher, the camera focused on a single drop of blood conglobulating on the apex of his patella. The drop careened off the patella and plunged into the earth, slavishly followed by the camera.   On impact, appropriate background sound was dubbed in, adding verisimilitude.   The effect was delicious beyond words.

Humorous definition of *mayhem*; examples illustrate the definition.

We also like to watch football because of our love of mayhem.   Mayhem designates absurd, gratuitous gore, which I will explain by alluding to Greek mythology.   Sisyphus, we read, was sentenced by the gods to push a boulder up a steep hill for eternity.   On reaching the brow of the hill, the boulder promptly rolls back down, compelling Sisyphus to push it back up again.   But what if

4

the boulder, on rolling down the hill, should bash Sisyphus on the noggin, spill blood, and knock him silly? That would be mayhem.

Recently, in a game between Los Angeles and Green Bay, I had the pleasure of witnessing some authentic mayhem. A linebacker from Green Bay was hit on the blind side by a Los Angeles offensive tackle and fell senseless as a cabbage. Enough blood was visible to qualify the hit as gory. But then something happened to elevate it to mayhem. The coach ran onto the field, took off the injured linebacker's helmet, and revealed the fellow's head to be perfectly bald! The mayhem was instantly clear, for it is tonsorial impertinence for the glabrous to play football. That little touch of blood and baldness was just deft enough to transmogrify ordinary gore into mayhem. The klieg lights blazed down, the fellow writhed with pain, the coach fussed with a tourniquet to stem the flow of blood, and shining implacably through all this frantic ministration

5

was a sizzling, inglorious bald head.    What
a game that was!

Mayhem and gore, these explain why Ameri-    6
can men love to watch football on television.    Satisying our appetites for these is
responsible for selling more television
sets, automobiles, and indigestion medications than all the combined forces of soap
operadom, cop stories, documentaries,
thrillers, and miscellaneous voyeuristic
tragedies.

## ARGUMENT

THE INEFFICIENT POSTAL SERVICE

The essay opens
with two shock-
ing statements to
captivate the
reader's attention.
In its classical po-
sition, at the end
of the first para-
graph, appears
the thesis in the
form of an argu-
mentative propo-
sition.

The next time someone sends you a package    1
or letter, you might not receive it; and if
you do receive it, the sender paid too much
money for postage.    Also, the package will
probably arrive later than it should.    Because the present postal service is too expensive and inefficient, private couriers
should be given the United States postal
service business.

The author's first major point is that the U.S. postal service is poorly managed. To support this point, the author offers the testimony of *Sixty Minutes*, an influential television news program.

The U.S. postal service is very poorly managed.  As the television news program Sixty Minutes recently explained, "Postal employees are still sorting the mail the same way Benjamin Franklin originally designed—by hand, stuffing each piece into one of many different pigeonholes."  In the bulk mail sorting centers, the mail is sorted in order to be sent to the post office nearest its final destination.  Once it has arrived at that post office, it is sorted again to be handed to the correct postman, and it is then delivered by him to the appropriate neighborhood block. Unfortunately, this repeated sorting requires exorbitant amounts of manpower.  To be more precise, it requires 667,000 people to sort and deliver the more than one hundred billion pieces of mail that go through the United States postal service annually.

2

The author introduces another major point, that the federal system could be improved. He states how his proposition would im-

The system could be modernized dramatically, but the federal government is so slow to change that nothing will be done for decades.  For instance, if these mail sorting

3

prove the status quo—private couriers would modernize the postal system and would increase efficiency through competition.

processes were computerized, the number of those thousands of employees could be cut back considerably.   The delivery time on the mail would be shortened, and the costs of handling would be decreased.   But such a dramatic change could be accomplished only if the postal service were a private industry.   It would even be feasible to have two or three separate postal services, along with other private couriers, all in competition with each other.   That way the postal employees that were laid off by the government could ban together to incorporate another postal service, thus creating even more competition.   After all, competition has always improved business efficiency.

The author introduces the third major point, that the U.S. postal service mismanages its money. The paragraph is well bolstered by facts about workers' salaries. The U.S. Postmaster General is quoted as authoritative testimony.

    The United States postal service also mismanages its money.   Profligate dollars are spent on unreasonable payroll raises and benefits.   The postal service seems to be unconscious of any cause—effect relationship between performance and pay.   Even the most bumbling worker is paid a good wage, and no one is ever fired.   The three major postal

4

workers' unions have pushed until the average salary for a worker is $22,000 per year
in wages and benefits, plus a cost-of-living
adjustment every six months.   William F.
Bolger, the U.S. Postmaster General, in discussing studies done by the postal service,
states, "The employees have been paid much
more than workers holding comparable jobs in
private industries and have contributed little to the agency's recent productivity
gains." Bolger also says, "Every two weeks
their payroll is over five hundred million
dollars." Today, the post office tax burden
is crippling and demoralizing the average
taxpayer.   In payroll alone, twenty million
dollars is spent every two weeks, which is
520 million tax dollars every year, paid by
us.   What is really appalling is that in the
fiscal year 1979, the postal service had a
surplus of 470 million dollars of taxpayers'
money, and then had the nerve to institute a
general postage rate increase! Since that
time, increases have proliferated until they
seem to happen every year.   By the way,

eighty—six percent of every postal dollar
goes for workers' salaries

The author's personal experience is cited in order to further strengthen his argument.

My personal experience with the postal
service has embittered me considerably.
Once I received an important letter three
weeks after the post date.    The letter had
to travel only 300 miles.    Another time a
relative of mine mailed me an expensive
clock, but upon arrival at my house it was
badly damaged, despite the fact that it had
been well wrapped.    My bad experiences have
been echoed by numerous experiences of relatives, friends, and acquaintances whose complaints I have listened to over the years.

5

Paragraphs 6 and 7 are filled with evidence to prove that private couriers already serve the public better than does the U.S. postal service and that additional private couriers would be even more efficient because they would create healthy competition. In paragraph 7, Consumer Reports is quoted as an authority.

To stop private couriers from taking
business from our inefficient postal service, the U.S. postal service has created
for itself a monopoly on first—class mail.
In 1960, the government passed a law called
"The Private Express Statute," which prevents private couriers from carrying first—
class mail.    First—class mail is considered
any letter bearing information to a specific
person.    The law considers "letters" any

6

standard written correspondence, payroll

checks, tickets, hunting and fishing licen-

ses, and many other items.    There are a few

exceptions to this monopoly.    Outside agen-

cies may deliver time-sensitive documents.

They can also deliver first-class mail any-

time, under any circumstances, provided that

first-class postage has been paid to the

postal service!

The few smaller private couriers that do          7

exist are much faster and more reliable than

the U.S. postal service.    Their services are

frequently more convenient to the consumer,

which enables them to charge high rates

since they have little or no competition.

Most of the private firms offer overnight

delivery and guarantee delivery by noon of

the next working day.    They also offer door-

to-door service, which the U.S. postal ser-

vice does not.    The postal service will usu-

ally have its express mail (best service

available) to its destination only by the

end of the next working day.    Private cour-

iers today offer great speed at a high price

because they have no competition.   They know

that most businesses and other consumers do

not mind paying high prices when they re-

quire a speedy delivery.   The United Parcel

Service (U.P.S.) is the exception to the

"faster therefore more expensive" rule.

Its rates are cheaper than first-class mail,

very close in fact to the U.S. postal ser-

vice's parcel post rate.   However, U.P.S. is

often faster than first-class mail and of-

fers door-to-door delivery.   According to

Consumer Reports, "From Washington, D.C., to

New York, for a two-pound package, U.P.S.

would charge $1.28 and would make a two-day

delivery; in contrast, the U.S. postal ser-

vice would charge $1.39 for a three- to ten-

day delivery.   Federal Express, another

large private courier, would charge $16.39

for a one- to two-day delivery."

The final para-
graph is a restate-
ment of the thesis
and appeals to all
people who are
practical and
would like to see
money saved.

Any person of a practical or money-saving         8

bent will conclude that it is in everyone's

best interest to eliminate the monopoly of

mail delivery created by the postal service

by delegating its business to smaller private couriers that could be in competition with each other, forcing rates down.   Such a system would be much better than continuing the large, mismanaged postal service we have now.

# GLOSSARY OF RHETORICAL TERMS

**abstract**     Words or phrases denoting ideas, qualities, and conditions that exist but cannot be seen. *Love*, for example, is an abstract term; so are *happiness*, *beauty*, and *patriotism*. The opposite of abstract terms are concrete ones—words that refer to things that are tangible, visible, or otherwise physically evident. *Hunger* is abstract, but *hamburger* is concrete. The best writing blends the abstract with the concrete, with concrete terms used in greater proportion to clarify abstract ones. Writing too steeped in abstract words or terms tends to be vague and unfocused.

**ad hominem argument**     An argument that attacks the integrity or character of an opponent rather than the merits of an issue. (*Ad hominem* is Latin for "to the man.") It is also informally known as "mud-slinging." See "Obstacles to Clear Thinking," by Richard Altick in Chapter 9.

**ad populem argument**     A fallacious argument that appeals to the passions and prejudices of a group rather than to its reason. An appeal, for instance, to support an issue because it's "the American Way" is an *ad populem* argument. For more, see Chapter 9, especially Richard Altick's "Obstacles to Clear Thinking."

**allusion**     A reference to some famous literary work, historical figure, or event. For example, to say that a friend "has the patience of Job" means that he is as enduring as the biblical figure of that name. Allusions must be used with care lest the audience miss their meaning.

**ambiguity**     A word or an expression having two or more possible meanings is said to be ambiguous. Ambiguity is a characteristic of some of the best poetry, but it is not a desired trait of expository writing, which should clearly state what the writer means.

**analogy**     A comparison that attempts to explain one idea or thing by likening it to another. Analogy is useful if handled properly, but it can be a source of confusion if the compared items are basically unalike.

**argumentation**     Argumentation is the writer's attempt to convince his reader to agree with him. It is based upon appeals to reason, evidence proving the argument, and sometimes emotion to persuade. Some arguments attempt merely to prove a point, but others go beyond proving to inciting the reader to action. At the heart of all argumentation lies a debatable issue.

**audience**     The group for whom a work is intended. For a writer, the audience is the reader whom the writer desires to persuade, inform, or entertain. Common sense tells us that a writer should always write to the level and needs of the particular audience for whom the writing is meant. For example, if you are writing for an unlettered audience, it is pointless to cram your writing with many literary allusions whose meanings will likely be misunderstood.

**balance**     In a sentence, a characteristic of symmetry between phrases, clauses, and other grammatical parts. For example, the sentence "I love Jamaica for its weather, its lovely scenery, and its people" is balanced. This sentence—"I love Jamaica for its weather, its lovely scenery, and because its people are friendly"—is not. See also **parallelism**.

**causal analysis**  A mode of developing an essay in which the writer's chief aim is to analyze cause or predict effect. For example, in "Why the Justice System Fails," Roger Rosenblatt's chief aim is to explain the criminal justice system's inability to deter crime.

**cliché**  A stale image or expression, and the bane of good expository writing. "White as a ghost" is a cliché; so is "busy as a bee." Some clever writers can produce an effect by occasionally inserting a cliché in their prose, but most simply invent a fresh image rather than cull one from the public stock.

**coherence**  The principle of clarity and logical adherence to a topic that binds together all parts of a composition. A coherent essay is one whose parts—sentences, paragraphs, pages—are logically fused into a single whole. Its opposite is an incoherent essay—one that is jumbled, illogical, and unclear.

**colloquialism**  A word or expression acceptable in informal usage but inappropriate in formal discourse. A given word may have a standard as well as a colloquial meaning. *Bug*, for example, is standard when used to refer to an insect; when used to designate a virus, i.e. "She's at home recovering from a *bug*," the word is a colloquialism.

**comparison/contrast**  A rhetorical mode used to develop essays that systematically match two items for similarities and differences. See the comparison/contrast essay examples in Chapter 8.

**conclusion**  The final paragraph or paragraphs that sum up an essay and bring it to a close. Effective conclusions vary widely, but some common tacks used by writers to end their essays include summing up what has been said, suggesting what ought to be done, specifying consequences that are likely to occur, restating the beginning, or taking the reader by surprise with an unexpected ending. Most important of all, however, is to end the essay artfully and quietly without staging a grand show for the reader's benefit.

**concrete**  Said of words or terms denoting objects or conditions that are palpable, visible, or otherwise evident to the senses. *Concrete* is the opposite of *abstract*. The difference between the two is a matter of degrees. *Illness*, for example, is abstract; *ulcer* is concrete; "sick in the stomach" falls somewhere between the two. The best writing usually expresses abstract propositions in concrete terms.

**connotation**  The implication or emotional overtones of a word rather than its literal meaning. *Lion*, used in a literal sense, denotes a beast (see **denotation**). But to say that Winston Churchill had "the heart of a lion" is to use the connotative or implied meaning of *lion*. See Chapter 10, "The Meaning of Words," especially "Politics and the English Language" and "A Semantic Parable."

**deduction**  Something inferred or concluded. Deductive reasoning moves from the general to the specific. For more, see "Introduction to Logic" by John C. Sherwood in Chapter 9.

| | |
|---|---|
| **denotation** | The specific and literal meaning of a word, as found in the dictionary. The opposite of *connotation*. |
| **description** | A rhetorical mode used to develop an essay whose primary aim is to depict a scene, person, thing, or idea. Descriptive writing evokes the look, feel, sound, and sense of events, people, or things. See Chapter 6 for instructions on how to write a descriptive essay. |
| **diction** | Word choice. Diction refers to the choice of words a writer uses in an essay or other writing. Implicit in the idea of diction is a vast vocabulary of synonyms—different words that have more or less equivalent meanings. If only one word existed for every idea or condition, diction would not exist. But since we have a choice of words with various shades of meaning, a writer can and does choose among words to express ideas. The diction of skilled writers is determined by the audience and occasion of their writing. |
| **division and classification** | A rhetorical mode for developing an essay whose chief aim is to identify the parts of a whole. A division and classification essay is often an exercise in logical thinking. See, for example, "Thinking as a Hobby," by William Golding in Chapter 8. |
| **documentation** | In a research paper, the support provided for an assertion, theory, or idea, consisting of references to the works of other writers. Different styles of documentation exist. Most disciplines now use the parenthetical style of documentation—see the sample research paper, "The Bilingually Handicapped Child," in the Appendix—where citations are made within the text of the paper rather than in footnotes or endnotes. |
| **dominant impression** | The central theme around which a descriptive passage is organized. For example, a description of an airport lobby would most likely use the dominant impression of rush and bustle, which it would support with specific detail, even though the lobby may contain pockets of peace and tranquility. Likewise, a description of Cyrano de Bergerac—the famous dramatic lover whose nose was horrendously long—would focus on his nose rather than on an inconspicuous part of his face. |
| **emotion, appeal to** | An appeal to feelings rather than to strict reason; a legitimate ploy in an argument as long as it is not excessively and exclusively used. See, for example, the essay by President Ronald Reagan, "Abortion and the Conscience of the Nation," which appeals to emotion in making its case against abortion. |
| **emphasis** | A rhetorical principle that requires stress to be given to important elements in an essay at the expense of less important elements. Emphasis may be given to an idea in various parts of a composition. In a sentence, words may be emphasized by placing them at the beginning or end or by judiciously italicizing them. In a paragraph, ideas may be emphasized by repetition or by the accumulation of specific detail. |
| **essay** | From the French word *essai*, or "attempt," the essay is a short prose discussion of a single topic. Essays are sometimes classified as formal or informal. A formal essay is aphoristic, |

structured, and serious. An informal essay (such as the essays by Caskie Stinnett and E. B. White in Chapter 7) is personal, revelatory, humorous, and somewhat loosely structured.

**evidence**   The logical bases or supports for an assertion or idea. Logical arguments consist of at least three elements: propositions, reasoning, and evidence. The first of these consists of the ideas that the writer advocates or defends. The logical links by which the argument is advanced make up the second. The statistics, facts, anecdotes, and testimonial support provided by the writer in defense of the idea constitute the evidence. In a research paper, evidence consisting of paraphrases or quotations from the works of other writers must be documented in a footnote, endnote, or parenthetical reference. See also **argumentation**.

**example**   An instance that is representative of an idea or claim or that otherwise illustrates it. The example mode of development is used in essays that make a claim and then prove it by citing similar and supporting cases. See, for example, the essay "Coincidences" in Chapter 7.

**exposition**   Writing whose chief aim is to explain. Most college composition assignments are expository.

**figurative**   Said of a word or expression used in a nonliteral way. For example, the expression "to go the last mile" may have nothing at all to do with geographical distance, but may mean to complete an unfinished task or job.

**focus**   In an essay, the concentration or emphasis upon a certain subject or topic.

**generalization**   A statement that asserts some broad truth based upon a knowledge of specific cases. For instance, the statement "Big cars are gas guzzlers" is a generalization about individual cars. Generalizations are the end products of inductive reasoning, where a basic truth may be inferred about a class after experience with a representative number of its members. One should, however, beware of rash or faulty generalizations—those made on insufficient experience or evidence. It was once thought, for example, that scurvy sufferers were malingerers, which led the British navy to the policy of flogging the victims of scurvy aboard its ships. Later, medical research showed that the lethargy of scurvy victims was an effect rather than the cause of the disease. The real cause was found to be a lack of vitamin C in their diet.

**image**   A phrase or expression that evokes a picture or describes a scene. An image may be either literal, in which case it is a realistic attempt to depict with words what something looks like, or figurative, in which case an expression is used that likens the thing described to something else (e.g., "My love is like a red, red rose").

**induction**   A form of reasoning that proceeds from specific instances to a general inference or conclusion. Inductive reasoning is the cornerstone of the scientific method, which begins by examining representative cases and then infers some law or theory to explain them as a whole. See the article "Introduction to Logic" in Chapter 9.

**interparagraph**   Between paragraphs. A comparison/contrast, for example, may be drawn between several paragraphs rather than within a single paragraph. For an example of an interparagraph comparison/contrast, see "Grant and Lee: A Study in Contrasts" in Chapter 8.

**intraparagraph**   Within a single paragraph. For an example of an intraparagraph comparison/contrast, see Emerson's essay "Conservatism and Liberalism" in Chapter 8.

**inversion**   The reversal of the normal order of words in a sentence to achieve some desired effect, usually emphasis. Inversion is a technique long used in poetry, although most modern poets shun it as too artificial. For examples of inversion, see Shakespeare's "That Time of Year" (Sonnet 73) in Chapter 4.

**irony**   The use of language in such a way that apparent meaning contrasts sharply with real meaning. One famous example (in Shakespeare's *Julius Caesar*) is Antony's description of Brutus as "an honorable man." Since Brutus was one of Caesar's assassins, Antony meant just the opposite. Irony is a softer form of sarcasm and shares with it the same contrast between apparent and real meaning.

**jargon**   The specialized or technical language of a specific trade, profession, class, or other group of people. Jargon is sometimes useful, but when used thoughtlessly it can become meaningless expression bordering on gibberish, as in the following sentence from a psychology text: "His male sibling's excessive psychogenic outbursts were instrumental in causing him to decompensate emotionally." A clearer statement would be the following: "His brother's temper eventually caused him to have a nervous breakdown."

**literal**   *Literal* and *figurative* are two opposing characteristics of language. The literal meaning is a statement about something rendered in common, factual terms: "A good writer must be aggressive and daring." The figurative meaning is couched in an image: "A good writer must stick out his neck." See **figurative**.

**logical fallacies**   Errors in reasoning used by speakers or writers, sometimes in order to dupe their audiences. Most logical fallacies are based on insufficient evidence ("All redheads are passionate lovers"); or irrelevant information ("Don't let him do the surgery; he cheats on his wife"); or on faulty logic ("If you don't quit smoking, you'll die of lung cancer"). See Richard Altick's "Obstacles to Clear Thinking," in Chapter 9.

**metaphor**   A figurative image that implies the similarity between things otherwise dissimilar, as when the poet Robert Frost states, "I have been acquainted with the night," meaning that he has suffered despair.

**mood of a story**   The pervading impression made on the feelings of the reader. For instance, Edgar Allan Poe often created a mood of horror in his short stories. A mood can be gloomy, sad, joyful, bitter, frightening, and so forth. A writer can create as many moods as his emotional range suggests.

**mood of verbs**    A verb form expressing the manner or condition of the action. The "moods of verbs" are *indicative* (statements or questions); *imperative* (requests or commands); and *subjunctive* (expressions of doubt, wishes, probabilities, and conditions contrary to fact).

**narration**    An account of events as they happen. A narrative organizes material on the basis of chronological order or pattern, stressing the sequence of events and pacing these events according to the emphasis desired. Narration is often distinguished from three other modes of writing: argumentation, description, and exposition. See "How to Write a Narration," Chapter 6.

**objective and subjective writing**    Two different attitudes toward description. In *objective* writing the author tries to present the material fairly and without bias; in *subjective* writing the author stresses personal responses and interpretations. For instance, news reporting should be objective whereas poetry can be subjective.

**pacing**    The speed at which a piece of writing moves along. Pacing depends on the balance between summarizing action and representing the action in detail. See "How to Write a Narration," Chapter 6.

**parallelism**    The principle of coherent writing requiring that coordinate elements be given the same grammatical form, as in Daniel Webster's dictum, "I was born an American; I will live an American; I will die an American."

**paraphrase**    A restatement of a text or passage in another form or other words, often to clarify the meaning. Paraphrase is commonly used in research papers to assimilate the research into a single style of writing and thereby avoid a choppy effect. See also **plagiarism**.

**personification**    Attributing human qualities to objects, abstractions, or animals: "'Tis beauty calls and glory leads the way."

**plagiarism**    Copying words from a source and then passing them off as one's own. Plagiarism is considered dishonest scholarship. Every writer is obligated to acknowledge ideas or concepts that represent someone else's thinking.

**point of view**    The perspective from which a piece of writing is developed. In nonfiction the point of view is usually the author's. In fiction the point of view can be first- or third-person point of view. In the first-person point of view, the author becomes part of the narration and refers to himself as "I." In the third-person point of view the narrator simply observes the action of the story. Third-person narrative is either *omniscient* (when the narrator knows everything about all of the characters) or *limited* (when the narrator knows only those things that might be apparent to a sensitive observer).

**premise**    An assertion or statement that is the basis for an argument. See **syllogism**.

**process**    A type of development in writing that stresses how a sequence of steps produces a certain effect. For instance, explaining to the reader all of the steps involved in balancing a checkbook would be a *process* essay.

| | |
|---|---|
| **purpose** | The commitment on the part of authors to explain what they plan to write about. Purpose is an essential part of unity and coherence. Most teachers require student writers to state their purpose in a statement of purpose, also called a *thesis*: "I intend to argue that our Federal Post Office needs a complete overhaul." |
| **red herring** | A side issue introduced into an argument in order to distract from the main argument. It is a common device of politicians: "Abortion may be a woman's individual right, but have you considered the danger of the many germ-infested abortion clinics?" Here the side issue of dirty clinics clouds the ethical issue of the right or wrong of having an abortion. See Richard Altick's "Obstacles to Clear Thinking," pp. 666–75. |
| **repetition** | A final review of all of the main points in a piece of writing; also known as *recapitulation*. In skillful writing, repetition is a means of emphasizing important words and ideas, of binding together the sentences in a passage, and of creating an effective conclusion. Its purpose is to accumulate a climactic impact or to cast new light upon the material being presented. |
| **rhetoric** | The art of using persuasive language. This is accomplished through the author's diction and sentence structure. |
| **rhetorical question** | A question posed with no expectation of receiving an answer. This device is often used in public speaking in order to launch or further discussion: "Do you know what one of the greatest pains is? One of the greatest pains to human nature is the pain of a new idea." |
| **satire** | Often an attack on a person. Also the use of wit and humor in order to ridicule society's weaknesses so as to correct them. In literature, two types of satire have been recognized: *Horatian satire*, which is gentle and smiling; *Juvenalian satire*, which is sharp and biting. |
| **simile** | A figure of speech which, like the metaphor, implies a similarity between things otherwise dissimilar. The simile, however, always uses the words *like, as,* or *so* to introduce the comparison: "*As* a jewel of gold in a swine's snout, *so* is a fair woman which is without discretion." |
| **slanting** | The characteristic of selecting facts, words, or emphasis to achieve a preconceived intent:<br>*favorable intent:* "Although the Senator looks bored, when it comes time to vote, he is on the right side of the issue."<br>*unfavorable intent:* "The Senator may vote on the right side of issues, but he always looks bored." |
| **specific** | A way of referring to the level of abstraction in words; the opposite of *general*. A *general* word refers to a group or a class whereas a *specific* word refers to a member of a group or class. Thus, the word *nature* is general, the word *tree* more specific, and the word *oak* even more specific. The thesis of an essay is general, but the details supporting that thesis are specific. See also **abstract** and **concrete**. |
| **standard English** | The English of educated speakers and writers. Any attempt to define standard English is controversial because no two |

speakers of English speak exactly alike. What is usually meant by "standard English" is what one's grammar book dictates.

**statement of purpose**    What an author is trying to tell his audience; the main idea that he claims to support in his essay. Traditionally, what distinguishes a statement of purpose from a **thesis** is wording, not content. A statement of purpose includes such words as "My purpose is . . ." or "In this paper I intend to . . ." A statement of purpose is often the lead sentence of an essay. See Chapter 3, "Purpose and Thesis."

**straw man**    An opposing point of view, set up so that it can easily be refuted. This is a common strategy used in debate.

**style**    The expression of an author's individuality through the use of words, sentence patterns, and selection of details. Our advice to fledgling writers is to develop a style that combines sincerity with clarity. See F. L. Lucas's "What Is Style?" in Chapter 2.

**subordination**    Expressing in a dependent clause, phrase, or single word any idea that is not significant enough to be expressed in a main clause or an independent sentence:
*lacking subordination:* John wrote his research paper on Thomas Jefferson; he was interested in this great statesman.
*with subordination:* Because John was interested in Thomas Jefferson, he wrote his research paper on this great statesman.

**syllogism**    In formal logic, the pattern by which a deductive argument is expressed:
All men are mortal (major premise)
John Smith is a man (minor premise)
Therefore John Smith is mortal (conclusion)

**symbol**    An object or action that in its particular context represents something else. For instance, in Ernest Hemingway's novel *Farewell to Arms* the rain represents impending disaster because when it rains something terrible happens.

**synonym**    A word or phrase that has the same meaning as another. For instance, the words *imprisonment* and *incarceration* are synonyms. The phrases "fall short of" and "miss the mark" are synonymous.

**syntax**    The order of words in a sentence and their relationships to each other. Good syntax requires correct grammar as well as effective sentence patterns, including unity, coherence, and emphasis.

**theme**    See **thesis**.

**thesis**    The basic idea of an essay, usually stated in a single sentence. In expository and argumentative writing, the thesis (or *theme*) is the unifying force that every word, every sentence, and every paragraph of the essay must support.

**tone**    In writing, *tone* is the reflection of the writer's attitude toward subject and audience. The tone can be personal or impersonal, formal or informal, objective or subjective.

Tone may also be expressed by a tone of voice, such as irony, sarcasm, anger, humor, satire, hyperbole, or understatement.

**topic sentence**  The *topic sentence* is to a paragraph what the *thesis* or *theme* is to the entire essay—that is, it expresses the paragraph's central idea.

**transition**  Words, phrases, sentences, or even paragraphs that indicate connections between the writer's ideas. These transitions provide landmarks to guide the reader from one idea to the next so that the reader will not get lost. The following are some standard transitional devices:

*time:* soon, immediately, afterward, later, meanwhile, in the meantime

*place:* nearby, on the opposite side, further back, beyond

*result:* as a result, therefore, thus, as a consequence

*comparison:* similarly, likewise, also

*contrast:* on the other hand, in contrast, nevertheless, but, yet, otherwise

*addition:* furthermore, moreover, in addition, and, first, second, third, finally

*example:* for example, for instance, to illustrate, as a matter of fact, on the whole, in other words

**understatement**  A way of deliberately representing something as less than it is in order to stress its magnitude. Also called *litotes*. A good writer will restrain the impulse to hammer home a point and will use understatement instead. An example is the following line from Oscar Wilde's play *The Importance of Being Earnest*:

"To lose one parent, Mr. Worthing, may be regarded as a misfortune; to lose both looks like carelessness."

**unity**  The characteristic in writing of having all parts contribute to an overall effect. An essay or paragraph is described as having *unity* when all of its sentences develop one central idea. The worst enemy of unity is irrelevant material. A good rule is to delete all sentences that do not advance or prove the thesis or topic sentence of an essay.

**voice**  The presence or the sound of self chosen by an author. Most good writing sounds like someone delivering a message. The aim in good student writing is to sound natural. Of course, the voice will be affected by the audience and occasion for writing. See Chapter 2, "The Writer's Voice."

# COPYRIGHTS AND ACKNOWLEDGMENTS

For permission to use the selections reprinted in this book, the authors are grateful to the following publishers and copyright holders:

ABINGDON PRESS    For "I Believe in God," excerpted from *I Believe* by Gerald Kennedy. Copyright renewal © 1986 by Mary Kennedy. Used by permission of the publisher, Abingdon Press.

APPLAUSE THEATRE BOOK PUBLISHERS    For *The Brute* by Anton Chekhov, translated by Eric Bentley, from *The Brute and Other Farces*. Copyright 1956, copyright renewed 1984. Reprinted by permission of Applause Theatre Book Publishers, 211 West 71st Street, New York, N.Y. 10023.

ATLANTA MAGAZINE    For "The Party's Over" by Vincent Coppola from the October 1987 issue of *Atlanta* Magazine. Adapted by permission of the publisher.

THE ATLANTIC MONTHLY    For "Farewell, My Unlovely" by Caskie Stinnett from the *Atlantic Monthly*. Copyright © 1976, by The Atlantic Monthly Company, Boston, Mass. 02116. Reprinted with permission of the *Atlantic Monthly* and the author.

LAURA BOHANNAN    For "Shakespeare in the Bush" by Laura Bohannan from *Natural History*, August–September 1966. Copyright © 1966 by Laura Bohannan. Reprinted by permission.

CAROL BRISSIE    For "The Right to Fail" from *The Lunacy Boom* by William Zinsser. Copyright 1969, 1970 by William K. Zinsser. Reprinted by permission of the author.

SUZANNE BRITT JORDAN    For "That Lean and Hungry Look" from *Newsweek*, October 9, 1978. Copyright © 1978 by Suzanne Britt Jordan. Reprinted by permission of the author.

BULLETIN OF THE ATOMIC SCIENTISTS    For "Preventing Nuclear War" by Roger Fisher from *The Bulletin of the Atomic Scientists*, March 1981. Reprinted by permission of *The Bulletin of the Atomic Scientists*, a magazine of science and world affairs. Copyright © 1981 by the Educational Foundation for Nuclear Science.

COMMONWEAL FOUNDATION    For "Mom and Pop Forgive Them" by John Garvey from *Commonweal*, December 2, 1983. Copyright © Commonweal Foundation. For "Buying and Selling Babies" by Michael Novak from *Commonweal*, July 17, 1987. Copyright © 1987 Commonweal Foundation. Both reprinted by permission.

CURTIS BROWN LTD.    For "R.M.S. *Titanic*" by Hanson W. Baldwin from the January 1934 issue of *Harper's*, published by Harper and Row. Copyright © 1933, 1961. For "Kitsch" by Gilbert Highet from *A Clerk of Oxenford* by Gilbert Highet. Copyright © 1954 by Gilbert Highet. Both reprinted by permission of Curtis Brown Ltd.

CURTIS PUBLISHING COMPANY    For "Thinking as a Hobby" by William Golding from *Holiday*, August 1961. Copyright © 1961 The Curtis Publishing Company. For "What Is Style?" by F. L. Lucas from *Holiday*, March 1960. Copyright © 1960 The Curtis Publishing Company. Reprinted with permission from *Holiday* magazine.

JOAN DAVES    For "I Have a Dream" by Martin Luther King, Jr. Copyright 1963 by Martin Luther King, Jr. Reprinted by permission of Joan Daves.

DOUBLEDAY    For "I Thought My Last Hour Had Come" by Robert Guillain, excerpted from *I Saw Tokyo Burning* by Robert Guillain. Copyright © 1980, 1981 by Doubleday, a division of Bantam, Doubleday, Dell Publishing Group, Inc. Reprinted by permission of the publisher.

ESTATE OF NORMA MILLAY ELLIS    For "Oh, oh, you will be sorry for that word!" by Edna St. Vincent Millay. From *Collected Sonnets*, Revised and Expanded Ed., Harper & Row, 1988. Copyright 1923, 1951 by Edna St. Vincent Millay and Norma Millay Ellis. Reprinted by permission.

FARRAR, STRAUS AND GIROUX, INC.    For "Salvation" from *The Big Sea* by Langston Hughes. Copyright © 1940 by Langston Hughes. Copyright © renewed 1968 by Arna Bontemps and George Houston Bass. Reprinted by permission of Farrar, Straus and Giroux, Inc.

of the State University of New York Press. Copyright © 1983 State University of New York Press. All rights reserved.

ST. MARTIN'S PRESS, INC. For "Do Animals Have Souls?" by James Herriot from *All Creatures Great and Small* by James Herriot, St. Martin's Press, Inc., New York. Copyright © 1972 by James Herriot. Reprinted by permission.

MAY SWENSON For "Pigeon Woman" by May Swenson. Copyright © 1962 by May Swenson, first published in *The New Yorker*. Reprinted with permission of the author.

JUDY SYFERS For "Why I Want a Wife" by Judy Syfers. Copyright 1970 by Judy Syfers. Reprinted by permission of the author.

ARTHUR C. TENNIES For "In Defense of Deer Hunting" by Arthur C. Tennies. Originally appeared in the *National Observer*, January 4, 1975. Reprinted by permission of the author.

HELEN W. THURBER For "The Catbird Seat" by James Thurber. Copyright © 1945 James Thurber. Copyright © 1973 Helen W. Thurber and Rosemary T. Sauers. From *The Thurber Carnival*, published by Harper & Row. Reprinted by permission.

TIME For "Baffle-Gab Thesaurus," from *Time*, September 13, 1968. Copyright 1968 Time Inc. All rights reserved. For "In New York: Be Kind to Your Mugger," by Timothy Foote from *Time*, February 21, 1983. Copyright 1983 Time Inc. All rights reserved. For "Mirror, Mirror on the Wall . . ." by John Leo from *Time*, March 6, 1978. Copyright 1978 Time Inc. All rights reserved. For "Why the Justice System Fails" by Roger Rosenblatt. Copyright 1981 Time Inc. All rights reserved. All reprinted by permission from *Time*.

UNIVERSAL PRESS SYNDICATE For "The Cruel Logic of Liberation" by Joseph Sobron. Taken from the "Joseph Sobron" column by Joseph Sobron. Copyright 1980 Universal Press Syndicate. Reprinted by permission. All rights reserved.

VERBATIM For "A History of the World" by Richard Lederer from *Verbatim®, the Language Quarterly*. © Copyright 1987 by *Verbatim®, the Language Quarterly*. Used by permission.

VIKING PENGUIN INC. For "The View from Eighty" by Malcolm Cowley from *The View from Eighty* by Malcolm Cowley. Copyright © 1976, 1978, 1980 by Malcolm Cowley. All rights reserved. For "Cystic Fibrosis" by Frank Deford from *Alex: The Life of a Child* by Frank Deford. Copyright © 1983 by Frank Deford. All rights reserved. For "Hell" by James Joyce from *A Portrait of the Artist as a Young Man* by James Joyce. Copyright 1916 by B. W. Huebsch. Copyright renewed 1944 by Nora Joyce. Definitive text copyright © 1964 by the Estate of James Joyce. All rights reserved. All reprinted by permission of Viking Penguin Inc.

THE VILLAGE VOICE For "How the Superwoman Myth Puts Women Down" by Sylvia Rabiner from the *Village Voice*, May 24, 1976. Reprinted by permission of the *Village Voice* © 1976.

VITAL SPEECHES OF THE DAY For "The Peace Movement" by Charlton Heston from *Vital Speeches of the Day*, October 15, 1983, vol. 15, no. 1, p. 20. Reprinted by permission of *Vital Speeches of the Day*.

WALLACE & SHEIL AGENCY, INC. For "Why I Write" by Joan Didion from *The New York Times Book Review*, December 6, 1976. Reprinted by permission of Wallace & Sheil Agency, Inc. Copyright © 1976 by Joan Didion. First appeared in *The New York Times Book Review*.

WASHINGTON POST WRITERS GROUP For "AIDS Research Does Deserve Funding, but There Are Other Fatal Diseases, Too" by Charles Krauthammer from the *Atlanta Constitution*, June 15, 1987. Copyright © 1987, Washington Post Writers Group. Reprinted with permission.

ARTHUR WEINBERG For "Why I Am an Agnostic" by Clarence Darrow from *Verdicts Out of Court*, edited by Arthur and Lila Weinberg, Quadrangle/The New York Times Book Company, 1963.

# ·· *INDEX* ··

A    8
B    9
C    0
D    1
E    2
F    3
G    4
H    5
I    6
J    7